Introduction

Despite the fact that 2008 has been the year where the term 'credit crunch' firmly entered consumers' vernacular, the London shopping scene is looking as multifaceted and exciting as ever. While the team behind Westfield London in Shepherd's Bush prepare to open what will become Europe's largest shopping mall from autumn 2008, there's concurrently been a resurgence of small-scale independent sellers and producers in the capital (*see p9* **From London, with love**). Since the last edition of this guide we have welcomed in several new independents, including Ryantown on Columbia Road, Lemon Balm on Camden's Parkway, the Big Green Bookshop in Wood Green, Lost in Beauty in Primrose Hill, Feather & Stich in Richmond and the impressive new Farringdon space for record shop Pure Groove. Opening a small business in London is always going to be a risky prospect, but the fact that so many enterprising folk are still prepared to take that risk is testamount to their faith that a sizeable number of city dwellers and visitors will be there to support them.

There may be a sense of the tightening of belts in light of economic doom and gloom, but, partly as a consequence of this, many of us are becoming more discerning when it comes to deciding who we want to swipe our plastic. Disillusionment with the throwaway trend exemplified by super-cheap clothing retailer Primark has deepened, and many of us are yearning for the return to better-quality products that will last longer than one season. As a consequence, there has been something of a return in high-street fashion shoppers' consciousness to the mid-range shops; 2008 saw Jigsaw make a full comeback after several years of rather mediocre wares, Cos go from strength to strength and the arrival of US import Banana Republic.

INDIE SCENE

But for many people, it's support for the independents that's the crucial bullet point on the shopping agenda, partly for ethical reasons, but also because of the quality of the shopping experience itself. So we've focused more than ever on the indies, from eccentric old faves such as Soho's Lina Stores to comparative newcomers like its neighbour Hurwundeki. The capital's independent fashion boutiques continue to increase, both in number and quality, and there's still a plethora of fascinating independent bookshops and record stores, despite a handful of losses every year (RIP Metropolitan Books and Reckless Records in 2008). The **Unique Selling Point** series in the guide highlights some of the most original of these independents, places where a sense of uniqueness and integrity – qualities rarely associated with chain shops – are central. In addition, our **Streetwise** series aims to flag up shopping streets containing a high number of independents – which make them some of the most enjoyable places in which to shop.

GOING GREEN

Hand in hand with support for independents has been the (necessary) growth of the more ethical and eco-minded brand of consumerism; from the plethora of cotton shopping bags now seen around town (all attempting to outwit one another with right-on slogans of the 'Plastic bags are rubbish' ilk) to the increase in stylish eco boutiques and concept stores packed with green and Fairtrade items, the era of eco shopping is more evident than ever. In fact, as this guide went to press, the Fairtrade Association was about to declare London an official Fairtrade city (*see p46* **Fair game**), the largest city in the world to achieve such status. However, the number of shops led by ethical and green principles are still in a minority, so for this reason we've highlighted those that are making strides in this arena by flagging them up with an (eco) symbol.

One good way to shop more ethically, of course, is to buy second-hand, and London's vintage and thrift shops are looking stronger than ever; Oxfam Designer opened on Westbourne Grove in summer 2008, and as we went to press a sister store to the East End Thrift Store, the Brick Lane Thrift Store, was opening at 68 Sclater Street, E1 (7739 0242). With all items under £10, the latter sells 'thrift' items in the true sense of the word. For those of you concerned about these challenged times, we've also tried to promote other ways of spending less while still being part of the consumer fray: boxes on buying a second-hand bike and a bespoke suit on the cheap, for example.

FLASH THE CASH

One area of London's shopping scene that's unlikely to be affected anytime soon by the credit crunch, however, is the luxury end. No gap in the market is left unplugged in the capital when it comes to filling the superflous needs of the city's moneyed classes. From high-end designer clothes shopping on Bond Street or in one of the city's famed department stores to bespoke suits on Savile Row, exotic fragrances from the likes of Miller Harris and Ormonde Jayne or an indulgent Balinese massage in new Knightsbridge spa Ushvani, London is still the place to flex that gold card. The steady increase in high-end 'concept stores' (which analysts of consumer habits believe will be an important aspect of shopping in the future), such as Dover Street Market, Shop at Bluebird and newcomer Couveture & the Garbstore, should provide some extra inspiration.

While London will always be one of the world's most exciting shopping spots, its size and diversity can make it an exhausting place too. By using this guide as a practical resource to narrow down what you're after – and consulting the **Where to shop** map on p6 – we hope that, as well as feeling inspired, you'll be well equipped to part with your pounds without losing your head.

Anna Norman, Editor

EDITION 14

timeout.com/shopping

One-Stop

Fashion

Health & Beauty

Home

Contents

Shops & Services

Leisure

Food & Drink

Babies & Children

Indexes & Map

Features

About the guide

No retail guide to a city of London's scale can be completely comprehensive; we have tried to select what we believe are the best of the capital's shops and services. If you feel we've missed somewhere exceptional or included a place that's gone downhill, please email us at guides@timeout.com.

Opening hours

Although many of the shops, companies and individuals listed in this guide keep regular store hours, others are small concerns run from private addresses or workshops that have erratic opening hours, or are open by appointment only. In such cases, the times given are a guide as to when to phone, not when to visit.

The opening times were correct at the time of going to press, but if you're going out of your way to visit a particular shop, always phone first to check (especially as stores are constantly launching and closing down in London). Many outlets extend their opening times in summer to benefit from tourist traffic and in the run-up to Christmas; others take their holidays in August and close altogether. Some are closed on bank holidays or have reduced opening times.

Abbreviations

The following credit card abbreviations are used: **AmEx**: American Express; **DC**: Diners Club; **MC**: MasterCard; **V**: Visa. Some larger shops and department stores also accept euros. In the fashion chapter, we have indicated whether shops sell menswear and/ or womenswear with the letters **M** and **W**, respectively. Childrenswear is represented by a **C**, babywear by a **B**.

Prices

While prices were accurate at the time of writing, they are subject to change.

Mail order & online

For online retailers, we have provided the web address only, as contact telephone numbers and additional ordering information can be found on the website. Many of the shops listed have ordering facilities on their sites.

Branches

We have included details for shops' London branches in the A-Z Index (p277). For shops with branches throughout the city, please see the phone directory for the location of your nearest. Note that branches may have different opening hours from the reviewed shop, so it is advisable to call to check times before visiting.

Subject index

The chapters are divided into easy-to-navigate subsections, but if you need to locate a specific item quickly, the Subject Index (p270) is a useful resource – especially as many shops fall into several categories.

Sponsors and advertisers

We would like to thank our sponsor, MasterCard, for its involvement in this guide. However, we would like to stress that sponsors have no control over editorial content. The same applies to advertisers: no shop has been included because its owner has advertised in the guide. An advertiser may receive a bad review or no review at all.

Published by
Time Out Guides Limited
Universal House
251 Tottenham Court Road
London W1T 7AB
Tel +44 (0)20 7813 3000
Fax +44 (0)20 7813 6001
email guides@timeout.com
www.timeout.com

Editorial
Editor Anna Norman
Copy Editors Sarah Barden, Daniel Smith, Sarah Thorowgood, Patrick Welch, Yolanda Zappaterra
Listings Editor Alex Brown
Researchers Alex Brown, Charlotte Middlehurst, Meryl O'Rourke, Gemma Pritchard, Kohinoor Sahota
Proofreader Tamsin Shelton
Indexer Jackie Brind

Managing Director Peter Fiennes
Editorial Director Sarah Guy
Series Editor Cath Phillips
Business Manager Dan Allen
Editorial Manager Holly Pick
Assistant Management Accountant Ija Krasnikova

Design
Art Director Scott Moore
Art Editor Pinelope Kourmouzoglou
Senior Designer Henry Elphick
Graphic Designers Gemma Doyle, Kei Ishimaru
Advertising Designer Jodi Sher

Picture Desk
Picture Editor Jael Marschner
Deputy Picture Editor Katie Morris
Deputy Picture Editor Lynn Chambers
Picture Researcher Gemma Walters
Picture Desk Assistant Marzena Zoladz
Picture Librarian Christina Theisen

Advertising
Commercial Director Mark Phillips
Sales Manager Alison Wallen
Advertising Sales Ben Holt, Alex Matthews, Jason Trotman, Rob Bates
Advertising Assistant Kate Staddon
Display Production Manager Sally Webb
Copy Controller Chris Pastfield

Marketing
Marketing Manager Yvonne Poon
Sales & Marketing Director, North America Lisa Levinson
Marketing Designers Anthony Huggins, Nicola Wilson

Production
Group Production Director Mark Lamond
Production Manager Brendan McKeown
Production Controller Damian Bennett
Production Coordinator Julie Pallot

Time Out Group
Chairman Tony Elliott
Group General Manager/Director Nichola Coulthard
Time Out Communications Ltd MD David Pepper
Time Out International Ltd MD Cathy Runciman
Group IT Director Simon Chappell
Circulation Director Polly Knewstub
Head of Marketing Catherine Demajo

Sections in this guide were written by
From London, with love Helen Jennings. **One-stop** *Department stores* Fiona McAuslan; *Shopping Centres, Arcades, Markets* Sarah Barden; *Concept Stores* Sarah Barden, Patrick Welch. **Fashion** *Boutiques & Emerging Designer* Sarah Barden, Mansel Fletcher, Keremi Gawade, Anna Norman (*Label watch* Helen Jennings, *Unique Selling Point* Hannah Kane); *International Designer & Classic* Sarah Barden, Mansel Fletcher, Keremi Gawade; *High Street* Caroline Hunter (*Fair game* Anna Norman, Richard Norman); *Jeans & Urban Casual* Patrick Welc (*Classic clobber* Dan Jones); *Bespoke & Tailoring* Mansel Fletcher; *Vintage* Lindsay Calder; *Weddings* Maggie Davis, Lindsay Macpherson; *Maternity* Sarah Barden, Sarah Thorowgood; *Lingerie & Swimwear* Emma Howarth; *Unusual Siz* Sarah Thorowgood; *Shoes* Helen Jennings (*Trainers* Matt Norman); *Accessories* Helen Jennings (*Enduring loves* Daniel Smith); *Jewellery* Kate Riordan (*In gold trust* Anna Norman); *Cleaning & Repairs* Sarah Barden. **Health & Beauty** *Heal & Beauty Shops* Fiona McAuslan, Anna Norman (*Natural selection* Anna Norman); *Beauty Salons & Spas* various; *Specialists* various (*Best foot forwar* Anna Norman; *Pretty in ink* Dan Jones, Rodolfo Schmidt, Patrick Welch); *Clinics* Sarah Barden; *Hairdressers* various (*High barnets* Matt Norman); *Opticians* Norman Miller (*Rekindling old frames* Dan Jones). **Home** *Furniture & Accessori* Lindsay Calder, Yolanda Zappaterra (*Out of the woodwork...* Fiona McAuslan, *Unique Selling Point* Emma Howarth); *Interiors* Ronnie Haydon; *Bathrooms & Kitchens, Antiques, 20th-century Design* Lindsay Calder; *Art & Craft* Yolanda Zappaterra; *Gardens & Flowers* Ronnie Haydon. **Leisure** *Books* Daniel Smith; *CDs & Records* Kate Hutchinson; *Electronics* Phillip Othen; *Erotic* Kate Hutchinson; *Gifts* Kate Riordan (*Museum pieces* Patrick Welch); *Art & Craft Supplies* Caroline Hunter; *Hobbies & Games* Sarah Barden; *Music* John Lewis *Parties* Emma Howarth; *Pets* Sarah Barden, Jan Fuscoe; *Photography* Norman Miller (*Plastic fantastic* Anna Norman); *Sport & Fitness* Matt Norman; *Statione* Sarah Barden, Caroline Hunter. **Food & Drink** *Food* Jenni Muir (*Unique Selling Point* Sarah Barden); *Drink* Richard Ehrlich. **Babies & Children** Ronnie Haydon **Shop talk interviews** Lindsay Calder (Sam Chatterton Dickson), Dan Jones (Lulu Kennedy), John Lewis (Kieren Hebden, Fergus Henderson), Anna Normar (Rebecca Lowrey Boyd). **Streetwise features** Sarah Barden (Ledbury Road), Katie Cordell (Columbia Road), Daniel Smith (Camden Passage, Mount Street Sarah Thorowgood (Ledbury Road). **Additional reviews written by** Shane Armstrong, Ismay Atkins, Yolanda Chiaramello, Alix Cordell, Ruth Jarvis, Rob Murray, Emma Perry, Holly Pick, Ros Sales, Elizabeth Winding.

The Editor would like to thank Edoardo Albert, Sarah Barden, Maggie Davis, Dan Jones, Cath Phillips, Lisa Ritchie, Ros Sales, Daniel Smith.

Map London Underground map supplied by Transport for London.

Cover image photography Rob Greig, artwork John Oakey.
Bertoia chair from the Conran Shop (www.conranshop.co.uk). Anglepoise lam from Heals (www.heals.co.uk). Shoe from LK Bennett (www.lkbennett.com). Bicycle from Dutch Bike (www.dutchbike.co.uk). Perfume from Laura Ashley (www.lauraashley.com). Glasses by Police (01923 249 491). Tilly bag by Ally Capellino (www.allycapellino.co.uk). Mirror from Chandeliers & Mirrors (www.chandeliersandmirrors.co.uk). Toy train from a selection at Hamleys (www.hamleys.com).

Photography by Michelle Grant, except: pages 4, 14, 15, 20, 29, 34, 56, 57 74, 75, 120, 122, 123, 154, 160, 172, 173, 176, 187, 196, 197, 207, 21 219, 223, 234, 243 Ming Tang-Evans; pages 9,10, 55, 103, 108, 231, 245 Marzena Zoladz; page 14 Scott Wishart; pages 14, 22, 26, 49, 53, 60, 61, 77, 79, 80, 120, 134, 138, 139, 168, 169, 176, 190, 207, 210, 213, 23 238, 251, 258, 260 Britta Jaschinski; page 51 Ed Marshall; page 88,97 Elisabeth Blanchet; page 111 Yolanda Chiaramello; page 168 Haris Artemis page 169 Piers Allardyce; pages 221, 257 Rob Greig; pages 234, 243 Helo Bergman; page 235 Oliver Knight; page 252 Scott Chasserot.
The following images were provided by the featured establishments/artists: pages 18, 19, 45, 95, 96, 126, 141, 147, 163, 166, 171, 195, 248.

Printer St Ives (Web) Ltd, Storeys Bar Road, Eastern Industrial Estate, Peterborough, PE1 5YS
Time Out Group uses paper products that are environmentally friendly, from well managed forests and mills that use certified (PEFC) Chain of Custody p in their production.

ISBN 978-1-905042-29-6
ISSN 1752-6167

Distribution by Seymour Ltd +44 (0)20 7429 4000
For further distribution details, see www.timeout.com

London overview

Where to shop

Make the most of your spending spree with our guide to the key retail areas.

MARYLEBONE

Wigmore Street brims with bathroom and kitchen showrooms, while the High Street offers a browsable mix of food, fashion, design and books. Head north for Church Street's cache of antiques.

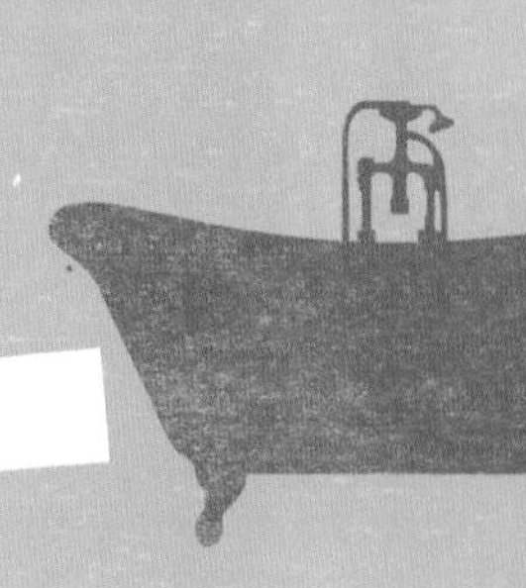

NOTTING HILL

Boutiques abound on Westbourne Grove and Ledbury Road. Portobello Road and Kensington Church Street overflow with posh antiques.

OXFORD STREET, REGENT STREET & SOHO

The backbone of London's retail scene. Oxford Street's chains peter out on elegant Regent Street, while Soho's indies cock a snook at them all.

MAYFAIR

Traditional home of tailors (Savile Row), shirtmakers (Jermyn Street), luxe labels and jewels (Bond Street).

SOUTH KENSINGTON & CHELSEA

Big international designers rule on Sloane Street, while the area around Brompton Cross has a clutch of modern furniture showrooms.

Upper Street
Camden Passage
ANGEL
EUSTON
Lamb's Conduit Street
Rosebery Avenue
Tottenham Court Road
CLERKENWELL & SHOREDITCH
Clerkenwell's contemporary furniture stores cater to local loft dwellers. Young and emerging designers set up shop further east near Brick Lane in Shoreditch, where you'll also find edgy art galleries.
COVENT GARDEN & BLOOMSBURY
Bibliophiles beat a path to Charing Cross Road and Cecil Court. Streetwear dominates on Carnaby Street and Seven Dials. Unlovely Tottenham Court Road is worth the trawl for electronics and homewares – just.
Clerkenwell Road
FARRINGDON
Shoreditch High Street
Bethnal Green Road
Cheshire Street
TOTTENHAM COURT ROAD
Monmouth Street
Shorts Gardens
Charing Cross Road
Brick Lane
COVENT GARDEN
LIVERPOOL STREET
LEICESTER SQUARE
River Thames

Classic London shops

From London, with love

Helen Jennings reports on the perseverance – and resurgence – of the capital's skilled artisans.

London's landscape is littered with signs of enterprises long departed. Staples Corner at the mouth of the M1 is named after the Staples Mattress Factory that opened there in 1926, and closed in 1986. Similarly, the 'Golden Mile' stretch of the Great West Road (A4) is home to several once glorious art deco factories. The Gillette Building was vacated in 2006, while the nearby Hoover Building is now a Tesco superstore. Driven out by the rising costs of London, countless companies have said goodbye to the Big Smoke.

However, with today's concerns about ethical shopping, consumers are starting to question global companies that use cheap foreign labour – and from this comes an emerging trend for local brands. Working on a smaller scale, an increasing number of skilled artisans are lovingly hand-making authentic products in the heart of the capital. 'When people come to London, they expect to find the best. It adds a huge amount of kudos to a product. That's why we base our business here.' So explains Robert Boyd-Bowman, proprietor of shirt-maker **Alexander Boyd** (*see p54*). The firm has supplied the smart shirt shops on Jermyn Street since 1913 and opened its own store on Artillery Lane in 2001. 'All the factories that were making shirts closed up in the 1980s when Thatcher came to power. She decided that globalisation was the thing, so everybody went abroad.' Boyd disapproves of loopholes in EU law that allow firms to appear British while having all their production offshore. 'Elsewhere in the world you have to put country of origin on your label, but in Europe you don't. So companies use a nice old-fashioned name, then just import stuff and sell it. It's a fraud because people are paying a premium for something they think is from England.'

Alexander Boyd is 100 per cent British. One of only two shirt-makers left in the country, its bespoke shirts are a cut above. Despite a price tag of £150, Boyd says there's always demand. 'Somebody might cut down on how many they buy when times get tough, but they won't go back to Marks & Spencer. We convert 90 per cent of people who walk into our shop because they can tell from the look of the outfit if it's their sort of shop.'

Boyd's friend – and kindred spirit – Michael Drake set up **Drakes** (*see p54*) in 1978 after spying a niche in the market for men's printed scarves and ties. 'Manufacturers were offering only small classic scarves in traditional tartans, so I developed a fashion item with a huge variety of colourful designs. It became an overnight success.' Now the UK's largest independent tie maker, Drakes makes everything at its premises in Clerkenwell. The ties are cut by hand and 18 separate checks ensure only perfect products leave the workshop. 'The Handmade in England label is the essence of our brand. It's unusual to manufacture in London, but if we didn't we couldn't guarantee quality.'

Up the road in Hackney is **Gina** (*see p73*): the last luxury label standing in an area that was once brimming with shoe factories. Mehet Kurdash started the business in 1954 and his sons Attila, Altan and Aydin still run the show from their factory off Kingsland Road. 'We've been here for some 40 years and employ over 50 people, many of whom have been with Gina for a long time,' says Aydin. Renowned for its sexy diamanté-encrusted shoes, the firm has an enviable A-list clientele thanks to its in-house production. Everything from the design concept right through to the last hand stitch happens at the Hackney HQ. 'Gina has always used the finest materials,' says Aydin. 'This

Junky Styling. *See p10.*

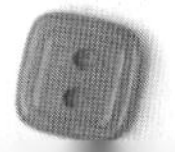

philosophy has passed the test of time; although the costs to produce in London are very high, Gina competes with the best in the world. We live and breathe London. It's this melting pot of cultures, images, ideas and feelings that gives Gina its distinguishable handwriting. That's why Gina remains made in London.' Gina's shops on Old Bond Street and Sloane Street create a decadent shopping experience that seems poles apart from the east London factory, yet that dichotomy sums up London's diverse appeal. For autumn/winter 2008/9, Gina's jewel-encrusted heels and python-skin boots will take you from dinner at Claridge's to a disco in Dalston in true style.

Annika Sanders and Kerry Seager of **Junky Styling** (www.junkystyling.co.uk) opened their shop at the Old Truman Brewery 11 years ago, long before it became a trendy retail destination. They've also been pioneers of recycled fashion. 'We have a team of sewers in the studio. Once trained in the deconstruct/ reconstruct process, they are invaluable to us,' Annika says. 'Every label should be transparent about how their products are made. Junky is special not only because it's made in London by Londoners, but because we meet our customers daily.' Also showing at Esthetica, London Fashion Week's sustainable fashion exhibition, there's no place like home for Annika and Kerry. 'London is the best place for us because our designs reflect the city's inhabitants. We hold a catwalk show and party for our customers twice a year too. It's all part of the service.'

It's not just the rag trade that continues to thrive in London. The **Brompton** folding bicycle (www.brompton.co.uk; *see also p223* **Cycling**) is a uniquely London invention that owes its name to one of the city's landmarks and, indeed, wouldn't have been born if it weren't for the tribulations its inventor Andrew Ritchie faced in the 1970s. 'He lived in a flat above the Brompton Oratory. Space was not something he had a lot of, so the desire to make a bike that folded up as compactly as possible most definitely informed his design,' says the firm's Katharine Horsman. 'As the first prototypes were actually made in his flat, it seemed appropriate to name the bike after its origins.'

Moving to a railway arch in Brentford in 1987, then to Chiswick Park in 1993, Brompton's current factory has nestled next to Kew Bridge station since 1998. The bike's 1,200 parts are assembled into a full-size machine that folds into a light, portable package. 'We rely heavily on our staff and have been building up a trained workforce for the last 20 years. While it may be cheaper to run a factory outside London, we wouldn't be able to transfer our staff. Plus the London connection is undoubtedly a unique selling point.'

Wallpaper manufacturer **Cole & Son** (*see p147*) also has an unrivalled London history. Founded in 1873 by John Perry, the current Harringay factory is only a few miles from the original premises in Islington. 'We hand-block, hand-flock and hand-screenprint on the original machinery. We also use modern technology and inks for our machine-printed papers – all under one roof,' says managing director Anthony Evans. 'The Cole & Son archive consists of over 2,000 designs and we can produce any of them to order.'

Employing ten artisans with over 200 years of experience between them, the firm also has a showroom at the Design Centre Chelsea Harbour and a royal warrant (its wallpaper currently hangs on the walls of Buckingham Palace). 'London is one of the greatest cities in the world and Cole & Sons has been part of it for over a century. Yes, rental costs are a worry, but the plus points always outweigh the minuses.' And if it's good enough for Her Majesty, well, it's good enough for us.

Drakes. *See p9.*

One-stop

One-stop

Liberty. *See p16.*

Harrods. *See p15.*

Borough Market (also right and below). *See p21.*

Department Stores

Fenwick

63 New Bond Street, W1A 3BS (7629 9161/www.fenwick.co.uk). Bond Street tube. **Open** 10am-6.30pm Mon-Wed, Fri, Sat; 10am-8pm Thur. Also open some Sundays during sales. **Credit** AmEx, MC, V.

Fenwick is less about discovering edgy new designers and more about quality, classics and wearability, with the style emphasis on luxurious smart casual. Designers new to the second-floor Designer Collections for autumn/winter 2008/9 include New York label Theory, for softly tailored daywear, feminine dresses from Tracey Reese, Rebecca Taylor's kittenish collection, plus new Italian names Pollini by Rifat Ozbek, Zhor & Nema and Piazza Sempione. On the third floor, in Weekend Collections, Erotokritos strikes a more playful note alongside jeans labels Ruby and Radcliffe. Diane von Furstenberg's beautiful colour-blocked briefcases and clutches light up the accessories and handbags department on the ground floor, alongside Sonia Rykiel's studded designs and J&M Davidson classics. Stella McCartney's new, colourful new underwear collection, meanwhile, is a welcome addition to the Lingerie department, as are the silk and lace confections from French label Elise Aucouturier. For men, the biggest draw is likely to be the sharply tailored separates by new addition Hardy Amies, as well as collections from Sonia Rykiel and Ralph Lauren. Beauty is also well served by most of the international perfume houses as well as the select make-up lines like Laura Mercier; and there's a walk-in Headmasters Blo Out bar on the ground floor, a Nails Inc nail bar and the Blink Bar for eyebrow threading, tinting and express waxing. A major rebuilding plan will see Fenwick expand by around 20% by 2010.

Fortnum & Mason

181 Piccadilly, W1A 1ER (7734 8040/ www.fortnumandmason.co.uk). Green Park or Piccadilly Circus tube. **Open** 10am-8pm Mon-Sat; noon-6pm Sun (food hall only). **Credit** AmEx, DC, MC, V.

In 2007, F&M revealed the outcome of a £24 million, two-year revamp. The results are stunning: the store has retained all that was marvellous about its Georgian past while changing just enough to position itself as a 21st-century shopping experience. A sweeping spiral staircase soars through the four-storey building, while light floods down from a central glass dome. The iconic F&M eau de nil blue and gold colour scheme with flashes of rose pink abound on both the store design and the packaging of the fabulous ground-floor treats, like the chocolates, biscuits, teas and preserves. The five restaurants, all redesigned by David Collins (of Wolseley fame), are equally impressive, with the ice-cream parlour a welcome addition. A new food hall in the basement, meanwhile, has a huge range of fresh produce and more wines than ever before, meaning F&M is no longer just a place for a picnic hamper or an eye-catching jar of pickle. Hard-to-find fragrances like Micallef or Women and Clive Christian (for both sexes) fill the extended perfume boutique, while homewares tend to be finishing touches like eau de nil linen and cashmere hot water bottles rather than essentials, though there's a good line of smart leather luggage. F&M is redolent of a time when luxury meant the highest degree of comfort rather than ostentation, but that's not to say it's beyond the means of a modest budget. The famous hampers start from £40 and the blended teas from £2.75.

Harrods

87-135 Brompton Road, SW1X 7XL (7730 1234/www.harrods.com). Knightsbridge tube. **Open** 10am-8pm Mon-Sat; noon-6pm Sun (browsing from 11.30am). **Credit** AmEx, DC, MC, V.

The distinctive terracotta façade with dark-green awnings stirs up some of the most divided feelings in the capital. For every tourist who comes out clutching their must-have Harrods teddy, there's a Londoner who sniffs at its vulgarity. It's true that all the glitz and marble can be a bit much, but in the store that boasts of selling everything, it's hard not to leave with at least one thing you'll like. The last year has seen various floors and departments with redesigns; new additions to the legendary food halls and restaurants include the Andronicas world of coffee on the fourth floor, where you can choose from over 60 different types of bean, roasted to your specification. There's also the 5J ham and tapas bar from Sanchez Romero Carvajal, Spain's oldest Jabugo ham-producing company. Flying in the face of the credit crunch, the new Luxury & Objet room showcases porcelain figurines, animals and vases from the likes of designers Loet Vanderveen, Jay Strongwater and Lladro. Similarly, the New Luxury Dining Room's brands like Versace, Christofle and Herend make the perfect adornment for the top table. It's on the fashion floors that Harrods really comes into its own, however, with well-edited collections from the heavyweights. New for autumn/winter 2008/9 is the eagerly awaited revival of Halston, the iconic 1970s design house, plus a boutique from Oscar de La Renta with opulent signature evening gowns and beautifully wearable day dresses. The lingerie boutique has been refurbished too, and now stocks exquisite designs from Alberta Ferretti, Agent Provocateur, Elle Macpherson and Roberto Cavalli. Menswear is also strong with directional tailoring from Bespoken. There's more subtle styling from new label Form by Bernie Ecclestone's daughter Petra. Andre 3000 of Outkast also makes his fashion debut with Benjamin Bixby hip collegiate styles. On the ground floor, the new Beauty Concierge service gives advice across all Harrods' treatments, services and products – essential for navigating the 250 or so brands on offer. Harrods' extravagence is much in evidence in the new pet bakery in the revamped pet department, which can sell you pet-friendly profiteroles, while the Pet Concierge service can source a rare breed from a reputable breeder.

Liberty. *See p16*.

Harvey Nichols

109-125 Knightsbridge, SW1X 7RJ (7235 5000/www.harveynichols.com). Knightsbridge tube. **Open** *Store* 10am-8pm Mon-Sat; noon-6pm Sun. *Café* 8am-10.30pm Mon-Sat; 8am-6pm Sun. *Restaurant* noon-3pm, 6-11pm Mon-Sat; noon-4pm, 6-11pm Sun. **Credit** AmEx, DC, MC, V.

Harvey Nics feels like it's coasting a little these days, with a shop that looks more like an identikit department store than the cutting-edge emporia that are some of its rivals. That said, you'll still find a worthy clutch of unique brands. In beauty, there's skin-firming Rodial and New York fave Bliss, with slick Gentlemen's Tonic for men. Accessories and shoes remain strong, with exclusive collections from Alejandro Ingelmo and, new for autumn/winter 2008/9, sexy heels from Camilla Skovgaard – alongside big names like Jimmy Choo. In womenswear, slinky and sophisticated dresses from Derek Lam and edgy styles from Les Chiffoniers are worthy exclusives. In menswear you'll find Balenciaga and Jil Sander as well as hip threads from Thom Browne and Limoland. There's a fine food hall on the fifth floor, filled with products in Harvey Nic's smart black and silver livery. Those with a taste for luxury can adjourn to the bar, which even has a private vodka tasting room.

John Lewis

300 Oxford Street, W1A 1EX (7629 7711/ www.johnlewis.co.uk). Bond Street or Oxford Circus tube. **Open** 9.30am-8pm Mon-Wed, Fri, Sat; 9.30am-9pm Thur; noon-6pm Sun. **Credit** AmEx, MC, V.

With a sensible ratio of quality to price for all its products, John Lewis retains its rightful crown as the retail world's safe pair of hands. Arguably the strongest selling point is the lower ground-floor cookware and white goods section, where an excellent range of kitchen staples is backed up by exemplary customer service. Well-informed staff will guide you to the right product for your purse, delivery is usually smooth and the after-care service, should you need it, admirable. The new food hall from Waitrose has speciality food galore, a walk-in cheese room and the plethora of check-out staff to keep the queues moving swiftly. Although the much-touted redesign of the ground-floor beauty hall hasn't quite transformed the store into the emporium of style the directors were hoping for, niche lines such as This Works and Bliss, alongside stalwarts like Benefit, MAC and Clarins, have upped the beauty ante. There's also an Elemis spa pod for express facials. Under the auspices of the new Director of Buying, Peter Ruis, fashion at John Lewis is fast becoming more directional, with hipper labels like Day Birger et Mikkelsen and BCBG Max Azria being added for autumn/winter 2008/9. The clutch of respectable classics is also still strong with Coast, Jaeger and Fenn Wright Mason among them. Other strengths include technology, schoolwear and homeware and the website is equally straightforward to use.
For branch see index.

Liberty

Regent Street, W1B 5AH (7734 1234/ www.liberty.co.uk). Oxford Circus tube. **Open** 10am-9pm Mon-Sat; noon-6pm Sun. **Credit** AmEx, DC, MC, V.

Shopping at Liberty is about more than just spending money; artful and arresting window displays, exciting new collections and luxe labels all make it an experience to savour for its own sake. Inside, atmospheric wood panelling provides the perfect foil for such fashion labels as Alexander McQueen, Gareth Pugh and PPQ, with new arrivals for autumn/winter 2008/9 including Spencer Hart menswear. The new shoe bar on the second floor includes exclusives from Nicholas Kirkwood, Rupert Sanderson, Giuseppe Zanotti and Stella McCartney. It's also strong on bags, with names like Marc Jacobs, Mulberry and Chloé featuring. The array of beautiful and original jewellery includes newcomer Lucy Hutchins's delicate and unusual necklaces and Stephen Dweck's dramatic pieces. The Rosa Clara Bridal Boutique consists of own-label styles and those by Karl Lagerfeld and Christian Lacroix. And despite being fashion forward, Liberty still respects its dressmaking heritage with an extensive range of cottons in the third-floor haberdashery department. Stationery also pays court to the traditional, with beautiful Liberty of London notebooks, address books, photo albums and diaries embossed with the art nouveau 'Ianthe' print. Interiors are equally impressive with regular exhibitions showcasing new and classic furniture designs on the fourth floor, alongside a dazzling permanent collection of 20th-century classics like Charles and Ray Eames's famous armchair and Le Corbusier's chaise. Meanwhile, a well-edited collection of homeware includes ethereal and romantic Astier de Villatte ceramics and beautiful silk and Egyptian cotton bedlinen. There's also a made-to-measure curtain service. New arrivals in the beauty depatment include Le Labo fragrances, mixed by hand, and fresh and modern scents from Eau d'Italie. Beauty lines include botanical extracts Malin & Goetz, with Zirh for men. With the launch in 2008 of a stand-alone store on Sloane Street, selling trademark leather accessories, scarfs, swimwear, jewellery and men's collections, and the launch of an online shop, Liberty shows no sign of slowing down.
For branch (Liberty of London) see index.

Selfridges

400 Oxford Street, W1A 1AB (0800 123 400/www.selfridges.com). Bond Street or Marble Arch tube. **Open** 9.30am-8pm Mon-Wed, Fri, Sat; 9.30am-9pm Thur; noon-6pm (browsing from 11.30am) Sun. **Credit** AmEx, DC, MC, V.

It's no surprise that Selfridges won the *Time Out* Shopping Awards 2008 for Best Department Store; its concession boutiques, store-wide themed events and collections from the hottest new brands make it a first port-of-call for stylish one-stop shopping, while useful floor plans make navigating the store easy-peasy. The basement is chock-full of hip home accessories and stylish but practical kitchen equipment (think Alessi, Le Creuset and Marco Pierre White for Russell Hobbs), while on the ground floor the Wonder Room – 19,000sq ft of luxury brands – goes from strength to strength. There are plenty of concessions worthy of note: Cycle Surgery on the first floor is a knowledgeable pitstop for two-wheelers, while Beautiful Blooms on the ground floor specialises in cut, scented English and French garden roses. Too many shoppers bypass these delights as they make a beeline for Selfridges's excellent fashion floors. With a winning combination of new talent, hip and edgy labels, smarter high street labels and mid and high end brands, the store stays at the head of the pack. In 2008, recent Kingston graduate and Student of the Year Sophie Hulme joined the hallowed second-floor womenswear halls with her dramatic first collection of luxury streetwear. Also new is Alexis Mabille's beautiful collection of androgynous tailoring inspired by Jane Birkin. Elsewhere, Simon Miller Jeans joins the already phenomenal jeans stable, while the new Halston boutique in Superbrands shows that Selfridges is not neglecting its big labels either. Menswear is also superb, with concepts like the b store pop-up shop continuing to excite customers. There's plenty anew too in the food hall, with great deli produce from London-based Baker & Spice and the appropriately named Australian raw food company Raw. March 2009 sees the 100th anniversary of the store, and while celebration plans are being kept under wraps, you can guarantee that whatever it unveils will be sensational.

Also check out...

Debenhams

334-348 Oxford Street, W1C 1JG (0844 561 6161/www.debenhams.com). Bond Street tube. **Open** 9.30am-8pm Mon, Tue, Sat; 10am-8pm Wed; 9.30am-9pm Thur-Fri; noon-6pm Sun. **Credit** AmEx, DC, MC, V.

Highlights here include the Designers at Debenhams range, plus cheaper capsule collections (like Ben de Lisi in womenswear and John Rocha in homewares). Also good for Fairtrade lines.

Branches: throughout the city.

House of Fraser

318 Oxford Street, W1C 1HF (0870 160 7258/www.houseoffraser.co.uk). Bond Street or Oxford Circus tube. **Open** 10am-8pm Mon-Wed, Sat; 10am-9pm Thur, Fri; 11.30am-6pm Sun. **Credit** AmEx, DC, MC, V.

Mainstream clothing, beauty and home brands. The Linea own label is good quality.
For branches see index.

Marks & Spencer

458 Oxford Street, W1C 1AP (7935 7954/ www.marksandspencer.co.uk). Bond Street or Marble Arch tube. **Open** 9am-9pm Mon-Fri; 8am-8pm Sat; noon-6pm Sun. **Credit** AmEx, DC, MC, V.

Some come for the undies, the food and designer Autograph collection, others for the regularly updated Limited Collection, plus bedlinen and luggage. All good quality and well priced. What would we do without it?

Branches: throughout the city.

Peter Jones

Sloane Square, SW1W 8EL (7730 3434/ www.peterjones.co.uk). Sloane Square tube. **Open** 9.30am-7pm Mon, Tue, Thur-Sat; 9.30am-8pm Wed; 11am-5pm Sun. **Credit** AmEx, MC, V.

John Lewis's posh Chelsea sibling.

Shopping Centres

Bluewater

Greenhithe, Kent DA9 9ST (0870 777 0252/www.bluewater.co.uk). Greenhithe rail. **Open** 10am-9pm Mon-Fri; 9am-9pm Sat; 11am-5pm Sun. **Credit** varies.

A consumer paradise or a modern-day monstrosity? The fact is that people either love Bluewater, with its 330 stores and restaurants, or they hate it. Beyond its austere exterior, it has to be admitted that it's a rather déjà vu experience, with its host of familiar names round every corner – but these doing include some of the great British staples like John Lewis, Marks & Spencer and House of Fraser. Well-known high street chain shops are grouped into three 'malls'; All Saints, Carluccio's, Jaeger, Joseph, Pringle, Reiss, Topshop and Urban Outfitters being some of the highlights. There's also a Molton Brown Day Spa and a bike hire unit. The artificial space is hardly atmospheric, but it does attract some 27 million visitors a year.

Brunswick

Hunter Street, Bernard Street & Marchmont Street, WC1N 1BS (7833 6066/www.brunswick.co.uk). Russell Square or Holborn tube/King's Cross tube/rail/ 59, 68, 91, 968 bus. **Open** varies; see website for info on individual shops. **Credit** varies.

Conceived as an experimental retail and social housing complex in the 1960s, the Brunswick was neglected throughout the 1980s and '90s. In 2006, however, the Grade II-listed centre was given a much-needed £24 million facelift by an architectural partnership that included the building's original designer, Patrick Hodgkinson. The concrete-heavy complex has retained its 1960s character but it is now brighter, whiter and considerably more popular. The retail outlets are largely of the high street chain variety (there's French Connection, Office, Space NK, Holland & Barrett, as well as Chocolat Chocolat), but on a summer evening the central walkway buzzes with shoppers and diners (at Giraffe, Carluccio's, Yo! Sushi and Strada, among other eateries) creating a lively continental vibe. And the crowning glory is still here – the arthouse Renoir cinema.

Cardinal Place

Victoria Street, SW1E 5JH (www.cardinal place.co.uk). Victoria tube/rail/11, 24, 148, 211, 507 bus. **Open** 8am-8pm Mon-Fri; 9am-6pm Sat; 11am-4pm Sun; see website for opening hours of individual shops. **Credit** varies.

This slickly impressive glass and metal building on the corner of Victoria Street and Bressenden Place and opposite Westminster Cathedral opened in 2004, bringing a much needed burst of new life to this rather drab part of Westminster. You'll find Topshop, L'Occitane, Zara and Hawes & Curtis, and there's a good range of eateries. The space also houses the sleekly designed 3,000sq ft SW1 Gallery (www.sw1gallery.co.uk).

Covent Garden Market

Between King Street & Henrietta Street, WC2E 8RF (0870 780 5001/www.covent gardenmarket.co.uk). Covent Garden, Embankment or Temple tube/Charing Cross tube/rail. **Open** 10am-7pm Mon-Sat; 11am-6pm Sun. **Credit** varies.

This London institution is too commercial and crowded to provide a characterful retail experience. The colonnaded 19th-century building houses mainly chain stores and tourist shops, although some independents are still holding their ground, such as Eric Snook's Toyshop and the specialist tobacconist/cigar shop Segar & Snuff Parlour (*see p256*).

Kingly Court

Carnaby Street, opposite Broadwick Street, W1B 5PW (7333 8118/www. carnaby.co.uk). Oxford Circus tube. **Open** 11am-7pm Mon-Sat; noon-6pm Sun. **Credit** varies.

Kingly Court has helped London's Carnaby Street to reclaim its 1960s reputation as the heart of swinging London (well, at least a vein of it, anyway). The three-tiered complex boasts a funky mix of established chains, independents, vintage and gift shops. The café-filled courtyard generates the most bustle, attracting custom to ground-level shops such as Marshmallow Mountain (*see p62*), which has a good selection of vintage shoes, clothes and bags, Lazy Oaf (trendy menswear), Henri Lloyd, Vans and Mnini (vintage-style gifts). There's more vintage clothing on the upper floors with Sam Greenberg, while Stromboli's Circus (formerly Twinkled, *see p60*) goes the whole hog with vintage homewares as well as clothes. Also check out the women's boutique BirdCage (*see p34*). Crafts get a look in on the second floor at Buffy's Beads (*see p205*) and All the Fun of the Fair (knitting supplies; *see p208*). There are also outposts of Triyoga and Walk-In Backrub , and decent beauty treatments (manicures, waxing, facials) can be had at the Beauty Lounge (no.1, 7734 6161,www.thebeauty lounge.co.uk).

Westfield London

Westfield London, W12 (www.westfield. com/london). Shepherd's Bush tube. **Open** 9am-9pm Mon-Fri; 9am-8pm Sat; noon-6pm Sun; see website for details of opening hours of individual shops. **Credit** varies.

Occupying 46 acres, and covering nine different postcodes, Westfield London will take the crown of Europe's largest shopping centre when it opens at the end of October 2008. The impressive site – which held the 1908 Olympics – cost around £1.6 billion to build and will house some 265 shops, including, of course, House of Fraser, Marks & Spencer (the biggest branch in the UK), Debenhams, Waitrose and Next, as well as lesser-known brands such as eco shoe retailer Terra Plana (*see p73*). Popular labels that have never had stand-alone stores in the UK, like Hollister and UGG, will have shops here, and you'll also find luxury fashion houses, with branches of Louis Vuitton, Armani and Mulberry. The 16-screen Cinema de Lux and gym will keep shoppers in search of extra-curricular activities busy, while Michelin-starred chefs Pascal Aussignac and Vincent Labeyrie can soothe away any shopping-induced stress with their gastronomic creations at Croque Gascon, in the centre's Eat Gallery. If they don't manage to tempt your taste buds, then one of the other 50 eateries surely will. Does London need a new mammoth shopping centre? It's a rather rhetorical question.

Whiteleys

151 Queensway, W2 4YN (7229 8844/ www.whiteleys.com). Bayswater or Queensway tube. **Open** 8.30am-midnight daily. **Credit** varies.

Shop until you drop at London's first official department store, considered the height of luxury when it was opened in 1911 (the original Whiteleys department store in Westbourne Grove burned down in 1897). Today's largely mainstream tenants are at odds with the refined Edwardian structure – its marble floors, huge glass atrium and impressive La Scala staircase mean the place sometimes gets used in film shoots (it features in both *Love Actually* and *Closer*). The mainly mid-range high street shops include Zara, Dune, Muji and Borders, and there's also an eight-screen Odeon cinema and a branch of the upmarket bowling chain All Star Lanes.

Also check out…

Bentall Centre

Wood Street, Kingston-upon-Thames, Surrey KT1 1TP (8541 5066/www.the bentallcentre-shopping.com). Kingston-upon-Thames rail. **Open** 9.30am-6pm Mon-Wed, Fri; 9.30am-8pm Thur; 9am-6.30pm Sat; 11am-5pm Sun. **Credit** varies.

Home to over 85 high street chains, this centre, with its glass atrium, links into Bentalls department store on every level.

Brent Cross Shopping Centre

Prince Charles Drive, NW4 3FP (8457 3997/www.brentcross.co.uk). Brent Cross tube then 210 bus/Hendon Central tube then 143, 326, 186 bus. **Open** 10am-8pm Mon-Fri; 9am-7pm Sat; noon-6pm Sun. **Credit** varies.

The UK's first enclosed shopping centre has a number of high-quality chains, including Kate Kuba and an Apple Store.

Canary Wharf Shopping Centres

Canada Place, Cabot Place & Jubilee Place, E14 5AB (7477 1477/www.mycanary wharf.com). Canary Wharf tube/DLR. **Open** 9am-6pm Mon-Wed; 9am-8pm Thur, Fri; 10am-6pm Sat; noon-6pm Sun. **Credit** varies.

A clutch of upper-end high street stores (Church's, Myla, Reiss, Bang and Olufsen et al) fill this centre's three main malls.

Centre Court Shopping Centre

4 Queens Road, SW19 8YA (8944 8323/ www.centrecourt.uk.net). Wimbledon tube/ rail. **Open** 9am-7pm Mon-Wed, Fri, Sat; 9am-8pm Thur; 11am-5pm Sun. **Credit** varies.

On the site of the old town hall, Centre Court comprises mainly high-street brands.

Duke of York Square

King's Road, between Sloane Square & Cheltenham Terrace, SW3 4LY. Sloane Square tube. **Open** varies. **Credit** varies.

This made-over military barracks houses upper-end high street and designer shops (Kate Kuba, Agnès B, Myla, Liz Earle skincare), plus a Patisserie Valerie and slick hairdresser Richard Ward (*see p110*).

Exchange Shopping Centre

High Street, SW15 1TW (8780 1056/www.theexchangesw15.com). East Putney or Putney Bridge tube/Putney rail. **Open** 9am-6pm Mon-Wed, Fri, Sat; 9am-8pm Thur; 11am-5pm Sun. **Credit** varies.

Pleasant local resource, best for necessities, high street clothes and home basics.

Lakeside

West Thurrock, Grays, Essex RM20 2ZP (01708 869933/www.lakeside.uk.com). Chafford Hundred rail. **Open** 10am-10pm Mon-Fri; 9am-9pm Sat; 11am-5pm Sun. **Credit** varies.

Lakeside packs in around 300 retailers; most high street names can be found.

N1 Islington

21 Parkfield Street, N1 0PS (7359 2674/www.n1islington.com). Angel tube. **Open** 10am-7pm Mon-Sat; 11am-5pm Sun. **Credit** varies.

High street fashion names dominate in this unremarkable but practical complex.

Plaza Shopping Centre

120 Oxford Street, W1D 1LT (7637 8811/www.plaza-oxfordst.com). Oxford Circus tube. **Open** 10am-7pm Mon-Wed, Fri, Sat; 10am-8pm Thur; noon-6pm Sun. **Credit** varies.

This unassuming centre has the usual high street fashion favourites as well as the odd independent boutique.

Thomas Neal Centre

29-41 Earlham Street, WC2H 9LD (7240 4741). Covent Garden tube. **Open** 10am-7pm Mon-Sat; noon-6pm Sun. **Credit** varies.

Small complex with a skate/surfwear slant.

Arcades

The capital's royal arcades are a throwback to the gentility of the 19th-century shopping experience, with many of the shops holding royal warrants for decades. By way of contrast, **Portobello Green** gives retail space to emerging designers and quirky one-offs.

Burlington Arcade

Mayfair, W1 (7630 1411/www.burlington-arcade.co.uk). Green Park tube. **Open** 9.30am-5.30am Mon-Fri; 10am-6pm Sat. **Credit** varies.

In 1819, Lord Cavendish commissioned Britain's very first shopping arcade – as history has it to 'stop ruffians from throwing quantities of rubbish' and disrupting the consumer experience. The Burlington is still London's most prestigious and traditional arcade (patrolled by 'Beadles' decked out in top hats and tailcoats). Highlights include collections of classic watches at Vintage Omega, Armour-Winston Ltd and David Duggan; men's and children's brightly patterned beachwear brand Vilebrequin; and Globe-Trotter and Mackintosh (iconic British luggage and rainwear). Jimmy Choo-trained shoe designer Beatrix Ong (*see p70*) also has a very attractive flagship here. New to the arcade in 2008 are Luponde Tea, with an array of organic and Fairtrade leaves from Tanzania, and the membership-only hairdressers Joe's Mayfair.

Piccadilly Arcade

Between Piccadilly & Jermyn Street, SW1 (www.piccadilly-arcade.com). Green Park or Piccadilly Circus tube. **Open** varies. **Credit** varies.

A colonnaded mall that stretches between Piccadilly and Jermyn Street, the Piccadilly Arcade opened in 1909 and houses 16 shops, with plenty of idiosyncratic choices. Pick our of the crop include Bayan Loutre for their high-quality skincare products, Benson & Clegg tailors and shirt-makers, Favourbrook (posh mens- and womenswear and accessories), Jeffery-West (*see p71*; a range of stylish men's footwear and unusual accessories) and the olde worlde chemist's A Maitland & Co.

Portobello Green Arcade

281 Portobello Road, under the Westway, W10 5TZ (www.portobellodesigners.com). Ladbroke Grove or Westbourne Park tube. **Open** varies. **Credit** varies.

From its unassuming – but prime – position sandwiched between Portobello Road and Ladbroke Grove, this arcade showcases a host of unusual mini-shops and emerging designer labels. The most established is Preen (*see p41*), with Poppy Valentine (*see p78*), Relax Garden (a branch of the trendy Shoreditch Japanese design store; *see p36*) also popular. Divette (cheeky lingerie), Baby Ceylon (delicate tops made from saris, vintage scarves), Sasti children's wear (*see p264*) and skincare and bath oil-specialist Zarvis (*see p94*) are also all well worth checking out.

Princes Arcade

38 Jermyn Street, SW1Y. Green Park tube. **Open** 9am-7pm Mon-Sat. **Credit** varies.

It's the smallest and least grand of the Piccadilly arcades but Princes is still well worth a visit for it houses the sumptuous Prestat chocolatier (creator of the chocolate truffle, and famously adored by Roald Dahl and the Queen) and Andy & Tuly, a traditional tailor and waistcoat-maker, known for its decadent window displays.

Royal Arcade

28 Old Bond Street, W1. Green Park tube. **Open** 10am-6pm Mon-Sat. **Credit** varies.

Old Bond Street's Royal Arcade caters for the rich and careless and for the dreamers among us who are happy just to window browse. You'll find the best hot chocolate powder courtesy of Charbonnel et Walker (chocolatier to the Queen) as well as the somewhat Dickensian Ormonde Jayne upmarket perfumery (*see p94*).

Royal Opera Arcade

30 Royal Opera Arcade, between Charles II Street & Pall Mall, SW1 (7839 2440). Piccadilly Circus tube or Charing Cross rail/tube. **Open** varies. **Credit** varies.

The oldest – and most in need of a face-lift – of London's covered arcades (1816-18) was designed by John Nash. Originally, the shops went down one side only, with access to the Opera on the other. Now, there's not much left besides an old-fashioned florist (Vive La Rose), Kiwifruits, selling goods to homesick New Zealanders, Debonair Menswear (a selection of ties, bow-ties, handkerchiefs) and the Stephen Wiltshire Gallery, showcasing urban drawings by the autistic genius.

Brunswick. *See p17.*

Concept Stores

Bermondsey 167

167 Bermondsey Street, SE1 3UW (7407 3137/www.bermondsey167.com). London Bridge tube/rail. **Open** 11am-8pm Tue-Sat; noon-4pm Sun. **Credit** AmEx, MC, V. **Sells** M, W.

Former Burberry designer Michael McGrath has poured his heart into Bermondsey 167, an intriguing, slick boutique that opened in south London in 2007. The shop's own-label (M2cG) shirts (made in Northern Ireland), fine merino wool sweaters (made in Italy), ties and scarves, and swimwear (from £50) are the main draw, but the unique, commission-only furniture, home accessories, jewellery and coconut-leaf lights are intriguing too; all are sourced from artists and artisans around the world, and particularly in South America. There's also a great range of trendy perspex Toy watches, beloved of celebs and fashionistas, and a tiny collection of womenswear items.

Beyond the Valley

2 Newburgh Street, W1F 7RD (7437 7338/ www.beyondthevalley.com). Oxford Circus tube. **Open** 11am-7pm Mon-Sat; 12.30-6pm Sun. **Credit** AmEx, MC, V. **Sells** M, W.

Set up in 2004 by three Central Saint Martins graduates, this concept boutique is a showcase for creations by hot new names. There's a casual-urban feel to the cutting-edge offerings, with own-label T-shirts and sweaters plus choice pieces by Call of the Wild, Yuko Yoshitake and French designer Shoboshobo. Affordable jewellery, by the likes of Zoe & Morgan and Miss Bibi, is another strong point. Next to the jewellery cabinet is a small room that acts as an impromptu event space showcasing the work of new artists and collaborations with design initiatives like Benetton's Fabrica. It's here too that the wallpaper samples are stocked, a fantastic range that includes many designs unique to the store, including a range of hand-finished designs by Louise Body (£58-£95), a new collaborative collection with Cole & Son and Jenny Wilkinson's fun paint-by-numbers range (£44). The homewares selection is small but well worth a look; highlights include flat-packed furniture from new product design collective Farm Designs and ceramics by Bosa for Fabrica.

Couverture & the Garbstore

188 Kensington Park Road, W11 2ES (7229 2178/www.couverture.co.uk/ www.garbstore.com). Ladbroke Grove tube. **Open** 10am-6pm Mon-Sat; (*Dec only*) noon-5pm Sun. **Credit** AmEx, MC, V.

Husband and wife team Emily Dyson and Ian Paley opened their new venture Couverture & the Garbstore in March 2008; Emily's Couverture shop was previously housed in Chelsea, while the Garbstore was a wholesale operation with a cult international fanbase. Couverture, upstairs, stocks clothes, accessories and jewellery, a large selection of choice kids' items, homewares, furniture and the odd vintage knick-knack. Both shops stock exclusive label collaborations, such as the back packs produced with Battle Lake in 2008. Garbstore, on the lower level, is the first stand-alone shop stocking Paley's vintage-inspired label for men; every item is made using old-school techniques from the 1940s and '50s (some of the garments, for instance, feature three-hole buttons that have to be hand-sewed onto the item). We're especially keen on the red and black check officer's shirt (£100) and the selection of denim (from £125). The shop also stocks trainers from New Balance and Terrem, macs from K-Way and T-shirts and sweatshirts from Australia's Rittenhouse, and is the exclusive UK stockist of Japan's Bedwin & the Heartbreakers label, as well as Mountain and Naval Research.

Dover Street Market

17-18 Dover Street, W1S 4LT (7518 0680/ www.doverstreetmarket.com). Green Park tube. **Open** 11am-6pm Mon-Wed; 11am-7pm Thur-Sat. **Credit** AmEx, MC, V. **Sells** M, W.

Comme des Garçons designer Rei Kawakubo's ground-breaking six-storey space combines the edgy energy of London's indoor markets – concrete floors, tills housed in corrugated-iron shacks, Portaloo dressing rooms – with rarefied labels. All 14 of the Comme collections are here, alongside exclusive lines such as Lanvin, Givenchy and Azzedine Alaïa. New for autumn/winter 2008/9 is the collection by NY high society fave Oscar de la Renta and the exclusive range by Stefano Pilati's Yves Saint Laurent Edition 24, a collection of keep-safe classics and limited-edition pieces in special colourways. Dover Street's biannual 'Tachiagari' event sees the store close while designers make changes to their concessions, ensuring the space is constantly evolving. There's a Hussein Chalayan area with exclusive pieces, and an area devoted to designer du jour Henry Holland. New jewellery areas include Tom Binns Couture on the first floor, and Solange Azagury-Partridge on the ground floor. Once you've taken it all in, have a sit-down in the Rose Bakery on the top floor.

Ganesha (eco)

3-4 Gabriel's Wharf, 56 Upper Ground, SE1 9PP (7928 3444/www.ganesha.co.uk). Waterloo tube/rail. **Open** 11.30am-6pm Tue-Fri; noon-6pm Sat, Sun. **Credit** (over £5) AmEx, DC, MC, V.

Jo Lawbuary and Purnendu Roy source goods from local co-operatives and small-scale producers in India, Bangladesh and beyond, to ensure every item in their store is fairly traded. There's a good selection of Fairtrade and recycled homewares (organic bedlinen; embroidered cushions from Bangladesh; lamps and colanders made from recycled tin), as well as wallhangings and clothes. New for 2008 are leaf plates – disposable plates made from sali leaves from forests in India (£4.99). Ganesha also offers a wedding service. Another branch opened recently in Covent Garden.

For branch see index.

Luna & Curious

198 Brick Lane, E1 6SA (7033 4411/ www.lunaandcurious.com). Aldgate East tube/Liverpool Street tube/rail. **Open** noon-6pm Thur-Sun. **Credit** MC, V. **Sells** W, M.

The stock here is put together by a collective of young artisans, from the vintage cocktail dresses sourced, restored and accessorised by

Shop talk
Lulu Kennedy

Lulu Kennedy, director of the Old Truman Brewery's new talent initiative Fashion East, lives in Bethnal Green.

'There's a tiny, exquisite perfumery on Elizabeth Street in Belgravia called **Les Senteurs** (*see p94*). They've got incredibly lovely staff and wonderful rare scents. I discovered my favourite perfume there, Carnal Flower. I love **Cutler & Gross** (*see p115*) for shades shopping – they've got the best sunglasses in London, and the best vintage frames. When I'm an old bag and my eyesight's failing I'll be rocking their chunky prescription frames!

'For art, I love **www.othercriteria.com**, which sells books and T-shirts as well as prints and limited editions by artists like Damien Hirst and Mat Collishaw.

'For fashion I visit the **Shop at Bluebird** (*see p20*), which stocks a few of Fashion East's young designers like Danielle Scutt, Marios Schwab and Richard Nicol, or I might pop into **Topshop** on Oxford Street (*see p46*). Most people think it's hell on a Saturday afternoon, but I love it!

'For music I love **Rough Trade East** (*see p189*), which is right on my doorstep. I'm in there most lunchtimes and I love the in-store gigs they put on. When I heard a whisper about a secret Radiohead gig there [in February 2008] I had palpitations. They only gave out 200 tickets, but of course, word got around and it was so rammed the police had to move on the thousands queuing outside, but the organisers rolled the gig over to 93 Feet East. It was... L-E-G-E-N-D-A-R-Y. Thank you Rough Trade East!'

stylist Susie Coulthard, to the quintessentially English teacups and ceramics of Polly George. Look out for jewellery by Rheanna Lingham who uses ceramics, feathers and old embroidery from military jackets to make necklaces, earrings and headbands. Also adorning the walls are intricate masks by Natasha Law. Prices are surprisingly reasonable for products so lovingly put together; immaculate vintage dresses are around £38, while a tea set can be had for around £200. For a quirky gift idea, the shop's T-Shirt Patisserie (www.tshirtpatisserie.co.uk) takes some beating – choose a plain tee, add the design of your choice and receive it hot off the press in beautiful packaging.

Muji

37-78 Long Acre Road, WC2E 9JT (7379 0820/www.muji.co.uk). Covent Garden. **Open** 10am-8pm Mon-Wed, Fri, 9am-8pm Sat; 10am-9pm Thur; 11.30am-6pm Sun. **Credit** AmEx, DC, MC, V. **Sells** M, W.

The Japanese concept store has long been a favourite of style-conscious Londoners when it comes to practical, affordable and aesthetically pleasing goods for the office, home or wardrobe. Stock runs the gamut from useful gadgets (umbrellas from £12.95; alarm clocks from £5) and stationery (a huge range of pens, notebooks, photo albums et al) to pleasingly plain bedroom furniture, storage units and furnishings. While you can't help feeling that £17.95 for a plastic shoebox is a little steep, the collection of vanity cases, hair grips and travel pots for creams and lotions is unbeatable in terms of usefulness. Bedlinen – in rather masculine and understated colours and styles – is reasonably priced and worth checking out, as are the durable laptop bags. The stylish kitchenware range is of good quality and particularly strong on glasses and tableware, while the clothing range is worth a look if you're not after anything wildly exciting – it's a good bet for simply cut macs, underwear basics and scarves, all in muted colours.
Branches: throughout the city.

Potassium (eco)

2 Seymour Place, W1H 7NA (7723 7800/ www.potassiumstore.co.uk). Marble Arch tube. **Open** 11am-7pm Mon-Sat. **Credit** AmEx, MC, V. **Sells** M, W.

It's stylish, modern and, believe it or not, all of its unique products are ethically sourced and environmentally friendly. There's a collection of clothes that moves with the seasons, accessories, candles, glasswear and even a minibar for sale (£325). Owner Karim Ladak – who earned his stripes working for Habitat and Ralph Lauren – is friendly and informed, making shopping here a memorable experience. Take your pick from wardrobe staples like organic cotton tees (around £12.95) or vegan bags from Mat & Nat made from recycled materials; on our last visit we fell for the pink handbag made from plastic bottles (£105). There are own-brand soy candles (£5.95), made in Canada as part of a return-to-work programme, and Penguin menswear from the US. The Dutch line Kuyichi has proved a big hit because of its fair-trade tag (jeans from £79, a summer bamboo halterneck dress for £125). For spring/summer 2009, look out for classic and sustainable womenswear by Brit designers Julia Smith, Makepiece and Agent ZuZu.

Shop at Bluebird

350 King's Road, SW3 5UU (7351 3873/ www.theshopatbluebird.com). Sloane Square tube. **Open** 10am-7pm Mon-Sat; noon-6pm Sun. **Credit** AmEx, MC, V. **Sells** M, W, C.

In an airy art deco garage on the King's Road you'll find this chic lifestyle boutique. Owners John and Belle Robinson (the people behind womenswear chain Jigsaw) may cite European concept stores such as Colette in Paris as inspiration, but there's none of the froideur associated with such temples to avant-garde design. On display in the 10,000sq ft space is a broad selection of designer clothing, shoes (from the likes of Rupert Sanderson), accessories, books, music (both CDs and vinyl) and the odd piece of furniture. The shop now also boasts a spa offering shoppers the chance to unwind with a variety of treatments. There's also a slew of hard-to-find niche skincare brands, including Ole Henriksen, Kali's Pearl and Kaeline, and organic make-up by Nvey. Fashion is wide-ranging; London-based designers Emma Cook and Richard Nicoll are to be found here, as are New York faves Alexander Wang and Proenza Schouler and Japanese heavyweights Junya Watanabe and Comme des Garçons. Look out for lesser-known labels as well, such as the Chloé-esque Madame à Paris and Isabel Marant. New womenswear for autumn/winter 2008/9 includes Ossie Clark, Chris Benz and store-exclusive Andy & Deb. The selection for men is equally enticing – new for spring/summer 2009 will be Marc Jacobs, Kitsune and PS by Paul Smith. Denim also features heavily, including hip brands 18th Amendment, Superfine and Earnest Sewn.
For branches see index.

Urban Outfitters

200 Oxford Street, W1D 1NU (7907 0815/ www.urbanoutfitters.co.uk). Oxford Circus tube. **Open** 10am-8pm Mon-Wed, Fri, Sat; 10am-9pm Thur; 11.30am-6pm Sun. **Credit** AmEx, MC, V. **Sells** M, W.

Urban Outfitters may hail from America but the London stores have strong traces of Cool Britannia. You'll find homewares, accessories and clothes for every occasion; step into the Oxford Street store and be greeted by an overwhelming mix of casualwear and kitschy pieces for gifts such as picture frames. Menswear is in the basement, with the first and second floors dedicated to more upscale womenswear covering a wide range of styles – from vintage and bohemian to classic. There's a good selection of jeans and denim (by Diesel, Lee, Cheap Monday). Prices climb as you go upstairs so look out for the sales periods when real bargains can be had. New highlights include a range of jewellery by Erickson Beamon and clothing by Luella. Among other favourites are labels like Vanessa Bruno, Athé, Anna Sui, Manoush, Thomas Burberry and Twenty8Twelve.
For branches see index.

Beyond the Valley. *See p19.*

Markets

For antiques markets and arcades, *see p160*.

Central

Borough Market

Southwark Street, SE1 1TL (7407 1002/ www.boroughmarket.org.uk). London Bridge tube/rail. **Open** 11am-5pm Thur; noon-6pm Fri; 9am-4pm Sat.

London's oldest market – dating back to the 13th century – is also the busiest, and the most popular for gourmet goodies. Here, traders satisfy the city's insatiable appetite for artisan cheeses and ham from acorn-fed pigs. If food is your thing, then Borough, with its abundance of beautifully displayed organic fruit and veg, cakes, bread, olive oil, fish, meat and booze, is the place to go. Our favourite stalls include Northfield Farm for rare-breed meat, Furness for fish and game, Elsey & Bent for fruit and veg and Flour Power City Bakery for organic artisan loaves. Leave home hungry to take advantage of the numerous free samples and be prepared for lengthy queues for the famous barbecued chorizo and rocket rolls from the Brindisa stand. Events, such as seasonal tasting days, run throughout the year and opening hours extend in the run-up to Christmas. Building work on a rail viaduct above the market is set to start in late 2008; some stalls will move to different spots.

Cabbages & Frocks

St Marylebone Parish Church Grounds, Marylebone High Street, W1 (7794 1636/ www.cabbagesandfrocks.co.uk). Baker Street tube. **Open** 11am-5pm Sat.

Held in the attractive cobbled yard of St Marylebone parish church, this market was started by food-loving fashionista Angela Cash. The Saturday afternoon crowd is drawn in by fashion retailers as well as mouthwatering grub. Stalls satisfy even the most demanding taste buds, with stuffed organic chicken, Jamaican rum cakes, flavoured olives and shortbreads. Choose to take your goods home or eat them on the spot. There's a range of retro and vintage clothing plus work from independent designers and craftspeople.

Camden Markets

Camden Market *192-200 Camden High Street, junction with Buck Street, NW1 (7267 3417/www.camdenmarkets.org). Camden Town tube.* **Open** 9.30am-5.30pm daily.

Camden Lock Market *Camden Lock Place, off Chalk Farm Road, NW1 (7485 7963/www.camdenlockmarket.com). Camden Town tube.* **Open** 10am-6pm Mon-Wed, Fri-Sun; 10am-7pm Thur.

Electric Ballroom *184 Camden High Street, NW1 (7485 9006/www.electric ballroom.co.uk). Camden Town tube.* **Open** 10am-3pm Fri, Sat.

Stables Market *off Chalk Farm Road, opposite junction with Hartland Road, NW1 (7485 5511/www.stablesmarket.com). Camden Town tube.* **Open** 10am-6pm daily.

Camden's sprawling collection of markets offers a real smörgåsbord of street culture. Wander past loitering goths and scowling punks to join the throng of tourists, locals and random celebs fighting it out at the vast and varied selection of shops and stalls. Saturdays are not for the faint hearted – crowds craving lava lamps, skull rings, fashion, interiors, music and vintage finds swarm about. To avoid the rough and tumble visit on a weekday, though weekends are better for variety and atmosphere. In the more relaxed Stables area the emphasis is on the art and exhibition space. A multi-million-pound redevelopment project will leave the place spic and span by the end of 2008. Currently, there are 46 stalls selling antiques and bric-a-brac at the Horse Tunnel Market here. At Camden Lock you'll find everything from corsets and childrenswear to Japanese tableware and delicious food stalls (Thai, Japanese, Mexican, you name it). Head to Camden (Buck Street) Market for cheapo jeans, T-shirts and accessories. Sadly, Canal Market was destroyed by a fire in February 2008 and remains closed until further notice. Note that Camden Town tube is exit-only at weekends – use Chalk Farm or Mornington Crescent for your return journey.

Portobello Road Market

Portobello Road, W10 & W11 (7727 3649/ www.rbkc.gov.uk/streettrading). Ladbroke Grove or Notting Hill Gate tube. **Open** *General* 8am-6.30pm Mon-Wed, Fri, Sat; 8am-1pm Thur. *Antiques* 8am-6.30pm Fri, Sat.

Portobello is actually several markets rolled into one: antiques start at the Notting Hill Gate end (between Chepstow Villas and Elgin Crescent); further up are food stalls (between Elgin Crescent and Talbot Road); and emerging designer and vintage clothes are found under the Westway flyover and along the walkway to Ladbroke Grove. A visit here is as much about soaking up the vibe as it is about shopping. Saturdays are manically busy so head out early, especially if you're serious about buying antiques. Friday is less hectic and one of the best days for sourcing clothes from up-and-coming fashion designers. Best of all are the fantastic shops lining the surrounding streets; escape the crowds with a browse round Ledbury Road's boutiques (*see p38* **Streetwise**) or head up to Westbourne Park Road for a pint of Guinness at the Cow (no.89).

Spitalfields Market

Commercial Street, between Lamb Street & Brushfield Street, E1 (7247 8556/ www.visitspitalfields.com). Liverpool Street tube/rail. **Open** *General* 10am-4pm Mon-Fri; 9am-5pm Sun. *Antiques* 9am-4pm Thur. *Food* 10am-5pm Wed, Fri, Sun. *Fashion* 10am-4pm Fri. *Records & books* 10am-4pm 1st & 3rd Wed of mth.

Recent redevelopment has given a new lease of life to this East End stalwart. The market now comprises the refurbished 1887 covered market and the adjacent modern shopping precinct. Around the edge of Old Spitalfields Market, enthusiastic stallholders sell grub from just about every corner of the world. Sunday is busiest (withdraw money before you arrive or you face a long, and often fruitless, cash machine queue); browsing options include creations by up-and-coming designers, vintage clobber, crafts, jewellery, books, sheepskin rugs and Brazilian flipflops. There's a new fine food market held three times a week in Crispin Place with over 20 traders, many of whom can also be found at Borough Market. A record market is held twice a month. Note that Spitalfields is not open on Saturdays.

Sunday (Up)Market

91 Brick Lane, The Old Truman Brewery (entrances on Brick Lane & Hanbury Street), E1 6QL (7770 6100/www.sunday upmarket.co.uk). Liverpool Street tube/rail. **Open** 10am-5pm Sun.

Another good reason to head out east on Sundays (and very easily combined with a trip to nearby Spitalfields, or Brick Lane, *see p22*), the Old Truman Brewery's buzzy (Up)Market boasts some 140 stalls toting edgy fashion from young designers (many fresh from fashion college), vintage gear, gifts, art and crafts and well-priced jewellery. Food stalls offer everything from dainty, pastel-coloured cupcakes to rich Ethiopian coffee, Japanese yakisoba, tapas and dim sum (a few of the vendors have lounging areas for customers too). There's a more relaxed vibe here than at Spitalfields and prices tend to be lower.

Also check out…

Berwick Street Market

Berwick Street, Rupert Street, W1. Piccadilly Circus or Tottenham Court Road tube. **Open** 9am-6pm Mon-Sat.

This buzzy street market, in an area better known for its lurid, neon-lit trades, is one of London's oldest, dating back to 1778. It's great for seasonal produce, cheap fabric and indie record shops.

Earlham Street Market

Earlham Street, WC2. Leicester Square tube. **Open** 10am-4pm Mon-Sat.

Cheap street fashion, T-shirts and the Wild Bunch flower stall (*see p173*).

Leadenhall Market

Whittington Avenue, off Gracechurch Street, EC3 (www.leadenhallmarket.co.uk). Bank tube/DLR. **Open** 7am-4pm Mon-Fri.

This vaulted-roofed Victorian structure built by Horace Jones (who also built the market at Smithfield) now houses a range of upmarket shops and restaurants. September's gastronomic Leadenhall Show is also worth investigating.

Leather Lane

Leather Lane, between Greville Street & Clerkenwell Road, EC4 (www.leatherlane market.co.uk). Chancery Lane tube. **Open** 10am-2.30pm Mon-Fri.

Lunchtime market selling cut-price clothing (skirts from a fiver) and household items (cheap towels and the like), plus flowers, fruit and veg.

Lower Marsh Market

Lower Marsh, from Westminster Bridge Road to Baylis Road, SE1 (7926 2530/ www.lower-marsh.co.uk). Waterloo tube/ rail. **Open** 8am-6pm Mon-Thur, Sat; 8am-7pm Fri.

A street market since Victorian times, there's some quality veg, women's clothes, decent jewellery and vintage shops.

Petticoat Lane Market

Middlesex Street, Goulston Street, New Goulston Street, Toynbee Street, Wentworth Street, Bell Lane, Cobb Street, Leyden Street, Strype Street, E1 (7364 1717/www.towerhamlets.gov.uk). Aldgate East tube/ Liverpool Street tube/rail. Open 8am-4pm Mon-Fri (Goulston Street, Toynbee Street & Wentworth Street only); 9am-2pm Sun.
Mainly tat (cheap clothes, leather, luggage, toys and electronic goods), but good for the odd one-off bargain.

South Bank Book Market

Riverside Walk, outside BFI Southbank, under Waterloo Bridge, SE1. Waterloo tube/rail. **Open** noon-7pm daily.
London's very own *bouquinistes*: endless second-hand books, maps and old prints on a collection of stalls on the South Bank.

Local

Brick Lane Market

Brick Lane (north of railway bridge), Cygnet Street, Sclater Street, E1; Bacon Street, Cheshire Street, E2 (7364 1717). Aldgate East tube. **Open** 8am-2pm Sun.
Tools, household goods and fruit and veg sold by the bowl are among the offerings at this busy East End market. Also worth a look are the fascinating makeshift stalls set up on blankets at the side of the road – dodgy old videos, broken dolls, CD players and dubiously acquired bicycles abound.

Broadway Market

Broadway Market, E8 4PH (07709 311869/www.broadwaymarket.co.uk). London Fields rail/236, 394 bus. **Open** 8.30am-4.30pm Sat.
Since its 2004 comeback, Broadway Market has gone from strength to strength, and is now a destination for fashionably attired food-lovers from Hackney and beyond. Spend a Saturday here and you'll find well-priced fresh fruit and veg, artisan cheeses, rare-breed meat, luscious cakes and top-notch snacking options in the form of an array of hot food stalls (Ghanaian food from Spinach & Agushi is worth making a beeline for). It also has stalls selling vintage and new designer threads, old Vogue patterns, flowers and hand-knits. The shops, restaurants and pubs that line the street are good for a browse too – in particular **Black Truffle** (*see p70*), **Fabrications** (*see p208*) and the **Broadway Bookshop** (*see p177*).

Columbia Road Market

Columbia Road, E2 (7364 1717). Bethnal Green tube, Liverpool Street tube/rail, then 26, 48 bus or Old Street tube/rail, then 55, 243 bus. **Open** 8am-2pm Sun.
One of London's most visually appealing markets, Columbia Road overflows with bucket fulls of beautiful flowers. There are bulbs, herbs, shrubs and bedding plants too. Alongside the market you'll find a host of independent galleries and shops selling pottery, perfume and the like. Turn up as things start to wind down at around 2pm for the best bargains, or as early as humanly possible if you want to guarantee yourself the pick of the crop. *See also p167 and p174* **Streetwise**.

Borough Market. *See p21.*

Greenwich Market

Off College Approach, SE10 (weekdays 7515 7153/weekends 8293 3110/www.greenwichmarket.net). Greenwich rail/Cutty Sark DLR. **Open** *Antiques & collectibles* 10am-5.30pm Mon-Tue, Thur-Sun; 11am-6pm Wed. *Village Market* Stockwell Street, 8am-5pm Sat, Sun. *Arts & crafts* 9.30am-5.30pm Sat, Sun.
Selling bric-a-brac, second-hand clothes, ethnic ornaments, CDs, crafts and jewellery galore at the weekends, Greenwich takes a different tack on Thursdays and Fridays with an excellent antiques and collectables market. Thursday is best for unearthing unusual finds and offers a selection of stalls dealing in antique jewellery, vintage clothes, old books, music and collectibles – the Calneva Vintage stall with its cool 1950s and '60s homewares, ceramics, lamps, handbags and compacts is just one such example.

Shepherd's Bush Market

East side of railway viaduct, between Uxbridge Road & Goldhawk Road, W12. Goldhawk Road or Shepherd's Bush tube. **Open** 8.30am-6pm Tue, Wed, Fri, Sat; 8.30am-1pm Thur.
There's a fantastic range of ethnic foodstuffs (Indian, Caribbean, African and Polish) at this gritty, multicultural market. Stalls selling fragrant spices, yams, coconuts, cassava, okra, falafel, mangoes and some of the freshest fish in the capital line the strip between Uxbridge and Goldhawk Roads. You'll also see vivid print fabrics, goatskin rugs, saris, home furnishings, electronic equipment, CDs and DVDs. Visit the nearby branch of TRAID (154 Uxbridge Road, 8811 2400) for its 'remade' items: second-hand goods transformed into fashionable gear.

Also check out...

Brixton Market

Electric Avenue, Pope's Road, Brixton Station Road, SW9 (7926 2530). Brixton tube/rail. **Open** 10am-6pm Mon, Tue; 10am-4pm Wed; 10am-6pm Thur, Sat.
Outdoor market and several arcades of stalls selling exotic fruit and veg, halal meats, fish, clothes, fabrics, household goods, reggae music, crafts and wigs.

Chapel Market

Chapel Street, N1. Angel tube. **Open** 9am-6pm Tue-Sat; 8.30am-4pm Sun.
Decent fruit and veg, fish, household goods, clothes, cheap CD and card stalls line this unpretentious street market.

Northcote Road Market

Northcote Road, SW11. Clapham Junction rail/319 bus. **Open** 10am-6pm Mon-Sat. *Antiques* 10am-6pm Mon-Sat; noon-5pm Sun.
Decent fruit and veg, flowers, ceramics, vintage clothes, plus the Antiques Market (no.155A, 7228 6850) and some excellent independent shops.

Queen's Market

Off the junction of Green Street & Queen's Road, E13. Upton Park tube. **Open** 9am-6pm Tue-Sat.
An extensive range of veg, fish, ethnic fabrics, CDs, homewares, and hair products.

Ridley Road Market

Ridley Road, off Kingsland High Street, E8. Dalston Kingsland rail/30, 38, 56, 67, 76, 149, 236, 242, 243, 277 bus. **Open** 9am-5pm Mon-Fri; 9am-5.30pm Sat.
Everything from domestic and exotic fruit

and veg, fish and meat to cheap clothes, household goods, toys, bric-a-brac and fabrics from Africa and India.

Roman Road Market

Roman Road, between Parnell Road & St Stephen's Road, E3 (7364 1717). Bow Road or Mile End tube/Bethnal Green tube/rail/8, S2 bus. **Open** 8am-6pm Tue, Thur, Sat.
Cheap gear rules here, from underwear to shoes. You'll also find homewares (towels, bedlinen) and lots of fruit and veg.

Southall Market

The Cattle Market, High Street, opposite North Road, Southall, Middx UB1 (8943 0979). Southall rail. **Open** *General* 9am-5pm Sat. *Furniture* 6am-noon Fri.
A cross between a traditional market and a visit to India: fresh produce, spices and sari fabrics. The poultry and horse markets have now closed, after 300 years of trade.

Walthamstow Market

Walthamstow High Street, E17 (8496 2880). Walthamstow Central tube/rail.
Open 8am-5pm Tue-Sat.
This is the longest market in Europe, with loads of fruit and veg stalls, a good selection of Asian and Caribbean products, fabric, flowers and more.

Whitecross Street Food Market

Whitecross Weekly Food Market, Whitecross Street, EC1 (7378 0422/www.whitecross streetmarket.co.uk). Old Street tube/rail.
Open 11am-5pm Thur, Fri.
Whitecross Street Market started in 2007 as a monthly operation, but fast turned into a weekly event. The workaholics of Clerkenwell and Hoxton descend upon this energetic collection of food stalls every Thursday and Friday for a slap-up lunch on the go. Luardo's, purveyor of Latin American street food, is a good bet, with its fluffy burritos; another hit with regulars is Mario and Carol's Italian food stall, where an order of classic Roman-style grub comes with friendly banter.

Best of the rest

North

Archway Market *Holloway Road and St John's Grove, N19.* **Open** noon-6pm Thur; 10am-5pm Sat.

Chalton Street Market *Chalton Street, NW1.* **Open** 9am-5pm Fri.

Church Street Market *Church Street, NW8.* **Open** 8am-6pm Mon-Sat.

Inverness Street Market *Inverness Street, NW1.* **Open** 9am-5pm daily.

Nag's Head Market *Seven Sisters Road (junction with Enkel Street), N7.* **Open** *General* 6am-5pm Mon, Tue, Thur. *Second-hand & antiques* 6am-3.30pm Wed. *New goods* 6am-5pm Fri; 6am-5.30pm Sat. *Flea Market* 7am-2pm Sun.

Plender Street Market *Plender Street, NW1.* **Open** 9am-5pm Mon-Sat.

East

Bethnal Green Road Market *Bethnal Green Road, E2.* **Open** 8am-6pm Mon-Sat.

Chrisp Street Market *Chrisp Street, E14.* **Open** 8am-6pm Mon-Sat.

Hoxton Street Market *Hoxton Street, N1.* **Open** 9am-5pm Mon-Sat.

Roman Road Square Market *Roman Road Square, E2.* **Open** 8am-6pm Mon-Sat.

Watney Street Market *Watney Street, E1.* **Open** 8.30am-6pm Mon-Sat.

Well Street Market *Well Street (Morning Lane to Valentine Road), E9.* **Open** 8.30am-5pm Mon-Sat.

Whitechapel Market *Whitechapel Road (Vallance Road to Cambridge Heath Road), E1.* **Open** 8am-6pm Mon-Sat.

South-east

Catford Market *Catford Broadway, SE6.* **Open** 9am-4pm Mon, Thur-Sat.

Choumert Road Market *Choumert Road, SE15.* **Open** 8am-5pm Mon-Sat.

Deptford Market *Douglas Way & Deptford High Street, SE8.* **Open** 9am-5pm Wed, Fri, Sat.

East Street Market *East Street, SE17.* **Open** 8am-5pm Tue-Fri; 8am-6.30pm Sat; 8am-2pm Sun.

Lewisham Market *Lewisham High Street, SE14.* **Open** 9am-5.30pm Mon-Sat; 9am-5pm Sun.

North Cross Road Market *North Cross Road, SE22.* **Open** 8am-5pm Mon-Sat.

Peckham Square Market *Peckham Square, SE15.* **Open** 8am-2pm Sun.

Woolwich Market *Beresford Square, SE18.* **Open** 9am-4pm Mon-Wed; 9am-1pm Thur; 9am-4.30pm Fri, Sat.

South

Broadway Market & Tooting Market *Upper Tooting Road, SW17.* **Open** 9am-5.30pm Mon, Tue, Thur; 9am-6pm Fri, Sat; 9am-3pm Wed.

Hildreth Street Market *Hildreth Street, SW12.* **Open** 8am-6pm Mon-Sat.

Nine Elms Market *New Covent Garden Market, Nine Elms Lane, SW8.* **Open** 8am-2pm Sun.

Partridges Food Market *Duke of York Square, SW3 4LY (www.partridges.co.uk/foodmarket). Sloane Square or South Kensington tube.* **Open** 10am-4pm Sat .

Wimbledon Stadium Market *Plough Lane, SW17.* **Open** 9am-2pm Sun.

South-west

North End Road Market *North End Road (Walham Grove to Lillie Road), SW6.* **Open** 9am-6pm Mon-Sat.

North-west

Kilburn Square Market *off Kilburn High Road, NW6.* **Open** 9am-5.30pm Mon-Sat; 11am-5pm Sun. (Note: closed for refurbishment from Jan 2008; expected to reopen in Apr 2008.)

Queen's Crescent Market *Queen's Crescent (Grafton Road to Malden Road), NW5.* **Open** 9am-5pm Thur, Sat.

Wembley Market *Stadium Car Park, Wembley, Middx HA9.* **Open** 9am-4pm Sun.

Willesden Market *Church Road, NW10.* **Open** 9am-5.30pm Wed, Sat.

Farmers' markets

For more information about farmers' markets in the capital (except where an alternative number is listed), contact **London Farmers' Markets** (7833 0338, www.lfm.org.uk).

Acton *Corner of Kings Street & Acton High Street, W3. Acton Town or Ealing Common tube.* **Open** 9am-1pm Sat.

Alexandra Palace *Entrance at Hornsey Gate, off Muswell Hill; or Campsbourne School, Nightingale Lane, off Priory Street, N8. Wood Green tube the W3 bus/Alexandra Palace rail.* **Open** 10am-3pm Sun.

Blackheath *Blackheath railway station car park, SE3. Blackheath rail/54, 89, 108, 202, 380 bus.* **Open** 10am-2pm Sun.

Clapham *Bonneville Primary School, Bonneville Gardens, off Abbeville Road, SW4. Clapham South tube.* **Open** 10am-2pm Sun.

Ealing *Leeland Road, W13. Ealing Broadway tube/rail then 83, 207, 607, 208, E8 bus/West Ealing rail.* **Open** 9am-1pm Sat.

Fulham *Farm Lane, by St John's Church, off North End Road, SW6. Fulham Broadway tube.* **Open** 10am-2pm Sun.

Islington *William Tyndale School, behind Town Hall, Upper Street, N1. Angel tube/Highbury & Islington tube/rail/38, 73, 56 bus.* **Open** 10am-2pm Sun.

Marylebone *Cramer Street car park, corner of Moxton Street, off Marylebone High Street, W1. Baker Street or Bond Street tube.* **Open** 10am-2pm Sun.

Notting Hill *Car park, behind Waterstone's, access via Kensington Place, W8. Notting Hill Gate tube/12, 27, 28, 52, 70, 94, 328 bus.* **Open** 9am-1pm Sat.

Oval *St Mark's Church, SE11 4PW (8297 5590). Oval tube.* **Open** 10am-3pm Sat.

Peckham *Peckham Square, Peckham High Street, SE15. Peckham Rye or Queens Road rail/12, 36, 171, 375 bus.* **Open** 9am-1pm Sun.

Pimlico Road *Orange Square, corner of Pimlico Road & Ebury Street, SW1. Sloane Square tube/11, 211, 239 bus.* **Open** 9am-1pm Sat.

Queens Park *Salusbury Primary School, Salusbury Road, NW6. Queens Park or Brondesbury Park tube.* **Open** 10am-2pm Sun.

Richmond *Heron Square, off Hill Street, Richmond, Surrey TW9 (8878 5132). Richmond tube/rail.* **Open** 11am-3pm Sat.

South Kensington *Bute Street, SW7 3EX (7833 0338/www.lfm.org.uk). South Kensington tube.* **Open** 9am-1pm Sat.

Stoke Newington *William Patten School, Stoke Newington Church Street, N16 (7502 7588/www.growingcommunities.org). Stoke Newington rail/73, 149, 243, 393, 726 bus.* **Open** 10am-2.30pm Sat.

Swiss Cottage *College Crescent, NW3.* **Open** 10am-4pm Wed.

Twickenham *Car park, Holly Road, Twickenham, Middx TW1. Twickenham rail.* **Open** 10am-4pm Sat.

Wimbledon *Wimbledon Park Primary School, Havana Road, SW19. Wimbledon Park tube/156 bus.* **Open** 9am-1pm Sat.

Fashion

Fashion

Alexander Boyd. *See p54.*

Hurwundeki. *See p30.*

Anna Lou of London (and right top and bottom). *See p82.*

Georgina Goodman. *See p70.*

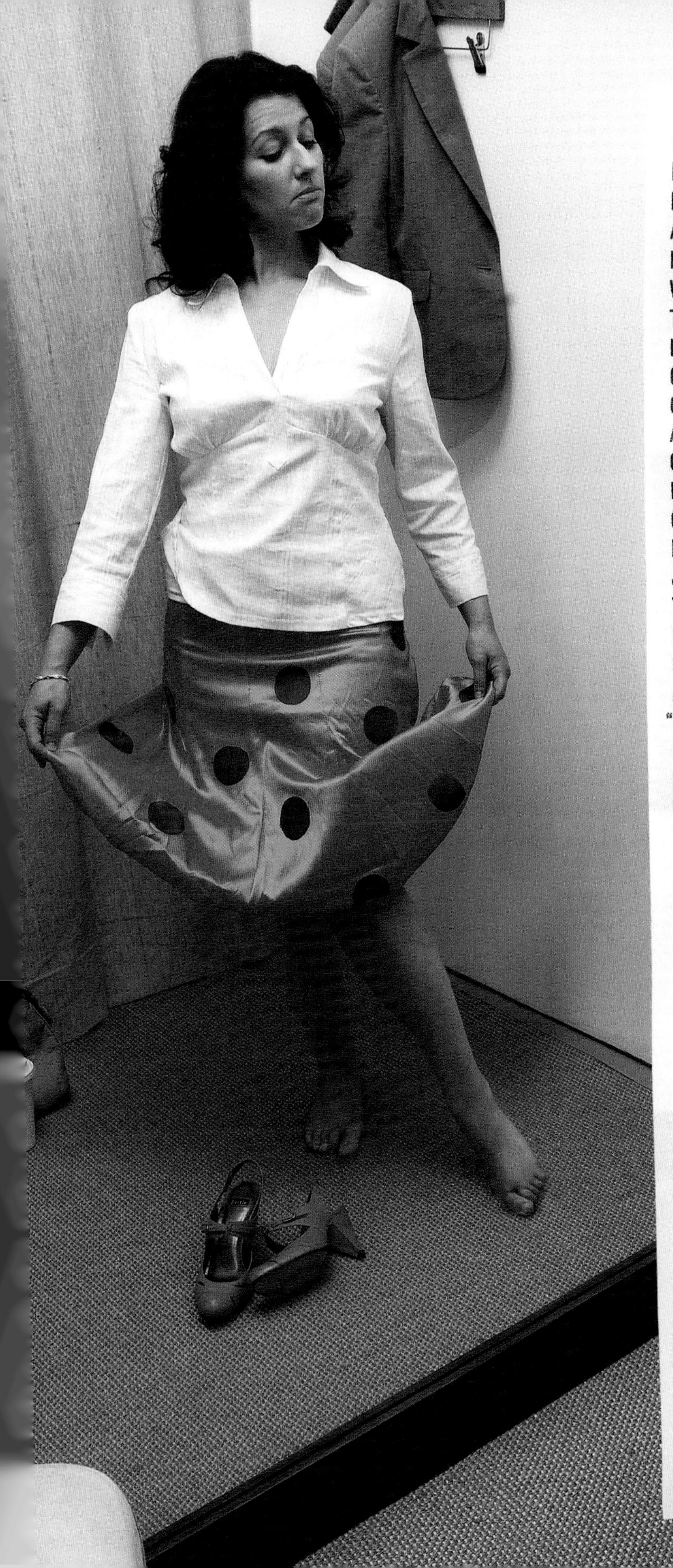
POLKADOT SKIRT, BOUGHT THE MORNING AFTER THE STAFF PARTY WHEN I WASN'T FEELING TOO WITH IT. I'D ONLY POPPED OUT TO GET A COFFEE WHEN ALL THE MEMORIES OF THE NIGHT BEFORE CAME FLOODING BACK - SQUEEKY JOANNE WITH THAT NEW BOY IN FINANCE. SHE GETS ALL THE ATTENTION. "IT'S THOSE OUTRAGEOUS OUTFITS," I SAID TO MYSELF. THE NEXT THING I KNEW, I WAS IN A DRESSING ROOM TRYING ON THIS SKIRT.
WELL, SOMEONE'S GOTTA GIVE JOANNE A RUN FOR HER MONEY: £95
KEEPING THE RECEIPT: PRICELESS

MasterCard
There are some things money can't buy.
For everything else there's MasterCard.

Boutiques & Emerging Designer

Online boutique **nina&lola** (www.ninaandlola.com) stocks offbeat and hard-to-find independent designers; it opened a temporary pop-up shop in Hoxton in summer 2008.

Men

A Butcher of Distinction

11 Dray Walk, Old Truman Brewery, E1 6QL (7770 6111). Liverpool Street tube/rail. **Open** 10am-7pm daily. **Credit** MC, V. **Sells** M.

A cornerstone of the trendy Brick Lane scene, Butcher of Distinction has done much to define its look, which remains determinedly casual – how better to telegraph the fact that, if you work at all, you work in a creative industry? The house style is laid-back and fashion-forward, so think sagging, narrowish jeans in quality denim from Sugar Cane or Studio D'Artisan, bubble jackets from Canada Goose, casual shirts from Steve Alan and work boots from Redwing or brogues from Tricker's.

Albam

23 Beak Street, W1F 9RS (3157 7000/ www.albamclothing.com). Oxford Circus tube. **Open** noon-7pm Mon-Sat; noon-5pm Sun. **Credit** AmEx, DC, MC, V. **Sells** M.

Late in 2007, Alastair Rae and James Shaw's excellent menswear line, Albam, jumped off the internet and into its first store on Beak Street. The label's refined yet rather manly aesthetic soon won it a loyal fanbase, dressing well-heeled gents, fashion editors and regular guys who appreciate no-nonsense style. With a focus on classic, high-quality design with a subtle retro edge (Steve McQueen has been cited as inspiration), the store is the label's unofficial clubhouse: airy and minimal, but unselfconsciously warm and friendly. Bestsellers like the Fisherman's Cagoule (£160) and Classic T-shirt (£25; *see also p51* **Classic clobber**) periodically sell out, having popped up in style mags and Saturday supplements the week before.

Designworks

42-44 Broadwick Street, W1F 7AE (7434 1968/www.designworkslondon.co.uk). Oxford Circus tube. **Open** 10.30am-7pm Mon-Fri; noon-7pm Sat. **Credit** AmEx, MC, V. **Sells** M.

This Anglo-Japanese shop is undeniably cool, but also friendly and approachable – not something London shoppers can take for granted. Nestling alongside Designwork's own-label clothes is a good selection of little-known brands including Swiss jeans by Kohzo Denim, bags and accessories by Chris & Tibor, crazy leather shoes by Alfredo Bannister, slim-fit leather jackets by Santa Croce and trilby hats by Misaharada Millinery. The look is strong, but comfortable and wearable.

Q by Santos & Mowen

10 Earlham Street, WC2H 9LN (7836 4365/www.qbysantosandmowen.com). Covent Garden or Leicester Square tube. **Open** 11am-7pm Mon-Sat; noon-6pm Sun. **Credit** AmEx, MC, V. **Sells** M.

This was the first shop in London to stock the cult Canadian label DSquared and remains a major stockist of the brand, which is never less than shamelessly figure-hugging. If your body is buff enough for DSquared you might also like Italian label Memine's body-conscious version of street fashion for men – all tight shorts and shirts. Other labels on offer range from high fashion (refined Italian label Alessandro Dell'Aqua) to grungey rock chic (American jeans and Tees label Affliction).

Also check out...

Duffer of St George

34 Shorts Gardens, WC2H 9PX (7836 3722/www.thedufferofstgeorge.com). Covent Garden tube. **Open** 10.30am-7pm Mon-Fri; 10.30am-6.30pm Sat; 1-5pm Sun. **Credit** AmEx, MC, V. **Sells** M.

Casual menswear institution that's slowly waning, but still relevant.

Palmer

771 Fulham Road, SW6 5HA (7384 2044). Parsons Green tube. **Open** 10am-6pm Mon-Sat; noon-5pm Sun. **Credit** AmEx, MC, V. **Sells** M.

Grown-up menswear, largely from Italy but edited to offer customers a distinctly London look. Sports jackets are a speciality.

For branch see index.

Twentyone the Green

21 The Green, N21 3NL (8882 4298/ www.twentyonethegreen.co.uk). Winchmore Hill rail. **Open** 10am-6.30pm Mon-Sat; 11am-1.30pm Sun. **Credit** AmEx, MC, V. **Sells** M.

A local shop for guys stocking a wide range of gear that takes in Nigel Hall, Jeffery-West shoes and PRPS jeans (from £325).

Zee & Co

454-456 Roman Road, E3 5LU (8983 3383/ www.zeeandco.co.uk). Mile End tube/ Bethnal Green tube/rail. **Open** 9.30am-6pm Mon-Sat. **Credit** MC, V. **Sells** M.

A funky mix of both street and relatively exclusive designer labels.

For branches see index.

Women

Aimé

32 Ledbury Road, W11 2AB (7221 7070/ www.aimelondon.com). Notting Hill Gate tube. **Open** 10.30am-7pm Mon-Sat. **Credit** AmEx, MC, V. **Sells** W.

Shoppers searching for a touch of Gallic chic on London's streets should make Aimé – the offspring of French-Cambodian sisters Val and Vanda Heng-Vong – their first port-of-call. Inside you'll find the crème de la crème of French designers, with labels like APC, Isabel Marant and Forte Forte. Look out for the first APC Madras diffusion line for autumn/winter 2008/9 in funky colours and prints, and a choice mix of patent Repetto ballet pumps. Check out also Faliero's range of tasteful scarves. Biker jackets and boots are set to be big news again as are all items inspired by the 1970s Jane Birkin look. Bath products and seductive home accessories, including Aimé's range of scented candles, are equally attractive. Next door, Petit Aimé stocks an adorable range of clothes for babies and children.

For branch (Petit Aimé) see index.

Austique

330 King's Road, SW3 5UR (7376 4555/ www.austique.co.uk). Sloane Square tube then 11, 22 bus. **Open** 11am-7pm Mon-Sat; noon-5pm Sun. **Credit** AmEx, MC, V. **Sells** W, C.

Opened by sisters Katie Cancin and Lindy Lopes, Austique displays a super-feminine collection of clothes, lingerie and accessories in a light, two-floor space. Unsurprisingly, given the name, there's a strong Antipodean influence, with designs from the likes of Thurley and Camilla & Marc, along with collections from Alice McCall and gorgeous dresses by Alice & Olivia. The shop also stocks its own label, Austique, offering an assortment of silk dresses, pyjamas and pretty ballet shoes. There's a lovely selection of jewellery from the likes of Alex Monroe, Zara Simon and You & Me, all in keeping with the girly feel of the clothes. Also worth a look are the shoes by Olivia Morris. Upstairs you'll find everything for the boudoir including a great range of knickers, negligees and camisoles.

Cochinechine

74 Heath Street, NW3 1DN (7435 9377/ www.cochinechine.com). Hampstead tube. **Open** 10am-6pm Mon-Sat; noon-6pm Sun. **Credit** AmEx, MC, V. **Sells** W.

Eftychia Georgilis's airy boutique brings an interesting selection of designer labels to Hampstead. Spread over two floors are hip, wearable clothes from boutique favourites 3.1 Phillip Lim, Vanessa Bruno and McQ, as well as lesser known but equally interesting names from around the world. New for autumn/winter 2008/9 is a Turkish knitwear label called Eternal Child, specialising in gorgeous shrugs and skirts from £100, and Shipley and Halmos who have perfected a type of geek chic with their tailored suits, dresses and cute shirts. Accessories include vibrant bags and clutches by Lelya (from £300) and Philip Roucou, both also new for autumn/winter 2008/9. The shop also stocks an extensive range of Comme des Garçons perfumes, candles and wallets.

Coco Ribbon

21 Kensington Park Road, W11 2EU (7229 4904/www.cocoribbon.com). Notting Hill Gate tube. **Open** 10.30am-6.30pm Mon-Fri; 10am-6pm Sat; 12.30-5.30pm Sun. **Credit** AmEx, MC, V. **Sells** W.

The boudoir of the girl who has it all, Coco Ribbon is a store for the girly girl who loves to pick out delicate trinkets in an intimate and romantic setting; think antique-style bedroom furniture lined with pretty lingerie, cashmere knits, princess slippers and scented candles. Founders Alison Chow and Sophie Oliver draw on their world travels and personal passions to bring us bejewelled kaftans, Grecian-style dresses and baby-doll tops among other pieces. Other lines on offer

Hub. *See p35.*

include jeans by J Brand, chi-chi designs by Jasmine di Milo and shoes by Repetto and Pedro Garcia. The shop's Panty Postman service delivers knickers to your door every three months, from £58 a year for two pairs (www.pantypostman.co.uk). It continues to expand its own label across the country, with lines in Harvey Nichols and other shops.

Crimson

7 Porchester Place, W2 2BS (7706 4146/ www.crimsonclothes.com). Marble Arch tube. **Open** 10.30am-6pm Mon-Sat. **Credit** AmEx, MC, V. **Sells** W.

Not far from the hubbub of Edgware Road, this flamboyant nugget of a shop is a pleasant surprise amid the backstreets of Bayswater. Opened in 2006 by the ebullient American Anmarie McDonald, it's packed with an offbeat mix of US labels you don't normally find in London. Clothes include New Orleans-based Trashy Diva's fitted silk print blouses (from £65) and 1940s-inspired cocktail frocks (from £85), as well as figure-hugging jersey dresses from Fee Gee, bright hoodies and T-shirts by My Little Big Eyes, and flowing tops fashioned from vintage saris by Ginger Lamb. Sarah Donegan's bags crafted from sumptuous recycled textiles are particularly popular and complete the eclectic mix.

The Cross

141 Portland Road, W11 4LR (7727 6760/ www.thecrossshop.co.uk). Holland Park tube. **Open** 11am-6pm Mon-Wed, Fri; 11am-7pm Thur; 11am-6pm Sat. **Credit** AmEx, MC, V. **Sells** W, C.

With its consistently strong fashion and accessories, the Cross remains one of the capital's most successful boutiques. A selection of kids' clothes (mostly by Quincy) and toys on the ground floor reflects the shop's main customer base – west London yummy (and often very starry) mummies. Downstairs, the eclectic compilation of designers takes in Easton Pearson, easy-to-wear separates and jersey dresses by Humanoid, oriental-influenced Dosa from LA, and designs in cashmere and silk by Queene & Belle, previous head designers at Pringle of Scotland. For eveningwear look to British designer Jenny Dyer, while jewellery is catered for by Pippa Small and Claire van Holthe. Sister shop Cross the Road at no.139 stocks This Works toiletries, stripy wool and embroidered cushions, quilts and statement floor lights.

Diverse

294 Upper Street, N1 2TU (7359 8877/ www.diverseclothing.com). Angel tube. **Open** 10.30am-6.30pm Mon-Sat; noon-5.30pm Sun. **Credit** AmEx, DC, MC, V. **Sells** W.

Islington stalwart Diverse does a fine job of keeping N1's style queens in fashion-forward mode. Despite the cool clobber, chic layout and striking window displays, this is the sort of place where you can rock up in jeans and scuzzy Converse and not feel uncomfortable trying on next season's See by Chloé. And while you're there, you might as well give that Marc by Marc Jacobs dress a try, and maybe a little something by Vanessa Bruno, and those Repetto ballet slippers are looking good, come to think of it. You get the picture. This is a well-edited collection of incredibly desirable garments, plus some original jewellery, accessories and shoes thrown in for good measure. There's plenty for the more feminine or classic dresser too, such as Diana von Furstenberg, tasteful Parisian label Isabel Marant, and Superfine jeans (from £145) and basics from C&C California. For autumn/winter 2008/9 Humanoid is well represented and there's gorgeous cashmere from CASH CA. Down the road at no.286, the menswear outpost stocks hip, laid-back lines such as APC, Marc by Marc Jacobs, Trovata and Unconditional.

For branch (menswear) see index.

Dragana Perisic

30 Cheshire Street, E2 6EH (7739 4484/ www.draganaperisic.com). Aldgate East tube/Liverpool Street tube/rail. **Open** 11am-6pm Wed-Sun; also by appointment. **Credit** MC, V. **Sells** W.

Dragana Perisic is the boutiquc of the Serbian designer of the same exotic name. The clothes (priced from £60 for a T-shirt to £450 for a coat) are mainly handmade and sold in short runs. Perisic favours natural fabrics – raw silks, wools and cottons in a subtle palette of creams, golds and greens – and likes to throw in surprise details, such as moveable pockets and detachable detailing; some garments are reversible. Jewellery, also designed by Perisic, complements the clothes and includes unusual pieces such as the fabric rosettes called 'Sussex Puffs' that Perisic became 'obsessed with'. Other accessories are from a small selection of hand-picked labels – new in are shoes by Esska, and fantastic handbags and purses made from leather offcuts by Dialogue (£18-£50).

Equa (eco)

28 Camden Passage, N1 8ED (7359 0955/ www.equaclothing.com). Angel tube. **Open** 10am-6.30pm Mon-Wed, Sat; 10am-7pm Thur; noon-5pm Sun. **Credit** AmEx, MC, V. **Sells** W.

Since it opened in 2005, this airy and calm boutique has become an Islington favourite thanks to its Fairtrade and organic fashion collections. It recently had a makeover and the rails are packed with feel-good clothing brands; old-timers Annie Greenabelle, Edun and Enamore (check out the beautiful lingerie sets, for £90), Veja Volley trainers, Debbi Little parachute dresses (£240), Terra Plana shoes, Mat & Nat vegan wallets and bags and organic cotton jeans from LA-based brand Del Forte (£135) all feature. Newer lines include lingerie from Eco-Boudoir (from around £40) and Ila, the new 100% organic line of beauty products.

Children's clothes, toiletries (from Timothy Han) and jewellery are also sold.

Feathers

42 Hans Crescent, SW1 0LZ (7589 5802). Knightsbridge tube. **Open** 10am-7pm Mon-Sat; noon-6pm Sun. **Credit** AmEx, MC, V. **Sells** W.

A browser's paradise, the joy of Feathers is the fact that lesser-known lines, like British label Brogden (specialising in parkas, jumpers and jackets) or Maria Rudman, sit alongside big-league pieces by Givenchy, Alexander McQueen and Rick Owens. Exclusive for autumn/winter 2008/9 are labels as diverse as eccentric duo Basso & Brooke, Derercuny, Antonio Marras and pieces by Peter Pilotto and Toga. There's a tendency towards unusual fabrics, and owner Suzanne Burstein's specially commissioned coats and throws in vintage Indian printed cotton are popular with the well-heeled boho clientele. Accessories are also very strong – See by Chloé bags, Linda Farrow vintage sunglasses and hats by Japanese label CA4LA. Much of the stock is £250-plus, but there are less expensive lines such as Velvet and LA label James Perse (for sporty basics).

For branch see index.

Handmade and Found

109 Essex Road, N1 2SL (7359 3898/ www.handmadeandfound.co.uk). Angel tube. **Open** 10.30am-6pm Tue-Sat. **Credit** MC, V. **Sells** W.

Now in its 12th year, this little find on Essex Road was given a makeover by retail guru Mary Portas on *Mary Queen of Shops* a couple of years back. Fans of the unique labels hunted out in Japan needn't worry – they're still here, but presented in a slightly different format. Portas consolidated all the clothes made on the premises under one label, Handmade, and all of those sourced

Unique Selling Point
Hurwundeki

'Pursuing beautiful things organic and natural to our lifestyle is the essence of Hurwundeki,' explains KI, owner and founder of the brand. KI had the novel (now copied) idea of fusing a vintage boutique and hair salon, establishing the Spitalfields boutique (*see p62*) in 2004. Five years later and the original East End unit now houses cherry-picked vintage alongside the Hurwundeki own label (for both mens- and womenswear), while the salon has moved around the corner to Puma Court, and there's a new West End outpost on Marshall Street (*see p35*), just off the perennially modish Carnaby Street.

The Marshall Street store, with exposed brick walls, stripped pine floorboards and paint-splattered concrete, is furnished with an assortment of lovingly sourced curios and antiques – all for sale – acting as props and display cabinets. On our last visit we spotted a granny chic Welsh dresser (£490). The idiosyncratic interior perfectly complements the rails of garments from the Hurwundeki label, a wearable and well-priced collection of quirky modern classics designed in east London by a creative team headed up by KI.

For autumn/winter 2008/9, the modern dandy is well catered for with a strong selection of waistcoats, such as the tweed 'Comte' (£39), best paired with one of the signature men's shirts (from £39) and an on-trend dapper Glen tartan check bow tie (£14) for the epitome of British heritage chic. Style-savvy London ladies frequent the store for affordable, design-conscious staples such as the Rocky lightweight black satin bomber (£45), an array of pencil skirts and fine jersey tank tops such as the Bracesops with kooky braces pre-attached (£18). Move towards the rear of the shop and, tucked under the vaulted brick arches, you'll find a small but covetable assortment of footwear – we're currently hankering after the particularly tasty Mushroom patent ladies' brogues (£69).

As creative director of the hair salon Jony Hallam commented, 'Hurwundeki's like one big family', and it certainly feels like that when you're sipping tea from china cups, munching shortbread and listening to Abba on an old gramophone while having your barnet expertly worked over. Cuts at Puma Court start at around the £35 to £50 mark while highlights start at £30 for a T-section on short hair rising to £95 for a full head on long hair.

Get in with these guys for an instant passport into east London's bohemian sub-culture – fashionable in any of the capital's postcodes.

from around the globe under the label Found. This makes for lots of pretty and modern womenswear you won't see anywhere else. Prices start at around £39 for a beautifully cut jersey smock or tunic dress. Japanese jeans for women by Sugar Cane (from £95) have proved a big hit in 2008 and are set to stay. 'Wearable' is a key adjective here, but touches of Japanese and Korean flair (a carefully placed pleat here, a bubble hem there), make everything feel like a one-off.

House of Weardowney

9A Ashbridge Street, NW8 8DH (7725 9694/www.weardowney.com). Edgware Road tube or Marylebone tube/rail. **Open** 10am-6pm Mon-Sat. **Credit** MC, V. **Sells** W.

Get stitched up at House of Weardowney, a mecca to all things woolly. Former models Amy Wear and Gail Downey – one-time knitwear designer for John Galliano – launched their label in 2004, and it's helped put handcrafted knit couture on runways and in wardrobes all over. As well as supplying knitting needles, patterns and yarns, its 'getUp boutique' reveals the brand's flirty designer knitwear featuring vintage-inspired frocks (their Racerback dress is £137), pashminas and hotpants, and, for men, oversized stripy wool boxers. The Grade II-listed building doubles up as a knitting school and has a seven-room guesthouse upstairs; lodgers tend to be from the fashion industry. Look out for the ever-expanding collection of modern and antique books on the craft.

Hoxton Boutique

2 Hoxton Street, N1 6NG (7684 2083/ www.hoxtonboutique.co.uk). Old Street tube/rail. **Open** 10.30am-6.30pm Mon-Fri; 11am-6pm Sat. **Credit** MC, V. **Sells** W.

This gallery-like store has been a favourite with crooked-fringed locals since it opened in 2000. The reason for its continued success is a host of niche labels; the owners make an effort to source interesting and emerging brands from around the world. In autumn/ winter 2008/9 you'll find choice garments from the likes of Paul & Joe Sister, Isabel Marant and Margo, as well as hard-to-get DR Denim and the shop's own +HOBO+ label. There's also a cabinet full of costume jewellery, plus pieces from British jewellery designer Jennifer Corker – a store exclusive.

KJ's Laundry

74 Marylebone Lane, W1U 2PW (7486 7855/www.kjslaundry.com). Bond Street tube. **Open** 10am-7pm Mon-Wed, Fri, Sat; 10am-8pm Thur; 11am-5pm Sun. **Credit** AmEx, MC, V. **Sells** W.

Owners Jane Ellis and Kate Allden stock a mix of lesser-known designers in their super-chic store, including Sydney's Ginger & Smart, S Sung from New York and Suzannah from the UK. Hidden behind the over-hyped high street this attitude-free boutique has lines you won't see all over town, and by manning the shop floor themselves, they can adapt their buying according to demand. There are leathers and separates by Mike & Chris (around £600), feminine dresses by NY designer Richard Ruiz (from around £250) and laid-back silk dresses by LA label Geren Ford. Look out also for easy-wear East by East West (from £50); the 1940s-influenced dresses and coats have an oriental simplicity.

Koh Samui

65-67 Monmouth Street, WC2H 9DG (7240 4280/www.kohsamui.co.uk). Covent Garden tube. **Open** 10.30am-6.30pm Mon-Wed, Fri, Sat; 10.30am-7pm Thur; noon-5.30pm Sun. **Credit** AmEx, DC, MC, V. **Sells** W.

Vintage pieces sourced from around the world share rail space with heavyweight designers at Koh Samui, resulting in a delightfully eclectic mix of stock. There really is something for everyone; choose from gorgeous, printed pieces from Antik Batik, Dries Van Noten and newly relaunched Ossie Clark, to simple, feminine clothing from current fashion editor faves 3.1 Phillip Lim (new to the store for autumn/winter 2008/9) and Derek Lam, and beautiful evening dresses by Marchesa. There are also slightly more affordable lines such as Parisian labels Vanessa Bruno and Manoush, and new for autumn/winter 2008/9 the label Sienna Miller designs with her sister: Twenty8Twelve. Look out for an extensive range of shoes by designers such as Rupert Sanderson, Marc Jacobs and Chloé. The shop also stocks jewellery by Claire O – whose skull and star charm bracelets and brooches are bang on for the current Gothic-punk trend – Mia Lia and Jessica Kanerva. There are plans in the pipeline for Koh Samui's own label.

Labour of Love

193 Upper Street, N1 1RQ (7354 9333/ www.labour-of-love.co.uk). Highbury & Islington tube/rail. **Open** 11am-6.30pm Mon-Sat; noon-5.30pm Sun. **Credit** AmEx, MC, V. **Sells** W.

This Islington gem stocks a delightful range of colourful clothing for those who want something a little bit different. Hand-picked by owner Francesca Forcolini, the shop stocks pieces by Peter Jensen, renowned for his witty prints, clothing bordering on the avant-garde by Ann-Sofie Back, whose collections are always delightfully tongue in cheek, wearable dressy jersey pieces from Erotokritos and footwear by Eley Kishimoto. Forcolini's own Labour of Love label goes from strength to strength; for autumn/winter 2008/9 it draws its inspiration from the circus. Expect to find playful yet wearable clothes at (just about) reasonable prices: key pieces include a star print knit twin set (£155 for the cardigan and £95 for the tank) and a cashmere wool jacket with silk pussy bow detail (£260), as well as the label's popular jazz shoes in six new patent colours. It's also a great place to browse for gifts. This season look out for Tatty Devine giant plastic knit zip necklaces and earrings, weird and wonderful jewellery by Erica Weiner and colourful knit and leather gloves by Cristine Bec.

Nancy Pop

19 Kensington Park Road, W11 2EU (7221 9797/www.nancypop.com). Ladbroke Grove tube. **Open** 10.30am-6.30pm Tue-Sun. **Credit** MC, V. **Sells** W.

From the heart of Notting Hill, Nancy Pop entices customers with its purple and white interior and own-brand designs that are fun, sophisticated and feminine. Friendly staff are only too happy to answer all your fashion-related questions or to help you build a new look. Outfits for every occasion are spread over the two floors. Get yourself a metallic Da Vinci cocktail frock for that hot date, for £298, or a black top with ruffles for a long weekend away, for £157. Look out also for established brands such as Alice McCall and Eley Kishimoto. You'll no doubt come across some new names here. Fresh in for autumn/winter 2008/9 are Dr Denim Jeans from Sweden, elegant shoes by Lotus and Lundgren & Windinge dresses. Back due to popular demand are creations by Margot and accessories by Joanna Louca.

Press

3 Erskine Road, NW3 3AJ (7449 0081). Chalk Farm tube. **Open** 10am-6.30pm Mon-Sat; noon-6pm Sun. **Credit** MC, V. **Sells** W.

Before opening her boutique in 2004, Melanie Press had solid retail credentials as former creative director of Whistles. The ultimate Primrose Hill chick's closet, Press sells a mix of designer labels such as Vera Wang's diffusion line Lavender, Marc by Marc Jacobs (both clothing and accessories) and Italian biker-chic label Belstaff, which has done some great Barbour-esque jackets for autumn-winter 2008/9, alongside pretty vintage pieces. Another addition are Golden Goose boots, made from 100% leather and already worn in for you (they've already garnered a long waiting list). The shop also stocks an impressive range of denim including cult jeans label J Brand and Wrangler. A second shop recently opened in St John's Wood, catering for more French-led tastes. Hip Parisian labels APC and Paul & Joe Sister are both stocked, while APC's Madras line by Jessica Ogden will launch for spring/summer 2009.

For branch see index.

Saltwater

98 Marylebone Lane, W1U 2QB (7935 3336/www.saltwater.net). Bond Street tube. **Open** 11am-6pm Mon-Wed; 11am-7pm Thur-Sat. **Credit** AmEx, MC, V. **Sells** W.

Tucked behind Marylebone High Street, the Saltwater boutique has a lovely, sunny seaside vibe – which makes sense, when you learn that the label's designer, Laura Watson, comes from Cornwall. The clothes, in natural fabrics with subtle, washed-effect patterns, from tree prints to polka dots, have an appealingly wearable feel that suits all ages. Shapes are simple and well cut, with lots of nice details such as pin-tucks and ribbon ties. The autumn/winter 2008/9 collection features great daywear pieces with a definite workwear feel; loose, mannish cord trousers (£60), regatta striped blazers (£155) paired with cute chemise blouses (£45) and knitted cardigans or jumpers. For eveningwear expect to find pretty velvet, silk or embellished dresses at reasonable prices (from £65). The shop also stocks a couple of other labels, including basic everyday pieces in soft jersey by American Vintage and more tailored clothing by Hartford.

Shop at Maison Bertaux

27 Greek Street, W1D 5DF (05601 151584/www.shopatmaisonb.com). Leicester Square or Piccadilly Circus tube. **Open** 11am-6.30pm Tue-Sat. **Credit** MC, V. **Sells** W.

S***R
GREATEST
HITS
THE
GRANT
www.swear-london.com

Jas M.B.

Label watch

The most covetable brands of the moment – and where to get your hands on them.

London's boutiques are a shopper's delight. Each one is a treasure trove where big-name labels nestle next to lesser-known ones in alluring surroundings. The sheer volume of designer fashion on offer is enough to make the faint-hearted dizzy. But there are some buzz brands you won't want to miss.

Naturally, London Fashion Week designers are well represented in the capital's most chi chi salons. Known for its austere aesthetic, **Meadham Kirchhoff** (available at Browns Focus) based its autumn/winter 2008/9 collection on power-dressing city women. Think skirt suits, structured knits and draped dresses. The motto of **Ashish** (Browns Focus, Sixty 6) could well be 'you can never have too many sequins', as his latest range of Vegas strip dresses and jazzy sportswear attests. **Nathan Jenden**, who cut his teeth at Diane von Furstenberg, looks to his dark side for winter 2008/9, as daintily dressed Goths come out to play. Also keep an eye out for recently revived retro brands **Biba** (Matches, Browns) and **Ossie Clark** (Browns, Koh Samui, Sixty 6) and growing label **Twenty8Twelve** (Sefton, Studio 8, Koh Samui), which comes courtesy of the Miller siblings Siena and Savannah.

New York designers also do battle on the rails of London's boutiques, with their no-nonsense, high-impact style. Since he launched in 2005, **3.1 Phillip Lim**'s understated collections have been a phenomenon and are still a high-end boutique fave (Browns, Sefton, Koh Samui, Start, as well as newcomer Feather & Stitch). For autumn/winter 2008/9, he offers uptown knits for women and geek chic for men. Likewise **Derek Lam**'s (Koh Samui, Browns, Matches) success lies in impeccably tailored pieces and sophisticated cocktail dresses that have 'waiting list' written all over them.

US brands also dominate in the designer denim stakes. Try **Earnest Sewn** (Start), courtesy of ex-Paper, Denim & Cloth designer Scott Morrison (check out the kick flares), **J Brand** (Browns Focus, Cochinechine, Coco Ribbon, Feather, Matches, Press, Sefton), and **18th Amendment** (Diverse, Browns, Matches, Press) – jean du jour of the best-dressed celebrities (Mischa Barton, Jessica Stam et al).

A plethora of covetable European designers without stand-alone shops in London can be found in many of the capital's boutiques. From Paris, **Vanessa Bruno** (Diverse, Cochinechine, Koh Samui, Start) chooses muted shades and delicate materials to produce her asymmetric tops, oversized cardigans and raw edged dresses. And **APC** (Aimé, Shop at Maison Bertaux, Diverse, Start, Press) excels at the classics – trench coats, pullovers, tennis shoes and scarves come in both boy's and girl's versions. Dutch womenswear label **Humanoid** (Folk, Diverse, the Cross and concept stores Shop at Bluebird (*see p20*) and Couverture (*see p19*) is all about comfortable luxury; its relaxed fits and elegant fabrics in muted shades make it one of our current faves. And Danish brand **Won Hundred** is also starting to make waves for its structured yet casual aesthetic and well-fitting jeans for both sexes; find it in Hub and Three Threads (for the latter, *see p49*).

Further afield, Kiwi **Karen Walker** (Austique, Diverse, Matches, Start, No-one, Question Air, nina&lola) specialises in high casual clothes inspired by such muses as Annie Hall and Amelia Earhart. Her seductively cute separates featuring twisted cartoons complement her hugely popular charm necklaces. And Indian designer **Manish Arora** (Austique, Sixty 6 as well as Dover Street Market, *see p19*) is famed for his kaleidoscopic colours and kitsch motifs. The autumn/winter 2008/9 warrior collection comes complete with crystal chain mail and Disney prints.

For eyewear, however, it has to be London label **Linda Farrow** (Feathers), which continues to pillage its archive from the 1970s and 1980s for its Vintage collection as well as collaborate with designers such as Bernhard Wilhelm, Jeremy Scott and Raf Simons on contemporary ranges.

From head to toe and east to west, the capital's boutiques have it licked.

This boutique started out in a small converted launderette, grew to inhabit the World According To... (now closed) on Brewer Street, and now exists happily beneath the charming pâtisserie Maison Bertaux in Soho. A nicer way to shop is hard to imagine; pluck a cream-filled fancy from the selection upstairs before wandering down to the candy-coloured, vintage-inspired boutique to peruse the rails. The store boasts a big selection of clothes and accessories by APC and Sonia by Sonia Rykiel, as well as Eley Kishimoto and Obey, a small selection of gorgeous jewellery and shoes by Repetto.

Sixty 6

66 Marylebone High Street, W1U 5JF (7224 6066). Baker Street tube. **Open** 10am-6.30pm Mon-Fri; 10am-6pm Sat; noon-5pm Sun. **Credit** AmEx, MC, V. **Sells** W.

The owner of this tiny Marylebone gem, former antiques dealer Jane Collins, has a knack for choosing clothes that are eye-catching and feminine without being showy; many items are distinguished by interesting trimmings or embellishments. A tempting mix of designers is in evidence, such as Temperley and Manish Arora, who designs special commissions for the store. New for autumn/winter 2008/9 is the revived Ossie Clark collection. There's a mid-range line-up too, with Malene Birger and Just In Case pieces displayed in combinations you might not have thought of putting together yourself. The shop also has the widest range of tops and dresses by Velvet we've seen in the capital, including unusual styles. Look out for accessories by Lara Bohinc, famed for her art deco-inspired pieces, and decorative bags by Jamin Puech, as well as choice vintage items. Collins is opening a second shop in St John's Wood in mid October 2008, which she hopes will be all the more experimental.

Souvenir

53 Brewer Street, W1F 9UY (7287 9877/ www.souvenirboutique.co.uk). Piccadilly Circus tube. **Open** 11am-7pm Mon-Wed, Fri, Sat; 11am-7.30pm Thur; noon-6pm Sun. **Credit** AmEx, MC, V. **Sells** W.

This Soho boutique, popular with the style-savvy media types who frequent the area, has a distinct *Sex & the City* feel. Buyer Anna Namiki has an eye for fun, girly fashion. As well as stocking Vivienne Westwood's Red Label, Viktor & Rolf and PPQ, the shop also stocks hip Parisian label Rue du Mail and Tsumori Chisato, a Japanese designer famed for her romantic designs and favoured by fashion darlings. New for autumn/winter 2008/9 is Spanish Central Saint Martins graduate Lorena de la Torre, who originally trained as a dancer, lending her designs a greater understanding of the female physique. Look out for shoes by Marc Jacobs and Chloé, a great selection of Vivienne Westwood bags, wallets and jewellery, as well as quirky Pop Art jewellery by Lady Luck Rules. Souvenir is celebrating its tenth anniversary in 2009, so be sure to check out the special displays.

Susy Harper

35 Camden Passage, N1 8EA (7704 0688/ www.susyharper.co.uk). Angel tube. **Open** 11am-6pm Tue, Wed; 11am-7pm Thur, Fri; 10.30am-6.30pm Sat; noon-5pm Sun. **Credit** MC, V. **Sells** W.

Designer Michelle Anslow originally started selling her label Susy Harper (her mum's maiden name) on a stall in Spitalfields Market; she's recently moved her shop/ studio from Cross Street to more foot traffic-friendly Camden Passage. Her simple, chic designs in silk, cotton, linen and wool draw on classic shapes – simple skirts, shifts, 1950s-style fitted frocks, short Harris Tweed coats – and sometimes feature unusual, vintage-look patterns, while the hand-dyed crinkly cotton tunics (from £42) in white, black, grey and seasonal colours are perennial staples. Kate Moss and Cate Blanchett (who can be seen in Susy Harper in *Notes on a Scandal*) are said to be fans.

Also check out...

A La Mode

10 Symons Street, SW3 2TJ (7730 7180). Sloane Square tube. **Open** 10am-6pm Mon-Sat. **Credit** AmEx, DC, MC, V. **Sells** W.

High-profile stockist of big-league designers such as Marni, Oscar de la Renta, Chloé, Marc Jacobs and Giambattista Valli.

Anna

126 Regent's Park Road, NW1 8XL (7483 0411/www.shopatanna.co.uk). Chalk Farm tube. **Open** 10am-6pm Mon-Sat; noon-6pm Sun. **Credit** AmEx, MC, V. **Sells** W.

A good mix of expensive designer fare and mid-range labels such as Velvet, Citizens of Humanity and American Vintage.

For branch see index.

Aquaint

18 Conduit Street, W1S 2XN (7499 9658/ www.ashleyisham.com). Oxford Circus tube. **Open** 10am-6pm Mon-Sat. **Credit** AmEx, MC, V. **Sells** W.

Owner/designer Ashley Isham's red-carpet creations sit alongside exclusive labels.

BirdCage

1st Floor, Kingly Court, Kingly Street, W1B 5PW (7494 3828/www.birdcage boutique.com). Oxford Circus or Piccadilly Circus tube. **Open** 11am-7pm Mon-Wed, Fri, Sat; 11am-8pm Thur; noon-6pm Sun. **Credit** MC, V. **Sells** W.

BirdCage's own line of clothes is made from natural fabrics; there are also feminine accessories and oriental knick-knacks.

Feather & Stitch

54 Hill Street, Richmond, Surrey TW9 1TW (8332 2717/www.featherand stitch.com). Richmond tube/rail. **Open** 10am-6pm Mon-Sat; 11am-5pm Sun. **Credit** AmEx, MC, V. **Sells** W.

This new Richmond boutique is packed with leftfield designers like Rebecca Taylor and Philip Lim protégé Grace Sun.

Frost French

22-26 Camden Passage, N1 8ED (7354 0053). Angel tube. **Open** 10am-7pm Mon-Sat; noon-7pm Sun. **Credit** AmEx, MC, V. **Sells** W.

Sadie Frost and Jemima French's designs often have a slightly quirky feel. Quality is good but the styles don't always impress.

Iris

73 Salusbury Road, NW6 6NJ (7372 1777/ www.irisfashion.co.uk). Queen's Park tube. **Open** 10am-6pm Mon-Wed; 10am-7pm Thur, Fri; 10am-6pm Sat; 10.30am-4.30pm Sun. **Credit** MC, V. **Sells** W, C.

Feminine fashion and cool kidswear targeted at trendy local mums.

For branch see index.

Musa

31 Holland Street, W8 4NA (7937 6282). High Street Kensington tube. **Open** 11am-6pm Tue-Sat. **Credit** MC, V. **Sells** W.

Bijou boudoir combining designer fare with hand-selected jewellery and accessories.

Mimi

309 King's Road, SW3 5EP (7349 9699/ www.mimilondon.co.uk). Sloane Square tube/11, 19, 22 bus. **Open** 10.30am-6.30pm Mon-Sat; noon-5pm Sun. **Credit** AmEx, MC, V. **Sells** W.

Designer labels and premium denim for the Chelsea party set.

Precious

16 Artillery Passage, E1 7LJ (7377 6668/ www.precious-london.com). Liverpool Street tube/rail. **Open** 11am-6.30pm Mon-Fri; noon-6pm Sat. **Credit** AmEx, MC, V. **Sells** W.

Owned by former Harvey Nichols buyer; stocks mid-priced designer labels.

Shoon

94 Marylebone High Street, W1U 4RG (7487 3001/www.shoon.com). Baker Street or Bond Street tube. **Open** 10am-6.30pm Mon-Sat; 11am-5pm Sun. **Credit** MC, V. **Sells** W, B.

Womenswear by brands like Hoss Intropia, Wall and Oska. Also bags by Orla Kiely and Oushka, and shoes from Chie Mihara.

Sublime

225 Victoria Park Road, E9 7HJ (8986 7243). Mile End tube then 277 bus. **Open** 10am-6pm Mon-Sat; 11am-4pm Sun. **Credit** MC, V. **Sells** W.

Stocks feminine, mid-range womenswear as well as fun gifts, upmarket toiletries and original 1950s furniture.

For branch see index.

Toast

133 Upper Street, N1 1QP (7704 8243/ www.toast.co.uk). Angel tube/Highbury & Islington tube/rail. **Open** 10.30am-6.30pm Mon-Sat; noon-6pm Sun. **Credit** MC, V. **Sells** W.

London store for the high-quality mail-order purveyor of casual women's clothing, nightwear and loungewear.

For branch see index.

Twenty8Twelve

172 Westbourne Grove, W11 2RW (7221 9287/www.twenty8twelve.com). Notting Hill Gate tube. **Open** 10am-6.30pm Mon-Sat; noon-5pm Sun. **Credit** AmEx, MC, V. **Sells** W.

On-trend label from the Miller sisters Siena and Savannah that's making a presence in boutiques such as Studio 8 and Sefton.

Folk

Men & women

b store

24A Savile Row, W1S 3PR (7734 6846/ www.bstorelondon.com). Oxford Circus tube. **Open** 10.30am-6.30pm Mon-Fri; 10am-6pm Sat. **Credit** AmEx, MC, V. **Sells** M, W.

Possibly London's trendiest clothes shop, b store's reputation remains unimpeachable – where else can you pick up clothes designed by this year's Saint Martin's graduates? Choose from emerging and more established designers, including Damir Doma, Opening Ceremony and Peter Jensen. The look is decidedly avant-garde – oversized bow ties and caped coats from Mjolk. The emphasis is more on men's fashion; in autumn/winter 2008/9, the b clothing menswear line – the company's first own-label range – is all about high-waisted pleated trousers worn with bomber jackets and gingham shirts. The cutting-edge house shoes collection has styles for both men and women, with prices hovering around the £160 mark.

Bamford & Sons (eco)

The Old Bank, 31 Sloane Square, SW1W 8GA (7881 8010/www.bamfordandsons.com). Sloane Square tube. **Open** 9am-6pm Mon-Tue, Thur, Fri; 9am-7pm Wed; 10am-6pm Sat; noon-5pm Sun. **Credit** AmEx, DC, MC, V. **Sells** M, W, C.

Bamford & Sons' beautiful four-floor flagship exudes a polished, luxurious vibe. Think muted shades, spot-on ethical credentials (lots of organic cotton and vegetable-dyed leather) and a refined sense of style. Prices are high, but then so is quality – these are clothes for the man who wears linen all summer and cashmere all winter. You'll find timeless, well-cut polos, shirts and suits, shoes, scarves and grown-up toys, such as customised iPods. A collection of boys' clothes is available on the top floor, while the basement is home to a branch of Daylesford Organic Café – you'll probably have to queue but the delicious food is well worth the wait.
For branches see index.

Browns

23-27 South Molton Street, W1K 5RD (7514 0000/www.brownsfashion.com). Bond Street tube. **Open** 10am-6.30pm Mon-Wed, Fri, Sat; 10am-7pm Thur. **Credit** AmEx, MC, V. **Sells** M, W.

For the ultimate fashion fix look no further than Joan Burstein's venerable store. Among the 100-odd designers jostling for attention at its five interconnecting shops are fashion heavyweights Chloé, Dries Van Noten, Balenciaga and Lanvin. Burstein has always championed the next-big-things from the fashion elite, so you'll also find designs from rising stars like Christopher Kane, Marios Schwab and Todd Lynn. Exclusive to Browns for autumn/winter 2008/9 are Parisian label du jour Balmain, Ossie Clark and Vince. The women's shoe salon, meanwhile, showcases fabulous footwear from Alaïa, Alexander McQueen and Christian Louboutin. The two-floor menswear section brings together an unrivalled collection of high-end designer gear, from Dior Homme to Miu Miu. Across the road, Browns Focus caters for a younger crowd, with more accessibly priced labels, such as 3.1 Phillip Lim, Alexander Wang and Ann-Sofie Back. New for autumn/winter 2008/9 is cult legging label Les Chiffoniers, shoes by Charlotte Olympia and ethical denim by Shakrah Chakra. Up at no.50, the sale shop, Browns Labels for Less (*see p43* **Sales & events**), is loaded with leftovers from the previous season.
For branches (including Browns Focus and Browns Labels for Less) see index.

Doors by Jas MB

8 Ganton Street, W1F 7PQ (7494 2288/ www.doorsbyjasmb.com). Oxford Circus tube. **Open** 11am-7pm Mon-Sat; 1-5pm Sun. **Credit** AmEx, MC, V. **Sells** M, W.

The distinctive aroma of treated leather pervades this dimly lit boutique off Carnaby Street, and with good reason. Jas Sehmbi stocks a variety of clothing and accessories labels, but the highlight is his luxury leather bags. Designs are wonderfully practical, with models like the Mono Tower, with its abundance of zippered pockets (£379), and the cavernous BT bag (the perfect size for hand luggage). You're invited to customise many models with your own leather and trim choices – options include ponyskin, cracked leather (with a deliberately distressed effect) and a selection of different colours. Other offerings in-store include clothing by Swedish labels Ann-Sofie Back and Acne, as well as Peter Pilotto and Chloe Sevigny for Opening Ceremony shoes and glasses.

Egg

36 Kinnerton Street, SW1X 8ES (7235 9315). Hyde Park Corner or Knightsbridge tube. **Open** 10am-6pm Tue-Sat. **Credit** AmEx, MC, V. **Sells** M, W.

Hidden away in a residential mews behind Knightsbridge, this exquisite shop is housed in a former dairy. There's an unconstructed, oriental feel to the clothing (owner Maureen Doherty used to work for Issey Miyake). The shapes may be simple, but the fabrics are luxurious: lots of natural linen, wispy silk and heavy, recycled wools. Sumptuously oversized Sine cashmere sweaters in deep colours will set you back over £600. There's also mens- and womenswear by Casey Vidalenc (the collaboration of Englishman Gareth Casey and Frenchman Philippe Vidalenc), which has a substantial, artisan feel; Dosa's simple, Asian-influenced lounge/ daywear; and handmade coats and jackets by Indian designer Gitika Goyal. Unusual jewellery, blanket-sized cashmere scarves and a selection of ceramics and glassware are displayed alongside the clothes. Prices reflect the high quality of the goods.

Folk

49 Lamb's Conduit Street, WC1N 3NG (7404 6458/www.folkclothing.com). Holborn tube. **Open** 11am-7pm Mon-Fri; noon-6pm Sat. **Credit** MC, V. **Sells** M, W.

Folk was born in 2001 and is the label of choice for guys who once dressed like skaters, then progressed to labels like Silas and are now after more quality, more respectability and less branding. The silhouette and the fabrics are comfortable but hip and slightly dishevelled – in a tasteful rather than grungey way (think gingham, quality knits and casual jackets). In autumn/winter 2008/9 we'd go for a narrow shirt in chambray, and wear it under a black gilet with Kicking Mule jeans from Colorado (which only Folk stocks) and Lulac boots in brown. Sister brand Shofolk offers stylish but comfortable shoes for men and women that have a hand-crafted feel (the moccasin-inspired styles are now very on-trend). This is the place to head to for Dutch womenswear label Humanoid, and women are also catered for with a good selection of Lee jeans. Keep a look out for the shop's excellent sample sales. Folk's big news this year is its concession in Liberty.

Hub

49 & 88 Stoke Newington Church Street, N16 0AR (7254 4494/www.hubshop.co.uk). Bus 73, 393, 476. **Open** 10.30am-6.30pm Mon-Sat; noon-5pm Sun. **Credit** MC, V. **Sells** M, W.

Hub stocks a well-edited selection of covetable mid-range designer labels, with See by Chloé and Sonia by Sonia Rykiel much in evidence. Spot a brace of trendy-looking yummy mummies in a Stokey café and chances are they'll have picked up their Acne skinny jeans or Cacharel blouses here; Cacharel's collaboration with Eley Kishimoto is a highlight of the autumn/winter 2008/9 stock. No.49 houses the womenswear; as well as the labels mentioned above, there are pieces by Thomas Burberry and Hoss Intropia, jeans by Lee, Won Hundred, coats from Mackintosh, lingerie from Princesse Tam Tam, Peter Jenson T-shirts and sweatshirts, Ally Capellino bags, affordable jewellery from the likes of Comfort Station, plus everyday knits and dresses with a quirky edge by co-owner Beth Graham. It's also a good bet for a choice selection of shoes (lots of F-Troupe) and scarves. Over the road at no.88, Hub Men stocks many of the same labels, as well as knits by John Smedley and a selection of items from Folk, Fred Perry, Barbour and more.

Hurwundeki

34 Marshall Street, W1F 7EU (7734 1050/ www.hurwundeki.com). Oxford Circus tube. **Open** noon-7.30pm Mon-Sat; noon-6pm Sun. **Credit** MC, V. **Sells** M, W.
See p30 **Unique Selling Point**.
For branch see index.

JW Beeton

48-50 Ledbury Road, W11 2AJ (7229 8874). Notting Hill Gate tube. **Open** 10.30am-6pm Mon-Sat; noon-5pm Sun. **Credit** AmEx, MC, V. **Sells** M, W.

Now in its 12th year, JW Beeton is one of the longest serving boutiques in this now crowded patch. Keen to cater for all sorts of budgets, owner Debbie Potts buys small quantities of European and international labels and sells them at non-extravagant prices. Recent updates include Diab'Less from Paris, Rützou from Denmark and funky knits from Brazilian label Cecilia Prado. A selection of bags, belts and shoes by the Jacksons is displayed in the front.

Kokon To Zai

57 Greek Street, W1D 3DX (7434 1316/ www.kokontozai.co.uk). Leicester Square or Tottenham Court Road tube. **Open** 11am-7.30pm Mon-Sat; noon-6pm Sun. **Credit** AmEx, MC, V. **Sells** M, W.

Kokon To Zai specialises in avant-garde, weird and wonderful fashion. The buyers are adept at picking up young designers from the nearby London College of Fashion and

Central Saint Martins, so you'll often see new names here first. The selection is constantly changing, but labels the shop continues to stock include darling of the nu-rave scene Cassette Playa, Bernhard Wilhelm and Vivienne Westwood. Ever present, however, is Marjan Pejoski, who made Björk's famous swan dress. Look out for his new line of jewellery too; quirky silver and diamond pieces start at £250. For offbeat streetwear look no further than the house label KTZ, which excels in T-shirts and sweats with wacky prints (from £40). A new homewares store opened in 2008 in west London.
For branch see index.

Laden Showroom

103 Brick Lane, E1 6SE (7247 2431/www.laden.co.uk). **Open** 11am-6.30pm Mon-Fri; 11am-7pm Sat; 10.30am-6pm Sun. **Credit** MC, V. **Sells** M, W.

The Laden Showroom's range of cutting-edge designer clothing from the hottest independent talent on the scene is second to none. There are some 55 designers to choose from, including Emily & Fin, for great cotton tops, skirts and dresses at very affordable prices, and Love Our Clothes, whose hip jump suits for autumn/winter 2008/9 are very on-trend. Peruse the bags and shoes section for cheap ballet pumps and Brazilian trainers. Some pieces are a bit of a case of trend as opposed to style led, but ideal for that just off to art college look. It's a great place to put together an interesting look on a shoestring budget.

Library

268 Brompton Road, SW3 2AS (7589 6569). South Kensington tube. **Open** 10am-6.30pm Mon, Tue, Thur-Sat; 10am-7pm Wed; 12.30-5.30pm Sun. **Credit** AmEx, DC, MC, V. **Sells** M, W.

Designer labels and rare books may seem an unlikely combination, but this fantastic emporium should convince you that it's an inspired one. Clothes by fashion giants like Alexander McQueen and Dries Van Noten hang alongside those of newer, edgy names like Austrian Carol Christian Poell. Casual clothes are also available, in the form of great jeans by PRPS and fancy sweat pants by Maharishi, for lazy weekends or evenings in a club. The staff are as smart and well presented as the merchandise, and don't forget to cast an eye over the bookshelves if you're visiting.

Matches

60-64 Ledbury Road, W11 2AJ (7221 0255/www.matchesfashion.com). Notting Hill Gate tube. **Open** 10am-6pm Mon-Sat; noon-6pm Sun. **Credit** AmEx, DC, MC, V. **Sells** M, W.

The pick of the crop of assorted designers are on show here. Get yourself kitted out in Bottega Veneta, Burberry, Stella McCartney, Chloé or Marc Jacobs, among other labels. Across the road at Matches Spy there's more casual gear to be had, such as Acne Jeans, Heidi Klein and Theory. On our last visit we spotted Lily Cole trying on clothes here – what better proof of cutting-edge fashion? The dedicated Diane von Furstenberg store at no.83 is also part of the empire.

Branches: (including Diane von Furstenberg, Matches Spy and MaxMara) throughout the city.

no-one

1 Kingsland Road, E2 8AA (7613 5314/www.no-one.co.uk). Old Street tube/rail. **Open** 11am-7pm Mon-Sat; noon-6pm Sun. **Credit** AmEx, DC, MC, V. **Sells** M, W.

On the style-setting axis between Old Street and Kingsland Road, this cutting-edge store is a favourite of Shoreditch locals and noncomformist style icons, including Roisin Murphy and Björk. Buyer Teresa Letchford is brilliant at spotting cool new labels, and was the first to champion Swedish denim label Cheap Monday in Britain, which it continues to sell alongside denim by Lee. The stock ranges from the latest Bi La Li womenswear, YMC men's clothing, reasonably priced feminine frocks by Mine (from £70), and kooky clothing by Henrik Vibskov. Shoes this season are catered for by Opening Ceremony and Bernhard Wilhelm (for women only). The shop has counters brimming over with vintage sunglasses, knitted accessories by local label Made With Hands, badges, wittily branded toiletries and cult magazines and books. Best of all, there's a newly enlarged café next door with good coffee and muffins the size of your head.

Relax Garden

40 Kingsland Road, E2 8DA (7033 1881/www.relaxgarden.com). Old Street tube/rail. **Open** noon-7pm Mon-Wed; noon-8pm Thur, Fri; noon-6pm Sat, Sun. **Credit** MC, V. **Sells** M, W.

This small boutique aims to bring lesser-known, affordable independent labels from abroad to the UK. Look out for LA-based GLAM, jersey knitwear by Italian label Northland and a wide selection of Japanese labels, including Fanaka. The shop's own label, Relax Garden, designed by owner Eriko Nagata offers reasonably priced, simple, feminine designs in silk and jersey. There's also a good selection of accessories, including shoes by Apex T, Rabeanco bags and pretty jewellery by London-based label Mille & Me. The shop is a good stopoff for cute hair clips, hairbands, vintage-style plastic earrings and patterned tights.
For branch see index.

Sefton

271 Upper Street, N1 2UQ (7226 9822/www.seftonfashion.com). Highbury & Islington tube/rail. **Open** 10am-6.30pm Mon-Wed, Sat; 10am-7pm Thur, Fri; noon-6pm Sun. **Credit** MC, V. **Sells** M, W.

At Sefton, high-end international designers sit alongside emerging labels. The ladies' branch at no.271 is brimming with reliably stylish names like Acne Jeans, Miss Bibi, Eley Kishimoto and 3.1 Phillip Lim, as well as Paul & Joe's diffusion line Sister, the Miller sisters' Twenty8Twelve range and lingerie by Princesse Tam-Tam. There are also hot accessories, including shoes by Rupert Sanderson, Vivienne Westwood and Costume National as well as a beautiful display of Miller Harris perfumes in a cabinet behind the till. Sefton is also an excellent bet for affordable gold-plated jewellery of the Alex Monroe ilk. Further up Upper Street, on the other side of the road (at no.196), is the menwear store. Check out the Comme des Garçons KAWS wallets and polka-dot undies – pieces by Marni, Edwin, YMC, Marc Jacobs and Alexander McQueen also all swing from Sefton's rails; a silver rainbow tie by the latter goes for £65.
For branch (menswear) see index.

Start

42-44 Rivington Street, EC2A 3BN (7729 3334/www.start-london.com). Old Street tube/rail. **Open** 10.30am-6.30pm Mon-Fri; 11am-6pm Sat; 1-5pm Sun. **Credit** AmEx, MC, V. **Sells** M, W.

Philip Start (founder of Woodhouse) and his wife Brix (former guitarist for punk rock band the Fall) own these his 'n' hers boutiques. In the women's store you'll find well-known, international brands Miu Miu, Marc by Marc Jacobs, Sonia, See by Chloé and Stella McCartney, alongside up-and-coming labels like 3.1 Phillip Lim, Richard Nicoll, David Szeto and Zoe Tee's. New for autumn/winter 2008/9 is Jean Pierre Braganza and Australian designer Josh Goot. There's also a hugely covetable range of accessories such as sunglasses by Cutler & Gross, an expanding shoe section and jewellery by Lucy Hutchings. Denim by Acne, Earnest Sewn and Paper Denim Cloth and hard-to-find skincare brands, such as Hei Poa, REN and, new for autumn/winter 2008/9, Olivina completes the shopping experience. Across the road at the men's store enjoy browsing rails of Jil Sander, Neil Barrett, APC and Balenciaga. A recently opened third store on Rivington Street houses the Mr Start label including suits, ties, shirts and a made-to-measure service (prices for the latter start at £750), as well as Mulberry bags and a selection of cashmere.
For branches (menswear and made to measure) see index.

Studio 8

83 Regent's Park Road, NW1 8UY (7449 0616/www.studio8shop.com). Chalk Farm tube. **Open** 10am-6pm Mon-Wed, Fri, Sat; 10am-7pm Thur; noon-5pm Sun. **Credit** AmEx, MC, V. **Sells** M, W.

One of three Studio 8 boutiques (the other two are in South Africa), this airy Primrose Hill shop has a pleasingly grown-up appeal. Set up by Marcelle Savage, a South African of eastern European and Middle Eastern origins, there's a global feel to the clothing and accessories lines carried here – Marithé & François Girbaud, Twenty8Twelve, Juicy Couture, Graham & Spencer, Elm, Ash shoes and Pauric Sweeney bags. Son Simon is at the helm where menswear is concerned and has selected a fine array, including Rogues Gallery, Roberto Collina, Haversack and Ash.

Also check out...

Bunka

4 Dartmouth Road, SE23 3XU (8291 4499/www.bunka.co.uk). Forest Hill rail. **Open** 10am-6pm Mon-Sat. **Credit** MC, V. **Sells** M, W.

Funky casualwear and accessories.

Question Air

229 Westbourne Grove, W11 2SE (7221 8163/www.question-air.co.uk). Notting Hill Gate tube. **Open** 10.30am-6pm Mon-Wed; 10.30am-6.30pm Thur-Sat; noon-5.30pm Sun. **Credit** AmEx, MC, V. **Sells** M, W.

Laid-back European and American labels and an exhaustive range of premium jeans.
For branches see index.

BirdCage
Oriental elegance expressed through
a beautiful collection of clothing, accessories,
gifts and homeware.
BirdCage invite you to stimulate your senses
with this distinctive theme.
1.13 Kingly Court (1st floor)
Kingly Street, London W1B 5PW
BirdCageBoutique.com
+44 (0) 20 7494 3828

Ledbury Road

A bit of glamour, a bit of boho: retail nirvana hits leafy Ledbury Road.

As fantasy high streets go, swankily bohemian Ledbury Road is up there with the best of them. Even for Notting Hill's most pampered, spoilt and well-heeled residents, shopping here is an unalloyed indulgence. With an impressive choice of high-end independents and a smart yet laid-back vibe, the street is made for unhurried browsing and is a welcome escape from the bustle of Westbourne Grove. Accessorise with a tall cappuccino, a cherubic child and someone else's credit card and you'll fit right in.

Passing elegantly refined residences and starting from the Westbourne Park end of the road, make **Matches** (*see p36*) your first stop for assorted luxe labels by Chloé, Balenciaga and Lanvin. Or, for sharply dressed guys, **Matches Menswear** has a host of brands including Marc Jacobs, Miu Miu, Paul Smith and Prada. **Matches Spy**, across the road, is also good for a more casual collection: think Marni and Acne Jeans along with other popular diffusion lines.

A bit further along, classy kids (or, rather, their mums) will be happy at chic **Caramel** (no.77, *see p263*) and classic **Petit Bateau** (no.73, *see p265*); the former also has its own range of shoes and accessories and a hair salon in the basement.

Next up, on the other side of the road, is the quirky and undefinable **JW Beeton** (*see p35*). Now in its 12th year, it's one of the longest serving boutiques in this now-crowded patch of town. Owner Debbie Potts buys up small quantities of international labels and sells them on at non-extravagant (for these parts) prices. Recent hits include Diablesse from Paris, Rützou from Denmark and funky knits from Brazilian Cecilia Prado. The selection appeals to a mixed bag of shoppers, and there's some kids and menswear as well as a selection of bags, belts and shoes by the Jacksons.

Keeping up with the steady stream of new businesses and shoppers in the immediate area, **Ottolenghi** (no.63, *see p242*) opened its doors to the hungry and foot-weary back in 2002. A quick glance at the window display and you can see why it's a winner when it comes to interior deli design. There's a selection of colourful Mediterranean, Middle Eastern and oriental dishes on offer alongside tempting pastries and tasty-yet-size-zero-conscious salads. If you're not ravenous (and not calorie-counting), meringues, cheesy biscuits and cakes will all set you back around £3.50. The designs next door come by way of **Anya Hindmarch** (no.63, *see p76)* and her exceedingly hip bags.

Over the road at **Bodas** (*see p67*) you'll find a simple and sexy underwear line, all made with high-quality fabrics, while at no.36 the floaty crepe frocks and fresh fragrances of **Ghost** (7229 1057, www.ghost.co.uk) are a recurrent favourite with the hippie-chic set.

In tribute to the many French settlers of Kensington and Chelsea, the road is also host to a clutch of top Gallic boutiques – shops that make dressing like a Parisienne easy. **Aimé** (no.32, *see p28*), founded by French-Cambodian sisters, has simple cardies from the étoile range by Isabel Marant, cute smock dresses by Antik Batik and Bardot-style ballet shoes by Repetto. Bath products, scented candles and quality home accessories are also a hit.

For a one-stop shop for gorgeous shoes, you can't go wrong at **Iris** (no.61, 7229 7229, *see p34*). The Milan-based boutique houses so many top designers – among them Chloé, John Galliano, Marc Jacobs, Victor & Rolf and Paul Smith, to name but a choice few – that you should find something that matches your newly purchased Ledbury Road designer outfit.

Next door at no.59, the indulgence continues at **Melt** (7727 5030, www.meltchocolates.com). Assailed by the enticing aroma of cocoa, you'll be hard pressed to avoid the temptation of taking a break from all the shopping frenzy to sample some mouth-watering chocolates, all lovingly handcrafted on the premises.

Where once antique shops lorded it over the road, nowadays you'll have to walk further up the block to see them; don't miss art deco specialist **B&T Antiques** (no.47, 7229 7001), which has a near cult following.

With an interior resembling a princess's boudoir, French designer Sophie Albou's **Paul & Joe** (nos.39-41, *see p41)* provides a seductive, yet girlie clothes collection. Think romantic, classic French tailoring with a contemporary edge: ruffled blouses, oversized knits and wide-leg trousers are hits, alongside impressive party dresses and a make-up range to match. Also worth a peek is **Paul & Joe Sister**, which offers a more casual range heavy on mini-dresses.

International Designer & Classic

Online retailer of designer clobber **Net-a-porter** (www.net-a-porter.com) has a same-day delivery service in London (for an extra charge).

At the time of going to press, cult brand **PPQ** (www.ppqclothing.com) was without a home, having closed its Conduit Street shop.

Men

Hackett

137-138 Sloane Street, SW1X 9AY (7730 3331/www.hackett.co.uk). Sloane Square tube. **Open** 9.30am-7pm Mon-Sat; 11am-5pm Sun. **Credit** AmEx, DC, MC, V. **Sells** M, C.

Jeremy Hackett's eponymous label makes no apology for its love of the upper echelon of British society – and its popularity speaks volumes about the perennial appeal of the Sloane look. Of course it helps that the clothes are reasonably priced, well made and designed with the shape and attitude of real men in mind. You won't find fashion intruding on Hackett's vision of the world – he's well aware that there are plenty of men who'll never wear a fluorescent T-shirt but still want to look sharp. If you've fallen for the classic British look but Savile Row prices are beyond you, this is the place to come. **Branches**: throughout the city.

London Home of Alfred Dunhill

Bourdon House, 2 Davies Street, W1K 3DJ (0845 458 0779/www.dunhill.com). Green Park or Oxford Circus tube. **Open** 10am-7pm Mon-Sat. **Credit** AmEx, DC, MC, V. **Sells** M.

Despite continual referencing of its century of British heritage, Dunhill shows no sign of becoming complacent. The big stories this year are that renowned British designer Kim Jones has been appointed Creative Director – a bold move given Jones's avant garde reputation – and the opening of this massive new shop in Mayfair. The London Home of Alfred Dunhill combines extensive retail space with a member's club (including bedrooms, bar and restaurant), a spa, cinema, barbers and a room dedicated to tailoring. If that's not enough to tempt you in, the keys to a pair of Bentley Flying Spurs are at the disposal of particularly favoured customers. **For branch see index**.

Nigel Hall

18 Floral Street, WC2H 9DS (7379 3600/ www.nigelhallmenswear.co.uk). Covent Garden or Leicester Square tube. **Open** 10.30am-6.30pm Mon-Wed; 10.30am-8pm Thur; 10.30am-7pm Fri, Sat; noon-6pm Sun. **Credit** AmEx, MC, V. **Sells** M.

Nigel Hall, with its no-nonsense sense of style, is fast becoming a staple. Clean, simple garments have a Riviera elegance, but Hall also gives them a fashionable edge. Knitwear is modern, straightforward and wearable, in a range of unfussy pastel hues. Trousers and jackets are gently fitted and appeal to those of a retro-preppy persuasion. But the clincher is the winning combination of affordable prices and high quality; the details are particularly impressive – stitching, hems and collars are every bit as sophisticated as grander brands that cost three times as much. The clothes are arranged by colour in the airy, store and the staff are smart and obliging .

Also check out...

Gant

107 New Bond Street, W1S 1ED (7629 3313/www.gant.com). Bond Street tube. **Open** 10am-6.30pm Mon-Wed, Fri, Sat; 10am-7pm Thur; noon-5pm Sun. **Credit** AmEx, DC, MC, V. **Sells** M.
For branches see index.

Women

Betty Jackson

311 Brompton Road, SW3 2DY (7589 7884/www.bettyjackson.com). South Kensington tube. **Open** 10.30am-6.30pm Mon-Fri; 10am-6pm Sat; noon-5pm Sun. **Credit** AmEx, DC, MC, V. **Sells** W.

Famous as the designer of Eddy and Patsy's outrageous costumes in the hit television comedy *Absolutely Fabulous*, Betty Jackson offers classic clothing with a large dose of chic. Key in autumn/winter 2008/9 is a painted poppy print featured on coats, dresses and skirts. Tapered trousers and bold colours for knitwear are also strong. Spring/summer 2009 is full of movement, and pieces are airy and light, with water embroideries, fluid fabrics, light textured jacquards and fine stripes setting the tone. Check out her cheaper range at Debenhams.

Hoss Intropia

213 Regent Street, W1B 4NF (7287 3569/ www.hossintropia.com). Oxford Circus tube. **Open** 10am-7pm Mon-Wed; 10am-8pm Thur-Sat; noon-6pm Sun. **Credit** AmEx, MC, V. **Sells** W.

Hoss Intropia's Regent Street flagship proved so successful that the Spanish label opened a second shop in Sloane Square in autumn 2007. It seems London can't get enough of the brand's individual, wearable designs. Expect clothing characterised by unusual fabrics, contrasting prints and vibrant colours. As well as useful basics, the autumn/winter 2008/9 collection boasts some fantastic dresses: look out for short and sassy sequined mini dresses, full-length silk gowns, smocks and knitted dresses. Other highlights include elegant black, beaded, pleated funnel-neck coats. Attention to detail is paramount, hence the use of hand embroidery, sequins, stones and beading. Prices vary considerably – a simple dress or trousers can be had for as little as £60 to £70, but more elaborate pieces are over £300. The accessories range has expanded significantly, with shoes, bags and jewellery. New for autumn/winter 2008/9 is a range of watches, starting at £149.
For branch see index.

Luella

25 Brook Street, W1K 4HB (7518 1830/ www.luella.com). Bond Street tube. **Open** 10am-6pm Mon-Wed, Fri, Sat; 10am-7pm Thur. **Credit** AmEx, MC, V. **Sells** W.

The opening of Luella's first stand-alone store in September 2007 coincided with her return to London Fashion Week, where she continues to show. The 1,400sq ft space – all wood panelling, old leather and pop culture references – houses Luella's ready-to-wear and accessories collections. She originally made her name with roomy, strappy, charm-laden bags, but her fun, sexy prom dresses have also been gaining momentum, with young London hipsters such as Alexa Chung and Lily Allen regularly snapped in them. The autumn/ winter 2008/9 main line takes a somewhat more gothic turn, inspired by witches and all things pagan. However – this being Luella – it's a witty affair and includes super-wearable smocked blouses, checked dresses, and a slew of covetable accessories including satchels and totes adorned with bells and ribbons. The trademark T-shirts (£79) are still strong.

Orla Kiely

31-33 Monmouth Street, WC2H 9DD (7240 4022/www.orlakiely.com). Covent Garden tube. **Open** 10am-6.30pm Mon-Sat; noon-5pm Sun. **Credit** AmEx, MC, V. **Sells** W.

Orla Kierly's individual mis-matching colour combinations made her a name in the fashion world, and graphic prints and layered textures adorn the Covent Garden flagship. The Dublin-born designer has been called a 'quiet force' in the industry but her designs speak loud and clear, from original laminate totes and purses (starting at £56) to leather bags. It may have been accessories that shot Kiely to fame, but her womenswear is attracting an increasing following. Stripy jackets, tops and flowery dresses are inspired by the 1960s and '70s. The quality of the fabrics is top-notch and garments are temptingly tactile, but they're not cheap.

Stella McCartney

30 Bruton Street, W1J 6LG (7518 3100/ www.stellamccartney.com). Bond Street or Green Park tube. **Open** 10am-6pm Mon-Wed, Fri, Sat; 10am-7pm Thur. **Credit** AmEx, DC, MC, V. **Sells** W.

It's been more than six years since Stella McCartney launched her label, and, with every collection stronger than the last, even her original doubters have become converts. Her easy-to-wear, luxe but sporty look has enduring appeal and is a hit with young Hollywood, off-duty supermodels and fashionistas with cash to flash. For autumn/winter 2008/9, expect to find McCartney's trademark sweater dresses, swing coats and inventive alternatives to fur; this time she has used felt and mohair. Poetic blouses, broderie anglaise dresses and leather platform boots feature heavily and are destined to work their way into many fashion-conscious wardrobes. Joining the main line, fragrance, skincare and sportswear collaboration with Adidas, is an expanded accessories line. McCartney's views on animal rights

Margaret Howell

are well known, so her bags, belts and shoes are made in cruelty-free fabrics such as satin, velvet, nylon and canvas.

Temperley London

6-10 Colville Mews, Lonsdale Road, W11 2DA (7229 7957/www.temperleylondon.com). Notting Hill Gate tube. **Open** 10am-6pm Mon-Wed, Fri; 10am-7pm Thur; 11am-6pm Sat. **Credit** AmEx, MC, V. **Sells** W.
British designer Alice Temperley had a vision: to create a label for the 'upwardly mobile romantic', a blending together of city chic and country living. The label has been dismissed by some as a load of sparkle and sequins, but it has become something of a mini institution, selling in over 37 countries and establishing itself as a firm favourite among famous partygoers – Sarah Jessica Parker and Helena Christensen have both sported the brand. At the Notting Hill boutique, fine lace and embroidery hang alongside intricate beadwork (qualities also represented in the Temperley bridalwear; *see p64* Temperley London Bridal Room). The collection for autumn/winter 2008/9 features lots of short and snappy frocks in vibrant colours for all those parties. The shop also stocks luxe bags and sunglasses.

Also check out...

Alberta Ferretti

205-206 Sloane Street, SW1X 9QX (7235 2349/www.aeffe.com). Knightsbridge tube. **Open** 10am-6pm Mon, Tue, Thur-Sat; 10am-7pm Wed. **Credit** AmEx, MC, V. **Sells** W.
Two-floor flagship of the Italian designer known for her delicate, feminine dresses.

Amanda Wakeley

80 Fulham Road, SW3 6HR (7590 9105/www.amandawakeley.com). South Kensington tube. **Open** 10am-6pm Mon, Tue, Thur-Sat; 10am-7pm Wed; 11am-5pm Sun. **Credit** AmEx, MC, V. **Sells** W.
Sexy clothes for grown-up women.

Betsey Johnson

29 Floral Street, WC2 9DP (7240 6164/www.betseyjohnson.com). Covent Garden tube. **Open** 10.30am-6.30pm Mon-Wed; 11am-7pm Thur-Sat; noon-5pm Sun. **Credit** AmEx, MC, V. **Sells** W.
Packed with Johnson's trademark dresses, accessories and limited-edition designs.

Chanel

278-280 Brompton Road, SW3 2AB (7581 8620/www.chanel.com). South Kensington tube. **Open** 10am-6pm Mon-Sat; 1-5pm Sun. **Credit** AmEx, DC, MC, V. **Sells** W.
For branches see index.

Chloé

152-153 Sloane Street, SW1X 9BX (7823 5348/www.chloe.com). Sloane Square tube. **Open** 10am-6pm Mon, Tue, Thur-Sat; 10am-7pm Wed. **Credit** AmEx, DC, MC, V. **Sells** W, C.
The sturdy bags and shoes are still objects of lust, while the girly smocks and boxy jackets have spawned countless copies.

Diane von Furstenberg

83 Ledbury Road, W11 2AG (7221 1120/www.dvf.com). Notting Hill Gate tube. **Open** 10am-6pm Mon-Sat; noon-6pm Sun. **Credit** AmEx, DC, MC, V. **Sells** W.
For branches see index.

Donna Karan

46 Conduit Street, W1S 2YW (7479 7900/www.donnakaran.com). Oxford Circus tube. **Open** 10.30am-6.30pm Mon-Wed, Fri; 10.30am-7pm Thur; 10am-6pm Sat; noon-5pm Sun. **Credit** AmEx, DC, MC, V. **Sells** W.

Ghost

36 Ledbury Road, W11 2AB (7229 1057/www.ghost.co.uk). Notting Hill Gate tube. **Open** 10.30am-6.30pm Mon- Fri; 10am-6pm Sat. **Credit** AmEx, MC, V. **Sells** W.
Tanya Sarne's antique-effect frocks.
For branches see index.

Jesiré

28 James Street, WC2E 8PA (7420 4450/www.jesire.net). Covent Garden tube. **Open** 10.30am-7.30pm Mon-Wed, Fri; 10.30am-8pm Thur; 10am-7.30pm Sat; noon-6pm Sun. **Credit** AmEx, MC, V. **Sells** W.
The flagship of the mid-priced label that's especially strong on nicely cut dresses.

Matthew Williamson

28 Bruton Street, W1J 6QH (7629 6200/www.matthewwilliamson.com). Green Park tube. **Open** 10am-6pm Mon-Wed, Fri, Sat; 10am-7pm Thur. **Credit** AmEx, MC, V. **Sells** W.
Whimsical clothes with an A-list fan base.

Miu Miu

123 New Bond Street, W1S 1EJ (7409 0900/www.miumiu.com). Bond Street or Oxford Circus tube. **Open** 10am-6pm Mon-Wed, Fri, Sat; 10am-7pm Thur. **Credit** AmEx, DC, MC, V. **Sells** W.

Moschino

28-29 Conduit Street, W1S 2YB (7318 0555/www.moschino.com). Oxford Circus tube. **Open** 10am-6pm Mon-Wed, Fri, Sat; 10am-7pm Thur. **Credit** AmEx, MC, V. **Sells** W.

Nanette Lepore

206 Westbourne Grove, W11 2RH (7221 8889/www.nanettelepore.com). Notting Hill Gate tube. **Open** 10am-6pm Mon-Wed, Fri, Sat; 10am-7pm Thur; noon-5pm Sun. **Credit** AmEx, MC, V. **Sells** W.
US designer with a colourful retro style.

Ross + Bute by Anonymous

57 Ledbury Road, W11 2AA (7727 2348/www.anonymousclothing.com). Notting Hill Gate tube. **Open** 10am-6pm Mon-Sat; noon-5pm Sun. **Credit** AmEx, MC, V. **Sells** W.
A feminine range specialising in lace detailing. Dresses, camisoles and shirts plus a range of separates and accessories.
For branch see index.

Sonia Rykiel

27-29 Brook Street, W1K 4HE (7493 5255/www.soniarykiel.com). Bond Street tube. **Open** 10am-6.30pm Mon-Wed, Fri, Sat; 10am-7pm Thur. **Credit** AmEx, MC, V. **Sells** W, C.

Theory

237 Westbourne Grove, W11 (7221 1626/www.theory.com). Notting Hill Gate tube. **Open** 10am-6pm mon-Wed, Fri; 10am-7pm Thur; noon-5pm Sun. **Credit** AmEx, MC, V. **Sells** W.

High-end NY label Theory opened its first UK store in 2008. Cuts are contemporary and simple. A second store is opening on Marylebone High Street in autumn 2008. **For branch see index**.

Men & women

Alexander McQueen

4-5 Old Bond Street, W1S 4PD (7355 0088/www.alexandermcqueen.com). Green Park tube. **Open** 10am-6pm Mon-Wed, Fri, Sat; 10am-7pm Thur. **Credit** AmEx, DC, MC, V. **Sells** M, W.

Alexander McQueen's only UK store is a groovy, contemporary space with curved lines and soft lighting. The ground floor is dedicated to womenswear and accessories, which spill into the lower-ground floor, where you'll also find some wickedly sharp men's tailoring, outrageously dapper footwear and manbags. The bags for women are equally delectable, especially the super-shiny Elvie tote. Perhaps this store and the backing of a multinational corporation (PPR) is finally blunting McQueen's famously confrontational attitude, because his collection for autumn/winter 2008/9 seems more wearable than ever. The beautiful Shetland wool overcoat would keep out the coldest of winds, but it's the rockabilly leather jacket that really caught our eye. Fans of the label on a tighter budget should seek out the diffusion line, McQ, which packs a gutsy McQueen punch, but at far more pocket-friendly prices (£130 for jeans).

Aquascutum

100 Regent Street, W1B 5SR (7675 8200/ www.aquascutum.co.uk). Piccadilly Circus tube. **Open** 10am-6.30pm Mon-Wed, Fri, Sat; 10am-7pm Thur; noon-5pm Sun. **Credit** AmEx, DC, MC, V. **Sells** M, W.

Balancing heritage alongside fashion is always a tricky business, but it's one that Aquascutum's CEO, Kim Winser, knows all about, having previously transformed Pringle. Aquascutum is rightly proud of its 155-year history and of the fact that it still makes some of its core pieces in Corby, Northamptonshire. But it also knows that heritage and tradition are no substitute for fashion when it comes to attracting new customers, and that's why Gisele has appeared in recent ad campaigns, and why jazz-loving designer Nick Hart creates the fashionable, mod-influenced Aquascutum LTD. range for men each season. More classic pieces are designed by Graeme Fidler, who's first Vintage collection of coats is available for winter 2008/9. The brand has also recently added women's tailoring to its men's made-to-measure service.

Joseph

77 Fulham Road, SW3 6RE (7823 9500/ www.joseph.co.uk). South Kensington tube. **Open** 10am-6.30pm Mon, Tue, Thur-Sat; 10am-7pm Wed; 1-6pm Sun. **Credit** AmEx, DC, MC, V. **Sells** M, W.

Subtly stylish rather than cutting edge, Joseph's long-legged trousers, oversized knitwear and sumptuous sheepskins are updated just enough to tempt loyal customers back for more each season. Pricewise, it hovers between upper-range high street brands and big catwalk names – trousers are generally over £150 and simple tops are around the £60 mark. As well as the Joseph main line, you'll find a selection of clothing and accessories by desirable, high-end labels such as Prada, Alaïa and Chloé. The menswear, around the corner at 74 Sloane Avenue (7591 0808), is in a similar vein – smart but relaxed tailoring and knitwear in luxurious fabrics.
Branches: throughout the city.

Margaret Howell

34 Wigmore Street, W1U 2RS (7009 9009/ www.margarethowell.co.uk). Bond Street tube. **Open** 10am-6pm Mon-Wed, Fri, Sat; 10am-7pm Thur. **Credit** AmEx, DC, MC, V. **Sells** M, W.

The thing that makes Howell's wonderfully wearable clothes so contemporary is her old-fashioned attitude to quality. She believes in making things well, in the UK and out of good fabric. These principles combine with her elegant designs to make for the best 'simple' clothes for sale in London. Her pared-down approach means prices can seem steep, but unlike cheap, throwaway fashion these are clothes to cherish, and which will get better with time – as will the new bags she's designed with Japanese label Porter. Her shops are also worth a visit for anyone interested in 20th-century British design – she now offers both vintage and reissued classics by Ercol, Anglepoise, Robert Welch and others.
For branches see index.

Mulberry

41-42 New Bond Street, W1S 2RY (7491 3900/www.mulberry.com). Bond Street tube. **Open** 10am-6pm Mon-Wed, Fri, Sat; 10am-7pm Thur. **Credit** AmEx, DC, MC, V. **Sells** M, W.

Having established its credentials as a bona fide fashion brand in recent years, Mulberry is now working to maintain the momentum. There's a new range of shoes designed by Jonathan Kelsey and a series of in-store collaborations. In autumn 2008, young artists from the Fred Gallery in the East End are involved in both an exhibition and in customising some of the brand's famous tote bags. Meanwhile, classic handbags like the Bayswater and Roxanne are constantly reinvented in new finishes, colours and materials, while this season's 'it' bag, the oversized Maggie, is set to be in high demand – Agyness Deyn has been using hers for months.
For branches see index.

Paul & Joe

39-41 Ledbury Road, W11 2AA (7243 5510/www.paulandjoe.com). Notting Hill Gate tube. **Open** 10am-6pm Mon-Sat; noon-5pm Sun. **Credit** AmEx, MC, V. **Sells** M, W, C.

French designer Sophie Albou's Paul & Joe is a seductive space with interiors that resemble a princess's boudoir and match the romantic, elegant and forward-thinking collections. Think classic French tailoring with a contemporary edge: structured jackets, wide-leg trousers, fringe and lace detailing, alongside impressive party dresses, all in flamboyant prints and feminine fabrics. And there's a make-up range to match. Albou named her brand after her two sons and aimed to introduce variety on to the menswear market (gents should visit the Floral Street branch). Men's garments are pensive and dandy-like. This is prêt-a-porter at its best, so invest to possess timeless pieces. In 2008/9, keep your eyes peeled for a limited-edition range in collaboration with fashion legend Pierre Cardin. Also worth a peek is Paul & Joe Sister, a more casual range featuring mini dresses and often stocked in boutiques.
For branches see index.

Paul Smith

Westbourne House, 120 & 122 Kensington Park Road, W11 2EP (7727 3553/ www.paulsmith.co.uk). Notting Hill Gate tube. **Open** 10am-6pm Mon-Fri; 10am-6.30pm Sat. **Credit** AmEx, DC, MC, V. **Sells** M, W, C.

Paul Smith's Notting Hill shop celebrated its tenth birthday in 2008; branded a 'shop in a house', customers step through its doors into a world of eccentricity. There are clothes for men, women and children, plus accessories, homewares and the odd piece of furniture, spread over four floors. The place is dotted with Sir Paul's collection of art and other objects, giving insight into the vision behind his quirky-classic tailoring. Womenswear is characterised by silhouette-enhancing garments, softened out with crinoline petticoats, silk bodices and painted taffeta. Masculine jackets are cut in traditional Prince of Wales checks, pinstripes and flannels. Menswear is a rich collection of tartans and checks with contrast detailing, satin lapels and velvet trims.
Branches: throughout the city.

Preen

5 Portobello Green, 281 Portobello Road, W10 5TZ (8968 1542). Ladbroke Grove tube. **Open** 11am-6pm Thur, Fri; 10am-6pm Sat. **Credit** MC, V. **Sells** M, W.

Tucked quite literally under the Westway overpass, Preen brings imaginative takes to traditional silhouettes – it's all about not trying too hard. The current collection is quintessentially Preen: urban, minimalist shapes and a tame colour palette cut with splashes of bombastic colour, such as cobalt blue, to stunning effect. Other highlights include typical Preen cocoon-shaped jackets, billowy shirtdresses, skirts with belts, slouchy trousers and hoodie knitwear. It was one of the first labels to produce a capsule collection for Topshop and still does. Look out for a great range of bags and shoes, plus the launch of an accessories range in spring 2009. Other London stockists include Selfridges, Harrods and Browns.

Pringle of Scotland

112 New Bond Street, W1S 1DP (7297 4580/www.pringlescotland.com). Bond Street tube. **Open** 10am-6.30pm Mon-Wed, Fri, Sat; 10am-7.30pm Thur. **Credit** AmEx, MC, V. **Sells** M, W.

Talented ex-Gucci designer Clare Waight Keller is really getting into her stride as Pringle's creative director. In autumn/ winter 2008/9 look out for glamorous metallic finishes and 1960s-style coats, all in restrained but desirable colours. Menswear is a series of classic British forms – double-

breasted suits, dinner jackets, corduroy trousers, reimagined in slim, sharp, contemporary shapes. If the runway fashion seems a bit racy, a range of traditional Scottish cashmere is always available.
For branch see index.

Vivienne Westwood
44 Conduit Street, W1S 2YL (7439 1109/ www.viviennewestwood.com). Oxford Circus tube. **Open** 10am-6pm Mon-Wed, Fri, Sat; 10am-7pm Thur; noon-5pm Sun. **Credit** AmEx, DC, MC, V. **Sells** M, W.
Vivienne Westwood is part of British fashion history, with over 30 years in the business and a damehood to her credit. Perhaps still best known for pioneering the punk look, she's since become one of Britain's most revered designers. Her pieces are recognisable for their voluminous quantities of fabric (frequently in her trademark tartan), and of course those signature corsets. The Conduit Street flagship houses the women's Gold Label main line, two diffusion ranges – Red Label and the more casual Anglomania – and menswear and accessories. The original World's End premises carries a smaller selection of clothing and the full range of accessories, as well as special-edition pieces, which are exclusive to the store. The small Davies Street salon stocks only the Gold Label and accessories, and provides a couture and bridal service.
For branches (including Worlds End) see index.

Also check out...

Agnès b
35-36 Floral Street, WC2E 9DJ (7379 1992/www.agnesb.com). Covent Garden or Leicester Square tube. **Open** 10.30am-6.30pm Mon-Wed, Fri; 10.30am-7pm Thur, Sat; noon-6pm Sun. **Credit** AmEx, MC, V. **Sells** M, W.
Stylishly low-key, retro-influenced French label. The men's knitwear, shirts and suits are especially covetable.
For branches see index.

Antoni & Alison
43 Rosebery Avenue, EC1R 4SH (7833 2141/www.antoniandalison.co.uk). Farringdon tube/rail/19, 38, 341 bus. **Open** 10.30am-6.30pm Mon-Fri. **Credit** AmEx, MC, V. Sells M, W, C.
Design duo known for witty slogan T-shirts.

Bottega Veneta
33 Sloane Street, SW1X 9NR (7838 9394/ www.bottegaveneta.com). Knightsbridge tube. **Open** 10am-6pm Mon, Tue, Thur-Sat; 10am-7pm Wed. **Credit** AmEx, DC, MC, V. **Sells** M, W.
For branch see index.

Burberry
21-23 New Bond Street, W1S 2RE (7968 0000/www.burberry.com). Bond Street tube. **Open** 10am-7pm Mon-Sat; noon-6pm Sun. **Credit** AmEx, DC, MC, V. **Sells** M, W, C.
Burberry continues to place great emphasis on its Britishness. Burberry's iconic macs remain investment pieces that will justify the heavy price tag (£700 plus). For the factory shop, *see p43* **Sales & events**.
For branches see index.

Christian Dior
31 Sloane Street, SW1X 9NR (7245 1300/ www.dior.com). Knightsbridge tube. **Open** 10am-6.30pm Mon, Tue, Thur-Sat; 10am-7pm Wed; noon-6pm Sun. **Credit** AmEx, DC, MC, V. **Sells** W.

Cordings
19 Piccadilly, W1J 0LA (7734 0830/www.cordings.co.uk). Piccadilly Circus tube. **Open** 9.30am-6.30pm Mon-Wed, Fri; 10am-7pm Thur; 10am-6pm Sat. **Credit** AmEx, DC, MC, V. **Sells** M, W.
Good quality countrywear from Eric Clapton's favourite outfitter. He liked the company so much he bought it in 2003.

Daks
10 Old Bond Street, W1S 4PS (7409 4040/ www.daks.com). Bond Street or Green Park tube. **Open** 10am-6pm Mon-Wed, Fri, Sat; 10am-7pm Thur. **Credit** AmEx, DC, MC, V. **Sells** M, W.
Venerable British label offering a contemporary, Giles Deacon-designed line for women, and a dandified collection for men by Bruce Montgomery.
For branch see index.

Dolce & Gabbana
6-8 Old Bond Street, W1S 4PH (7659 9000/www.dolcegabbana.it). Green Park tube. **Open** 10am-6pm Mon-Wed, Fri, Sat; 10am-7pm Thur. **Credit** AmEx, DC, MC, V. **Sells** M, W.
For branches (including D&G) see index.

Emilio Pucci
170 Sloane Street, SW1X 9QG (7201 8171/www.emiliopucci.com). Knightsbridge tube. **Open** 10am-6pm Mon, Tue, Thur-Sat; 10am-7pm Wed. **Credit** AmEx, DC, MC, V. **Sells** M, W.
The iconic swirly prints adorn everything from dresses to wallets.

Etro
14 Old Bond Street, W1X 3DB (7495 5767/www.etro.it). Green Park tube. **Open** 10am-6pm Mon-Sat. **Credit** AmEx, DC, MC, V. **Sells** M, W.
Rich, clashing fabrics (especially paisley) are the signature of this Italian fashion house.

Fendi
20-22 Sloane Street, SW1X 9NE (7838 6288/www.fendi.com). Knightsbridge tube. **Open** 10am-6pm Mon, Tue, Thur, Fri; 10.30am-7pm Wed; 10.30am-6pm Sat. **Credit** AmEx, DC, MC, V. **Sells** M, W.

Giorgio Armani
37 Sloane Street, SW1X 9LP (7235 6232/ www.giorgioarmani.com). Knightsbridge tube. **Open** 10am-6pm Mon, Tue, Thur-Sat; 10am-7pm Wed. **Credit** AmEx, MC, V. **Sells** M, W.
For branches (Emporio Armani, Armani Collection) see index.

Gucci
18 Sloane Street, SW1X 9NE (7235 6707/www.gucci.com). Knightsbridge tube. **Open** 10am-6pm Mon, Tue, Thur-Sat; 10am-7pm Wed. **Credit** AmEx, DC, MC, V. **Sells** M, W.
For branches see index.

Hermès
179 Sloane Street, SW1X 9QP (7823 1014/www.hermes.com). Knightsbridge tube. **Open** 10am-6pm Mon-Sat. **Credit** AmEx, DC, MC, V. **Sells** M, W.
For branches see index.

Issey Miyake
52 Conduit Street, W1S 2YX (7851 4620/ www.isseymiyake.com). Oxford Circus tube. **Open** 10am-6pm Mon-Sat. **Credit** AmEx, MC, V. **Sells** M, W.
For branches (including Pleats Please) see index.

Jaeger
200-206 Regent Street, W1R 6BN (7979 1100/www.jaeger.co.uk). Oxford Circus tube. **Open** 10am-7pm Mon-Wed, Fri, Sat; 10am-8pm Thur; noon-6pm Sun. **Credit** AmEx, DC, MC, V. **Sells** M, W.
Once synonymous with middle England, now a byword for classic British chic. The hipper Jaeger London diffusion label has given the brand a kickstart.
For branches see index.

Jean Paul Gaultier Boutique
171-175 Draycott Avenue, SW3 3AJ (7584 4648/www.jpgaultier.com). South Kensington tube. **Open** 10am-6pm Mon, Tue, Thur-Sat; 10am-7pm Wed. **Credit** AmEx, DC, MC, V. **Sells** M, W, .

Lucien Pellat-Finet
51 Elizabeth Street, SW1W 9PP (7259 9995/www.lucienpellat-finet.com). Sloane Square or Victoria tube. **Open** 10am-6pm Mon-Fri; 11am-4pm Sat. **Credit** AmEx, MC, V. **Sells** M, W, C.
Rock'n'roll cashmere in wild colours and even wilder patterns – think marijuana leaves and skulls.

Louis Vuitton
17-18 New Bond Street, W1S 2RB (7399 4050/www.vuitton.com). Piccadilly Circus tube. **Open** 10am-7pm Mon-Sat. **Credit** AmEx, DC, MC, V. **Sells** M, W.
The London flagship.

Maison Martin Margiela
22 Bruton Place, W1J 6NE (7629 2682/ www.maisonmartinmargiela.com). Bond Street or Green Park tube. **Open** 11am-7pm Mon-Sat. **Credit** AmEx, MC, V. **Sells** M, W.
The Belgian designer's pieces are both innovative, eccentric and luxurious. If you're pockets aren't deep enough, check out the cheaper urban line MM6.

Marc Jacobs
24-25 Mount Street, W1K 2RR (7399 1690/www.marcjacobs.com). Bond Street or Green Park tube. **Open** 11am-7pm Mon-Sat; noon-6pm Sun. **Credit** AmEx, MC, V. **Sells** M, W, C.
Opened in 2006, the London flagship stocks mens-, womens- and childrenswear as well as the coveted bags and shoes.

Marni
26 Sloane Street, SW1X 9NE (7245 9520/ www.marni.com). Knightsbridge tube. **Open** 10am-6pm Mon, Tue, Thur-Sat; 10am-7pm Wed. **Credit** AmEx, DC, MC, V. **Sells** M, W, C.

Nicole Farhi
158 New Bond Street, W1S 2UB (7499 8368/www.nicolefarhi.com). Green Park tube. **Open** 10am-6pm Mon-Wed, Fri; 10am-7pm Thur; 10am-6.30pm Sat; 11am-5pm Sun. **Credit** AmEx, DC, MC, V. **Sells** M, W.
Stylish, comfortable classics, such as airy linens, chunky knitwear, woollen suits and luxurious coats in sheepskin and cashmere.
Branches: throughout the city.

Prada
16-18 Old Bond Street, W1X 3DA (7647 5000/www.prada.com). Green Park tube. **Open** 10am-6pm Mon-Wed, Fri, Sat; 10am-7pm Thur; noon-5pm Sun **Credit** AmEx, DC, MC, V. **Sells** M, W.
For branch see index.

Ralph Lauren
1 New Bond Street, W1S 3RL (7535 4600/ www.polo.com). Green Park tube. **Open** 10am-6pm Mon-Wed, Fri, Sat; 10am-7pm Thur; noon-5pm Sun. **Credit** AmEx, DC, MC, V. **Sells** M, W.
For branches see index.

Selina Blow
1 Ellis Street, SW1X 9AL (7730 2077/ www.selinablow.com). Sloane Square tube. **Open** 10am-6pm Mon-Fri; 11am-6pm Sat. **Credit** AmEx, MC, V. **Sells** M, W, C.
The British-Sri Lankan designer creates tailored pieces in flamboyant textiles. Unique accessories, such as contemporary footwear hand-embroidered in Pakistan, are sold alongside her collection.

Ted Baker
9-10 Floral Street, WC2E 9HW (7836 7808/www.tedbaker.co.uk). Covent Garden tube. **Open** 10am-7pm Mon-Wed, Fri, Sat; 10am-8pm Thur; noon-6pm Sun. **Credit** AmEx, MC, V. **Sells** M, W.
Former Glasgow shirtmaker Ted Baker's contemporary suits have legions of fans.
Branches: throughout the city.

Yohji Yamamoto
14-15 Conduit Street, W1S 2XJ (7491 4129/www.yohjiyamamoto.co.jp). Oxford Circus or Piccadilly Circus tube. **Open** 10am-6pm Mon-Sat. **Credit** AmEx, MC, V. **Sells** M, W.

Yves Saint Laurent: Rive Gauche
33 Old Bond Street, W1X 4HH (7493 1800/ www.ysl.com). Green Park tube. **Open** 10am-6pm Mon-Wed, Fri, Sat; 10am-7pm Thur. **Credit** AmEx, DC, MC, V. **Sells** M, W.
The cult bags and shoes (including styles you won't see elsewhere) as well as the sleek, grown-up clothes.
For branch see index.

Knitwear

See also p31 **House of Weardowney**.

Ballantyne
153A New Bond Street, W1S 2TZ (7495 6184/www.ballantyne.it). Green Park tube. **Open** 10am-6pm Mon-Wed, Fri, Sat; 10am-7pm Thur. **Credit** AmEx, DC, MC, V. **Sells** M, W.
Established in 1921 in Scotland, and once the realm of safe cashmere knits, Ballantyne's head office is now in Milan. The new management have brought Italian design flair to the brand, but at the same time held on to to its fine manufacturing traditions. That's why the famous intarsia diamond sweaters retail for around £800 – each one requires hours of hand-work by the Scottish craftsmen that make them. Ballantyne's fashion credentials are being strengthened with a range of handbags and men's accessories, but the cashmere remains the main attraction.

Also check out...

Belinda Robertson
4 West Halkin Street, SW1X 8JA (7235 0519/www.belindarobertson.com). Hyde Park Corner or Knightsbridge tube. **Open** 10am-6.30pm Mon-Fri; 10am-6pm Sat. **Credit** AmEx, MC, V. **Sells** M, W.
Fashion-led Scottish cashmere.

Brora
344 King's Road, SW3 5UR (7352 3697/ www.brora.co.uk). Sloane Square tube/11, 19, 22 bus. **Open** 10am-6pm Mon-Sat; noon-5pm Sun. **Credit** AmEx, MC, V. **Sells** M, W, C.
Well-priced, classic Scottish cashmere and more for upmarket mums, dads and their cossetted kids.
For branches see index.

John Smedley
24 Brook Street, W1K 5DG (7495 2222/ www.johnsmedley.com). Bond Street tube. **Open** 10am-6pm Mon-Wed, Fri, Sat; 10am-7pm Thur.; noon-5pm Sun. **Credit** AmEx, MC, V. **Sells** M, W.
A cult British knitwear label with sweaters, tops and polo shirts for everyone, whether in cashmere, merino wool or organic, unbleached cotton.

Sales & events

Designer sample sales and discount shops for every savvy shopper's diary and address book.

Browns Labels for Less
50 South Molton Street, W1K 5RD (7514 0052/www.brownsfashion.com). Bond Street tube. **Open** 10am-6.30pm Mon-Wed, Fri, Sat; 10am-7pm Thur. **Credit** AmEx, MC, V. **Sells** M, W.
This Browns (*see p35*) offshoot has end-of-season lines from high-end designers, at impressive discounts.

Burberry Factory Shop
29-53 Chatham Place, E9 6LP (8328 4287). Hackney Central rail. **Open** 10am-6pm Mon-Sat; 11am-5pm Sun. **Credit** AmEx, DC, MC, V. **Sells** M, W, C.
A vast range of excess stock at up to 70% off. Classic men's macs can be had for around £199.

Designer Sales UK
The Bridge, Atlantis, 1st Floor, 146 Brick Lane, E1 6QL (mailing list 01273858464/during sale week 7247 8595/www.designersales.co.uk). Liverpool Street tube/rail. **Dates** see website. **Credit** MC, V. **Sells** M, W.
Stock from over 70 designers such as PPQ, Biba, Betty Jackson and See by Chloé. Also has a permanent online sale at www.designersales.biz.

Designer Warehouse Sales
5-6 Islington Studios, N7 7NU (7697 9888/www.designerwarehousesales.com). **Dates** see website. **Credit** MC, V. **Sells** M, W.
Separate mens- and womenswear sales are held throughout the year, featuring Coco de Mer, Hussein Chalayan and Nicole Farhi, to name but a few.

London Fashion Weekend
Natural History Museum, Cromwell Road, SW7 5BD (tickets 0870 890 0097/www.londonfashionweekend.co.uk) South Kensington tube. **Dates** Feb, Sept 2009. **Credit** MC, V. **Sells** M, W.
A host of familiar names at the twice-yearly sample sales held in conjunction with London Fashion Week. Tickets from £10. The location can be subject to change.

Paul Smith Sale Shop
23 Avery Row, W1X 9HB (7493 1287/www.paulsmith.co.uk). Bond Street tube. **Open** 10.30am-6.30pm Mon-Wed, Fri, Sat; 10.30am-7pm Thur; 1-5.30pm Sun. **Credit** AmEx, DC, MC, V. **Sells** M.
Previous season's stock with 30%-50% off. Note: it's strictly menswear.

Secret Sample Sale
www.secretsamplesale.co.uk. Held six times a year at various locations around London; brands include Belstaff, Missoni and Celine, reduced by up to 80%.

carhartt
CARHARTT FLAGSHIP STORE
15 - 17 EARLHAM ST.
COVENT GARDEN
LONDON
WC2H 9LL
WWW.THECARHARTTSTORE.CO.UK
THE CARHARTT STORE
56 NEAL ST.
COVENT GARDEN
LONDON
WC2H 9PA
THE CARHARTT STORE
59 - 61 OLDHAM ST.
NORTHERN QUARTER
MANCHESTER
M1 1JR
THE CARHARTT WAREHOUSE
18 ELLINGFORT RD.
HACKNEY
LONDON
E8 3PA
carhartt®
Work In Progress Textilhandels GmbH - authorized distributor for
carhartt and carhartt logo are registered trademarks of Carhartt Inc., Dearborn, Mi 48121, U.S.A.

High Street

For US chains **Urban Outfitters** and **American Apparel**, *see p20* and *p48*, respectively.

Abercrombie & Fitch

7 Burlington Gardens, W1S 3ES (0844 412 5750/www.uk.abercrombie.com). Oxford Circus or Piccadilly Circus tube. **Open** 10am-7pm Mon-Sat; noon-6pm Sun. **Credit** AmEx, DC, MC, V. **Sells** M, W.

This is a case of having to be seen to be believed. The US clothing brand's 2007 arrival horrified the neighbours. The way *not* to impress the Savile Row set that it's now geographically a part of: with banging tunes and a topless male model standing in the doorway at all times. Indeed, with its dimmed lighting and weird scent, the place feels more like a bizarre, posh club than a shop. Despite this, or maybe because of it, A&F's logo-heavy sweaters, jeans and polos (to be worn with collars turned up, of course) are mighty popular with the Sloane Square set.

All Saints

57-59 Long Acre, WC2E 9JL (7836 0801/ www.allsaints.co.uk). Covent Garden tube. **Open** 9.30am-9pm Mon-Wed, Fri; 9.30am-10pm Thur; 10am-9pm Sat; noon-6pm Sun. **Credit** AmEx, MC, V. **Sells** M, W.

With its distressed denim, leather and glitzy sequinned asymmetric dresses, All Saints provides edgy glamour with a dose of knowingly trashy bling. The shop's exposed brickwork and pumping music help to boost its credentials among European visitors and trendy twentysomethings. In 2008, the look for ladies focused on graffiti print T-shirts with unfinished hems, short, multilayered skirts and floaty, patterned dresses. A small but distinctive selection of heels completes the look. For men, there are fitted leather jackets, a wide range of denim jeans, tailored shirts and karate-style plimsolls.
Branches: throughout the city.

Banana Republic

224 Regent Street, W1B 3BR (7758 3550/ www.bananarepublic.eu). Oxford Circus tube. **Open** 10am-8pm Mon-Wed, Fri; 10am-9pm Thur; 9am-9pm Sat; noon-6pm Sun. **Credit** AmEx, MC, V. **Sells** M, W.

The 17,000sq ft store on Regent Street covers two vast floors. Men are well catered for with a sea of neatly stacked fine-knit V-necks, military shirts, neutral-toned cords and classic chinos. For women there are classic wardrobe staples and chic accessories. Autumn/winter 2008/9 sees the launch of the 30th anniversary collection, which updates classic pieces three decades on; think little black dresses in silk jersey or black lace, and cleverly tailored crisp white shirts. For men there are tweed jackets with skinny ties and an array of dark grey trenchcoats, tuxedos and cable-knit sweaters.

Comptoir des Cotonniers

8 South Molton Street, W1K 5QQ (7495 1464/www.comptoirdescotonniers.com). Bond Street tube. **Open** 10am-7pm Mon-Sat; noon-5pm Sun. **Credit** AmEx, MC, V. **Sells** W, C.

Despite being a relatively new kid on the block, this chic French label already has ten branches in some of the capital's most prestigious shopping areas and is fast becoming a popular choice for classic, unfussy clothing. The emphasis is on quality and wearability, with the autumn/winter 2008/9 collection offering diaphanous blouses, tailored high-waisted trousers, belted safari-style jackets and shirt-dresses in crisp cottons. The brand excels at subtle detailing with pleats, oversize buttons and unusual hemlines. The childrenswear collection and the stores' campaigns fronted by mothers and daughters promote clothes that span generations. With prices averaging £80 for dresses and skirts, it ain't cheap, but with its fine-quality fabrics, tailored styles and excellent finishes, you may decide it's worth the money.
Branches: throughout the city.

COS

222 Regent Street, W1B 5BD (7478 0400/ www.cosstores.com). Oxford Circus tube. **Open** 10am-8pm Mon-Wed, Fri, Sat; 10am-9pm Thur; noon-6pm Sun. **Credit** AmEx, MC, V. **Sells** M, W.

H&M (*see p47*) created a buzz when it opened this flagship store in 2007; since then, the brand has gone from strength to strength. Catering for those who have grown tired of fighting their way through a frenzy of teenagers at the sale rails, COS (which stands for Collection of Style) is the antithesis to H&M's throwaway trend-led fashion. But what was supposed to be a grown-up sister of H&M actually looks more like Gap's posh sibling. The slick, well laid-out store houses an impressive range of simple, classic separates and coats, jackets and eveningwear in good-quality fabrics and both neutral and vibrant colours. Recent collections have focused on simple shift dresses, classic narrow leg suits for men, and unfussy boxy tops and skirts for women. Prices start at around £50 for a dress and £80 for jackets; men's suits average between £200 and £250.

French Connection

396 Oxford Street, W1C 1JX (7629 7766/ www.frenchconnection.com). Bond Street tube. **Open** 10am-8pm Mon-Wed, Fri; 10am-9pm Thur; 10am-7pm Sat; noon-6pm Sun. **Credit** AmEx, DC, MC, V. **Sells** M, W.

Now considered an old-timer on the list of high street brands, French Connection has worked hard over the past couple of years to free itself from the shackles of its FCUK identity – and it appears to have succeeded. Designs for autumn/winter 2008/9 are a mix of mature and on-trend, with unfussy separates and outerwear in a range of good-quality fabrics at the smarter end, and men's lumberjack shirts at the more casual end. Dresses and eveningwear in sequinned and glittery fabrics, shift dresses and oversize capes are among the offerings for girls. The classic T-shirts and knitwear remain firm favourites, and its good selection of denim jeans and cotton workwear trousers complement every wardrobe.
Branches: throughout the city.

Jigsaw

126-127 New Bond Street, W1S 1DZ (7491 4484/www.jigsaw-online.com). Bond Street tube. **Open** 10am-6.30pm Mon-Wed, Fri, Sat; 10am-7.30pm Thur; noon-6pm Sun. **Credit** AmEx, MC, V. **Sells** W, C.

Shop talk Rebecca Lowrey Boyd

Rebecca Lowrey Boyd (aka Top Bird) flew from her native Sydney – where she'd been an editor of glossy mags – in February 2007. She's currently nesting in the Big Smoke, from where she writes her London shopping blog Wee Birdy (www.weebirdy.com).

'I love wandering along streets with a number of independent boutiques. My favourite is Cheshire Street in east London. **Shelf** (*see p203*) has an amazing collection of design-led products. **Labour & Wait** (*see p129*) is also here; I love its earthy quality. I used to live on Kingsland Road and loved walking along the canal to **Broadway Market** (*see p22*) on Saturdays for a wander around the stalls as well as the shops that line the street.

'The whole craft trend has really exploded now. Online there's **Etsy** (www.etsy.com). Rob Ryan sells a lot of his stuff here and has also set up shop on Columbia Road (*see p166* **Ryantown**).

'**Liberty** (*see p16*) is my favourite department store. It's a beautiful shopping experience and I love the sense of history.

'When I first moved here it was all about **Topshop** (*see p46*), but **Cos** (*see p45*) is my favourite on the high street now. I also really like **Jigsaw** (*see p45*) for accessories and I'm looking forward to seeing what **Whistles** (*see p47*) is doing now that Jane Shepherdson's taken over.

'I've just bought a load of stuff in the sale at **Start** (*see p36*). They've got a great line-up with all my favourite labels. I sign up to get messages on their secret sales – which really are secret.

Fair game

As this guide went to press in October 2008, the **Fairtrade London Campaign** (www.fairtradelondon.org.uk) was all set to formally announce that the Big Smoke has now become the world's largest official Fairtrade city – the result of a five-year campaign launched by former mayor Ken Livingstone, and given its final push by his successor Boris Johnson. To achieve this status (it's one of some 500 official Fairtrade communities worldwide), a certain number of the city's boroughs had to individually reach five goals set by the Fairtrade Foundation, the overall aims of which were for Fairtrade products to be readily available in local shops and eateries and be used by a number of workplaces, educational establishments and community organisations. Some 900 retailers (as well as around 600 restaurants) across 21 London boroughs now sell a selection of Fairtrade items. 'The people of London are demanding change in order to tip the balance of trade in favour of the producer,' says Sophi Tranchell, chair of the Fairtrade London Steering Group.

The term 'Fairtrade' has now entered the British vernacular. But what does it actually entail? The familiar logo that's found on numerous products (mostly food and drink, but increasingly clothes and bedlinen) guarantees that producers in developing countries get a fair price for their products as well as receiving a community premium that they can choose how to invest. This is all underwritten by the international Fairtrade Labelling Organisation with its system of monitoring and inspection.

An important recent breakthrough has been the availability of clothes made from Fairtrade cotton – a vital support for cotton farmers working in some of the world's poorest countries, such as Mali in West Africa, who face unfair competition from massively subsidised North American cotton farmers. Several

of the big chains are now stocking Fairtrade cotton products, including **Marks & Spencer** (*see p16*) and **Debenhams** (*see p16*), which is trialling a range of menswear, and **Topshop** (*see p46*), which also stocks other fashion lines led by Fairtrade principles, but which don't always have official Fairtrade status, such as **Where** (www.wherefashion.co.uk) and **Annie Greenabelle** (www.anniegreenabelle.co.uk). The Fairtrade mark only certifies that the cotton is Fairtrade, however – it doesn't regulate the subsequent production process. But a number of specialist firms are committed to ethical trading at every stage of the clothing supply chain: style-conscious brands such as **People Tree** (www.peopletree.co.uk), **Ascension** (www.ascensionclothing.co.uk), **Gossypium** (www.gossypium.co.uk) and **Epona** (www.eponaclothing.com). Keep a look out for brands such as these in the increasing number of ethically led shops around the capital, from the dedicated stalwarts such as **Oxfam** (*see p63*) and **Ganesha** (*see p19*) to fashion-led stores such as Angel's eco-boutique **Equa** (*see p29*) and the ethically aware concept store **Potassium** (*see p20*) in Marble Arch, which stocks Dutch fairly traded denim label Kuyichi. Childrenswear shops are also ahead when it comes to fair trade – a natural progression given that many were early stockists of related organic products due to their baby-friendly nature; Bethnal Green's **Finnesse** (*see p259*), Stoke Newington's **Born** (*see p261*) and Camden's **Blue Daisy** (*see p262*) all sell stylish fair trade baby clothes and accessories from the likes of PeopleTree. **Shepherds bookbinders**, meanwhile, is now stocking high-quality fair trade Bengali paper.

So, there's no longer any excuse for apathy, or argument about lack of choice. Use your spending power to make a difference.

With its classic lines, simply cut separates and luxurious fabrics, Jigsaw feels every inch the grown-up of high street fashion; and after keeping something of a low profile over the past few years, it's now firmly back on the radars of the capital's style-conscious thirtysomethings. While designs seem to vary little from season to season, there's the occasional surprise, such as the bronze sequinned cardigan and a banana yellow trench coat, which both appear in its autumn/winter 2008/9 collection. Influences for 2008/9 are drawn from Surrealist art, 1950s film icon Tippi Hedren and vintage YSL, resulting in a range that uses bold, bright colours and retro-style fabrics, like crepes and damasks, to full effect. Cashmere-mix cardigans start at £50, while wool-mix coats go from £150.
Branches: throughout the city.

Reiss

Kent House, 14-17 Market Place, W1H 7AJ (7637 9112/www.reiss.co.uk). Oxford Circus tube. **Open** 10am-6.30pm Mon-Wed, Fri, Sat; 10am-7.30pm Thur; noon-6pm Sun. **Credit** AmEx, MC, V. **Sells** M, W.

Bridging a cavernous gap between high street and high-end fashion, Reiss is the place to shop if you like your clothing well made and directional. With its mix of tailored suits and separates and glamorous after-dark and special-occasion dresses, it's not hard to figure out why this shop is popular. The layout of the shop is clean, uncluttered and well organised, with friendly staff readily available to offer advice. The look for autumn/winter 2008/9 is typically smart, classy and trendy with menswear offering heavyweight dark denim, crisp shirts with epaulettes and chunky knits in neutral colours. For ladies, there are flirty shift dresses with exquisite lace details and ruching in the finest of fabrics. Our two grumbles with Reiss are its harsh no-refunds policy and the fact that a large number of items are labelled dry-clean only.
Branches: throughout the city.

Topman

214 Oxford Street, W1W 8LG (7636 7700/www.topman.com). Oxford Circus tube. **Open** 9am-9pm Mon-Sat; 11.30am-6pm Sun. **Credit** AmEx, DC, MC, V. **Sells** M.

Topman is as on-trend as the high street gets for guys. And while it's true that on a Saturday this flagship resembles something of a teenage Hades – blaring music and endless queues – everyone here knows that they're on to a good thing. Well-cut jeans for all shapes and sizes are cheap (from £20) and always popular, while on our last visit the bestseller was a Mark Ronson-style 1960s wool skinny jacket (£100). Other offerings range from brightly coloured print T-shirts to knitted polos (£25) and faux leather jackets (from £55). September 2008 saw the launch of the yearly capsule collections by young designers. Lens offers clothing by the likes of Dexter Wong, Another Boy and Casper Harup-Hanfen. A Black Trouser project, where designers Tim Hamilton and Patrick Ervell (to name a few) add their own twist to the staple black trouser, is also in the pipeline.
Branches: throughout the city.

Topshop (eco)

214 Oxford Street, W1W 8LG (7636 7700/www.topshop.com). Oxford Circus tube. **Open** 9am-9pm Mon-Sat; 11.30am-6pm Sun. **Credit** AmEx, DC, MC, V. **Sells** W.

Philip Green's fashion emporium still rules the high street, despite increasing competition and the loss of Jane Shepherdson to Whistles. With another successful Kate Moss range and celebrity fans from Kate Middleton to Coleen Rooney, Topshop manages to convince legions of teens to thirtysomethings that it has something for every female. And it's not hard to see why, with three floors of trend-led clothes. The basement houses concessions from young, independent designers like Alice McCall, Will Broome, Crafty Couture, Once Upon a Time and Sweet & Sour. The boutique section on the lower ground floor offers more individual concept-driven designs with work by designers like Danielle Scott. Add to this a vintage section, a café, shoe department, Daniel Hersheson's Blow Dry Bar, style advice, screens showing pop videos, and there isn't much left to wish for. Look out for the TRAID (Textile Recycling for Aid and International Development) collection banks. The downsides? Changing-room rage, an endless queue for returns and some rather low quality fabrics. If you lack the stamina to fight your way through the throng, Topshop To Go will bring a selection of clothing to your home or office.
Branches: throughout the city.

Whistles

12 St Christopher's Place, W1M 5HB (7487 4484/www.whistles.co.uk). Bond Street tube. **Open** 10am-7pm Mon-Fri; 10am-6pm Sat; noon-5pm Sun. **Credit** AmEx, MC, V. **Sells** W.
All eyes are on Whistles now that Jane Shepherdson is at the helm. The shop has traditionally had a loyal following among well-heeled women looking for feminine, practical styles. With its floaty fabrics and eclectic mix of separates, the overall feel is a sort of suburban Bohemia. Prices are higher than the usual high street outlet but, with an emphasis on quality and finishing, these well-made pieces should last a lifetime. Staple items include blouses in soft fabrics, loose knits, drop-waist gathered skirts and pencil skirts. As well as its own label, this impressive flagship stocks others such as Antik Batik, Michael Stars, Odd Molly, Pink Soda and Diablesse. Prices start from around £60 for knitwear, £100 for dresses and £195 for coats.
Branches: throughout the city.

Also check out...

Benetton

255-259 Regent Street, W1B 2ER (7647 4220/www.benetton.com). Oxford Circus tube. **Open** 10am-8pm Mon-Wed, Fri, Sat; 10am-8.30pm Thur; 11.30am-6pm Sun. **Credit** AmEx, MC, V. **Sells** M, W, B, C.
Branches: throughout the city.

Burton

375-383 Oxford Street, W1C 2JS (7495 6282/www.burton.co.uk). Bond Street tube. **Open** 9am-9pm Mon-Sat; noon-6pm Sun. **Credit** AmEx, DC, MC, V. **Sells** M.
Arcadia-owned chain (now with a new logo) offering affordable officewear for men.
Branches: throughout the city.

Coast

12 St Christopher's Place, W1U 1NQ (7486 0911/www.coast-stores.co.uk). Bond Street tube. **Open** 10am-6pm Mon-Wed, Fri, Sat; 10am-7pm Thur; noon-5pm Sun. **Credit** AmEx, DC, MC, V. **Sells** W.
Smart office-to-evening outfits and occasion wear made from quality materials.
Branches: throughout the city.

Dorothy Perkins

189 Oxford Street, W1D 2JY (7494 3769/ www.dorothyperkins.com). Oxford Circus tube. **Open** 9am-8pm Mon-Wed, Fri, Sat; 9am-9pm Thur; noon-6pm Sun. **Credit** AmEx, MC, V. **Sells** W.
Branches: throughout the city.

Esprit

178-182 Regent Street, W1R 5DF (7025 7700/www.esprit.com). Oxford Circus or Piccadilly Circus tube. **Open** 10am-8pm Mon-Sat; noon-6pm Sun. **Credit** AmEx, DC, MC, V. **Sells** M, W, B, C.
Branches: throughout the city.

Fenn Wright Manson

95 Marylebone High Street, W1U 4RQ (7486 6040/www.fennwrightmanson.com). Baker Street or Bond Street tube. **Open** 10am-7pm Mon-Wed, Fri; 10am-7.30pm Thur; 10am-6.30pm Sat; 11.30am-5.30pm Sun. **Credit** AmEx, DC, MC, V. **Sells** W.
Quality, grown-up suits and safe dresses in good fabrics.
For branches see index.

Gap

376-384 Oxford Street, W1C 1JY (7408 4500/www.gap.com). Bond Street tube. **Open** 9.30am-9.30pm Mon-Wed; 9.30am-10pm Thur, Fri; 9.30am-9pm Sat; 11am-6pm Sun. **Credit** AmEx, MC, V. **Sells** M, W, B, C.
Branches: throughout the city.

H&M

261-271 Regent Street, W1B 2ES (7493 4004/www.hm.com). Oxford Circus tube. **Open** 9am-9pm Mon-Sat; 11.30am-6pm Sun. **Credit** MC, V. **Sells** M, W.
Branches: throughout the city.

Hobbs

84-88 King's Road, SW3 4TZ (7581 2914/ www.hobbs.co.uk). Sloane Square tube. **Open** 10am-7pm Mon, Thur, Fri; 10.30am-7pm Tue; 10am-7.30pm Wed; 10am-6.30pm Sat; noon-6pm Sun. **Credit** AmEx, DC, MC, V. **Sells** W.

Banana Republic. *See p45.*

FASHION

Contemporary and slightly quirky takes on classic items, plus well-made shoes.
Branches: throughout the city.

Karen Millen

229-247 Regent Street, W1B 2EW (7629 1901/www.karenmillen.com). Oxford Circus tube. **Open** 10am-8pm Mon-Wed, Fri; 10am-8.30pm Thur; 10am-7.30pm Sat; 11am-6pm Sun. **Credit** AmEx, MC, V. **Sells** W.
Branches: throughout the city.

Kew

11-12 James Street, W1U 1EE (7495 4646/www.kew-online.com). Bond Street tube. **Open** 10.30am-7pm Mon-Wed, Fri, Sat; 10.30am-8pm Thur; noon-6pm Sun. **Credit** MC, V. **Sells** W.
Jigsaw's cheaper offshoot.
Branches: throughout the city.

Mango

235 Oxford Street, W1D 2LP (7534 3505/ www.mango.com). Oxford Circus tube. **Open** 10am-8.30pm Mon-Wed, Fri, Sat; 10am-9.30pm Thur; 11.30am-6pm Sun. **Credit** AmEx, DC, MC, V. **Sells** W.
Branches: throughout the city.

Miss Selfridge

214 Oxford Street, W1W 8LG (7927 0188/ www.missselfridge.co.uk). Oxford Circus tube. **Open** 9am-9pm Mon-Sat; 11.30am-6pm Sun. **Credit** AmEx, DC, MC, V. **Sells** W.
Topshop's funky little sister.
Branches: throughout the city.

Monsoon

5-7 James Street, WC2E 8BH (7379 3623/ www.monsoon.co.uk). Covent Garden tube. **Open** 10am-8pm Mon-Sat; 11am-6pm Sun. **Credit** AmEx, MC, V. **Sells** W, B, C.
Boho-inspired high street fave that also encompasses eveningwear and kids' clothes; head to the Long Acre branch for menswear.
Branches: throughout the city.

Next

15-17 Long Acre, WC2E 9LD (7420 8280/ www.next.co.uk). Covent Garden or Leicester Square tube. **Open** 10am-8pm Mon-Wed, Fri, Sat; 10am-9pm Thur; 11.30am-6pm Sun. **Credit** AmEx, DC, MC, V. **Sells** M, W, B, C.
Branches: throughout the city.

New Look

500-502 Oxford Street, W1C 2HW (7290 7860/www.newlook.co.uk). Marble Arch tube. **Open** 9am-10pm Mon-Fri; 9am-8pm Sat; noon-6pm Sun. **Credit** AmEx, MC, V. **Sells** M, W.
Disposable fashion. Collaborations with the likes of Lily Allen have upped its cool.
Branches: throughout the city.

Noa Noa

14A Gees Court, St Christopher's Place, W1U 1JW (7495 8777/www.noa-noa.com). Bond Street tube. **Open** 10am-6.30pm Mon-Wed, Fri, Sat; 10am-7pm Thur; noon-5pm Sun. **Credit** AmEx, MC, V. **Sells** W.
Well-priced Danish womenswear.
For branches see index.

Oasis

12-14 Argyll Street, W1F 7NT (7434 1799/www.oasis-stores.com). Oxford Circus tube. **Open** 10am-8pm Mon-Wed, Fri; 10am-9pm Thur; 10am-7pm Sat; 10am-6pm Sun. **Credit** AmEx, MC, V. **Sells** W.
Well-made, oft-vintage-inspired clothes for young women; strong on dresses.
Branches: throughout the city.

Principles

38 The Poultry, EC2R 8AG (7710 0075/ www.principles.co.uk). Bank tube/DLR. **Open** 8am-8pm Mon-Fri. **Credit** AmEx, MC, V. **Sells** W.
Convincing, low-priced catwalk looks.

River Island

301-309 Oxford Street, W1C 2DN (0844 395 1011/www.riverisland.com). Bond Street or Oxford Circus tube. **Open** 10am-8pm Mon-Sat; 11am-6pm Sun. **Credit** AmEx, DC, MC, V. **Sells** M, W.
Branches: throughout the city.

Warehouse

19-21 Argyll Street, W1F 7TR (7437 7101/ www.warehouse.co.uk). Oxford Circus tube. **Open** 10am-8pm Mon-Wed, Fri; 10am-9pm Thur; 10am-7pm Sat; 11am-6pm Sun. **Credit** AmEx, DC, MC, V. **Sells** W.
Branches: throughout the city.

Zara

333 Oxford Street, W1C 2HY (7518 1550/ www.zara.com). Oxford Circus tube. **Open** 10am-8pm Mon-Wed, Fri, Sat; 10am-9pm Thur; noon-6pm Sun. **Credit** AmEx, DC, MC, V. **Sells** M, W, B, C.
Branches: throughout the city.

Budget

Uniqlo

311 Oxford Street, W1C 2HP (7290 7701/ www.uniqlo.co.uk). Oxford Circus tube. **Open** 10am-8pm Mon-Wed; 10am-9pm Thur- Sat; noon-6pm Sun. **Credit** AmEx, MC, V. **Sells** M, W.
Uniqlo ferociously attempted to rebrand in 2007, with celeb envoys like Chloe Sevigny, a Terry Richardson ad campaign and the opening of two new stores on Oxford Street. The ongoing UT T-shirt project – with designs from the likes of Cassette Playa and French – has attempted to keep up the momentum, but the jury's still out as to whether Uniqlo is more than simply a Japanese Gap or not; useful staples aside, most of the clothes here are unremarkable. Still, the cut-price pure cashmere and the simple, well-cut selvedge jeans are great.
Branches: throughout the city.

Also check out…

Primark

499-517 Oxford Street, W1K 7DA (7495 0420/www.primark.co.uk). Marble Arch tube. **Open** 9am-9pm Mon-Fri; 9am-8pm Sat; noon-6pm Sun. **Credit** AmEx, MC, V. **Sells** M, W, B, C.
Branches: throughout the city.

TK Maxx

57 King Street, W6 9HW (8563 9200/ www.tkmaxx.co.uk). Hammersmith tube. **Open** 10am-8pm Mon-Fri; 9am-7pm Sat; 11am-5pm Sun. **Credit** AmEx, DC, MC, V. **Sells** M, W, B, C.
Branded clothing at up to 60% off the RRP.
Branches: throughout the city.

Jeans & Urban Casual

Urban Outfitters (*see p20*), **Slam City Skates** (*see p228*) and **Tuesday** (*see p229*) are also good for urban casual clothing, while many boutiques stock high-end jeans from the likes of 18th Amendment and J Brand; *see pp28-36*. Online retailer **oki-ni** (www.oki-ni.com) sells limited-edition items from cult labels.

American Apparel (eco)

3-4 Carnaby Street, W1F 9PB (7734 4477/ www.americanapparel.net). Oxford Circus tube. **Open** 10am-8pm Mon-Sat; noon-6pm Sun. **Credit** AmEx, DC, MC, V. **Sells** M, W, C.
Ethically minded US-import American Apparel opened its first shop in London three years ago; since then, it's expanded at breakneck speed. The colourful, vaguely kinky, 1980s-inspired garb (leggings, figure-hugging jersey dresses, spandex leotards, skinny jeans, tracksuit bottoms and a large range of tops) seems to have captured the spirit of the times – at least as far as London's twentysomethings are concerned – with simple cuts, comfortable materials and very affordable prices. The company first conquered with the well-fitting cotton tees, then the nigh-on-perfect hoody and, most recently – in spite of their tendency to sag – with its nudge nudge, wink wink retro briefs.
For branches see index.

Bread & Honey

205 Whitecross Street, EC1Y 8QP (7253 4455/www.backin10minutes.com). Old Street tube/rail. **Open** 10am-6.30pm Mon-Wed, Fri; 10am-7pm Thur; 11am-6pm Sat. **Credit** AmEx, MC, V. **Sells** M, W.
Given its petite size and off-centre location, this French-owned men and women's boutique does surprisingly well. The reason being that the selection of goods – the interesting but not ostentatious end of streetwear – is well selected and the staff friendly and frank. On our last visit we were given a definite 'no' verdict on a T-shirt, surely not something that happens all too often. Menswear is particularly strong – look out for pieces by Baracuta and fine-knit sweaters by Modern Amusement. Women are catered for with pieces by Marimekko, Emily & Finn and Laura Lees.

Cinch

5 Newburgh Street, W1F 7RB (7287 4941/ www.eu.levi.com). Oxford Circus tube. **Open** 11am-6.30pm Mon-Sat; 1-5pm Sun. **Credit** MC, V.
Levi's Cinch store is the geeky-cool little brother of the flagship round the corner on Regent's Street, stocking anything that's too exclusive or expensive for its mainstream sibling. Denim enthusiasts come here for Levi's conceptual RED line as well as its vintage collection that harks back to the label's 1873 origins, or maybe just back to 1994 and that Stiltskin advert of lore. Think classic white T-shirts in cuts that correspond to the decade they came out in

Three Threads

and USA-made vintage dry jeans. The latter are justifiably popular, though some pairs come in ridiculously baggy cuts. We'd rather play it safe with the 1947 501s classic fit.

CP Company & Stone Island

46 Beak Street, W1F 9RJ (7287 7734/www.cpcompany.co.uk/www.stoneisland.co.uk). Oxford Circus or Piccadilly Circus tube. **Open** 10am-6pm Mon-Wed, Fri, Sat; 10am-7pm Thur. **Credit** AmEx, MC, V. **Sells** M, W, C.

This snazzy, well-lit Soho store is home to both CP Company upstairs and Stone Island in the basement. The latter's forte is functional, well-made knitwear and outerwear for men, while CP Company has refined this functional formula making pieces for men, women and even children. Neither come cheaply: £550 for a CP Company overcoat, for example, but the quality of the fabric and attention to detail are a cut above your average casualwear brand. A Covent Garden store is due to open in autumn 2008.

DPMHI

2-3 Great Pulteney Street, W1F 9LY (7494 7550/www.dpmhi.com). Oxford Circus or Piccadilly Circus tube. **Open** 11am-7pm Mon-Sat; 11am-8pm Thur. **Credit** AmEx, MC, V. **Sells** M, W.

DPMHI is a lifestyle store sprung from the loins of parent brand Maharishi – the influence of which is felt throughout. T-shirts by the likes of Rockers NYC and Wood Wood stand out as do collaboration threads with the likes of the Andy Warhol foundation, but the array of baggy jeans, shorts and hoodies feels uninspiring. Girls are offered a small selection of Maharishi tops and there's a large range of trendy MediCom toys, but best, sartorially speaking, are the Pointer-esque trainers. Staff are friendly and there's ample room for browsing, but because of the endless grafitti, trendy retro vending machines and, our bête noire, fashion label-designed skateboard decks on the walls, it feels like it's trying a bit too hard.

For branch (Maharishi) see index.

Fred Perry

Unit 6-7, Thomas Neal Centre, Seven Dials, WC2H 9LD (7836 4513/www.fredperry.com). Covent Garden tube. **Open** 10.30am-7pm Mon-Sat; noon-6pm Sun. **Credit** MC, V. **Sells** M, W.

The 1930s Wimbledon-winning tennis star who packaged his own style as a brand is still considered the polo shirt's founding father by many. This remains a fine place to pick up a discreetly logoed classic shirt but has also managed to move with the times, supplementing muted palettes with oversize argyle, abstract prints and quirky detailing. There's also a range of limited editions from the likes of Paul Weller. The Harrington jackets (£150) and dandyish cardigans are both a hit, but for a real treat try the bespoke polos (£75) that can be personally embroidered: a great gift for boyfriends, brothers or even discerning dads.

For branches see index.

Goodhood

41 Coronet Street, N1 6HD (7729 3600/www.goodhood.co.uk). Old Street tube. **Open** 11am-7pm Tue-Sat. **Credit** AmEx, DC, MC, V. **Sells** M, W.

Stock for this boutique-like store is selected by streetwear obsessives/owners Kyle and Jo with items weighted towards Japanese independent labels. We like the Gregory Japan rucksacks that you won't otherwise find outside of Tokyo; these and the Black Dollars Tees are store exclusives. Knits from Australia's Rittenhouse, T-shirts from PAM and pieces from Copenhagen's Wood Wood are also popular picks. This is one of the rare places that stocks local fashion heroine Cassette Playa, though her clothes aren't cheap (up to £176 for a sweatshirt). An R Newbold–Paul Smith collaboration is lined up for autumn 2008/9, while a cabinet full of reasonably priced watches and jewellery makes this a great place for pressies for hard-to-please hipster boyfriends and girlfriends.

Hideout

7 Upper James Street, W1F 9DH (7437 4929/www.hideoutstore.com). Piccadilly Circus or Oxford Circus tube. **Open** 11am-7pm Mon-Fri; 11am-6.30pm Sat. **Credit** MC, V. **Sells** M.

This small but central streetwear store has a New York feel to it – unsurprising as much of the stock, such as Supreme, comes from the Big Apple. There are also cool labels from Sydney, Japan and London. All the streetwear staples are in attendance – hoodies, polos, sneakers and caps – and the quality and design of the garments are a definite cut above. Labels like Pharell, William's Ice Cream or Billionaire Boys Club justify their slightly above-average pricing.

Imperious Rex!

75 Roman Road, E2 0QN (8981 3392/www.imperiousrex.com). Bethnal Green tube. **Open** noon-7pm Mon-Fri; 10am-6pm Sat; noon-5pm Sun. **Credit** AmEx, MC, V. **Sells** M, W.

True, this hyper-trendy T-shirt boutique is a little out of the way, and it's also one of the smallest shops we know – if you could swing a cat in here you'd knock all the stock off the walls. But a schlep here is rewarded with the crème de la crème of independent, mainly US streetwear brands, with Tees, hoodies and tops from Rocksmith, Mishka, Sixpack France and DIM MAC keeping the place busy since early 2008. Staff, or rather the other guy in the room with you, is the knowledgeable, chirpy TC, the owner, who'll be happy to talk you through what's hot in LA, New York or Paris. Girls can choose from an expanding selection of tops from the likes of Darkhouse and Coup De Grace but will often end up leaving with an oversized boys Tee. Best of all, you'll be hard pressed to find anything over £25. A gem.

Interstate

17 Endell Street, WC2H 9BJ (7836 0421). Covent Garden tube. **Open** 11am-6.45pm Mon-Fri; 11am-6.30pm Sat; noon-6pm Sun. **Credit** MC, V. **Sells** M.

Interstate was a central London staple for denim, polos and overcoats long before the likes of Urban Outfitters muscled in on the scene and it's still as popular as ever. Denim and workwear are the focus, and it's packed with a decent range of sizes and well-chosen brands. There's a stack of Tees and polos but its real appeal lies in its selection of jackets and parkas from the likes of Spiewak, Woolrich and Penfield, or as a place to pick up a sturdy pair of jeans from Japan's Edwin or Sweden's Nudie. Staff are helpful, if a little hawk-eyed, but overall the place is laid-back and unpretentious compared to some of its Covent Garden competitors.

Three Threads

47-49 Charlotte Road, EC2A 3QT (7749 0503/www.thethreethreads.com). Old Street tube/rail. **Open** 11am-7pm Mon-Sat; noon-5pm Sun. **Credit** MC, V.

Despite its trendy location (it's a stone's throw from the Bricklayer's Arms), the Three Threads manages to be both laid-back and friendly. Decent background tunes, sofas, a fridge full of beer and chatty, down-to-earth staff collude to create an experience more akin to lounging than shopping. The well-stocked shop is particularly good for shoes, stocking a carefully edited range that takes in Loakes, for an unpretentious British brogue, Clarks Originals and the largest range of Pointers in town. There's a good choice of T-shirts too, with many of the labels – Tonite, Suburban Bliss or Alakazam (£25-£35) – run by mates of the store. Ultra-practical raincoats from Sweden's Fjall Raven (£100), shirts from Denmark's Won Hundred (£70-£90) and classic Americana-inspired Maiden Noire are further draws. For women, there are tops and dresses from New York's Built By Wendy (£145), blouses from YMC (£105) and bags by local fave Mimi. Commendably, much of the stock is from labels that take pride in manufacturing their clothing nationally – brands such as Post NY (made in New Jersey) and New Balance (from Cumbria).

Trilogy

33 Duke of York Square, King's Road, SW3 4LY (7730 6515/www.trilogystores.co.uk). Sloane Square tube. **Open** 10am-7pm Mon-Sat; noon-6pm Sun. **Credit** AmEx, DC, MC, V. **Sells** W.
This upmarket jeans emporium is the joint venture of three friends who saw the need for a one-stop denim shop. That means premium, cult and budget denim all under one roof, with sizes and styles for all budgets. The premium labels dominate the rails, however, with fit-focused brands like current fave J Brand, Radcliffe, Citizens of Humanity and Paper Denim & Cloth. The buyers are keen to track down exclusive finds, while staff are well trained and happy to bring refreshments to the chandelier-lit changing rooms. Labels like Patrizia Pepe, Twenty8Twelve, Juicy Couture and See by Chloé break up the denim a bit. A new branch opened in Marylebone in 2008.
For branch see index.

Also check out...

A Bathing Ape 'Busy Workshop'

4 Upper James Street, W1F 9DG (7494 4924/www.bape.com). Piccadilly Circus tube. **Open** 11am-7pm Mon-Fri; 11am-6.30pm Sat. **Credit** AmEx, MC, V. **Sells** M.
This small Soho shop is the only European stockist of cult Japanese label Bathing Ape. T-shirts are displayed like works of art.

Adidas Originals Store

9 Earlham Street, WC2H 9LL (7379 4042/www.adidas.com). Covent Garden tube. **Open** 10.30am-7pm Mon-Sat; noon-6pm Sun. **Credit** AmEx, MC, V. **Sells** M, W.
Casual clothes and trainers.
For branch see index.

American Classics

20 Endell Street, WC2H 9BD (7831 1210/www.americanclassicslondon.com). Covent Garden tube. **Open** 11am-6.30pm Mon-Sat; 12.30-5.30pm Sun. **Credit** AmEx, MC, V. **Sells** M, W.
Classic US garb since 1981: Redwing Boots, Vintage Levi's, Lee and super-comfy Buzz Rickson UCLA sweatshirts.

Belstaff

12-13 Conduit Street, W1S 2XQ (7495 5897/www.belstaff.com). Oxford Circus or Piccadilly Circus tube. **Open** 10am-6pm Mon-Sat. **Credit** AmEx, MC, V. **Sells** M, W, C.
Rugged urban range inspired by motorcycle gear, known for its jackets and boots.

Boxfresh

13 Shorts Gardens, WC2H 9AT (7240 4742/www.boxfresh.co.uk). Covent Garden or Leicester Square tube. **Open** 10.30am-6.30pm Mon-Wed, Fri, Sat; 10.30am-7pm Thur; noon-6pm Sun. **Credit** AmEx, MC, V. **Sells** M, W.
Boxfresh has lost some of its kudos, but its sweats, polos and jackets still go down well with young, casual Brighton types.

Carhartt

15-17 Earlham Street, WC2H 9LL (7836 1551/www.carhartt-europe.com). Covent Garden or Tottenham Court Road tube. **Open** 11am-7pm Mon-Wed, Fri, Sat; noon-6pm Sun. **Credit** MC, V. **Sells** M, W.
It may have had its heyday, but Carhartt is still a good bet for stylish streetwear basics in hardwearing materials.
For branch (Carhartt Factory Store) see index.

Diesel

130 New Bond Street, W1S 2TB (7520 7799/www.diesel.com). Bond Street tube. **Open** 10am-7pm Mon-Wed, Fri, Sat; 10am-8pm Thur; noon-6pm Sun. **Credit** AmEx, MC, V. **Sells** M, W.
For branches see index.

Donna Ida

106 Draycott Avenue, SW3 3AE (7225 3816/www.donnaida.com). South Kensington tube. **Open** 10am-7pm Mon-Fri; 10am-6.30pm Sat; 1-6pm Sun. **Credit** AmEx, DC, MC, V. **Sells** M, W.
The latest hot looks from J Brand, 4 Stroke, Made in Heaven and New York label Siwy.

Evisu

9 Savile Row, W1S 3PF (7734 2540/www.evisu.com). Oxford Circus or Piccadilly Circus tube. **Open** 10am-6pm Mon-Wed, Fri; 10am-7pm Thur; 11am-6pm Sat. **Credit** AmEx, MC, V. **Sells** M, W.
Japanese denim line.

Fenchurch

36 Earlham Street, WC2H 9LH (7240 1880/www.fenchurch.com). Covent Garden or Leicester Square tube. **Open** 10am-7pm Mon-Sat; noon-6pm Sun. **Credit** AmEx, MC, V. **Sells** M, W.
Play it safe, logo-based tees, coats and hats. Roomy cuts on the jeans and sweaters nod to the brand's 1990s skater origins.

Full Circle

13-15 Floral Street, WC2E 9DH (7395 9420/www.fullcircleuk.com). Covent Garden tube. **Open** 10am-7pm Mon-Wed, Fri, Sat; 10am-8pm Thur; noon-6pm Sun. **Credit** AmEx, MC, V. **Sells** M, W.
Fashion-forward parkas, hooded vests and functional staples in clean, cool colours.

Henri-Lloyd

48 Carnaby Street, W1F 9PX (7292 0080/www.henrilloyd.com). Oxford Circus tube. **Open** 10am-6.30pm Mon-Sat; 11am-5pm Sun. **Credit** AmEx, MC, V. **Sells** M, W.

Howies

42 Carnaby Street, W1F 7DY (7287 2345/www.howies.co.uk). Oxford Circus tube. **Open** 10am-7pm Mon-Sat; 10am-8pm Thur; 11am-5pm Sun. **Credit** DC, MC, V. **Sells** M, W.
The ethical brand's first stand-alone store. Stylish outdoor clothing, with good jeans, sweaters and jackets, and lots of stripes.

J Simons

2 Russell Street, WC2B 5JD (7379 7353). Covent Garden tube. **Open** 10.15am-6.30pm Mon-Thur; 10.15am-6pm Fri; 10.15am-5.30pm Sat; 12.30-4.30pm Sun. **Credit** AmEx, MC, V. **Sells** M.
All-American preppy menswear essentials, with a good range of Harrington jackets.

Lacoste

223 Regent Street, W1B 2EQ (7491 8968/www.lacoste.com). Oxford Circus tube. **Open** 10am-7pm Mon-Wed, Fri, Sat; 10am-8pm Thur; noon-6pm Sun. **Credit** AmEx, MC, V. **Sells** M, W, C.
For branches see index.

Lee

13-14 Carnaby Street, W1F 9PL (7434 0732/www.lee.com). Oxford Circus tube. **Open** 10am-7pm Mon-Wed, Fri, Sat; 10am-8pm Thur; noon-6pm Sun. **Credit** MC, V. **Sells** M, W.
The London flagship. Look out for Powell (his) and Norma (hers) skinny jeans.

Mambo

39 Shelton Street, WC2H 9HJ (7438 9800/www.mambo.com.au). Covent Garden tube. **Open** 10am-7pm Mon-Sat; 11.30am-5.30pm Sun. **Credit** AmEx, MC, V. **Sells** M, W.
For branch see index.

Miss Sixty

31 Great Marlborough Street, W1V 1HA (7434 3060/www.misssixty.com). Oxford Circus tube. **Open** 10am-7pm Mon-Sat; noon-6pm Sun. **Credit** AmEx, MC, V. **Sells** M, W.
For branches see index.

New Era

72-74 Brewer Street, W1F 9JG (0845 600 5950/www.neweracap.co.uk). **Open** 10am-7pm Mon-Wed, Fri, Sat; 10am-7.30pm Thur; noon-6pm Sun. **Credit** AmEx, MC, V. **Sells** M, W.
London's flagship cap store carries a huge range of baseball caps, including the Major League Baseball (MLB) range.

Original Levi's Store

174-176 Regent Street, W1B 5TJ (7292 2500/www.eu.levi.com). Oxford Circus tube. **Open** 10am-7pm Mon-Wed, Fri, Sat; 10am-8pm Thur; noon-6pm Sun. **Credit** AmEx, MC, V. **Sells** M, W, C.
The London flagship of the world-renowned jeans label.
For branches see index.

Pepe Jeans

26-27 Carnaby Street, W1F 7DY (7439 0523/www.pepejeans.com). Oxford Circus tube. **Open** 10am-7pm Mon-Sat; noon-6pm Sun. **Credit** AmEx, MC, V. **Sells** M, W.
Branches: throughout the city.

Quiksilver

229 Regent Street, W1B 4EG (7493 5900/www.pepejeans.com). Oxford Circus tube. **Open** 10am-7pm Mon-Wed; 10am-8pm Thur-Sat; noon-6pm Sun. **Credit** AmEx, MC, V. **Sells** M, W, C.
For branches see index.

Stüssy

19 Earlham Street, WC2H 9LL (7836 9418/www.stussystore.co.uk). Covent Garden tube. **Open** 11am-7pm Mon-Sat; 1-5.30pm Sun. **Credit** MC, V. **Sells** M, W.

Menswear

Classic clobber

Iconic gear with wardrobe staying power.

As trends flutter in and out of fashion, there are a handful of simple, classic styles that have real tenacity. The following five iconic pieces have clung diligently to the wardrobes of the most fashionable men, from the cool Mod-favoured Harrington to smoking-room staple the velvet slipper.

In the 1960s, finely turned out Mods would slip on a **Harrington**, pootle down to Brighton on gleaming Italian scooters, roll around with the Rockers and get their heads kicked in. The Mod badge of honour, this simple blouson jacket with bright tartan lining, has meandered through fashion, its progress marked by pop culture references and celebrity wearers. Designed by Manchester men's outfitters Baracuta in the 1930s, the Harrington was adopted by skinheads in the late '70s, worn by Steve McQueen and popularised by bands like the Clash. These days, the Harrington has settled into its position as an iconic Brit classic, something designer **Margaret Howell** (*see p41*) made good use of in her spring/summer 2008 collection in a collaboration with the jacket's original creator. Baracuta (www.baracuta-g9.com) is still churning out the classic style, the G9 (pictured above), and **J Simon** in Covent Garden (*see p50*) is packed with choice picks from the range; **Bread & Honey** (*see p48*) is another good port-of-call.

Before his weight gain and love affair with butter in *Last Tango in Paris*, Marlon Brando was the wearer of man's most important garment: the **white T-shirt**. And, boy, did he look cool. All bulges and brawn in *A Streetcar Named Desire* in 1951 and saucily grease-smudged in *The Wild One* in 1953, Brando unwittingly made the T-shirt the epitome of manliness. Still a staple of every man's wardrobe, it's strangely difficult to find a simple, unadulterated shirt of the type Brando might have cruised around the waterfront in. For a classic fit, without clever puff-paint splatters, rips or girly capped sleeves, try a classic store like **Marks & Spencer** (*see p16*). Vintage-feel pieces can be had from **American Apparel** (*see p48*) or **Albam** (*see p28*); Alastair Rae and James Shaw, owners of the latter, sell a super-soft jersey tee, the result of their obsession with creating the perfect classic T-shirt.

London's style-set may be eager to out-do themselves with outlandish outfits, but others show their rebellious streak in a subtler way. With a quick flash of ankle you can dazzle the hoards with a **jaunty sock**. Apricot and silver lurex from **Tabio** (www.tabio.com), fine **Missoni** stripes, eye-popping candy hues from **Pantherella** (www.pantherella.co.uk)

Albam

or a pom-pom knee-high pair from **Holland & Holland**: each pair a fine-knit, polka-dotted 'fuck you' to the establishment.

A quick stroll down Jermyn Street, home to shirtmakers **TM Lewin** (*see p54*) will also reveal the royal warranted **Turnbull & Asser** at nos.71-72 (*see p54*). Established in 1885, T&A's bespoke shirts are created with 28 individual measurements from a collection of nearly 700 different fabrics. James Bond was certainly a valued customer. If the bespoke fee is a little steep for your wedding/funeral/bar mitzvah, try the high street. **Marks & Spencer** (*as above*) stocks an array of cotton shirting (from £25) and offers an online made-to-measure service from £30. Look out for Prince of Wales collars – thick wide wedges leaving room for a plump double Windsor knotted tie – or the Duke of York: far narrower, with a sharp downturn.

Once firmly planted under the breakfast bar, **slippers** have been brushed off and spruced up, and are now popping up in the collections of young designers. For its autumn/winter 2008/9 collection, **House of Holland** (www.houseofholland.co.uk) proffered an electric purple pair of plaid slippers embroidered with designer Henry Holland's faux coat-of-arms (in stores late 2008), and they were also a hit at Florence fashion expo the Pitti Uomo fair in January 2008. More than a few buyers, exhibitors and fey male fashion journalists have been spotted sporting embroidered velvet slip-ons with hard soles.

Get ahead and start wearing them now with classic styles from **Trickers** (www.trickers.com) and black velvet hard-soled slippers with a crown embroidered in gold (£95) from **Church's Shoes** (*see p70*).

Bespoke & Tailoring

What's in a word? When the word is 'bespoke', not much, it seems, after an Advertising Standards Authority ruling in 2008 that allowed a retailer of machine-made suits to advertise them as bespoke – to the annoyance of Savile Row stalwarts. The ASA went with the argument that, although modern-day customers would expect a bespoke suit to be tailored to their measurements, most wouldn't expect it to be completely handmade. So how do you know if a place offers the real deal? It's simple: a real bespoke suit is *entirely* handmade... so just ask.

Tailors

See also p54 **Alexander Boyd** and **Dege & Skinner**.

Anderson & Sheppard

32 Old Burlington Street, W1S 3AT (7734 1420/www.anderson-sheppard.co.uk). Green Park or Piccadilly tube. **Open** 8.30am-5pm Mon-Fri. **Credit** AmEx, MC, V.

Though not technically on Savile Row (it's located one street away), A&S is famous for its legendary house style, which is soft and light, without much padding and cut a little looser than is usual. The 'drapey' results are wonderfully comfortable, although to some eyes they lack shape – it's not exactly a fashionable look right now. Until it is, you can always make do with a bespoke tie.

Brian Russell & Co

6 Sackville Street, W1S 3DD (7287 4880/ www.brianrusselltailors.co.uk). Piccadilly tube. **Open** by appointment 9.30am-5pm Mon-Fri. **Credit** MC, V.

Glamorous Lebanese lady Fadia Aoun is now head cutter here, having taken over from Russell, who died in 2007. Aoun's versatility means customers can choose between a Scholte cut (the drapey house style at Anderson & Sheppard, *see above*) and something more structured. Having worked for Stella McCartney at Chloé, Aoun is as good a tailor for women as she is for men, yet her prices are cheaper than those on Savile Row.

Charlie Allen

1 Cooper's Yard, N1 1RQ (7359 0883/www. charlieallen.co.uk). Angel tube/Highbury & Islington tube/rail. **Open** by appointment 10am-6.30pm Mon-Sat. **Credit** AmEx, MC, V.

The hugely likeable Charlie Allen, Islington's chief tailor, pays attention to every detail of an outfit, not just the suit. His eye for shirts, cufflinks, belts and even socks goes into turning out the perfect ensemble. Bespoke starts at £1,200, although Allen also offers a made-to-measure service from £750.

Chris Kerr

52 Berwick Street, W1F 8SL (7437 3727/ www.eddiekerr.co.uk). Oxford Circus tube. **Open** 8am-5.30pm Mon-Fri; 8.30am-1pm Sat. **Credit** MC, V.

Chris Kerr, son of legendary 1960s tailor Eddie Kerr, is the man to see if Savile Row's prices or attitude aren't to your liking. The versatile Kerr has no house style; instead he makes every suit to each client's exact specifications – and those clients include Johnny Depp and David Walliams. Whether you need something for a wedding, the office or even for the country, Kerr will patiently talk you through the details in his Soho workroom. His relaxed approach and modest prices make this the ideal place to commission your first bespoke suit.

Gieves & Hawkes

1 Savile Row, W1S 3JR (7434 2001/ www.gievesandhawkes.com). Green Park or Piccadilly Circus tube. **Open** 9.30am-6.30pm Mon-Thur; 9am-6pm Fri; 10am-6pm Sat; 11am-5pm Sun. **Credit** AmEx, DC, MC, V.

Four centuries on and this isn't just a great shop, it's a history lesson for anyone interested in the development of men's clothes. Despite having held royal warrants without interruption for 200 years (the Queen, the Duke of Edinburgh and Prince Charles are all customers) Gieves continues to innovate. There are two custom services available: personal tailoring (a made-to-measure service) and bespoke, which is the real deal, and commensurately expensive.

For branch see index.

Henry Poole & Co

15 Savile Row, W1S 3PJ (7734 5985/ www.henrypoole.com). Green Park or Piccadilly Circus tube. **Open** 9am-5.15pm Mon-Fri. **Credit** AmEx, MC, V.

Poole's clientele list reads like a *Who's Who* of world history: Napoleon III, Haile Selassi and 'Buffalo' Bill Cody feature on it, as do Winston Churchill and the Prince of Wales. Established in 1806, it was the first place to set up on 'The Row' and in 1865 Poole invented the modern dinner suit (the tuxedo) by lopping the tails off a tailcoat on the instruction of the then Prince of Wales. Suits here cost from £2,800.

John Pearse

6 Meard Street, W1F 0EG (7434 0738/ www.johnpearse.co.uk). Piccadilly Circus tube. **Open** 10am-7pm Mon-Fri; noon-7pm Sat. **Credit** AmEx, MC, V.

Many consider John Pearce the Godfather of British bespoke. His playful eccentricity rests on the foundations of his classic tailoring apprenticeship, after which he opened legendary 1960s boutique Granny Takes a Trip, offering flower-power dandyism to the likes of Cream, Hendrix and the Stones. Sir Mick remains a customer and has since been joined by George Clooney and Brad Pitt. Tucked away down a Soho alley, Pearse's shop retains a renegade spirit; his trademark work includes bespoke denim jackets and casual cotton suits, but if the materials are wild, the craftsmanship is always first class. Bespoke suits cost around £2,000.

Kilgour

5 & 8 Savile Row, W1S 3PE (7734 6905/ www.8savilerow.com). Oxford Circus or Piccadilly Circus tube. **Open** 9am-6pm Mon-Wed, Fri; 9am-7pm Thur; 10.30am-6pm Sat. **Credit** AmEx, DC, MC, V.

Kilgour has undergone a revolution steered by its creative director Carlo Brandelli. The sleek, modern shop – which includes the new, minimalist space at 5 Savile Row – sets the tone for a brand that is now more a fashion house than a tailor, although there are still old-fashioned tailors on site. The suits, which are keenly priced, have very little structure or lining, making them lightweight and well suited to life in today's overheated offices. Don't miss the sleek accessories: shirts, coats, handkerchiefs, socks, luggage, ties and shoes.

Mark Powell

12 Brewer Street, W1R 3FS (7287 5498/ www.markpowellbespoke.co.uk). Piccadilly Circus tube. **Open** by appointment Mon-Sat. **Credit** MC, V.

Bullet-headed Mark Powell is proud of his East End roots and his brash take on tailoring. His starry clientele list tells its own story – Usher, Goldie and Ian Wright are all fans – but no one epitomises the Mark Powell look better than the man himself.

Nick Tentis

14 Hampden House, 2 Weymouth Street, W1W 5BT (7355 3399/www.nicktentis. com). Great Portland Street tube. **Open** by appointment 10am-6pm Mon-Fri. **Credit** AmEx, MC, V.

Tentis's suits are always sharp, but despite attracting the attention of crime writer Jake Arnott they never descend into the clichés of *Lock Stock* gangster chic. Sharply turned out Tentis skilfully executes his slim, slightly 1960s silhouette, with its narrow lapels and slender trousers, in fine fabrics. If you don't need a whole new outfit but like the look, then pick up one of his neat jackets.

Norton & Sons

16 Savile Row, W1S 3PL (7437 0829/ www.nortonandsons.co.uk). Oxford Circus or Piccadilly Circus tube. **Open** 9am-5.30pm Mon-Fri; 1-5.30pm Sat. **Credit** AmEx, MC, V.

Oxford MBA graduate Patrick Grant took over Norton & Sons three years ago, and while his outlook is modern he's kept the fundamentals of his business very traditional. Norton only makes bespoke clothes (which is reassuring now that most Savile Row houses do ready-to-wear), including shirts, sweaters and soft leather bags. The house cut is classic and crisp, but, this being bespoke, every style and request can be accommodated, whether it's a Dior Homme-esque skinny suit or a full, six-piece shooting suit in bespoke tweed. Prices, unsurprisingly, are steep.

Oliver Benjamin

8 Kingly Street, W1B 5PQ (7734 3334/ www.oliverjbenjamin.co.uk). Oxford Circus or Piccadilly Circus tube. **Open** 11am-7pm Mon-Fri; 11am-6pm Sat. **Credit** AmEx, MC, V.

The Benjamin empire now has four London outposts, and is building its success on the sound foundations of keen pricing and approachable style. Suits with waisted jackets and flat-fronted trousers are particularly accessible, starting at just under £600, but his Italian-made shirts are worth a look too. If

Alexander Boyd. See p54.

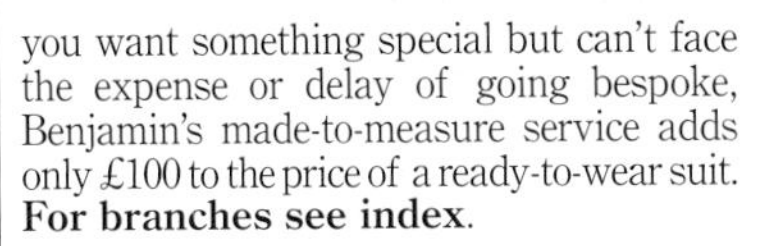

you want something special but can't face the expense or delay of going bespoke, Benjamin's made-to-measure service adds only £100 to the price of a ready-to-wear suit.
For branches see index.

Richard Anderson

Sherborne House, 13 Savile Row, W1S 3PH (77340001/www.richardanderson ltd.com). Oxford Circus or Piccadilly Circus tube. **Open** 9am-5pm Mon-Fri; by appointment Sat. **Credit** AmEx, MC, V.
Although the new kid on the block (he only opened here in 2001), Anderson is traditional through and through. He expresses his exuberance through the use of eye-catching patterns, in the form of Tango orange, or grass-green jackets, diagonal pinstripes and the windowpane check on his house tweed. Despite the loud colours, shapes and styles remain classic, and the accessories – ties, socks, cufflinks and sweaters – are top quality. Anderson makes suits for women as well as men, and a lot of shooting suits. Prices are steep – bespoke is around £3,000 – but ready-to-wear is available from £1,076.

Richard James

29 Savile Row, W1S 2EY (7434 0605/ www.richardjames.co.uk). Green Park or Piccadilly Circus tube. **Open** 10am-6pm Mon-Wed, Fri; 10am-7pm Thur; 11am-6pm Sat. **Credit** AmEx, DC, MC, V.
After 14 years as Savile Row's rebel, Richard James is now espousing the old-fashioned values that define the street through his bespoke shop. Confusingly, there are now four levels of quality to choose from, starting at ready-to-wear and rising in price up to full bespoke. Not that this is limited to suits – even socks can be customised.
For branch (Richard James Bespoke) see index.

Rubinacci

96 Mount Street, W1K 2TB (7499 2299/ www.marianorubinacci.it). Green Park or Marble Arch tube. **Open** 10am-6pm Mon-Wed, Fri; 10am-7pm Thur; 10am-2.30pm Sat. **Credit** AmEx, DC, MC, V.
It makes good sense that one of Italy's most revered tailors has a London outpost because the Rubinacci family are true anglophiles – even their Naples HQ is called London House. Inside the Mount Street shop there's a great range of shirts, ties, polos, soft jackets, trousers, shorts and sweaters, all in luxurious fabrics and in brighter colours than a British tailor might countenance. The ultimate, however, is to order a bespoke suit or jacket – the results should be world class.

Threadneedleman Bespoke Tailors

187A Walworth Road, SE17 7RW (7701 9181/www.threadneedlemantailors.co.uk). Elephant & Castle tube/rail. **Open** 10am-6pm Mon-Sat. **Credit** MC, V.
Veteran tailor George Dyer cuts bespoke suits at bargain prices in his Elephant & Castle shop. Note, however, that with suits starting at £650, customers – who include Suggs and mod-obsessed style journalists Robert Elms and Paolo Hewitt – don't (and shouldn't expect to) get Savile Row service.

Timothy Everest

35 Bruton Place, W1J 6NS (7629 6236/ www.timothyeverest.co.uk). Bond Street tube. **Open** 10am-6pm Mon-Fri;11am-5pm Sat. **Credit** AmEx, MC, V.
One-time apprentice to local legend Tommy Nutter – who dressed everyone from the Beatles to Jack Nicholson in *Batman* – Everest is a big name among London tailors and has his own broad range of stars from the Kaiser Chiefs' Ricky Wilson to Davids Cameron and Beckham. Everest has an irreverence about his clothes that informs both the relaxed cut and the colours, but his genius is to deploy this with restraint.
For branch see index.

Udeshi

8 Davies Street, W1K 3DW (7495 1333/ www.udeshi.co.uk). Green Park or Bond Street tube. **Open** 11am-6pm Mon-Fri; noon-5pm Sat. **Credit** AmEx, MC, V.
One-time City boy Udeshi only sells from his Mayfair shop, and makes contemporary men's clothes in the best, old-fashioned ways, so exclusivity is guaranteed. There's everything a man needs here, and if the ready-to-wear doesn't fit, made-to-measure and bespoke services are also available. Look out for his rare, vintage fabrics – suitings and shirtings are available.

Welsh & Jefferies

20 Savile Row, W1S 3PR (7734 3062/ www.welshandjefferies.com). Piccadilly Circus or Oxford Circus tube. **Open** 9am-5pm Mon-Fri. **Credit** AmEx, DC, MC,V.
Malcolm Plews, the approachable head cutter at Welsh & Jefferies, is considered by other Savile Row tailors to be one of the street's greatest talents – high praise indeed. The W&J house style is a classic, elegant English cut, beautifully executed in the purest of bespoke traditions, and the customer service is as good as the finished product.

Also check out...

George's Tailors

50 Wightman Road, N4 1RU (8341 3614). Manor House tube. **Open** 8am-7pm Mon-Sat. **No credit cards**.
Savile Row-trained George Christodoulou is known for his sharp, mod-inspired handmade suits, from £600.

FASHION

Huntsman
11 Savile Row, W1S 3PF (7734 7441/www.h-huntsman.com). Green Park or Piccadilly Circus tube. **Open** 9am-5.30pm Mon-Fri; 10am-5pm Sat. **Credit** AmEx, MC, V.
One of the most expensive tailors on Savile Row; house tweeds are particularly beautiful.

Jonathan Quearney
7 Windmill Street, W1T 2HY (7631 5132/ www.jonathanquearney.com). Goodge Street tube. **Open** 9am-5.30pm Mon-Fri; by appointment Sat. **Credit** AmEx, MC, V.
Contemporary Savile Row-trained tailor.

Shirts & ties

Piccadilly's **Jermyn Street** is still synonymous with shirt-makers.

Alexander Boyd
52 Artillery Lane, E1 7LS (7377 8755/ www. alexanderboyd.co.uk). Liverpool Street tube/rail. **Open** 8.30am-7.30pm Mon-Fri; by appointment Sat. **Credit** MC, V. **Sells** M.
As part of Rayner & Sturges, Britain's second oldest shirt-maker, it's no surprise that almost everything on sale at Alexander Boyd is made in Britain. The emphasis is on bespoke: shirts of course but also suits and shoes (by Eric Cook) – but fine ready-to-wear shirts and accessories are also available.

Dege & Skinner
10 Savile Row, W1S 3PF (7287 2941/ www.dege-skinner.co.uk). Oxford Circus or Piccadilly Circus tube. **Open** 9.15am-5.15pm Mon-Fri; 9.30am-12.30pm Sat; also by appointment. **Credit** MC, V. **Sells** M.
Dege & Skinner has a good reputation as a tailor, but a great reputation as a shirt-maker, because Robert Whittaker cuts the shirts with a skill that's hard to find in London any more. Shirts are available in a wide range of fabrics (including bamboo), but equally impressive are the dressing gowns.

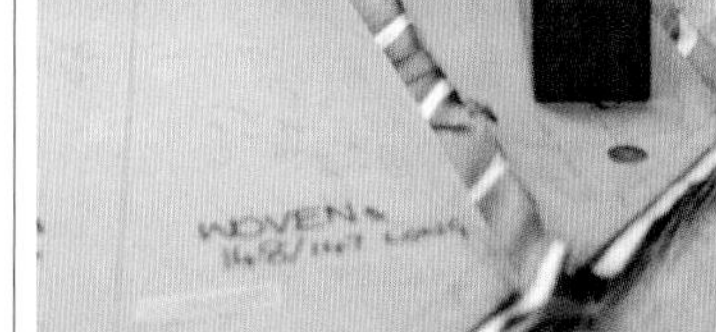

Emmett London
380 King's Road, SW3 5UZ (7351 7529/ www.emmettlondon.com). Sloane Square tube. **Open** 10am-6.30pm Mon-Sat; noon-5.30pm Sun. **Credit** AmEx, DC, MC, V. **Sells** M.
Robert Emmett opened his first London shop in 1992; his USP is to stock very limited numbers (25) of each pattern. Jazzier than classic Jermyn Street shirts, but without the dubious flamboyance of the fashion labels, his designs are perfect for anyone looking for something a tad different. If his regular sizes (from £79) don't fit, try made-to-measure.
For branches see index.

Sean O'Flynn
7 Sackville Street, W1S 3DE (7437 0044/ www.seanoflynnshirtmaker.co.uk). Piccadilly Circus tube. **Open** 9am-6pm Mon-Fri; also by appointment. **Credit** AmEx, MC, V. **Sells** M, W.
O'Flynn learnt his craft at Huntsman and then New & Lingwood, and still makes shirts the old-fashioned way. Every customer has his or her own paper pattern, cut by O'Flynn himself, and the shirts are made up on the premises – making this genuinely bespoke. There's such a vast range of fabrics to choose from that O'Flynn's gentle guidance is often invaluable. Shirts start at £160.

Also check out...

Anne Fontaine
151 Fulham Road, SW3 6SN (7584 7703/ www.annefontaine.com). South Kensington tube. **Open** 10am-6.30pm Mon-Sat; noon-5pm Sun. **Credit** AmEx, MC, V. **Sells** W.
Every imaginable take on the white shirt.
For branches see index.

Drakes

Budd
1-3 Piccadilly Arcade, SW1Y 6NH (7493 0139). Piccadilly Circus tube. **Open** 9am-5.30pm Mon-Thur; 9am-5pm Fri; 10am-5pm Sat. **Credit** AmEx, DC, MC, V. **Sells** M.
London's friendliest shirt shop – and an incomparable one at that – sells bespoke and ready-to-wear as well as cotton batiste pyjamas, madder silk ties and socks.

Drakes
www.drakes-london.com/7608 0321.
High-quality silk ties (including bespoke), plus cashmere scarves and shawls – all handmade in England.

Emma Willis
66 Jermyn Street, SW1Y 6NY (7930 9980/ www.emmawillis.com). Green Park tube. **Open** 10am-6pm Mon-Sat. **Credit** AmEx, MC, V. **Sells** M, W.
Jermyn Street's queen of shirts. Her stand-out products are shirts made from an exclusive heavy oxford silk (£190).

Hilditch & Key
73 Jermyn Street, SW1Y 6NP (7930 5336/ www.hilditchandkey.co.uk). Green Park or Piccadilly Circus tube. **Open** 9.30am-5.30pm Mon-Sat. **Credit** AmEx, MC, V. **Sells** M.
Venerable shirt-maker much loved by one Karl Lagerfeld and a lot more soberly dressed gentlemen besides.
For branch see index.

Pink
85 Jermyn Street, SW1Y6JD (7930 6364/ www.thomaspink.co.uk). Piccadilly Circus tube. **Open** 10am-6pm Mon-Wed, Fri; 10am-7pm Thur; 10am-6.30pm Sat; noon-5pm Sun. **Credit** AmEx, DC, MC, V. **Sells** M, W, C.
Branches: throughout the city.

TM Lewin
106-108 Jermyn Street, SW1 6EQ (7839 3372/www.tmlewin.co.uk). Piccadilly Circus tube. **Open** 9am-7pm Mon-Fri; 10am-7pm Sat; 11am-5pm Sun. **Credit** AmEx, MC, V. **Sells** M, W.
Branches: throughout the city.

Turnbull & Asser
71-72 Jermyn Street, SW1Y 6PF (7808 3000/www.turnbullandasser.co.uk). Green Park tube. **Open** 9am-6pm Mon-Fri; 9.30am-6pm Sat. **Credit** AmEx, DC, MC, V. **Sells** M.
The pre-eminent Jermyn Street shirt-maker (established 1885) is due to open a new shop in late 2008, in the City.

Waistcoats

African Waistcoat Company
33 Islington Green, N1 8DU (7704 9698/ www.africanwaistcoatcompany.com). Angel tube. **Open** 10am-6pm Wed, Sat; noon-6pm Sun; also by appointment. **Credit** MC, V.
The garments in Old Etonian Calum Robertson's cupboard-sized shop at the end of Camden Passage are unique: a marriage of African and Savile Row traditions and craftsmanship. The speciality is smart waistcoats made from West African cottons

Made in China

Mansel Fletcher finds out whether you can cut costs without cutting corners in the world of bespoke suits.

'We work hard,' says Vic Vasandani of Hong Kong tailor **Raja Fashions**, and he's not exaggerating. While he spends long days seeing clients all over Britain, his tailors are beavering away in China. I'm standing in a hotel room by Paddington Station, wearing a half-finished suit, which I ordered only seven days earlier. It's a suit in seersucker cotton, and it's a bit of an extravagance because, although it'll be just the thing for hot summer days, I'm unlikely to get much wear out of it.

Or at least it would be an extravagance if the suit wasn't so cheap – it costs around £250, a tenth of what I'd pay for it on Savile Row. The idea of going bespoke for the price of an M&S suit seems ridiculous, but that's what Raja Fashions offers. It's worth bearing in mind that M&S suits are made in a factory, by the thousand and almost entirely by machine. To create a bespoke suit, however, a trained tailor must measure the customer, fabrics must be chosen and details discussed. These specifications are then given to a cutter who creates a paper pattern unique to that customer. The fabric from the suit is then cut according to the paper template, and handed to the coat maker and the trouser maker, who sew each item individually.

Raja can make suits this cheap for two reasons. The first is that the Shanghainese workforce is based on the Chinese mainland where wages are low. The second is that because the company makes 20,000 suits a year, it can buy fabrics at very low prices. Everything, however, depends on the quality of the product – even £250 is a lot for a bad bespoke suit.

The first thing to say is that anyone new to bespoke might struggle; style is in the eye of the beholder, but to my mind the advice young Vishal Daswani (company director and son of the founder Raj Daswani) offered me regarding the style and cut of my suit was bad. He wears his own suit trousers like baggy jeans, low on the hip and three inches too long in the leg. It took some effort to persuade him that I was quite set on a classic look. My fitting was also worrying, in that the suit was still a long way from being right, which made Daswani's suggestion that I might miss out the fitting seem ridiculous. The picking of fabrics and colours felt a bit hurried too, leading to the still-lingering fear that I had perhaps made the wrong choice of lining.

Then there was a cock-up with the couriers, who ruined the suit on its way to London. But amazingly, and to Raja's credit, only two weeks later a replacement was ready, so the overall time frame was still only one month from measurement to finished suit (my last two Savile Row suits took more than six months). As for the final cut and fit, it's good (but not great), although I had to open up a jacket buttonhole and the sleeves are fractionally too short. Both these deficiencies will be adjusted free of charge by Raja as soon as I can get the suit back to them. but, as with the styling and the fitting, it will have been down to me to get it right, and had I less experience the suit would be notably imperfect.

For many bespoke customers the client/tailor relationship, the sense

of occasion and the collaborative consideration given to all the details are part of the pleasure of ordering a handcrafted suit. None of these are present here, but that's hardly surprising given the low prices.

Do not go in expecting style advice or the chance to linger over decisions about colours. This is a production line, albeit a friendly one, and you need to know exactly what you want in terms of cut and fabrics. If you are firm about these and are willing to persevere until you get them just right, then Raja Fashions is a good budget option. It can't possibly stand comparison with Savile Row, but it certainly beats anything available at the same price on the high street. *www.raja-fashions.com.*

and silks known as *aso oke*, which means high-status or 'up country' cloth in Yoruba, and is traditionally worn to mark special occasions. Patterns range from centuries-old Yoruba patterns to contemporary designs. Robertson makes regular trips to Nigeria to add to a range that takes in over 30 dazzling designs. As well as the peacockish waistcoats (starting at £149), the shop offers a selection of traditional robes, scarves and beads.

Shoes

See also p70 **Grenson**.

Caroline Groves

37 Chiltern Street, W1U 7PW (7935 2329/www.carolinegroves.co.uk). Baker Street tube. **Open** by appointment Thur, Fri. **Credit** MC, V.

The gorgeous textures, flowing shapes, vintage trims and exhuberant colours of Caroline Groves' shoes are probably what attract clients like Noel Fielding and Kristen Scott Thomas. Prices start at £1600.

Foster & Son

83 Jermyn Street, SW1Y 6JD (7930 5385/www.wsfoster.com). Green Park tube. **Open** 10am-6pm Mon-Sat. **Credit** AmEx, MC, V.

One of London's, if not the world's, oldest bespoke shoemakers, with a heritage that dates back to 1840. Staff pride themselves on their specialist knowledge and craftsmanship; master last-maker Terry Moore is considered by some to be the greatest last-maker in London. Bespoke luggage is also available.

Gaziano & Girling

12 Savile Row, W1S 3PQ (01536 511022/www.gazianogirling.com). Oxford Circus or Piccadilly Circus tube. **Open** by appointment only. **Credit** AmEx, MC, V.

The old-fashioned world of bespoke shoes was given a shake-up in 2004 when a new brand was created by Tony Gaziano and Dean Girling. Its shoes combine the finest English shoemaking with contemporary design.

George Cleverley

13 Royal Arcade, W1S 4SL (7493 0443/www.gjcleverley.co.uk). Piccadilly Circus or Green Park tube. **Open** 9am-6pm Mon-Fri; 10am-5pm Sat. **Credit** AmEx, MC, V.

From bijou premises, George Glasgow, Cleverley's MD, has been making traditional English shoes for 30 years.

Vintage & Second-hand

See p217 for **Prangsta Costumiers** and **Contemporary Wardrobe**; for **American Retro**, *see p204*. For second-hand childrens' clothes and equipment, *see p265*.

Absolute Vintage

15 Hanbury Street, E1 6QR (7247 3883/ www.absolutevintage.co.uk). Liverpool Street tube/rail. **Open** noon-7pm Mon-Sat; 11am-7pm Sun. **Credit** AmEx, MC, V. **Sells** M, W.

On entering Absolute Vintage, women look slightly giddy. Where to start? The wall of shoes? The racks of handbags? It's a dilemma. There are over 1,000 pairs of shoes here, arranged in size (even size eight), colour and era, from ladylike 1940s suede courts, through to the white high-heeled cast-offs of the 1980s Essex girl. Men can be shod here too, in brown country brogues or lizard-skin pimp numbers. Stock is priced to sell – we spotted a pair of Rayne 1960s silver sling-backs for £18. And you can easily kit yourself out in an entire outfit for £50. Day dresses, of mixed vintage and arranged by colour, are generally £15, as are cotton maxis, with known labels priced higher. Slinky '70s disco dresses, starting at £18, are a bargain and '80s posh frocks with labels such as Frank Usher go for £25. A matching clutch bag shouldn't be a problem; they are stacked in their hundreds, priced from £8. It's all about the look here rather than labels, but you can happen on something more special. Around the corner, sister store Blondie (Unit 2, 114-118 Commercial Street, 7247 0050) has a more boutiquey atmosphere and an edited selection, ideal for those who don't want to trawl through the rails.

Annie's Vintage Clothes

12 Camden Passage, N1 8ED (7359 0796). Angel tube. **Open** 11am-6pm Mon, Tue, Thur, Fri; 9am-6pm Wed, Sat; 11am-3pm Sun. **Credit** AmEx, MC, V. **Sells** W, C.

Annie Moss provided dresses for the original *Brideshead Revisited* TV series back in the 1980s, and a visit to her shop is rather like walking into Julia Marchmain's closet. Everything is sheer, floaty and ethereal – there are delicate fans, genteel parasols and indulgent dressing table accessories. Knockout flapper dresses are the speciality here, usually French, but originally bought by wealthy English women. The paler dresses are currently popular with brides, and are good value compared to modern off-the-peg frocks. We spotted a pretty jade green embroidered flapper dress for £390. For a more traditional choice, there's a rail of wedding dresses from the Victorian period and slinkier bias cut numbers from the 1930s, priced from £95 to £400. Most day dresses date to the 1930s and '40s, but you'll also find examples of later vintage too, such as 1950s appliqué skirts from around £50 and Mrs Robinson-style silk slips for £58. There is a good selection of accessories – particularly chic hats – as well as 1920s shoes, swimwear and even baby clothes.

Appleby

95 Westbourne Park Villas, W2 5ED (7229 7772/www.applebyvintage.com). Royal Oak tube. **Open** 11am-6pm Mon-Sat. **Credit** AmEx, MC, V. **Sells** W.

Not keen on the whiff of the past? Then head to the fragrant, boutique-like Appleby, where glamorous Jane Appleby-Deen has a select stock of beautiful – and pristine – vintage clothes. She acknowledges that her stock is not cheap, but here you get what you pay for. When we last dropped by, highlights included a rare deco print shirt by Ossie Clark (£500), a crazy 1970s Pucci sunhat (£150) and a pair of green suede platform boots by Terry de Havilland (£1,000). Always in stock are good 1930s chiffon and '40s crêpe tea dresses, from £300 to £500. You can depart with change from £100, however: cute 1960s dresses can be found for £75, as can good (non-label) party shoes.

Bang Bang

21 Goodge Street, W1T 2PJ (7631 4191). Goodge Street tube. **Open** 10am-6.30pm Mon-Fri; 11am-6pm Sat. **Credit** MC, V. **Sells** W.

It's all down to luck and timing at this lunch-break browser's fave. More dress agency than vintage shop, top-end labels such as Dries Van Noten and Moschino hang alongside mediocre high street pieces. Sharp eyes are rewarded: in the past we've spotted a well-priced Ossie Clark gown in the mix. Nearly new shoes sport labels such as Gina, Costume National and Miu Miu, and there are usually plenty for larger feet too. The turnover of stock is fast, so it's worth popping in regularly. The shop often takes designers' samples; on our last visit there was a superb haul from the new Biba collection, including suede platforms, and a fabulous lurex maxi dress for £180. There's also a sister store on Berwick Street, with similar vintage womenswear on the ground floor and menswear in the basement. **For branch see index.**

Beyond Retro

110-112 Cheshire Street, E2 6EJ (7613 3636/www.beyondretro.com). Liverpool Street tube/rail. **Open** 10am-6pm daily. **Credit** MC, V. **Sells** M, W.

Winner of the best vintage shop in our 2008 Shopping Awards, this East End institution has a loyal following of fancy dress-seekers, hard-up students and offbeat musicians. But you can create almost any look you want here – that's the beauty of it. The vast former warehouse is crammed with around 10,000 items of stock, helpfully arranged by colour. Much of it is unremarkable, but if you have the time and patience to flick through the rails you can find just what you're looking for, and literally dress yourself from top to toe. On our last visit we spotted vintage corsets and suspender belts (from £4), silk slips (£9) and an explosion of net petticoats. And that's before we even reached the rails of clothes. It all here: tartan, leopard print, flower power and lace. We saw great Polynesian-print maxi dresses (£16), frou-frou prom dresses for around £95 and vintage kimonos (£45). In a raised section you'll find 1930s to '60s dresses (from £50) with handwritten labels suggesting what you might like to wear them with. Lace and satin wedding dresses hang from on high. For men, there are sharp '70s suits, trilbies, waistcoats and a vast array of T-shirts and denim. Not everything is in great nick, but it's priced accordingly and ideal if you're after an instant wear-once look.

For branch see index.

Birgit Israel

279 Fulham Road, SW10 9PZ (7376 7277/www.birgitisrael.com). South Kensington tube. **Open** 10am-7pm Mon-Sat. **Credit** AmEx, MC, V. **Sells** W.

Former stylist Birgit Israel's own label now dominates the mix here, with a select display of customised vintage clothes, but the assistant promised much more behind the scenes, so do ask if you are looking for something in particular. We spotted 1930s full-length chiffon dresses and extremely good quality accessories. A deco-era clutch bag with a Bakelite clasp was supremely elegant – and a cool £600. You'll need a thick vintage wallet to match your pristine tastes: this is the Fulham Road, after all. But head here if you tend to be squeamish about second-hand clothes – it doesn't look remotely like a vintage shop. Popular with slender Kensington and Chelsea types, the boutique's fresh, white interior is scented with own-label candles and has a decent-sized changing area at the back. *See also p161.*

Blackout II

51 Endell Street, WC2H 9AJ (7240 5006/ www.blackout2.com). Covent Garden or Tottenham Court Road tube. **Open** 11am-7pm Mon-Fri; 11.30am-6.30pm Sat. **Credit** AmEx, MC, V. **Sells** M, W.

Popular with fashion-savvy students, this Covent Garden treasure trove is great for a focused browse. The bijou space is jam-packed with vintage attire for men and women. You can find everything here from gloves to swimming costumes. Clothing dates from the 1920s to the '80s and prices are reasonable. There are rails of 1950s cotton day dresses from £55, as well as lovely prom and cocktail dresses for under £100. Check out the cabinets of costume jewellery, with 1950s earrings that Pat Butcher would die for. Lucite bags from the same era are piled up on shelves above the dress rails. Head downstairs for skirt and dress suits and a very good range of vintage shoes (from £40) and ladylike handbags (£45). Men are catered for too with suits, shirts, trilbies and swathes of ties.

Butler & Wilson

189 Fulham Road, SW3 6JN (7352 8255/www.butlerandwilson.co.uk). South Kensington tube. **Open** 10am-6pm Mon, Tue, Thur-Sat; 10am-7pm Wed; noon-6pm Sun. **Credit** AmEx, MC, V. **Sells** W.

The costume jewellery range, for which the brand is famous, is at ground level, along with original pieces by Stanley Hugler. But to the left of the jewellery showroom, a gated stairway leads to vintage heaven. Up here, rails of beaded dresses that once shimmied to the charleston are ready to party once more (£1,000-£2,500). You'll also find ultra-feminine Edwardian white lace dresses, bought by brides-to-be, from around £500. And if you've ever fancied delivering the line 'I'll just change into something more comfortable', then one of the exotic silk kimonos should do the job. There are later vintage surprises here too. We spotted a black and red Ossie Clark dress, identical to the one Celia Birtwell wore in Hockney's famous portrait of the couple, *Mr and Mrs Clark and Percy*, for £998. Collectable 1950s novelty bags – such as raffia animals – are another Butler & Wilson strength.

For branch see index.

Cenci

4 Nettlefold Place, SE27 0JW (8766 8564/ www.cenci.co.uk). West Norwood rail. **Open** 11am-6pm Mon-Sat, 1st Sun of mth; also by appointment. **Credit** AmEx, DC, MC, V. **Sells** M, W, C.

Massimo Cenci began his vintage business in Florence in the 1970s, and after a decade in Covent Garden, he and his American wife

Annie's Vintage Clothes

Didi began operating from this south London warehouse. They have over 3,000sq ft of space, filled with men's, women's and children's clothing that's priced to sell, most dating from the 1940s to 1960s. Smart '60s childrenswear is particularly popular these days, with designers such as Ralph Lauren buying for inspiration. Although the stock comes from all over the world, the emphasis is Italian and American. The huge array of bargain accessories ranges from boxy patent-leather granny bags to sleek clutches and leather satchels for men.

Circa Vintage Clothes

64 Fulham High Street, SW6 3LQ (7736 5038/www.circavintage.com). Putney Bridge tube. **Open** 10am-6pm Mon-Fri; 10am-5pm Sat; also by appointment. **Credit** MC, V. **Sells** W.

Collectable labels such as Ossie Clark, Missoni, Leonard and Pucci hang beautifully from the rails in this chic boutique (which is just a few doors along from men's vintage shop Old Hat, *see p59*). On our last visit, highlights included a 1970s Alice Pollock cream trouser suit (£550) and a 1930s full-length net dress with appliqué flowers (£450). Otherwise, £300 is the average price for 1930s georgette and '50s day dresses. If you're looking for an LBD with clout, then there's an entire rail devoted to particularly elegant cocktail dresses from the 1940s and '50s that will certainly turn heads. Upstairs, past Molly the schnauzer, is Circa's bridal range, inspired by classic vintage designs (see www.circabrides.com). The bridal service is by appointment only, and gowns are priced under £2,000.

Cloud Cuckoo Land

6 Charlton Place, Camden Passage, N1 8AJ (7354 3141). Angel tube. **Open** 11am-5.30pm Tue-Sat. **Credit** MC, V. **Sells** W.

This fun little shop has a great selection of very wearable dresses from the 1930s to 1970s. Stock is feminine and quirky: elegant 1930s full-length silk slips, '40s crêpe cocktail gowns and '50s circle skirts. Cotton day dresses are priced at £50, and elegant mink evening capes at £75. There are often some good '70s labels here too, such as John Varon, Bus Stop and Janice Wainwright. On a recent visit we saw a superb 1960s Susan Small black satin duster coat, beautifully lined, for £95. At the back of the shop you'll find accessories, coats and jackets, plus a good selection of wraps, scarves, shawls and '50s novelty bags. The cheerful owner is happy to make suggestions if you're after a particular vintage look.

Dolly Diamond

51 Pembridge Road, W11 3HG (7792 2479/www.dollydiamond.com). Notting Hill Gate tube. **Open** 10.30am-6.30pm Mon-Fri; 9.30am-6.30pm Sat; noon-6pm Sun. **Credit** AmEx, MC, V. **Sells** M ,W.

A visit to Dolly Diamond reminds us of the sitcom *Goodnight Sweetheart*. One minute you're in the 21st century, then you step through the door into the 1940s. You almost expect to be asked for ration coupons. The shop has a delightfully old-fashioned feel, with its neat displays and vintage bra mannequins. When Elton John held his 1940s-themed 60th birthday bash, some of the guests came here to buy their kit. It's also popular with classic car enthusiasts who dress in post-war fashions for the glamorous Goodwood Revival weekend. The stock doesn't disappoint, whether it's a glam 1940s grosgrain gown (£225) or a cute burlesque hat (£65). There are men's clothes too, with 1940s dinner jackets costing from £85 and shirts from £30. At the back of the store you'll find a rail of vintage bridalwear, which takes in accessories and headdresses, and offers a custom alteration service on all its exquisite vintage gowns. Prices start at around £250 for a slinky 1930s number.

East End Thrift Store

Unit 1A, Watermans Building, Assembly Passage, E1 4UT (7423 9700/www.theeastendthriftstore.com). Stepney Green tube. **Open** 11am-6pm Mon-Wed, Sun; 11am-7pm Thur-Sat. **Credit** MC, V. **Sells** M, W.

How we ever lived without the East End Thrift Store is a mystery. The clue's in the name – 'thrift' rather than 'vintage', which means you get essentially all the fab gear of yesteryear at prices that would get Del Boy all a-quiver. Most of the stock is around the £7-£10 mark, but if you splash £15 you could get the one-of-a-kind turquoise evening dress with marabou trim on its hem, which we spotted on our last excursion, or a Gloria Vanderbilt bomber jacket, also £15. It might not be as pretty as some of the other vintage shops, but the stripped warehouse space has a certain functional charm all of its own.

For branch see index.

Emporium

330-332 Creek Road, SE10 9SW (8305 1670). Cutty Sark DLR. **Open** 10.30am-6pm Wed-Sun. **Credit** MC, V. **Sells** M, W.

This Greenwich boutique focuses on mostly British vintage clothing from the 1950s to 1970s. You'll find some recognisable names in the '70s evening gowns, but owners Jackie and John Hale choose pieces for their quality and design rather than labels, and the result is a diverse collection of high-end clothing and accessories, from quirky handbags to classic men's tailoring. Stock is well priced – you can pick up a little 1960s shift dress for £25. Don't miss the brilliant range of 1970s sunglasses.

The Girl Can't Help It

Alfie's Antique Market, 13-25 Church Street, NW8 8DT (7724 8984/www.thegirlcanthelpit.com). Edgware Road tube/ Marylebone tube/rail. **Open** 10am-6pm Tue-Sat. **Credit** AmEx, MC, V. **Sells** M, W.

Named after the Jayne Mansfield film, the Girl Can't Help It is blonde bombshell territory. A cream lace dress worn by Monroe herself is on display – and for sale if you have £5,000 and a 23-in waist. The look is classic Hollywood, personified by co-owner Sparkle Moore, an exuberant New Yorker with a flowing platinum mane and scarlet lips. She and her partner (professional name, Cad Van Swankster) source almost all of their stock from the US, because it's better quality and more opulent than austere post-war British garb. Always in stock are classic 1940s suits from Lili Ann of California (from £375) and 1950s circle skirts (£100-£350), decorated with everything from kitsch kittens to Mexican-style patterns. If you're after the total look you'll get it here, right down to the lingerie. On our last visit we saw a girdle with a beautiful art deco satin panel (£139) and silk knickers embroidered with 'Don't Touch' (far too flimsy to mean it). For retro bathing, you'll find 1950s swimsuits that once frolicked in the Pacific, from £95. There's a great range of glam accessories from cute velvet opera hats to straw bags covered in bunches of plastic cherries. Van Swankster presides over the suave menswear – Hawaiian shirts (from £50), gabardine jackets, slick 1940s and '50s suits, pin-up ties and camp accessories, such as tiki-themed bar glasses.

Lost 'n' Found Vintage Clothing

25 Stables Market, Chalk Farm Road, NW1 8AH (7482 2848). Camden Town tube. **Open** 11am-6pm Mon-Fri; 10am-7pm Sat, Sun. **Credit** AmEx, MC, V. **Sells** M, W.

If you only have time for one vintage stop in Camden Market, then head to this fun shop. Over two levels, it's perfect rummaging territory, with great music to accompany your browsing. Upstairs you'll find rails of dresses, furs, menswear and a wall of shoes and boots. The shop is well organised and stock is competitively priced, making it an ideal source for one-off party gear and cheap vintage clobber to wear every day. There are no big labels here, but a patient search through the rails will unearth worthwhile pieces. We spotted a 1960s Samuel Sherman wool dress (£35) and a floral Marion Donaldson day dress (£18). Cotton maxi dresses are priced from £18 and 1950s cocktail dresses from £50. Bags are good value too; there are elegant '60s handbags at £20 and '70s tooled leather shoulder bags at £35. Men will be happy here too, with shirts, biker jackets and denims. When we last visited it even had proper pipe band kilts for £45.

Marcos & Trump

146 Columbia Road, E2 7RG (7739 9008). Liverpool Street tube/rail. **Open** noon-6pm Fri; noon-5pm Sat; 8.45am-3.45pm Sun. **Credit** MC, V. **Sells** W.

This brilliantly edited collection of vintage and new pieces gives you the space and time to examine every item without feeling overwhelmed by mountains of stock. Especially good for retro dresses. *See also p174* **Streetwise**.

Mensah

291 Portobello Road, W10 5TD (8960 8520/www.mensah.uk.com). Ladbroke Grove tube. **Open** 10am-6pm Tue-Sat; 11am-5pm Sun. **Credit** AmEx, MC, V. **Sells** W.

Run by former 1980s catwalk model Herbie Mensah and his wife Sarah, this lovely boutique stocks vintage labels such as Biba, Pucci, Halston and Alaïa alongside contemporary designers – it's the sole stockist of handmade one-offs by Mrs Jones, the celebrity stylist who designed the white hooded playsuit for Kylie's 'Can't Get You Out of My Head' video. The Mensahs pick out elegant examples from different decades; good-quality vintage pieces dating from the 1960s onwards are surprisingly affordable. On our last visit we spotted a sexy 1970s Jean Muir dress for £250 and a '60s Biba satin gown (£150).

Old Hat

66 Fulham High Street, SW6 3LQ (7610 6558). Putney Bridge tube. **Open** 10.30am-6.30pm Mon-Sat. **Credit** MC, V. **Sells** M.

David Saxby's menswear emporium is perfect for those with lord of the manor pretensions but without the trust fund to match. You practically need pliers to free the tightly packed suits from their rails, but it's worth persevering as Savile Row suits can be had for under £100 – beyond a bargain when you consider that originals can cost upwards of £3,000. Look in the inside jacket pocket, and you'll usually find the name of the chap it was originally made for. All the gentlemanly requisites are here: top hats, tailcoats, silk scarves, overcoats and moleskin trousers, and the shop is a favourite with those off to retro events such as the Goodwood Festival of Speed. Saxby also has a branch in Tokyo, and recently opened his own-label menswear shop a couple of doors down at no.62, selling traditional tweed suits, overcoats and cords for off-duty gents.

One of a Kind

259 Portobello Road, W11 1LR (7792 5853/www.1kind.com). Ladbroke Grove tube. **Open** 10am-6pm daily. **Credit** AmEx, DC, MC, V. **Sells** M, W, C.

Lindsay Lohan reportedly shelled out £10,000 in one visit here, selecting dresses and accessories sporting labels such as Chanel, Dior and YSL. No wonder owner Jeff Ihenacho plans to open a shop in LA. There are photographs of Jeff posing with various celebs in the window, and you certainly need an A-lister's wallet to shop here. Fashionistas are fans too – Alice Temperley was expected when we last dropped in. Rare pieces are kept in a 'secret' room in the back, to be viewed by appointment. During our last peek, Jeff revealed sequined Pucci harem pants and an early '70s YSL lace gown. One of a kind, indeed.

Orsini Gallery

76 Earl's Court Road, W8 6EQ (7937 2903/www.orsini-vintage.co.uk). Earl's Court or High Street Kensington tube. **Open** 11am-7pm Mon-Sat; noon-6pm Sun. **Credit** AmEx, MC, V. **Sells** W.

This well-stocked shop is popular with well-heeled local residents seeking outfits for events of 'the Season' such as the Chelsea Flower Show and Ascot. In a slightly off-the-radar patch of Kensington, its owner Sophie Bulley has a glamorous selection of posh frocks from the 1920s to 1970s. There are swishy '20s flapper dresses (£320), wispy 1930s chiffons (£300-£400) and 1960s evening gowns in pastel silks from around £250. Pucci and the 'French Pucci', Leonard, are a draw for collectors, with dresses priced between £385 and £650. Well-preserved handbags go from £65 to £245 (£585 for Chanel). In a side room there are rails of more affordable '50s and '60s cocktail dresses with more ordinary, but good-quality, labels such as Susan Small. Bulley also offers a made-to-measure service – the Orsini Collection – for cocktail, evening and wedding dresses, using vintage *Vogue* patterns.

Palette London

21 Canonbury Lane, N1 2AS (7288 7428/www.palette-london.com). Highbury & Islington tube/rail. **Open** 11am-6.30pm Mon-Wed, Fri, Sat; 11am-7pm Thur; 11am-5.30pm Sun. **Credit** MC, V. **Sells** W.

Owner Mark Ellis knows instinctively what flatters certain body shapes, and he's a great stylist too – for example, using a wide 1980s belt to cinch in a gorgeous '30s dress, then completing the look with a great pair of heels. The boutique has a 50/50 mix of vintage and contemporary designers, selected to complement each other. Look out for Viennese designer Anna Aichinger, who trained with Viktor & Rolf and creates wonderful 1940s-inspired dresses and pencil skirts. Vintage glamour comes courtesy of legendary labels such as Pucci and Courrèges, US designers like Pauline Trigère and Norma Kamali and home-grown talents Ossie Clark, Biba and Janice Wainwright. Highlights from our last visit were a 1981 Chloé crêpe shift (£490) and vintage Courrèges sunglasses, still with original tags (£125). Prices are mid to high end, but the quality is superb. And you can guarantee that you'll walk out with something supremely flattering.

Persiflage

2nd Floor, Alfie's Antique Market, 13-25 Church Street, NW8 8DT (7724 7366). Edgware Road tube/Marylebone tube/rail. **Open** 10.30am-5.45pm Tue-Sat. **No credit cards. Sells** M, W.

A visit to Gwyneth Trefor-Jones's shop is always a treat. Stock is ever-changing, with no strict adherence to a particular period, so you never know what you'll find. One thing's for certain, though – it will be a bargain. She turns over cheaply, mainly because she enjoys fashion students coming to visit the shop (she gives discounts to Saint Martins students). When we last visited, we spotted a very pretty 1970s Janice Wainwright skirt and bolero, with her Poland Street label – a steal at £45 – as well as maxi dresses by the likes of Marion Donaldson for £40. An embroidered black silk Victorian jacket was only £55. Trimmings, however, are Trefor-Jones's real passion – beads, buttons, sequins and the like – and there are drawers full of goodies, divided up into £3 bags. A few years ago she bought up the entire stock of a button shop in the East End. She has become well known in the Far East, where there is a fascination with buttons, and even keeps a fold-up chair for Japanese husbands to employ while their wives browse.

Radio Days

87 Lower Marsh, SE1 7AB (7928 0800/ www.radiodaysvintage.co.uk). Waterloo tube/rail. **Open** 10am-6pm Mon-Sat; also by appointment. **Credit** MC, V. **Sells** M, W.

This charming shop is pure nostalgia. Hits of yesteryear such as 'Diamonds Are a Girl's Best Friend' play in the background, and, in winter, a gas fire warms your tootsies while you leaf through the 1940s and '50s frocks. To the rear are rails of day and evening dresses, coats, suits and lots of beaded evening tops. Prices are fair, with 1940s black dresses at £55 and beaded bags for £25. Men are catered for too, with dinner suits, great hats and heavy coats. The front area is filled with accessories for the home – and, yes, reconditioned radios from the 1940s and '50s (£65 and up) feature in the melange, along with great Bakelite telephones and magazines (such as 1960s gents' mag *Parade*, £5). There are even saucy vintage birthday cards.

Rellik

8 Golborne Road, W10 5NW (8962 0089/ www.relliklondon.co.uk). Westbourne Park tube. **Open** 10am-6pm Tue-Sat. **Credit** AmEx, DC, MC, V. **Sells** W.

Rellik (the Trellick Tower is opposite) is often cited as a favourite among the Kates and Siennas of the celebrity world, but neither the shop nor its price tags are intimidating. It's big enough for a lingering browse and small enough to get advice should you need it. Run by three former Portobello market stallholders – Fiona Stuart, Claire Stansfield and Steven Philip – their different tastes mean there's a good mix of pieces by the likes of Lanvin, Halston, Vivienne Westwood, Bill Gibb, Christian Dior and Ossie Clark. Philip's passion is the 1980s (Westwood, Alaïa) and he's popular with pop stylists (Kylie wore Rellik vintage in her Showgirl tour). Other diverse items spotted on a recent visit were a Courrèges wool shift (£285), a YSL cape (£280) and a wispy chiffon Zandra Rhodes gown (£484). There are earlier pieces too – a stunning '30s black silk dress and bolero was £275. One wall of the shop is dedicated to glam accessories to complete your outfit, such as enormous Hermès sunglasses (£120).

Rokit

42 Shelton Street, WC2 9HZ (7836 6547/ www.rokit.co.uk). Covent Garden tube. **Open** 10am-7pm Mon-Sat; 11am-6pm Sun. **Credit** AmEx, MC, V. **Sells** M, W.

As Rokit's flagship store – there's also one in Camden and two in Brick Lane – this branch stocks the most comprehensive selection of second-hand items, from tutus and military gear to cowboy boots and sunglasses. You won't find many well-known labels here, but it's still worth a rummage; on a recent visit we unearthed a Gunne Sax prairie dress and a Marimekko day dress, which were a steal at £15 each. There are also scarves, belts and hats galore. For men there are Doherty-style trilbies, waistcoats and shirts, as well as the usual male Americana. The shop at 107 Brick Lane is more boutiquey.

For branches see index.

Shikasuki

67 Gloucester Avenue, NW1 8LD (7722 4442/www.shikasuki.com). Camden Town or Chalk Farm tube. **Open** 11am-7pm Mon-Sat; noon-7pm Sun. **Credit** AmEx, MC, V. **Sells** M, W.

Shikasuki has yards of dress rails to sift through at your leisure, with pristine vintage clothes, beautifully displayed and helpfully labelled. Could this be the perfect vintage shop? Perhaps. Rachel Ducker's boutique is bright and welcoming and her extensive stock, although not cheap, is priced to match the quality. Tags are carefully marked with the decade of the garment, and each piece is graded from A to E depending on its condition – although most are in excellent nick. Accessories are on the ground floor, along with a bespoke hat service from milliner Emily London, while downstairs there are two rooms packed with fabulous frocks. The smaller room has a mostly boho mix, with a large selection of 1960s and 1970s cotton maxi dresses from the US label Gunne Sax (as worn by Hillary Clinton when she married Bill). The next room is more glamorous. We pulled out a 1960s mint green column dress embellished with pearls (£195) and a '70s shimmering sequin number by Oleg Cassini (£175). On the stairs, there's an impressive amount of Ossie Clark, mostly priced at around £700. The changing room, with its black floors and mirror-ball walls, is rather fabulous. Don't miss the Cheapasuki sale rail where stock is regularly marked down.

The Shop

1 & 3 Cheshire Street, E2 6ED (7739 5631). Liverpool Street tube/rail. **Open** 11am-6pm Tue-Sat; 9.30am-5pm Sun. **Credit** MC, V. **Sells** M, W.

The Shop is in fact two shops on Cheshire Street; Sharon Selzer's son Michael opened up at no.1 in spring 2008. His domain, which looks like an old-fashioned gentleman's outfitters, has everything from tailored suits to brothel creepers. In true Selzer tradition everything is priced to sell, suits from as little as £50 and ties from £5. There are even vintage swimming trunks. Sharon, at no.3, has rails of frocks, with great-value maxi dresses for £20, including '60s and '70s labels like Dollyrockers and Troubadour, as well as a selection of wedding gowns. True bargain territory.

Stromboli's Circus

Unit 1.5, Kingly Court, Carnaby Street, W1B 5PW (7734 1978/www.circus vintage.com). Oxford Circus tube. **Open** 11am-7pm Mon-Wed, Fri, Sat; 11am-8pm Thur; noon-6pm Sun. **Credit** AmEx, MC, V. **Sells** M, W, C.

Formerly known as Twinkled, this vintage one-stop shop feels a million miles away from Carnaby Street and its glut of jeans shops. Up here, in pleasant Kingly Court, Doris Day chirps away in the background and a Homemaker china set (the collectable, mid-century line made by Ridgway Potteries for Woolies in the 1950s) is laid out for lunch on the 1950s kitchen table. You could bring your mother or grandmother here to reminisce (and tut at the prices of the stuff they chucked out years ago). Over half of the shop is dedicated to clothes; you won't find many big-name labels, but it's a good bet for 1960s and '70s frocks from the likes of Kati and the increasingly popular Jean Varon. Prices are reasonable, despite the central location, so you could easily kit yourself out with an entire evening outfit, shoes included, for under £100. Vintage stockings sit in old suitcases along with Butterwick patterns. For men, there are suits, ties and leather jackets on offer. You'll also find bags, shoes, jewellery and glassware, along with a rail full of 1950s and '60s curtains.

Beyond Retro. *See p57.*

Thea Vintage

16 Stables Market, Chalk Farm Road, NW1 8AH (7482 5002). Camden Town tube. **Open** 11am-7pm Mon-Fri; 9.30am-7pm Sat, Sun. **Credit** MC, V. **Sells** M, W.

Located in Camden's Stables Market, there are several brilliant vintage shops. Thea Vintage is a small but on-trend unit with seasonally appropriate stock. You'll find colourful skinny jeans for £20 and polka-dot PVC cropped macs that'll weather spring showers for £15. A word of advice, however: some of the stock is actually new, but 'vintage inspired'. Obviously, this can be a false economy, so it's worth being a savvy shopper and digging around for the designer labels to ensure quality. We unearthed a pair of Jacques Vert coral pumps for £27 and a D&G vest for £15.

Tin Tin Collectables

Ground Floor, Alfie's Antique Market, 13-25 Church Street, NW8 8DT (7258 1305/ www.tintincollectables.net). Edgware Road tube/Marylebone tube/rail. **Open** 10am-6pm Tue-Sat. **Credit** AmEx, MC, V. **Sells** W.

Owner Leslie Verrinder says his shop stocks 'the dress that the gauche girl in the corner would wear' – though his frocks often take a twirl on the red carpet. He provided the diaphanous robe sported by Keira Knightley at her 21st birthday party as well as the dress she wore in the fountain scene in *Atonement*. There's an emphasis on unusual, less flashy pieces; to find them Verrinder scours antiques markets all over the country. Era-spanning stock includes elaborate turn-of-the-century gowns, 1920s beaded flapper dresses and ladylike '40s tweed suits. The focus, however, is on the 1920s and '30s, with a rail of wonderful chiffon dresses – so floaty that they look as if they might blow away in the wind (from £285). Complete the look with pretty 1930s shoes (from £90) and a bag from the tempting, well-priced selection. In the 'special drawer' there are all sorts of extraordinary trinkets. A favourite on a recent visit was a pair of 1930s honeymoon garters, still boxed, showing a policeman with his hand up for 'stop'. Everything here is in superb condition.

Vintage Modes

Grays Antiques Market, 1-7 Davies Mews, W1K 5AB (7409 0400/www.vintagemodes.co.uk). Bond Street tube. **Open** 10am-6pm Mon-Fri. **Credit** AmEx, MC, V. **Sells** W.

This award-winning shop is home to four vendors: Gillian Horsup, Susie Nelson, June Victor and David Wightman, all of them catering to a different niche. The tantalising mix here has attracted the likes of the Royal Opera (hats for *Fidelio*) as well as film makers (*Mrs Henderson Presents*). Stock spans 100 years of fashion history; you'll find demure Victorian corsets, 1930s satin wedding gowns, chic '50s cocktail dresses, slinky '70s disco dresses and ruched '80s party frocks. Despite the proximity to Bond Street, prices are not sky high. On a recent browse we saw a 1950s Worth silk day dress (£345), a '70s Yuki pleated gown (£225) and an '80s Bruce Oldfield evening dress (£270). Otherwise you can pick up a good non-label party dress for £150. You'll also find pairs of shoes from the 1940s as well as hats, veils and accessories. Gillian Horsup sells vintage jewellery, including art deco, celluloid and Bakelite pieces, as well as vintage bags and compacts.

Virginia Antiques

98 Portland Road, W11 4LQ (7727 9908/ www.virginiaantiques.co.uk). Holland Park tube. **Open** 11am-6pm Mon-Fri; by appointment Sat. **Credit** AmEx, DC, MC, V. **Sells** W.

Few vintage stores share the magical quality of Virginia Bates's elegant Holland Park shop. Step down into the basement and enter a lingerie dreamland; the room is draped with satin and lace petticoats and nightdresses, and even the ceiling is tented in ruched muslin. An embroidered curtain leads into another area filled with dark and sparkly gowns. Bates selects exquisite Victorian to 1940s-era pieces, all in perfect condition. Most of the eveningwear is French, as the best beadwork was made in Paris. Prices aren't cheap – ranging from £350 for a Victorian petticoat to £3,000 for a beaded 1920s flapper dress – but the quality is excellent. A heavenly place.

What Goes Around Comes Around

Unit 36, Stables Market, Chalk Farm Road, NW1 8AH (7424 9621). Camden Town tube. **Open** noon-6pm Mon-Fri; 10.30am-6.30pm Sat, Sun. **Credit** MC, V. **Sells** M, W.

At one time only specialising in rare vintage trainers, this shop now also sells a good selection of 1940s to '80s clothing and accessories, including some customised 1980s rock T-shirts for £22 and a 50-strong collection of vintage Vivienne Westwood. But it's still a sure-fire bet for limited-edition and rare kicks, many in their original boxes. We spotted a pair of Reebok Insta Pumps for around £100.

What the Butler Wore

131 Lower Marsh, SE1 7AE (7261 1353/ www.whatthebutlerwore.co.uk). Lambeth North tube/Waterloo tube/rail. **Open** 11am-6pm Mon-Sat. **Credit** MC, V. **Sells** M, W.

This intimate shop is an ideal place to be introduced to reasonably priced vintage clothes. Everything is in good condition and impeccably clean – with the local dry-cleaners tending to the stock. Its friendly owner Bridget Duffy focuses on the 1960s and '70s, but there are a few earlier and later pieces in the mix too. This is not vintage for the sake of it: clothes are selected carefully, and are pretty and wearable. To the rear, further stock includes maxi dresses by the likes of Gina Fratini and Jean Varon, and 1940s day dresses for £45. Shoes are a particular forte, with styles from the 1960s to '80s in all sizes and hues.

Also check out...

Dreamtime

6 Pierrepont Row, Camden Passage, N1 5ED (07804 261082). Angel tube. **Open** 8am-4pm Wed; 1-5pm Fri; 10am-5pm Sat. **No credit cards**. **Sells** W.

Has an interesting range stock of vintage hats, quirky jewellery and dresses, mainly from the 1930s and '40s.

Episode
26 Chalk Farm Road, NW1 8AG (7485 9927/www.episode.eu). Camden Town or Chalk Farm tube. **Open** 11am-7pm daily. **Credit** MC, V. **Sells** M, W.
A branch of the Dutch second-hand and vintage wholesale company that focusses on 1970s and '80s mens- and womenswear. They also have childrenswear on occasion.

L'Homme Designer Exchange
50 Blandford Street, W1U 7HX (7224 3266). Baker Street or Bond Street tube. **Open** 11.30am-5pm Mon-Sat. **Credit** AmEx, MC, V. **Sells** M.
Nearly new designer labels for men.

Hunky Dory Vintage
226 Brick Lane, E1 (7729 7387/www.myspace.com/welovevintageclothing). Liverpool Street tube/rail. **Open** 11am-7pm Tue-Sun. **Credit** MC, V. **Sells** M, W.
Open since summer 2008 and selling a hand-selected range of vintage spanning the 1930s to the 1980s.

Hurwundeki
98 Commercial Street, E1 6LZ (7392 9194/www.hurwundeki.com). Liverpool Street tube/rail. **Open** 11am-7.30pm Mon-Fri; 10am-7pm Sat, Sun. **Credit** MC, V. **Sells** M, W.
A select range of items dating from the Victorian era to the 1960s. *See also p30* **Unique Selling Point**.
For branch see index.

I Dream of Wires
68a Cheshire Street, E2 6EH (7739 4481/www.idreamofwires.co.uk). Liverpool Street tube/rail. **Open** 11am-7pm daily. **Credit** AmEx, MC, V. **Sells** M, W.
Stylist Lou Winwood and her partner Pete Voss opened this eccentric store in early 2008; selling retro fashions, toys, annuals and more, with an emphasis on the 1980s.

Lazooli
46 High Road, N2 9PJ (8883 1117/www.lazooli.co.uk). East Finchley tube/143, 263 bus. **Open** 10am-6pm Tue-Fri; 10am-5pm Sat. **Credit** AmEx, MC, V. **Sells** M, W.
A combination of vintage and dress-agency stock means you never know what you might find in this cheery shop.

Marshmallow Mountain
Ground Floor, Kingly Court, 49 Carnaby Street, W1B 5PW (7434 9498/www.marshmallowmountain.com). Oxford Circus or Piccadilly Circus tube. **Open** 11am-7pm Mon-Wed, Fri, Sat; 11am-8pm Thur; noon-6pm Sun. **Credit** AmEx, MC, V. **Sells** W.
Stocks a carefully-chosen selection of both clothing and accessories in a modern and boutique-like setting.

Mint Vintage
20 Earlham Street, WC2H 9LN (7836 3440/ww.mintvintage.co.uk). Covent Garden tube. **Open** 11am-7pm Mon-Wed; 11am-8pm Thur-Sat; noon-6pm Sun. **Credit** MC, V. **Sells** M, W.

ModernAge Vintage Clothing
65 Chalk Farm Road, NW1 8AN (7482 3787/www.modern-age.co.uk). Chalk Farm tube. **Open** 11am-6pm daily. **Credit** MC, V. **Sells** M, W.
Good selection for men and women. We liked the 1960s velvet capes by Quad and '70s suede trenchcoats.

Pop Boutique
6 Monmouth Street, WC2H 9HB (7497 5262/www.pop-boutique.com). Covent Garden tube. **Open** 11am-7pm Mon-Sat; 1-6pm Sun. **Credit** AmEx, MC, V. **Sells** M, W.
As well as a few rails of some genuine old clobber, Pop also has its own fun vintage-inspired label.

Retro Man/Retro Woman
20, 28, 32 & 34 Pembridge Road, W11 3HL (7792 1715/7221 2055/www.mveshops.co.uk). Notting Hill Gate tube. **Open** 10am-8pm daily. **Credit** AmEx, MC, V. **Sells** M, W.
You can buy, sell or swap your unwanted clothes at this sprawling used designerwear emporium.
For branch (Retro Clothing) see index.

Sheila Cook
28 Addison Place, W11 4RJ (7603 3003/www.sheilacook.co.uk). Holland Park tube. **Open** by appointment daily. **Credit** AmEx, MC, V. **Sells** W.
Cook has moved from Portobello to a new space in Holland Park; clothes, costumes and textiles from the late 1700s to the 1970s.

Still...
61D Lancaster Road, W11 1QG (7243 2932/www.still-shop.co.uk). Ladbroke Grove tube. **Open** 11am-6pm Mon-Sat; noon-4pm Sun. **Credit** MC, V. **Sells** W.
Vintage stock, complemented by the shop's own retro-inspired label, hand-embroidered by women in India.

Vintage Hart
96 Church Road, SE19 2LZ (07982 184657/www.vintagehart.co.uk). Crystal Palace rail. **Open** noon-8pm Fri; noon-6pm Sat, Sun. **Credit** AmEx, MC, V. **Sells** W.
This shop is actually in the White Hart pub; it sells 1950s to '80s ladieswear, with pretty '50s frocks from £40.

Wow Retro
179 Drury Lane, WC2B 5QF (7831 1699/www.wowretro.co.uk). Covent Garden tube. **Open** 11am-7pm Mon-Sat; noon-5pm Sun. **Credit** MC, V. **Sells** M, W.
This Drury Lane shop has frocks galore and some labels, but check clothes carefully – some are in less-than-mint condition.

Dress agencies

Catwalk
52 Blandford Street, W1U 7HY (7935 1052). Baker Street or Bond Street tube. **Open** 12.30-6pm Mon; 11.30am-6pm Tue-Fri; 11.30am-5pm Sat. **Credit** MC, V. **Sells** W.

Dress Box
8 Cheval Place, SW7 1ES (7589 2240). Knightsbridge or South Kensington tube. **Open** 10am-6pm Mon-Fri; 10.30am-6pm Sat, Sun. **Credit** AmEx, DC, MC, V. **Sells** M, W.

The Dresser
10 Porchester Place, W2 2BS (7724 7212/www.dresseronline.co.uk). Marble Arch tube. **Open** 11am-6pm Mon-Fri; 11am-5pm Sat. **Credit** MC, V. **Sells** M, W.

Pandora
16-22 Cheval Place, SW7 1ES (7589 5289/www.pandoradressagency.com). Knightsbridge or South Kensington tube. **Open** 10am-7pm Mon-Sat; noon-6pm Sun. **Credit** AmEx, MC, V. **Sells** W.

Salou
6 Cheval Place, SW7 1ES (7581 2380). South Kensington or Knightsbridge tube. **Open** 10am-6pm Mon-Sat; noon-6pm Sun. **Credit** MC, V. **Sells** W.

Charity shops

Barnado's
7 George Street, W1U 3QH (7935 2946/www.barnados.org.uk). Marylebone tube/rail. **Open** 10am-6pm Mon-Sat. **Credit** MC, V. **Sells** M, W.
Tucked away on George Street, just off Thayer Street, this branch of Barnado's has (until now) been a well-kept secret among West End professionals. On a recent scouting mission we found an array of workwear, including a smart pinstripe business suit for £29.95, and Kurt Geiger brogues for a mere £8.15.
Branches: throughout the city.

British Red Cross Shop
69-71 Old Church Street, SW3 5BS (0845 054 7101/www.redcross.org.uk). Sloane Square tube then 11, 19, 22 bus. **Open** 10.30am-6pm Mon-Sat. **Credit** MC, V. **Sells** M, W, C.
Buying from charity shops is all to do with location. It's simple: the more affluent the area, the better the stock. The Red Cross shop in Chelsea is the place where many designer neighbours – like Manolo Blahnik and Catherine Walker – donate unwanted items. Previous visits have yielded such fab finds as Chanel bags and an Yves Saint Laurent shirt.
Branches: throughout the city.

Cancer Research UK
24 Marylebone High Street, W1U 4PQ (7487 4986/www.cancerresearchuk.org). Baker Street tube. **Open** 10am-6pm Mon-Fri; 10am-5pm Sat; 11am-5pm Sun. **Credit** MC, V. **Sells** M, W.
Designer fashion and accessories, often in mint condition, can be found here.
Branches: throughout the city.

Crusaid
19 Churton Street, SW1V 2LY (7233 8736/www.crusaidshop.com). Pimlico tube or Victoria tube/rail. **Open** 10am-6pm Mon-Sat; 11am-3pm Sun. **Credit** MC, V. **Sells** M, W.

Sales & events

Unearth something special at one of the capital's vintage happenings.

Anita's Vintage Fashion Fairs

Battersea Arts Centre, Lavender Hill, SW11 5TN (8325 5789/ www.vintagefashionfairs.com). Clapham Junction rail. **Dates** 12 Oct, 30 Nov 2008 (see website for future dates). **Admission** £5; £2.50 students.

The six annual fairs are among London's best for vintage fashion. Attended by fashion editors and designers, they're a great place to pick up designer brands like Biba, Westwood, Christian Dior, Yves Saint Laurent and a host of others. Prices range from £5 to £500.

Biba Lives Auctions

01932 568678/www.bibalives.com/www.wellersauctions.com. **Dates** see website.

Several large vintage auctions a year through Surrey auctioneers Wellers. Smith-Hughes, a long-haul stewardess for 23 years, sources 1930s eveningwear and accessories, '40s two-piece fitted suits and dresses, cocktail dresses from the '50s, minis from the '60s, and '70s polyester and flares. Collections are sourced from all over the world and the likes of Kate Moss and Stella McCartney are fans. All items are restored and cleaned before they're given a Biba Lives label as a stamp of approval.

Christie's South Kensington

85 Old Brompton Road, SW7 3LD (7930 6074/www.christies.com). South Kensington tube. **Dates** see website.

Costume, Textiles & Fans sales take place about four times a year, with collectors' items like bonnets, knickerbockers and 18th-century clothing to be had. There are also biannual sales of 1940s to '80s clothes by leading designers like Westwood and Dior.

Frock Me!

Chelsea Town Hall, King's Road, SW3 5EZ (7254 4054/www.frockmevintagefashion.com). Sloane Square tube. **Dates** 26 Oct, 14 Dec 2008 (see website for additional dates). **Admission** £3.

Some 50 specialists set up their stalls at these fairs, which were launched five years ago by Matthew Adams and which are now held about six times a year. Dealers sell clothes from every era, from the 1920s 'flapper' style to 1950s glamour pieces, '80s retro-chic or classic 1960s trends. Prices range from £2 to several hundred.

Kerry Taylor Auctions

Unit C25, Parkhall Road Trading Estate, 40 Martell Road, SE21 8EN (8676 4600/www.kerrytaylorauctions.com). West Norwood rail. **Dates** 4 Dec 2008 (see website for future dates).

Kerry Taylor headed up the Costume & Textile department at Sotheby's auction house, before leaving in 2003 to set up her own business. There are eight auctions a year – six held in Dulwich and two at Sotheby's in Bond Street. Expect choice items spanning several centuries, from 18th-century christening robes to Thierry Mugler suits.

Vintage Fashion, Textiles & Accessories Fair

Dulwich College, Dulwich Common, SE21 7LD/Hammersmith Town Hall, King Street, W6 9JU (8543 5075/www.pa-antiques.co.uk). **Dates** see website. **Admission** £5-£10.

These popular Sunday vintage fairs are held around every five to six weeks at Dulwich College and in Hammersmith Town Hall.

A gem of a charity shop stocking lots of designer items. In particular, look out for Nicole Farhi; every couple of months the designer makes a generous donation.

Octavia Housing & Care

57 Kensington Church Street, W8 4BA (7937 5274/www.octaviahousing.org.uk). High Street Kensington tube. **Open** 10am-6pm Mon-Sat; noon-5pm Sun. **Credit** MC, V. **Sells** M, W.

The former Notting Hill Trust shop stocks the cast-offs of well-heeled locals, and there are some great designer finds to be had. A burgundy taffeta Oscar gown worn by Keira Knightley was sold for thousands of pounds on eBay after being exhibited in the shop window here.

Branches: throughout the city.

Oxfam

245 Westbourne Grove, W11 2SE (7229 5000/www.oxfam.org.uk). Notting Hill Gate tube. **Open** 10am-6pm Mon-Sat; noon-4pm Sun. **Credit** MC, C. **Sells** M, W.

Only the best clothes donated to Oxfam make their way to one of three west London 'boutique' stores, which sell second-hand labels (Miu Miu skirts for £50, say, or Stella McCartney for £90) – prices are higher than your average charity shop, but the clothes are better. As well as vintage designer gear, they sell customised pieces by fashion-school designers and Fairtrade fashion labels.

Branches: throughout the city.

Retromania

6 Upper Tachbrook Street, SW1V 1SH (7630 7406/www.faracharityshops.org). Victoria tube/rail. **Open** 10am-6pm Mon-Sat; 11am-5pm Sun. **Credit** MC, V. **Sells** M, W, C.

This is a charity shop with a difference. It is part of FARA, the Romanian orphan charity, but only vintage donations are sold here. The shop's well-to-do benefactors clearly have some good clear-outs. As well as posh frocks, there are also shoes, belts and bags galore as well as a small selection of menswear – including military outfits. Worth a regular rummage.

Salvation Army

9 Princes Street, W1B 2LQ (7495 3958/ www.salvationarmy.org.uk). Oxford Circus tube. **Open** 10am-6pm Mon-Sat. **Credit** MC, V. **Sells** M, W.

Two floors of thrift, tucked away from the chaos of Oxford Street. On the ground floor, the shoe selection includes labels such as Charles Jourdan and there's an abundance of 1970s dresses and skirts. Upstairs has a more boutiquey feel, with luxurious finds such as floor-length fake-fur coats and evening bags filling the rails – the latter can be snapped up for less than a tenner.

Branches: throughout the city.

TRAID

61 Westbourne Grove, W2 4UA (7221 2421/www.traid.org.uk). Bayswater tube. **Open** 10am-6pm Mon-Sat; 11am-5pm Sun. **Credit** MC,V. **Sells** M, W.

A favourite of both fashion stylists and journalists, TRAID (Textile Recycling for Aid and International Development) offers superior second-hand clothing for a worthy cause. The small, boutique-like shop has a vintage clothing section as well as its renowned remade threads.

Branches: throughout the city.

Trinity Hospice

31 Kensington Church Street, W8 4LL (7376 1098/www.trinityhospice.org.uk). High Street Kensington tube. **Open** 10.30am-5.30pm Mon-Sat; 11am-5pm Sun. **Credit** MC, V. **Sells** M, W.

Great for its ladies' clothing and accessories, this branch always has a good selection of handbags and shoes by the likes of Louis Vuitton and Ferragamo.

Branches: throughout the city.

Weddings

London has some of the best and most original bridal shops in the UK. These stores tend to operate on an appointment-only basis and booking ahead is essential. Also bear in mind that it can take up to a year to order a dress. Go along with a positive attitude, a strong idea of your budget and what you want, and an honest friend. Ask about fittings, alterations and extras to avoid any nasty financial surprises later on.

Vintage shops are an excellent starting point for brides and grooms; **Annie's Vintage Clothes** (*see p56*) and **Virginia** (*see p61*) have some great gowns and accessories for brides-to-be, **Circa Vintage Clothes** (*see p58*) offers a vintage-inspired bridal range (www.circabrides.com), and **Heirloom Couture** reworks old dresses into beautiful bridal gowns.

For wedding dresses at low prices, try **Bhs**, **Evans** (*see p69*) and **Marks & Spencer**'s (*see p16*) new bridal range; for all. **Lipman & Sons** (22 Charing Cross Road, WC2H 0HR, 7240 2310) is a friendly and well-priced suit hire chain with several branches in London. **Moss Bros Hire** (27-29 King Street, WC2E 8JD, 7632 9700, www.mossbros.co.uk) also offers safe suit options. One-stop wedding shop **Confetti** (0870 774 7177, www.confetti.co.uk) is good for affordable stationery, table decorations and planning advice.

FASHION

Dresses

Basia Zarzycka

52 Sloane Square, SW1W 8AX (7730 1660/www.basia-zarzycka.com). Sloane Square tube. **Open** 10am-6pm Mon-Sat. **Credit** AmEx, MC, V.

Not for shrinking violets, Basia Zarzycka's kaleidoscopic shop in Sloane Square is stuffed with the most opulent accessories in London: feathery fascinators, sparkly tiaras and statement costume jewellery. Basia herself overseas all bridal commissions (from £10,000) and specialises in coloured gowns, extravagant gems and couture detailing.

Browns Bride

12 Hinde Street, W1U 3BE (7514 0056/ www.brownsfashion.com). Bond Street tube. **Open** by appointment 11am-6pm Mon-Sat. **Credit** MC, V.

Combining high-octane designer names with hands-on personal service, Browns Bride sets the trends when it comes to wedding dresses. It's all about big-name designers here, such as Oscar de la Renta, Monique Lhuillier and Carlos Miele. Many of the ranges on offer are exclusive to Browns and prices start at the £2,000 mark, going up to around £12,000. New for spring/summer 2009 is the highly regarded Mira Zwillinger. Accessories are also available including Christian Louboutin's much coveted bridal shoes. Book an appointment and prepare to part with vast sums of cash.

Caroline Castigliano

62 Berners Street, W1T 3NN (7636 8212/ www.carolinecastigliano.co.uk). Oxford Circus tube. **Open** by appointment 10am-6.30pm Tue-Sat; 11am-8pm Thur. **Credit** AmEx, MC, V.

This well-established bridal shop (there's also a branch in Knightsbridge) offers in-depth consultations as well as thorough fittings. Providing all the major silhouettes, including fish-tail, hourglass, A-line and full-circle, the aim here is to provide your dream dress so each frock you see hanging on the rails can be altered to your precise requirements. Fittings are fun, with wine and props including veils and bouquets so you get a feel for what you'll actually look like on the big day. Staff recommend ordering a year in advance. Prices from £3,500 to £13,000.

Heirloom Couture

Studio 18, Walters Workshops, 249-251 Kensal Road, W10 5DB (8969 4013/ www.heirloomcouture.com). Kensal Green rail/tube. **Open** by appointment 9am-6pm Mon, Tue, Thur, Fri; 9am-8pm Wed; 10am-4pm Sat. **No credit cards**.

With a background in couture embroidery, Rachel Spencer's expertise in traditional techniques and finishes allows her to perfectly restore, alter or reinvent precious vintage gowns for a modern-day bride. Heirloom Couture also works with vintage inspiration to create one-off bespoke pieces from £2,000, and Spencer's Parisian-style studio showcases a capsule collection of vintage gowns from £700 and original ready-to-wear dress styles from £1,800. For time-pushed (or perfectionist) brides, Heirloom Couture's personal service will track down or create the perfect accessories to complete the look.

Jacqueline Byrne

18 Arlington Way, EC1R 1UY (7833 0381/www.jacquelinebyrne.co.uk). Angel tube. **Open** by appointment 10am-7pm Mon-Sat. **Credit** AmEx, MC, V.

Offering a uniquely personal experience, Jacqueline Byrne works closely with the client in the design process, incorporating the bride-to-be's individual style and tastes to produce a bespoke creation from £1,500. Combining artisan touches (think intricate beading, handmade lace and hand-dyed fabric) with figure-flattering devices such as weighted hems and built-in foundation garments, the results are guaranteed to make any bride feel a million dollars.

Jenny Packham

75 Elizabeth Street, SW1W 9PJ (7730 2264/www.jennypackhambride.com). Sloane Square tube/Victoria tube/rail. **Open** by appointment 10am-6pm Tue-Sat. **Credit** AmEx, MC, V.

With a string of design accolades to her name and a devoted celebrity following, Packham's brand of contemporary bridal glamour is in high demand. Appointments start with a lengthy discussion to determine exactly what the bride is looking for, and staff are experts in advising on styles to flatter. New this year is a range of crystal-adorned 1920s heels – a collaboration between Packham and footwear designer Emmy (*see p65*), as well as tiaras by Polly Edwards and jewellery by Coleman Douglas.

Luella's Boudoir

33 Church Road, SW19 5DQ (8879 7744/ www.luellasboudoir.co.uk). Wimbledon tube/ rail. **Open** 11am-7pm Tue, Wed; 11am-8pm Thur; 11am-6pm Fri; 10am-6pm, Sat; noon-5pm Sun. **Credit** AmEx, MC, V.

A one-stop shop for every bride and bridesmaid, Luella's Boudoir features a handpicked selection of the best accessories, lingerie, shoe and jewellery designers. Labels are constantly updated and include Jason Jennings, Phillipa Scott, Olivia Morris and milliner Caroline Morris. The staff's wedding expertise is second to none and the shop offers a made-to-order bridesmaid collection with a choice of over 200 colours (from £180) and the option of bespoke from £280.

Mirror Mirror

37 Park Road, N8 8TE (8348 2113/ www.mirrormirror.uk.com). Finsbury Park tube/rail. **Open** 10am-6pm Mon-Sat. **Credit** MC, V.

Both branches of this pretty boutique stock an exceptional array of styles and designers (such as Pronovias, Luci Dibella and the Curvy Collection – which goes up to size 24) as well as Mirror Mirror Couture where bespoke gowns can be individually created to fit and flatter (from £2,700). Expertly trained staff eschew the hard sell in favour of a more personal and intimate approach, and brides are encouraged to take their time in making a decision.

For branch see index.

Morgan Davies

62 Cross Street, N1 2BA (7354 3414/ www.morgandavieslondon.co.uk). Angel tube/Highbury & Islington tube/rail. **Open** by appointment 9.30am-6pm Mon-Sat. **Credit** DC, MC, V.

The boudoir-like interior of this Islington boutique is flanked with stunning gowns, all of them classic with a contemporary twist. Designers stocked include Alan Hannah, Stephanie Allin and Beverly Lister. Shop manager Annalize has the remarkable ability to pick the perfect dress for your physique; keep your mind open, it's often not the one you expect. After initial fittings, you're looked after in the atelier over the road on Upper Street where the seamstresses ensure you're fitted to absolute perfection.

Temperley London Bridal Room

6-10 Colville Mews, Lonsdale Road, W11 2DA (7229 7957/www.temperley london.com). Notting Hill Gate tube. **Open** by appointment 10am-6pm Mon-Wed; 10am-7pm Thur; 11am-6pm Sat. **Credit** AmEx, MC, V.

Tucked away in a quiet Notting Hill mews, Alice Temperley's bridal room delivers superb service and an unparalleled attention to detail – offering champagne at appointments and even retailoring the dress to cocktail length after the big day to ensure you get as much wear as possible. As well as the extensive showroom of ready-to-wear creations in the label's signature romantic and ethereal style, from autumn 2008, Temperley will be offering a fully bespoke service, giving a lucky few the opportunity to work with Alice herself to design a dream gown (from £10,000).

Vera Wang Bridal Salon at Selfridges

Selfridges, Lower Level, 400 Oxford Street, W1A 1AB (7318 3095/www.verawang.com/www.weddingshop.com). Bond Street tube. **Open** by appointment 10am-5.30pm Mon-Sat; noon-4.30pm Sun. **Credit** AmEx, DC, MC, V.

The name Vera Wang is synonymous with bridal and anyone taking more than a quick browse around the Selfridges Salon would concede that the designer's reputation for the highest end of luxury is well deserved. Prices start from £2,400 for a classic design, rising steeply for the higher-end Luxe couture line or any bespoke details. Fittings are expertly performed in the designer's Chelsea boutique, where the stunning made-to-order bridesmaids range (from £245), in soft silks and with Grecian draping, can also be viewed.

Also check out...

Amanda Wakeley Sposa

80 Fulham Road, SW3 6HR (7590 9108/www.amandawakeley.com). South Kensington tube. **Open** by appointment 9am-5pm Mon-Sat. **Credit** MC, V.
Understated glamour in beautiful fabrics.

Collette Dinnigan

26 Cale Street, SW3 3QU (7589 8897/www.collettedinnigan.com). South Kensington tube. **Open** 10am-6pm Mon-Sat. **Credit** AmEx, DC, MC, V.
A modern, fresh and chic bridal range.

Johanna Hehir

10-12 Chiltern Street, W1U 7PX (7486 2760/www.johanna-hehir.com). Baker Street tube. **Open** by appointment 11.30am-6pm Mon-Fri; 10am-5pm Sat. **Credit** MC, V.

Pronovias

94 Bond Street, W1S 1SH (7518 8470/www.pronovias.com). Bond Street tube. **Open** by appointment 10am-7pm daily. **Credit** AmEx, DC, MC, V.

Ritva Westenius

28 Connaught Street, W2 2AS (7706 0708/www.ritvawestenius.com). Marble Arch tube. **Open** by appointment 9am-6pm Mon-Sat; 9am-7pm Thur. **Credit** MC, V.

Stewart Parvin

14 Motcomb Street, SW1X 8LB (7235 1125/www.stewartparvin.com). Hyde Park Corner or Knightsbridge tube. **Open** by appointment 10am-6pm Tue-Sat. **Credit** AmEx, MC, V.

Suzanne Neville

29 Beauchamp Place, SW3 1NJ (7823 9107/www.suzanneneville.com). Knightsbridge tube. **Open** by appointment 10am-4.45pm Mon-Thur; 10am-5.30pm Fri, Sat. **Credit** AmEx, MC, V.

Wedding Dress Shop

174 Arthur Road, SW19 8AQ (8605 9008/www.theweddingdressshop.co.uk). Wimbledon Park tube. **Open** by appointment 10am-5pm Tue-Sat. **Credit** MC, V.

Temperley London Bridal Room

Shoes

Many footwear designers, including **Emma Hope**, **Gina** and **Jimmy Choo**, have bridal collections; for these and others, *see pp70-75*.

Beatrix Ong

4 Burlington Arcade, W1J 0PD (7499 4089/www.beatrixong.com). Piccadilly Circus or Green Park tube. **Open** 10am-6pm Mon-Sat. **Credit** AmEx, MC, V.

As you'd expect from someone who honed her craft at Jimmy Choo, Beatrix Ong's designs are exceptionally beautiful, seriously covetable and (perhaps more surprisingly) very comfortable. Upstairs in the boutique, brides-to-be are treated to tea and cakes while they browse the white satin bridal collection and the mainline range (all of which can be hand-dyed or remade in another material to match a swatch of fabric). Prices start at around £250 and, for a unique touch, the leather sole can be personalised with a name, date or even a poem. *See also p70.*

Emmy

65 Cross Street, N1 2BB (7704 0012/www.emmyshoes.co.uk). Highbury & Islington tube/rail. **Open** by appointment 10.30am-5.30pm Tue, Thur-Sat; 11.30am-6.30pm Wed. **Credit** MC, V.

This Islington shoemaker, located over the road from bridal shop Morgan Davies (*see p64*), provides exquisite custom-made shoes in a variety of heel heights and shapes – you get to have them made up to your specifications. Choose from round toes, pointed toes, peep-toes and sandals in a range of dizzyingly pretty designs.

Also check out...

Hanna Goldman

Studio 4, 10-13 Hollybush Place, E2 9QX (7739 2690/www.hannagoldman.couk). Bethnal Green tube/rail. **Open** by appointment 11am-7pm Mon-Sat. **No credit cards.**

FASHION

Maternity

Several high street chains offer trend-led maternity lines, including **Topshop** and **H&M**; **American Apparel** is also a good choice for style-conscious expectant-mums because of its abundance of stretchy, high-quality cotton items. Also worth checking out is **Lilliput**'s (*see p261*) Crave concession, while those on a budget should visit **Mamas & Papas** (*see p261*), which is great for inexpensive basics like vests and kaftan-style tops, and **Merry Go Round** (21 Half Moon Lane, SE24 9JU, 7737 6452), which offers previously owned, end-of-line and new maternity wear. Many of the shops listed below also sell baby clothes and gifts.

Blooming Marvellous

725 Fulham Road, SW6 5UL (7371 0500/ www.bloomingmarvellous.co.uk). Parsons Green tube. **Open** 9.30am-5.30pm Mon-Sat; 11am-5pm Sun. **Credit** AmEx, MC, V.

Created to fill a gap in the market for mothers-to-be in search of fashionable clothes, Blooming Marvellous is a useful resource for maternity basics. Styles are practical, colours neutral and prices reasonable. There's nothing here that has the wow factor, but you'll be able to get a pair of stretch jeans for just £29.99 and practical staples like lingerie (from £9.99) and breastfeeding tops. Complete your wardrobe with useful linen dresses (£39.99), smocks, wrap tops and T-shirts. There's nightwear and swimwear too, a large range of kids' clothes and toys, and bedroom and nursery accessories – all of which have been approved by a mothers' testing panel.

For branches see index.

Blossom Mother & Child

164 Walton Street, SW3 2JL (0845 262 7500/www.blossommotherandchild.com). South Kensington tube. **Open** 10am-6pm Mon-Sat; noon-5pm Sun. **Credit** AmEx, MC, V.

Nestled in Walton Street since 2003, this softly scented maternity wear specialist is a calming place for hot and bothered mothers-to-be, and can count Gwyneth Paltrow among its many style-conscious customers. The pretty shop is a one-stop haven of reassurance and advice on everything from nursing bra sizes to local maternity wards and, as well as visiting during business hours, you can pop in in the evenings for a private appointment. Clothes are designed to flatter the temporarily full-frontal look; the broad collection ranging from more affordable own-label day- and eveningwear (jeans around £135; dresses around £125) and sexy swimwear through to their popular customised jeans (J Brand, Paige), and a wide selection of high end designs by the likes of Sonia Rykiel, See by Chloé and Temperley. The lingerie collection includes Michael Stars, Cadeau and 1 et 1 font 3. There are plenty of things for the baby too – weeny newborn clothes by Aztec and Tiny Te and Angel Baby toiletries, lotions and potions. Blossom is such a success story that as we were going to press another branch was due to open on Marylebone High Street. The main maternity collection, however, will remain at the Walton Street branch.

Bumpsville

33 Kensington Park Road, W11 2EU (7727 1213/www.bumpsville.com). Notting Hill or Westbourne Park tube. **Open** 10am-6pm Mon-Sat; 11am-5pm Sun. **Credit** AmEx, MC, V.

The offspring of funky boutique the West Village, Bumpsville is the place to visit if you're an expectant mother striving for colour and flair. Striking own-label patterned shirt-dresses are the shop's forte (£189), but there are also sequinned T-shirts in different shades (£99), along with super-flattering Earl jeans (£150). The shop also stocks some great toys and gifts (an egg box of socks for £35, say, or a cool kids' drum for £24) and the bright and beautiful Sprogsville range of children's clothes (adorable cord dungarees, £25).

For branches (West Village) see index.

Crave Maternity

207 King's Road, SW3 5ED (7349 9822/ www.cravematernity.co.uk). Sloane Square tube. **Open** 10am-6pm Mon, Tue, Thur-Sat; 10am-7pm Wed; noon-5pm Sun. **Credit** MC, V.

This flagship store in the heart of Chelsea offers a host of solutions to all sorts of bump-dressing dilemmas. There are some versatile skirts (from £25) in linen and pull-on jersey, cotton jackets (£49), camisoles, knitwear, swimwear (£35) and accessories. Look out for a range of simple but stylish maternity clothes called Lisa B Essentials – courtesy of model Lisa Barbuscia – silk print dresses come in at £59, trousers start at £79 and an evening dress is around £140.

Elias & Grace

158 Regent's Park Road, NW1 8XN (7449 0574/www.eliasandgrace.com). Chalk Farm tube. **Open** 10am-6pm Mon-Sat; noon-6pm Sun. **Credit** MC, V.

The Primrose Hill fashion set needn't compromise on style with this haven of Vivienne Westwood, Stella McCartney and Luella designs at their fingertips. While Elias & Grace is ideal for special-occasion clothes, be warned that not everything is maternity and some are just items that have been adapted over a prosthetic bump, so may not take the extra weight on breasts, arms, back and thighs into consideration. But with its adorable baby clothes upstairs (Petit Bateau, Quincy Maan) and racks of beautiful pregnancy clothes downstairs (Matthew Williamson dresses; James maternity jeans £175), this is the first stop for the mum-to-be with cash to flash. The shop also stocks a fantastic array of health and beauty products from the likes of Hema and This Works.

Emily Evans

8 Hollywood Road, SW10 9HY (7352 7600/ www.emilyevansboutique.com). Earl's Court tube. **Open** 10am-6pm Mon-Sat; noon-5pm Sun. **Credit** AmEx, MC, V.

Opened in 2002, this swanky maternity shop has a decidedly starry following – Kate Moss, Gwen Stefani and Laura Bailey are among the names who've chosen its designs during their nine months. Its own-label collection, which launched in 2006, offers amazingly flattering and stylish evening and day dresses. Tiny9, a children's collection for newborns to nine-year-olds, launched in 2007.

Formes

33 Brook Street, W1K 4HG (7493 2783/ www.formes.com). Bond Street tube. **Open** 10.30am-6.30pm Mon-Wed, Fri, Sat; 10.30am-7.30pm Thur; noon-5pm Sun. **Credit** AmEx, MC, V.

Formes was one of the first companies to make maternity wear remotely trendy. It's consistently reliable for sedate but chic designs, such as sleek, discreet tailored trousers, layered tops, wraparound cardis and ribbed polo necks. The tough skinny jeans have plenty of give at the top.

For branches see index.

JoJo Maman Bébé

68 Northcote Road, SW11 6QL (7228 0322/ www.jojomamanbebe.co.uk). Clapham Junction rail. **Open** 9.30am-5.30pm Mon-Sat; 11am-5pm Sun. **Credit** MC, V.

Affordable and practical, with occasional flashes of French chic, JoJo is one of the most user-friendly maternity ranges around. Bestsellers include jeans (still only £29 and have been for years), easy-to-wear wrap dresses, kaftans and capsule office wear (linen shirts, trousers, dresses). There's loads of choice, loads of style and nothing much over £45 – the most expensive thing is a beautiful silk dress for £70. Even so, only a selection of its huge stock is in-store – visit the website for further lines. It's also a good source of clothes for babies and children, gifts and nursery items (*see also p259*).

For branches see index.

Also check out...

Harry Duley

01747 855023/www.harryduley.co.uk.

Contemporary cotton basics, including an ingenious supportive 'belly band' (£15).

Isabella Oliver

0844 844 0448/www.isabellaoliver.com.

Chic specialist.

Maternity Co

42 Chiswick Lane, W4 2JQ (8995 4455/ www.thematernityco.com). Turnham Green tube. **Open** 10am-5.30pm Mon-Sat; 11am-5pm Sun. **Credit** MC, V.

Mothernature

01782 824242/www.mothernature bras.co.uk.

A wide range of maternity bras online.

Mums 2 Be

3 Mortlake Terrace, Mortlake Road, Kew, Surrey TW9 3DT (8332 6506/ www.mums-2-be.co.uk). Kew Gardens tube/rail. **Open** 10am-5.30pm Mon-Sat. **Credit** MC, V.

Pretty Pregnant

102 Northcote Road, SW11 6QW (7924 4850/www.prettypregnant.co.uk). Clapham Junction rail. **Open** 10am-6pm Mon-Sat; 11am-5pm Sun. **Credit** MC, V.

A good selection of flattering dresses, jeans, cardigans, jackets and lingerie at this welcoming Clapham Junction shop.

Lingerie & Swimwear

Lingerie sections in many of London's department stores (*see pp15-16*) make great browsing grounds for underwear and bikinis. Our faves are **Liberty** and **Selfridges**; the latter stocks Parisian brand **Princesse Tam Tam** (www.princesstamtam.com), which can also be found in boutiques like **Hub** (*see p35*). The ingenious Panty Postman service run by **Coco Ribbon** (*see p28*) delivers two pairs of stylish own-label smalls to your door every quarter. **Austique** (*see p28*) is another good bet for boudoir-style lingerie.

See also p201 **Erotic**.

Lingerie

Agent Provocateur

6 Broadwick Street, W1V 1FH (7439 0229/www.agentprovocateur.com). Oxford Circus or Tottenham Court Road tube. **Open** 11am-7pm Mon-Wed, Fri, Sat; 11am-8pm Thur; noon-5pm Sun. **Credit** AmEx, MC, V. **Sells** W.

First port of call for the glamorous, decadent and fashion-forward lingerie fan, Agent Provocateur designs some of the most desirable bras, briefs and babydolls around. It's been 14 years since the first AP opened in Soho, and the brand now boasts an international reputation. Slip into the seductively lit shop, complete with saucy pink-uniformed staff, and lose a happy hour flipping through rails of wispy tulle and luxurious silk. It's a fine place to stock up on honeymoon fripperies (note for men: you cannot go wrong with a gift from this place); there's also a brilliant bridal range. Designs for autumn/winter 2008/9 are suitably hot, featuring sheer, flesh-coloured bras, briefs, thongs and bodies with black barbed wire embroidery and PVC bows ('Maschina', from £65), frou-frou black babydolls and tie-side knickers. Nipple tassels, slips, waspies and corsets are also all on the menu.

For branches see index.

Alice & Astrid

30 Artesian Road, W2 5DD (7985 0888/ www.aliceandastrid.com). Notting Hill Gate tube. **Open** 10am-6pm Mon-Fri; 11am-6pm Sat. **Credit** AmEx, MC, V. **Sells** W.

This bright and breezy boutique exudes a care-free summery vibe. Rails are lined with simple and beautiful lingerie (camis, soft-cup bras and french knickers), nightwear, beachwear and ready-to-wear separates (cotton halter dress, £98) in soft cotton, delicate silk chiffon and baby alpaca (cosy wrap-around knits come in at £185). Alice & Astrid's exclusive prints (sweet birds, flowers and polka dots) are showcased to perfection in a palette of fresh pinks, blues, greens and white. A trousseau collection is planned for summer 2009, drawing on archive shapes and bestsellers, recreated in creamy satins and vintage lace for brides. Also on offer are Heyland & Whittle hand-pressed soaps, Poppy Rocks handmade jewellery (beautiful boho charm bracelets, £75), sparkly sandals and cute cards and wrapping paper.

Bodas

38B Ledbury Road, W11 2AB (7229 4464/ www.bodas.co.uk). Notting Hill Gate tube. **Open** 10am-6pm Mon-Sat; noon-4pm Sun. **Credit** AmEx, MC, V. **Sells** W.

There's a time and a place for seductive peepholes, tie-side knickers and marabou mules – and we implore you to go forth and enjoy it. The rest of the time, boutiques such as Bodas are a real godsend. Head here for simple, well-cut and super-flattering bras and knickers. There are smooth padded bras (£40) in invisible 'maquillage' (a dark pink that works much better than nudes) for the perfect line under a flimsy frock, and sheer white soft-cup bras (£35) for stylish comfort. Matching knickers start at around £11 (in sheer, Tactel and cotton) and the lovely nightwear encompasses chic white pyjamas, nightdresses and kimonos. Great for cut-above essentials and wardrobe basics.

For branch see index.

Bordello

55 Great Eastern Street, EC2A 3HP (7503 3334/www.bordello-london.com). Old Street tube/rail. **Open** 12.30-7.30pm Tue, Wed, Fri, Sat; 12.30- 9.30pm Thur. **Credit** MC, V. **Sells** W

Naughty but definitely nice, Bordello London brings a touch of decadent, old-fashioned glamour (think heavy drapes framing the windows and rich red walls) to Shoreditch. Seductive yet welcoming, the boutique stocks luxurious and original lingerie designs by the likes of Damaris, Mimi Holliday, Myla, Buttress & Snatch and Pussy Glamore. Summer 2008 saw the introduction of Australian swimwear label Jemma Jube, while bikinis by Flamingo Sands will be added in 2009. With an edgy vibe that appeals to East End glamazons, first-daters and off-duty burlesque stars alike, Bordello has top-drawer inspiration in spades. Fabulous corsetry is also on offer, including designs by Velda Lauder (Dita is a fan).

Myla

74 Duke of York Square, King's Road, SW3 4LY (7730 0700/www.myla.com). Sloane Square tube. **Open** 10am-6.30pm Mon-Sat; noon-5pm Sun. **Credit** AmEx, MC, V. **Sells** W.

Since it was founded in 1999, the luxury lingerie brand Myla has acquired a devoted following (its lace and freshwater pearl g-string acquired particular infamy after being featured in a classic Samantha *Sex and the City* scene). There are now five London stores and various concessions around town, which makes getting one's hands on the label's stylish, high-quality bras, knickers, toys and accessories a breeze. Seasonally updated collections always include fashion-forward colours and designs, though classics, such as the signature silk and lace couture range (bras £119, thongs £49) are always in stock. There's a lovely swimwear range, elegant nightwear (classic silk satin pyjamas come in at £169) and accessories such as candles (£29), silk-bow nipple tassels (£39) and blindfolds (£39). The brand is also known for its elegant and subtle sex toys (Myla Spot vibrator, £79).

For branches see index.

Rigby & Peller

22A Conduit Street, W1S 2XT (7491 2200/ www.rigbyandpeller.com). Oxford Circus tube. **Open** 9.30am-6pm Mon-Wed, Fri, Sat; 9am-7pm Thur. **Credit** AmEx, MC, V. **Sells** W.

Unquestionably the Rolls-Royce of the bra-fitting world, Rigby & Peller – corsetière to the Queen, no less – offers a professional, service-oriented experience in its Mayfair boutique (there are other branches in Knightsbridge and Chelsea). Once you've seen the difference these properly fitting undergarments make, there'll be no returning to the grab-and-go guesswork and the greying rejects from the back of the drawer. Either arrive early or make an appointment if you want to be measured (it takes 45 minutes), and come prepared to splash some cash. Not because it's outrageously expensive – prices are, in fact, pleasingly affordable (bras start at around £30) – but because you'll be dying to get your hands on the array of fabulous items. Brands include Spanx, Berlei, Lejaby, La Perla, Aubade and Fantasie as well as own-brand designs (a R&P swimwear range is set to launch in summer 2009). Sports, mastectomy and maternity bras are available too.

For branches see index.

Also check out...

Aware

25 Old Compton Street, W1D 5JN (7287 3789/www.awarelondon.com). Leicester Square or Tottenham Court Road tube. **Open** 11am-8pm Mon-Sat; noon-8pm Sun. **Credit** MC, V. **Sells** M.

Men's designer undies. The women's arm, Amelie's Follies, sells European lingerie.

For branch (Amelie's Follies) see index.

Bravissimo

28 High Street, W5 5DB (8579 6866/ www.bravissimo.com). Ealing Broadway tube/rail. **Open** 10am-5.45pm Mon-Sat; 11am-5pm Sun. **Credit** MC, V. Sells W.

A selection of feminine bras amd swimwear in bigger cup and back sizes.

For branches see index.

Calvin Klein

65 New Bond Street, W1F 1RN (7495 2916/www.ck.com). Bond Street tube. **Open** 10am-6.30pm Mon-Wed, Fri, Sat; 10am-7pm Thur; noon-5pm Sun. **Credit** AmEx, MC, V. **Sells** M, W.

For branches see index.

Top five
Bra-fitting services

Calvin Klein. *See p67.*
John Lewis. *See p16.*
Rigby & Peller. *See p67.*
Selfridges. *See p16.*
La Senza. *See p68.*

Bodas. See p67.

Damaris
www.damaris.co.uk.
Damaris Evans's signature 'peep bottom' knickers have many fans. We also love the cheaper, and equally seductive, diffusion line Mimi Holliday.

Figleaves
www.figleaves.com.
Online lingerie superstore.

Miss Lala's Boudoir
148 Gloucester Avenue, NW1 8JA (7483 1888/www.misslalasboudoir.co.uk). Chalk Farm tube. **Open** 9am-5pm daily. **Credit** MC, V. **Sells** W.
Fabulous boutique packed with deliciously frothy, unusual and luxurious brands.

La Perla
163 Sloane Street, SW1X 9QB (7245 0527/www.laperla.com). Knightsbridge tube. **Open** 10am-6pm Mon, Tue, Thur-Sat; 10am-7pm Wed. **Credit** AmEx, DC, MC, V. **Sells** M, W.
Exclusive Italian label.

Phoebe Carlyle
8 Holland Street, W8 4LT (7938 2121/ www.phoebecarlyle.com). High Street Kensington tube. **Open** 10.30am-6.30pm Mon-Sat; noon-6pm Sun. **Credit** AmEx, MC, V. **Sells** M, W.
Upmarket brands like Araks, Aubade, Huit and Kenzo, plus nightware and accessories.

La Senza
162 Oxford Street, W1D 1NG (7580 3559/ www.lasenza.co.uk). Oxford Circus tube. **Open** 10am-7pm Mon-Wed, Fri, Sat; 10am-8pm Thur; noon-6pm Sun. **Credit** AmEx, DC, MC, V.
Branches: throughout the city.

Tallulah
65 Cross Street, N1 2BB (7704 0066/www.tallulah-lingerie.co.uk). Angel tube/Highbury & Islington tube/rail/Essex Road rail. **Open** by appointment Mon; 11am-6pm Tue-Fri; 10.30am-6.30pm Sat; 12.30-5pm Sun. **Credit** MC, V. **Sells** W.
Well-edited boutique collection.

Swimwear

Biondi
55B Old Church Street, SW3 5BS (7349 1111/www.biondicouture.com). Sloane Square tube. **Open** 10.30am-6.30pm Mon-Sat. **Credit** MC, V. **Sells** W, C.
For the ultimate indulgence and buckets of beach confidence, this luxury bikini boutique offers a fantastic bespoke service. Check out the array of shapes, styles, patterns and colours with the online 'bikini designer', then pop in and let the team make your dream one- or two-piece a reality. Obviously, this all comes at a price, but slightly less extravagant is the made-to-measure option (from £250), where staff produce tailored items from existing shapes and materials. There's also a great ready-to-wear selection of beachwear and swimwear from the likes of Vix, Fisico and Anna & Boy.

Heidi Klein
174 Westbourne Grove, W11 2RW (7243 5665/www.heidiklein.com). Notting Hill Gate tube. **Open** 10am-6pm Mon-Sat; noon-5pm Sun. **Credit** AmEx, MC, V. **Sells** M, W.
A whiff of the divine aroma of own-brand coconut candles at this glamorous beachwear store is enough to transport you to a world where stress-free grooming (there's an on-site beauty salon offering waxing, tanning, facials and manicures), sampling beauty products (this is one of only two stockists of the fabulous St Barth's range in the capital) and choosing the latest Missoni bikini are numbers 1, 2 and 3 on your to-do list. Own-brand bikinis start at £120 and come in classic black and white, with a choice of fashion-forward colours too (gold was a popular buy in 2008). Also on offer are bikinis by cult brands Lenny, and Vix and Eres, Tom Ford eyewear and a host of own-brand kaftans, sandals and cover-ups. Robes and flip flops in every dressing room add to the VIP feel. A finer place to buy a bikini we can't imagine.
For branch see index.

Odabash
48B Ledbury Road, W11 2AJ (7229 4299/ www.odabash.com). Notting Hill Gate tube. **Open** 10am-6pm Mon-Sat; noon-5pm Sun. **Credit** AmEx, MC, V. **Sells** M, W, C.
Slink into ultra-glam Odabash (unbelievably white, white carpets, driftwood lamps, low-key R&B on the stereo) and even if the best you can hope for this summer is a week in a caravan in Wales, you'll feel like there's a yacht with your name on it somewhere. Frankly, nothing less would do justice to the swanky animal print kaftans (from £130), amazingly flattering bikinis (£129-£175), sparkly flip flops and beachy-glam jewellery. The autumn/winter 2008/9 collection features fabulous coral and circle prints and an array of unusual shades – olive, salmon, tobacco brown – that'll guarantee you stand out on the beach. There's even a bling cut-out one-piece covered in crystal (but still OK to swim in) if you have £450 to spare. A range of Odabash flip flops launches in 2009 too. Children get their own range of swimsuits, bikinis and kaftans. The shop's late summer sale is a fantastic way to stock up on high-quality swimwear on the cheap.

Pistol Panties
75 Westbourne Park Road, W2 5QH (7229 5286/www.pistolpanties.com). Westbourne Park tube. **Open** noon-6pm Tue-Sat; 1-5pm Sun. **Credit** MC, V. **Sells** W.
If the eye-catching window displays – hip, colourful one- and two-pieces strung up on washing lines – don't draw you in, the flattering cuts certainly will. Started up by British/Columbian designer Deborah Fleming, Pistol Panties proved an instant success (her entire first collection was snapped up by Selfridges), attracting a loyal following for its fresh take on swimwear classics. We love the retro pink and white polka dot bikini and cool cutaways (Tatiana one-piece, £165). Bright, oversized beach bags, cover-ups (asymmetric dress, £199), flip flops and beachy jewellery are also on offer as are candles by True Grace. Friendly and refreshingly honest staff will steer you in the direction of the perfect beachwear for you.

Also check out...

Exotica Brazil
15 Gloucester Arcade, 128 Gloucester Road, SW7 4SF (7835 0669/www.exoticabrazil.com). Gloucester Road tube. **Open** 11am-7pm Mon-Sat. **Credit** AmEx, DC, MC, V. **Sells** W, C.
Bright, teeny-weeny bikinis and sexy lingerie.
For branch see index.

Favelashop
12-18 Hoxton Street, N1 6NG (3222 0042/ www.favelashop.com). Old Street tube/rail. **Open** 11am-6pm Mon-Sat. **Credit** MC, V. **Sells** W.
Brazilian bikinis and pretty lingerie.

Sand In My Toes
www.sandinmytoes.com.
Online beachwear specialist.

Vilebrequin
56 Fulham Road, SW3 6HH (7589 0073/ www.vilebrequin.com). South Kensington tube. **Open** 10am-6pm Mon, Tue, Thur-Sat; 10am-7pm Wed. **Credit** AmEx, MC, V. **Sells** M.
Quality, vividly patterned swimming trunks.
For branch see index.

Unusual Sizes

On the high street, **New Look** has a line called Inspire, which comes in sizes 16-28, while **Topshop**, **Dorothy Perkins** and **Next** all cater for both small and tall girls; **Principles** has a Petite range for women under 5ft 3in (in sizes 6-16); for all, *see pp45-48*. Stylish Marylebone High Street shop **Shoon** (*see p34*) also stocks several brands that will suit larger female figures, including luxurious labels **Wall** (www.wall-london.com), which also has a stand-alone shop in Notting Hill, **Oska** and **Hebbeding**. All offer elegant, contemporary styles that won't make you look frumpy.

Evans

538-540 Oxford Street, W1C 1LS (7499 0434/www.evans.co.uk). Marble Arch tube. **Open** 9am-8pm Mon-Wed, Sat; 9am-9pm Thur, Fri; noon-6pm Sun. **Credit** AmEx, DC, MC, V. **Sells** W.

The traditional home of 'outsized' clothing, Evans' strapline is 'cut to curves'. Staff offer excellent advice on the best styles for different body shapes, and sizes stretch from 14 to 32. There are also petite (5ft 3in and under) and tall (5ft 10in and above) ranges. New for 2008 was a bridalwear range. In the lingerie section, bras go up to a 50H. Prices are also pleasing, with trousers from £25 and dresses from £20. Shoes are available in wide-fitting styles and up to a size 10 and there's also a selection of wide-fitting rings and jewellery to match.

Branches: throughout the city.

High & Mighty

145-147 Edgware Road, W2 2HR (7723 8754/www.highandmighty.co.uk). Marble Arch or Edgware Road tube. **Open** 10am-6pm Mon; 9am-6pm Tue, Wed, Fri, Sat; 9am-7pm Thur; noon-4pm Sun. **Credit** AmEx, DC, MC, V. **Sells** M.

High & Mighty opened its first shop on Edgware Road some 50 years ago, trading as Northern Outsize Menswear. Since then its contemporary and classic styles for men who struggle to fit into conventional high street sizes have gone from strength to strength. Catering to men over 6ft 2 in, most trousers go up to 38in leg, and waist sizes up to 60in. Alongside its own labels there's a choice of brands such as Polo Ralph Lauren, Ben Sherman, Pierre Cardin, Lee Cooper and Umbro. Covering most wardrobe necessities, there are accessories and shoes as well. Prices tend to be reasonable – £50 for a jumper, say, or £79 for Ben Sherman jeans.

Long Tall Sally

21-25 Chiltern Street, W1U 7PH (7487 3370/www.longtallsally.com). Baker Street tube. **Open** 9.30am-6pm Mon-Wed, Fri; 9.30am-7pm Thur; 9am-6pm Sat; noon-5pm Sun. **Credit** AmEx, DC, MC, V. **Sells** W.

Providing sartorial solutions for many a long-legged lass for over 30 years, Long Tall Sally's collections focus on comfortable, conventional and well-cut styles rather than high fashion. Prices are mid range (dresses around £55, jeans £45, shirts £30), and there are clothes for every occasion. Tailored for ladies over 5ft 8in, trousers stretch from 34in to 38in, sleeves are longer, waists are cut lower and everything is offered in sizes 10-20. 2008 saw the launch of a series of collections named after cities: look out for the Oxford and Milan ranges, with lots of basics in neutral tones. Shoes come in sizes 7-11.

Also check out...

Ann Harvey

266 Oxford Street, W1N 9DC (7408 1131). Oxford Circus tube. **Open** 10am-7pm Mon-Wed, Fri, Sat; 10am-8pm Thur; noon-6pm Sun. **Credit** AmEx, MC, V. **Sells** W.

Well-tailored, youthful classics in sizes 16-28.

Branches: throughout the city.

Base

55 Monmouth Street, WC2H 9DG (7240 8914/www.basefashions.com). Covent Garden tube. **Open** 10am-6pm Mon-Sat. **Credit** AmEx, DC, MC, V. **Sells** W.

A nice collection of upmarket, continental designerwear in sizes 16-28.

Beige

44 New Cavendish Street, W1G 8TR (7935 8999/www.beigeplus.com). Bond Street or Oxford Circus tube. **Open** 10am-6pm Mon-Wed, Fri; 10am-7pm Thur; 10am-6pm Sat; noon-6pm Sun. **Credit** AmEx, DC, MC, V. **Sells** W.

Upmarket line of clothing aimed at women over 35 (in sizes 16-26).

For branches see index.

Elvi

92 New Bond Street, W1S 1SQ (7629 6284/ www.elvi.co.uk). Bond Street tube. **Open** 9.30am-8pm Mon-Wed, Fri, Sat; 9.30am-9pm Thur; 11.30am-6pm Sun. **Credit** AmEx, MC, V. **Sells** W.

Trendy, affordable womenswear that comes in sizes 16-26. They also have concessions in department stores such as Debenhams, House of Fraser and John Lewis.

Marina Rinaldi

39 Old Bond Street, W1S 4QP (7629 4454). Green Park tube. **Open** 10am-6pm Mon-Wed, Fri, Sat; 10am-7pm Thur. **Credit** AmEx, MC, V. **Sells** W.

Max Mara's plus size division (up to size 28).

Rochester Big & Tall

90 Brompton Road, SW3 1ER (7838 0018/ www.rochesterclothing.com). Knightsbridge tube. **Open** 9.30am-6pm Mon, Tue, Thur-Sat; 9.30am-7pm Wed; noon-5pm Sun. **Credit** AmEx, DC, MC, V. **Sells** M.

Caters for men from 6ft 1in, who require large sizes (42-74in chest, 36-72in waist).

SimplyBe.co.uk

www.simplybe.co.uk.

Online womenswear range with styles for every occasion, available in sizes 16-30.

Sixteen 47

www.sixteen47.com.

Named because 47% of all UK females wear a size 16 or over, Dawn French and Helen Teague's online womenswear comes in sizes 16-47.

Tallgirls.co.uk

www.tallgirls.co.uk.

Don't be fooled by the name, this online store offers fashionable clothes for tall men and women. There's also a range of footwear in sizes 8-12 for women and 12-15 for men.

Vivace

2 Bridge Street, Richmond, Surrey TW9 1TQ (8948 7840/www.vivace.co.uk). Richmond tube/rail. **Open** 10am-5.30pm Mon-Sat. **Credit** MC, V. **Sells** W.

Women's fashion in sizes 16-22, from suits and casuals to party wear, in natural fabrics.

Shoes

Many of the shops listed above also stock shoes in large sizes. For children's shoes, *see p265*.

Magnus

44 Chiltern Street, W1U 7QP (7224 3938/ www.magnusshoes.com). Baker Street tube. **Open** 10am-5.30pm Mon-Wed, Fri, Sat; 10am-7pm Thur. **Credit** MC, V. **Sells** W.

A company that moves with the seasons, Magnus does stylish and traditional shoes in sizes 12-16 for men and 8-12 for women. The women's store on Chiltern Street stocks fashionable high heels (around £70), boots (around £100) and Mustang trainers (£50). The sale room at the back often has end of season bargains. The men's shoes, which are available online and in the Hampstead branch (7435 1792), include everything from wellington boots (£50) to rugby boots (around £80).

For branch see index.

Also check out...

After 8 Shoes

42 Old London Road, Kingston, Surrey KT2 6QF (8546 8519/www.after8shoes.co.uk). Kingston rail. **Open** 10am-5pm Wed-Sat; noon-4pm Sun. **Credit** MC, V. **Sells** W.

Wide variety of women's shoes starting at size 8 and going up to 12 in selected styles.

Crispins

28-30 Chiltern Street, W1U 7QG (7486 8924/www.crispinsshoes.com). Baker Street tube. **Open** 10am-6pm Mon-Wed, Fri, Sat; 10am-7pm Thur. **Credit** DC, MC, V. **Sells** W.

Trendy shoes for sizes 6-10 in narrow AA, and sizes 8½-12 in standard width (C).

House of Sole

8 Chiltern Street, W1U 7PU (7486 7789/ www.houseofsole.co.uk). Baker Street tube. **Open** 10am-6pm Mon-Wed, Fri, Sat; 10am-7pm Thur. **Credit** AmEx, MC, V. **Sells** M, W.

Providing fashion-led footwear in sizes 8-12 for women and 12-18 for men.

Little Shoe Shop

71 York Street, W1H 1BJ (7723 5321/ www.thelittleshoeshop.com). Baker Street tube. **Open** 10am-5pm Mon-Wed, Fri, Sat; 10am-7pm Thur. **Credit** MC, V. **Sells** W.

Shoes in miniscule sizes; its own range comes in 12½-3, and in C and D widths.

Shoes

For bespoke footwear, including by **Caroline Groves**, *see p55*; for unusual sizes, *see p69*; for children's shoes, *see p265*.

Many of the shops listed in the **Boutiques** chapter (*see pp28-36*) stock a select range of stylish shoes; both **b store** (*see p35*) and **Folk** (*see p35*) have their own lines of directional models for men and women. The **Three Threads** (*see p49*) is also excellent for men's shoes, with the biggest range of Pointers in town. **Topshop** (*see p46*), **Selfridges** and **Liberty** (for both, *see p16*) are also good first ports-of-call with huge ranges.

Beatrix Ong

4 Burlington Arcade, W1J 0PD (7499 4089/7449 0480/www.beatrixong.com). Piccadilly or Green Park tube. **Open** 10am-6pm Mon-Sat. **Credit** AmEx MC, V. **Sells** W.

One year on and Beatrix Ong's beautiful Burlington Arcade (*see p18*) boutique has truly found its feet in Piccadilly. The chandelier-lit white space makes a suitably luxurious backdrop to the ex-Jimmy Choo designer's elegant women's shoes. Known for her timeless styles that can be worn from season to season, here she sells limited editions alongside the main collection on the ground floor while upstairs tea and cakes are served to private clients and brides-to-be in search of their dream slipper (*see p65*). Key styles for autumn/winter 2008/9 include the Berkshire (£338) shoe-boot, chunky heeled Fettes (£308) and sensible lace-up Cambridge (£268). Ong also launches her first collection of men's shoes in September 2008 featuring loafers and brogues.

For branch see index.

Black Truffle

52 Warren Street, W1T 5NJ (7388 4547/ www.blacktruffle.com). Warren Street tube. **Open** 11am-6.30pm Mon-Sat. **Credit** AmEx, MC, V. **Sells** M, W, C.

Black Truffle was recently voted one of the best shoe shops in *Time Out* magazine's Shopping Awards 2008 and for good reason. Selling some quirky yet wearable footwear for women, men and kids, the original Broadway Market shop proved so popular that this second, more upscale central London outlet was added in 2006. The range of stock is impressive with brands including Arche, Chie Mihara, Melissa, Rosa Mosa, Jocomomola and Repetto.

For branch see index.

British Boot Company

5 Kentish Town Road, NW1 8NH (7485 8505/www.britboot.co.uk). Camden Town tube. **Open** 10am-7pm daily. **Credit** AmEx, MC, V. **Sells** M, W, C.

The British Boot Company was the first UK retailer for Dr Martens and became a favourite haunt of bands such as the Sex Pistols, the Buzzcocks and Madness in their late 1970s heyday. As well as the aforementioned DMs, the BBC offers all manner of big-soled, mean-looking, hard-wearing boots and shoes from the likes of Solovair, Gladiators, Grinders, NPS and Tredair. This is also one of the few outlets where you can get your hands on George Cox, the British brand famed for its brothel creepers and winklepickers and newer Robot shoes. The shop even sells vintage versions for true Cox aficionados.

Christian Louboutin

23 Motcomb Street, SW1X 8LB (7245 6510/www.christianlouboutin.fr). Knightsbridge tube. **Open** 10am-6pm Mon-Fri; 11am-6pm Sat. **Credit** AmEx, MC, V. **Sells** W.

Celebrity favourite Christian Louboutin has been making truly exquisite footwear since 1992. He's recently branched out into making equally covetable bags and creates catwalk shoes for everyone from Rodarte to Richard Nicoll. His London boutique brings a little drop of Paris to the big smoke and stocks key looks from his autumn/winter 2008/9 collection including the sky-high Bouclette platform, the Ms Turner-inspired fringed Forever Tina boot and the patent Cotton Club wedge. Prices (from £300) aren't for the faint-hearted, but perfection doesn't come cheap.

For branch see index.

Church's Shoes

201 Regent Street, W1B 4NA (7734 2438/ www.church-footwear.com). Oxford Circus tube. **Open** 10am-7pm Mon-Fri; 10am-6.30pm Sat; noon-6pm Sun. **Credit** AmEx, MC, V. **Sells** M, W.

The Regent Street flagship of this old English shoemaker (est. 1873) looks rather like a gentlemen's club – all dark, polished wood and the smell of expensive leather. There's a small army of impeccably turned-out staff on hand to guide you through the range, which is still produced at the factory in Northampton (each shoe undergoes 250 different stages and takes a total of eight weeks to complete). The quality and comfort levels are second to none; shoes come in a choice of five fittings. The current collection covers everything from a traditional Oxford dress shoe to some rather more daring blue leather brogues. A true gentleman, however, wouldn't be comfortable reclining without a pair of Church's slippers embroidered with a rose, crown or fox's face.

Branches: throughout the city.

Duo

25A Savile Row, W1S 2ES (7494 1817/ www.duoboots.com/www.duoshoes.co.uk). Oxford Circus tube. **Open** 10am-6pm Mon-Sat; 11am-5pm Sun. **Credit** DC, MC, V. **Sells** W.

Not a shop but a fitting room is where you go to view Duo's extensive range of women's styles, then get measured up by a member of its well-trained staff – which are known to the shop's fans as Fitting Angels. Where Duo truly excels though is with its ranges of boots. Calf widths span from 30cm right up to 50cm and come in sizes 2 to 10 to ensure customers find a pair that will fit the foot and leg exactly. Your Angel will then help you place your order online and your purchase is delivered promptly to your door. Et voila!

Emma Hope

53 Sloane Square, SW1W 8AX (7259 9566/www.emmahope.co.uk). Sloane Square tube. **Open** 10am-6.30pm Mon, Tue, Thur-Sat; 10am-7pm Wed; noon-5pm Sun. **Credit** AmEx, MC, V. **Sells** M, W.

Emma Hope is one in a million. Having cut her teeth at Laura Ashley, her own-name designs nod to current trends yet remain every inch a reflection of her own dainty tastes. Her unisex Joe sneakers are popular thanks to their natty juxtaposition of unusual uppers such as velvet (£189) and embroidered silk (£259) with stripes and simple rubber soles. Her straw weave and metallic leather ballet pumps are also bestsellers, while for evening there's a wide selection of slender courts and slingbacks.

For branches see index.

French Sole

6 Ellis Street, SW1X 9AL (7730 3771/ www.frenchsole.com). Sloane Square tube/ 19, 22, 137 bus. **Open** 10am-6pm Mon-Sat; 10am-6.30pm Wed; noon-5pm Sun. **Credit** AmEx, MC, V. **Sells** W.

French Sole is destination number one for ballet pumps. Designer Jane Winkworth has won awards for her fancy ballerina shoes and offers up a dazzling array of styles to suit everyone. From the simple Harriet style in ostrich skin to the square-toed Hope and from the Chanel-esque quilted Paris to the two-tone pointed Sandra with patent trim, the beauty here is in the detail. Also on offer are driving shoes, boots and loafers with prices from £195 and new for autumn/winter 2008/9 is the fur-lined Renaissance collection.

For branches see index.

Georgina Goodman

44 Old Bond Street, W1S 4GB (7493 7673/www.georginagoodman.com). Green Park tube. **Open** 10am-6pm Mon-Wed, Fri, Sat; 10am-7pm Thur. **Credit** AmEx, DC, MC, V. **Sells** M, W, C.

Georgina Goodman's smart flagship store, which opened in 2008, brings new blood to Old Bond Street. The RCA graduate launched her label back in 2001 crafting made-to-measure footwear from a single piece of untreated leather – and a couture service is still available. Since then, she has gone on to design for everyone from Alexander McQueen to Evans, and began ready-to-wear in 2004. Her personal touch remains thanks to the inscription 'Made in Love' on the sole of every mainline shoe. Her autumn/winter 2008/9 range – a dramatic mix of textures and colours – is inspired by Picasso's first wife, the Russian ballet dancer Olga Koklova.

Grenson

The ANdAZ, Liverpool Street, EC2M 7QN (7618 5050/www.grenson.co.uk). Liverpool Street tube. **Open** 9am-6pm Mon-Fri. **Credit** AmEx, DC, MC, V. **Sells** M.

Even though Grenson was established way back in 1866, the classic men's shoe brand only opened its first shop in 2007. The smart atelier can be found in the AN*d*AZ (formerly the Great Eastern Hotel) and aims to bring back an air of the old-fashioned concierge service – arranging bespoke fittings, shoe polishing and fixing and delivery of new or repaired shoes to your hotel room or office.

For autumn/winter 2008/9 designer Tim Little has extended the two ready-to-wear ranges, Rose and Rushden, with four new looks (£140-£165).

Jeffery-West

16 Piccadilly Arcade, SW1Y 6NH (7499 3360/www.jeffery-west.co.uk). Green Park or Piccadilly Circus tube. **Open** 10am-6pm Mon-Wed, Fri, Sat; 10am-7pm Thur. **Credit** AmEx, MC, V. **Sells** M.

With its playboy vampire's apartment feel (red walls, velvet curtains, a papier-mâché devil's head), this gothic Piccadilly store is the perfect showcase for Marc Jeffery and Guy West's rakish shoes. Made to exacting traditional standards in Northampton, each shoe comes with a twist, such as hand-burnished uppers, diamond broguing or a cleft heel, and are much loved by modern-day dandies about town. Classic shoes include the Punched Gibson in polished burgundy (£210) and the Center Seam Sylvian boot with pointed toe and higher heel (£275). Shoes go from £205 to £230, boots from £215 to £275.

For branch see index.

Kate Kuba

22-24 Duke of York Square, King's Road, SW3 4LY (7259 0011/www.katekuba.co.uk). Sloane Square tube. **Open** 10am-6.30pm Mon-Sat; noon-6pm Sun. **Credit** AmEx, MC, V. **Sells** W.

Grown-up glamour is the order of the day at Kate Kuba. Since opening its first shop in Muswell Hill back in 1992, eight more outlets across London have established its reputation for sophisticated, sexy shoes. Whether you need a strappy sandal for a wedding or a nautical but nice wedge for daytime, Kate Kuba has it covered. The autumn/winter 2008/9 collection reinvents the Mary Jane with an extra high heel, and has a good number of croc and suede uppers, patent platforms and industrial-style buckles. The shoe-boot is also central, with styles including the buckled-up Cindy (£125) and pointed-toe Celeste (£125).

Branches: throughout the city.

Kurt Geiger

198 Regent Street, W1B 5TP (3238 0044/ www.kurtgeiger.com). Oxford Circus tube. **Open** 10am-7pm Mon-Wed, Fri, Sat; 10am-8pm Sat; noon-6pm Sun. **Credit** AmEx, DC, MC, V. **Sells** M, W.

Kurt Geiger has become the uncrowned king of the high street shoe chains in London with its swanky products found in all the classiest department stores (Liberty, Selfridges, Harrods). Its mirror-clad Regent Street flagship store and nearby South Molton Street branch remain the best places to see the full collection, however.

For branches see index.

Lollipop London

114 Islington High Street, N1 8EG (7226 4005/www.lollipoplondon.com). Angel tube. **Open** 11am-6pm Mon-Wed; 11am-7pm Thur-Sat; noon-5pm Sun. **Credit** DC, MC, V. **Sells** W.

This petite boutique has more girly charm than you can shake a stick at. Owner Laura Allnatt and her lollipop ladies have sourced interesting lines from some of the world's best independent designers. Displays see newer labels such as Wilomena and Talie sit alongside established favourites such as the Jackson Twins, Chie Mihara, Beatrix Ong, Lulu Guinness and Scorah Pattullo. And spanking new in store for August 2008 was Lollipop's own-brand Laura J London by Cordwainers graduate Rachele Davies. Form an orderly queue for the Elsie flat jazz shoe (£165).

For branch see index.

Manolo Blahnik

49-51 Old Church Street, SW3 5BS (7352 3863/www.manoloblahnik.com). South Kensington tube or Sloane Square tube then 11, 19, 22 bus. **Open** 10am-5.30pm Mon-Fri; 10.30am-4.45pm Sat. **Credit** AmEx, MC, V. **Sells** W, M.

Manolo Blahnik CBE has become one of the most prestigious shoe designers in the world. You have to buzz to gain admittance but once inside the service is impeccable as you rub shoulders with women happy to pay a month's rent for a pair of his timeless shoes. Best known for his killer heels, Blahnik's designs run the gamut from flat slip-ons to boots and he also launched his first men's collection in 2008. For autumn/winter 2008/9 devotees will fight for the pom-pom festooned Compulsa sandal (£550), the cut-out ankle boot Preura (£900) or the tartan lace-up Zione (£430).

For branch see index.

Men's Traditional Shoes

171 Camberwell Road, SE5 0HB (7703 4179). Elephant & Castle tube/ 12, 35, 40, 45, 68, 171, 176 bus. **Open** 9.30am-5pm Mon-Sat. **Credit** DC, MC, V. **Sells** M.

There are no prizes for guessing what Men's Traditional Shoes sells. It's an old-fashioned shop that has only had three owners since it opened in 1861. A trip here pays off, as the out-of-the-way location means the shop can sell stylish brogues, Oxfords and loafers for about £30-£50 less than you pay in the West End (prices are around £80-£200). Loakes are perennially popular, while other labels include Trickers, Benson's, Church's and Northampton stalwarts Crockett & Jones. The shop also sells industrial steel-capped work boots and Dr Martens.

For branch see index.

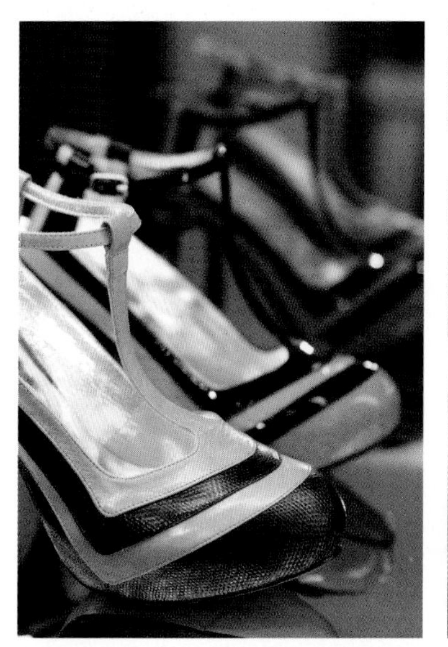

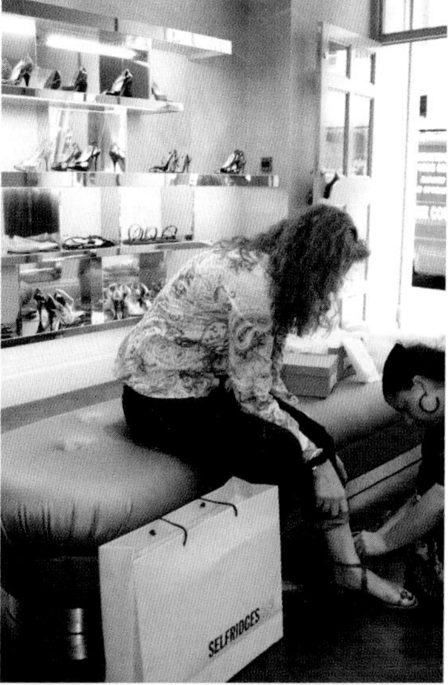

Georgina Goodman

FASHION

Old Curiosity Shop

Old Curiosity Shop

13-14 Portsmouth Street, WC2A 2ES (7405 9891). Holborn tube. **Open** 10am-7pm Mon-Sat. **Credit** MC, V. **Sells** M, W.

Built around 1567, this building can justifiably lay claim to being the oldest shop premises in central London – though whether it actually inspired the Charles Dickens novel of the same name is anyone's guess (Dickens lived in nearby Bloomsbury and was known to have visited the shop). These days, Japanese designer Daiko Kimura creates handmade shoes in the basement workshop. His avant-garde styles for men and women start at around £200. Duck as you go in to avoid bumping your head on the ceiling beams.

Oliver Sweeney

66 New Bond Street, W1S 1RW (7355 0387/www.oliversweeney.com). Bond Street tube. **Open** 10am-7pm Mon-Sat; noon-6pm Sun. **Credit** AmEx, DC, MC, V. **Sells** M.

Oliver Sweeney makes beautiful men's shoes from his gallery-like New Bond Street store. For autumn/winter 2008/9 he gives classic styles such as the brogue, Chelsea boot and loafer fresh twists including metal stud detailing, a toe-shape inspired by the clean lines of a Ford Mustang and new colourways including petrol blue and wine. Prices typically range from £125 to £260.
For branches see index.

Poste

10 South Molton Street, W1K 5QJ (7499 8002/www.friendsofposte.com). Bond Street tube. **Open** 10am-7pm Mon-Wed, Fri, Sat; 10am-8pm Thur; 11.30am-6pm Sun. **Credit** AmEx, MC, V. **Sells** M.

South Molton Street is full of shoe shops but here, with records on the walls and big squashy sofas, male shoppers can feel right at home trying on shoes from the likes of Alexander McQueen, Vivienne Westwood, Prada, Dior, Dries Van Noten, Miu Miu and Swear. The shop's own-name brand does a fine job of keeping up with the competition this autumn/winter 2008/9 with a collection of simple silhouettes in burgundy and aubergine leathers as well as sheepskin-lined boots and rustic lace-ups. For the brand's women's shoes, head to Poste Mistress (*see below*).

Poste Mistress

61-63 Monmouth Street, WC2H 9EP (7379 4040/www.office.co.uk). Covent Garden tube. **Open** 10am-7pm Mon-Wed, Fri, Sat; 10am-8pm Thur; 11.30am-6pm Sun. **Credit** AmEx, DC, MC, V. **Sells** W.

The women's answer to the men's shoe store Poste (*see above*) offers higher class footwear in a decadent, retro boudoir setting. The store was undergoing a facelift as this guide went to press, to ensure its decor is fit for the stock, which, as well as its own-brand range, includes designer favourites Paco Gil, Dries Van Noten, Eley Kishimoto, Chie Mihara, Miu Miu and Vivienne Westwood.

Rupert Sanderson

33 Bruton Place, W1J 6NP (0870 750 9181/www.rupertsanderson.co.uk). Bond Street or Green Park tube. **Open** 10am-6pm Mon-Fri; 11am-6pm Sat. **Credit** AmEx, MC, V. **Sells** W.

Made in Italy (at his own factory in Bologna) but staying true to his English roots, Rupert Sanderson names every pair of his shoes after a daffodil with trans-seasonal styles including the Glitter court, the Helsa peeptoe and Wave sandal. The current 'it' shoes are his two stylised brothel creepers – called Jupiter and Thunderbolt (both £595) – both of which come in a huge array of psychedelic pony skins, leopard and zebra print suedes and shiny leathers.
For branch see index.

Russell & Bromley

24-25 New Bond Street, W1S 2PS (7629 6903/www.russellandbromley.co.uk). Bond Street tube. **Open** 10am-6.30pm Mon-Wed, Fri, Sat; 10am-7.30pm Thur; 11am-5pm Sun. **Credit** AmEx, DC, MC, V. **Sells** M, W.

This British high street stalwart maintains a fashion-forward outlook, offering classy takes on catwalk trends. Girls with parties to attend will find the requisite glitz in designs by US brands Stuart Weitzman and Beverly Feldman, while city slickers can smarten things up with shoes by Church's (*see p70*) and Barker. The top-notch (though pricey) on-site repair service is worth noting. **Branches**: throughout the city.

Sniff

1 Great Titchfield Street, W1W 8AU (7299 3560/www.sniff.co.uk). Oxford Circus tube. **Open** 10am-7pm Mon-Fri; 10am-6.30pm Sat; noon-6pm Sun. **Credit** AmEx, MC, V. **Sells** W.

Owned by Sean Farrell, a former director at Office, Sniff aims to provide an alternative to your average high street shoe store, selling a range of shoes for men and women that covers every eventuality from sports to parties. There's a well-balanced mix of brands, established (Paco Gil, Birkenstock, Ed Hardy, French Sole) as well as up-and-coming, such as British designer Miss L Fire whose eccentric autumn/winter 2008/9 collection includes wedges covered in a strawberry motif and 1970s snakeskin platforms with bows on the front. Sniff also stocks the covetable Argentinian brand Mishka, while the in-house label offers safely trendy styles at reasonable prices.
For branches see index.

Terra Plana (eco)

64 Neal Street, WC2H 9PQ (7379 5959/ www.terraplana.com). Covent Garden tube. **Open** 10am-7pm Mon-Sat; noon-6pm Sun. **Credit** AmEx, MC, V. **Sells** M, W.

Winners of Drapers' Ethical Footwear Retailer of the Year award 2008 and the *Observer* Ethical Fashion Product of the Year 2007, Terra Plana has set its sights on original, fashionable yet ecologically sound shoes. All of autumn/winter 2008/9 collection is constructed using traditional artisan methods and includes ankle boots, cowboy boots and mid-heeled shoes made from recycled Saami quilts. The Worn Again range is particularly virtuous – it's 99% recycled (using everything from T-shirts to leather car seat scraps and second-hand rubber), and a donation is made to Climate Care to help offset the carbon footprint incurred by each sale. On-trend bohemians, however, will go especially mad for the Vivo and Dopie ranges with their ultra-thin, puncture-resistant soles that mimic a barefoot stroll.

For branch see index.

Tracey Neuls

29 Marylebone Lane, W1U 2NQ (7935 0039/www.tn29.com). Bond Street tube. **Open** 11am-6.30pm Mon-Fri; noon-5pm Sat; noon-5pm Sun. **Credit** AmEx, MC, V. **Sells** W.

Footwear hangs from the ceiling on chains, nestles on top of wooden stools and sits in fireplaces in Tracey Neuls' intimate and stylish studio shop on Marylebone Lane. The Cordwainers-trained Canadian is known for challenging the footwear norm with her unconventional yet comfortable designs and uses her equally conceptual shop to show off her wares. The eponymous mainline (from £300) concentrates on black for autumn/winter 2008/9 with her signature solid leather heels polished, slicked and even burnt. Her TN-29 brand (around £220) combines old and new so that vegetable tanned leathers are paired with perspex, felt and hand-painted details. September 2008 saw Neuls introduce a third label called Homage, which offers her classic shapes with new rubber soles at a more affordable price (from £150).

Also check out...

Aldo

3-7 Neal Street, WC2H 9PU (7836 7692/ www.aldoshoes.com). Covent Garden tube. **Open** 10am-8pm Mon-Sat; noon-6pm Sun. **Credit** AmEx, MC, V. **Sells** M, W.

A Canadian company that recreates catwalk glamour at pavement prices. Also stocks a line of handbags and accessories.

Branches: throughout the city.

Bally

116 New Bond Street, W1S 1EN (7491 7062/www.bally.com). Bond Street tube. **Open** 10am-6.30pm Mon-Wed, Fri, Sat; 10am-7pm Thur; noon-6pm Sun. **Credit** AmEx, MC, V. **Sells** M, W.

This renowned Swiss brand makes sleek, well-crafted footwear for style-conscious men and women.

Bertie

36 South Molton Street, W1K 5RH (7493 5033/www.bertieshoes.com). Bond Street tube. **Open** 10am-7pm Mon-Wed, Fri, Sat; 10am-8pm Thur; noon-6pm Sun. **Credit** AmEx, MC, V. **Sells** W.

A British brand with a good selection of trend-led, affordable styles.

For branch see index.

Birkenstock

70 Neal Street, WC2H 9PR (7240 2783/ www.birkenstock.co.uk). Covent Garden tube. **Open** 10.30am-7pm Mon-Wed, Fri, Sat; 10.30am-8pm Thur; noon-6pm Sun. **Credit** AmEx, MC, V. **Sells** M, W, C.

This is the only UK shop dedicated entirely to these famous ergonomic sandals.

For branch see index.

Camper (eco)

8-11 Royal Arcade, 28 Old Bond Street, W1S 4SQ (7629 2722/www.camper.com). Green Park tube. **Open** 10am-6pm Mon-Wed, Fri, Sat; 10am-6.30pm Thur. **Credit** AmEx, DC, MC, V. **Sells** M, W.

The successful Mallorcan brand is still going strong, with its environmentally conscious and funky footwear for all.

For branches see index.

Clarks

476 Oxford Street, W1C 1LD (7629 9609/www.clarks.co.uk). Marble Arch tube. **Open** 10am-8pm Mon-Fri; 10am-7pm Sat; noon-7pm Sun. **Credit** AmEx, MC, V. **Sells** M, W.

Sensible shoes from the family-friendly retailer that invented the iconic desert boot and the Wallabee.

Branches: throughout the city.

Dr Martens

17-19 Neal Street, WC2H 9PU (7240 7555/www.drmartens.com). Covent Garden tube. **Open** 10am-7pm Mon-Wed; 10am-8pm Thur-Sat; 11am-6pm Sun. **Credit** AmEx, MC, V. **Sells** M, W.

This bare-bricked flagship store sells both original and new versions of the archetypal rock 'n' roll boot.

Dune

18 South Molton Street, W1Y 1DD (7491 3626/www.dune.co.uk). Oxford Circus tube. **Open** 10am-7pm Mon-Wed, Fri, Sat; 10am-8pm Thur; noon-6pm Sun. **Credit** AmEx, MC, V. **Sells** W.

Designer shoes interpreted in a fresh way for the high street.

For branches see index.

Faith

192-194 Oxford Street, W1D INS (7580 9561/www.faith.co.uk). Oxford Circus tube. **Open** 10am-9pm Mon-Sat; noon-6pm Sun. **Credit** MC, V. **Sells** M, W.

Finsk, Gil Carvalho and Olivia Morris all provide exciting FaithSolo collections for this chain in autumn/winter 2008/9.

For branches see index.

Gina

189 Sloane Street, SW1X 9QR (7235 2932/www.gina.com). Knightsbridge tube. **Open** 10am-6pm Mon, Tue, Thur-Sat; 10am-7pm Wed. **Credit** AmEx, MC, V. **Sells** W.

Glitzy diamanté heels much loved by WAGs, pop stars and screen starlets. Prices start at around £300. *See also pp9-10* **From London, with love**.

For branch see index.

Iris

124 Draycott Avenue, SW3 3AH (7584 1252/www.iris-shoes.it). South Kensington tube. **Open** 10am-6.30pm Mon, Tue, Thur-Sat; 10am-7pm Wed; 1-6pm Sun. **Credit** AmEx, DC, MC, V. **Sells** W.

This high-end boutique stocks shoes from top designers such as John Galliano, Chloé, Marc Jacobs and Victor & Rolf.

For branches see index.

Jimmy Choo

32 Sloane Street, SW1X 9NR (7823 1051/ www.jimmychoo.com). Knightsbridge tube. **Open** 10am-6pm Mon, Tue, Thur-Sat; 10am-7pm Wed; noon-5pm Sun. **Credit** AmEx, MC, V. **Sells** W.

Kylie, Sophie Dahl, Jennifer Lopez and countless other celebrities all adore Jimmy Choo's high-maintenance stiletto heels. Prices start from around £300.

For branch see index.

John Rushton

93 Wimpole Street, W1G 0EQ (7629 1888/www.johnrushtonshoes.com). Bond Street tube. **Open** 10am-6pm Mon-Fri; 10am-5.30pm Sat. **Credit** AmEx, DC, MC, V. **Sells** M.

English brands like Alfred Sargent, Cheaney and Chatham from £135 to £200. New for 2008 is its own-brand of trad styles.

LK Bennett

43 King Street, WC2E 8JY (7379 9890/ www.lkbennett.com). Covent Garden tube. **Open** 10.30am-7.30pm Mon-Wed, Fri, Sat; 10.30am-8pm Thur; noon-6pm Sun. **Credit** AmEx, MC, V. **Sells** W.

Quintessentially English shoes, which have an elegant, feminine charm.

Branches: throughout the city.

Natural Shoe Store

21 Neal Street, WC2H 9PU (7836 5254/ www.thenaturalshoestore.com). Covent Garden tube. **Open** 10am-6pm Mon, Tue; 10am-7pm Wed, Fri; 10am-8pm Thur; 10am-6.30pm Sat; noon-5.30pm Sun. **Credit** AmEx, DC, MC, V. **Sells** M, W.

The small parent shop of the Birkenstock store (*see p73*) specialises in comfortable shoes by brands like Trippen and Arche.

For branches see index.

Number 22

22 Carnaby Street, W1F 7DB (7734 1690/ www.swear-london.com).Oxford Circus tube. **Open** 11am-7pm Mon-Sat; 1-6pm Sun. **Credit** AmEx, MC, V. **Sells** M, W.

Swear's bold designs, plus models by People's Market. The collaborative collections with DIE and Fred Perry fly off the shelves.

Office

57 Neal Street, WC2H 4NP (7379 1896/ www.office.co.uk). Covent Garden tube. **Open** 10am-8pm Mon-Fri; 10am-7.30pm Sat; 11.30am-6.30pm Sun. **Credit** AmEx, DC, MC, V. **Sells** M, W.

Safely trendy styles at affordable prices.

Branches: throughout the city.

Patrick Cox

129 Sloane Street, SW1X 9AT (7730 8886/www.patrickcox.co.uk). Sloane Square tube. **Open** 10am-6pm Mon, Tue, Thur-Sat; 10am-7pm Wed. **Credit** AmEx, MC, V. **Sells** M, W.

Patrick Cox has been making tongue-in-cheek shoes for over 20 years now; a long list of celebs are fans of his sassy but kitsch styles.

Pied à Terre

19 South Molton Street, W1K 5QX (7629 1362/www.piedaterre.co.uk). Bond Street tube. **Open** 10am-7pm Mon-Wed, Fri, Sat; 10am-8pm Thur; noon-6pm Sun. **Credit** AmEx, DC, MC, V. **Sells** M, W.

Fashion-led, mid-priced footwear with a good range of sophisticated styles.

For branches see index.

Pretty Ballerinas

34 Brook Street, W1K 5DN (7493 3957/ www.prettyballerinas.com). Bond Street tube. **Open** 10am-7pm Mon-Sat; noon-6pm Sun. **Credit** AmEx, DC, MC, V. **Sells** W, C.

With shops in Brook Street, Knightsbridge and the City, Pretty Ballerinas is snapping at the (10mm) heels of French Sole.

For branches see index.

Rene Caovilla

37 Old Bond Street, W1S 4QN (7499 9802/www.renecaovilla.com). Green Park tube. **Open** 10am-6pm Mon-Sat. **Credit** AmEx, MC, V. **Sells** W.

Only the most exotic, delicate (and eye-wateringly expensive) Italian creations are sold at this chandelier-clad boutique.

Robert Clergerie

67 Wigmore Street, W1U 1PY (7935 3601/ www.robertclergerie.com). Bond Street tube. **Open** 10.30am-6pm Mon-Wed, Fri, Sat; 10am-7pm Thur. **Credit** AmEx, DC, MC, V. **Sells** M, W.

Striking shoes characterised by their simplicity, bold colours and functionality – handmade in limited quantities in France.

For branch see index.

Scorah Pattullo

www.scorahpattullo.com

London-based label Scorah Pattullo creates bold, fashionable shoes, available online or in selected boutiques.

Sergio Rossi

207A Sloane Street, SW1X 9QX (7811 5950/www.sergiorossi.com). Knightsbridge tube. **Open** noon-6pm Mon, Tue, Thur-Sat; noon-7pm Wed. **Credit** AmEx, DC, MC, V. **Sells** W.

'Flat' is a dirty word at Sergio Rossi's – shoes here come with death-defying heels in python skin, high-gloss patent and suede.

Shipton & Heneage

117 Queenstown Road, SW8 3RH (7738 8484/www.shipton.com). Queenstown Road rail/137 bus. **Open** 9am-6pm Mon-Fri; 10am-4pm Sat. **Credit** AmEx, MC, V. **Sells** M, W.

Men's Oxfords, brogues, loafers and boots – made in Northampton with Goodyear soles. Women's boots, deck shoes and loafers too.

For branch see index.

Sole

72 Neal Street, WC2H 9PA (7836 6777/ www.sole.co.uk). Covent Garden tube. **Open** 10.30am-7pm Mon-Wed, Fri, Sat; 10.30am-8pm Thur; noon-6pm Sun. **Credit** AmEx, MC, V. **Sells** M, W, C.

Stocks a huge range of brands including Adidas, Diesel, Fly and Esska. Especially good for casual and outdoor styles.

Branches: throughout the city.

Tod's

35-36 Sloane Street, SW1X 9LP (7235 1321/www.tods.com). Knightsbridge tube. **Open** 10am-6pm Mon-Fri; 10.30am-6pm Sat. **Credit** AmEx, MC, V. **Sells** M, W.

Best known for luxurious driving moccasins in a variety of materials.

For branch see index.

Trainers

The last couple of years have seen the closure of cool stalwarts such as **Foot Patrol**, **Slammin' Kicks** and **My Trainers**. Carnaby Street and Neal Street still have the highest concentration of trainer shops in London. For the latest lines from the sneaker giants, visit **Nike Town** (*see p222*), the **Puma** flagship (*see p75*) and the **Adidas Performance Store** (415-419 Oxford Street, W1C 2PG, 7493 1886); retro fiends should make a beeline for **Adidas Originals** (*see p50*) and **What Goes Around Comes Around** (*see p61*), with the latter specialising in rare vintage trainers. Skate shops **Slam City Skates** (*see p228*) and **Tuesday** (*see p229*) are good for limited-edition Nike SB's and Vans.

Adidas Concept Store (No.6)

6 Newburgh Street, W1F 7RQ (7734 9976/www.adidas.com/conceptstores). Oxford Circus tube. **Open** 10.30am-6.30pm Mon-Sat; 1-5pm Sun. **Credit** AmEx, MC, V.

With a small stock of limited-edition lines displayed in a compact, bijou space, this store is not the first to try to sell trainers as works of art. However, don't let the pretension detract from the fact that there are some decent sneakers here, many of them selected from the seasonal Adidas Consortium series, which involves slight design modifications and original colour schemes on classic Adidas trainers like Trimm Trabs, Forest Hills and Sambas. You'll find that the costs are modified too, with prices higher than average – around the £70 mark.

Gloria's

Old Truman Brewery, 6 Dray Walk, Brick Lane, E1 6QL (7770 6222/www.superdeluxe.net). Aldgate East tube. **Open** noon-7pm Mon; 11am-7pm Tue-Fri, Sun; 10am-7pm Sat. **Credit** MC, V.

Appropriately enough, for a store located in the image-conscious Old Truman Brewery, this independent sneaker dealer trades on its combination of 1970s and '80s nostalgia coupled with a fair dose of contemporary Shoreditch silliness. The space is decked out with retro classic items such as a Space Invaders machine, chopper bikes and some world-famous New York graffiti prints, and the trainer range follows suit with models including the early Nike Air Jordan lines, vintage Nike Dunks, New Balance 580s, reissued Vision Streetwear and various Adidas and Puma throwbacks. The selection may seem quite small – especially given the relatively large size of the store – but there is an entire

Sniff. *See p72.*

wall devoted to Vans and a few lesser-seen, newer brands like JB, Silas and Run Athletics, the brand set up by Joseph Simmons of Run DMC and his Def Jam-founder brother Russell.

Kazmattazz

39 Hoxton Square, N1 6NN (7739 4133/ www.kazmattazz.com). Old Street tube. **Open** 10.30am-6.30pm Mon-Thur; 10.30am-9pm Fri, Sat; 11am-4pm Sun. **Credit** AmEx, MC, V.

An essential stop for both hardened trainer fanatics and anyone looking for rare pumps. Past treats found among the piles of boxes have included pairs of brown-and-white, as well as purple-and-grey, Adidas Flavours of the World as well as kicks from Greedy Genius, and new stuff comes in every week, sourced from all over the world. It also stocks more standard Nike, Puma, Converse and Vans models.

Meteor Sports

408-410 Bethnal Green Road, E2 0DJ (7739 0707/www.mrsneaker.com). Bethnal Green tube. **Open** 9.30am-6pm Mon-Fri; 10am-7pm Sat, Sun. **Credit** MC, V.

This old-skool trainer shop has been one of the best independents for a number of years now and is well worth making a trip to if you're looking for something a little different – especially if you're a Nike head and a fan of the classic 1980s styles. It's the colour schemes rather than the trainer models that make up most of the out-of-the-ordinary stock, with countless variations of Air Force Ones and Air Max. Some of these variations are exclusives and can be found in the glass cabinets, which have also been home to original early Nike Air Jordans and Blazers. There's a set of racks of discount sneakers, but the regular stock is sold at above-average prices with plenty of pairs for over £100.

Offspring

60 Neal Street, WC2H 9PP (7497 2463/ www.office.co.uk). Covent Garden tube. **Open** 10am-7pm Mon-Wed, Fri, Sat; 10am-8pm Thur; 11.30am-6pm Sun. **Credit** AmEx, DC, MC, V.

One of the best of the Neal Street trainer dealers for the variety and originality of its stock; here you'll find all sorts of rarely seen kicks from alternative brands such as Yohji Yamamoto, Oki-Kutsu, Spring Court and YMA. Most of these are canvas sneakers in low-key designs similar to Converse All Stars or the Fred Perry range, both of which are also well represented. Completing the picture is a well-chosen spread of the usual suspects: Adidas, Puma, Nike et al. At the other end of the spectrum are several styles of Veja trainers, a Fairtrade brand launched in 2005.

For branch see index.

Size?

33-34 Carnaby Street, W1V 1PA (7287 4016/www.size-online.co.uk). Oxford Circus tube. **Open** 10am-7.30pm Mon-Wed, Fri, Sat; 10am-8pm Thur; noon-6pm Sun. **Credit** AmEx, DC, MC, V.

This hot-spot for London trainer fiends is unbeatable simply for its sheer variety of sneaker brands and colour combinations, thus making the too-cool-to-smile staff a necessary evil for punters looking for something a bit different. Old-school styles abound – there's no better place to pick up all-time classics like Puma Clydes, Adidas Gazelles and Nike Super Blazers. There are countless alternatives to the industry giants, like the more subdued Pointer and Tretorn kicks, an array of British New Balance trainers, plus Asics, skate shoes from Vans, Lakai and DVS and, upstairs, an entire floor dedicated to Converse. The staff at the Neal Street branch are friendlier.

For branches see index.

Also check out...

Focus

58 Neal Street, WC2H 1PA (7836 5860). Piccadilly Circus. **Open** 10am-7pm Mon-Sat; 11am-6.30pm Sun. **Credit** MC, V.

It may be middle-of-the-road in its range of stock, but this store makes up for it with its below-average pricing. It's also good for kids' sizes.

Foot Locker

363-367 Oxford Street, W1C 2LA (7491 4030/www.footlocker.eu). Bond Street tube. **Open** 10am-9pm Mon-Sat; noon-6pm Sun. **Credit** AmEx, MC, V.

This huge branch of the US sportswear store king has a massive quantity of trainers – you'd be hard pushed to find another place with a more extensive selection of contemporary street and sports styles from all the major brands.

Branches: throughout the city.

JD Sports

268-269 Oxford Street, W1RLD (7491 7677/www.jdsports.co.uk). Oxford Circus tube. **Open** 9am-8pm Mon-Wed; 9am-9pmThur, Fri, Sat; 10am-6pm Sun. **Credit** AmEx, MC, V.

This brash chain stocks a huge range of mainstream models from all of the major brands, with myriad exclusive colourways and patterns.

Branches: throughout the city.

Onitsuka Tiger

15 Newburgh Street, W1F 7RX (7734 5157/www.onitsukatiger.co.uk). Oxford Circus tube. **Open** 11am-7pm Mon-Sat; 1-6pm Sun. **Credit** MC, V.

The company behind the Asics brand has gone back to its roots at this store which specialises in the original Tiger designs that the Japanese manufacturer first made its name with back in the 1960s.

Puma

51-55 Carnaby Street, W1F 9QE (7439 0221/www.puma.com). Oxford Circus tube. **Open** 10am-7pm Mon-Sat. **Credit** MC, V.

Puma's London flagship.

Rbk

51 Neal Street, WC2H 9PQ (7240 8689/ www.reebok.com). Covent Garden tube. **Open** 10am-7pm Mon-Sat; noon-6pm Sun. **Credit** AmEx, MC, V.

Another global brand flagship store that stocks undoubtedly the broadest range of Reebok trainers available in the capital; if you like garish colours you'll be in heaven here.

Vans

47 Carnaby Street, W1F 9PT (7287 9235/www.vans.eu). Oxford Circus tube. **Open** 10am-7pm Mon-Wed, Fri, Sat; 10am-8pm Thur; noon-6pm Sun. **Credit** MC, V.

The original skate trainers are still going strong and there's no better place to get them than the brand's flagship store. You can find classic Chukkas and Slip-Ons plus a lot of the new designs and there's also a good women's range upstairs.

Accessories

For sunglasses, *see pp115-117* **Opticians**. For ties, *see p54* **Shirts & ties**. Hip shoe shop **Black Truffle** (*see p70*) sells a range of bags and accessories for men and women.

General

The following sell a good mix of jewellery, bags, belts and the like; good high street bets include **Banana Republic**, **Jigsaw** and **Reiss** (for all, *see pp45-47*). The latter rolled out a line of dedicated accessories stores in spring 2008.

Comfort Station

22 Cheshire Street, E2 6EH (7033 9099/ www.comfortstation.co.uk). Liverpool Street tube/rail. **Open** 11am-6pm Tue-Sun. **Credit** AmEx, MC, V.

Artist turned designer Amy Anderson's lady-like retail space opened its doors in 2004. Offbeat touches such as birds painted on the door and a piano-cum-display cabinet, provide the ideal environment to showcase her handmade accessories. Alongside the beautiful, ethically made bags and bone china crockery covered in wonderfully weird collaged prints is her jewellery line. For autumn/winter 2008/9 there's a heraldic theme with recurring symbols including hearts, crowns, horses, medals and stags made from silver, gold, porcelain and black onyx. These emblems of power are fastened with chains, festooned with pearls and drip from earrings and necklaces. Prices start at £40 for jewellery and £150 for bags.

The Jacksons

5 All Saints Road, W11 1HA (7792 8336/ www.thejacksons.co.uk). Westbourne Park tube. **Open** 10am-6pm Mon-Fri; 11am-6pm Sat. **Credit** AmEx, DC, MC, V.

Run by twins Joey (the business brains) and Louise (the arty one), the Jacksons first launched in 1995 and has been both a London Fashion Week and Notting Hill staple ever since. All stock is ethically made and the brand works closely with Fairtrade organisations in developing companies, which means that the canvas bag or beaded belt you buy will be both beautiful to look at and give you that feel-good factor. Whether made by a skilled Masai tribeswoman or by Louise in the shop's studio space, each accessory exudes a cultural richness and hand-finished timeless charm. From dog collars to shoes with signature red soles, the Jacksons have it licked.

Swaine Adeney Brigg

54 St James's Street, SW1A 1JT (7409 7277/www.swaineadeney.co.uk). Green Park tube. **Open** 10am-6pm Mon-Sat. **Credit** AmEx, DC, MC, V.

See p79 **TRAD BOX**.

Tatty Devine

57B Brewer Street, W1F 9UL (7434 2257/www.tattydevine.com). Piccadilly Circus tube. **Open** 11am-7pm Mon-Sat; noon-5pm Sun. **Credit** MC, V.

Harriet Vine and Rosie Wolfenden's eccentric accessories include their plastic fantastic jewellery and, for autumn/winter 2008/9, the Attack of the 50ft Jewellery collection includes such oddities as giant pencil necklaces, bobby pin brooches and glow in the dark eyeball earrings. For men there are similarly fun cufflinks, and you can get an acrylic name necklace made up for £25. They also host art and craft exhibitions.

For branch see index.

Also check out…

Accessorize

22 The Market, Covent Garden, WC2H 8HB (7240 2107/www.accessorize.co.uk). Covent Garden tube. **Open** 10am-7.30pm Mon-Sat; 10.30am-6pm Sun. **Credit** AmEx, MC, V.

Cheap 'n' cheerful accessories from the Monsoon camp, often with an art deco feel. **Branches**: throughout the city.

Asprey

167 New Bond Street, W1S 4AR (7493 6767/www.asprey.com). Bond Street or Green Park tube. **Open** 10am-6pm Mon-Sat. **Credit** AmEx, DC, MC, V.

The very best British luxury goods, since 1781. Don't forget your cheque book.

Fur Coat No Knickers

Top Floor, Kingly Court, Carnaby Street, W1B 5PW (07814 002 295/www.furcoat noknickers.co.uk). Oxford Circus tube. **Open** 11am-7pm Mon-Sat; noon-6pm Sun. **Credit** MC, V.

A treasure trove for vintage bags, hats and jewellery. Alas, no fur coats – or knickers.

Lotus

11 Pont Street, SW1X 9EH (7235 3550/ www.lotuslondon.com). Sloane Square tube. **Open** 10am-6.30pm Mon-Sat. **Credit** AmEx, MC, V.

Embellished, beaded jewellery, bags, kaftans and cashmere made by artisans in India.

Bags & leather goods

Ally Capellino

9 Calvert Avenue, E2 7JP (7613 3073/www. allycapellino.co.uk). Liverpool Street tube/ rail. **Open** noon-6pm Wed-Fri; 10am-6pm Sat; 11am-4pm Sun. **Credit** AmEx, MC, V.

Ally Capellino's stylishly understated unisex bags, wallets and purses have developed something of a cult following since the brand was set up in 1980, and are now stocked in an increasing number of boutiques around town. This east London store on up-and-coming Calvert Avenue houses the full range; prices start at around £39 for a cute leather coin purse, rising to two or three hundred for the larger, more structured models, such as the Bossy large shoulder bag (£330) in lovely tanned brown leather. The classic Jeremy waxed cotton satchels will set you back £162 (£134 for the small size); we're coveting the pillar-box red version. For autumn/winter 2008/9 there's a lovely collection of womens' leather clutches in the classic Capellino muted colour palette, priced at £180 for the large size. The laptop bags, launched in summer 2008, are sold exclusively in Apple stores (*see p197*).

Anya Hindmarch

15-17 Pont Street, SW1X 9EH (7838 9177/www.anyahindmarch.com). Sloane Square tube. **Open** 10am-6pm Mon, Tue, Thur-Sat; 10am-7pm Wed. **Credit** AmEx, MC, V.

There's much more to Anya Hindmarch than her gimmicky I'm Not A Plastic Bag, which hit the headlines in 2007. The high-end label has recently opened two stores on New Bond Street and Sloane Street and excels in It-bags that sit the right side of celebrity naff (Jake Gyllenhaal and Reese Witherspoon are both fans). For autumn/winter 2008/9 Hindmarch was inspired by the linear feel of architecture. Grab a Perry for daytime in cream, chocolate and black, or an oversize Piano clutch for evening (£695 a piece). Her Be a Bag service allows you to have your own images printed on a choice of totes, washbags and shoppers.

For branches see index.

Augustina

11 West Halkin Street, SW1X 8JL (7823 1188/www.augustinaboutiques.com). Knightsbridge tube. **Open** 10am-6pm Mon-Sat. **Credit** AmEx, MC, V.

Augustina hand-selects up-and-coming bag and accessory brands from around the globe that you just don't find in department stores. Instead of a Marc Jacobs tote, try one by Joy Gryson, who incidentally used to design for Jacobs (and it shows). Instead of a generic Prada sack, how about a sleek shopper by Andrea Brueckner or a python pouch by Carlos Falchi? Other exclusives by Treese, B Romanek, Rebecca Minkoff or Anna Corinna ensure the shop is brimming with irresistible finds. Augustina also has its own fragrances and leather goods plus a line of jewellery called the Farms Collection. These adorable charms come in silver (£125) or gold (£175) and allow you to choose between a hen, goat, foal, horse, fawn, rooster or unicorn.

Bagman & Robin

47 Exmouth Market, EC1R 4QL (7833 8780/www.bagmanandrobin.com). Angel tube then 38 bus/Farringdon tube/rail then 68 bus. **Open** 11am-6pm Mon-Sat. **Credit** AmEx, MC, V.

Don't let the ever-so-tasteless name put you off because Bagman & Robin – aka Marco Araldi and Keng Wai Lee – make delightfully different, limited-edition bags. For autumn/winter 2008/9 a new line of clutches made from Japanese vintage obi and kimono fabrics (£105) sits alongside patent lacquered leather day bags (£85) and some colourful oilcloth totes (£70). New this season is their first collection of contemporary jewellery featuring chunky necklaces and bangles (prices from £35).

Bill Amberg

21-22 Chepstow Corner, W2 4XE (7727 3560/www.billamberg.com). Notting Hill Gate tube. **Open** 10am-6pm Mon-Sat. **Credit** AmEx, MC, V.

When you walk into Bill Amberg's flagship store the smell of expensive leather fills your nostrils. Lovingly displayed around the two-floor corner shop are the brand's covetable men's and women's bags – everything from a classic briefcase to an about-town shopper in seasonal colours – plus accessories you never knew you needed (a leather-lined

jewellery box for £395). It also offers a pampered pets collection, leather goodies for babies (you'll wish you could fit into the sheepskin snuggler) and a gentlemen's sports range including footballs, boxing gloves and rifle straps. Each item exudes a refined yet fashionable luxury, but if you are after something super special, such as a leather-lined room, try the bespoke service.

Connolly

41 Conduit Street, W1S 2YQ (7439 2510/ www.connollylondon.com). Oxford Circus tube. **Open** 10am-6.30pm Mon-Wed, Fri, Sat; 10am-7pm Thur. **Credit** AmEx, DC, MC, V.
Connolly is the type of store where the old adage 'If you have to ask the price, you can't afford it' applies. The British luxury label has a long history of upholstering prestige cars such as Aston Martin and is the sole supplier of leather to Rolls-Royce. It's also responsible for the red leather seats in the Houses of Parliament. Since opening its flagship in 1995, the brand has proved its accessories credentials too by making the sorts of goods only the really rich 'need', such as a gentleman's tool kit (£1,800), suit carrier (£640), weekend bag (£2,500) and Krug champagne case (£850). A collection of leather overcoats and chic mens- and womenswear also ensures you can be head-to-toe Connolly whether you own your own sports car or not.

Elliot Rhodes

79 Long Acre, WC2E 9NG (7379 8544/ www.elliotrhodes.com). Covent Garden tube. **Open** 10am-7.30pm Mon-Sat; noon-5pm Sun. **Credit** AmEx, MC, V.
The belt shop to end all belt shops. At Elliot Rhodes you can assemble your own waist-cincher from a choice of over 450 straps and 1,000 interchangeable buckles. The mind-boggling mix-and-match approach ensures your belt is unique (a simple belt costs from £60, fancy ones around £500). Buckles might come in the shape of hearts, flowers, or fish, be covered in semi-precious stones or have a motif such as the Virgin Mary, skulls or a sacred heart. Straps range from mock croc to very real python. A new shop has opened on Duke of York Square.
For branch see index.

J&M Davidson

42 Ledbury Road, W11 2AB (7313 9532/ www.jandmdavidson.com). Notting Hill Gate tube. **Open** 10am-6pm Mon-Sat; noon-5pm Sun. **Credit** AmEx, MC, V.
Anglo-French couple John and Monique Davidson's bags and leather accessories are made in their own Bolton factory and the brand's slightly retro aesthetic has stood them in good stead for over 20 years. The two-floor shop in the heart of Westbourne Park faces some stiff competition from the neighbouring fashion boutiques but holds its own thanks to the calming vibe and good-quality leather. Bag styles steer clear of trends, and although one won't come cheap, it won't date either. Small leather goods include belts, purses and wallets.

Lulu Guinness

3 Ellis Street, SW1X 9AL (7823 4828/ www.luluguinness.com). Sloane Square tube. **Open** 10am-6pm Mon-Fri; 11am-6pm Sat. **Credit** AmEx, MC, V.
Lulu Guinness celebrates 20 years of making fun and feminine bags in 2009. Known for her nostalgic novelties and whimsically shaped totes, the anniversary collection French Kiss is as frou frou as ever. Inspired by romantic cinema and the actress Anna Karina, the recurring motif of lips dominates the range. There's a perspex or snakeskin lips clutch and a snakeskin or soft leather Amelie, an oversized frame purse with a chain handle. Quilting, prints and embroidery add to the collection's appeal, while the palette of red, black and silver, hot pink and green gives a nod to Pop Art. Lulu Guinness also offers jewellery, sunglasses, vanity cases and umbrellas covered in her customary shoes and flower patterns; the shop now has a corner crammed with bedlinen and cushions.
For branch see index.

Mimi

40 Cheshire Street, E2 6EH (7729 6699/ www.mimimika.com). Liverpool Street tube/ rail. **Open** 10am-6pm Tue-Thur; 11am-6pm Fri-Sun. **Credit** MC, V.
Mimi Berry studied fashion at Central Saint Martins and had a popular stall at Spitalfields Market before she opened her bag shop on Cheshire Street in 2001. She began by making a choice selection of slouchy leather carry-alls in unconventional colours but these days her collection covers a wider array of understated designs, taking in more structured styles. Must-haves include large metallic beach bags, the Baby Lou handbag, the Jack shopper and the Ella clutch, while the Musette (£98) has become the handbag of choice for east London's style-conscious gals. There are manbags aplenty too plus purses and accessories such as the Patrick Oyster card holder. Prices range from about £90 to about £250.

Pickett

32-33 & 41 Burlington Arcade, W1J OPZ (7493 8939/www.pickett.co.uk). Green Park tube. **Open** 9am-6pm Mon-Fri; 10am-6pm Sat. **Credit** AmEx, DC, MC, V.
Pickett prides itself on hand-making all of its upmarket leather goods on British soil. The very English company wouldn't win any fashion races but its comprehensive range of traditional products have a timeless quality that's worth investing in. Prices for a men's attaché case start at £755 and briefcases from £225. By comparison a wallet is a snip at £90. Women's bags come in similarly classic shapes including the Sian clutch (£275) and Birkin-esque Helen (£415). Stuck for a gift for the millionaire who has everything? Then buy a leather scrabble set for £1,095 or one of its splendid umbrellas with Malacca cane handles. Its sedate Burlington Arcade shop also has a Bespoke Room.
For branches see index.

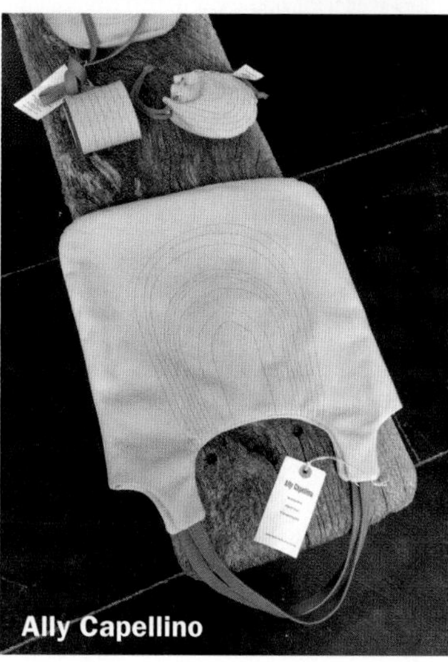

Ally Capellino

Poppy Valentine

Unit 16, Portobello Green Arcade, 281 Portobello Road, W10 5TZ (8964 1350/ www.poppyvalentine.com). Ladbroke Grove tube. **Open** 10am-5.30pm Tue-Sat. **Credit** AmEx, MC, V.

Claire Read's shop in Ladbroke Grove is a little like stepping back in time. The designer sources original fabrics – florals from the 1940s, graphic prints from the 1950s, hippie patterns from the 1960s and psychedelic abstracts from the 1970s – and turns them into retro-inspired bags. If vintage isn't your thing, the contemporary range is made from vegetable tanned nappa leather and modern printed textiles.

Susannah Hunter

7 Rugby Street, WC1N 3QT (7692 3798/ www.susannahhunter.com). Holborn tube. **Open** 10am-6pm Mon-Fri; noon-4pm Sat. **Credit** AmEx, MC, V.

Hunter's ethos is that bags should be portable works of art and her bright white shop acts as a gallery dedicated to them. If you don't like flowers, look away now – her designs are fixated on florals. Leather cut-outs in muted pastel shades are appliquéd on to roomy day bags, deep shoppers, overnight carry-alls and delicate evening clutches. Prices range from £140 for a purse to £770 for the overnight bag, and every piece is handmade in Hunter's studio. The shop also carries a small but smart range of furnishings (chairs and screens) bearing Hunter's painterly roses, lilies and daisies.

Also check out...

Coccinelle

13 Duke of York Square, King's Road, SW3 4LY (7730 7657/www.coccinelle.com). Sloane Square tube. **Open** 10am-7pm Mon-Sat; noon-6pm Sun. **Credit** AmEx, DC, MC, V.
Sleek Italian handbags for uptown girls.

Custom Leather

Unit 72, Camden Lock, Chalk Farm Road, NW1 8AF (7482 1407/www.htleather.co.uk). Camden Town tube. **Open** noon-5.30pm Wed-Fri; 11am-6pm Sat, Sun. **Credit** MC, V.
Hard-wearing bags covering the gamut of classic styles. Bespoke service is available.

Doors By Jas M.B.

8 Ganton Street, W1F 7QP (7494 2288/ www.doorsbyjasmb.com). Oxford Circus tube. **Open** 11am-7pm Mon-Fri; noon-7pm Sat, Sun. **Credit** AmEx, MC, V.
Effortlessly cool British-made bags using the finest Italian leathers.

Globe-Trotter

54-55 Burlington Arcade, W1J 0LB (7529 5950/www.globe-trotterltd.com). Green Park tube. **Open** 10am-6pm Mon-Sat. **Credit** AmEx, MC, V.
The indestructible steamer-trunk luggage that accompanied the Queen on honeymoon.

Jocasi

19 Fouberts Place, W1F 7QE (7734 2828/ www.jocasi.com). Oxford Circus tube. **Open** 10am-7pm Mon-Sat; 10am-8pm Thur; 11.30am-6pm Sun. **Credit** AmEx, MC, V.
Brightly coloured leather bags and belts featuring bold buckles and braiding.

Ollie & Nic

20 Fouberts Place, W1F 7PL (7494 4214/ www.ollieandnic.com). Oxford Circus tube. **Open** 10am-7pm Mon-Wed, Fri, Sat; 10am-8pm Thur; noon-6pm Sun. **Credit** AmEx, MC, V.

O&N's new flagship houses the brand's stylish bags in tweed, leather and velvet. **For branch see index.**

Hats

For baseball caps, *see p50* **New Era**. Vintage shops are often good bets for hats; *see pp56-63.*

Bates the Hatter

21A Jermyn Street, SW1Y 6HP (7734 2722/www.bates-hats.co.uk). Piccadilly Circus tube. **Open** 9am-5.15pm Mon-Fri; 9.30am-4pm Sat. **Credit** AmEx, DC, MC, V. *See p79* **Enduring loves**.

Bernstock Speirs

234 Brick Lane, E2 7EB (7739 7385/ www.bernstockspeirs.com). Aldgate East tube. **Open** 11am-6pm Tue-Fri; 11am-5pm Sat, Sun. **Credit** AmEx, MC, V.

Paul Bernstock and Thelma Speirs first met at Middlesex Polytechnic in 1979 and have been attiring east London's best-dressed heads since 1981. Everyone from Boy George to Kylie Minogue has bought one of their bonnets – creative reworkings of classic styles. The autumn/winter 2008/9 collection includes veiled visors, bobble hats with bows, trilbys with a zip detail brim and beanies in corduroy and tartan. Having just revamped its Brick Lane shop, the brand also provides catwalk hats for London Fashion Week designers Peter Jensen and Modernist.

CA4LA

23 Pitfield Street, N1 6HB (7490 0055/ www.ca4la.com). Old Street tube/rail. **Open** 11am-7pm daily. **Credit** MC, V.

CA4LA (pronounced 'Ka-shi-la') is big in its native Japan. Collaborating with designers, artists and musicians from around the world, hats by the likes of Eley Kishimoto, Puma and Maximo Park all grace the shops' shelves. The London store (the only one outside Japan) opened in 2006 and sells a huge variety of cutting-edge headwear including bejewelled baseball caps, polka-dot flatcaps, flapper-style headbands and trilbys covered in Warhol prints. Stock changes frequently, so there's always an excuse to pop in and prices range from the everyday affordable to the special occasion splurge.

Philip Treacy

69 Elizabeth Street, SW1W 9PJ (7730 3992/www.philiptreacy.co.uk). Sloane Square tube. **Open** 10am-6pm Mon-Fri; 11am-5pm Sat. **Credit** AmEx, MC, V.

Philip Treacy competes only with Stephen Jones (*see below*) for the title of London's most fashionable milliner. Much-loved by the late, great fashion editor Isabella Blow, he established his first studio in the basement of her house on Elizabeth Street in 1991 and his petite shop has since become a Belgravia hotspot a few doors down. Known for his ornate, attention-grabbing creations that often don't resemble a hat at all, designers like Karl Lagerfeld and Alexander McQueen have called on his services. Autumn/winter 2008/9 ranges from leopard-print trilbys and logo-embroidered baseball caps for men to fantastically feathered fascinators and neon berets for women.

Also check out...

Fred Bare

118 Columbia Road, E2 7RG (7729 6962/ 01904 624579/www.fredbare.co.uk). Bethnal Green tube. **Open** 9am-2.30pm Sun. **Credit** AmEx, DC, MC, V.
Traditional styles with a funky twist for men and women; vintage trimmings are often used.

Gabriela Ligenza

5 Ellis Street, SW1X 9AL (7730 2200/ www.gabrielaligenza.com). Sloane Square tube. **Open** 10am-6pm Mon-Sat. **Credit** AmEx, MC, V.
Sophisticated and sculptured women's hats handmade in Florence.

Hectic Hat Hire

236 Munster Road, SW6 6BX (7381 5127/ www.hectichathire.co.uk). Fulham Broadway or Parsons Green tube. **Open** 10am-5pm Mon, Tue, Thur, Fri; 10am-1pm Wed, Sat; also by appointment. **Credit** AmEx, MC, V.
Need a hat for a special occasion? Look no further than Hectic.

James Lock

6 St James's Street, SW1A 1EF (men's 7930 8874/women's 7930 2421/www.lockhatters.co.uk). Green Park tube. **Open** 9am-5.30pm Mon-Fri; 9.30am-5pm Sat. **Credit** AmEx, DC, MC, V.
Hats for the great and good since 1676.

Siggi Hats

48 Fulham High Street, SW6 3LQ (7736 2030/www.siggihats.co.uk). Putney Bridge tube. **Open** 9am-5.30pm Mon-Fri; by appointment Sat. **Credit** MC, V.
Made-to-measure hats fit for trips to Ascot or the mother of the bride.

Stephen Jones

36 Great Queen Street, WC2B 5AA (7242 0770/www.stephenjonesmillinery.com). Holborn tube. **Open** 11am-6pm Tue, Wed, Fri; 11am-7pm Thur. **Credit** AmEx, MC, V.
Hugely influential, innovative milliner who's worked with the likes of John Galliano and Comme des Garçons.

Umbrellas

See also p76 **Swaine Adeney Brigg** and *p77* **Lulu Guinness**.

James Smith & Sons

53 New Oxford Street, WC1A 1BL (7836 4731/www.james-smith.co.uk). Holborn or Tottenham Court Road tube. **Open** 9.30am-5.15pm Mon-Fri; 10am-5.15pm Sat. **Credit** AmEx, MC, V.
See p79 **Enduring loves**.

T Fox & Co

118 London Wall, EC2Y 5JA (7628 1868/ www.tfox.co.uk). Moorgate tube/rail. **Open** 9am-6pm Mon-Fri. **Credit** AmEx, MC, V.
See p79 **Enduring loves**.

Classic London shops

Enduring loves

These capital stalwarts are as traditional as talking about the weather.

Some things in London are timelessly traditional, and should remain so: Nelson's Column, Big Ben, the Changing of the Guard and, of course, worrying about the weather. The same applies to London's shops, whether it's Jermyn Street's experts in fine gentleman's clothing or the cigar shops around St James's. Paying homage to these bastions of traditional British life, here is a selection of our favourites that are still going strong in the 21st century.

James Smith & Sons

James Smith & Sons (*see p78*) is one of the most visually striking of these characterful survivors. In the niche market of superior quality umbrellas, the store is unrivalled thanks to its lovingly crafted products, all built to last. This charming shop opened in 1830 and its original Victorian fittings are still intact. To say that it sticks out like a sore thumb would be an understatement, but it's impossible to imagine New Oxford Street without it.

Alongside the expected traditional brollies (such as a classic City umbrella with a hickory crook), there are high-tech folding models and sun parasols – including a dainty beechwood-handled number that's designed for weddings. Walking sticks and canes are the shop's other speciality, each one cut to the correct length for the customer. Furthermore, if you buy an umbrella here and the elements do get the better of it, James Smith has a repairs service to put it right again. The shop's staff are clearly proud to be carrying on a brand with such a long history.

T Fox & Co

Protection from the elements is clearly a priority on any traditional gent's agenda: **T Fox & Co** (*see p78*) also began as an umbrella makers, back in 1868, though they have expanded their range since then. Today, with its leaping fox logo a sure-fire stamp of quality, it also provides smart shirts, ties, shoes and leather goods (wallets, briefcases and the like). Located on the edge of the City, the shop caters to power-broking businessmen out to impress with their attire and accessories. A bespoke tailoring service is also available, but the real treat is a trip to the shop itself: the ground-floor's attractive modernist interior is complemented by a Victorian clubroom upstairs.

Bates the Hatter

Once, a man was not considered fully dressed if he went out without his hat. Having kept the tradition of gents' hats alive on Jermyn Street for over a century, **Bates the Hatter** (*see p78*) clearly knows its niche, advising customers: 'Always wear a hat in inclement and sunny weather.' And sure enough, the shop sells headwear that covers all weather conditions: the straw panama is perfect for summer, while the deerstalker is ideal for those winter hunting expeditions. Well-crafted flat caps are a timeless classic, and chaps would do well to keep Bates in mind for formal occasions – Steed from *The Avengers* would be proud to wear the company's bowler hat, and the classy black top hat is a stunner in grey or black. This old-fashioned shop, with its wonderful topper-shaped sign, is one of London's finest surviving gems.

Swaine Adeney Brigg

This purveyor of equestrian goods has an impressive 250-year pedigree, and is a firm favourite with the upper echelons of society – not to mention their horses. Continuing the obsession with the weather, **Swaine Adeney Brigg** (*see p76*) is perhaps most highly reputed for its umbrellas. A classic, solid oak brolly is £195, while the top-of-the-range version, with a solid silver handle, goes for £775.

Bates

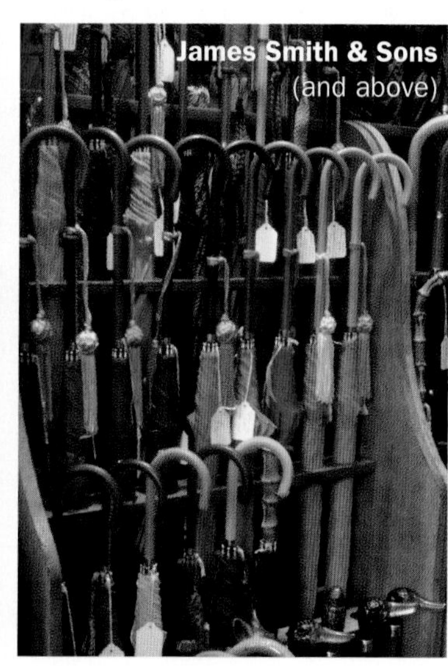
James Smith & Sons (and above)

Jewellery

See also p76 **Comfort Station** and **Tatty Devine**. Shops such as **Paul Smith** (*see p41*), **Beyond the Valley** (*see p19*), **Paul & Joe** (*see p41*), **Diverse** (*see p29*), **Sefton** (*see p36*) and **Goodhood** (*see p49*) have glass cabinets displaying some lovely, affordable pieces by an eclectic range of designers.

@work

156 Brick Lane, E1 6RU (7377 0597/ www.atworkgallery.co.uk). Aldgate East tube/Liverpool Street tube/rail. **Open** 11am-6pm Mon-Sat; 10.30am-5.30pm Sun. **Credit** MC, V.

It's been a decade since this innovative but affordable East End showcase opened its doors, and three years since a second similarly eclectic shop opened in Pimlico. All things contemporary and experimental take centre stage, as many of the designers are recent graduates of jewellery design courses. Sarah Hickey's elegant pieces are inspired by ancient talismans and amulets, while Katie Clarke's offerings are more off-the-wall, fashioned out of brightly hued feathers. Meanwhile, Casey Rogers has created a cute line of brooches featuring dogs and cats screenprinted onto gingham and chintz. For budding designers or complete beginners, there are courses in silver jewellery-making, and bride and groom to-be can attend make-it-yourself wedding ring workshops. Prices from £7.

For branch see index.

Ben Day

18 Hanbury Street, E1 6QR (7247 9977/ www.benday.co.uk). Liverpool Street tube/rail. **Open** 11am-6pm Tue-Fri; 11am-5pm Sat, Sun. **Credit** AmEx, MC, V.

Ben Day has built up a loyal following for his exquisite, opulent creations – a showcase of colour and luxury. Day's workshop lies below the shop itself, in an original Huguenot building in Spitalfields – the perfect setting for his almost medieval designs, which feature flawless South Sea pearls, smooth pebbles of rich amethyst or heavy drops of vivid green chysoprase. All the pieces are handmade one-offs, adding to the air of rarified exclusivity; for those who want something even more personal, Day will undertake bespoke work, including wedding rings. Men are not forgotten, with a range of accessories that includes unusual cufflinks and signet rings (from £350).

Carolina Bucci

4 Motcomb Street, SW1X 8JU (7838 9977/ www.carolinabucci.com). Knightsbridge tube. **Open** 10am-6pm Mon-Sat. **Credit** AmEx, MC, V.

Carolina Bucci might well have gold running through her veins – born in Florence, a city famous for the stuff, she comes from a line of jewellers dating back to 1885. A thousand or so miles from the Ponte Vecchio, but not so far in spirit, in May 2007 she opened her first boutique here. Known especially for her delicate bracelets and necklaces (in a variety of gold colours and prices – from £200 up to £7,000) her influences are truly global in scope – from Japan to Mexico, the Caribbean and, of course, Italy. There are also some unusual changes in pace; take, for example, the bold Woven collection, with its range of chokers, belts, blankets and scarves incorporating gold threads woven into luxurious fabrics (a blanket will set you back from £8,000 to £12,000). As well as the collections showcased in the store, there's also a bespoke service.

Cox & Power

35C Marylebone High Street, W1U 4QA (7935 3530/www.coxandpower.com). Baker Street tube. **Open** 10am-6pm Mon-Sat. **Credit** AmEx, DC, MC, V.

Cox & Power is still turning out top-end, mould-breaking and beautifully crafted designs, and selling them out of a stylish, minimalist shop on Marylebone High Street. The design team, headed up by Tony Power, has plenty of new ideas. The men's range has been extended to include hand-forged bangles (£375) and a pair of stunning cufflinks in carved silver where one is matte, the other polished (£275). Other fresh designs include an almost industrial take on the traditional claw-set diamond ring, updated by an ultra-plain, matte band (£5,750). Another eye-catcher is the Nine Diamonds cocktail ring, studded with white, gold and tawny diamonds (£10,000). Wedding and commitment rings can be customised according to taste: choose the shape, finish and colour of the gold – white, yellow or even red (from £295).

Dower & Hall

39 Brushfield Street, E1 6AA (7377 5544/www.dowerandhall.com). Liverpool Street tube/rail. **Open** 10.30am-6.15pm Mon-Fri; 11.30am-5pm Sat, Sun. **Credit** AmEx, DC, MC, V.

Husband-and-wife duo Dan Dower and Diane Hall met while studying jewellery design at college in the 1980s. The pair haven't rested on their laurels. New design collections appear all the time: one of the latest, named Rainforest, was inspired by a trip to Vietnam and Cambodia. The result is intricately carved silver palm leaves dotted with bursts of colour in the form of garnets – the Silver Leaf bracelet is £375. Another collection plucked from nature is Waterlily,

ec one

which mixes carved silver flowers with the cool colours of amazonite, citrine and topaz. The blue topaz, pearl and silver bead bracelet costs £110. Charms are a big seller here and you can create your own customised bracelet or pendant (£45 each) by hand-picking from an array of 135 silver charms (£30 each). Those with more cash might like the contemporary precious collection from £435.

ec one

41 Exmouth Market, EC1R 4QL (7713 6185/www.econe.co.uk). Farringdon tube/rail. **Open** 10am-6pm Mon-Wed, Fri; 11am-7pm Thur; 10.30am-6pm Sat. **Credit** AmEx, MC, V.

Whether it's precious luxury or a witty costume piece you're after, you'll probably find it in one of ec one's three London branches – in Exmouth Market, Westbourne Grove or Chiswick. With husband and wife team Jos and Alison Skeates at the helm, the stores run the gamut of jewellery design with consummate ease. Over 50 designers are showcased; new arrivals include Amanda Coleman's cute cupcake stud earrings (£27) and Rose Morant's bold stacks of wooden bangles lacquered in juicy colours (£45 for seven in orange). For something a little more subtle, try Monica Vinader's delicate gold-plated chain hung with pink and white opals (£93) or Alex Monroe's summery Buttercup ring in gold (£108). Elegant wedding bands and engagement rings come courtesy of the in-house design team, Niessing, or Henrich & Denzel. The latter combines bands of rose gold and platinum for £1,863.

For branches see index.

Electrum Gallery

21 South Molton Street, W1K 5QZ (7629 6325). Bond Street tube. **Open** 10am-6pm Mon-Fri; 10am-6pm Sat. **Credit** AmEx, DC, MC, V.

Talent-spotting new jewellery design brains is made easy at Electrum Gallery, where a good deal of stock is conveniently under one roof. Now under new management, Electrum's brand new sister gallery is the mixed-media (glass, ceramics and textiles) Contemporary Applied Arts (*see p165*). At the South Molton Street shop, around 100 designers are represented at any one time, so the range of styles and budgets is huge. Gerda Flöckinger CBE works with fused 18ct yellow gold (from £700), while Jo Hayes-Ward uses computer aided design to create works in stainless steel and aluminium as well as precious metals. A new star arrival to Electrum's sparkling firmament is Mette Jenson, whose bold, sculptural designs are crafted out of natural and stained beechwood and silver (£245 for a bracelet).

Fiona Knapp

178A Westbourne Grove, W11 2RH (7313 5941/www.fionaknapp.com). Westbourne Park or Notting Hill Gate tube. **Open** 11am-6pm Mon-Wed, Fri; 10am-6pm Sat; 11am-4pm Sun. **Credit** AmEx, DC, MC, V.

New Zealand-born Fiona Knapp is a gemmologist, and a rather glamorous one at that, so it's no surprise that her jewellery is bold, beautiful and expensive. Her shop – with its matte black walls, chandeliers and vivid turquoise carpet – is the perfect showcase for glossy sparklers. Working with dramatic coloured stones, Knapp has made her name with daring designs for both sexes that are inspired by the architectural (like churches and city skylines) as well as the natural world. The Sea Urchin design has proved lastingly popular: a large fire opal set in yellow gold will set you back £2,980. A rare Paraiba tourmaline, weighing in at 37.5 carats, surrounded by rose-cut diamonds is £27,000, but this is top whack: most pieces cost between £3,000 and £5,000.

Jess James

3 Newburgh Street, W1F 7RE (7437 0199/ www.jessjames.com). Oxford Circus or Piccadilly Circus tube. **Open** 11am-6.30pm Mon-Wed, Fri; 11am-7pm Thur; 11am-6pm Sat. **Credit** AmEx, MC, V.

Opened in 1988 as a riposte to the snobbery of well-to-do jewellers that barred customers from their doors if they weren't dressed conservatively, Jess James is just as innovative today. A hip clientele pops in to browse through in-house designs, including glittering eternity bands of diamond and pink sapphire, and an eclectic group of designers, from celebrity favourite Shaun Leane to lesser-known names such as Tina Lilienthal and Jana Reinhardt. Leane's statement bangles of turquoise resin with either gold or silver caps go from £165; in contrast is Lucy Jade Sylvester's intricate work inspired by nature, including an exotic beetle bangle (£95) and a highly detailed oak twig ring made from 9ct gold and finished off with ethereal moonstones (£370). Watches are also a strong point.

Kabiri

37 Marylebone High Street, W1U 4QE (7224 1808/www.kabiri.co.uk). Baker Street tube. **Open** 10am-6.30pm Mon-Sat; noon-5pm Sun. **Credit** AmEx, MC, V.

This independent's admirable mission statement is to showcase the best in jewellery, regardless of its price, provenance or how well known the designer is – in fact, many careers of hitherto unknown makers have been launched here, such as those of Ana de Costa and Lauren Hassey. In the fun camp is Alex & Chloe: the 'Don't Say Non' necklace in neon pink acrylic and silver is £46. Just as kitsch and covetable is a chain hung with a gold and enamel pistol by Miss Bibi, priced at £135. For those with deeper pockets there are treasures like New York-based Conroy & Wilcox's elegantly retro Russian emerald and 18ct gold ring, costing £1,330. Just one of many new designers in stock is Californian-trained gemmologist Jen Tozer, whose delicately strange bird's wing brooch is made from cultured pearl (£640).

Kirt Holmes

16 Camden Passage, N1 8ED (7226 1080/ www.kirtholmes.com). Angel tube. **Open** 11am-6pm Tue-Thur; 10am-6pm Sat; 11am-7pm Fri; noon-4pm Sun. **Credit** AmEx, MC, V.

Kirt Holmes is a popular fixture on Camden Passage, where Holmes's own handiwork is complemented by French designer Corpus Christi and Alex Monroe's feminine fripperies. A selection of vintage jewellery dating from the 1920s comes courtesy of Eclectica (once a near-neighbour on Camden Passage, now an online shop, *see p84*). Holmes's trademark chain mail and beading is still very much in evidence, though it evolves with each collection. One striking new design is a chain mail necklace of silver mesh with a scattering of black haematite beads that resembles an elegant shirt collar when worn (£265). Holmes is going more geometric, with precisely cut translucent haematite shards as pendants (£338). Earrings start at £120.

Lara Bohinc

149F Sloane Street, SW1X 9BZ (7730 8194/www.larabohinc107.co.uk). Sloane Square tube. **Open** 10am-6pm Mon-Fri; 10am-7pm Wed; noon-5pm Sun. **Credit** MC, V.

Lara Bohinc is going up in the world after moving premises from gritty(ish) Hoxton Square to the salubrious environs of Sloane Street. Postcode aside, the Slovenian-born designer's creations remain glossy and sleek with a high-fashion edge. Wearing a statement piece takes guts: one dominant theme is inspired by the high-carat bling of the ancient Egyptians, with chunky yellow gold or lacquered brass collars called Nefertiti (from £379) and a stunning pendant named for the sun god Ra (£175). Another bold theme that demonstrates Bohinc's originality and flair is the Solaris collection, where spheres of onyx, diamond and stark white agate cluster together resembling orbiting planets (from £780). Ultra-stylish bags, belts and sunglasses along similar lines complete the look.

Lesley Craze Gallery

33-35A Clerkenwell Green, EC1R 0DU (7608 0393/www.lesleycrazegallery.co.uk). Farringdon tube/rail. **Open** 10am-5.30pm Tue-Sat. **Credit** AmEx, DC, MC, V.

This Clerkenwell gallery is an internationally renowned showcase for jewellery (some 60 designers), metalwork and textiles with a thriving and ever-evolving programme of events. On the jewellery front, Yoko Izawa is proving popular with his curvaceous, juicy-coloured and affordable rings (£38 each), unexpectedly made out of knitted lycra and nylon. Another UK designer, Josephine Cullen, creates dramatic rings out of Whitby jet, usually associated with ornate Victorian mourning jewellery but in Cullen's hands transformed into something elemental, especially when combined with threads of gold or tiny, winking black diamonds (£238).

Nicholas James

16-18 Hatton Garden, EC1N 8AT (7242 8000/www.nicholasjames.com). Chancery Lane tube/Farringdon tube/rail. **Open** 10am-5.30pm Mon-Fri; 10am-5pm Sat. **Credit** AmEx, MC, V.

Owned by Nicholas Fitch (James is in fact his middle name), this minimalist shop exudes sophistication even in classy Hatton Garden, London's famous jewellery quarter. Predominantly working with platinum and white diamonds, the designs are simple but never boring: a deceptively simple rose-cut diamond sits in an ultra-modern, sharp-edged setting (£3,695). Meanwhile, designs experimenting with more colour include rose gold rings embellished with natural brown diamonds (from £795). Over at 9 Cross Street, Fitch has opened a gallery to showcase other designers' work, whether international or home-grown, in addition to his own creations.

For gallery see index.

Solange Azagury-Partridge

187 Westbourne Grove, W11 2SB (7792 0197/www.solangeazagurypartridge.com). Notting Hill Gate or Westbourne Park tube. **Open** 11am-6pm Mon-Sat. **Credit** AmEx, DC, MC, V.

Flamboyance and originality are what this designer does best so it's perhaps no coincidence that she didn't receive any formal training. The Kinetic range boasts plenty of high-wattage sparkle, with rings in the shapes of Catherine wheels, mazes, mirror balls and stars – all of them generously sprinkled with diamonds (from £7,200). Quite different is the Enamels range, where highlights are rings emblazoned with blocks of ice-cream coloured enamel and a Union Jack of royal blue enamel and rubies (£14,000). Yet more avant-garde is the Beauties range (from £820), where a gold ring has been manipulated into script spelling out the word 'sexy'.

Theo Fennell

169 Fulham Road, SW3 6SP (7591 5000/ www.theofennell.com). South Kensington tube. **Open** 10am-6pm Mon-Sat. **Credit** AmEx, DC, MC, V.

Seriously luxe jewellery meets rock'n'roll at Theo Fennell; you'd never guess he'd been on the scene for more than 20 years. Signature motifs include serpents, devils and arrow-pierced hearts: an Ampoule pendant of white brilliant-cut diamonds topped off with a black diamond snake will set you back £5,000; a Bitten Apple pendant in green tsavorite and diamond is £2,400. Silverware and men's jewellery – equally unsuitable for the faint of heart – are also available: the horn-shaped white gold and pave-cut ruby cufflinks (from £2,750 a pair) are sure to turn heads in a morning business meeting.

For branch see index.

Wint & Kidd

5 The Courtyard, Royal Exchange, EC3V 3LQ (7908 9990/www.wintandkidd.com). Bank tube. **Open** 10.30am-5.30pm Mon-Fri. **Credit** AmEx, MC, V.

Memorably named for the villains in *Diamonds Are Forever*, Wint & Kidd specialises in white and 'fancy' diamonds – that is, the rare coloured varieties. Its 'Brivka Moment' is a charming, not to mention sensible, service (named after the paper that certified diamonds come wrapped in). Select a loose stone, present it to the one you love and return to the shop together to design the setting around it. It's not all bespoke rings – there are also fabulous ready-to-wear pieces. A glittering bracelet studded with alternating pink and white diamonds worthy of Marilyn Monroe in *Gentlemen Prefer Blondes* costs a cool £13,450; at the other end of the financial spectrum are pretty sea horse and ladybird pendants shimmering with tiny diamonds for £500.

For branch see index.

Wright & Teague

35 Dover Street, W1S 4NQ (7629 2777/ www.wrightandteague.com). Green Park tube. **Open** 10am-6pm Mon-Fri; 10am-5pm Sat. **Credit** AmEx, MC, V.

Gary Wright and Sheila Teague met at St Martins and set up their business in 1984. After a decade on Grafton Street, they settled into this revamped 'e-boutique' on Dover Street. Despite the Mayfair setting, a large portion of the jewellery is affordable, with a set of silver Gala bangles with charms costing from £240, and a ring depicting Pegasus from £150. Staying in a mythological vein is the Cybele pendant for £150 – a round disc of silver cross-hatched to resemble the surface of the moon and named after the goddess of nature and fertility. If you can afford to go higher, the Delphi ring in yellow gold set with an amethyst pear is W&T's version of a solitaire ring and costs £1,100. Pendants, rings and bracelets are also available for men and children.

Also check out...

Alex Monroe

9 Ilisse Ward, SE17 3QA (7703 8507/ www.alexmonroe.com). Elephant & Castle tube. **Open** 10am-6pm Mon-Fri. **No credit cards.**

Monroe's whimsical jewellery is fashioned from silver and gold-plated silver, and features toadstool necklaces and bumblebee charm bracelets (from £72).

Anna Lou of London

11 Newburgh Street, W1F 7RW (7434 1177/www.annalouoflondon.com). Oxford Circus tube. **Open** 10.30am-7pm Mon-Sat; noon-5pm Sun. **Credit** DC, MC, V.

Trend-led bright colour and bold design with plenty of sparkle.

Boodles
1 Sloane Street, SW1X 9LA (7235 0111/ www.boodles.com). Knightsbridge tube.
Open 10am-6pm Mon-Sat. **Credit** AmEx, DC, MC, V.
Established in 1798, Boodles now combines classic design with contemporary flair.
For branches see index.

Butler & Wilson
189 Fulham Road, SW3 6JN (7352 3045/www.butlerandwilson.co.uk). South Kensington tube. **Open** 10am-6pm Mon-Sat; 10am-7pm Wed; noon-6pm Sun. **Credit** AmEx, MC, V.
B&W has long branched out from antiques and art deco to include semi-precious stones and, since 2007, a men's collection.
For branches see index.

Cartier
175-176 New Bond Street, W1S 4RN (7408 5700/www.cartier.com). Green Park tube. **Open** 10am-6pm Mon-Sat. **Credit** AmEx, DC, MC, V.
Jewellery and watches for those with serious cash to splash.
For branches see index.

Dinny Hall
200 Westbourne Grove, W11 2RH (7792 3913/www.dinnyhall.com). Notting Hill Gate tube. **Open** 10am-6.30pm Mon-Wed, Fri; 10am-7pm Thur; 10am-6pm Sat; noon-5pm Sun. **Credit** AmEx, MC, V.
Dinny Hall's collections are elegant, affordable and very wearable. She has also has concessions in Liberty and Selfridges.

Erickson Beamon
38 Elizabeth Street, SW1W 9NZ (7259 0202/www.ericksonbeamon.com). Sloane Square tube. **Open** 10am-6pm Mon-Fri; 11am-5pm Sat. **Credit** AmEx, MC, V.
Eclectic, sparkly, fashion-led show-stoppers are the order of the day here.

French's Dairy
13 Rugby Street, WC1N 3QT (7404 7070/ www.frenchsdairy.com). Holborn or Russell Square tube. **Open** 11am-6pm Mon-Fri; 11am-4pm Sat. **Credit** AmEx, MC, V.
Behind the beautifully tiled frontage lies a lovely collection of bold, contemporary jewellery by the likes of Philippe Ferrandis and Anton Heunis.

Garrard
24 Albemarle Street, W1S 4HT (0870 871 8888/www.garrard.com). Bond Street or Green Park tube. **Open** 10am-6pm Mon-Fri; 10am-5pm Sat. **Credit** AmEx, MC, V.
Money is no object if you're shopping at this venerable store, with gems as big as gobstoppers set in platinum and gold.
For branch see index.

Georg Jensen
15 New Bond Street, W1S 3ST (7499 6541/www.georgjensen.com). Bond Street or Green Park tube. **Open** 10am-6pm Mon-Sat. **Credit** AmEx, DC, MC, V.
Original designs that move from sleek minimalism to a more vintage aesthetic with the 2008 Heritage Collection. Also has a men's collection.
For branch see index.

Anna Lou of London

Gill Wing
182 Upper Street, N1 1RQ (7359 4378/ www.gillwing.co.uk). Highbury & Islington tube/rail. **Open** 10am-6pm Mon-Sat; noon-5pm Sun. **Credit** MC, V.
Contemporary designers, including Grainne Morton, who works with 'found' material.

Jacqueline Rabun
32 Grosvenor Crescent Mews, SW1X 7EX (7245 0524/www.jacquelinerabun.com). Hyde Park tube. **Open** 10.30am-6pm Mon-Fri; noon-5pm Sat. **Credit** AmEx, MC, V.
Features Jacqueline Rabun's own designs as well as pieces she designs for Georg Jensen.

Links of London
28 Ludgate Hill, EC4M 7DR (7236 5564/ www.linksoflondon.com). St Paul's tube.
Open 9.30am-6pm Mon-Fri. **Credit** AmEx, DC, MC, V.
Links' Sweetie bracelet has become a classic. Extensive range of silver charms.
Branches: throughout the city.

Mappin & Webb
132 Regent Street, W1B 5SF (080 8141 0505/www.mappin-and-webb.co.uk). Piccadilly Circus tube. **Open** 10am-6pm Mon-Sat; 10am-7pm Thur; 11am-5pm Sun. **Credit** AmEx, DC, MC, V.
Founded in back in 1774, this famous and traditional jeweller is still going strong.
For branch see index.

Mikala Djørup
2 Gabriel's Wharf, 56 Upper Ground, SE1 9PP (7021 0011/www.djorup.net). Waterloo tube/rail. **Open** 11am-4.30pm Tue, Wed; 11am-6pm Thur-Sat; by app't Sun. **Credit** AmEx, MC, V.
Danish designer Djørup's diminutive shop is stocked with her own distinctive designs. Commissions are welcome.

Mikimoto
179 New Bond Street, W1S 4RJ (7629 5300/www.mikimoto.co.uk). Green Park tube. **Open** 10am-5.30pm Mon-Fri; 10am-5pm Sat. **Credit** AmEx, DC, MC, V.
Exquisite cultured pearls by the world-renowned specialists.

Nude Contemporary Jewellery
36 Shepherd Market, W1J 7QR (7629 8999/www.nudejewellery.co.uk). Green Park tube. **Open** 11am-7pm Mon-Fri; 11am-6pm Sat (longer hours in summer). **Credit** AmEx, DC, MC, V.
Stocking hard-to-find and up-and-coming designers from home and abroad.

Stephen Einhorn

210 Upper Street, N1 1RL (7359 4977/ www.stepheneinhorn.co.uk). Highbury & Islington tube/rail. **Open** 10am-6pm Mon-Sat. **Credit** MC, V.

Original designs that occasionally mix up precious metal and ancient wood, plus bespoke jewellery and commitment rings.

Stephen Webster Boutique

1A Duke Street, W1U 3EB (7486 6576/ www.stephenwebster.com). Bond Street tube. **Open** 10am-6pm Mon-Fri. **Credit** MC, V.

Decadent statement jewellery from this past Luxury Designer of the Year.

Secrets Shhh

41 Duke of York Square, Sloane Square, SW3 4LY (7259 9400/www.secrets-shhh.eu). Sloane Square tube. **Open** 10am-7pm Mon-Sat; noon-6pm Sun. **Credit** AmEx, DC, MC, V.

The secret being that the diamonds used are actually simulated – which makes them cheaper and arguably more ethical.

For branch see index.

Sweet Pea

77 Gloucester Avenue, NW1 8LD (7449 9393). Chalk Farm tube. **Open** 10am-6pm Mon-Fri; 10.30am-5pm Sat. **Credit** AmEx, MC, V.

This gorgeous treasure box stocks designers like Alex Monroe and Laura Lee in addition to its own dainty pieces.

Tiffany & Co

25 Old Bond Street, W1S 4QB (7409 2790/ www.tiffany.com/uk). Green Park tube. **Open** 10am-6pm Mon-Wed, Fri; 10am-7pm Thur; 10am-6pm Sat. **Credit** AmEx, MC, V.

World-famous luxury jeweller best known for its distinctive pale mint packaging and heart pendants.

For branches see index.

William Prophet Gallery

11 Lower Marsh, SE1 7RJ (7928 7123/www.williamprophet.com). Waterloo tube/rail. **Open** 9.30am-6pm Mon-Sat. **Credit** MC, V.

Fun, contemporary designs punctuated with spots and slashes of bright colour.

Antique & vintage

Berganza

88-90 Hatton Garden (entrance in Greville Street), EC1N 8PN (7404 2336/www.berganza.com). Chancery Lane tube/ Farringdon tube/rail. **Open** 10am-5pm Mon-Sat. **Credit** AmEx, MC, V.

Among the look-at-me sparkle and glitter of Hatton Garden, Berganza has a more subtle appeal, with its array of antique and period stones and displaced heirlooms rescued from home and abroad. Most of the stock comes in the form of rings, each displayed in its threadbare velvet box in the shop window next to a traditional hand-written provenance label. Georgian, Victorian, Edwardian and art deco styles are all represented, in addition to a selection of stylish 1940s and '50s one-offs. The website contains useful histories of each period, as well as showcasing the evolving selection of treasures on offer. Prices start from just over £200.

Eclectica

www.eclectica.biz

The Angel shop closed a couple of years ago but you can still buy Eclectica's vintage costume jewellery online and from Kirt Holmes (*p80*) and John Lewis Oxford Street (*p15*).

Merola

195 Fulham Road, SW3 6JL (7351 9338/ www.merola.co.uk). South Kensington tube. **Open** 10am-6pm Mon, Tue, Thur-Sat; 10am-7pm Wed; 2-6pm Sun. **Credit** AmEx, MC, V.

The bang-up-to-date jostle for space with covetable vintage pieces, such as Kenneth Lane's fabulous retro earrings.

Engraving

ACS Engraving

Basement, 49 Maddox Street, W1S 2PQ (7629 2660/www.acs-engraving.co.uk). Oxford Circus tube. **Open** 9.30am-5pm Mon-Thur; 9.30am-4.30pm Fri. **No credit cards.**

Bennett & Thorogood

Stand 109, Basement, Grays Antique Market, 58 Davies Street, W1K 5LP (7408 1880). Bond Street tube. **Open** 10am-4.30pm Mon-Fri. **No credit cards.**

Watches

P Cyrlin & Co

Stand 141, Grays Antiques Market, 58 Davies Street, W1K 5AB (7629 0133/www.cyrlin.co.uk). Bond Street tube. **Open** 11am-4pm Mon-Fri. **Credit** AmEx, DC, MC, V.

Vintage watches by Rolex, Cartier, Patek Philippe and the like, with many hard-to-find limited-editions, priced at £2,000-£4,000.

Vintage Watch Company

24 Burlington Arcade, W1J 0EA (7499 2032/www.vintagewatchcompany.com). Green Park tube. **Open** 10.30am-5.30pm Mon-Sat. **Credit** AmEx, MC, V.

Vintage Rolex specialist (Patek Philippe watches are also sold), including Oysters and rare Sport Rolexes: prices start at £2,100.

Watches of Switzerland

16 New Bond Street, W1S 3SU (7493 5916/ www.watches-of-switzerland.co.uk). Bond Street or Green Park tube. **Open** 10am-5.30pm Mon-Sat. **Credit** AmEx, DC, MC, V.

Sells, services and repairs luxury Swiss timepieces. Breitling, Longines, Omega and Chopard are among the 29 brands sold.

Branches: (including Jaeger-LeCoultre Boutique, Rolex Boutique) throughout the city.

In gold we trust

The uncertainty of the world economic outlook in 2008, coupled with the traditional reliance on gold as a safe investment, meant that Reuters was predicting record gold prices as this guide went to press, estimating that the metal's value will have risen by around 30 per cent by the end of 2008.

Both the bling and vintage trends of the past few years have meant a renewal in the popularity of gold among people who might have previously associated it with Ratners' sovereign rings, Elizabeth Duke at Argos (as name-checked by Goldie Lookin Chain), motherly conservatism or the latino gangster image (à la Tony *Scarface* Montana); today, the fashion crowd's penchant for chunky chains and bracelets and the film-star vintage jewellery look epitomised by **Lara Bohinc** (*see p80*) means gold is the metal *du jour* once again – silver just doesn't have the same sexiness, and, in excess, is in danger of eliciting the Goa new-age hippie look. The bling trend may have now waned, yet gold looks set to stay as the metal of choice for many designers.

However, with current swings in the price of gold, designers are turning to more lightweight designs to appeal to the shopper with shallower pockets, sometimes using hollowed-out gold or gold together with non-traditional materials like coloured plastics or wood. And with gold mainstream once more, the range of affordable gold-plated pieces has increased hugely, with the cabinets of on-trend boutiques and concept stores such as **Sefton** (*see p36*) and **Beyond the Valley** (*see p19*) displaying gold-plated pendants, rings, earrings and bracelets from the likes of **Zoe & Morgan** (www.zoeandmorgan.com) and **Alex Monroe** (*see p82*). Traditional jewellers, as well as contemporary places like **ec one** (*see p80*), can also gold-plate silver (or other) jewellery for you, either in-house or by out-sourcing; you'll pay around £25 to gold-plate a thin chain with a small pendant (or to replate once the gold has worn off).

Just don't forget the fake tan (pale skin and gold don't mix well).

Camden Passage

Angel's pedestrianised crooked alley mixes 19th-century charm with some seriously stylish boutiques.

One of the attractions of antiques and boutique shopping is that very special thrill of a unique or unusual find, and visitors to Islington's Camden Passage are unlikely to be disappointed on that score: expect to stumble across anything from Marmite-flavoured chocolates and Nigerian waistcoats to Regency candle snuffers and 1940s bicycle spokes. The alleyway, running between Islington High Street (near Angel tube) and the southern tip of Essex Road, is a glorious throwback to 19th-century London, with Victorian lamp-posts, wonky paving, smart traditional shopfronts and a time-warp pub, the Camden Head.

Antiques dealers, active throughout the week but especially energetic on Saturdays, hawk their curiosities from shops and showrooms along the alley, such as the gloriously camp **Jewels by Count Alexander** (www.countalexander. co.uk), or from stalls, like those around **Pierrepont Arcade** (*see p161*), set back in nooks and crannies. There are lots on the corner of Charlton Place and opposite the Camden Head. You really can't miss them, so here's our pick of the best of the other shops.

Coming from Angel tube, you'll first pass some lovely gems on connecting Islington High Street, among them cute but pricey shoe boutique **Lollipop** (*see p71*), which stocks strappy heels and stylish pumps from the likes of the Jackson Twins and Chie Mihara. On Camden Passage proper, your first stops might include **Christina's Boxes** (no.8, 07780 961663), purveyor of tasteful lacquered antique boxes, and **Esme** (no.6, 7704 9617), for unique antique jewellery. The nearby **Japanese Gallery** at no.23 sells and displays 18th- and 19th-century oriental prints, while **Vincent Shoe Store** (no.19) stocks fun and hard-wearing children's shoes from Sweden.

Keep ambling north to find **Kirt Holmes** (no.16, *see p81*); his chain mail-style jewellery is perennially popular, and his smart monochrome shop – which also stocks pieces by Alex Monroe and Eclectica – is a chic standout from the chaos that can prevail elsewhere along the alley. On the other of the street, on the corner of Charlton Place, you'll find **Dominic Crinson** (no.27, *see p149*), for beautifully patterned and extremely contemporary wall tiles. The ladies' vintage collection at **Annie's** (no.12, *see p56*), diagonally opposite, is particularly strong on wedding dresses from the Victorian era to the 1950s, and she's got a fab stock of pretty '30s tea dresses; Kate Moss is said to be a fan. Which brings us nicely on to **Frost French**, the first standalone boutique of Kate's pal, Sadie (no.22-26); rumours were flying that the brand was in trouble as this guide went to press, but for now, at least, it makes an appropriate neighbour to two similarly stylish clothes shops: **Susy Harper** (no.35, *see p28*), who recently moved her Cross Street store here, selling upmarket, structured-yet-floaty linen womenswear, and ethical boutique **Equa** (no.28, *see p29*). The designers you'll find at the latter – such as Annie Greenabelle, Eden and Wildlife Works – use organic materials and fairtrade practices in their products, and the shop celebrated its third birthday in 2008 with a smart refurb.

Check out the life-size suit of armour outside the **Furniture Vault** (no.50), before moving on to a profoundly more modern gentleman's outfitters, the **African Waistcoat Company** (no.33, *see p54*). Here, traditional, bright and eye-catching fabrics hand-woven by Nigeria's Yoruba weavers are perfectly tailored to fit around any waist by the Old Etonian owner Calum Robertson.

For some gastronomic respite, your eating and drinking options along Camden Passage include the **Elk in the Woods** (no.39), for a hearty main or a sandwich or snack (the french fries and halloumi and beetroot sandwiches are recommended) and a decent pint; **Macondo** (no.20), for healthy and not-so-healthy Latin American snacks; and, if you get here early – which you'll need to do if you want to make the most of the antiques – the **Breakfast Club** (no.31), which is a consistent winner on the breakfast front.

Make sure you save some of your daily calorie-count for **Paul A Young Fine Chocolates** (no.33; *see p239*), however. In autumn 2008, this chocolatier was promoting a limited edition range of British-themed flavours, including worcester sauce and port and stilton – choices for the less adventurous are just as delicious.

For more details on these and other shops in Camden Passage, visit www.camdenpassageislington.co.uk.

Cleaning & Repairs

Dry-cleaners

The **Textile Services Association (TSA)/Dry-Cleaning Information Bureau** (8863 7755, www.tsa-uk.org) will help you find a reputable local launderer or dry-cleaner, and provide advice on how to complain about a member dry-cleaner.

Blossom & Browne's Sycamore

73A Clarendon Road, W11 4JF (7727 2635/ www.blossomandbrowne.com). Holland Park tube. **Open** 8.30am-5.30pm Mon-Wed, Fri; 8.30am-4.30pm Thur; 8.30am-3pm Sat. **Credit** MC, V.
With royal warrants aplenty, you know your clothes are in good hands. Prices aren't too steep and there's a collection and delivery service (if you set up an account).
For branches see index.

Celebrity Cleaners

9 Greens Court, W1F 0HJ (7437 5324). Piccadilly Circus tube. **Open** 8.30am-6.30pm Mon-Fri. **No credit cards.**
Dry-cleaners to West End theatres and the ENO; an expert in specialist fabrics.
For branches see index.

Jeeves of Belgravia

8 Pont Street, SW1X 9EL (7235 1101/ collection & delivery service 8809 3232/www.jeevesofbelgravia.co.uk). Knightsbridge or Sloane Square tube. **Open** 8.30am-7pm Mon-Fri; 8.30am-6pm Sat. **Credit** AmEx, MC, V.
Jeeves isn't cheap, but you get what you pay for, and pick-up and delivery are free. Knitwear from £16.50.
Branches: throughout the city.

Lewis & Wayne

13-15 Elystan Street, SW3 3NU (7589 5075/www.lewiswayne.co.uk). South Kensington tube. **Open** 8am-5pm Mon-Fri; 8.30am-12.30pm Sat. **Credit** MC, V.
Long-standing dry-cleaners specialising in vintage clothes, textiles and wall hangings.
For branch see index.

Master Cleaners

189 Haverstock Hill, NW3 4QG (7431 3725/ www.themastercleaners.com). Belsize Park tube. **Open** 8am-7pm Mon-Wed, Fri; 8am-6pm Thur, Sat; 10am-4pm Sun. **Credit** AmEx, MC, V.
Specialises in wedding dresses, designer and vintage garments. A day dress costs from £11.50, or £17.50 using the gentler, greener F-clean process.

Peters & Falla

281 New King's Road, SW6 4RD (7731 3255). Parsons Green tube. **Open** 8.30am-6.15pm Mon-Fri; 9.30am-5.30pm Sat. **Credit** MC, V.
Established dry-cleaners that gives leathers and suedes a new lease of life; from £45 for a leather jacket. It also does repairs.
For branches see index.

Valentino

56B New Oxford Street, WC1A 1ES (7436 1660). Tottenham Court Road tube. **Open** 8.30am-6pm Mon-Fri; 9am-1pm Sat.
Good value dry cleaner specialising in suede, leather and delicate designer pieces.

Washington Dry Cleaners

18 Half Moon Street, W1J 7BF (7499 3711). Green Park tube. **Open** 8am-6pm Mon-Fri; 9am-1pm Sat. **No credit cards.**
Competitively priced all-round dry-cleaner.
For branch see index.

Laundries

White Rose Laundries

16 Hinde Street, W1U 2BB (7935 6306/ www.whiteroselaundries.co.uk). Bond Street tube. **Open** 8am-7pm Mon-Fri; 9am-4.30pm Sat; 11am-3pm Sun. **Credit** MC, V.
For branches see index.

Repairs & alterations

British Invisible Mending Service

32 Thayer Street, W1U 2QT (7935 2487/ www.invisible-mending.co.uk). Bond Street tube. **Open** 8.30am-5.30pm Mon-Fri; 10am-1pm Sat. **No credit cards.**
For 70 years, this family business has been perfecting its reweaving techniques (threads are extracted from a hidden section of the garment). From £40 per hole (plus VAT).
For branch see index.

Designer Alterations

220A Queenstown Road, SW8 4LP (7498 4360/www.designeralterations.com). Queenstown Road rail. **Open** 9am-6pm Mon-Wed, Fri; 9am-8pm Thur; 10am-4pm Sat. **Credit** MC, V.
Julia Dee's 15-year-old company employs some 20 tailors to restyle, alter and repair your favourite items. A wardrobe 'rehab' service is offered (from £20).
For branch see index.

First Tailored Alterations

85 Lower Sloane Street, SW1W 8DA (7730 1400). Sloane Square tube. **Open** 9am-6pm Mon-Sat. **Credit** MC, V.
This traditional tailor is particularly good with delicate fabrics like chiffon and silk.
For branch see index.

KS Tailoring Services

Lower Ground Floor, 13 Savile Row, W1S 3NE (7437 9345). Green Park or Piccadilly Circus tube. **Open** 9.30am-5.30pm Mon-Fri; 10am-2pm Sat. **No credit cards.**
Known for its alteration of suits and shirts.
For branch see index.

Manuela Alterations

Oriel Court, Heath Street, NW3 6TE (7431 9283). Hampstead tube. **Open** 10am-6pm Mon-Fri; 10am-5pm Sat. **No credit cards.**
Regulars are full of praise for the speedy, good-value shortening and hemming services offered here.
For branch see index.

Stitchcraft

3rd Floor, 7 South Molton Street, W1K 5QG (7629 7919/www.stitchcraftalterations.co.uk). Bond Street tube. **Open** 9am-5pm Mon-Fri; 10am-4pm Sat. **No credit cards.**
Alterations, tailoring, remodelling – you name it, it does it. Reasonable rates too.
For branch see index.

Shoe repairs

The well-regarded chain **Timpson** (www.timpson.co.uk) has several branches in the city and **Russell & Bromley** (*see p72*) also has its own repairs service.

Fifth Avenue Shoe Repairers

41 Goodge Street, W1T 2PY (7636 6705). Goodge Street tube. **Open** 8am-6.30pm Mon-Fri; 10am-6pm Sat. **Credit** (over £20) AmEx, DC, MC, V.
Shoe and bag repairs, as well as key cutting in an old-fashioned environment.
For branch see index.

KG Shoes

253 Eversholt Street, NW1 1BA (7387 2234/www.cobbler.co.uk). Mornington Crescent tube. **Open** 8am-6pm Mon-Fri; 9am-1pm Sat. **No credit cards.**
For branch see index.

Michael's Shoe Care

4 Procter Street, WC1V 6NX (7405 7436). Holborn tube. **Open** 8am-6.30pm Mon-Fri. **Credit** AmEx, DC, MC, V.
For branches (including Fenchurch Shoe Care) see index.

Sole-Man

1 White Horse Street, W1Y 7LA (7355 2553). Green Park tube. **Open** 8am-6pm Mon-Fri; 9am-3pm Sat. **No credit cards.**
For branch see index.

Well Heeled

443 Bethnal Green Road, E2 9QH (7739 3608). Bethnal Green tube. **Open** 7am-5pm Mon-Fri; 8am-4pm Sat. **No credit cards.**
Proprietor Ken Holmes is strictly a needle and thread man – you won't catch him solving problems with a slick of glue. Great value service too.
For branch see index.

Specialists

Cashmere Clinic

Flat 5, 53 Redcliffe Gardens, SW10 9JJ (7584 9806). South Kensington tube. **Open** by appointment Mon-Fri. **No credit cards.**
Help is at hand if your knitwear needs some tender loving care. If the moths have munched on your favourite jumper, it'll cost £15 per hole to sort it.
For branch see index.

General Leather Company

56 Chiltern Street, W1U 7QY (7935 1041/ www.generalleather.co.uk). Baker Street tube. **Open** 10am-6pm Mon-Fri; 10am-5pm Sat. **Credit** AmEx, MC, V.
Top designer and manufacturer offers tailoring and repairs, plus leather wall tiles.
For branch see index.

Health & Beauty

Health & Beauty

Lemon Balm (and left). *See p93.*

Eye Company. *See p116.*

Ortigia. *See p95.*

Spa Illuminata (and left). *See p99.*

Health & Beauty Shops

Cosmetics & skincare

Becca

91A Pelham Street, SW7 2NJ (7225 2501/ www.beccacosmetics.com). South Kensington tube. **Open** 10am-6pm Mon-Sat. **Credit** AmEx, MC, V.

With its rich brown colour scheme and seductive lighting, Becca has a luxurious, decadent feel. Australian founder Rebecca Morrice Williams, a former make-up artist, launched the brand when she couldn't find the perfect foundation, and is still very 'hands-on' in her approach. The focus is on achieving a radiant complexion, with a three-step system that begins with primer – a key product here, available in Hydrating or Mattifying versions (£30) – and a tinted base of Luminous Skin Colour or Shimmering Skin Perfecter (£32). We're big fans of the Beach Tint (£19) 'crème stain' for cheeks and lips, which imparts a dewy, natural-looking glow. The final step is a dusting of very fine finishing powder (£28). New for autumn 2008 is the smudge-proof, waterproof Ultimate Mascara (£17), which can be removed with warm water. Make-up artists are on hand to give you a revamp (from £45) or lesson (£90; £45 redeemable against products), and there's a bridal service. Becca caters for all skin colours and complexions.

Benefit

9-11 Foubert's Place, W1F 7PZ (7287 8645/ www.benefitcosmetics.com). Oxford Circus tube. **Open** 10am-7pm Mon-Wed, Fri, Sat; 10am-8pm Thur; noon-6pm Sun. **Credit** AmEx, MC, V.

You can almost wear a full face of Benefit make-up and still look the natural beauty – this kitschly packaged range, the brainchild of San Fran-based twins Jean and Jane Ford, is the place for anyone looking to tuck a few beauty cheats up their sleeve. Benefit's most celebrated product, Benetint (£22.50), the ruby liquid that brings a healthy glow to cheeks of any skin colour, now has a sister product in Posietint (£22.50), for a cute fresh-faced look that knocks off years. Beauty bag stalwarts also include Bad Gal mascara, which wins hands down over dearer brands, and Lemon Aid colour-corrective eyelid primer – brilliant for reviving computer reddened eyes. Equally effective is the new industrial strength Erase Paste concealer (£18.50). Alongside these tools are a range of shadows, blushes and lipsticks. New fragrance B Spot (£26.50) adds the finishing touch. Brow shaping, eyelash and brow tints are offered at shop-floor stations; bigger waxing jobs are undertaken downstairs.
For branches see index.

Cosmetics à la Carte

19B Motcomb Street, SW1X 8LB (7235 0596/www.cosmeticsalacarte.com). Knightsbridge tube. **Open** 10am-6pm Mon-Sat. **Credit** AmEx, MC, V.

Cosmetics à la Carte, in the same hands for 30 years, has enjoyed a steady following from local Sloane families throughout its lifetime; grandmothers bring their teenage granddaughters here for their first make-up lesson, thirtysomethings drop in for a seasonal make-up bag refresher, while brides-to-be visit in preparation for the big day. The small, stylish shop offers 'made-to-measure' make-up (it was the first company to do so) and skincare. Gone are the days of buying an eyeshadow trio because you like two of the shades. The click-in Colourbox system here allows you to fill up a palette with whichever shade you fancy (eye, lip and cheek colours cost between £10 and £25). And we're big fans of the Rose Dew Hyrating Primer (£30) to smooth out fine lines. Having trouble finding your perfect foundation? If one of the ready-made shades (£30) doesn't match your complexion perfectly, you can have one specially mixed for £45. Make-up artists are on hand to give advice, even if you don't opt for one of the renowned lessons (£40-£175). New for 2008/9 is the Skin Veil primer (£30) and Cover Tint mineral make-up (£30).

Dr Boo

22 North Cross Road, SE22 9EU (8693 4823/www.drboo.co.uk). East Dulwich rail. **Open** 10am-6pm Mon-Sat; 11am-5pm Sun. **Credit** AmEx, MC, V.

Set up in September 2005 by actress Kazia Pelka and her writer husband Brian Phillips, Dr Boo is an ever-expanding one-stop shop for local yummy mummies. The front of the shop is given over to cult health and beauty brands: there's a range of Susan Posnick and Becca make-up (a Becca representative comes in monthly for lessons costing £10, redeemable against products), Blink mascara, Tweezerman tools, REN and Dr Hauschka toiletries, plus harder-to-find lines like Suki organic toiletries and MOP haircare. Geo F Trumper grooming products are stocked for men, while the Mama Mio lotions are a stretchmark-preventing treat for pregnant women.

Fresh

92 Marylebone High Street, W1U 4RD (7486 4100/www.fresh.com). Baker Street tube. **Open** 10am-7pm Mon-Wed, Fri, Sat; 10am-8pm Thur; noon-5pm Sun. **Credit** AmEx, MC, V.

Boston-based company Fresh does a very fine line in sophisticated health and beauty products, made with premium ingredients and dressed up in irresistible packaging. Co-founders Lev Glazman and Alina Roytberg are pioneers of sugar as a beauty ingredient, and the sensual Sugar range is among the brand's most covetable; the heavenly Brown Sugar Body Polish (£42/400g) contains real brown sugar crystals and essential oils, while the SPF15 Sugar lip treatment combines reparative oils and natural waxes with the sweet stuff. Products certainly don't come cheap but the quality is clearly high. The most indulgent purchase has to be a pot of Crème Ancienne (£155/100g); it's made entirely by hand in a monastery in the Czech Republic and is so rich that it banishes any dryness instantaneously. Pretty apothecary-style eaux de parfum (£47.50/100ml) are also available, in enticing flavours such as Tobacco Caramel and Redcurrant Basil, and for autumn/winter 2008/9 the brand is launching a new make-up collection inspired by the wanton 'aristocratic indulgence of the 18th century' (Firebird mascara £17; Imperial Bedroom Face Pallete £32) plus a range of anti-ageing skincare products – we loved the rich-but-not-greasy Black Tea Age-delay face cream (£75/30ml) with its distinctive scent. Fresh's Fig Apricot scent is now ten years old and, to celebrate the anniversary, the brand has launched two new products for the range: a delectable bath and shower gel (£16.50/300ml) and a body cream (£42/200g).

HQ hair & beautystore

2 New Burlington Street, W1S 2JE (0871 220 4141/www.hqhair.com). Oxford Circus tube. **Open** 10am-6pm Mon, Sat; 10am-7pm Tue, Fri; 10am-8pm Wed, Thur. **Credit** AmEx, MC, V.

The wealth of products within this store, teamed with knowledgeable advice from in-house experts – not least Dominic Webb the products guru – mean you're sure to find just what you're looking for. It's a store that doubles-up as a salon offering hairdressing and beauty services including waxing, spray tanning and even the odd holistic health treatment like Hopi ear candles treatment. Product lines are extensive with the clutch of new arrivals including YonKa, the French skin care range, Frederic Fekkai hair products and Slikit cordless ceramic straightening irons, plus the luxury make-up range Becca. As well as the original website, there's one dedicated to the boys: www.hqman.com.

Korres

124 King's Road, SW3 4TR (7581 6455/ www.korres.com). Sloane Square tube. **Open** 10am-7pm Mon-Sat; noon-6pm Sun. **Credit** AmEx, MC, V.
See p95 **Natural selection**.

Liz Earle Skincare

38-39 Duke of York Square, King's Road, SW3 4LY (7730 9191/www.lizearle.com). Sloane Square tube. **Open** 10am-7pm Mon, Thur-Sat; 10.30am-7pm Tue; 11am-5pm Sun. **Credit** AmEx, MC, V.
See p95 **Natural selection**.

Lost in Beauty

117 Regent's Park Road, NW1 8UR (7586 4411/www.lostinbeauty.com). Chalk Farm tube. **Open** 10.30am-7pm Mon-Fri; 10.30am-6.30pm Sat; noon-5.30pm Sun. **Credit** AmEx, MC, V.

Kitted out with vintage shop fittings, this chic new Primrose Hill boutique stocks a well-edited array of beauty brands, including Phyto, Australian brand Jurlique (newly repackaged), Caudalie, Dr Hauschka Rodial, REN, ZO1 sun-care products and Butter London nail polish with supremely covetable colours; other cult brands stocked include Becca make-up, the retro-packaged Rosebud Salve, Chantecaille make-up and skincare, Bumble & Bumble hair products and Belmacz Oyster Pearl translucent face powder. Make-up artist Georgie Hamed (a regular on glossy fashion shoots) offers private lessons and parties. Prices start from £60 and head upwards. There's also a choice selection of vintage jewellery.

Lucy Backhouse

136 Crouch Hill, N8 9DX (8342 8020). Finsbury Park tube/rail then W7 bus. **Open** 9am-6pm Tue-Fri; 10am-6pm Sat; noon-4pm Sun. **Credit** MC, V.

Walking through this shop's doors is a little like wandering into a dressing room in a pre-revolution court of Versailles. The emphasis at the newly named Lucy Backhouse (previously called Joy, the shop has now taken on the name of its owner) is on femininity with deep aubergine coloured walls and mirror-lined shelves displaying suitably pretty wares. Scent lines from E Coudray, Miller Harris and Ombre Rose, among others, reflect the ethos, while the beauty lines are generally natural (think REN, Neal's Yard and Earth Friendly Baby). There are also soya-based candles and Backhouse herself gives facials and massages in the on-site therapy rooms or at your home.

Neal's Yard Remedies (eco)

15 Neal's Yard, WC2H 9DP (7379 7222/ www.nealsyardremedies.com). Covent Garden or Leicester Square tube. **Open** 10am-7pm Mon-Sat; 11am-6pm Sun. **Credit** AmEx, MC, V.

A forerunner of the organic movement in the early 1980s, Neal's Yard has retained a loyal following, despite competition from younger companies with similar ideologies. The prettily packaged products, in their distinctive blue-glass bottles to safeguard the ingredients, smell delicious without being overpowering, and prices are fairer than many organic products. Made in an eco-factory in Dorset, they run the gamut from lovely French soaps, hand washes and bath oils to sun creams, deodorants and essential oils, plus a mother-and-baby range. There's also a dispensary for a huge range of dried herbs. Our top picks are the quick-absorbing Orange Flower Facial Oil (£20), the gently foaming Palmarosa Facial Wash (£12) and the Melissa Hand Cream (£10). New for 2008 is a range of remedies designed to 'feed the skin from within', including the Mahonia Clear Skin Formula (£8), a tonic to be taken orally, and the Organic Beauty Oil (£10), containing essential fatty acids to improve skin elasticity and hydration. By the end of 2008, Neal's Yard will have 16 London stores, most with luxury treatment rooms offering a wide range of therapies.

Branches: throughout the city.

Organic Pharmacy (eco)

369 King's Road, SW10 0LN (7351 2232/www.theorganicpharmacy.com). Sloane Square tube, then 11, 22 bus. **Open** 9.30am-6pm Mon-Sat; noon-6pm Sun. **Credit** AmEx, MC, V.

Organic Pharmacy has gone from strength to strength with the recent opening of its fourth new store in Great Marlborough Street. The secret is its commitment to sourcing and creating products free from artificial preservatives, petrochemicals and harsh detergents. When you consider that the average lipstick user consumes five pounds (450g) of lipstick throughout her life, using products from the Organic Glam range makes sense. There are mineral eye shadow shimmers (£18) and lipsticks (£16.95), plus a recently introduced range of pencil eyeliners (£15) – ideal for sensitive eyes. Skincare products include the award winning Carrot Butter cleanser (£26.95) and a Mother and Baby Care range. A clinic staffed by trained homeopaths offers health assessments, food-intolerance testing and other treatments. There's also a line of supplements and tinctures including Immune Support (£10.99).

For branches see index.

Ortigia

55 Sloane Square, SW1W 8AX (7730 2826/www.ortigia-srl.com). Sloane Square tube. **Open** 10am-6.30pm Mon-Sat. **Credit** AmEx, MC, V.

See p95 **Natural selection**.

Screenface

48 Monmouth Street, WC2H 9EP (7836 3955/www.screenface.com). Leicester Square tube. **Open** 10.30am-6.30pm Mon-Sat; noon-5pm Sun. **Credit** AmEx, MC, V.

Professional make-up artists seek out Screenface for its high-quality, long-lasting make-up and tools of the trade. Fardel face and body paints, Blink mascara, Lord & Berry eye and lip liners and Screenface's own range of make-up are to be found here (eyeshadow £7.95; lipsticks £8.95). Haircare is of a similarly high standard (Joico, Fudge, Phyto), as are the make-up brushes and other tools. Special effects are big business: fake blood, adhesives and removers, plus all types of facial hair, from handlebar moustaches to mutton chops.

For branch see index.

Shu Uemura

24 Neal Street, WC2H 9QU (7240 7635/ www.shuuemura.com). Covent Garden tube. **Open** 10.30am-7pm Mon-Sat; noon-5pm Sun. **Credit** AmEx, MC, V.

There's a decidedly luminous and modern feel to the Shu Uemura boutique on Neal Street with its extensive palette of eyeshadows (from £13), concealers (from £15) and foundations. Alongside the bright trademark colours and subtle but equally excellent neutrals you'll find make-up tools worthy of the professionals. The company's world-renowned false-eyelashes border the main mirror; new in 2008 is the Tokyo lash bar with 12 new pairs (from £11), the icing on the cake to any party outfit. Because 'beautiful make-up starts with beautiful skin', there's also a skincare range including the cleansing oil, a beauty editors' favourite. The Iyashi (which means 'harmony') basement space offers a calm area in which to enjoy a trademark facial or eyelash extension. It also houses the smart Atelier, where you're taught how to apply the crazy colours on sale upstairs.

Space NK

8-10 Broadwick Street, W1F 8HW (7287 2667/www.spacenk.com). Oxford Circus, Piccadilly Circus or Tottenham Court Road tube. **Open** 10am-7pm Mon-Wed, Fri, Sat; 10am-8pm Thur. **Credit** AmEx, MC, V.

With some 24 stores across London, and more in the offing, Space NK could have easily swerved off the rails into soulless

Lemon Balm. See p93.

super-chain territory. The fact that it hasn't pays testament to founder Nicky Kinnaird's commitment to unearthing the latest cult beauty products from across the world. And not just any old products either – at Space NK, you can count on a meticulously edited range of top-quality items, produced by specialists in their field. You'll find winners such as the legendary cleanser from celebrated facialist Eve Lom (£78); perfect lipsticks by dedicated lip colour specialist Poppy King (aka Lipstick Queen); skincare by dermatologist Dr Brandt; By Terry make-up and skincare from Terry de Gunzburg, who created YSL's celebrated light-reflective concealer Touche Eclat; and a UK exclusive of coveted scented candles by NY's hottest florist, Belle Fleur. On the eve of its 15th birthday, Space NK is showing no signs of resting on its laurels. New lines of products are added all the time – recent additions include Elemental Herbology, Dayna Decker candles and super-high-end facecare from RéVive, whose Peau Magnifique will set you back an eye-watering £1,100 – and autumn 2008 will see the launch of Space NK's own line of fine fragrances and beauty products. For details of Spa NK, see *p99*.
Branches: throughout the city.

This Works

18 Cale Street, SW3 3QU (7584 1887/ www.thisworks.com). South Kensington tube. **Open** 10am-5pm Mon-Sat. **Credit** MC, V.
This Works, created by International Beauty Director for Condé Nast Asia Kathy Phillips, uses 100% pure essential oils in its cleanly packaged, sensual and effective products which are also free from parabens and petro-chemicals. The Enjoy Really Rich body lotion (£30/200ml) with shea butter and aloe vera is one of the best body lotions we've sampled. The equally good Active Oil (£35 for 30ml) for faces is ideal for those who find traditional moisturisers too heavy and is effective on oily skin. Recent introductions to the range include Perfect Cleavage (£35/50ml), which promises to plump and tone the neck, and Tired Eye serum, a blend of aloe vera, marine extracts and cucumber, which will have your peepers shining.

WholeMan

67 New Bond Street, W1S 1UA (7629 6659/ www.wholeman.co.uk). Bond Street tube. **Open** 10am-7pm Mon-Fri; 10am-6pm Sat; 11am-5pm Sun. **Credit** AmEx, MC, V.
Eveything about this New Bond Street boys' boutique is chic and sleek. It tends to 'body maintenance for men' and if the range of products is anything to go by, it really is a revolution in male beauty. On the ground floor you'll find hair and skincare products (unfussy brands such as Kiehl's and Perricone), displayed alongside Jean Paul Gaultier's make-up for men, plus the shop's own range of supplements. Developed in association with Dr Rajendra Sharma, medical director of the Diagnostic Clinic, these include formulas for male potency. Up the sweeping marble staircase are treatment rooms done up in masculine black and stone, with Bose docks to park your own iPod and an adjoining wet room so you can shower off every trace of massage oil. Wet shaves in reclining barber's chairs take place behind wooden screens off the chill-out area.

Body Shop

268 Oxford Street, W1C 1DS (7629 9365/ www.bodyshop.co.uk). Oxford Circus tube. **Open** 9.30am-8pm Mon-Sat; 11am-6.30pm Sun. **Credit** AmEx, MC, V.
Branches: throughout the city.

Brummells of London

www.brummelsoflondon.com
Named after dandy Beau, this men's website has classy products from the likes of Aqua di Parma and Shiseido Men.

Crabtree & Evelyn

Unit 3, The Piazza, WC2E 8RA (7836 3110/www.crabtree-evelyn.co.uk). Covent Garden tube. **Open** 10am-7pm Mon-Wed, Sat; 10am-7.30pm Thur; 11am-6pm Sun. **Credit** MC, V.
This US-born brand has some lovely ranges, including the paraben-free Naturals Collection and a selection of candles.
Branches: throughout the city.

Kiehl's

29 Monmouth Street, WC2H 9DD (7240 2411/www.kiehls.com). Covent Garden or Leicester Square tube. **Open** 10.30am-7.30pm Mon-Sat; noon-5pm Sun. **Credit** AmEx, MC, V.
London flagship of the New York skincare company. The lip balms and rich Crème de Corps (from £22.50) are cult products.
For branch see index.

Lush

Unit 11, The Piazza, WC2E 8RB (7240 4570/www.lush.com). Covent Garden tube. **Open** 10am-7pm Mon-Sat; 11am-6pm Sun. **Credit** AmEx, MC, V.
Strong-smelling products made with natural ingredients, in deli-style packaging (complete with use-by dates).
Branches throughout the city.

MAC Cosmetics

109 King's Road, SW3 4PA (7349 0022/ www.maccosmetics.com). Sloane Square tube. **Open** 10am-6.30pm Mon-Sat; noon-5.30pm Sun. **Credit** AmEx, MC, V.
Hour-long lessons on party looks (£25), or more hands-on 90-minute tutorials (£50). Redeemable against any purchase.
For branches see index.

Mankind.co.uk

www.mankind.co.uk
Premium male grooming products.

Molton Brown

18 Russell Street, WC2B 5HP (7240 8383/ www.moltonbrown.co.uk). Covent Garden tube. **Open** 10am-7pm Mon-Fri; 10am-6pm Sat; 11am-5pm Sun. **Credit** AmEx, MC, V.
A favourite body brand in hotel bathrooms, MB offers skin- and haircare products based on exotic plant extracts and essential oils.
Branches: throughout the city.

L'Occitane

149 Regent Street, W1B 4JD (7494 0467/ www.loccitane.com). Oxford Circus or Piccadilly Circus tube. **Open** 10am-7pm Mon-Wed, Fri, Sat; 10am-8pm Thur; 11am-5pm Sun. **Credit** MC, V.
Well packaged bath and body products, inspired by the flora of southern France.
Branches: throughout the city.

Origins

42 Neal Street, WC2H 9PS (7836 9603/ www.origins.com). Covent Garden tube. **Open** 10am-6.30pm Mon-Wed, Fri, Sat; 10am-7pm Thur; noon-6pm Sun. **Credit** AmEx, MC, V.

Pixi

22A Foubert's Place, W1F 7PW (7287 7211/www.pixibeauty.com). Oxford Circus tube. **Open** 11am-7pm Mon-Sat; noon-5pm Sun. **Credit** AmEx, MC, V.
Pretty candy-coloured lip glosses, sleek colour palettes and sparkly pots of glitter sit alongside sheer foundations at this cute pistachio-coloured boutique.

Zest

18 Broadwick Street, W1F 8HS (7437 3846/ www.zestessentials.com). Oxford Circus tube. **Open** 9am-7pm Mon-Fri; 10am-6.30pm Sat. **Credit** MC, V.
Pharmacy-cum-beauty shop selling men's, women's and baby skincare products. It now sells MBT trainers too.

Afro hair & beauty

Keep a place in your diary for the annual, and essential, **Afro Hair & Beauty** exhibition (7498 1795, www.afrohairshow.com). It's been running for over a quarter of a century and is held each May at Alexandra Palace.

Pak's

25-27 & 31 Stroud Green Road, N4 3ES (7263 2088/www.pakcosmetics.com). Finsbury Park tube/rail. **Open** 9am-8pm Mon-Sat; 10am-6pm Sun. **Credit** MC, V.
Established 27 years ago, Pak's is an Aladdin's cave of African and Afro-Caribbean hair and beauty products, with many exclusive and hard-to-find ranges. The flagship is a shop of two halves; the Wig Centre, on the left, offers an extensive array of wigs, weaves and extensions, both synthetic and human, alongside fake ponytails and hair pieces. Colours range from natural blond to black as well as kaleidoscopic blues, reds and pinks. The right-hand side Hair Centre is stocked to the rafters with hair and beauty products. Alongside names like Bedhead and Aveda are excellent moisturising haircare ranges Soft n' Free and Soft & Beautiful and various relaxers. Hair serums, oils, shines and polishers are a particular strength. Men are also catered for with shaving oils, aftershaves and ingrowing hair treatments. The store also has a wide range of combs, brushes, straightening irons and rollers.
For branches see index.

Also check out...

AfroEuro Hair & Beauty

209 Uxbridge Road, W13 9AA (8579 9595). West Ealing rail/207 bus. **Open** 9am-6pm Mon-Sat; 11am-5pm Sun. **Credit** MC, V.
Afro and European hair and beauty products, including permanent and clip-on hair extensions. A salon upstairs offers facials, manicures and waxing.

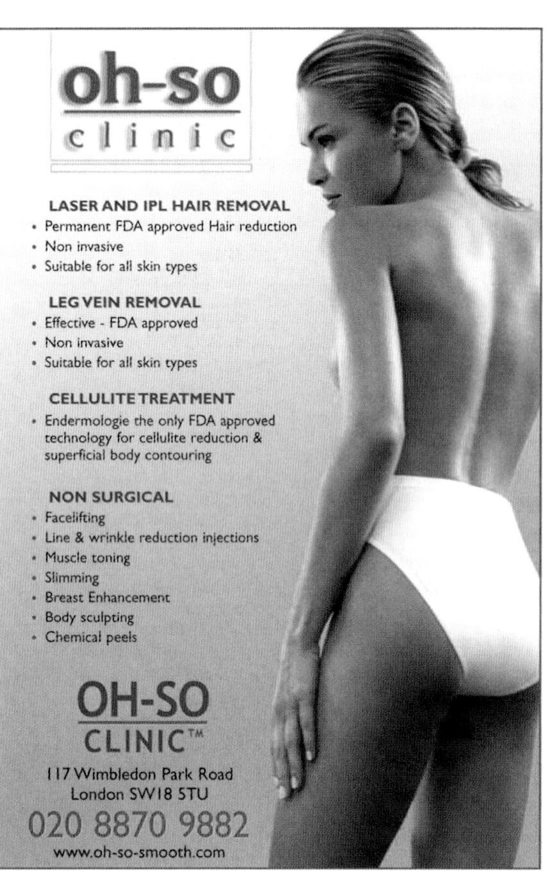
oh-so
clinic
LASER AND IPL HAIR REMOVAL
• Permanent FDA approved Hair reduction
• Non invasive
• Suitable for all skin types
LEG VEIN REMOVAL
• Effective - FDA approved
• Non invasive
• Suitable for all skin types
CELLULITE TREATMENT
• Endermologie the only FDA approved technology for cellulite reduction & superficial body contouring
NON SURGICAL
• Facelifting
• Line & wrinkle reduction injections
• Muscle toning
• Slimming
• Breast Enhancement
• Body sculpting
• Chemical peels
OH-SO
CLINIC™
117 Wimbledon Park Road
London SW18 5TU
020 8870 9882
www.oh-so-smooth.com

ZARVIS
LONDON

KORRES
NATURAL
PRODUCTS
124 KING'S
ROAD
CHELSEA,
SW3 4TR
FACE_BODY_HAIR_COLOR
ATHENS
KORRES
RECEIVE 20% DISCOUNT AT THE KORRES STORE
WHEN YOU QUOTE 'TIME OUT'.
Offer valid until March 31st 2009. Not valid in conjunction
with other offers or promotions.

Skin & Tonic
604 Roman Road, Bow, London E3 2RW
0208 980 5492
PAMPERED
PRIORI
ST.TROPEZ
The Ultimate Tan

Herbalists

Chinalife

101-105 Camden High Street, NW1 7JN (7388 5783/www.acumedic.com). Camden Town tube. **Open** 9am-8pm Mon-Sat; 9am-6pm Sun. **Credit** AmEx, MC, V.

Created with the aim of bridging the gap between Eastern and Western healthcare, Chinalife is a modern holistic health shop with wooden shelves piled high with a selection of teas, supplements and aromatherapy oils. Stylishly packaged skincare and body ranges feature all-natural active ingredients: some familiar (gingko and ginseng), others, like the anti-ageing reishi or moisture-boosting Chinese angelica, less well known in the West. We particularly like the herbal foot bath (£2.50), the flower water sprays (£3) and the jasmine face mask for dry skin (£3.95). Tea-lovers are spoilt for choice, with an impressive array of medicinal blends and flower- and berry-filled sachets. A chic tea bar also offers exotic concoctions infused with pomegranate syrup and crushed rosebuds and fragrant, spice-infused lattes. At the shop's rear, canvas panels suspended from the ceiling create an airy room where a therapist can help you feel right as rain with an energising lifestyle package, where acupuncture and Chinese Meridian massage (£55/hr) fullfil their promises. Next door at the AcuMedic clinic, a team of experts from China can offer solutions to just about anything, from infertility through to smoking addiction.

DR Harris

29 St James's Street, SW1A 1HB (7930 3915/www.drharris.co.uk). Green Park or Piccadilly Circus tube. **Open** 8.30am-6pm Mon-Fri; 9.30am-5pm Sat. **Credit** AmEx, MC, V.

In a city overtaken by characterless chain pharmacies, DR Harris has remained unfazed – it's hung on tight to its identity since 1790 and even boasts a royal warrant. A visit is much like stepping back through a door into times past. Polished wooden cabinets are filled with bottles and jars with old-fashioned shaving brushes and manicure kits. Its own elegantly packaged products have appealing names; there's Almond Oil Skinfood (£11.95/50ml), Bay Rum Aftershave (£18.95) and Old English Lavender Cologne (£25.95/100ml). Keep your eyes peeled too for Marvis toothpaste and Roger & Gallet soaps. Traditional it may be, but DR Harris appeals to modern sensibilities – none of the products are tested on animals and beauty editors continue to clamour over cult favourites such as the bright blue Crystal Eye Gel.

G Baldwin & Co

171-173 Walworth Road, SE17 1RW (7703 5550/www.baldwins.co.uk). Elephant & Castle tube/rail. **Open** 9am-5.30pm Mon-Sat. **Credit** AmEx, MC, V.

This old-school apothecary, specialising in natural products, from oils and balms to herbs, has been open on the Walworth Road since 1844. Swing by for top-notch dispensing advice and you might bump into long-time customers Michael Caine or Terence Stamp. Products include health tinctures, supplements, barks and flower remedies. You can also buy soap-making mould kits (£24.49, makes 6 bars) and a range of unfragranced Baldwin bases to make your own face creams, shampoos or shower gels.

Lemon Balm (eco)

76 Parkway, NW1 7AH (7267 3334/ www.lemonbalmonline.com). Camden Town tube. **Open** 10am-7pm Mon-Fri; 10am-6pm Sat. **Credit** (shop) MC, V.

This natural health and beauty shop/ complementary therapies clinic opened in spring 2008. The lovingly arranged shop has a fresh and soothing vibe and is stocked with a plethora of high-quality herbal and organic skincare brands – such as local company Circaroma (based in Islington), Figs & Rouge, Ruby Red, Trilogy and Long Barn – as well as bath and beauty products, aromatic flower-water sprays from the company's own label, natural soaps (including organic liquid soaps from Ecosopia; the almond version is sublime), room sprays made with essential oils, top-notch eco candles and house-blended herbal teas (try the Skin Tea to clarify skin and hair or Wild Meadow Tea if you have a spot of indigestion). Owner Paula Grainger trys hard to stock brands from small-scale producers based in the UK. Lemon Balm is also a lovely space in which to search for a unique and indulgent present; gift sets come in three sizes, priced from £13 to £40. The clinic offers massage, aromatherapy, acupuncture, reflexology, homeopathy and more from independent therapists, as well as Western herbal medicine from Grainger herself.

Nelsons

73 Duke Street, W1K 5BY (7629 3118/ www.nelsonspharmacy.com). Bond Street tube. **Open** 9am-6.30pm Mon-Fri; 10am-5.30pm Sat. **Credit** MC, V.

There's a cure for every ailment at this homeopathic pharmacy – which was the first of its kind when Ernst Louis Ambrecht opened it in 1860. In the 1930s, Dr Edward Bach began to sell his famous Bach Original Flower Remedies here. On other shelves you'll find pills and potions such as Menopause Care Tincture (£15), Pills for Brain Fatigue (£6.60) and Tennis Elbow Bursitis (£6.60). If you don't find what you're after, the friendly pharmacist will talk over symptoms and tailor-make a medicine for you using the vast 'potency bank' of more than 2,000 remedies. There's a peaceful clinic in the basement for massages, food-sensitivity testing, Alexander Technique lessons and homeopathy.

Sen

59 South Molton Street, W1K 5SN (7629 2243/www.senhealth.com). Bond Street tube. **Open** 11am-7pm Mon-Fri; 10am-7pm Sat; noon-6pm Sun. **Credit** AmEx, MC, V.

Sen's stylish and modern London boutiques look East for inspiration. Herbs have been used in traditional Chinese medicine for over 5,000 years to maintain the body's equilibrium and at Sen there are supplements and tablets to tackle all manner of ailments. Essential oil-infused foot soaks, massage oils and bath products are towards the rear of the shop, along with a splendid selection of teas, ranging from lychee, peppermint and jasmine to more unusual formulas – we were intrigued by the blend designed to promote and preserve luxuriant tresses. You can pop in for a takeaway fruit juice or stay on for an express massage and acupuncture session, with prices from £30 for a 20-minute shoulder, back and neck massage.

For branches see index.

Also check out...

Ainsworths

36 New Cavendish Street, W1G 8UF (7935 5330/www.ainsworths.com). Bond Street tube. **Open** 9am-6pm Mon-Fri; 9am-4pm Sat. **Credit** MC, V.

Manufacturer of around 3,300 traditional homeopathic remedies.

Culpeper

236D Fulham Road, SW10 9NB (7352 5603/www.culpeper.co.uk). Fulham Broadway tube. **Open** 9am-7pm Mon-Fri; 10am-6pm Sat; 11am-5pm Sun. **Credit** MC, V.

The oldest chain of herbal shops in England, Culpeper has aromatherapy-based skincare and hair products, candles, supplements and remedies.

For branch see index.

Farmacia Santa Maria Novella

117 Walton Street, SW3 2HP (7460 6600). South Kensington tube. **Open** 10am-6pm Mon-Sat. **Credit** AmEx, MC, V.

The minuscule London outpost of the famed Florentine pharmacy, founded by Dominican friars in 1221, sells beautifully packaged lotions, perfumes and soaps.

Perfumeries

See also above **Farmacia Santa Maria Novella.**

Angela Flanders

96 Columbia Road, E2 7QB (7739 7555/ www.angelaflanders-perfumer.com). Liverpool Street tube/rail then 26, 48 bus/ Old Street tube/rail then 55 bus. **Open** 9am-3pm Sun; by appointment Mon-Thur. **Credit** AmEx, MC, V.

Perhaps thanks to her former job as a costume designer, entering Angela Flanders' shop is a little like stepping back in to Victorian London. The small perfumery is redolent of her own creations, all of which are simply presented in packaging that exudes an air of Victoriana. The 15 signature scents, available in eau de toilette, eau de parfum, perfumed candles, room sprays, fragrant burning oils and perfumed lamp grains, include the woody Coromandel, vanilla-scented Parchment and summery Hesperides. There's also a range of colognes for men and women based on historic scents, scented accessories like linen water and moth bags made of French herbs, plus a bespoke perfume service in which Angela will create a scent unique to you.

L'Artisan Parfumeur

36 Marylebone High Street, W1U 4QD (7486 3435/www.artisanparfumeur.com). Baker Street tube. **Open** 10am-6.30pm Mon-Sat; noon-5pm Sun. **Credit** AmEx, MC, V.

It's no surprise to find that the heritage of L'Artisan Parfumeur is Parisian. The pretty Marylebone store is discreet, stylish and unique. Scents are grouped by 'family' ('Fresh' includes Ananas Fizz, a youthful pineapple scent, while 'Precious Wood' features scents like the spicy Timbuktu). Fragrances are aranged in tealight holders filled with scented muslin, which allow the perfume notes to breathe more easily than a tester spray. What's more, all the fragrances are designed to be used by both sexes. New scents are regularly added to the collection: new in autumn 2008 is the heady and tropical Fleur de Liane (£70/100ml), while additions to the organic body care Jatamansi range – scented with rose and bergamot – include a new candle (£34) and shower gel (£20).
For branches see index.

Diptyque

195 Westbourne Grove, W11 2SB (7727 8673/www.diptyqueparis.com). Notting Hill Gate tube. **Open** 10am-6pm Mon-Sat; noon-5pm Sun. **Credit** AmEx, MC, V.
Diptyque was filling the air with perfume when scented candles were but a twinkle in its competitors' eyes. Four decades on and its candles are still the standard bearers. With the 54 scented versions is a selection of colognes ranging from delicate to heady. New on the shelves in 2008 were L'Eau de L'Eau (£75/200ml) – a lightly scented water with notes of Italian green mandarine, clove leaves and cinnamon – and summery L'Eau de Néroli (£75/200ml), with Italian bergamot, neroli and orange blossom. In autumn 2008, Diptyque will launch a bodycare line in the bestselling fragrances Philosykos, L'Ombre dans L'eau and Tam Dao.

Jo Malone

150 Sloane Street, SW1X 9BX (7730 2100/ www.jomalone.co.uk). Sloane Square tube. **Open** 9.30am-6pm Mon, Tue, Sat; 9.30am-7pm Wed-Fri; noon-5pm Sun. **Credit** AmEx, MC, V.
Jo Malone's worldwide business began from the trademark facials she used to give 20 years ago and the sense of touch in beauty care still plays an important part in her empire: step into any store and you'll be treated to a complimentary hand massage to help you choose a fragrance, while the famous facials (plus body treatments) are still available (both for £125). Scentwise, the trademark 'fragrance combining' is designed to enable you to wear various scents at once to create one that's unique to you. Recent additions include Verbenas of Provence, a light and clean citrus fragrance, and the youthful nectarine blossom and honey.

Miller Harris

21 Bruton Street, W1J 6QD (7629 7750/ www.millerharris.com). Bond Street or Green Park tube. **Open** 10am-6pm Mon-Sat. **Credit** AmEx, MC, V.
Lyn Harris, creator of Miller Harris, uses only the finest natural materials in her unisex eaux de parfum (£70/100ml), eaux de toilette (£58/100ml), body oils (£28/100ml) and body lotions (£30/250ml); this, plus the gorgeous packaging, makes the perfumes some of the best quality and most covetable on the market, and have earned her a slew of discerning fans. Harris, who undertook years of formal training in both Paris and Grasse, sources raw ingredients from all over the world. Her iris comes from Florence, the violet leaf from France, jasmine from Egypt, while the particular orange flower she favours is Tunisian. Harris eschews the idea of a signature scent, instead using the phrase 'wardrobe of scents' to describe her philosophy of choosing scents depending on mood and occasion. Perfumes from the original range of 12, divided up by 'family', are still some of the bestsellers; all are completely individual and evocative – we're big fans of Fleur Oriental Geranium Bourbon and Figue Amère. Recent additions to the range have been the Noix de Tubéreuse Fragrance Balm (£34), plus a unique selection of top-quality blended black and oolong teas (£16/50g tea caddy) – a natural progression for Harris given their fragrant qualities. A bespoke service is available, for those with money to burn.
For branch see index.

Ormonde Jayne

12 The Royal Arcade, 28 Old Bond Street, W1S 4SL (7499 1100/www.ormondejayne.com). Green Park tube. **Open** 10am-6pm Mon-Sat. **Credit** AmEx, MC, V.
Antique gold wallcoverings and black glass chandeliers give the Ormonde Jayne store a sumptuous new look that befits the rich scents created by Linda Pilkington. Pilkington is passionate about her trade, sourcing ingredients herself in the Far East and Africa. All components are free from mineral oils, parabens and GM products, and staff are happy to discuss which scents would best suit you. There are just ten to choose from; our favourites include the elegant Champaca, with pink pepper and bamboo, and Ormande Woman (both £58/50ml for the eau de parfum). An extended range of scents is now available in the form of Parfum d'Or Naturel (£46/15ml) – concentrated, alcohol-free gold perfume purées with a base of natural sugars; smooth it over the décolletage and shoulders for an incandescent effect with a lasting fragrance. There are also body lotions, bathing oils and candles.

Roja Dove Haute Parfumerie

Urban Retreat, 5th Floor, Harrods, 87-135 Brompton Road, SW1X 7XL (7893 8797/ www.rojadove.com). Knightsbridge tube. **Open** 10am-8pm Mon-Sat; noon-6pm Sun. **Credit** AmEx, DC, MC, V.
Roja (pronounced Roger) Dove is a man who takes scent so seriously he asked an air steward not to come near him as her perfume was so offensive. From his dark and sumptuous perfumed eyrie in Harrods' Urban Retreat (*see p99*), the self-styled 'Professeur des Parfums' discovers clients' signature scents from an array of quality and, not surprisingly, very expensive scents in his collection. Some, like perfumes from Lalique, Nina Ricci, Acqua di Parma and Jean Patou, will be familiar, while others, like those from the Different Company, Piver and Clive Christian (who boasts the world's most expensive perfume) may provide ground for discovery. A one-hour consultation with the man himself is £250 (not redeemable against products); with a member of the team it's £50 (and redeemable).

Les Senteurs

71 Elizabeth Street, SW1W 9PJ (7730 2322/www.lessenteurs.com). Sloane Square tube/Victoria tube/rail. **Open** 10am-6pm Mon-Sat. **Credit** AmEx, DC, MC, V.
The shelves of James Craven's pretty Victoria boutique are laden with wares by prestigious perfumers, including stalwarts like Annick Goutal, Creed and Diptyque, and lesser-known makes such as Frédéric Malle's Editions de Parfums. One of the shop's attractions is the care given to those selecting gifts for others. Craven builds up a profile of the intended recipient by asking questions about looks, personality, favourite colours and even food. Les Senteurs always supplies a sample with each sale so that the perfume can be tested before the bottle is opened.

Studio Perfumery

170 Regent's Park Road, NW1 8XN (7722 1478). Chalk Farm tube. **Open** 10am-6pm Mon-Sat; noon-6pm Sun. **Credit** AmEx, MC, V.
Linda Read's invitingly pretty Primrose Hill shop presents a carefully selected collection of scents and candles. Welcome additions this year include Isabey's Gardenia, (£95 for 50ml) a glamorous and decadent scent first created in 1925. Studio Perfumery also does a fine line in candles: particularly noteworthy are the new candles and matching room scents (both £40) from interior designer (of the Champs-Elysées' Ladurée store fame) Jacques Garcia.

Also check out...

Floris

89 Jermyn Street, SW1Y 6JH (7930 2885/ www.florislondon.co.uk). Piccadilly Circus or Green Park tube. **Open** 9.30am-6pm Mon-Fri; 10am-6pm Sat. **Credit** AmEx, MC, V.
Traditional British perfume house known for conservative but reliable scents like Lily of the Valley and Night-scented Jasmin.

Parfums de Nicolaï

101A Fulham Road, SW3 6RH (7581 0922/ www.pnicolai.com). South Kensington tube. **Open** 10am-1pm, 1.30-6pm Mon-Sat. **Credit** AmEx, MC, V.
Patricia de Nicolaï comes from the Guerlain family and fragrances are produced in the company's Orléans factory.

Penhaligon's

125 Regent Street, W1B 4HT (7434 2608/ www.penhaligons.co.uk). Piccadilly Circus tube. **Open** 10am-7pm Mon-Wed, Fri, Sat; 10am-8pm Thur; noon-6pm Sun. **Credit** AmEx, MC, V.
Penhaligon's treads a neat line between heritage – founder William Penhaligon was barber to Queen Victoria's court – and the quiet luxury of today's scents.
Branches: throughout the city.

Zarvis London

4 Portobello Green, 281 Portobello Road, W10 5TZ (8968 5435/www.zarvis.com). Ladbroke Grove tube. **Open** by appointment Mon, Tue; noon-6pm Wed-Sat. **Credit** AmEx, MC, V.
All Vivian Zarvis's perfumes, bath products and scented accessories are made in England using natural ingredients.

Botanical beauty

Natural selection

Three growing brands with a flora-inspired ethos have now set up shop in the capital.

Beauty brands selling themselves as 'natural' are as common in the capital these days as free newspapers. But the following three growing brands stand out, not only for their sensual, incredible-smelling and effective products made from premium plant ingredients (pertaining to specific regions of Europe in the first two cases), but also for their gorgeous packaging, reasonable prices and no-nonsense approach. What's more, all three now have stand-alone shops in west London that demand a visit – both to check out the range of products, and for the beautifully designed interiors.

Skincare products from Greek brand **Korres** (*see p89*) are becoming a common feature of beauty boutiques and department stores like Liberty. With a heritage leading back to Athens's first homeopathic pharmacy, the company uses only naturally derived, nourishing ingredients, eschewing the use of synthetic materials such as petroleum-derived mineral oils and silicones. Products are based on Greek kitchen ingredients – such as coriander, honey, thyme, watermelon and yoghurt – and smell utterly irresistible; we're big fans of the Coriander Shower Gel (£7/250ml), Fig Body Butter (£11.50/150ml) and Yoghurt Cooling Gel (£15/150ml). As well as being attractively packaged, the accessibly priced products also deliver on their promises – which are refreshingly realistic in the first place. Korres' stylish shop on the King's Road features a beautiful oak counter and flooring, warm and helpful staff and an excellent range of gift boxes (£13.50-£23.50), as well as the full array of its skincare, make-up and haircare ranges.

Sicilian brand **Ortigia** (*see p90*) is currently making something of a splash in the capital for its exotically presented soaps and skincare, which come in handmade packaging covered in designs inspired by Italian palazzos, mosaics and tiles (making them perfect for gifts). Ortigia uses plants indigenous to Sicily to create its luxurious but well-priced toiletries; aromatic ingredients such as lavender, pomegranate, Sicilian lime, orange blossom and bergamot (the essential oil derived from the bitter orange tree) feature heavily, with base materials such as olive oil and almond oil strengthening the natural agenda.

All the products are highly aromatic; the new Bergamotto collection, including Bath & Shower Gel (£3.50/75ml), Body Milk (£20/300ml) and Hand Cream (£13/75ml), is sure to be a bestseller, and we love the classically packaged Almond Milk body cream (£18/250ml). The firm's first stand-alone London boutique opened in spring 2008 in a fittingly elegant building in Sloane Square.

Isle of Wight-based former beauty writer **Liz Earle** launched her eponymous skincare brand in 1995, but it's only since the opening of her shop on Duke of York Square (*see p89*) in 2007 that it's become better known to beauty editors and savvy shoppers. Based on botanical ingredients, most grown organically or harvested from sustainable wild sources, the streamlined range of products is, like Korres and Ortigia, pleasingly gimmick-free, as well as being notable for its absence of mineral oils and liquid paraffin waxes.

Items are lovingly arranged in the spacious, well-staffed and fresh-feeling shop (think dove-grey tones, slate, greenery and wood), which is full of helpful leaflets and books on skincare and green beauty. The new Superskin Moisturiser (£30/50ml) for mature skin contains cranberry and borage seed oils and rosehip oil to nourish and restore skin, while the Instant Boost Skin Tonic Spritzer (£10.75/200ml) uses the naturally active ingredients of pure aloe vera, camomile, cucumber and essential oils. Cleanse & Polish Hot Cloth Cleanser (a cream used with a muslin cloth; £12.25 for a starter kit) has an avid following. The selection of 'minis' (from £4.25) in the shop are a great way to introduce yourself to the range, and facials are also available (signature facial, £85/90mins).

Ortigia

Beauty Salons & Spas

London's hairdressers (*see pp106-113*) are offering an ever-growing list of beauty treatments. For the new spa at concept store **Shop at Bluebird**, *see p20*.

Agua

Sanderson Hotel, 50 Berners Street, W1T 3NG (7300 1414/www.sandersonlondon.com). Oxford Circus or Tottenham Court Road tube. **Open** 9am-9pm daily. **Credit** AmEx, MC, V.

Treatments: aromatherapy, body treatments, facials, manicures, massages, pedicures, swiss shower, waxing.

A labyrinth of high white curtains, this is London's most space-age, contemporary-feeling spa. Before your treatment you'll be taken into the communal area to chill out with a few magazines until your therapist comes to collect you. Treatments are carried out in cubicles separated by drapes – meaning that they're not as private-feeling as some would like; afterwards, however, you can cocoon yourself in one of the private booths with comfy beds, TVs and a refreshments menu. The Eve Lom facial (from £85) and Hot Stone massage (£115) are as popular as ever, but it's the Thai Yoga Massage (from £95/60mins) that really stands out here.

Ark Health & Beauty

146 Holland Park Avenue, W11 4UE (7243 8889/www.arkhealthandbeauty.com). Holland Park tube. **Open** 10am-7pm Mon, Fri; 10am-8pm Tue-Thur; 9.30am-6pm Sat; 11am-5pm Sun. **Credit** MC, V.

Treatments: aromatherapy, body treatments, eyebrow reshaping & tinting, eyelash tinting, facials, manicures, massages, osteopathy, pedicures, reflexology, reiki, waxing.

Our favourite branch of Shula Starkey's small chain is a blond wood and white-walled haven in Holland Park's posh stretch of shops and cafés. Products from the classy Dermalogica and Aromatherapy Associates ranges are used in treatments, and are also for sale. There's a popular manicure/pedicure area offering basic and luxury options, incorporating exfoliation, extended massage and hot mitts and booties. The treatment rooms are modestly proportioned, but smart and suitably soothing. An aromatherapy massage begins with a consultation to assess how the client is feeling; we had a morning appointment, so the therapist advised focusing on oils for light relaxation rather than a knock-out effect. The massage skipped arm and torso work to incorporate a mini facial using rose and frankincense oil; the result was an express ticket to La-La Land. Deep-breathing techniques and reviving oils brought the blissful treatment to a close. For those battling with the problems of very dry skin, the deep-moisturising massage, using Swedish techniques and a rich cream spiked with fragrant oils, is an enjoyable and practical alternative.

For branches see index.

Beauty Works West

8-9 Lambton Place, W11 2SH (7221 2248/www.beautyworkswest.com). Notting Hill Gate tube. **Open** 9.30am-8.30pm Mon-Fri; 10am-6pm Sat, Sun. **Credit** MC, V.

Treatments: body treatments, Endermologie, eyelash perming & tinting, facials, IPL hair removal, manicures, make-up, massages, non-surgical facelifts, pedicures, reflexology, threading, waxing.

Although terms such as 'celebrity' and 'red carpet' are daubed over the treatment menu like bronzing powder, this is a cheerful and unpretentious salon that welcomes clients with little dishes of fruit and nuts. Blending beauty and science is the aim, so high-tech gadgetry is incorporated into several treatments: this is the place to come for non-surgical facelifts, photo-rejuvenation and hair-removal treatments using laser technology or mesotherapy (one of several therapies devised by anti-ageing expert Dr Sister). Opt for the Ling facials if you want a thorough clean-out, while the Rodial A-List facial is one to get you looking your best just before a special event; an oxygen pipe is run over the face and neck to plump up the skin, followed by a facial massage with luscious unguents (our therapist's hands were as soft as a satin pillow). The high-tech treatment beds are a pleasure in themselves.

Bharti Vyas Holistic Therapy & Beauty Centre

24 Chiltern Street, W1U 7QU (7935 5312/www.bharti-vyas.com). Baker Street tube. **Open** 9am-6pm Mon, Tue, Thur, Sat; 9am-7pm Wed, Fri. **Credit** MC, V.

Treatments: alternative therapies, anti-cellulite treatments, body treatments, body wraps, electrolysis, eyebrow shaping & tinting, eyelash tinting, facials, holistic beauty therapies, laser hair removal, lymphatic drainage, massages, reflexology, threading, waxing.

Bharti Vyas's holistic principles have earned her widespread acclaim and a a star-studded client list. A visit to her Chiltern Street salon certainly lives up to the hype. The treatment rooms have recently been given a much-needed lick of paint: the icing on the cake at this salon, which puts its customers first. The treatments combine complementary therapies with modern technology, and the therapists take time to understand and tailor them to your lifestyle and requirements. The Harmonising Treatment (£120/90mins) aims to rebalance bodies strained by 21st-century stress and incorporates everything from a full-body massage and organic face mask to lymphatic drainage boosts, which inflate and deflate to boost circulation. While the latter may look rather outlandish, the whole experience left us feeling indulged and transformed.

Bliss London

60 Sloane Avenue, SW3 3DD (7590 6146/www.blisslondon.co.uk). South Kensington tube. **Open** 9.30am-8pm Mon-Fri; 9.30am-6pm Sat; noon-6pm Sun. **Credit** AmEx, MC, V.

Treatments: body treatments, eyelash tinting, facials, manicures, massages, micro-dermabrasion, pedicures, self-tanning, waxing.

Chic, sleek and results-focused, Bliss is a spa that means business. Turn up early to take full advantage of the nibbles in the relaxation area – and seriously, what's not to like about a spa that offers chocolate brownies, cheese, crackers and wine as pre-facial sustenance? – before settling into one of the stylishly minimal treatment rooms for some pampering. Signature treatments include the fabulous Blissage massages (from £90/60mins), hot salt scrubs (£95) and shrink wraps (£100), but it's the facials that really stand out. The triple oxygen treatment (£145/85mins) is astoundingly effective, combining intensive cleansing, extractions, masks and a good going over with an oxygen spray. The results were immediately visible and the resulting glow lasted over a week. Best of all, no time is wasted – a relaxing arm massage is given while a mask does its job, for example – so you really do get what you pay for.

Body Experience

50 Hill Rise, Richmond, Surrey TW10 6UB (8834 9999/www.bodyexperience.co.uk). Richmond tube/rail. **Open** 9am-8.30pm Mon-Thur; 9am-7.30pm Fri, Sat; 9am-5.30pm Sun. **Credit** AmEx, MC, V.

Treatments: body treatments, facials, makeovers, manicures, massages, pedicures, reflexology, self-tanning, waxing.

Attention to detail is unwavering at this chic Richmond day spa, from the orchids in the elegant, airy therapy rooms to the plush purple robes and generous array of cleansers and moisturisers in the changing rooms. Thanks to its Antipodean ownership, the spa has a subtle Australian influence – so woody, aromatic outback herbs are burnt to 'dispel negative energy' before treatments begin, and Li'Tya products, made from native Australian plant extracts, are offered alongside spa stalwarts Elemis, Shiseido, La Thérapie and Thalgo. A Kodo Melody massage with Maggie (£65/hr) was one of the best massages we've ever had, easing out the most recalcitrant of knots with wonderful thoroughness. Post-treatment, you can linger over a complimentary herbal tea and luscious fruit salad in the relaxation room with its chaises longues and lovely little walled terrace.

Cowshed

119 Portland Road, W11 4LN (7078 1944/www.cowshedclarendoncross.com). Holland Park tube. **Open** 9am-8pm Mon-Fri; 9am-7pm Sat; 10am-5pm Sun. **Credit** AmEx, MC, V.

Treatments: body treatments, eyebrow shaping & tinting, eyelash tinting, facials, manicures, massages, pedicures, prenatal treatments, self-tanning, waxing.

It's an innovative concept: fill your tum with a good square meal and have yourself a facial all-in-one. That's the deal at the Holland Park outpost of Babington House's indulgent Cowshed. The decor on the ground floor resembles a country house kitchen showroom, with a food counter crammed with cakes and a line of white leather chairs (each with their own mini retro TV), where manicures (£28/30mins) and pedicures (£45/60mins) are given and received. We had – and would recommend – a no pain, no gain Cowshed full-body massage with Kazumi (£65/60mins), using own-brand organic essential oils to ease away our aches and pains.

Elemis Day Spa

2-3 Lancashire Court, W1S 1EX (7499 4995/www.elemis.com). Bond Street tube. **Open** 9am-9pm Mon-Sat; 10am-6pm Sun. **Credit** AmEx, MC, V.
Treatments: body treatments, detox treatments, facials, manicures, massages, mud & steam treatments, pedicures, prenatal treatments, self-tanning.
Still one of the best beauty spas in town, Elemis is a little oasis of quiet luxury. Barefoot therapists offer water before leading you to individually styled and scented rooms, where the magic begins. A newly created body facial uses hot and cold stones to relax and stimulate alternately during a 55-minute massage (£80 at the Elemis Day Spa/£65 at salons and spas). As with all treatments, it starts with foot-cleansing with lime-scented mitts, followed by skin brushing, some chakra-aligning breathing and a massage (muscle-easing, moisturising or de-stressing). A cooling gel is applied and hot stones are introduced to apply deep pressure (to encourage lymphatic drainage and boost circulation). Then a 25-minute anti-ageing booster facial takes place – all using natural products. Elemis treatments, including facials, wraps and massages, are now available at John Lewis and Selfridges, and at Heathrow's Terminal 5: perfect for a reinvigorating pep-up after a long-haul flight.

Guinot

17 Albemarle Street, W1S 4HP (7491 9971/www.guinotuk.com). Green Park tube. **Open** 9.30am-6.30pm Mon, Wed, Fri; 9.30am-8pm Tue, Thur; 9.30am-5pm Sat. **Credit** AmEx, MC, V.
Treatments: anti-cellulite treatments, body treatments, facials, massages, prenatal treatments, self-tanning.
With old-school elegance and country house charm – if such a thing can be found in the centre of Mayfair – Guinot is the sort of salon frequented by ladies who get facials before luncheon. Luckily, it also welcomes the rest of us. With its plush carpets, spacious treatment rooms and trompe l'oeil ceiling in the waiting parlour, this salon deliberately turns its back on the modern world so that you can too, if only for a relaxing hour or two. Hydradermie is Guinot's signature facial, a treatment developed by French biochemist Rene Guinot in the 1960s. The idea is that the therapist massages various unguents (selected according to skin type) deep into the face using a machine that employs a small galvanic current. Fear not, it doesn't hurt. In fact, it's very relaxing unless the machine goes anywhere near your fillings, in which case you briefly experience a strange metallic taste. The results were impressive: rejuvenating and long-lasting.

Health Club at One Aldwych

One Aldwych, WC2B 4RH (7300 0600/ www.onealdwych.com). Covent Garden tube. **Open** 6am-10pm Mon-Fri; 8am-8pm Sat, Sun. **Credit** AmEx, MC, V.
Treatments: body treatments, facials, manicures, massages, pedicures, prenatal treatments, reflexology, self-tanning, waxing.
Make your way through the sumptuous foyer of the One Aldwych hotel and you're directed downstairs to the equally sumptuous Health Club, a world of rare luxury in the tourist hell of Covent Garden. The two-floor space is super-modern and the three silk-panelled treatment rooms, designed by Mary Fox Linton, are stuffed with relaxing textures, sounds, smells and colours; the gorgeous 18m pool, sauna and steam room create a sense of calm. One Aldwych was the first London hotel to feature the full line of Natura Bissé treatments and products, with bespoke UK exclusive treatments such as the Luminous Vitamin C Ritual facial (£90) and the Frozen Marine DNA facial (£170). We sampled the latter, emerging two hours later into the grey London rain feeling like we were on a Caribbean beach. The 90-minute treatment involved a three-step exfoliation, face mask and massage – on top of gentle arm, leg and head massages – to leave our entire body feeling supple, glowing and full of vitality. Any treatment lasting more than an hour entitles spa users to use of the pool facilities, so bring your cozzie and book yourself in at one of the most relaxing addresses in town.

Hydrohealing

216A Kensington Park Road, W11 1NR (7727 2570/www.hydrohealing.com). Ladbroke Grove tube. **Open** 10am-8pm Mon-Sat; 11am-6pm Sun. **Credit** AmEx, MC, V.
Treatments: aromatherapy, body treatments, colonic irrigation, detox treatments, facials, massages, prenatal treatments, reflexology.
There are plenty of therapies worth investigating at this Notting Hill 'hydro spa', set up by a pair of entrepreneurial pharmacists, and they all involve that most underrated of resources: water. Treatments range from colonic irrigation to anti-cellulite treatments, but what this place really excels at is bespoke treatments. The latest detox programme combines prepared juices and meals with colonics (or non-invasive acupuncture) to aid weight loss, while a facial micro-dermabrasion – not quite as scary as it sounds – consists of cool jets of water to pummel the skin around the lymph glands and stimulate a sluggish system, and then a gentle peel of the top layer of your skin. We experienced a slight tingling sensation after the application of a rehydrating face mask by natural skincare range REN, and while this goes to work clients are treated to a fabulous head massage. Following all that action, our skin was plump and glowing – this one is definitely a pre-party winner.

Spa Illuminata. *See p99.*

Incredible You

40 Moreton Street, SW1V 2PB (7821 1020/www.incredibleyou.co.uk). Pimlico tube. **Open** 10am-8pm Mon-Fri; 10am-6pm Sat, Sun. **Credit** MC, V.
Treatments: acupuncture, aromatherapy, body treatments, Chinese herbal therapy, eyebrow & eyelash shaping & tinting, facials, manicures, massages, nutrition advice, pedicures, reflexology, tanning, waxing.

Linda Carter shares her name with the original Wonder Woman – and those who have experienced her own-designed rejuvenating facials (devotees include Angelina Jolie, Julianne Moore and even Sean Connery) might think that more than a coincidence. A qualified acupuncturist with over 22 years' experience, Carter is also a beauty therapist, cosmetologist, doctor of Chinese medicine and, erm, ordained inter-faith minister, and she brings all these disciplines together to create holistic treatments. After an initial consultation, a stimulating back, neck, shoulder and head massage precedes the Environ facial. The acupuncture treatment, with premium Japanese gold needles, follows, awakening the muscles, getting the blood circulating and catalysing collagen and elastin production. Our 'bespoke' treatment included a few needles applied to the belly (to stimulate a diagnosed sluggish digestive system). While best carried out as part of a course, the single two-hour session left our skin smooth, plump and refined. Carter's calm approach (and line-free face) are testament to her qualifications.

Jurlique Day Spa

300-302 Chiswick High Road, W4 1NP (8995 2293/www.apotheke20-20.co.uk). Chiswick Park or Turnham Green tube.
Open 10am-8pm Mon-Fri; 9.30am-6pm Sat; 10am-6pm Sun. **Credit** AmEx, MC, V.
Treatments: aromatherapy, body treatments, detox treatments, facials, hydrotherapy, manicures, massages, naturopathy, pedicures, reflexology, waxing.

The London home of Australia's leading organic and herbal skincare range, this non-gimmicky day spa is a mecca for those seeking purity and simplicity in their beauty and relaxation treatments. Clients ascend a scented stairway to a bright, no-nonsense reception area before being led to blue-toned rooms decorated with landscape photos. The facials are wonderful. Therapists spend time analysing the skin and explaining why they will use each selected product. For our biodynamic facial this meant two masks for an oily T-zone and dehydrated cheeks. A long time was spent on firm but gentle massage (you'll probably drift off to sleep). Afterwards, head to the relaxation room with its aromatherapy oil burner, views on to a little roof terrace and easy-reading books or mags. Tea and coffee were offered instead of the usual herbal brews – making this place refreshingly un-preachy.

May Fair Spa

May Fair Hotel, Stratton Street, W1J 8LT (7915 2826/www.radissonedwardian.com). Green Park tube. **Open** 9am-9pm Mon-Thur; 9am-8pm Fri-Sun. **Credit** AmEx, MC, V.
Treatments: body treatments, facials, massages, sauna, steam room, tanning.

Behind the elbows and choke of Piccadilly, beneath the belly of the May Fair Hotel, lies this sleek, minimalist spa. The salon is underground, but makes its complete lack of daylight into a virtue, using black and grey marble to create a Pharoah's tomb-like stillness that is calming indeed. Before a chosen treatment, clients are invited to use the relaxation room with its herbal teas, heated resin recliners and health-giving nibbles. They're also encouraged to start the detox process in the steam and sauna rooms before their therapist whisks them off to a treatment room. Prescriptive facials begin with a straight-talking analysis of your skin as the therapist scrutinises damage under a UV light. The treatment is then tailored to individual needs. It's not just a more youthful face that you gain from a visit here, but a general sense of well-being – as long as you leave enough time to make full use of the facilities.

Ritual Rooms

13 New Quebec Street, W1H 7RR (0870 085 5066/www.ritualrooms.com). Marble Arch tube. **Open** 10am-9pm Mon-Fri; 9am-7pm Sat. **Credit** AmEx, MC, V.
Treatments: body treatments, eye treatments, facials, hairdressing, manicures, massages, pedicures, waxing.

Taking comfort from life's little rituals goes one luxurious step further in this smoothly discreet Portman Village pampering centre. Much is made of the tailoring of the R&R. Clients are shown into the relaxation room – all dark polished wood, fairy lights and Classic FM's smoothest mixes – to shake off the London dust and have a snack and a drink. Once refreshed, they descend the twinkly lit stairs to complete the ritual in a warm and ingeniously appointed therapy room. From the multi-positional bed they can be completely topped and tailed. For hair treatments, the head end is lowered and a basin unfolded from a wall unit. There's no need to move from the reclining position for your facial, hot-stone massage, manicure, pedicure or waxing. There's a wide range of facials, using the Anne Sémonin beauty range, which blends essential oils and trace elements in a nourishing menu of oils, creams, serums and toners. The made-to-measure 90-minute facial (which we chose for stressed, dry skin) involved massaging in a whole roster of unguents, including a refreshing frozen serum for firming up the saggy bits. It was a blissful and sleep-inducing experience – so much so, it took cold water and a shot of raspberry sorbet to help us face the outside world. Ritual Rooms clients often buy their hours in advance, so that they can come in on a regular basis and benefit from lower per-hour rates. Another RR speciality is a Little Miss menu of hairdressing, manicures, pedicures and gentle facials for youngsters aged from 14.

Savana Urban Spa

45 Hereford Road, W2 5AH (7229 8300/ www.savanaspa.com). Bayswater or Notting Hill Gate tube. **Open** noon-9pm Mon; 10am-9pm Tue-Fri; 10am-7pm Sat, Sun. **Credit** MC, V.
Treatments: body treatments, complementary therapies, eye treatments, eyebrow shaping & tinting, eyelash tinting & perming, facials, manicures, massages, meditation, pedicures, Pilates, waxing, yoga.

Step into the basement of this spa and distance yourself from the big, bad world outside. The emphasis here is on restoring balance to body and mind via massage, complementary health and natural spa and beauty treatments. Set up by two massage therapists cum City high-fliers, the urban spa boasts a male clientele of around 30-40%, perhaps because lots of treatments have a masculine allure, like the jet lag relief treatment (£140/2hrs). On our last visit, we tried a therapeutic full-body massage (£75/55mins) and an Eminence Organic balancing facial (£100/75mins); the latter, in particular, was both refreshing and relaxing. It's not quite as private as it could be, however, and sitting in a gown in the communal waiting room feels like a mild anti-climax after a solo pampering session, but bowls of fresh fruit, lemon-flavoured water and the chance to choose your own music more than make up for it. Savana also hosts corporate hospitality and team-building events for investment banks, law firms and other companies. New for 2008 are the kids' spa parties, where five- to 16-year-olds can have their nails painted, learn how to give massages and apply face packs.

Scin

27 Kensington Park Road, W11 2EU (3220 0121/www.scin.uk.com). Ladbroke Grove tube. **Open** 9am-7pm Mon, Tue, Thur-Sat; 9am-8pm Wed; noon-5pm Sun. **Credit** AmEx, DC, MC, V.
Treatments: anti-cellulite treatments, body treatments, eyebrow shaping & tinting, facials, manicures, massages, pedicures, self-tanning, waxing.

Safe in the hands of Anna and Nicky Noble's sister-act pampering team you'll be hard pushed not to find instant escapism from the hustle and bustle of London life. The upstairs area, where the manicures and pedicures take place, is a laboratory-like white space; the dimly lit relaxation-inducing basement, meanwhile, contains five treatment rooms, a spray-tanning room and a hydrotherapy bath (perfect for unwinding before a massage). The shop stocks a variety of organic and natural products including Jo Wood Organics, Dermalogica and Scin's own brand. Treat yourself to a quick-fix session if you're on the go, or prolong your stop for a more indulgent experience. On our last visit we tried a treatment package (there are several available) that included hydrotherapy, a full-body massage and a pedicure (£65); the massage worked wonders, soothing away tension to the rhythm of chilled music, and we left feeling incredibly well groomed. The spa appeals to both men and women.

Shymala Ayurveda Spa

152 Holland Park Avenue, W11 4UH (7348 0018/www.shymalaayurveda.com). Holland Park tube. **Open** 9am-7pm Mon-Sat. **Credit** AmEx, MC, V.
Treatments: body treatments, detox treatments, facials, health consultations, massages, meditation, reiki, waxing, yoga.

An exotic sanctuary encased in a stately white stucco facade, the Shymala Ayurveda

Spa is the offspring of Shymala Gopal, who got her inspiration from a visit to an Ayurvedic retreat in Kerala. Clean lines and sleek fittings, set against hot pink walls and artefacts imported from Chennai, give the spa the feel of a boutique hotel. The Ayurvedic lifestyle is taken seriously here; a visit starts with a consultation with an Ayurvedic doctor who recommends the most suitable treatments. These include the Udvartana (£100/60mins), a vigorous rubdown-cum-scrub with an exfoliating herbal paste that helps eliminate toxins and reduce cellulite, and a sumptuous Cleopatra Bath in milk, Ayurvedic herbs, essential oils and flower petals. After your treatment, relax in the steam room and sauna while you sip herbal tea. The facilities are small but immaculate, and you are provided with a robe and slippers and an unlimited supply of fluffy white towels.

Spa at Brown's

Brown's Hotel, Albemarle Street, W1S 4BP (7518 4009/www.brownshotel.com). Green Park tube. **Open** 9.30am-8pm daily. **Credit** AmEx, DC, MC, V.
Treatments: aromatherapy, body treatments & wraps, detox treatments, eyebrow shaping & tinting, facials, hairdressing, makeovers, manicures, massages, non-surgical facelifts, pedicures, pre/postnatal treatments, waxing.
Browns Hotel has an air of a gentlemen's club about it, which might explain why half the clients at its downstairs spa are men – but there's nothing old-school about the spa, which is cool, contemporary and calming. As well as a wide range of massages and facials using products such as Dr Sebagh, Carita, Natura Bissé, Mama Mio and Aromatherapy Associates, the bijou spa (three treatment rooms, one double suite for couples) also has a seasonally changing 'menu'. For summer 2008 it featured a 'fruity' pedicure: while sipping a vanilla daiquiri or blueberry smoothie, a 90-minute treatment (£85) included a lower-leg massage with blueberries, foot-soaking in warm milk, a pressure-point foot massage and paraffin foot wrap – all followed by a professional pedicure. And it's not a gimmick: our friendly and knowledgeable therapist, Shareen, explained the benefits of nature's abundant resources – blueberries are delicious anti-oxidants, lactic acids aid exfoliation, vanilla cream is soothing and smoothing (in addition to its wonderful scent). It's reassuring to know you're in such safe, and soft, hands.

Spa at Mandarin Oriental

Mandarin Oriental Hyde Park, 66 Knightsbridge, SW1X 7LA (7838 9888/ www.mandarinoriental.com). Knightsbridge tube. **Open** 7am-10pm daily. **Credit** AmEx, DC, MC, V.
Treatments: aromatherapy, body treatments, facials, massages, pre/postnatal treatments, reflexology.
You might feel you have to dress up to enter the portals of this immaculate hotel, but once you're inside the spa the atmosphere is impeccably serene and the only dress code is robe-optional. The design is suave granite luxury, with sensual touches in the scents, lighting and carefully placed orchids, and sculptures based on the male and female body. You are encouraged to enjoy the Heat & Water Oasis – spa pool, 'sanarium' (humid sauna) and steam room – before your treatment appointment (the Oasis can't be accessed by non-residents without one). Allow a good 45 minutes as the spa pool runs a 20-minute jet sequence. Your therapist will pick you up in the relaxation room, togged out with sybaritic recliners with built-in headphones and personal spotlights. The spa is known for its Advanced Time Rituals (£240), whereby you book a two-hour time slot rather than specific treatments: you consult with your therapist what best suits your needs and mood that day. Treatments might include a shiatsu-inspired ginger ritual, an 'Oriental harmony' four-handed massage (book this in advance) or Padabhyanga foot therapy. The staff are experts, and draw a loyal local clientele. Products are from Espa.

Spa Illuminata

63 South Audley Street, W1K 2QS (7499 7777/www.spailluminata.com). Bond Street or Green Park tube. **Open** 10am-6pm Mon, Sat, Sun; 10am-7pm Tue, Fri; 10am-9pm Wed, Thur. **Credit** AmEx, DC, MC, V.
Treatments: body treatments, facials, makeovers, massages, manicures, pedicures, self-tanning, steam treatments, waxing.
Elegantly clad in pale marble, Illuminata's stylish Mayfair premises ooze expensive understatement. Offering both Carita and Décleor treatments gives the spa broad appeal; Décleor tends towards the holistic, using essential oils, while Carita's focus is on anti-ageing, results-oriented treatments, such as the Pro-Lift Firming facial (£125), which promises a non-surgical facelift experience. The Décleor Classic Aromatic facial (£90/60mins) was very relaxing, with gentle massages and a blissful spell under a warm, moisturising wheatgerm and linseed mask, resulting in wonderfully radiant and plump-looking skin. The one-hour Aromassage (£88) is the ideal choice if you want the results of a proper massage without the discomfort – the masseuse applied just the right amount of pressure to tension spots. For extra relaxation, book a Sound Therapy session, during which your bed emits deep vibrations in time with the calming music, or a Jasmine Steam Treatment (£55/45mins) in the soothing blue-tiled steam room. For the cash-rich but time-poor, there's a range of express options, including mini manicures, eyebrow shaping and a makeover (£50/30mins) in the swanky private make-up room.

Spa NK

40 Hans Crescent, SW1 0LZ (7581 2518/ www.spacenk.co.uk/category/spa.do). Knightsbridge tube. **Open** 10am-7pm Mon-Sat; 11am-5pm Sun. **Credit** AmEx, MC, V.
Treatments: aromatherapy, body treatments, detox treatments, eyebrow shaping & tinting, eyelash tinting, facials, lymphatic drainage, massages, prenatal treatments, self-tanning, waxing.
The newest Spa NK offers a peaceful retreat beneath the chic Knightsbridge Space NK store (although the original Spa NK at Westbourne Grove is still the flagship outfit). From the enticing array of top-quality facials using hard-to-come-by skincare (from Dr Sebagh to Peter Thomas Roth), we opted for a classic Eve Lom facial (£155/90mins). The combination of lymphatic massage, acupressure, thorough extractions and soothing products made a visible difference to our stressed-out skin. A dimly lit relaxation area provides a space to chill until you're ready to face the world again. As well as opening some 60 stores around the UK, Belfast-born beauty-junkie founder Nicky Kinnaird has also penned a book, *Awaken your senses: change your life*, so you can keep up the good habits after your visit to the spa.
For branches see index.

Tri-Dosha at the Rejuvenation Clinic

Baglioni Hotel, 60 Hyde Park Gate, SW7 5BB (7368 5923/www.therejuvenation clinic.co.uk). High Street Kensington tube. **Open** 9am-9pm Mon-Sat; 10am-8pm Sun. **Credit** MC, V.
Treatments: Ayurvedic treatments including meditation, nutritional therapy, spirituality and yoga.
Western and Asian techniques combine to restore youthful skin through anti-ageing treatments and complementary therapies at this elegant spa. There are four treatment rooms, a VIP couple's room, steam room and jacuzzi as well as hair and make-up artists to tend to your every need (in your room, if you're a hotel guest). Try the popular Shirodara Tri-Dosha Third-Eye treatment, where warm oil is poured on to the forehead to put you into a near meditative state of relaxation. You can also also pick up products, from Espa, SkinCeutical, Jo Woods, Philip Kingsley and Obagi, that promise to leave your skin glowing. Over at the Harley Street clinic, the bravest results-focused spa-goers can test out the latest laser treatment, Fraxel. Pioneered by celebrity favourite Dr Mario Luca Russo, it aims to renew the skin from the inside out, promoting fresher-looking skin that's free from acne marks, pigmentation or age scars. It costs around £750 for one session.

Urban Retreat

5th Floor, Harrods, 87-135 Brompton Road, SW1X 7XL (7893 8333/ www.harrods.com). Knightsbridge tube. **Open** 10am-8pm Mon-Sat; 11.30am-6pm Sun. **Credit** AmEx, DC, MC, V.
Treatments: anti-cellulite treatments, body treatments, botox, chiropody, electrolysis, hairdressing, laser treatments, makeovers, manicures, massages, micro-dermabrasion, nail extensions, non-surgical facelifts, pedicures, reflexology, self-tanning, semi-permanent make-up, waxing.
This beauty emporium in Harrods (other branches can be found across the country) is so vast, it's easy to lose oneself among the beautiful bottled perfume collection, the nail bar and the exclusive 'medical' wing. It prides itself on its holistic and natural qualities, using aromatherapy and massage to really help you engage with the products and sink into sheer bliss. Our facial (from £65/hr), designed by Anastasia Ahilleos and using the spa's own-brand products (also available from larger Boots nationwide) left us feeling nurtured and rejuvenated. Urban Retreat is surprisingly accessible given its swanky location, but doesn't skimp on the luxuries such as warm towels and great

service. And you can prolong your pamper by sampling the delicious smoothies in the East Dulwich Deli afterwards.

Ushvani

1 Cadogan Gardens, SW3 2RJ (7730 2888/ www.ushvani.com). Knightsbridge tube.
Open 10am-7pm Mon; noon-9pm Fri; Tue-Thur, Sat call for details. **Credit** AmEx, MC, V.
Treatments: body treatments, foot treatments, massages.
There's an emphasis on South-east Asian healing traditions, philosophies and ingredients at this new Knightsbridge spa. Malay- and Balinese-style massages, wraps and scrubs (using the likes of coconut milk, kaffir lime, hibiscus and banana and honey) are the focus, though they're planning to offer facials too. Allow plenty of time: massages (£150-£240) take a minimum of 90 minutes, except for the slightly shorter pregnancy option. Treatments are designed for both sexes, though only women can use the steam room, pool and 'tropical rain and experience showers'. The place is serene, all soothing honey and gold tones, with lattice-work screens, Malaysian sculptures and the aroma of ginger, nutmeg and pandan leaves whisking you to a world far removed from the grime and gloom of London.

West One Beauty

60 Chiltern Street, W1U 7RB (7486 1415/ www.westonebeauty.co.uk). Baker Street tube. **Open** 8am-8pm Mon-Fri; 9am-6pm Sat; 10am-6pm Sun. **Credit** AmEx, MC, V.
Treatments: body treatments, facials, manicures, pedicures, self-tanning, waxing.
Beauty therapist Sally Medcalf opened this spa after working in the industry for more than 20 years. She specialises in skin problems and deep-cleansing treatments, with a range of prescriptive facials – you decide how much time to spend on each problem area, and the therapist will suggest treatments to suit your needs. Try the Karin Herzog oxygen facial, the anti-ageing Smoothie (both £60/60mins) or the CoCo2 Chocolate: £75 for 75 minutes of pampering luxury, complete with a back massage and hand treatment and a chocolatey gift.

Also check out...

Angel Therapy Rooms

16B Essex Road, N1 8LN (7226 1188/ www.angeltherapyrooms.com). Angel tube.
Open noon-8pm Wed, Thur; 11am-7pm Fri; 11am-6pm Sat; 11am-5pm Sun. **Credit** MC, V.
Treatments: acupuncture, body treatments, facials, manicures, massages, nutritional therapy, pedicures, reflexology, waxing.
Set in a lovely Victorian townhouse, Angel Therapy Rooms offers a range of organic treatments. The superb signature Holistic Facial blends reiki, reflexology and intense massage techniques (£95/75mins).

Aveda Lifestyle Institute

174 High Holborn, WC1V 7AA (7759 7355/www.aveda.com). Holborn or Tottenham Court Road tube. **Open** 9.30am-7pm Mon-Wed; 8am-8pm Thur, Fri; 9am-6.30pm Sat; 11am-5pm Sun. **Credit** AmEx, MC, V.
Treatments: body treatments, complementary therapies, eye treatments, facials, hairdressing, manicures, massages, pedicures, self-tanning, waxing.
The flagship offers a full beauty menu, from hairdressing to luxurious spa treatments using the environmentally sensitive own-brand range.
For branch see index.

Berkeley Spa

The Berkeley, Wilton Place, SW1X 7RL (7201 1699/www.the-berkeley.com). Knightsbridge tube. **Open** 8am-9pm Mon-Fri; 9am-7pm Sat, Sun. **Credit** AmEx, DC, MC, V.
Treatments: facials, manicures, massages, pedicures, waxing.
Posh hotel spa with famous rooftop pool.

Cucumba

12 Poland Street, W1F 8QB (7734 2020/ www.cucumba.co.uk). Oxford Circus tube.
Open 10am-8pm Mon-Fri; 11am-7pm Sat. **Credit** AmEx, MC, V.
Treatments: facials, manicures, massages, pedicures, reflexology, threading, waxing.
This 'urban pit stop' in Soho offers quick-fixes and more extended pampering; try the super-duper snooze booth combo – you'll get a half-hour massage followed by a half-hour siesta for £56.

Elizabeth Arden Red Door Spa

29 Davies Street, W1K 4LW (7629 4488/ www.reddoorspas.com). Bond Street tube.
Open 10am-7pm Mon; 9am-7pm Tue, Sat; 9am-8pm Wed-Fri; 10am-6pm Sun. **Credit** AmEx, DC, MC, V.
Treatments: aromatherapy, body treatments, electrolysis, facials, hairdressing, makeovers, manicures, massages, micro-dermabrasion, non-surgical facelifts, pedicures, reflexology, self-tanning, waxing.
Reliable, long-established spa with hair salon and make-up studio.

Groom

49 Beauchamp Place, SW3 1NY (7581 1248/www.groomlondon.com). Knightsbridge tube. **Open** 10am-7pm Tue, Wed, Fri; 10am-8am Thur; 9am-6pm Sat; also by appointment. **Credit** AmEx, DC, MC, V.
Treatments: facials, manicures, massages, pedicures, waxing.
Time-saving packages, such as the Weekly Groom Hour (£105) are performed by two therapists. There's a branch in Selfridges.

Ironmonger Row Baths

1-11 Ironmonger Row, EC1V 3QF (7253 4011/www.aquaterra.org). Old Street tube/ rail. **Open** 6.30am-9.30pm Mon-Fri; 10am-6pm Sat, Sun. *Sauna: Mixed* 6.30am-9pm Mon; 6.30am-8pm Tue-Thur; 6.30am-7pm Fri; 9am-5.30pm Sat; noon-5pm Sun. *Turkish baths: Men* 9am-9.30pm Tue, Thur; 9am-6.30pm Sat. *Women* 9am-9.30pm Wed, Fri; 10am-6.30pm Sun. *Mixed* 2-9.30pm Mon. **Credit** AmEx, MC, V.
Treatments: body scrubs, massages, reflexology, reiki.
At this 1930s Turkish bath a day's use of the hot rooms, steam room and pool is £7.70 (non-members). Treatments are extra.

Langham Health Club & Spa

1C Portland Place, W1B 1JA (7973 7550/ www.langhamhotels.com). Oxford Circus tube. **Open** 6.30am-10pm Mon-Fri; 8am-8pm Sat, Sun. **Credit** AmEx, MC, V.
Elegant hotel spa with 16m mosaic pool, gym, steam rooms and sauna; the spa area is currently under refurbishment, so no treatments will be offered until mid 2009.

Natéclo

14 Portobello Green, 281 Portobello Road, W10 5TZ (07814 025 796/www.portobello designers.com). Ladbroke Grove tube. **Open** by appointment Mon-Sat. **No credit cards.**
Treatments: body treatments, eyelash tinting, facials, massages, self-tanning, waxing.
Kristy Nguyen carries out most of the treatments at her Portobello Green spa herself. It's a simple affair, with facials, body massages and treatments taking place in a single room. The oriental-style interior inspires peace and tranquillity, so that blocking out the outside world is easy. Facials (£65/hr for the signature option) combine steam, extraction, soothing organic oils and a warm wax mask.

Cowshed. *See p96.*

Pacifica Day Spa

1 Courtnell Street, W2 5BU (7243 1718/ www.pacificadayspa.co.uk). Notting Hill Gate tube. **Open** 10am-9pm Mon-Fri; 10am-7pm Sat, Sun. **Credit** AmEx, MC, V.
Treatments: body treatments, eyebrow shaping & tinting, facials, manicures, massages, pedicures, self-tanning, waxing.
Ladies who lunch love it, and rightly so. Bamboo, mini waterfalls and plenty of greenery will transport you away from your hectic urban lifestyle.

Parlour

3 Ravey Street, EC2A 4QP (7729 6969/ www.theparlouruk.com). Liverpool Street or Old Street tube/rail. **Open** 11.30am-8pm Mon-Thur; 10.30am-7pm Fri; 10am-5pm Sat. **Credit** MC, V.
Treatments: body treatments, eyebrow shaping & tinting, eyelash tinting, facials, hairdressing, hair treatments, manicures, massages, pedicures, self-tanning, waxing.
This friendly Shoreditch salon has been tending to the locks and beauty requirements of locals for over five years. Indulge in a 'hair smoothie' made from MOP's organic products (from £20). If your feet need a little TLC, have a pedicure: options include chocolate foot masks, peppermint soaks and lemon zings (from £40/45mins).

Porchester Spa

The Porchester Centre, Queensway, W2 5HS (7792 3980/www.courtneys.co.uk/ centres/porchester/the-porchester-spa). Bayswater tube. **Open** *Women* 10am-10pm Tue, Thur, Fri; 10am-4pm Sun. *Men* 10am-10pm Mon, Wed, Sat. *Mixed* 4-10pm Sun. Last admission 2hrs before closing. **Credit** AmEx, MC, V.
Treatments: body treatments, eyebrow tinting, eyelash tinting, facials, manicures, massages, pedicures, waxing.
The Grade II-listed Porchester Spa's marble and green-tiled relaxation room is an art deco delight, while downstairs lies a warren of steam rooms and a sauna. Treatments include shmeisse massages (£25), using a soapy raffia brush, and must be booked ahead. Admission is £20.35 for non-members, or £28.25 per couple on Sundays.

Sanctuary

12 Floral Street, WC2E 9DH (0870 063 0300/www.thesanctuary.co.uk). Covent Garden tube. **Open** 9.30am-6pm Mon, Tue; 9.30am-10pm Wed-Fri; 9.30am-8pm Sat, Sun. **Credit** AmEx, DC, MC, V.
Treatments: aromatherapy, body treatments, body wraps, dry flotation, facials, heat treatments, hot stone therapy, manicures, massages, pedicures, reflexology.
Not exactly cheap but timelessly popular all the same, this women-only spa has two pools, a sauna, a hammam, whirlpool, the famous koi carp lounge and a sleep retreat. A day pass is £69 (Mon-Thur) or £79 (Fri-Sun), excluding treatments.

Skin & Tonic

604 Roman Road, E3 2RW (8980 5492). Bow Road tube/Bow Church DLR/8 bus. **Open** 10am-6pm Mon, Tue; 10am-7pm Wed, Fri; 10am-8pm Thur; 9am-5pm Sat. **No credit cards.**
Treatments: body treatments, botox, collagen clinic, eyebrow shaping & tinting, eyelash tinting, facials, makeovers, massages, non-surgical facelifts, pedicures, self-tanning, steam treatments, sunbeds, waxing.
Chatty and seriously cheap East End salon (£25 for a Hollywood – all off – bikini wax).

Spa at Chancery Court

252 High Holborn, WC1V 7EN (7829 7058/www.spachancerycourt.co.uk). Holborn tube. **Open** 8am-9pm daily. **Credit** AmEx, MC, V.
Treatments: body treatments, bridal hair & make-up, eyebrow shaping, facials, manicures, massages, pedicures, reflexology, waxing.
A chic retreat offering sauna, steam rooms and adjustable daybeds with individual headphones in the relaxation room. Watch out for the launch of the men's spa menu.

Spa InterContinental

InterContinental London, 1 Hamilton Place, Park Lane, W1J 7QY (7318 8691/ www.spaintercontinental.com). Hyde Park Corner tube. **Open** 10am-6pm Mon, Sat, Sun; 9am-9pm Tue-Fri. **Credit** AmEx, MC, V.
Treatments: body treatments, eyebrow shaping and tinting, eyelash tinting, facials, manicures, massages, pedicures, self-tanning, waxing, wet shaves.
Lose and then re-find yourself in the hydrotherapy showers and the dry-flotation room. There are Elemis and La Thérapie treatments and for £180 you can indulge body to toe for two hours with the signature English Rose treatment.

Spa London

York Hall Leisure Centre, Old Ford Road, E2 9PJ (8709 5845/www.spa-london.org). Bethnal Green tube/rail. **Open** *Men* 11am-9.30pm Mon; 10am-9.30pm Thur. *Women* 10am-9.30pm Tue, Wed, Fri; 9am-7.30pm Sat. *Mixed* 9am-7.30pm Sun. **Credit** MC, V.
Treatments: body treatments, eyebrow & eyelash tinting, facials, make-up, manicures, massages, pedicures, self-tanning, waxing.
We didn't like losing the Turkish baths that made way for Spa London, but there's no denying it's good value for money – and rather sleek to boot. After paying admission (£21 for non-members) you can relax in the steam rooms, Turkish hot rooms, sauna, monsoon showers and relaxation room, or book for one of the reasonably priced treatments or massages.

Men only

Gentlemen's Tonic

31A Bruton Place, W1J 6NN (7297 4343/www.gentlemenstonic.com). Green Park tube. **Open** 10am-7pm Mon, Fri; 10am-8pm Tue, Wed; 10am-9pm Thur; 10am-6pm Sat; 11am-6pm Sun. **Credit** AmEx, MC, V.
Treatments: aromatherapy, facials, eyebrow & eyelash shaping & tinting, hairdressing, massages, reflexology, reiki, teeth whitening, waxing, wet shaves.
Gentlemen's Tonic offers an extensive array of male grooming services, from hand and facial treatments to Swedish massage. After four years of beard growth, our chosen 'tonic' could only be the wet shave (£32). The enthusiastic master barber, Mark Nimki, led the way into his old-world-meets-modern booth. After a brief chat, the barber's chair reclined to horizontal. Any thoughts of Sweeney Todd vanished as almond oil was applied to soften the bristles, followed by a hot towel and a cream-lathered badger-hair brush. Then the master went to work with his cut-throat. Whether it's once a week, once a month or a gift for Father's Day, a visit here is a must.
For branch see index.

Jason Shankey

19 Jerdan Place, SW6 1BE (7386 3900/ www.jasonshankey.com). Fulham Broadway tube. **Open** noon-7pm Mon; 10am-7pm Tue, Fri; 11am-8pm Wed, Thur; 10am-6pm Sat; 11am-4pm Sun. **Credit** MC, V.
Treatments: facials, hairdressing, manicures, massages, waxing, wet shaves.
Jason Shankey is a barber's shop with a difference. Although half of the business is straightforward haircuts (a shampoo, cut and rinse costs £25), waxing, massage and facials are offered in three treatment rooms on the first floor. Situated in an old Fulham townhouse, the salon has a friendly feel that is unintimidating and masculine without being overtly blokeish. You're free to help yourself to a beer from the fridge in the tiny lounge, but this is more *GQ* reader than lager lout territory.

Nickel Spa

27 Shorts Gardens WC2H 9AP (7240 4048/ www.nickelspalondon.co.uk). Covent Garden tube. **Open** noon-6pm Mon; 10am-7pm Tue, Wed, Sat; 10am-8pm Thur, Fri; noon-5pm Sun. **Credit** AmEx, MC, V.
Treatments: aromatherapy, body treatments, eyebrow & eyelash tinting, facials, manicures, massages, pedicures, waxing.
Nickel is a mini haven in Covent Garden. The staff are knowledgeable and do everything in their power to make you feel at ease. The list of treatments available is extensive and reasonably priced: expect to pay £35 for a standard facial, £20 for a manicure, £25 for a pedicure and £60 for a back, crack and sack waxing. The five treatment rooms, situated in the basement, ring to a soundtrack of pan pipes – surprisingly relaxing. We opted for a deep tissue massage (£60/60mins) and found the experience extremely pleasurable and professional; what more could a boy ask for? You can also pick up plenty of products in the reception area, from morning-after rescue gel (£24) to Silicon Valley anti-ageing cream (£42). It's a popular place, so book ahead.

Refinery

60 Brook Street, W1K 5DU (7409 2001/ www.the-refinery.com). Bond Street tube. **Open** 10am-7pm Mon, Tue; 10am-9pm Wed-Fri; 9am-6pm Sat; 11am-5pm Sun. **Credit** AmEx, MC, V.
Treatments: aromatherapy, body treatments, facials, hairdressing, manicures, massages, pedicures, reflexology, self-tanning, waxing, wet shaves.
One of the first male grooming salons, and still thriving. New treatments include micro-dermabrasion facials and 'intimate' waxing (£45-£120).

Specialists

Eyebrow threading

Blink Eyebrow Bar

Fenwick, 63 New Bond Street, W1A 3BS (7408 0689/www.blinkbrowbar.com). Bond Street tube. **Open** 10am-6.30pm Mon-Wed, Fri, Sat; 10am-8pm Thur. **Credit** MC, V.

Blink's innovative threading bars offer a speedy walk-in service, though you can also book appointments in advance. The majority of therapists here were trained in India. Eyebrows take 15 minutes and cost £17. There are also Blink bars in Selfridges and Harvey Nichols.

Kamini Salon

14-16 Lancer Square, off Kensington Church Street, W8 4EP (7937 2411). High Street Kensington tube. **Open** 10am-7.30pm Tue-Fri; 10am-6pm Sat. **Credit** MC, V.

With over 25 years' experience in the beauty business, eyebrow obsessive and celebrity favourite Kamini Vaghela delivers a deft, relatively painless service and long-lasting results. She has an infallible eye for what arch will best suit your face shape, and charges £45 per session.

Facialists

Gennie Monteith

Studio 1, 106 Draycott Avenue, SW3 3AE (7225 2200/www.genniemonteith.com). **Open** by appointment 9.30am-8pm. **No credit cards.**

Facialist Gennie Monteith is fanatical about facials, seeing them as a (admittedly) low-profile way in which to empower women, through giving them skincare knowledge; in her in-depth consultations she gives thorough advice on the right skincare to suit clients' needs, recommending products for daily use. In her practice Monteith mixes ingredients to create her own 'bespoke' products for her facials, using organic materials in their most natural state wherever possible. A typical session might include micro-dermabrasion followed by a healing homeopathic tincture, activated by light therapy to aid collagen renewal; 'acupuncture' with a special light wand to clear your meridians; and an oxygen mask to boost micro-circulation. The results are certainly impressive.

Vaishaly Clinic

51 Paddington Street, W1U 4HR (7224 6088/www.vaishaly.com) Baker Street tube. **Open** 9am-6pm Mon-Sat. **Credit** AmEx, MC, V.

Vaishaly Patel has been tending the visages of the rich and famous for years, training under Bharti Vyas before moving to Martyn Maxey's salon in the mid 1990s. Her signature facial has won numerous devotees, including the youthful-looking forty-somethings Elle Macpherson and Nigella Lawson. Tailored to the individual, the hour-long treatments at this sleek clinic incorporate deep cleansing, extraction, micro-dermabrasion and, especially, facial massage to boost circulation. Patel believes in treating the skin as naturally and gently as possible, eschewing the use of lots of different products. She also highlights the power of a well-groomed eyebrow to lift the face, and offers expert threading. Her diary is pretty full these days, but she's trained three facialists in her methods. A facial costs £125/hr with Patel or £95 with one of her staff. You can carry on the good work at home with her range of products, also sold at Harvey Nichols and Browns.

Foot care

Margaret Dabbs Foot Clinic/Spa

Until Nov 2008: *36 Weymouth Street, W1G 6NJ.* From Nov 2008: *7 New Cavendish Street, W1G 8UU (7487 5510/ www.margaretdabbs.co.uk). Baker Street or Regent's Park tube.* **Open** 9am-5pm Mon-Fri. From Nov 2008: hrs to be confirmed; call or visit website for details. **Credit** MC, V.

See p104 **Best foot forward.**

Also check out...

Chiropody

40 Upper Street, N1 0PN (7226 3781). Highbury & Islington tube/rail. **Open** 9am-7pm Mon-Fri; 9am-6pm Sat; 11am-5pm Sun. **Credit** MC, V.

Handily located on Upper Street, this is the footcare centre formerly known as Scholl. **For branch see index.**

Footopia

1st Floor, Peter Jones, Sloane Square, SW1W SEL (7259 0845). Sloane Square tube. **Open** 9.30am-7pm Mon, Tue, Thur-Sat; 9.30am-8pm Wed; 11am-5pm Sun. **Credit** MC, V.

Pedicures and podiatry (from £50) are the specialities of this tootsie-temple, which uses Karin Herzog's range of oxygen patented products. Manicures (from £27.50) are also available.

Foot Pad

30-32 Lamb's Conduit Street, WC1N 3LE (7404 6942/www.footpad.co.uk). Holborn or Russell Square tube. **Open** 10.30am-6pm Mon-Fri. **Credit** MC, V.

No-nonsense chiropody.

Make-up services

Many cosmetic shops, including **Becca** (*see p89*), **Cosmetics à la Carte** (*see p89*), **MAC Cosmetics** (*see p91*), **Pixi** (*see p91*), **Shu Uemura** (*see p90*) and new beauty boutique **Lost in Beauty** (*see p89*), offer makeovers for an extra charge. Beauty guru **John Gustafson** does consultations three days a week on the third floor of **Fenwick** (*see p15*). The fee is reasonable (£100, of which £50 can be redeemed against products), which partly explains the waiting list of up to five years. If you want to add your name to the queue, phone 7409 9823. Celebrity make-up artist **Daniel Sandler** heads a team at **Urban Retreat** in Harrods (*see p99*); prices start at £50 for a 60-minute consultation (redeemable against his products), or £300 with the man himself for a 90-minute make-up lesson.

Facemakeup.co.uk

www.facemakeup.co.uk.

One of a team of 100 make-up artists will visit you at home (from £62.50) for a lesson on bridal or party make-up or simply for tips and suggestions on how to spruce up your look. MAC, Chantecaille, Stila, NARS, Bobbi Brown and Laura Mercier are among their favoured products.

James Miller

8998 4763/mobile 07787 532545/ www.jamesmakeup.com. **Phone enquiries** 10am-8pm daily. **No credit cards.**

As well as his celebrity portfolio, the personable James Miller caters to private clients. Miller excels at transforming you into an enhanced yet natural-looking version of yourself, which makes him particularly in demand for weddings. Miller arrives with his kit and prices start at £95; a make-up lesson (90mins/2hrs) is £150.

Massage

Lavender Hill Slam Beauty

119 Lavender Hill, SW11 5QL (7585 1222/www.siambeauty.co.uk). Clapham Junction rail. **Open** 9.30am-11pm daily. *Massage* 11am-10pm daily. **Credit** MC, V.

We salute this no-frills gem for its long opening hours and amazing value for money. Thai or Swedish massage costs a mere £30 for an hour, while other treatments are equally cheap: a brow shape is yours for a paltry fiver, while hour-long Decleor or Dermalogica facials cost from £25.

For branch see index.

Micheline Arcier

7 William Street, SW1 9HL (7235 3545/ www.michelinearcier.com). Knightsbridge tube. **Open** 9.30am-6.30pm Mon-Wed; 10.30am-7.30pm Thur; 10am-6pm Fri; 9am-6pm Sat. **Credit** MC, V.

Inspired by French aromatherapist Jean Valnet and Marguerite Maury, who was one of the first to use essential oils in massage, Micheline Arcier opened her own clinic in 1981. It's now managed by her daughter Marie-Christine and holds a royal warrant. The quality of the oils – completely natural and not tested on animals – is guaranteed, and staff are thoroughly trained to treat clients with kind and holistic care. Most treatments are preceded by a half-hour consultation (£25); the list includes facials, reflexology and pregnancy aromatherapy, and body massages (£60/hr).

Pure massage

3-5 Vanston Place, SW6 1AY (7381 8100/ www.puremassage.com). Fulham Broadway tube. **Open** 11am-9pm Mon-Fri; 10am-9pm Sat; 11am-6pm Sun. **Credit** MC, V.

Pretty in ink

Tattooing has always been part of human culture; for better or worse we've been drawing on ourselves and each other throughout history. Groups as diverse as the Maoris, Egyptian priestesses and the Japanese criminal fraternity, the Yakuza, have adopted tattoos as a form of self-expression. The Romans and Greeks marked their slaves with tattoos; in 18th-century Japan tattooing was a form of punishment; and the Nazis branded concentration camp prisoners with a dehumanising number.

Nowadays it's a more positive tale, with skin (or body) art, as it's increasingly called, more mainstream than ever, and with many tattooists now seen as bona fide artists, with international followings and long waiting lists. In London there are now over 100 places where you can 'get inked'; this, however, has led to concern among the more established artists that the industry's integrity will suffer.

And, ironically for an industry that still gets so much bad press from middle England, integrity and reputation are what this business is founded on: you can't just pick up a needle and start working. As in the crafts of lore, long apprenticeships under somebody established are the only way in.

So where to head to? When you've decided what you want, and that you definitely want it (most reputable places will dissuade people who are in on a whim), have a look at some portfolios in one of the following establishments. And for anyone who has already endured an epidermal disaster, all the following studios also do cover-ups.

The Family Business

Into You (144 St John Street, EC1V 4UA, 7253 5085, www.into-you.co.uk) in Clerkenwell specialises in traditional and Japanese work and piercings. It's been running for 15 years and is well respected. Likewise, Kentish Town's **Flamin' Eight** (2 Castle Road, NW1 8PP, 7267 7888, www.flamineight.co.uk) is an award-winning studio with a retro feel, which has been open for some ten years. **The Family Business** (58 Exmouth Market, EC1R 4QE, 7278 9526, www.thefamilybusinesstattoo.com) is an original, spacious studio – the most impressive we've visited, with decor that incorporates Catholic paraphernalia – that claims to offer 'tasteful tattooing for first-timers, old-timers and serious collectors'. It's large enough to accommodate six resident artists (including the celebrated Saira Hunjan) at the same time. Meanwhile, Soho's small **Frith Street Tattoo** (18 Frith Street, W1D 4RQ, 7734 8180, www.frithstreettattoo.co.uk) houses seven in-house artists and five guests.

Other places to try are popular and professionally run **Happy Sailor Tattoo** in Shoreditch (17 Hackney Road, E2 7NX, 7033 9222, www.happysailortattoo.com) and the arty **Shangri-La Tattoo** on neighbouring Kingsland Road (no.52, E2 8DP, 7739 3066). Run by former arts student Lesley Chan, the latter has its own exhibition space and also sells prints and art books.

If you want your markings made at the same place as the rock and rollers, however, head to **New Wave Tattoo** in Muswell Hill (157 Sydney Road, N10 2NL, 8444 8779, www.newwavetattoo.co.uk); Liam Gallagher, Marc Almond and members of the Stereophonics have all submitted to the inked needle at Lal Hardy's studio.

Beata Aleksandrowicz and Jean-Marc Delacourt, evangelical believers in the healing power of touch, say that 'the world could be more beautiful with more relaxed faces around'. Emerging from the therapy rooms after a 45-minute back massage certainly engenders more benign feelings toward the world. From the bright, white reception area, clients are led downstairs to a series of softly lit, sparely appointed massage rooms. The next step is to drift away on a tide of plinky mood music as one of the Aleksandrowicz-trained therapists kneads, strokes, unravels knots and tensions and sends tense, stiff, stressed bodies to a better place. There are programmes for pregnancy and back problems as well as 15-minute chair-based introductory sessions (£15) and baby massage. Beata's groundbreaking Face Therapy, meanwhile, works on connective tissue and 're-educating the muscles' to release tension. The result is a smoother jawline, defined cheekbones and a happy glow.

For branch see index.

Also check out...

Rejuvenation Centre

132 Commercial Street, E1 6NG (7247 8464/www.therejuvenationcentre.com). Liverpool Street tube/rail/Old Street tube. **Open** 9am-8pm Mon-Fri; 9am-2pm Sat, Sun. **Credit** AmEx, MC, V.

Massages here are geared towards increasing and balancing energy levels.

Relax

65-67 Brewer Street, W1F 9UP (7494 3333/www.relax.org.uk). Piccadilly Circus tube. **Open** 10am-9pm Mon-Sat; noon-8pm Sun. **Credit** AmEx, MC, V.

At ground level, you can have an express chair massage and tea at the bar, or choose from a range of lie-down options upstairs.

For branch see index.

Walk-in Backrub

14 Neal's Yard, WC2H 9DP (7836 9111/www.walkinbackrub.co.uk). Covent Garden tube. **Open** 10.30am-7pm Mon-Sat; noon-6pm Sun. **Credit** AmEx, MC, V.

Stress-busting sessions on ergonomically designed leather chairs. A ten-minute backrub costs £9.75; for 30mins it's £27.

For branches see index.

Nails

As well as the specialists listed here, most beauty salons also offer manicures and pedicures; for details, *see pp96-101*.

Urban Retreat in Harrods (*see p99*), in particular, has a dedicated nail expert in the form of Leighton Denny and his crack team.

Iris Chapple

3 Spanish Place, W1U 3HX (07956 307392). Baker Street or Bond Street tube. **Open** by appointment 8am-5pm Tue-Sat. **No credit cards**.

Visiting Iris Chapple is a treat in so many ways. The fact that you end up with a superb nail treatment is of paramount importance and her decades of experience mean you needn't worry on that score. But before she became a nail expert (her pedicures are as famous as her manicures), she was a club singer, so – as she expertly trims, buffs, creams, smoothes, files, softens, moisturises, files again and finally applies base coat, two layers of (in our case) brilliant red polish and top coat – you can get her to tell you about her days at the famous Windmill club and the infamous Cabaret Club (remember the Profumo Affair?). Undoubtedly one of the most interesting manicures we've ever had and, at the end of it, a set of truly spectacular nails. Chapple's prices belie her skills, but don't (she was quite firm on this point) arrange to do anything for at least an hour afterwards.

Also check out...

Amazing Nails

Mane Line Hair Salon, 22 Weighhouse Street, W1K 5LZ (07775 780744). Bond Street tube. **Open** by appointment 10am-6pm Mon-Sat. **Credit** MC, V.

Amazing Nails offers solid manicures and pedicures that won't break the bank – though you'll have to phone first to make an appointment; don't just turn up. A half-hour manicure costs £28, while a 45-minute pedicure is £28.50.

California Nail Bar

78 Heath Street, NW3 1DN (7431 8988/ www.california-nail-bar.co.uk). Hampstead tube. **Open** 10am-7pm Mon-Sat; 11am-6pm Sun. **Credit** MC, V.

This reliable nail bar charges £15 for a simple manicure with polish; if you're faking it, a full set of gel nails costs £35. **For branch see index**.

Hawkeye

5 Silver Place, off Beak Street, W1F 0JR (7287 1847/www.hawkeyehair.com). Oxford Circus tube. **Open** 10am-8pm Tue-Fri; 10am-6pm Sat. **Credit** MC, V.

The hour-long 'Pure Indulgence Experience' (£34) includes a manicure and full arm massage, though you can just pop in for a speedy shape and paint (£13).

Problem skin

The Sher System

30 New Bond Street, W1S 2RN (7499 4022/www.sher.co.uk). Bond Street tube. **Open** 9am-5.30pm Mon-Fri. **Credit** AmEx, MC, V.

Now in her early seventies, Helen Sher is living proof that the Sher System of products – cleansers, serums, anti-blemish solutions, as well as a collection of natural-looking make-up – can help keep the plastic surgeon at bay. There are no gimmicks here – one of the key components of the Sher System's ideology is water, which, Sher stresses, stimulates circulation, regulates the natural balance of the skin and revitalises, rehydrates, oxygenates and detoxifies it. Her holistic approach takes in dietary advice and supplements. Our problem skin started to clear up within days of using the products, but if you need more proof, check out the before and after shots of clients on the website. A consultation costs from £75. New for 2008/9 is Sher's latest product, designed for use in the office or the tube; called Silver Mist Spray (£12/50ml), it contains ultra-fine particles of colloidal silver, and a light spritz of the stuff helps to keep your skin hydrated and bacteria-free.

Waxing

Katie Young's

Unit 12, Hoxton Walk, Hoxton Street, N1 6RA (7739 9271). Old Street tube/rail. **Open** 10am-5pm Mon; 10am-6pm Tue, Wed; 10am-7pm Thur, Fri; 9am-6pm Sat.

This cheap-and-cheerful Hoxton salon provides good-quality waxing at bargain rates, charging from £12 for a half-leg wax.

Ki Mantra Urban Life Spa

5 Camden Passage, N1 8EU (7226 8860/ www.kimantra.co.uk). Angel tube. **Open** 11am-8pm Mon; 10am-8pm Tue-Sat; 11am-6pm Sun. **Credit** (over £10) MC, V.

Waxing prices are surprisingly reasonable at this Islington salon, located just off Upper Street: a half-leg wax is £15, a bikini £10, and a full leg and bikini £25. Weekends tend to be busy, so try to book ahead.

Otylia Roberts at Greenhouse

142 Wigmore Street, W1U 3SH (7486 5537/www.otyliaroberts.co.uk). Bond Street tube. **Open** 10am-6pm Mon; 10am-7pm Tue; 9.20am-7pm Wed, Thur; 10am-5.40pm Fri; 9.30am-4.30pm Sat. **Credit** MC, V.

Queen of the Brazilian, Polish-born Otylia Roberts uses beeswax-based hot wax instead of strips. Less painful, and with better results, but it's pricier: from £34 for a half leg (the Brazilian is £49, while a Hollywood is £51).

Strip

112 Talbot Road, W11 1JR (7727 2754/ www.2strip.com). Westbourne Park tube. **Open** 10am-8pm Mon-Thur; 10am-6pm Fri, Sat; noon-5pm Sun. **Credit** MC, V.

The therapists at Strip use Lycon wax, which promises – and, say our sources, delivers – a less painful wax; treatment rooms also feature distracting plasma-screen TVs. Prices aren't too steep, with a bikini costing from £22. The lengthy menu also has plenty of options for men, from back waxes to 'Male Brazilians'.

Best foot forward

As this guide went to press, preparations were in full swing for the November 2008 opening of Europe's first dedicated foot spa. The initiative of chiropodist Margaret Dabbs, the spa will be housed in spacious, interior-designed premises on New Cavendish Street (*see p102* **Margaret Dabbs Foot Spa**), round the corner from Dabbs's rather more drab (but nevertheless characterful) foot clinic. The latter will close – it's being incorporated into the new space – once the spa has opened.

Continuing Dabbs's focus on the fusing of health and beauty when it comes to TLC for the tootsies, the spa will house a team of podiatrists – to take care of the thorough surgical pedicures to banish dead skin and debris (£75/45mins or £120/45mins with Margaret herself), diagnosis of fungal infections and soothing oxygen treatments. There will also be a beauty team, to see to the more luxurious foot massages, soaks and traditional pedicures (using the latest colour ranges from make-up brand Essie; manicures will also be available). Podiatrists will also be able to refer clients to other foot experts where necessary. Dabbs's approach seems to appeal to both sexes, with plenty of men among her regular clients.

Dabbs's own-label 'Beauty for the Feet' range of products has been extended to coincide with the opening of the spa. It includes Hydrating Foot Soak (£20/200ml) and Intensive Treatment Foot Oil (£20/200ml), which is designed to deal with cracked skin and uses emu oil, the ancient Australian Aboriginal healer, as a key ingredient (the company donates to the Spinifex Foundation's Schools for Settlements programme). As well as being sold in the spa, the range is available from Boots.

Clinics

Alive + Well

61 Shelton Street, WC2H 9HE (7379 5531/www.aliveandwell.co.uk). Covent Garden tube. **Open** 8.30am-9pm Mon-Fri. **Credit** AmEx, MC, V.
Treatments: acupuncture, aromatherapy, astrotherapy, colonic hydrotherapy, deep tissue and Ayurvedic massage treatments, hypnotherapy, homeopathy, nutritional therapy, osteopathy, reflexology, shiatsu, yoga.
With its cool white interior, chocolate-brown carpet, leather sofas and modern artwork, you'd be forgiven for confusing Alive + Well with a chic hotel. Now in its fourth year, this holistic clinic in the heart of Covent Garden is thriving and, even though two new rooms were added in 2008, you'll have to book well in advance to get a slot. Friendly osteopath Simon Freeman set up the practice after running a busy Soho clinic for 12 years and working with professional football teams. Helen Johnson – once a therapist to Princess Diana – is now working here one day a week, combining her expertise in osteopathy and homeopathy to relieve physical and emotional trauma. There's no mistaking the quality of the treatments, and the emphasis is on tailoring therapies to individual needs. It's not especially cheap: osteopathy consultations begin at £60/45mins, massages from £60/hr.

Balance the Clinic

250 King's Road, SW3 5UE (7565 0333/ www.balancetheclinic.com). Sloane Square tube. **Open** 9am-7pm Mon, Tue, Fri; 9am-8pm Wed, Thur; 9am-6pm Sat; 10am-5.30pm Sun. **Credit** MC, V.
Treatments: acupuncture, anti-cellulite treatments, body treatments, colonic hydrotherapy, detox treatments, eyebrow shaping & tinting, eyelash perming and tinting, facials, homeopathy, laser hair removal, lymphatic drainage, manicures, massages, naturopathy, nutritional advice, osteopathy, pedicures, reflexology, semi-permanent make-up, tanning treatments, waxing.
As the name suggests, this swish Chelsea clinic aims to provide a balanced set of therapies and procedures to help clients deal with the rigours of modern life. From facials to naturopathy to laser-assisted lipo, to macrolane breast enhancements, the emphasis is on tailor-made, life-enhancing treatments. In fact, Balance boasts the UK's largest colonic hydrotherapy practice, with prices starting at £80 for 60 minutes, or opt for a session with experienced nutritional therapist and iridologist Amanda Griggs (£115 for initial consultation).

Brackenbury Natural Health Clinic

30 Brackenbury Road, W6 OBA (8741 9264/www.brackenburyclinic.com). Goldhawk Road tube. **Open** 9am-6pm Mon-Sat (but can take appointments 8am-8pm). **No credit cards**.
Treatments: acupuncture, Alexander technique, allergy testing, Bowen Technique, Chinese medicine, chiropody, colonic hydrotherapy, counselling, cranio-sacral therapy, holistic birth, homeopathy, hypnotherapy, life coaching, massages, nutritional advice, osteopathy, Pilates, psychotherapy, reflexology, shiatsu, tui na (Chinese massage).
Quiet, long-established clinic with solid credentials. Treatments from £45.

Food Doctor

76-78 Holland Park Avenue, W11 3RB (7792 6700/www.thefooddoctor.com). Holland Park tube. **Open** 9am-6pm Mon, Wed, Thur, Fri; 9am-8pm Tue; also by appointment. **Credit** MC, V.
A consultation at nutritionist Ian Marber's clinic will teach you exactly what to eat, what to avoid and how to keep fit while leading a busy life. Ian first got interested in nutrition when he started to suffer from coeliac disease (gluten intolerance). Since then, he has dedicated his life to learning about food and passing on his knowledge to others. A consultation with the man himself will set you back £125, or £95 for a session with one of the three associate nutritional therapists. Some clients come with problems such as irritable bowel syndrome, PMS or eczema; others want to lose weight or simply eat more healthily. The Food Doctor is also open one or two Saturdays a month; phone for dates.

Hale Clinic

7 Park Crescent, W1B 1PF (7631 0156/ www.haleclinic.com). Great Portland Street or Regent's Park tube. **Open** 9am-9pm Mon-Fri; 9am-5pm Sat. **Credit** (shop only) AmEx, MC, V.
Treatments: acupuncture, African rhythms massage, age defiance facials, Alexander Technique, allergy testing, Bach flower remedies, Chakra balancing, chiropody, crystal therapy, colonic hydrotherapy, endometriosis therapy, hypnotherapy, hydrotherapy, feng shui, iridology, kinesiology, Jungian analysis, massages, non-surgical facelifts, nutrition, osteopathy, physiotherapy, psychotherapy, reflexology, reiki, spiritual healing, trichology.
The list of treatments at the home of all things alternative is endless. There are 100 practitioners – including 20 trained doctors – affiliated to the clinic. Opened in 1988 by the Prince of Wales, the aim at the Hale is to combine complementary and traditional medicine to solve health problems. Despite its grand Nash terrace premises, the interior is more shabby-genteel doctor's surgery than super-smart centre. The large basement shop stocks a wide range of supplements, skincare and books.

Joshi Clinic

57 Wimpole Street, W1G 8YW (7487 5456/www.thejoshiclinic.com). Bond Street tube. **Open** 9.30am-7pm Mon-Fri; by appointment 9.30am-2pm Sat. **Credit** MC, V.
Treatments: acupuncture, allergy testing, massage, chiropody, colonic hydrotherapy, clinical hypnosis, cranial osteotherapy, deep tissue massage, endermologie, GP clinic, holistic detox, homeopathy, Mesotherapy, nutrition, osteopathy, personal training, physiotherapy, Pilates, reflexology, spiritual healing, weight management.
Wanting to lose a few pounds to fit into that party frock, or merely to kick-start a diet? Nish Joshi's fusion of Ayurvedic principles and orthodox medicine has helped hone the svelte silhouettes of Kate Moss, Gwyneth Paltrow and Patsy Kensit, among others. Healing and purifying are at the heart of his work, but treatments here also focus on balancing the body's alkaline and acid levels, with the famous 21-day detox. Look out also for Joshi's latest venture – the Joshi Clinic Wellness Centre, in Marylebone – and for his column on solutions to all sorts of health problems in the *Telegraph*.
For branch see index.

Ashlins Natural Health

181 Hoe Street, E17 3AP (8520 5268/ www.ashlins.co.uk). Walthamstow Central tube/rail. **Open** 9am-9pm Mon-Fri; 9am-5pm Sat; 11am-5pm Sun. **No credit cards**.
Treatments: acupuncture, Alexander Technique, aromatherapy, Ayurvedic massage, Bach flower remedies, chiropody, chiropractic treatments, colonic hydrotherapy, counselling, craniosacral therapy, deep tissue massage, kinesiology, Indian head massage, nutritional therapy, personal training, psychotherapy, reflexology, reiki, shiatsu, sound meditation, sports injury therapy, Thai yoga, yoga.
This friendly health centre offers most of the popular alternative/natural therapies.

Common Sense

7 Clapham Common Southside, SW4 7AA (7720 8817/www.southlondon naturalhealthcentre.com). Clapham Common tube. **Open** 9am-10pm Mon-Fri; 9.30am-6.30pm Sat; 10am-4pm Sun. **Credit** (tanning and flotation only) MC, V.
Treatments: acupuncture, aromatherapy, body mirror healing, Bowen Technique, colonic irrigation, cranial osteopathy, flotation, homeopathy, hypnotherapy, Indian head massage, massages, meditation, metamorphic technique, nutrition, osteopathy, Pilates, reflexology, reiki, reverse therapy, tai chi, tanning.
This Clapham complementary therapy centre promises to provide a solution to all your therapeutic needs, be they relaxation, detoxification, realignment, pain relief or addiction support. It houses the London Flotation Centre on the top floor.

Diagnostic Clinic

50 New Cavendish Street, W1G 8TL (7009 4650/www.thediagnosticclinic.com). Bond Street tube. **Open** 9am-6pm Mon-Fri. **Credit** MC, V.
Treatments: health screens, homeopathy, naturopathy, nutritional therapy, osteopathy, natural remedies.
An integrated medicine clinic offering unique health screenings that are sometimes probing and personal but can get to the root of problems. The medical director is Dr Rajendra Sharma, author of *The Family Enclyclopaedia of Health*.

Life Centre

15 Edge Street, W8 7PN (7221 4602/ www.thelifecentre.com). Notting Hill Gate tube. **Open** 8am-9.30pm Mon-Fri; 8.15am-7.30pm Sat, Sun. **Credit** MC, V.
This famed Notting Hill establishment is rated as one of the best yoga centres in London. It also has a good range of treatments.

Hairdressers

Children's haircuts can be had at **Mini Kin**, **Caramel Baby & Child**, **Frogs & Fairies**, **Their Nibs** and the **Little Trading Company** (for all, *see pp259-268*).

For the **Hurwundeki** hair salon, *see p30* **Unique Selling Point**.

Andrew Jose

1 Charlotte Street, W1T 1RB (7323 4679/ www.andrewjose.com). Tottenham Court Road tube. **Open** 9am-7pm Mon-Wed; 9am-9pm Thur, Fri; 9am-6pm Sat; 10.30am-5pm Sun. **Credit** AmEx, MC, V.

It's easy to find a buzzy, busy West End salon that will make you feel you're at the cutting edge of hairstyling, less so to find one whose modern, wearable cuts are equally on-trend. Andrew Jose offers exactly this kind of service. The corner location ensures a bright and light-filled space, while the staff are friendly and expertly adept. A cut and blow-dry begins with a discussion of hair type and possible options, including how to achieve and maintain healthy, glossy hair and is followed by a wash that's also a gentle neck and head massage. Our cut resulted in a gentle, soft style – exactly what we wanted. A cut with the lovely Jose starts at £150, but it's £35 for a junior stylist. A half-head of highlights is £92 and semi-permanent colour £55.

Bloww

4 Regent Place, W1B 5EA (7292 0300/ www.bloww.com). Piccadilly Circus tube. **Open** 10am-7pm Tue, Fri; 10am-9pm Wed, Thur; 9am-6pm Sat. **Credit** AmEx, MC, V.

If you want a dramatic setting for a haircut, then this funky, two-store space is for you; what's more, director Paul Merritt was salon manager on reality TV show *The Salon*. Decorative touches like antique desks and bold splashes of colour ensure the basic black and white interiors aren't too antiseptic. Natter with friendly staff and describe the exact look you're after; our never-before-coloured, rather dull haircut was given a gorgeous makeover with a half head of highlights that brought out the chestnut in our natural colour while adding warm touches of gold and honey, and the blow-dry that finished it off made the hair look and feel fantastic. Downstairs, a series of luxurious rooms offer a wide range of beauty treatments, among them mud therapy and flotation body treatments. Cuts start at £60 for women and £40 for men.

Top five Blow-drys

Brooks & Brooks. *See above.*
Headmasters Blo Out Bar at Fenwick. *See p15.*
Hersheson's Blow Dry Bar at Topshop. *See right and p46.*
Michaeljohn. *See p109.*
Scissors Palace. *See p113.*

Brooks & Brooks

13-17 Sicilian Avenue, WC1A 2QH (7405 8111/www.brooksandbrooks.co.uk). Holborn tube. **Open** 9am-7pm Mon, Tue; 9am-8pm Wed-Fri; 10am-5.30pm Sat. **Credit** MC, V.

Jamie and Sally Brooks and their team of stylists have won London Hairdresser of the Year three times in recent years. It's not hard to see why; the team is made up of consummate professionals. Consultations are thorough, taking into account skin tone and face shape. Prices are reasonable, starting from £35 for a ladies' cut and blow-dry, while new 'express' treatments from Kerastase address specific needs of different hair types, and start from just £12.50. On our latest visit, senior stylist Melanie did wonders sorting out a mess of previous layers, leaving our barnet looking much more sleek and shapely. Recent additions to the salon are a dedicated boudoir area downstairs designed for bridal parties, and the Catwalk Blow Out – a blow-dry with a sexy, sassy finish; the cost is £25, while a blow-dry lesson will set you back £50.

Charles Worthington

7 Percy Street, W1T 1DH (7631 1370/ www.cwlondon.com). Tottenham Court Road tube. **Open** 8am-7.45pm Mon-Thur; 10.15am-6.45pm Fri; 9.15am-5.45pm Sat; 10am-4.45pm Sun. **Credit** AmEx, MC, V.

Inside Charles Worthington's airy, elegant flagship salon, all is blissfully calm and well ordered. Despite the packed appointments book, stylists take time over in-depth pre-cut and colour consultations – making this an excellent choice if you're contemplating a major chop and change. With an unerring eye for colour and gift for visualising which cut will best suit your face shape, Italian master stylist Massy is highly recommended (and often booked up weeks in advance): his blow-drys transform even the most unruly of mops into sleek, satisfyingly swishy tresses. Friendly staff are happy to chat, or leave you to work through a stack of magazines; a nominal charge (£2) brings unlimited refreshments, from tea and brownies to champagne cocktails and smoked salmon blinis.

For branches see index.

Daniel Hersheson

45 Conduit Street, W1F 2YN (7434 1747/www.danielhersheson.com). Oxford Circus tube. **Open** 9am-6pm Mon-Wed, Sat; 9am-8pm Thur, Fri. **Credit** AmEx, MC, V.

Despite its upmarket location and pedigree – it sits in pole position between Vivienne Westwood and Donna Karan – this airy, modern two-storey salon isn't at all snooty. Although often away on shoots, the father and son team are keen to remain accessible to 'ordinary' clients in their two London salons, but you're in good hands with every member of the team. Cuts start at £55 (men's from £35), though you'll pay more than that for a cut by Daniel or Luke (£250 and £125 respectively); a half head of highlights starts at £135. The salon has a cutting-edge approach to hairdressing, using and selling a high-tech range of own-brand hair tools (dryers, straightening irons, waving tongs, ceramic brushes), also sold at Selfridges and Liberty, and the salon launched a UK exclusive of the Permanent Blow Dry treatment from Brazil (from £200) in 2008. The more showy Harvey Nics branch has a high-concept spa and full menu of beauty treatments. There's also a blow-dry bar in Topshop (7927 7888; *see p46*).

For branch see index.

Errol Douglas

18 Motcomb Street, SW1X 8LB (7235 0110/www.erroldouglas.com). Knightsbridge tube/Victoria tube/rail. **Open** 9am-6pm Mon; 9am-7pm Tue-Sat. **Credit** MC, V.

The award-winning Errol Douglas, who swoops through his Knightsbridge salon in white, knows a thing or two about creating show-stopping hair. Be warned: try him once and he's very hard to give up. It comes as no surprise that he's been nominated for British Hairdresser of the Year 12 times and in 2008 he collected an MBE from Her Majesty herself, joining an exclusive band of hairdressers such as Charles Worthington and Nicky Clarke. His starry clientele includes Uma Thurman, Christina Ricci and Naomi Campbell. At his classy but comfy Knightsbridge salon, the focus is on giving great cuts, quality extensions, staightening and superb Afro care. A cut and blow-dry will set you back anything from £50 to £185 with Errol himself, while a half head of highlights or lowlights starts at £80.

Fish

30 D'Arblay Street, W1F 8ER (7494 2398/ www.fishweb.co.uk). Leicester Square tube. **Open** 10am-7pm Mon-Wed, Fri; 10am-8pm Thur; 10am-5pm Sat. **Credit** MC, V.

This former fishmonger celebrates 21 years in the business this year and, thanks to a constant stream of Soho regulars, there's no sign that the hairdryers will be hung up any time soon. Equal parts hip hairdresser and chatty barbershop, the Paul Burfoot-owned salon is comfortable and on the right side of scruffy, with clean white tiles and slightly wonky picture frames downstairs clashing with retro hairdressing photographs and posters, and mirrors full of faded postcards, upstairs. Donna and Angie (both from New Zealand) are outstanding cutters who labour over your tresses with care. Cuts are relatively cheap – £41 for a girl's cut and blow-dry and £34 for gents. Look out for Fish hair products for men and women, available in Boots.

Fordham Soho

47 Greek Street, W1D 4EE (7287 8484/ www.fordhamwhite.com). Tottenham Court Road tube. **Open** 10am-7pm Mon, Tue; 10am-8pm Wed-Fri; 10am-6pm Sat. **Credit** AmEx, DC, MC, V.

With the departure of Ben White (who took off with several members of the team), Sean Fordham is now going it alone. The salon previously known as Fordham White has kept its trendy yet unpretentious vibe and upmarket facilities – including the free refreshments (including wine), electronic reclining chairs and, for those who simply can't go for an hour without checking Facebook, Wi-Fi throughout. The new band of staff are of the same high standard, and prices are reasonable, starting at £47 for a senior stylist (£37 for men) and going up to

Tommy Guns.
See p110.

High barnets

Beehives, bouffants, quiffs and other retro styles.

Dressing down and the natural look might be all right for some, but, spurred on by the recent burlesque trend, a growing number of Londoners are hankering after the glamorous and glitzy hair-dos of yesteryear. Vintage clothes shops are to be found all over town, but where do you go for a Jackie Kennedy bouffant, an Audrey Hepburn beehive or a Bettie Page fringe? The answer is to one of the several specialist retro hair salons that have set up in the capital over the past year or so.

At **Nina's Hair Parlour** (*see p111*) in Marylebone, specialists in vintage hairstyling for men and women, the emphasis is on the big, bold and beautiful, inspired by both the burlesque look and the Hollywood glamour of the 1940s and '50s. The original hood dryers complete the time-warped experience and, pleasingly, the cuts start from just £38, with a cut and set from £45 – so you don't need to be earning glamorous wages. At **It's Something Hell's** (*see p111*) in Kingly Court, just off Carnaby Street, you'll find resident Miss Betty, another retro stylist catering to glamour girls and femme fatales, while her French colleague and compatriot, the switchblade wielding Mr Ducktail, leans more towards the bad boy look. This is where to come if your inspiration is more James Dean than Humphrey Bogart, and where a rockabilly cut will set you back £20 and a 'switchblade kut deluxe', £35.

It's Something Hell's

Over in the east, against a super-cool backdrop of black brick walls, and with theatrical dressing room mirrors, is **Pimps & Pinups** (*see p110*) offering 'classic hairdressing with the latest styles': the salon aims to combine the decadent styles of the post-war era with the cutting-edge trends of the Shoreditch set. A simple cut starts at £34 and £40 for men and women respectively, while the speciality retro hair-up service costs £40 per hour. Amy Winehouse, eat your heart out!

£80 for a director (£55 for men). The salon has always been great with colour and this is where Sean intends the focus of the new Fordham Soho to be. Scheduled to open in autumn 2008 is a brand-new Redken colour bar in place of the downstairs beauty salon.

4th Floor

3rd & 4th Floors, 4 Northington Street, WC1N 2JG (7405 6011/www.4thfloor.co.uk). Chancery Lane tube. **Open** 9am-7pm Mon-Fri; 9am-6pm Sat. **Credit** AmEx, MC, V.

Everything about 4th Floor is impressive – from the beautiful, airy, light warehouse space (over the third and fourth floors) populated by old barber's chairs, retro chairs, chunky sculptures and interesting light fittings, to the views over Clerkenwell from the floor-to-ceiling windows; then there's the reliably fabulous cuts and colouring, and the reasonable prices. Stylist Leigh is – as all Richard Stepney's staff are – friendly yet professional, instantly assessing what needs to be done with the mop of hair before her and aiming for top-notch results. Prices start at £43 for men, £48 for women, rising to £76/£81 if owner Richard tends your tresses. Colour starts from £45 for a semi-permanent to £115 for a full head of highlights. For cutting and colouring this is one of the best and most reasonably priced options in London.

Franco & Co

117 St John Street, EC1V 4JA (7253 8188/www.franco.co.uk). Farringdon tube/rail. **Open** 10am-8pm Mon-Fri; 10am-5pm Sat. **Credit** AmEx, MC, V.

Australian stylist Brent Barber and Zimbabwean manager Rejoice Phiri run this Clerkenwell hair and beauty salon with friendly efficiency, creating an ambience that's bright and on-trend without being off-puttingly high-fashion. Which isn't to say their cuts aren't high-fashion; Brent, a recipient of the British Hairdresser of the Year award when he was with Brooks & Brooks, has a ton of experience in editorial and fashion shoots, but here puts the client's wishes firmly to the fore. The open space, with bare bricks and wooden floorboards, lends itself to easy conversation, so discussing the cut and care of your hair doesn't mean shouting over the sound system. The result? A sleek, manageable style and beautifully conditioned hair, for the very reasonable price of £60 (cuts start at £40 with a junior stylist). Beauty treatments take place in the two basement rooms, and anyone getting their hair done gets a £10 voucher towards one.

Gina Conway Aveda Salon

62 Westbourne Grove, W2 5SH (7229 6644/www.ginaconway.co.uk). Bayswater or Notting Hill Gate tube. **Open** 10am-5pm Mon, Sun; 10am-7pm Tue; 9am-9pm Wed-Fri; 9am-7pm Sat. **Credit** AmEx, MC, V.

Set in a beautiful 19th-century former bank, the Westbourne Grove branch of Gina Conway is sublime – with an ornate domed ceiling, and Scandinavian-style wood, glass and lighting. First-timers have to fill in a comprehensive questionnaire – covering everything from the colours you wear to your styling preferences – to determine which look will suit them best. Afterwards, all customers get a scalp massage to ease away the woes. On our last visit the stylist recommended a classic cut with a sexy edge and delivered as promised – we left with a glossy barnet and versatile cut that was easy to manage afterwards. A cut and blow-dry starts at £48, a full head of highlights at £105. You can also have a facial, massage and pretty much any beauty treatment imaginable here, all with Aveda products. **For branch see index.**

Hair & Jerome

5 Artillery Passage, E1 7LJ (7375 0044/www.hairandjerome.co.uk). Liverpool

Street tube/rail. **Open** 10am-9pm Mon-Thur; 10am-8pm Fri; 9am-6pm Sat. **Credit** MC, V.
Located in a lovely little street between Liverpool Street and Spitalfields, Jerome Hillion's salon is as noteworthy for its eclectic interior – think Victoriana mixed with retro kitsch – as its haircuts. The unisex salon is popular with both City boys and fashionistas alike, and has been known to host fashion-related events (like the Cross & Spot menswear sample sale in July 2008). Jerome's flair with hair means that an eclectic and steady flow of regulars are treated like friends, safe in the knowledge that they're being attended to by some of the best scissor-wielding hands in London. A ladies' cut and blow-dry goes from £43 with a 'style adviser' to £89 with Jerome himself; a men's cut and finish varies between £31 and £46; a half head of highlights, meanwhile, costs from £68.

hob

Unit 3B, 28 Jamestown Road, NW1 7BY (7485 7272/www.hobsalons.com). Camden Town tube. **Open** 9am-6pm Mon; 9am-8pm Tue-Fri; 8.30am-6pm Sat; 10am-5pm Sun. **Credit** AmEx, MC, V.
Overlooking the dinky aquatic charms of Camden Lock, the interior of the latest branch of the hob chain seems strangely out of place resembling, as it does, a 1970s cruise-liner – lots of chrome, wooden 'deck' floors and black leather upholstery. From small beginnings (hob stands for Hair On Broadway, after the first salon to open in Mill Hill 25 years ago), this chain has quietly become something of a success story – a mini Tony & Guy of north London hoving into view. Our stylist's friendly and professional air of competence and advice on cut were reassuring on our visit; hob is well known in the industry for its training programmes (the hob academy is located in the Camden branch). As well as the usual cuts and colour services, there's a separate hair treatment room offering intensive conditioning using Alterna products (plus a massage while you wait) and a chemical-free straightening service.
For branches see index.

Jo Hansford

19 Mount Street, W1K 2RN (7495 7774/ www.johansford.com). Bond Street or Green Park tube. **Open** 8.30am-6pm Tue-Fri; 8.30am-5.30pm Sat. **Credit** MC, V.
Jo Hansford opened her salon in 1993 and colour has become her niche (an appointment with the *grande dame* herself will cost you £150). The smart Mayfair premises are everything an upmarket salon should be: professional, plush and comfortable, and offering a reliable service. Frequented by a long list of high-profile clients – including the Duchess of Cornwall and Elizabeth Hurley, who trust only Hansford herself with their locks – it's testament to the quality of her highly professional staff just how relaxed and welcoming the salon is to those who don't make the pages of *Hello* and *Vogue*. For a more affordable colour option ask for Jacklyn Smith (from £95 for a tint) or go to the charismatic Steve Carr for a natty new haircut (from £75). We've been to this salon many times and can't fault it.

Karine Jackson

24 Litchfield Street, WC2H 9NJ (7836 0300/www.karinejackson.co.uk). Leicester Square tube. **Open** 10am-7pm Mon, Fri; 10am-9pm Tue, Thur; 10am-8pm Wed; 9am-6pm Sat. **Credit** AmEx, MC, V.
Her Soho salon may be a simple affair, with cuts and colours upstairs, and treatment rooms downstairs, but Karine Jackson is really rather special. After all, Jackson was London Hairdresser of the Year 2007 (shortlisted for 2008), has a L'Oreal Colour Specialist Degree under her belt, and also happens to be downright friendly. Clients can sip a wine or beer (even champagne) during an initial consultation, and we felt confident enough in her skills to go for a total restyle. Our locks were lopped and layered to accentuate cheekbones and face shape, and the blonde quotient was upped. While the colour locked in, we enjoyed a complimentary nail polish. Jackson is a big fan of organic colour, promising that it will last (providing customers use gentle shampoos) and that locks will remain in tip-top condition. The resulting cut and colour certainly didn't disappoint. The salon offers beauty services for men as well as women.

Klinik

65 Exmouth Market, EC1R 4QL (7837 3771/www.theklinik.com). Angel tube/ Farringdon tube/rail. **Open** 9am-8pm Mon-Fri; 9am-6pm Sat. **Credit** MC, V.
This tiny yet fun salon shows work in progress through cameras suspended over each chair, with pictures on small, retro monitors next to each client mirror. Expect a friendly and open service, with all the activity going on in one room – there's no 'behind the scenes area' – creating a vibe of warm intimacy. Our cut (despite being delivered on to hair that had previously been cut at home) was adventurous and stylish, creating a side fringe that hung perfectly; the colour was a natural-looking blonde success. A downside was that unswept cuttings from a previous chop lingered, but that was our only gripe – Klinik is a great little find. Watch this space to see what happens when it moves further down the road in autumn 2008. All the team are senior stylists, so pricing remains simple; cuts start at £44 and colour at £62.

Lounge Soho

26 Peter Street, W1F 0AH (7437 3877/ www.theloungesoho.co.uk). Piccadilly Circus tube. **Open** 10am-7pm Mon, Sat; 10am-8pm Tue, Wed, Fri; 10am-9pm Thur; noon-5pm Sun. **Credit** AmEx, MC, V.
Nestled between the red light district and the buzz of Berwick Street Market lies this cosy salon. Owner and former DJ Joe Mills prides himself on his 'music of the month' wall – hand-picked, often pre-label release eclectic sounds hum soothingly around your ears as you sit back and let the pampering commence by the skilled snippers here. The decor is a cross between a Manhattan loft and a sleek contemporary hotel, complete with Wi-Fi and Shiatsu back massage washchairs. There's a colour bar too (from £50 for women) where you can see your own tailor-made shade being concocted before your eyes. Creative stylists' prices for women's cuts are £50, men's £40.

Mahogany

17 St George Street, W1S 1FJ (7629 3121/ www.mahoganyhair.co.uk). Oxford Circus tube. **Open** 9.15am-6.15pm Mon, Tue, Sat; 9.15am-8pm Wed-Fri. **Credit** AmEx, MC, V.
An oasis of calm slap bang in central London, Mahogany is the kind of upmarket yet unpretentious salon that inspires total confidence. Getting your hair done here is a pleasure. This is largely down to the skilled staff, who are both solicitous with offers of drinks and mags, and willing to listen carefully to clients and respond with honest and helpful suggestions. From the colourist came the idea of adding some caramel tones to our tired blonde highlights. From the director cutter: a clear explanation of two different ways to cut a fringe, and how each would have a different effect. We emerged satisfied, with smooth and silky tresses and natural-looking colour. Highlights start at £107 for half a head, and a cut and blow-dry will set you back £52 with a stylist, rising to £100 with the company's founder and its international creative director, Richard Thompson.

Michaeljohn

25 Albemarle Street, W1S 4HU (7629 6969/www.michaeljohn.co.uk). Green Park tube. **Open** 9am-6pm Mon; 8.30am-7pm Tue-Fri; 8.30am-6pm Sat. **Credit** AmEx, MC, V.
A Mayfair classic delivering great cuts to ladies who lunch. The client list reads like a celebrity *Who's Who*; Twiggy, Cherie Blair and Anna Wintour have all had their tresses seen to here. The salon's dream-team is composed of Max Coles, known for his wizardry with scissors, and master colourist Steve Cope, as well as the pioneer of the 'permanent blow-dry', former Daniel Hersheson star Gil Goncalces (from £200). Appointments start from £30 for a wash and blow-dry, rising up to £153 for cuts by senior stylists. Downstairs, indulge in tranquillity treatments such as manicures and facials, as well as threading and eyelash extensions. An advanced system for hair and tattoo removal is also available. Michaeljohn is having a major makeover in time for Christmas 2008.

Nyumba

6-7 Mount Street, W1K 3EH (7408 1489/ www.nyumbasalon.com). Bond Street tube or Green Park tube. **Open** 9am-6pm Mon-Wed, Fri, Sat; 9am-8pm Thur. **Credit** AmEx, MC, V.
If you're seeking a perfectionist to tend to your locks, then make an appointment with Michael Charalambous. His aptly named House of Hair & Beauty isn't just a hairdressers; it's a complete pampering centre, and you'll be welcomed with delicious eats from the café. When it came to the biz, our highlights (from £80), although a good shade lighter than past colourings, were expertly matched to our skin colouring, while a pedicure (from £35) turned ugly flip-flop feet into dainty softened tootsies and made the waiting time for the colour to set fly by. The finale was the cut. Michael prides himself on drawing out the best features of your face with his styling, analytically approaching each

strand and where it falls on your bone structure. The resulting side fringe and flattering layering instantly brought a tired look bang up to date. The blow-dry was rather Sloaney in style, but soon remedied once back on familiar ground. It's easy to see why the salon has a celebrity following. A cut and blow-dry starts at £95.

Patrick Lüdde Salon & Spa

22 Maddox Street, W1S 1PW (7495 9040/ www.patrickludde.com). Oxford Circus tube. **Open** 9am-6pm Mon-Wed, Sat; 9am-8pm Thur, Fri. **Credit** AmEx, MC, V.

Luxembourg's own celebrity snipper, globe-trotter Patrick Lüdde, settled in Mayfair after a stint as artistic director in Fortnum & Mason's salon. The attractively laid-out premises feature curved shelves of product lines (Kerastase, Thalco, George Michael – the long-hair specialist – not the crooner) leading on to a handsome mirrored salon and therapy rooms. Co-director Neil Ward is responsible for the more hirsute clientele; he runs the UK's only George Michael Long Hair Clinic, addressing the tangled issues of maintaining healthy, shiny hair. House specialities include expert colouring services (a half head of highlights from £85) and deep-conditioning one-hour thermal treatments, which leave hair unrecognisably silky and textured after a stint under a space-age lamp. Those short of time benefit from a 12-minute hot-towel wrap with cream conditioner – we can vouch for the efficacy. Thalgo facials and body wraps are available, as is a whole range of prettifying bespoke beauty services and massage.

Pimps & Pinups

14 Lamb Street, E1 6EA (7426 2121/ www.pimpsandpinups.com). Liverpool Street tube/rail. **Open** 10am-8pm Mon-Fri; 10am-6pm Sat, Sun. **Credit** MC, V.

See p108 **High barnets**.

Richard Ward

82 Duke of York Square, SW3 4LY (7730 1222/www.richardward.co.uk). Sloane Square tube. **Open** 9am-7pm Mon, Tue, Thur-Sat; 9am-8pm Wed. **Credit** MC, V.

Nicknamed 'Golden Scissors' by the fashion set, Richard Ward's talent seeps through his 5,000sq ft Chelsea salon, full of ladies who lunch, models and celebs. The salon's colouring system, Cento, is the latest word in natural-colour technique (from £80 for a half head of highlights) and Philippe Starck-designed workstations in the Colour Zone are equipped with mini TVs to spare you from boredom. Failing that, there's a snacks menu so you can treat yourself to a sandwich or a citron pressé while you wait. Senior stylist Karen (£85 for a cut and blow-dry) neatened up our split ends and dry strands, delivering on the salon's promise of 'innovative yet wearable couture hair'.

Taylor Taylor

137 Commercial Street, E1 6BJ (7377 2737/www.taylortaylorlondon.com). Liverpool Street tube/rail. **Open** 10am-8pm Mon-Wed; 10am-9pm Thur; 10am-7pm Fri; 10am-6pm Sat, Sun. **Credit** MC, V.

Decked out with chandeliers, chaises longues and a massive bird-cage, this Shoreditch salon adds a much-needed dose of glamour to E1. Offering affordable cuts and beauty treatments, it's the kind of place you'll want to hang out in afterwards thanks partly to the inviting bar where cocktails come free with your hair-do. It's also reassuringly friendly and affordable – £49 to £120 for women's cutting and styling, £39 to £100 for men, £78 for a half head of highlights. The original, and more intimate, Cheshire Street branch recently had a revamp, with crystal and mother-of-pearl walls, and new features like the gold-tiled hair-washing room.

For branch see index.

Tommy Guns

65 Beak Street, W1F 9SN (7439 0777). Piccadilly Circus tube. **Open** 10am-8pm Mon-Fri; 10am-6pm Sat. **Credit** AmEx, MC, V.

A stalwart in both Soho and Shoreditch, and currently celebrating its tenth year in the business, TG is a very cool prospect indeed. The stylish Soho space, complete with retro fittings, is filled with youthful colourists and cutters and there's a friendly, relaxed buzz to the place. We're never disappointed with our cuts here; on our last visit, stylist Natalie took the trouble to really think through how to transform a mess of layers into a stylish and manageable barnet; her superb cutting skills meant a look that lasted and a noticeable improvement in the condition of our hair. Men's cuts start from £39 (£49 for women) while colour begins at £35 for a vegetable rinse, £48 for a tint, £70 for a T-section and up to £125 for full highlights.

For branches see index.

Lounge Soho. See p109.

Windle

41-45 Shorts Gardens, WC2H 9AP (7497 2393/www.windlehair.com). Covent Garden tube. **Open** 10am-6pm Tue; 10am-7.15pm Wed, Thur; 10.30am-7.15pm Fri; 9.30am-5.30pm Sat. **Credit** MC, V.

Drawing a hip local crowd, this salon has been a firm favourite since ex-Vidal Sassoon school principal Paul Windle opened the doors of the industrial-looking, friendly space in 1988. Known for its original haircuts, consultations are thorough so the stylists can establish what is right for you. That's not to say fashion doesn't play an important role – Windle has a long history of mutually rewarding relationships with high-profile catwalk stylists. There's also a strong emphasis on training here, and you get the sense that staff loyalty is consequently strong. On our last visit, we were given a semi-permanent colour treatment to cover emerging grey hairs; this combined with some subtle highlights resulted in a shiny, natural-looking style, with the colour improving after several washes. Cuts start at £50 and colour from £55. The salon is also the distributor for the excellent eponymous haircare range of New York salon Bumble & Bumble.

Also check out...

Anita Cox Hair & Beauty

40 Battersea Rise, SW11 1EE (7223 8888/ www.anitacox.co.uk). Clapham Junction rail. **Open** 10am-7pm Mon, Fri; 10am-8pm Tue-Thur; 10am-6pm Sat; 10am-5pm Sun. **Credit** MC, V.
For branches see index.

Arena

89 Lower Marsh, SE1 7AB (7928 4880). Waterloo tube/rail. **Open** 9am-7pm Mon-Fri; 9am-4pm Sat. **Credit** AmEx, MC, V.

Aveda Institute

174 High Holborn, WC1V 7AA (7759 7355/www.aveda.co.uk). Holborn tube. **Open** 9.30am-7pm Mon-Wed; 8am-8pm Thur, Fri; 9am-6.30pm Sat; 11am-5pm Sun. **Credit** AmEx, MC, V.
For branch (Aveda Lifestyle Salon) see index.

Bar Hairdressing

44-46 St John Street, EC1M 4DF (7253 9999/www.barhairdressing.com). Farringdon tube/rail. **Open** 10am-8pm Mon-Fri; 10am-5pm Sat. **Credit** MC, V.

Cello

92 York Street, W1H 1QX (7723 7447/ www.cellohair.com). Baker Street tube/ Marylebone tube/rail. **Open** 9am-6pm Mon, Sat; 9am-8pm Tue-Fri. **Credit** AmEx, DC, MC, V.

Cobella

3rd Floor, Selfridges, 400 Oxford Street, W1A 1AB (0870 900 0440/www.cobella.co.uk). Bond Street or Marble Arch tube. **Open** 9.30am-8pm Mon-Wed, Fri, Sat; 9.30am-9pm Thur; 11.30am-6pm Sun. **Credit** AmEx, MC, V.
For branch see index.

Diverse Hair

280 Upper Street, N1 2TZ (7704 6842/ www.diversehair.co.uk). Angel tube/ Highbury & Islington tube/rail. **Open** 11am-7pm Mon; 10am-7pm Tue-Fri; 9am-6pm Sat; 11am-5pm Sun. **Credit** MC, V.

The Hairdressers

70 Amwell Street, EC1R 1UU (7713 0515/ www.thehairdresserslondon.com). Angel tube. **Open** 10.30am-7pm Mon-Wed, Fri; 10am-8pm Thur; 10am-6pm Sat. **Credit** MC, V.

It's Something Hell's

Unit 2.16, Kingly Court, off Carnaby Street, W1 (7287 0241/www.myspace.com/ something_hells). Oxford Circus or Piccadilly Circus tube. **Open** 11am-7pm Mon-Sat; 10am-6pm Sat, Sun. **Credit** MC, V.
See p108 **High barnets.**

James Lee Tsang

49 Eastcastle Street, W1W 8DZ (7580 0071). Oxford Circus tube. **Open** 9am-8pm Mon-Fri; 10am-7pm Sat. **Credit** MC, V.

John Frieda

75 New Cavendish Street, W1W 6XA (7636 1401/www.johnfrieda.com). Oxford Circus tube. **Open** 9am-6pm Mon-Sat. **Credit** MC, V.
For branch see index.

Kell Skött Haircare

93 Golborne Road, W10 5NL (8964 3004/ www.kellskotthaircare.com). Ladbroke Grove tube. **Open** 10am-6pm Mon; 9am-6pm Tue, Fri; 9am-9pm Wed, Thur; 8.30am-6pm Sat. **Credit** MC, V.

Nicky Clarke

130 Mount Street, W1K 3NY (7491 4700/www.nickyclarke.com). Bond Street tube. **Open** 9am-5pm Mon; 9am-8pm Tue, Wed; 9am-6pm Thur-Sat. **Credit** AmEx, MC, V.

Nina's Hair Parlour

1st Floor, Alfie's Antiques Market, 13 Church Street, NW8 8DT (7723 1911/ www.ninasvintageandretrohair.com). Edgeware tube/Marylebone tube/rail. **Open** 11am-8pm Tue-Fri; 10am-6pm Sat. **No credit cards.**
See p108 **High barnets.**

Mr Topper's

13A Great Russell Street, WC1B 3NH (7631 3233). Tottenham Court Road tube. **Open** 9am-7pm Mon-Sat; 11am-6pm Sun. **No credit cards.**
Branches: throughout the city.

Saco

71 Monmouth Street, WC2H 9JW (7240 7897/www.sacohair.com). Leicester Square tube. **Open** 9.30am-6.30pm Mon-Wed, Sat; 10am-8pm Thur, Fri. **Credit** MC, V.

Scissors Palace
122 Holland Park Avenue, W11 4UA (7221 4004). Holland Park tube. **Open** 9am-9pm Mon, Thur; 9am-6pm Tue, Wed; 9am-7.30pm Fri, Sat; 11am-6pm Sun. **Credit** MC, V.

Sejour
3-5 Bray Place, SW3 3LL (7589 1100/ www.sejour.co.uk). Sloane Square tube. **Open** 9am-6pm Mon; 8.30am-6pm Tue, Sat; 8.30am-8pm Wed; 8.30am-7pm Thur, Fri. **Credit** MC, V.

Toni & Guy
28 Kensington Church Street, W8 4EP (7937 0030/www.toniandguy.co.uk). High Street Kensington tube. **Open** 10am-8pm Mon-Fri; 9am-7pm Sat; 11am-6pm Sun. **Credit** AmEx, DC, MC, V.
Branches: throughout the city.

Trevor Sorbie
27 Floral Street, WC2E 9DP (0844 445 6901/www.trevorsorbie.com). Covent Garden or Leicester Square tube. **Open** 9am-7pm Mon, Tue; 9am-8pm Wed; 9am-8.30pm Thur, Fri; 9am-6pm Sat. **Credit** AmEx, MC, V.

Unruly Studio
100 Westbourne Studios, 242 Acklam Road, W10 5JJ (8964 9200/www.unrulystudio.co.uk). Ladbroke Grove or Westbourne Park tube. **Open** 10am-10pm Mon-Fri; 10am-6pm Sat; by appointment Sun. **Credit** MC, V.

Vidal Sassoon
45A Monmouth Street, WC2H 9DG (7240 6635/www.vidalsassoon.com). Covent Garden or Leicester Square tube. **Open** 9.30am-6.30pm Mon-Thur; 9.30am-5.45pm Fri; 8.45am-5pm Sat; 10.15am-3.30pm Sun. **Credit** AmEx, MC, V
For branches see index.

Willie Smarts
11 The Pavement, SW4 OHY (7498 7771/ www.williesmarts.com). Clapham Common tube. **Open** 9.30am-8pm Mon, Fri; 2-9.30pm Tue; 9.30am-9.30pm Wed; 11am-8pm Thur; 9.30am-6pm Sat. **Credit** MC, V.
For branch see index.

Afro

See also p106 **Errol Douglas**.

Aquarius
9 Stroud Green Road, N4 2DQ (7263 2483). Finsbury Park tube/rail. **Open** 9.30am-5pm Mon, Tue, Fri; 9.30am-6pm Thur; 8.30am-4pm Sat. **Credit.** MC, V.

Back to Eden
14 Westmoreland Road, SE17 2AY (7703 3173). Elephant & Castle tube/ rail. **Open** 10.30am-6.30pm Tue-Sat.
No credit cards.

Barbers

There are countless barbers across London, but these are some of the most outstanding. *See also p111* **Mr Topper's**. For male grooming emporia **Gentlemen's Tonic**, **Jason Shankey**, **Nickel Spa** and the **Refinery**, *see p101*.

F Flittner
86 Moorgate, EC2M 6SE (7606 4750/ www.fflittner.com). Moorgate tube/rail. **Open** 8am-6pm Mon-Wed, Fri; 8am-6.30pm Thur. **Credit** AmEx, MC, V.
It could almost still be 1904 inside this gorgeous relic of old-fashioned barbery. Hidden from bustling Moorgate behind beautifully frosted 'Saloon' doors is a simple, handsome room, where discerning City gents have been getting their trims for over a century. Most of the fittings are original, including the wonderful sinks and mirrors, but the owner knows how to make discreet allowances for the high-tech where necessary (check out the snazzy website and the clever cast-no-shadows lighting). Staff are skillful and dedicated, performing razor-sharp shaves as well as straightforward haircuts (£13.50-£22).

Geo F Trumper
9 Curzon Street, W1J 5HQ (7499 1850/ www.trumpers.com). Piccadilly Circus/Green Park tube. **Open** 9am-5.30pm Mon-Fri; 9am-1pm Sat. **Credit** AmEx, DC, MC, V.
A Mayfair institution since 1875, Geo F Trumper is still considered the finest traditional barber shop in London. Oak-panelled walls covered with hunting prints, and distinguished old men reclining on green leather chairs create the vibe of gentlemen's club, while red velvet curtains serve as partitions between booths. Yet despite the old-school trappings, Trumper caters for the New Man too. Morrissey has been known to drop in for a haircut, and the *GQ*-reading crowd appreciate the wet shaves. Barbers snip away carefully as opposed to shearing you like a sheep with an electric razor. And they talk to you in dulcet tones, which adds to the feeling of being pampered. Don't leave without trying the grooming products – the West Indian lime hair cream gives great texture and smells good enough to eat.

Murdock
340 Old Street, EC1V 9DS (7729 2288/ www.murdocklondon.com). Old Street tube/ rail. **Open** 10am-7pm Mon-Wed, Fri; 10am-8pm Thur; 10am-5pm Sat. **Credit** AmEx, MC, V.
Slap-bang on one of the East End's main arteries, Murdock is a barbers for the Hoxton generation. Nowadays, that includes everyone from bankers strolling up from the City to the white-plimsolled Shoreditch brigade. What keeps the place fully booked is decent-value haircuts and luxurious wet shaves by staff who take their time and know their stuff. On our last appointment (£28.50), chirpy chappy Ray declared that Murdock didn't 'do 15-minute haircuts' before talking us through ours in meticulous detail – an hour later the result was one of the best we've had. The wet shaves (£32.50-£38.50) are ideal for men who want to be pampered but aren't yet ready for a spa treatment. There's a selection of hard-to-get colognes and shaving products too, from the likes of Santa Maria Novella and DR Harris.

Pall Mall Barbers
27 Whitcomb Street, WC2H 7EP (7930 7787/www.pallmallbarbers.com). Piccadilly Circus tube. **Open** 9am-7pm Mon-Fri.
No credit cards.
In central London you generally have to choose between cheapo choppers that make you feel like you're being sheared or trendy salons where you feel like you're on a fashion shoot, and pay high for the privilege. So this barbers – tucked in a side street behind the horrors of Leicester Square – is a great find. There's been a barbers on this spot since 1896; moving on with the times, its current incarnation remains sympathetic to its origins. It may be small, but much of the original character – oak panels, old sinks – remain, and on our last visit two new chairs were being added and the shop extended to accommodate a total of six hairdressers. Professional haircuts come at very reasonable prices (£13.50 for a cut, £22.50 for a wet shave). Add in the aesthetics, the friendly service and the refreshingly unpretentious vibe, and Pall Mall is a hit with everyone from mens' magazine editors to local office folk.

Also check out...

Barber at Alfred Dunhill
2 Davies Street, W1K 3DJ (7853 4440/ www.pankhurstbarbers.com). Bond Street tube. **Open** 10am-7pm Mon-Sat. **Credit** AmEx, MC, V.

Sadlers Wells Barber Shop
110 Rosebery Avenue, EC1R 4TL (7833 0556). Angel tube. **Open** 8am-6pm Mon-Sat. **Credit** MC, V.

Truefitt & Hill
71 St James's Street, SW1A 1PH (7493 2961/www.truefittandhill.com). Green Park tube. **Open** 8.30am-5.30pm Mon-Fri; 8.30am-5pm Sat. **Credit** AmEx, MC, V.

Problem hair

Philip Kingsley
54 Green Street, W1K 6RU (7629 4004/ www.philipkingsley.co.uk). Bond Street or Marble Arch tube. **Open** 8.30am-6pm Mon, Tue, Thur, Fri; 8.30am-8pm Wed; 8.30am-5.30pm Sat. **Credit** MC, V.
Kingsley has been in the business for over 40 years and is an authority on hair health. Consultations start at £180, treatments £62.

London Centre of Trichology
37 Blandford Street, W1U 7HB (7935 1935/www.london-centre-trichology.co.uk). Baker Street or Bond Street tube. **Open** 10am-6pm Mon-Fri. **Credit** AmEx, MC, V.
The centre focuses mainly on thinning hair in men and women; scalp disorders are also treated. Prices from £17 for a shampoo.

Scalp & Hair Clinic
108 St John's Hill, SW11 1SY (7924 2195/ www.scalp-hair.co.uk). Clapham Junction rail. **Open** 9am-6pm Thur, Fri; 8.30am-2pm Sat. **No credit cards**.
The scalp experts here are all members of the Institute of Trichologists. An initial consultation is £60; treatments start at £30.

Opticians

Chains **Dollond & Aitchison** (223 Regent Street, W1B 2EB, 7495 8209, www.danda.co.uk), **Optical Express** (316 Regent Street, W1R 5AF, 7436 5029, www.opticalexpress.com), **Specsavers** (Unit 6, 6-17 Tottenham Court Road, W1T 1BG, 7580 5115, www.specsavers.com) and **Vision Express** (263-265 Oxford Street, W1C 2DF, 7409 7880, www.visionexpress.com) offer a wide range of frames, including budget-friendly options.

Arthur Morrice

11 Beauchamp Place, SW3 1NQ (7584 4661/www.arthurmorrice.com). Knightsbridge tube. **Open** 10am-6.30pm Mon-Fri; 10am-6pm Sat. **Credit** AmEx, DC, MC, V.

More a complement than a rival to street neighbour 36, this shop has undergone a makeover, swapping the previous Old World walnut look for a sleeker modern interior. The range takes in a mix of familiar names and less common labels, with popular names like ic! Berlin, Chrome Hearts and Anne et Valentin balanced by rare designs from Badgley Mischka featuring real feathers and Swarovksi pearls. Horn frames by Hoffman are a new arrival. Expect to pay around £300, though prices go up to £2,500. An eye test will set you back about £35.

For branches see index.

Cutler & Gross

16 Knightsbridge Green, SW1X 7QL (7581 2250/www.cutlerandgross.com). Knightsbridge tube. **Open** 9.30am-7pm Mon-Sat; noon-4pm Sun. **Credit** AmEx, MC, V.

Fashion is as important as focal length at this long-established Knightsbridge outlet, which introduces new themed collections twice a year. Contrasting with last year's Warhol-inspired 'New Rave' look, the latest theme sees a return to classic retro styling under the title 'Belle du Jour', with prices from £200. Also popular are light-but-sturdy buffalo horn frames, handmade to ensure top quality, from £499. The iconic Vintage eyewear range, meanwhile, draws rock and film stars to the fabulous sister shop at no.7, which has period gems dating back to the 1920s. Current bestsellers include 1960s Persols, '70s Porsche and '80s Cazals with prices from £200 to £3,000.

For branch see index.

Eye Contacts

10 Chalk Farm Road, NW1 8AG (7482 1701). Camden Town tube. **Open** 10.30am-6pm Mon-Sat; 11am-6pm Sun. **Credit** AmEx, MC, V.

Tucked away in the lee of the Camden Lock railway bridge, this relaxed optician's has been tending to the optically challenged of NW1 since Camden's 1980s heyday. Spec-themed stained-glass windows provide a nice touch of colour to an otherwise pared-back bare-brick space housing a small but well-chosen frame selection. Orgreen, Alain Mikli and ic! Berlin are displayed alongside less familiar designers such as Belgium's Mix and Etnia from Spain. British designs include Cutler & Gross (*see above*) and Booth & Bruce. Eye tests cost £22.50.

Kirk Originals

29 Floral Street, WC2E 9DP (7240 5055/www.kirkoriginals.com). Covent Garden tube. **Open** 11am-7pm Mon-Sat; noon-5pm Sun. **Credit** AmEx, MC, V.

Set up by Jason Kirk after he found some glasses made by his uncle 70 years ago, this shop takes a witty approach to the art of specs. Kirk's own-brand frames dominate, mixing simple old-school styling with bright colours. Ranges include a Heroes selection named after members of a fictional Kirk family tree, such as Olaf 'The Shadow' Kirk; gold-coloured flecks bring a dazzling twinkle to the Saturn range. Kirk also stocks the hard-to-find French brand Histoire-de-Voir as well as Anne Et Valentin, Michel Henau and Christian Roth. Prices start from £189.

Mallon & Taub

35D Marylebone High Street, W1U 4QB (7935 8200/www.mallonandtaub.com). Baker Street or Regent's Park tube. **Open** 10am-6.30pm Mon-Wed, Fri, Sat; 10am-7pm Thur; noon-5pm Sun. **Credit** AmEx, MC, V.

Stylish slate flooring and fresh flowers add panache to a shop whose stated aim is 'dress the eyes and have fun doing so'. Knowledgeable staff talk customers through eye-care issues as well as new developments – new high-tech varifocals, perhaps, or glasses geared for high-energy sport. Specs on offer include A-list favourites Chrome Hearts, the brightly coloured Face à Face range and vintage designs by Oliver Goldsmith. It's also one of the few UK outlets to stock the über-hip Less Than Human line. Bling-lovers can spend up to £6,000, but there are plenty of stylish offerings available for under £200.

Michel Guillon Vision Clinic & Eye Boutique

35 Duke of York Square, SW3 4LY (7730 2142/www.michelguillon.com). Sloane Square tube. **Open** 10am-7pm Mon-Thur, Sat; 9.30am-7.30pm Fri. **Credit** AmEx, MC, V.

Michel Guillon's Abe Rogers-designed interior provides a welcome blast of colour in an otherwise bland shopping precinct. The striking blue cabinets house a changing range of designer frames that includes Japanese Yellow Plus, Sama's retro-style two-tone creations and titanium offerings from Germany's Markus T. Those after a more natural look have a fine selection of Guillon's own-brand buffalo horn frames to choose from. But the real USP here is the quality of eye care, which draws on Guillon's 25 years of scientific research to provide a comprehensive service that includes extra eye checks and nutritional advice. Guillon is also an expert in contact lens research, providing lenses for people normally unable to wear them. Sporty types too can benefit from the shop's dynamic vision testing, designed to improve visual reactions. Frames start at £150, rising to ten times that for bespoke. The rigorous eye test regime means prices start at £55.

Opera Opera

98 Long Acre, WC2E 9NR (7836 9246/www.operaopera.net). Covent Garden tube. **Open** 10am-6pm Mon-Sat. **Credit** MC, V.

Dispensing for three decades from its corner site near the Royal Opera, this family-run business exudes an old-fashioned sense of pride in optical craftsmanship, and even has its own factory turning out the shop's Harpers range. Control of production not only allows touches like old-fashioned hinges, but also means the shop is geared for bespoke frames – whether to replicate some treasured old specs or copy something spotted in a magazine. Buffalo horn frames are about to be introduced and prices start at £160.

Spex in the City

1 Shorts Gardens, WC2H 9AT (7240 0243/www.spexinthecity.com). Covent Garden or Leicester Square tube. **Open** 11am-6.30pm Mon-Fri; 11am-6pm Sat; 1-5pm Sun. **Credit** MC, V.

Old wooden floorboards and panelled walls lend an air of distinction to this small and friendly Seven Dials outlet, run by Gillian Caplan. A carefully chosen range includes frames by European designers Orgreen, Reiz and Alain Mikli plus Brits Booth & Bruce and Oliver Goldsmith. Also check out Caplan's expanding line of own-brand frames. Prices are very reasonable with frames from £80, though the average is £200 to £280. Eye tests are just £22.

36 Opticians

36 Beauchamp Place, SW3 1NU (7581 6336/www.36opticians.co.uk). South Kensington or Knightsbridge tube. **Open** 10am-6pm Mon-Sat. **Credit** AmEx, MC, V.

Poor sight certainly has its compensations if it leads you to Ragini Patel and Sveta Khambhaita's appealing Knightsbridge outlet. There's an eclectic range of over 4,000 frames, stretching from simple offerings for a bargain £45 to exclusive limited-edition handmade beauties by US designer Barton Pereira (as worn by Angelina Jolie, among others). Bold styling and colours mark frames from the likes of Theo, whose range by designer Christoph Broich featured in *Sex and the City*. Tom Ford introduces a splash of retro 1980s-style, while Hoffman provides the bling with diamond-studded one-off frames for up to £5,000. A growing range of cool accessories includes stylish lorgnettes (the opera-style glasses with a handle on one side) and spectacle loops made of stone. Check-ups (including a glaucoma test) are £35.

Also check out…

Auerbach & Steele

129 King's Road, SW3 4PW (7349 0001/www.auerbach-steele.com). Sloane Square tube. **Open** 10am-6.30pm Mon-Fri; 10am-6pm Sat; noon-5pm Sun. **Credit** AmEx, MC, V.

State-of-the-art computer technology and some unusual designer frames, including styles by Philippe Starck.

Bromptons

202A Kensington High Street, W8 7RG (7937 5500). High Street Kensington tube. **Open** 9.30am-6.30pm Mon-Wed,

Fri; 9.30am-7.30pm Thur; 9.30am-6pm Sat; 11am-6pm Sun. **Credit** AmEx, MC, V.
High ceilings, polished wooden floors and helpful, non-pushy staff make shopping here a treat.

Charles Frydman
82 Mare Street, E8 3SG (8985 2479). Bethnal Green tube/rail. **Open** 10am-5.30pm Mon-Wed, Fri; 10am-4pm Sat. **No credit cards.**
Original 1970s frames at ridiculously low prices, as well as personal service.

Crawford Street Opticians
7A Wyndham Place, 37 Crawford Street, W1H 1PN (7724 8033/www.crawfordstreetopticians.com). Baker Street tube/Marylebone tube/rail. **Open** Call for details. **Credit** AmEx, MC, V.
A good selection of specialist frames and sunglasses, plus a range of accessories by Albert Bijoux.

David Clulow
185 King's Road, SW3 5EB (7376 5733/www.davidclulow.com). Sloane Square tube. **Open** 10am-6.30pm Mon, Tue, Thur-Sat; 10am-7pm Wed; noon-6pm Sun. **Credit** AmEx, DC, MC, V.
Branches: throughout the city.

Eye Company
159 Wardour Street, W1F 8WH (7434 0988/www.eye-company.co.uk). Oxford Circus or Tottenham Court Road tube. **Open** 10.30am-6.30pm Mon-Wed, Fri; 10.30am-7.30pm Thur; 11am-6pm Sat. **Credit** AmEx, DC, MC, V.
Hip store with a select range of mint-condition vintage frames as well as stylish own-brand frames designed by in-house experts.

Eye Level Opticians
37 Upper Street, N1 0PN (7354 9277/www.eyelevelopticians.co.uk). Angel tube. **Open** 10am-6pm Mon-Fri; 10am-5pm Sat; noon-5pm Sun. **Credit** AmEx, MC, V.
Designer frames include Philippe Starck, Paul Smith and German brand Freudenhaus.

Eye to Eye
3A Montpelier Street, SW7 1EX (7581 8828/www.eyetoeyeopticians.co.uk). Knightsbridge tube. **Open** noon-6pm Mon; 10am-6pm Tue-Fri; 10am-5.30pm Sat. **Credit** AmEx, MC, V.

Iris Optical
6 Maguire Street, SE1 2NQ (7407 7951/www.irisoptical.co.uk). Tower Hill tube/London Bridge tube/rail. **Open** 9am-7pm Mon-Fri. **Credit** MC, V.
For branches see index.

Optix at Broadgate
1-2 Exchange Arcade, 175 Bishopsgate, EC2M 3WA (7628 0330/www.optixuk.com). Liverpool Street tube/rail. **Open** 9.30am-6pm Mon-Fri. **Credit** AmEx, MC, V.

S Squared Eyecare
33 Lower Marsh, SE1 7RG (7633 0680/www.s2eyecare.com). Waterloo tube/rail. **Open** 9am-6pm Tue, Thur-Fri; 10.30am-7pm Wed; 1030am-4pm Sun. **Credit** AmEx, DC, V.

Schuller Opticians
44 Lamb's Conduit Street, WC1N 3LB (7404 2002/www.schulleropticians.co.uk). Holborn tube. **Open** 9.30am-5.30pm Mon-Fri; 9.30am-4pm Sat. **Credit** AmEx, MC, V.
For branches see index.

Sight Station
www.sightstation.com
Stylish prescription frames online.

20/20 Optical Store
216-217 Tottenham Court Road, W1T 7PT (7596 2020/www.20-20.co.uk). Goodge Street or Tottenham Court Road tube. **Open** 9am-8pm Mon-Fri; 9am-7pm Sat; 11.30am-6pm Sun. **Credit** AmEx, MC, V.
Spot on for choice.

Contact lens specialists

See also p115 **Michel Guillon Vision Clinic.**

Andrew Gasson Contact Lenses
6 De Walden Street, W1G 8RL (7224 5959/www.andrewgasson.co.uk). Baker Street or Bond Street tube. **Open** 9am-6pm Mon-Thur; 9am-5pm Fri. **Credit** MC, V.
A fellow of the British College of Optometry and Royal Society of Medicine, Gasson gives ultra-thorough eye exams using the latest technology and stocks a huge range of lenses.

Rekindling old frames

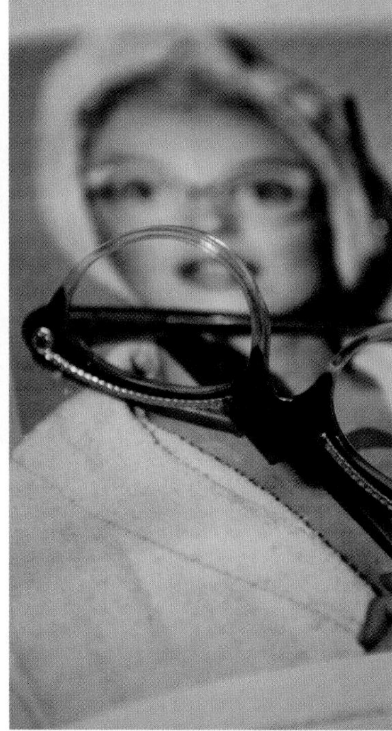

Eye Company

Chunky, vintage NHS-style glasses are perched on noses everywhere you look. A marked increase of goggle-eyed style in the capital points to a trend that's never quite out of fashion, and understandably so. What else could so subtly advertise your superior intelligence (or conceal your lack thereof)? Vintage frames can reference any number of studious figures and brilliant, creative wits; David Hockney and Truman Capote spring to mind (although Ronnie Corbett sadly follows). Yet these days it's all about music stars Lightspeed Champion and Hot Chip, and if thick-framed glasses are riding on a wave of cool, it's the need for a one-off, completely unique pair of affordable frames that has encouraged the myopic to hunt out vintage styles. From scuffed tortoise shell Wayfarers, to some clever retro reissues and a nod to *The Talented Mr Ripley* (an enduring reference for designers obsessed with academia), vintage frames are big news across the capital.

Opera Opera (*see p115*) on Long Acre houses a selection of dorky NHS-inspired frames that spans drag queen inspired cat's eye styles, Terry Richardson-style aviators, excellent vintage one-offs and a bespoke service to round off. Classic London eyewear brand **Cutler & Gross** (*see p115*) has a vintage selection of '50s through to '80s styles, and having honed the art of the horn-rimmed frame, it even offers styles in its nearby flagship that are hand-crafted from the real thing, making each pair unique. Local opticians also often have a wealth of well-priced dead stock, and the tiny **Charles Frydman** (*see p116*; its exterior marked by a pair of enormous faded spectacles) has retro-like styles. **Topman** (*see p46*) also has a few adroit frames in store that look startlingly like the real thing. **Retrospecs** (www.retrospecs.co.uk) and Ebay store **Dead Men's Spex** (www.deadmensspex.com) are other excellent resources for ocular delights, stocking vintage NHS frames; both can fit prescription lenses to order at prices significantly lower than the high street. The **Eye Company** (*p116*) is another excellent option, as is online shop **Klasik** (www.klasik.org), with some pre-war sunnies. Cheaper still are frames discovered at illicit car boot sales and at the bottom of a charity shop's bargain buckets, their lenses popped out and replaced by opticians who wonder what all the fuss is about.

NF Burnett Hodd

7 Devonshire Street, W1W 5DY (7636 2444/www.nfburnetthodd.com). Great Portland Street tube. **Open** 8.30am-5.30pm Mon, Wed-Fri; 8.30am-6.15pm Tue. **Credit** MC, V.

Hodd and his team are known for their success in overcoming problems that have previously ruled out contact lenses. The latest equipment is used to check eye health.

Get Lenses

www.getlenses.com

Sunglasses

For vintage sunnies try **Cutler & Gross** (*see p115*) and **Hurwundeki** (*see p30*). **Jigsaw** (*see p46*) has also recently had some good vintage-style sunglasses.

Klasik.org

www.klasik.org

Vintage sunglasses and frames; there's also a stall at Spitalfields Market (*see p21*).

Sunglass Hut

356 Oxford Street, W1C 1JL (7629 8934/www.sunglasshut.co.uk). Bond Street tube. **Open** 10am-8pm Mon-Fri; 10am-7pm Thur; 11.30am-5.30pm Sun. **Credit** AmEx, MC, V.

Designer sunglasses from Ray-Ban, Prada, Versace, Bulgari and the like.

Branches: throughout the city.

Sunglassesuk.com

www.sunglassesuk.com

Large range of designer models.

Home

Home

Water Monopoly (also right). *See p153.*

Angel Flowers. *See p171.*

Twentytwentyone (and centre right). *See p125.*

Labour & Wait. *See p129.*

Furniture & Accessories

Contemporary

Aram

110 Drury Lane, WC2B 5SG (7557 7557/ www.aram.co.uk). Covent Garden or Holborn tube. **Open** 10am-6pm Mon-Wed, Fri, Sat; 10am-7pm Thur. **Credit** AmEx, MC, V.

Back in the 1960s, design champion Zeev Aram introduced the likes of Alvar Aalto, Marcel Breuer, Le Corbusier and Arne Jacobsen to UK homes through his long-gone King's Road store. This impressive five-storey space replaced it, stocking furniture, lighting, textiles and other home accessories. Alongside the classics, Aram also stocks contemporary works by both established designers – Ronan and Erwan Bouroullec, Hella Jongerius and Massimo Morozzi – and emerging ones. Lighting comes from top manufacturers such as Artemide and Flos, furniture from brands like Herman Miller and Hitch Mylius. Head to the basement for funky accessories and tableware. Aram is the biggest stockist of Interlübke's storage systems, the only UK stockist of authorised Eileen Grey designs, and often stocks some special editions.

Aria

Barnsbury Hall, Barnsbury Street, N1 1PN (7704 1999/www.ariashop.co.uk). Angel tube/ Highbury & Islington tube/rail. **Open** 10am-6.30pm Mon-Wed, Fri, Sat; 10am-7pm Thur; noon-5pm Sun. **Credit** AmEx, DC, MC, V.

Aria has now settled into an atmospheric new space in Islington's Barnsbury Hall. Many of the building's original features have now been restored and they contrast beautifully with the über-modern lines of contemporary furniture and homewares. High-quality designers' pieces are here, as are more unusual pieces like Fornasetti's black and white handpainted wall plates (£99), the new Bourgie table light by Ferruccio Laviani (£199) and Naughtone's metal and glass Trace tables (from £600). This mix, teamed with a very nice in-store café, makes Aria a pleasure to visit. Chairs are a speciality, with Stark and Patrick Jouin well represented. Smaller stand-outs include a pretty Taika plate (£27) and a witty Teapot mug (£10.95) that would make a great gift, especially if it had some of Aria's very tempting selection of toiletries (Cowshed, Savon de Marseilles) nestled inside it.

Atelier Abigail Ahern

137 Upper Street, N1 1QP (7354 8181/ www.atelierabigailahern.com). Angel tube/ Highbury & Islington tube/rail. **Open** 10am-6pm Mon-Sat; noon-5pm Sun. **Credit** AmEx, MC, V.

This tiny interiors shop may not have a huge range, but what it lacks in quantity is more than made up for in quality. The selection is both inventive and original, with much of it from emerging international designers. A beautiful Kathy Dalwood concrete cast, part of a collection that focuses on historical characters, reinterprets 18th-century haute porcelain but retains mould lines from the casting process, indicating contemporary concerns about texture (from £300). British graduate Andrew Oliver is similarly playful, but with very different results; his new lighting range (from £700) is a delightful addition to his drunken table range, unique one-off furniture pieces inspired by practical experimentation with salvaged furniture. Textiles are particularly strong; as well as some striking merino wool ottomans (£755), there are Impressionist paintings transposed on to linen by Argentinian-born artist Haby Bonomo (from £65). Colour ranges are muted but striking, summing up a store that's a delightful departure from the sparse lines of many design stores.

B&B Italia

250 Brompton Road, SW3 2AS (7591 8111/www.bebitalia.com). South Kensington tube. **Open** 10am-6pm Mon-Sat; noon-5pm Sun. **Credit** AmEx, MC, V.

Few London interiors stores exhibit the pzazz of B&B Italia; if you've ever fancied yourself as a catwalk model, the long runway that guides you into the cavernous showroom offers plenty of opportunity to try out a few moves. B&B's sleek furniture is displayed in classic room-sets that are bigger than most London flats. Over its 40 years, the Italian brand has maintained a strong interest in working with inventive designers – 2008 saw new versions of Patricia Urquiola's Back and Lazy 100 chairs, and a raft of additions to Antonio Citterio's Maxalto range, including a new thermo-treated ash wood variant to the Apta collection of storage units, tables and book-cases. Alongside these traditionally proportioned pieces are more sculptural forms – Jean-Marie Massaud's Terminal 1 Daybed, for example, is a great example of a contemporary chaise longue.

Conran Shop

Michelin House, 81 Fulham Road, SW3 6RD (7589 7401/www.conran.co.uk). South Kensington tube. **Open** 10am-6pm Mon, Tue, Fri; 10am-7pm Wed, Thur; 10am-6.30pm Sat; noon-6pm Sun. **Credit** AmEx, MC, V.

While Terence Conran pioneered the idea of modernism in Britain back in the 1960s, he's always had an impressively sharp eye for the decorative too, and nowhere is this more evident than at the Fulham Road flagship. The shop recently celebrated its 21st birthday with a selling exhibition, 21 Products at the Conran Shop, which saw 21 suppliers produce 21 exclusive designs. With such world-renowned manufacturers as Hitch Mylius, Magis, Alessi, Flos and Wedgwood either reinterpreting classics, or diversifying into something they wouldn't normally do, results are as striking as you'd expect – with examples like the platinum glazed teapot by Jars (£195) and a 12in transparent globe with mirror printing by Authentics (£99) show. Much stock is exclusive and Conran mixes them in among classics to create inspirational room settings on the ground floor. The basement is home to a vast array of lighting, tableware and accessories and a great range of inventive kids' things.

For branch see index.

Designers Guild

267-271 (store) & 275-277 (showroom) King's Road, SW3 5EN (7351 5775/www.designersguild.com). Sloane Square tube then 11, 19, 22 bus. **Open** *Store* 10am-6pm Mon-Sat; noon-5pm Sun. *Showroom* 10am-6pm Mon-Sat. **Credit** AmEx, MC, V.

Interior designer Tricia Guild launched this shop in 1970 when it quickly became the best of its type, with colourful fabrics and wallpapers offering modern takes on traditional patterns. The store now also has a great selection of homewares, including a range of 98 paint colours selected to complement the fabrics, wallpapers, home furnishings, tableware, rugs, stationery and all the other design-led accessories. It also stocks a great range of contemporary and vintage furniture, which you can choose to cover with fabrics from the vast Designers Guild range or select from other brands such as Jasper Conran and William Yeoward, even combining different fabrics on the same piece. Cushions go from around £50, while bedlinen starts at £60 for a single duvet set.

Do Shop

47 Beak Street, W1F 9SE (7494 9090/ www.do-shop.com). Oxford Circus or Piccadilly Circus tube. **Open** 10am-6.30pm Mon-Wed, Fri, Sat; 10am-8pm Thur; noon-6pm Sun. **Credit** MC, V

When former banker Andrew Ying opened this Soho shop in 2006, it immediately proved a hit for its original selection of lifestyle ideas and products in natural materials. Mattia Cimadoro's quirky but stylish Tu Tu wall clock consists of two separate lime green cubes (£250), while German design company Dekoop's City Lights tealight holders (£17.50) use metal and plastic to cast a shimmering shadow of a city skyline. Idiosyncrasy is the buzz word here. There are dog- and cat-shaped cushions by NY outfit Pillow Pillow Pillow based on photos of beloved pooches and kitties sent in by adoring owners (from £45). Lighting is also a strong point; the sculptural birch planes of the Secto & Octo lighting by Seppo Koho are deservedly popular (from £190), while Hung-Ming Chen's cute laser-cut metal bird light can be clipped on to any light bulb to form an instant lampshade (£35).

Eco (eco)

213 Chiswick High Road, W4 2DW (8995 7611/www.eco-age.com). Turnham Green tube. **Open** 10am-6pm Mon-Sat; 11am-5pm Sun. **Credit** AmEx, DC, MC, V.

Founded by Nicola Giuggioli, with help from his sister Livia and her actor hubbie Colin Firth, Chiswick's green-minded lifestyle shop was opened to prove that ecologically sound items can also look fantastic. It's a hotspot for all things green; from solar panels, washing machines, TV sets, sustainably sourced designer homewares, ecological paints by earthBorn (£16.91 for 2.5 litres), wallpaper by the likes of Joanna Basford and Giles Miller and even toys. There are plenty of surprises here – who'd have thought a blanket or a towel (£24 for a bath towel) could be made from bamboo? But if you've only a few quid to spare, pencils made from recycled CD cases are just £2 and Maison Belle cleaning fluid starts at £3.95. The basement design consultancy advises amateur eco warriors.

Ella Doran Design

46 Cheshire Street, E2 6EH (7613 0782/ www.elladoran.co.uk). Bethnal Green or Liverpool Street tube/rail. **Open** 10am-6pm Mon-Fri; noon-5pm Sat; 11am-5pm Sun. **Credit** AmEx, MC, V.

Ella Doran's striking placemats and coasters feature a colourful range of photos – from the iconic Routemaster bus bells and American diner booths – to exotic vintage plates and lots of flora and fauna. The prints appear on bigger things too though, among them cushions, tote bags and even made-to-measure blinds (from £200). A recent addition is Brushwood, a delicate woodland scene that appears on everything from the blinds to drapes (£175), tea cosies (from £20) and mugs (£8).

Geoffrey Drayton

85 Hampstead Road, NW1 2PL (7387 5840/www.geoffreydrayton.com). Warren Street tube. **Open** 10am-6pm Mon-Sat. **Credit** MC, V.

Geoffrey Drayton has been pioneering modern furniture, lighting and homewares in London for almost five decades. The shop's success is partly down to the knowledgeable staff and partly to a terrific range of high-end, made-to-order classic furniture from the world's best brands and designers. B&B Italia, Fontana Arte, Interlübke, Kartell, Knoll, Vitra and Ycami are all stocked, along with smaller makers like E15 and Rexite. Limited editions crop up regularly; the most recent is a new version of Charlotte Perriand's LC3 armchair (£3,325 plus VAT), designed to her own specifications in a combination of tan leather, natural linen and powder blue frame. Tord Boontje's extraordinary Little Field of Flowers rug for Nani Marquina is crafted from New Zealand wool and is worth its price tag of £930, but there are much cheaper pieces – among them the pretty Pantone salt and pepper mills (£15.50 each) by Typhoon.

Graham & Green

4 Elgin Crescent, W11 2HX (7243 8908/ www.grahamandgreen.co.uk). Ladbroke Grove tube. **Open** 10am-6pm Mon-Sat; 11.30am-5.30pm Sun. **Credit** AmEx, MC, V.

If every neighbourhood had a shop like Graham & Green, we'd all be living in homes filled to the rafters with unusual and beautiful accessories. Classic and comfortable modern garden furniture is displayed outside, alongside a range of varnished steel French café chairs and tables designed in 1934 by Xavier Pauchard (from £90). Inside, myriad delights are spread over two floors. Stock is eclectic; the range of mirrors takes in Venetian, Louis Philippe-style, bone inlay and huge wooden antique gilt Trianon, then there's Scandic silver lanterns, Moroccan tea sets, silk kaftans, Indian semi-precious jewellery and Mongolian cushions and throws. Trinkets, toys, home accessories and clothing make gift shopping a lot of fun – not least because you're likely to find things here you don't see anywhere else – like the gorgeous range of Love mugs (£9.95), the pretty ceramic clocks with animal motifs (£18) and the Indian carved marble doorstops (£39.95).

For branches see index.

HOME

Twentytwentyone. *See p125.*

Habitat

121 Regent Street, W1B 4TB (0844 499 1134/www.habitat.co.uk). Oxford Circus or Piccadilly Circus tube. **Open** 10am-7pm Mon-Wed, Fri, Sat; 10am-8pm Thur; noon-6pm Sun. **Credit** AmEx, MC, V.

We're yet to be impressed by Habitat's mix of affordable modern homewares housed in this Grade II-listed building, with much of it dwarfed by its opulent setting. On the ground floor, room settings look lost against the towering racks of tableware; an ascent up through the bedding, textiles and soft furnishings to the new kids' section doesn't alleviate the sense of dowdiness. Still, odd individual items shine – literally, in the case of the gleaming red Masai audio-visual unit in lacquered high gloss (£349); others are more quietly compelling, like new armchair Ella (£699) – an elegant, three-tone upholstered piece. There's a big emphasis on ethnic styling; the carved palonia wood range is earthy and heavy, and worlds away from the stark lines we associate with Conran's original modernist themes.

Branches: throughout the city.

Heal's

196 Tottenham Court Road, W1T 7LQ (7636 1666/www.heals.co.uk). Goodge Street tube. **Open** 10am-6pm Mon-Wed; 10am-8pm Thur; 10am-6.30pm Fri; 9.30am-6.30pm Sat; noon-6pm Sun. **Credit** AmEx, MC, V.

Heal's may be the grand old dame of interiors stores, but its happy combination of excellent sourcing, helpful staff and a layout that's constantly being reinvented means it manages to stay relevant. Regular exclusives make the stock feel fresh; look out for British designer John Reeves's limited-edition purple console table from the Louis range (£595) – a fresh take on baroque furniture. It's part of the store's Discovers range – an initiative that shows Heal's commitment to sourcing new designers. Other gems include the 1950s-inspired Flow sideboard by Kay + Stemmer (£1,795) and the covetable new range of bedlinen by Orla Kiely. The store's ground floor is the most fun for casual browsers, offering a cornucopia of table- and kitchenware, toiletries and gift items, plus a terrific lighting department boasting such delights as Tom Dixon's Beat pendant shades range (from £155). First and second floors house the bulk of the furniture, and for mid-century modernist fans, there's a great selection of vintage Danish furniture.

For branches see index.

Lifestyle Bazaar

10 Newburgh Street, W1F7RN (7734 9970/www.lifestylebazaar.com). Oxford Circus tube. **Open** 11am-7pm Mon-Wed, Sat; 11am-8pm Thur; noon-5pm Sun. **Credit** AmEx, MC, V.

Lifestyle Bazaar specialises in a selection of small homeware items, which are perched on or around larger pieces such as storage systems, lighting and chairs. There are lots of bright ideas, with products sourced from around the world. New from Milan in 2008 came Patrick Jouin's polycarbonate Thalya chairs, while the Ready Meals earthenware plates by young British design outfit Soop Groop are equally colourful, depicting classic British meals like beans on toast and fish and chips (£11). There's a nice selection by big-name designers too, including Stark and Marcel Wanders, but this is definitely a place to discover new names and, with any luck, pick up future design classics.

Marimekko

16-17 St Christopher's Place, W1U 1NZ (7486 6454/www.marimekko.com). Bond Street tube. **Open** 10am-6.30pm Mon-Wed, Fri, Sat; 10am-7pmThur; noon-5pm Sun. **Credit** AmEx, DC, MC, V.

The signature Marimekko look – Maija Isola's Unikko (poppy) pattern – is as familiar to design fans as an Eames chair, but a visit to this store shows that there's far more to the company than this ubiquitous design. Established by Finnish Armi Ratia 50 years ago, it continues to source and commission bold and beautiful textiles from emerging European designers. Upholstered tub chairs and chaises longues provide great frames on which to exhibit the constantly expanding range of fabrics. There are lots of figurative patterns, many of which have been applied to a bright and bold range of home- and tableware. Many of Marimekko's designs feature on its kids' range of bedding, towels and luggage.

Mar Mar Co

16 Cheshire Street, E2 6EH (7729 1494/ www.marmarco.com). Aldgate East tube/ Liverpool Street tube/rail. **Open** by appointment Mon-Thur; 11am-5pm Fri, Sun; 1-5pm Sat. **Credit** MC, V.

Mar Mar Co seems to have cleverly squeezed the whole world into its tiny space on oh-so-trendy Cheshire Street. This is due entirely to the roving eyes of its owners, Danish Marianne Lumholdt and Brit Mark Bedford, who scour France, Scandinavia, the UK, Holland and the US for contemporary homewares and gifts from emerging new designers. Everything here is functional yet contemporary, with much of it made from natural materials. On a recent visit we were tempted by pretty much everything in the shop, but in particular Tse & Tse's porcelain pendant lamps (from £99.50), Kähler ceramic vases (from £19.50) and Eno's marble tableware (from £11.50).

Mint

70 Wigmore Street, W1U 2SF (7224 4406/ www.mintshop.co.uk). Bond Street tube. **Open** 10.30am-6.30pm Mon-Wed, Fri, Sat; 10.30am-7.30pm Thur. **Credit** AmEx, DC, MC, V.

Mint feels like a Dalí painting come to life, with its handpicked and specially commissioned furniture, glasswear, textiles and ceramics arranged like an avant-garde curiosity shop. Owner Lina Kanafani fills her two-level space with international designs, and form and colour play a large part in her selections. One of the latest coups is Kiki Van Eijk's cool chaise longue (POA). Much of Mint's stock could be considered as art with a capital 'a', a fact reflected in the prices. Louise Hindsgavl's porcelain stunning one-off piece Everyday Scenario, Surgery Suggestion (£1,400), would be hard to define as anything other than sculpture. The vintage pieces add to the sense of the unique, and there are plenty of smaller, more affordable items too; we fell in love with Katie Lilly's limited-edition hand-decorated plates (£60).

Nicole Farhi Home

17 Clifford Street, W1S 3RQ (7494 9051/ www.nicolefarhi.com). Green Park or Piccadilly Circus tube. **Open** 10am-6pm Mon-Wed, Fri, Sat; 10am-7pm Thur. **Credit** AmEx, DC, MC, V.

A short hop away from Saville Row, Nicole Farhi Home is as elegant as anything you'd find in that haven of smart tailoring. There are other similarities too: texture, weave and colour dominate a space where your eye is constantly drawn towards objects of beauty. Fat-bottomed chunky dark green tumblers (£12) give way to the delicately pretty Dip tableware (£16.50 for a mug), its pistachio greens, pale yellows and pinks are enticing. Cushions and throws are luxurious, with ostrich feathers, fur and knitted loops of merino wool. Vintage furniture, mirrors as well as extraordinary antiques make the space feel very special – an 18th-century hand-painted commode was so beautiful, its £11,000 price tag almost seemed reasonable.

For branches stocking homewares (Westbourne Grove) see index.

One Deko

111-113 Commercial Street, E1 6BG (7375 3289/www.onedeko.co.uk). Liverpool Street tube/rail. **Open** 10.30am-6pm Mon-Fri; noon-5pm Sat; 10.30am-5.30pm Sun. **Credit** MC, V.

One Deko is a breath of fresh air in the soaring steel and glass environs of the City. Stuffed to the gills with oversized sofas, chic Italian and Spanish lighting, furniture from Calligaris and Fama and vases and tableware from smaller design groups, it's a rich and colourful mix. Wit and charm abound; a doormat seen one way up reads 'come in' – turn it round 90 degrees and it reads 'go away' (£19.95). The furniture range is small but covers most tastes, with solid design principles to the fore in the lean sleek sofas and more adventurous armchairs that reference 1970s cool – the Swing Chair (£525) is one for budding Bonds everywhere. Storage is a strong point and covers the gamut from mid 20th-century style to contemporary, but we were more taken by Suck UK's lit-up steel-and-glass tube map coffee table (£1,895) and the cute Momiji mugs (£7.95), each with a few words of wisdom that shine through once you've finished your cuppa.

For branch see index.

Places & Spaces

30 Old Town, SW4 0LB (7498 0998/www.placesandspaces.com). Clapham Common tube. **Open** 10.30am-6pm Tue, Wed, Fri, Sat; 10.30am-7pm Thur; noon-4pm Sun. **Credit** MC, V.

A visit to this store is like wandering around a three-dimensional design encyclopedia. The shop has its own brand of wallpaper, in collaboration with graphic design studio Absolute Zero Degrees, which features strong but delicate designs (from £60 a roll); hundreds of fun accessories and tableware, like the Mustachio Self Portrait Mirror, featuring a cut-out moustache (£39); and the big hitters: Marcel Breuer and BarberOsgerby tables, a fantastic range of chairs and sofas – from Eames, Hans Wegner, Marc Newson, Jasper Morrison, Ross Lovegrove and Zanotti – and an impressive selection of lighting from the likes of Achille Castiglioni, George Nelson and Tom Dixon. Our eye was caught by Mark Cox's Proud floor lamp, spotted last year and still making an impact by displaying objects of your choice in a bell jar.

SCP

135-139 Curtain Road, EC2A 3BX (7739 1869/www.scp.co.uk). Old Street tube/rail. **Open** 9.30am-6pm Mon-Sat; 11am-5pm Sun. **Credit** MC, V.

SCP attempts to showcase the very best of contemporary furniture, lighting and homewares. Overseeing it is Sheridan Coakley, who sources globally and stocks a clutch of respected designers – among them Robin Day, Terence Woodgate, Matthew Hilton, Konstantin Grcic, James Irvine and Michael Marriott. Furniture and storage solutions are all bold lines and slick minimalism, exemplified by Kay + Stemmer's Foxtrot coffee table in oak (£595) or wenge stain (£615) and Jasper Morrison's Plan modular system of cabinets from Cappellini. Accessories broaden out to take in everything from the highly decorative – like the beautiful serving glass Groove collection by Simon Moore (from £45) – to the fun and quirky: we loved Reiko Kaneko's Egg soldier cup (£9.99), which has four sword-wielding soldiers attacking the egg. SCP now has exclusive UK rights to retail the George Nelson Bubble lights by Modernica. Produced by Howard Miller until 1979, these shades are part of the permanent collection of the Museum of Modern Art in New York – you can own one for £255.

For branches see index.

Skandium

247 Brompton Road, SW3 2EP (7584 2066/www.skandium.com). South Kensington tube. **Open** 10am-6.30pm Mon-Wed, Fri, Sat; 10am-7pm Thur; 11am-5pm Sun. **Credit** AmEx, DC, MC, V.

With two shops in London – a two-storey space in Marylebone and this 700sq m flagship – Skandium fans are spoilt for choice. Most people know the store for its home- and tableware, but there's also classic furniture from manufacturers like Asplund, Artek, Fritz Hansen, Swedese, Carl Hansen and Knoll and even broader European wares from the likes of German design house Vitra. Lighting comes courtesy of top names like Louis Poulsen, Secto, Le Klint and Normann Copenhagen. Everywhere you go your eye is drawn back to that gorgeous range of tableware, including a new black and white addition to the range of Iittala's fairytale-like Taika by Klaus Haapaniemi. There are all sorts of fabrics; the vibrant Jobs Handtryck nature motif prints (from £90/m) contrast beautifully with the more graphic serenity of the Sandberg range (from £57/m). What makes Skandium special, however, is its commitment to excellence in contemporary design; Arne Jacobsen's 1969 Vola mixer tap in 18 colours is stocked, as are vacuum cleaners, bird tables, hooks and phones that ensure attention to detail across the home.

For branch see index.

Supernice

106 Columbia Road, E2 7RG (7613 3890/ www.supernice.co.uk). Liverpool Street or Old Street tube/rail/55, 26, 48 bus. **Open** noon-5pm Sat; 9.30am-3pm Sun. **Credit** MC, V.

Opened a couple of years ago by ex-Selfridges homewares buyer Louise Sandor, Supernice is branching out from the Blik surface graphics (from £15) and the zany Tepper Jackson range of vinyl travel accessories that were its starting point. Thomas Paul has been added to the mix – with pillows and melamine tableware in attractive colours and simple patterns; from Russian dolls to puffer fish and a dizzying array of abstracts and colourways, the cushions (£85) and melamine plates and trays (from £6) will all stand the test of time. Inke Heiland's limited-edition vintage wallpaper, meanwhile, features animal silhouettes (from £12.95).

Suzy Hoodless

10 Clarendon Cross, W11 4AP (7221 8844/www.suzyhoodless.com). Holland Park tube. **Open** 9.30am-6.30pm Mon-Fri. **No credit cards.**

When you've worked on prestigious retail projects (like the art direction for Selfridges' window display), helped Swedish architect Thomas Sandell design a *Wallpaper** house during the Salone de Mobile in Milan and spent years on interiors shoots, you'd hope that the creation of your own interiors retail space would be a doddle – and so it's proved for Suzy Hoodless. The design consultant stocks a finely edited selection of antiques, 20th-century classics and inspirational pieces sourced globally alongside her own slick yet feminine designs for furniture, rugs and wallpapers. Products are pricey – a cashmere and merino wool throw produced in collaboration with Johnstons of Elgin is £565, while a Hoodless-designed rug is £525/sq m – but the quality and personality of the pieces are outstanding, and the shop a delight to wander around.

Twentytwentyone

274 Upper Street, N1 2UA (7288 1996/ www.twentytwentyone.com). Angel tube/ Highbury & Islington tube/rail. **Open** 10am-6pm Mon-Fri; 10am-5.30pm Sat; 11am-5pm Sun. **Credit** AmEx, MC, V.

Twentytwentyone was voted the capital's best furniture and homewares shop by *Time Out* magazine in 2008, for its mix of vintage originals, reissued classics and contemporary designs. Big-name brands such as Arper, Artek, Cappellini, DePadova, Flos, Swedese and Vitra are stocked, but founders Simon Alderson and Tony Cunningham are also keen to foster new talent, recently launching Ten/twentytwentyone – ten designs created by ten leading British designers. Eco-issues figure large: Artek's bent bamboo Bambu range looks as good as the vintage pieces stocked. Stock is divided between two locations; the River Street showroom houses most of the larger items, while the Upper Street outpost is brilliant for home accessories and gifts – pick up a Yoan David porcelain fortune chicken for £15.

For branch see index.

Unto This Last

230 Brick Lane, E2 7EB (7613 0882/ www.untothislast.co.uk). Liverpool Street or Old Street tube/rail. **Open** 10am-6pm daily. **Credit** MC, V.

Nestled snugly in an old East End workshop that exudes Dickensian quaintness, this small furniture maker produces a distinctive range of birch plywood and laminate pieces, transforming raw materials into decidedly modern furniture. Named after the 1862 John Ruskin book advocating the principles of local craftsmanship, Unto This Last does exactly that – combining simple design with sophisticated computer software to produce well-priced cabinets, bookcases, chairs and beds, plus a small range of accessories like tealight holders (from £3), fruit bowls (£15) and placemats (from £5). The finished products have a beautifully fluid, organic appearance, and are bold enough to act as statement pieces. We particularly liked the Square shelves (from £180) that can be free-standing or wall-mounted. Look out too for the undulating Wavy Bench (£280) and the 4ft Standing lamp (£90).

Viaduct

1-10 Summers Street, EC1R 5BD (7278 8456/www.viaduct.co.uk). Farringdon tube/rail. **Open** 9.30am-6pm Mon-Fri; 10.30am-4pm Sat. **Credit** MC, V.

Housed in an impressive 1930s industrial space, Viaduct oozes design quality, and is the sole UK agent for leading European companies Driade, e15, Maarten Van Severen, MDF Italia, Montis and xO. The emphasis is on contemporary homewares, but there's a good range of unusal classics too; Meret Oppenheim's gold leaf and brass bird-legged Traccia side table for Simon (£1,595) is here, as is Christophe Pillet's bright Sunlight chair for Cappellini and the wonderfully surreal high-heeled Sillon Leda chair by Salvador Dalí for BD Ediciones (£16,334). Fans of Driade and Moooi will relish the selection of smaller objects, such as Boris Sipek's arresting Celine vase in white porcelain and red glass (£1,309) and Marcel Wanders's gorgeously tactile Ming and Sponge vases (from £80). So vast is the range of lighting, furniture and accessories that much of it can't be displayed, so the showroom often mixes things up, making the space and objects feel vibrant and fresh on each visit.

Wawa

3 Ezra Street, E2 7RH (7729 6768/www.wawa.co.uk). Liverpool Street tube/rail then 26, 48 bus. **Open** by appointment Mon-Fri; 10am-2.30pm Sun. **Credit** AmEx, MC, V.

Wawa sells bright and bold made-to-order sofas designed and handmade by Richard Ward, whose love of curves, lines and colour is obvious in his work (think contemporary takes on old classics). Each sofa is unique and upholstered with great attention to detail using hand-tied springs. Prices start at around £680 for an armchair, rising to around £2,000 for a chaise longue; choose your fabric from the large collection that takes in ranges by the Designers Guild, Andrew Martin and Lelieve. Lucy Wassell works in the same studio and creates textiles to commission. The shop also stocks a gorgeous selection of plates and trays, as well as mirrors, lamps and lampshades, plus the covetable Mimi bags that are now so ubiquitous around these parts. Head to the showroom on a Sunday in order to have a mooch around the flower market afterwards.

Also check out…

Alessi

22 Brook Street, W1K 5DF (7518 9091/www.alessi.com). Bond Street tube. **Open** 10am-6.30pm Mon-Wed, Fri, Sat; 10am-7pm Thur; noon-6pm Sun. **Credit** AmEx, MC, V.

The flagship store for the iconic and witty Italian tableware line.

Alma Home

8 Vigo Street, W1S 3HJ (7439 0925/www.almahome.co.uk). Piccadilly Circus tube. **Open** 10am-6pm Mon-Sat. **Credit** MC, V.

Superior contemporary leather furniture.

Andrew Martin

200 Walton Street, SW3 2JL (7225 / 5100/www.andrewmartin.co.uk). South Kensington tube. **Open** 9am-6pm Mon-Fri; 10am-6pm Sat. **Credit** AmEx, MC, V.

Bold, contemporary and also masculine and classic, furniture and fabrics.

BoConcept

158 Tottenham Court Road, W1T 7NH (7388 2447/www.boconcept.co.uk). Goodge Street or Warren Street tube. **Open** 10am-6pm Mon-Wed, Fri, Sat; 10am-8pm Thur; noon-6pm Sun. **Credit** MC, V.

Affordable, understated modern wares.

For branch see index.

Carpenters Workshop Gallery

3 Albemarle Street, W1S 4HE (3051 5939/www.cwgdesign.com). Green Park tube. **Open** 10am-6pm Mon-Fri; 10am-4pm Sat. **Credit** MC, V.

Furniture that stretches the definition of the word to its creative boundaries, not to mention the budget of a small house.

Chaplins

477-507 Uxbridge Road, Pinner, Middx HA5 4JS (8421 1779/www.chaplins.co.uk). Pinner tube/Hatch End rail. **Open** 10am-6pm Mon-Sat. 11am-4pm Sun. **Credit** AmEx, MC, V.

Slick upmarket space showcasing a huge range of furniture from European designers.

Wawa

Charles Page
61 Fairfax Road, NW6 4EE (7328 9851/ www.charlespage.co.uk). Finchley Road or Swiss Cottage tube/31 bus. **Open** 9.30am-5.30pm Mon-Fri; 10am-6pm Sat; noon-5pm Sun. **Credit** MC, V.
Solid, top-quality furnishings.

Chest of Drawers
281 Upper Street, N1 2TZ (7359 5909/ www.chestofdrawers.co.uk). Angel tube/ Highbury & Islington tube/rail. **Open** 10am-6pm daily. **Credit** AmEx, MC, V.
Modern wooden furniture specialist.
For branch see index.

Dutch by Design
www.dutchbydesign.com
Great site featuring products by the likes of Moooi, Marcel Wanders and Droog.

Dwell
264 Balham High Road, SW17 7AN (0870 060 0182/www.dwell.co.uk). Balham tube/rail. **Open** 10am-7pm Mon-Sat; 11am-5pm Sun. **Credit** AmEx, MC, V.
Affordable modern interior items.
For branches see index.

Espacio
82 Tottenham Court Road, W1T 4TF (7637 1932/www.espacio.co.uk). Goodge Street or Tottenham Court Road tube. **Open** 10am-6.30pm Mon-Wed, Fri, Sat; 10am-7pm Thur; noon-5pm Sun. **Credit** MC, V.
Impressive collection from some of Europe's leading manufacturers.
For branch see index.

European Design Centre
77 Margaret Street, W1W 8SY (7323 3233/www.edcplc.com). Oxford Circus tube. **Open** 9am-6pm Mon-Fri; 10am-5pm Sat. **Credit** AmEx, MC, V.
Imported products at good prices.

Find That Chair
0151 285 0975/www.findthatchair.com.
Chairs, tables, accessories and classic designs from leading brands.

Freud
198 Shaftesbury Avenue, WC2H 8JL (7831 1071/www.freudliving.com). Covent Garden or Leicester Square tube. **Open** 11am-7pm Mon-Fri; 11am-5pm Sat. **Credit** MC, V.
Simple tableware and frames, plus repro Rennie Mackintosh chairs and retro fans.

Furniture Union
65A Hopton Street, SE1 9LR (7928 5155/ www.thefurnitureunion.co.uk). Southwark tube/rail. **Open** 9am-6pm Mon-Fri; 11am-6pm Sat. **Credit** MC, V.
Decent-sized studio with a strong collection of seating and accessories.

IKEA
2 Drury Way, North Circular Road, NW10 0TH (8233 2233/www.ikea.co.uk). Stonebridge Park tube then shuttle bus/ 92, 112, 206, 232, PR2 bus. **Open** 10am-midnight Mon-Fri; 9am-10pm Sat; 11am-5pm Sun. **Credit** MC, V.
For branches see index.

Indish
16 Broadway Parade, N8 9DE (8342 9496/www.indish.co.uk). Finsbury Park tube/rail then W3, W7 bus. **Open** 10.30am-5.30pm Mon-Sat; 12.30-4.30pm Sun. **Credit** MC, V.
Cool home accessories for Crouch Enders.

Interni
51-53 Fairfax Road, NW6 4EL (7624 4040/www.interni.co.uk). Finchley Road tube/Swiss Cottage tube. **Open** 9am-5.30pm Mon-Fri; 10am-6.30pm Sat. **Credit** DC, MC, V.
Furniture design exuding Italian style.

Isokon Plus
www.isokonplus.com
Has some classics and modernist pieces by Ernest Race, Marcel Breuer, BarberOsgerby, Michael Sodeau and Simon Pengelly.

Kelly Hoppen
175-177 Fulham Road, SW3 6JW (7351 1910/www.kellyhoppen.com). South Kensington tube. **Open** 10am-6pm Mon-Sat. **Credit** AmEx, DC, MC, V.
Renowned interior designer offering a simple design style fusing East and West.

Ligne Roset
23-25 Mortimer Street, W1T 3JE (7323 1248/www.ligne-roset-westend.co.uk). Goodge Street or Oxford Circus tube. **Open** 10am-6pm Mon-Wed, Fri, Sat; 10am-8pm Thur; noon-5pm Sun. **Credit** AmEx, MC, V.
Easy-living contemporary collections.

Living Space
36 Cross Street, N1 2BG (7359 3950/ www.livingspaceuk.com). Angel tube or Highbury & Islington tube/rail. **Open** 10am-6pm Mon-Sat; noon-5pm Sun. **Credit** AmEx, DC, MC, V.
High-end European furniture and lighting.
For branch see index.

Poliform
278 King's Road, SW3 5AW (7368 7600/ www.poliformuk.com). Sloane Square tube/South Kensington tube. **Open** 10am-6pm Mon-Sat. **Credit** AmEx, DC, MC, V.
Italian collection in minimalist settings.

Pop UK
278 Upper Richmond Road, SW15 6TQ (8788 8811/www.popuk.com). East Putney tube/Putney rail. **Open** 10am-6pm Mon-Sat; noon-5pm Sun. **Credit** AmEx, DC, MC, V.
High-end wares from top European brands and designers in an airy space.

Roche-Bobois
421-425 Finchley Road, NW3 6HJ (7431 1411/www.roche-bobois.com). Finchley Road tube. **Open** 10am-6pm Mon-Sat; noon-5pm Sun. **Credit** MC, V.
Chic French furniture.
For branch see index.

Tablemakers
153 St John's Hill, SW11 1TQ (7223 2075/www.individuallymade.com). Clapham Junction rail. **Open** 9.30am-5pm Mon-Sat. **Credit** MC, V.
Handmade solid wood furniture.

Willer
12 Holland Street, W8 4LT (7937 3518/ www.willer.co.uk). High Street Kensington or Notting Hill Gate tube. **Open** 10am-6pm Mon-Sat; other times by appointment. **Credit** AmEx, MC, V.
Stocking a selection of haute tableware and other objects.

Zara Home
129 Regent Street, W1B 4HT (7432 0040/ www.zarahome.com). Piccadilly Circus tube. **Open** 10am-7pm Mon-Wed, Fri, Sat; 10am-8pm Thur; noon-6pm Sun. **Credit** AmEx, DC, MC, V.
A broad range of affordable homewares that include tableware, bedlinen, bathroom linen and accessories.
For branches see index.

Retro, global & traditional

Brissi
196 Westbourne Grove, W11 2RH (7727 2159/www.brissi.co.uk). Notting Hill Gate tube. **Open** 10am-6.30pm Mon-Sat; noon-6pm Sun. **Credit** DC, MC, V.
Brissi is rather like a grander take on the White Company. The look is rustic simplicity combined with château chic; Bordeaux meets the Hamptons. Its elegant, but unstuffy range includes lots of white: china, blankets, towels, furniture. This provides a perfect neutral backdrop for the rest, such as a freestanding tin-coated slipper bath (£3,600) or a rather decadent silver daybed (£3,400). Home accessories are carefully chosen, and the silver and pewter range, in particular have pleasing antique/vintage designs. Lovely glass jars with pewter lids are £29 and silver-plated double champagne buckets with handles are £135. Brissi also has a paints range, the trademark shade being its Parisian Grey.
For branches see index.

Labour & Wait
18 Cheshire Street, E2 6EH (7729 6253/ www.labourandwait.co.uk). Aldgate East tube/Liverpool Street tube/rail. **Open** by appointment Fri; 1-5pm Sat; 10am-5pm Sun. **Credit** MC, V.
This retro-stylish store sells the sort of things everybody would have had in their kitchen or pantry 60 years ago: functional domestic goods that have a timeless style. Spend any time here and you'll be filled with the joys of spring cleaning. Who'd have guessed that a scrubbing brush (made of wood and Tampico fibre) for £8.50 could be so appealing? For the desk proud, there's a pig and goat hair bristle computer brush (£15), while for the kitchen there are some great simple classics like a steel-wall mounted bottle opener (£7.50) and enamel jugs and pans in retro pastels. You can garden beautifully with ash-handled trowels, pale suede gauntlets and a dibber and label set. Our favourite, though, is the chubby flowerpot brush. There are some great old-fashioned gifts for children, such as a pinhole camera kit (£22) and vintage-style satchels, plus a lovely range of notebooks. Hard to leave empty handed.

Lisa Stickley

74 Landor Road, SW9 9PH (7737 8067/ www.lisastickleylondon.co.uk). Clapham North tube/rail. **Open** 10am-6pm Mon-Fri. **Credit** MC,V.

Stickley's homely shop is stocked with quirky nostalgic homewares that will bring a smile to your face. Her collections have names like Mushy Peas, Teatime and Shortbread and encompass all sorts, from plastic-coated coin purses to washbags. The pretty, yet sturdy enamelware is by Garden Trading. Cushions, tea towels and aprons are handprinted with simple illustrations and genuine postcard messages; one reads, 'I went to the boat show in Southampton. Free for a pensioner. Everyone else paid £1.60. What a life.' The collection is also available at Heal's, Liberty and Selfridges.

Mandala

408-410 St John Street, EC1V 4NJ (7833 1074). **Open** 10.30am-6.30pm Mon, Tue, Sat; 10.30am-7pm Wed-Fri; 11.30am-5.30pm Sun. **Credit** MC, V.

Mandala aims to bring a touch of Zen into our hectic urban lives. Taking its name from the ancient eastern symbol for the circle of life, the company uses reclaimed timber for its pieces, which are made in Indonesia by Javanese master craftsmen. Wood is either sustainably managed, or it comes from old buildings, boats and even bridges. Furniture is light and elegant rather than dark and chunky. Beds come in simple contemporary designs (from £835) but it's the four posters that are the draw, such as the exotic Shanghai four poster (£1,295) or the elegant black satin lacquer Bhutan (£1,795). It also makes dining sets, daybeds and occasional furniture. Attractive homewares complete the look, with cushions, teapots, trays and candles. Mandala also has a bespoke service.

Nina Campbell

9 Walton Street, SW3 2JD (7225 1011/ www.ninacampbell.com). Knightsbridge or South Kensington tube. **Open** 10am-6pm Mon-Sat. **Credit** AmEx, MC, V.

Campbell displays are always elegant and eclectic, never formal or stale. The Walton Street shop stocks a small selection of her furniture along with home accessories and antiques. Her delightful chairs and sofas are built in the UK, and the range often inspired by antique pieces that Campbell owns herself. Her designs can cover every surface of a home; her popular wallpapers are sold through Osborne & Little, her rugs are distributed by the Rug Company and her paints are sold at the Paint Library. There's plenty to entice in the shop itself; scented candles (£25), the jewel-coloured Henry tumblers (£36) and Limoges China dessert plates with Campbell's birdcage design (£45). A wedding list service is available.

Roullier White

125 Lordship Lane, SE22 8HU (8693 5150/www.roullierwhite.com). East Dulwich rail. **Open** 11am-6pm Mon-Sat; 11am-5pm Sun. **Credit** AmEx, MC, V.

Roullier White combines practicality and elegance with a sense of fun. For the kitchen,

Out of the woodwork...

London's bespoke furniture-makers can turn your visions into three-dimensional realities.

It might not come at IKEA prices, but bespoke furniture needn't break the bank. Commissions can be as simple as a built-in wardrobe or as complex as a custom-made wood and glass staircase. The best joiners can create front door jambs, built-in beds or fireplace surrounds, and can line a room with inlaid bookshelves – even create your dream kitchen or bathroom.

Choose your designer with care, however. It's wise to be clear about what you want and establish your budget as soon as possible as this will influence the materials used and the complexity of the final product. Always ask for references and to see examples of the designer's work. If the commission is part of a larger project (redeveloping a house, for example) get them on board as early as possible so that their work is integral to the overall design.

Furniture designer **Alex Hellum** (01992 550021, alexhellum.com) uses traditional craftsmanship to create his excellent wood designs. The emphasis is on unique, beautifully finished and ingenious solutions to everyday situations. Recent commissions have included constructing a square dining table to match a set of vintage Hans Wegner Wishbone chairs, and site-specific built-in storage to house an iron, ironing board and other utility items in separate compartments. He's based in Hertfordshire but is willing to travel to London. The initial consultation should be by phone.

Ryan Fowler of **Fowlers Carpentry** (www.fowlerscarpentry.co.uk) undertakes commissions on basic carpentry projects, including bespoke fitted wardrobes, desks, shelves, entertainment units, and fitted kitchens. A one-metre unpainted fitted wardrobe with double doors in MDF and soft wood will cost in the region £500 to £600. He works mainly in north and central London but can travel further afield if necessary.

Well-respected south-east London company **Greenwich Woodworks** (8694 8449, www.greenwich woodworks.co.uk) specialises in high-quality bespoke kitchens in Shaker, Georgian, Victorian and contemporary styles. Bedroom, bathroom and study commissions are executed with equal skill. Prices reflect quality with kitchens averaging £28,000, though some projects have been completed for under £15,000. A one-metre fitted wardrobe in maple wood or similar will cost around £1,800 to £2,500, though prices for dark woods can be more expensive. Initial consultation is by phone.

James Whitehall (07786 513 936, www.jameswhitehall.co.uk) is one of the best finds in London. The furniture designer/maker and bespoke joiner produces excellent quality work matched by affordable prices. Cost depends on design and materials, but a one-metre fitted wardrobe in MDF will cost roughly £700 to £800, with prices for wood veneers like walnut costing more. His bespoke wardrobes can also be fitted with accessories like sensor-activated lights and he also designs and makes one-off bespoke pieces including sideboards and desks. His bespoke kitchens start from around £500 per linear per metre (for basic spray painted kitchen cupboards) and he can also make doors for pre-bought units. Recent commissions have included a walnut veneered wardrobe and a matching bed with under-bed storage.

Last but not least, is **Ray Clarke** (07903 184 914, www.rayclarke upholstery.com). If you've ever been to Cargo you've probably already parked your derrière on some of Clarke's upholstery. His trademark seating is both eye-catching and accomplished; key pieces include pool hall bar stools and an office chair reupholstered in leather. But he's at home working with all kinds of materials, including fabric and vinyl. Typical residential commissions include reupholstering vintage chairs (£45 for a drop in seat exclusive of fabric costs), built in banquette kitchen seating, respringing antique sofas and chairs, and upholstering bed headboards.

there's the purely functional, like onion-chopping goggles (£15). Then there are beautifully packaged natural household cleaners by Isabella Smith, including lavender and mint limescale removing gel. You'll find top-quality towels, linen and china as well as super-high thread count bedlinen. Among the quirkier items, we loved the solid brass lion doorknocker, made from the same mould as the knocker at 10 Downing Street (£45). The shop ingeniously tracked down the foundry that made the 1780s original and discovered they still had the mould. The Victorian shop fittings and haberdashery units used to display the stock are also for sale.

Story

4 Wilkes Street, E1 6QF (7377 0313/ 07949 827966). Liverpool Street tube/rail. **Open** 1-6pm Sun; also by appointment. **Credit** AmEx, MC, V. **Sells** M,W.
Tucked away behind a curtain of ivy on a Spitalfields side street and only open on Sunday afternoons, Anne Shore and Lee Hollingworth's Story is the ultimate secret hunting ground, and the territory of stylists and interiors designers looking for inspiration. Among the expertly sourced reclaimed fabrics you'll find hanging glass tea-light holders, candles and plenty of interesting decor ideas, as well as vintage clothing and cool jewellery.

Tobias & the Angel

68 White Hart Lane, SW13 0PZ (8878 8902/www.tobiasandtheangel.com). Hammersmith tube then 209 bus/ Barnes Bridge rail. **Open** 10am-6pm Mon-Sat. **Credit** MC, V.
This lovely shop has the kind of interior many of us strive to create at home: careful, but unfussy, cosy yet airy. The furniture, a sleeker Scandinavian take on English country, is all handmade to measure in its workshop in Surrey. Constructed in solid pine, the range includes tables, chairs, drawer units, chicken-wire linen cupboards, desks and benches – painted in a choice of colours and priced per square foot. The freestanding furniture, such as the superb housekeeper's cupboard, provides a flexible alternative to a fitted kitchen. Chairs and sofas are covered in antique and vintage cloth, which is also for sale in lengths. The accessories are particularly attractive, from pretty cushions to delightful cat doorstops. The place also has a good selection of lamps. Come Christmas, it's the place to head to for unusual decorations for the tree.

Also check out…

Caravan

3 Redchurch Street, EC2 7DJ (7033 3532/ www.caravanstyle.com). Liverpool Street tube. **Open** 11am-6pm Tue-Fri; 1-5pm Sat-Sun. **Credit** MC, V.
See p134 **Unique Selling Point**.

Cath Kidston

8 Clarendon Cross, W11 4AP (7221 4000/ www.cathkidston.co.uk). Holland Park tube. **Open** 10am-6pm Mon-Sat; noon-5pm Sun. **Credit** AmEx, MC, V.
There are numerous ways to embrace the nostalgic Cath Kidson lifestyle with her retro floral/stripey/dotty prints covering everything from washbags to tableware.
Branches: throughout the city.

Couch Potato Company

23 Hampton Road, Twickenham, Middx TW2 5QE (8894 1333/www.couchpotato company.com). Strawberry Hill rail. **Open** by appointment Mon; 9.30am-5.30pm Tue-Fri; 10am-5.30pm Sat. **Credit** MC, V.
Has some comfy seating plus classic reissues, including Knoll Tulip chairs and Eames loungers – but only the authorised versions, so you can be sure they are top quality.

Linley

60 Pimlico Road, SW1W 8LP (7730 7300/ www.davidlinley.com). Sloane Square tube. **Open** 10am-6pm Mon-Thur; 10am-5pm Fri, Sat. **Credit** AmEx, MC, V.
Handmade furniture at high prices. There's a more affordable accessories range.
For branch see index.

Lombok

204-208 Tottenham Court Road, W1T 7PL (7580 0800/www.lombok.co.uk). Goodge Street tube. **Open** 10am-6pm Mon-Wed; 10am-8pm Thur; 10am-6.30pm Fri; 10am-7pm Sat; noon-6pm Sun. **Credit** MC, V.
Indonesian teak for a colonial look, made in Asia and Africa. Attractive accessories include well-priced lamps and linens.
Branches: throughout the city.

Oka

60 Sloane Avenue, SW3 3DD (7590 9895/ www.okadirect.com), South Kensington tube. **Open** 9.30am-6pm Mon, Tue, Thur-Sat; 9.30am-7pm Wed; noon-6pm Sun. **Credit** AmEx, MC, V.
Colonial chic for Chelsea types. Rattan and bamboo feature strongly and there's a good range of attractive home accessories.
For branches see index.

Sofa Workshop

84 Tottenham Court Road, W1T 4TG (7580 6839/www.sofaworkshop.com). Goodge Street tube. **Open** 9.30am-6pm Mon-Wed, Fri, Sat; 9.30am-7.30pm Thur; noon-6pm Sun. **Credit** AmEx, MC, V.
Extensive range, excellent advice and good aftercare at this well-established company.
Branches: throughout the city.

Tann-Rokka

123 Regent's Park Road, NW1 8BE (7722 3999/www.tannrokka.com). Chalk Farm tube. **Open** 10am-6pm daily. **Credit** AmEx, MC, V.
Oriental and vintage homewares are the fortes of this laid-back, stylish shop in the former Primrose Hill train station.

Repairs & re-upholstery

See also p139 **Richard Morant** and *p143* **Fabrics & soft furnishings**.

Capital Crispin Veneer

12 & 13 Gemini Business Park, Hornet Way, E6 7FF (7474 3680/www.capital crispin.com). Gallions Reach DLR. **Open** 8.30am-5pm Mon-Fri. **Credit** MC, V.
Over 150 different types of wood veneer are sold by the leaf; as little or as much as you want. Individuals tend to buy for marquetry and restoration.

David Scotcher Interiors

285 Upper Street, N1 2TZ (7354 4111). Angel tube/Highbury & Islington tube/ rail. **Open** 10.30am-6.30pm Tue-Sat. **Credit** MC, V.
Reupholstery and restoration of antique furniture; the shop also sells sofas, chairs and soft furnishings.

E&A Wates

82-84 Mitcham Lane, SW16 6NR (8769 2205/www.eawates.com). Streatham Common rail/57, 133 bus. **Open** 9am-6pm Mon-Wed, Fri, Sat; 9am-7pm Thur. **Credit** MC, V.
Established in 1900, this furniture store also undertakes restoration work. Virtually anything can be tackled.

Fineline Upholstery

63 New King's Road, SW6 4SE (7371 7073). Fulham Broadway tube. **Open** 10.30am-5.30pm Mon-Fri; by appointment Sat. **Credit** MC, V.
Fineline will make bespoke sofas to the customer's design and dimensions as well as reupholstering just about anything you care to bring in.

JS Polishing

366 City Road, EC1V 2PY (7278 6803). **Phone enquiries** 8am-6pm Mon-Fri. **No credit cards**.
JS Polishing are the experts that restored the hardwood panelling at Hampton Court after a fire. They will also deal with more everyday damage, like fine scratches on tables.

K Restorations

PO Box 20514, NW8 6ZT (7722 2869/ www.antiqueleathers.com). **Phone enquiries** 8.30am-5.30pm Mon-Fri. **Credit** MC, V.
Leather restoration work for desktops, club chairs and other furniture.

Pilgrim Payne & Company

Units 12-14, Wharfside, Rosemont Road, Wembley, Middx HA0 4PE (8453 5350). Alperton tube. **Open** 8am-6pm Mon-Fri; 8am-1pm Sat. **Credit** MC, V.
Alongside reupholstery, the company offers a professional on- or off-site carpet, curtain and tapestry cleaning service.

Urban Sprawl

Unit W11, Metropolitan Business Centre, Enfield Road, N1 5AZ (7923 2292/www. urbansprawl.co.uk). Dalston Kingsland rail. **Open** by appointment only; phone to arrange a home visit. **Credit** MC, V.
This small business makes made-to-measure removable covers for sofas and chairs, plus foam, feather and fibre cushions.

William Fountain & Co

68A Cobden Road, E11 3PE (8558 3464/ www.williamfountain.co.uk). Leytonstone tube. **Open** 8am-6pm Mon-Fri. **No credit cards**.
Reupholstery, French polishing and also antique restoration are all done on site in its workshops.

Unique Selling Point
Caravan

Stylist and author Emily Chalmers's Redchurch Street boutique is a treasure trove of cool interiors ideas, vintage finds and unusual decorative pieces. Think billowing parachute skirts, a rainbow of glossy French industrial lamps, battered leather suitcases and gold angel wings for decorating candles. And right in the middle of it all, you'll find a vintage-clad Chalmers chatting animatedly to a stream of customers, who run the gamut from East End fashion fiends to older couples drawn in by the shop's timeless feel and stunning vintage teapots.

'It was a very natural progression for me to open Caravan,' says Chalmers. 'A stylist gathers and organises things for a shoot, a shop owner does just that for a shop.' But her achievement is much more than a series of attractively displayed objects. She has a passion for boutiques with personality, where the character of the owner shines through – and this is Caravan to a tee. From its freshly whitewashed walls – the shop relocated from Spitalfields in summer 2008 – to its hotchpotch display cabinets, Caravan showcases its owner's magpie tendencies and eye for detail.

And Spitalfields' loss is definitely Redchurch Street's gain. 'I enjoyed a very happy three years in Old Spitalfields Market,' says Chalmers. 'But I've always loved this street. It's edgy, inspiring and fresh – a total antidote to the commercialisation that's swept through Spitalfields over the last few years.'

She's right. Redchurch Street, though mere minutes from the heart of super-glossy Spitalfields, has a pleasingly anarchic, grimy appeal. There's a strip pub opposite Caravan's new location, hip upholsterer Squint (www.squintlimited.com) is just across the way on Shoreditch High Street and cool galleries are springing up on every spare corner. There's even an element of the commercial creeping in here too: Shoreditch House (www.shoreditchhouse.com) is up the road, while Conran's Boundary restaurant, rooms and bar is set to open on nearby Boundary Street in late 2008.

Constantly evolving environments are just one source of inspiration for Chalmers. In fact, there's very little she doesn't get excited about. 'I love colour and pattern, and mixing old and new,' she says. 'And I love the quality of production you get with vintage items – and the idea that something has had another life.'

Vintage gems aside, Chalmers's shop is full of quirky and affordable finds such as tiny cameo brooches, woollen knitted dog toys for cats (£9.50) and light-reactive singing birds (£16.95). 'Everything we sell is an item I particularly like. I love our big, black crows (£18.50), for example – they look great on a window ledge,' she says. A browsing ground for interior designers, gift-hunters, party planners and vintage aficionados, Caravan is bursting with ideas and fantastically offbeat takes on style and design (concrete bulb-shaped pendant lights at £45, for example). Why bother with pricey interior designers and style tomes when all the benefits of a stylist's keen eye are here for the taking?

For listing, *see p133*.

Beds

Alphabeds
92 Tottenham Court Road, W1T 4TL (7636 6840/www.alphabeds.co.uk). Warren Street tube. **Open** 10am-6pm Mon-Wed, Fri, Sat; 11am-7pm Thur; 11am-5pm Sun. **Credit** MC, V.
Huge range of self-assembly beds.

And So To Bed
15 Orchard Street, W1H 9AE (7935 0225/ www.andsotobed.co.uk). Baker Street or Bond Street tube. **Open** 10am-6pm Mon-Sat; 11am-5pm Sun. **Credit** AmEx, MC, V.
Wooden, brass, cast- and forged-iron beds. Lit bateau bedsteads are a speciality. The shop also sells its own-label high-quality bed linen.
For branch see index.

City Beds
17-39 Gibbins Road, E15 1HU (8534 3097/www.citybeds.co.uk). Stratford tube/ rail/DLR. **Open** 8.30am-5pm Mon-Sat. **Credit** MC, V.
Keenly priced bed outlet.
For branch see index.

Daniel Spring
158 Columbia Road, E2 7RG (7923 3033/ www.springmetalbeds.com). Liverpool Street or Old Street tube/rail. **Open** 10am-2.30pm Sun; also by appointment. **Credit** MC, V.
Stainless steel and polished iron bed specialist. Beds are made in its London Fields workshop.

Feather & Black
83 Tottenham Court Road, W1T 4SZ (7436 7707/www.featherandblack.com). Goodge Street or Warren Street tube. **Open** 10am-6pm Mon-Wed; 10am-8pm Thur; 10am-6.30pm Fri; 9.30am-6.30pm Sat; noon-6pm Sun. **Credit** MC, V.
A wide range of iron, wooden and chic upholstered beds.
For branches see index.

Futon Company
169 Tottenham Court Road, W1T 7NP (7636 9984/www.futoncompany.co.uk). Warren Street tube. **Open** 10am-7pm Mon-Sat; 11am-5pm Sun. **Credit** MC, V.
As well as standard futon beds, you'll find handy sleepover futons that roll up or fold into cubes for occasional guests.
For branches see index.

London Wall Bed Company
13 Roslin Square, Roslin Road, W3 8DH (8896 3757/www.wallbed.co.uk). Acton Town tube/South Acton rail. **Open** 9.30am-5.30pm Mon-Fri; by appointment Sat, Sun. **Credit** MC, V.
These wall beds discreetly disappear into wardrobes and bookcases. The company has fitted them in all sorts of locations, from boats to fire stations.

Hästens
99 Crawford Street, W1H 2HN (7723 2925/www.hastenswestend.co.uk). Baker Street tube. **Open** 9.30am-5.30pm Mon-Sat. **Credit** MC,V.
This Swedish manufacturer's high-quality beds are guaranteed for 25 years. Book a sleep consultation to find your perfect bed.
For branch see index.

Savoir Beds
104 Wigmore Street, W1U 3RN (7486 2222/www.savoirbeds.co.uk). Bond Street tube. **Open** 10am-6pm Mon-Sat. **Credit** MC, V.
The Savoir No.2 was first commissioned for the Savoy Hotel in 1905. You can still buy it (from £5,828). The newer, more affordable No.4 starts at £2,914.

Simon Horn
555 King's Road, SW6 2EB (7731 1279/ www.simonhorn.com). Fulham Broadway tube. **Open** 10am-6pm Mon-Sat. **Credit** MC, V.
Simon Horn is best known for his nursery furniture that can be transformed as your child grows up; lit bateau cots convert into a child's single bed, then to a small sofa.

Orthopaedic

Back Shop
14 New Cavendish Street, W1G 8UW (7935 9120/www.thebackshop.co.uk). Baker Street or Bond Street tube. **Open** 10am-5.30pm Mon-Fri; 10.30am-5pm Sat. **Credit** AmEx, MC, V.
Ergonomic seating solutions for home and office, plus accessories such as lumber support rolls and seat wedges.

Back 2
28 Wigmore Street, W1U 2RN (7935 0351/www.back2.co.uk). Bond Street tube. **Open** 9am-6pm Mon-Fri; 10am-6pm Sat; noon-5pm Sun. **Credit** AmEx, MC, V.
Ergonomic chairs, sofas and mattresses to ensure both a good day's work and a good night's sleep.

Bed & table linen

Austrian Bedding Company
205 Belsize Road, NW6 4AA (7372 3121/ www.austrianbedding.com). Kilburn Park tube. **Open** 10am-5.30pm Mon-Fri; 10am-5pm Sat. **Credit** MC, V.
Austrian-born Isolde Lawlor was the first person to introduce duvets to Ireland, some 40 years ago. Until the late 1960s duvets were something of a continental oddity for us Brits. Lawlor, who started business in London in the 1980s, sells top-quality Austrian and German duvets and pillows, along with Italian bedlinen. Duvets can be made to specific sizes, and the aftercare service means you can have extra or less weight, should your duvet not suit your personal thermostat. The friendly staff offer a cleaning and recovering service for duvets and pillows; it costs £29 to clean a double duvet plus £82 for a new cover (cleaning a pillow is £9.50, recovering £10).

Cabbages & Roses
3 Langton Street, SW10 0JL (7352 7333/ www.cabbagesandroses.com). Sloane Square tube then 22 bus. **Open** 9am-5.30pm Mon-Sat. **Credit** MC, V.
This well-presented shop displays a pretty selection of country-style home accessories. Cotton and linen mix tablecloths come in nostalgic floral patterns with names like *Ditzy pink* and *India rose* and cost from £78. There are matching napkins (£10) and even aprons, for oven to table chic. You'll also find useful household accessories, including laundry bags and floral cotton or oilcloth shoppers. Also worth checking out is the ever-changing stock of vintage homewares, including china, mirrors and furniture and French linen sheets.
For branch see index.

White Company
12 Marylebone High Street, W1U 4NR (7935 7879/mail order 0870 900 9555/ www.thewhitecompany.com). Baker Street or Bond Street tube. **Open** 10am-7pm Mon-Sat; 11am-5pm Sun. **Credit** MC, V.
Best known to most of us for its mail-order business and enticing sale catalogues, the company's appealing high street stores are worth a visit to see the range and have a squeeze of the goose-down pillows. Furniture now features, but the company still produces excellent-quality bedding. A wide range of fabrics and finishes is available, from pure linen pillowcases (from £30) to fine-rib cotton bedspreads (from £60) and hand-embroidered cotton percale duvet covers (from £65). Shop assistants are well informed about their products, and so can offer plenty of advice on thread counts and togs.
For branches see index.

Also check out…

Cologne & Cotton
39 Kensington Church Street, W8 4LL (7376 0324/www.cologneandcotton.com). High Street Kensington tube. **Open** 10am-7pm Mon-Sat; noon-5pm Sun. **Credit** AmEx, MC, V.
Pretty toile de Jouy quilts, waffle blankets, mohair throws as well as good range of bedlinen. There are duvets for all seasons, nursery bedding and luxury toiletries.
For branches see index.

Descamps
6 Marylebone High Street, W1U 4NJ (7935 0070/www.descamps.com). Baker Street or Bond Street tube. **Open** 9.30am-6.30pm Mon-Wed, Sat; 9.30am-7pm Thur, Fri; 11am-5pm Sun. **Credit** AmEx, MC, V.
English outpost of the chic French boudoir and bath specialist. The flagship store is on two levels.
For branch see index.

Peacock Blue
www.peacockblue.co.uk
Fresh, simply patterned bedlinen. Think ginghams, stripes and retro florals.

Kitchen equipment & tableware

Bodo Sperlein
Unit 1.05, Oxo Tower Wharf, Barge House Street, SE1 9PH (7633 9413/www.bodo sperlein.com). Blackfriars tube/rail. **Open** 10am-6pm Mon-Fri; noon-5pm Sat. **Credit** AmEx, DC, MC, V.
German-born Sperlein trained at Camberwell College of Art before going on to launch this successful ceramics range. Nowadays

HOME

he's fêted by the likes of *Vogue* and has a string of high-profile commissions from companies such as Lladro. He designed Agent Provocateur's pink porcelain perfume bottle, as well as a range for Swarovski. But it was his beautifully delicate domestic ceramics that got him noticed in the first place. His organically shaped china – all handmade in the UK – includes the heavily publicised Red Berry range of tableware (£22 for a mug), which was followed by a Black Berry collection. There is also a commission-only range of lighting and Sperlein has created a pewter Solaris tea strainer (£29), manufactured in Sheffield. The brand is stocked at other stores, such as Liberty and Vessel, but we recommend a visit to this showroom to get an idea for the full range.

Divertimenti

227-229 Brompton Road, SW3 2EP (7581 8065/www.divertimenti.co.uk). Knightsbridge or South Kensington tube. **Open** 9.30am-6pm Mon, Tue, Thur, Fri; 9.30am-7pm Wed; 10am-6pm Sat; noon-5.30pm Sun. **Credit** AmEx, MC, V.
Cooks will salivate in this fantastic store. If you need something to blanch, zest, grate, glaze or dust, then you're almost guaranteed to find it here. There's a good range of top-quality kitchen classics like the Waring Juice Extractor and the Kitchen Aid Artisan, and a dazzling array of knives; professional sets in a fabric roll by Wusthof are perfect for any wannabe Gordons. Attractive chunky earthenware is another speciality – the Mediterranean colours of the Poterie Provençal give an instant hit of sunshine. Venture downstairs for staggeringly pricey cookers by La Cornue (from £8,000), plus copper pans, enormous mortar and pestles, super-thick wooden chopping boards and old-fashioned ice-cream scoops. The baking section is exhaustive. If you don't think you merit fancy cooking tools yet, then enlist in its cookery school to hone your skills.
For branch see index.

Summerhill & Bishop

100 Portland Road, W11 4LN (7221 4566/ www.summerillandbishop.com). Holland Park tube. **Open** 10am-6pm Mon-Sat. **Credit** AmEx, MC, V.
A favourite of the River Cafe's Ruth Rogers, this lovely shop has an interesting selection of kitchenware from around the world. The wonderfully cluttered interior is great for a rummage. There are knives from Japan, steel pans from Italy and pots from Lebanon. June Summerill and Bernadette Bishop also sell more decorative kitchen items including pretty antique table linens, glass cake stands and attractive rustic pottery. There are brooms, colanders and bottle brushes for the more practically minded.

Vessel

114 Kensington Park Road, W11 2PW (7727 8001/www.vesselgallery.com). Notting Hill Gate tube. **Open** 10am-6pm Mon-Sat. **Credit** AmEx, MC, V.
Nadia Demetriou Ladas's store-cum-gallery space displays an impressive collection of contemporary tableware. With an emphasis on Italian and Scandinavian glass, as well as a smattering of the best of British design, every product is chosen for its top-quality and innovative form. Alongside classics such as Georg Jensen's stainless steel and porcelain Helena tea service (£189) and Orrefors crystal Light Stones tealight holders by Lena Bergstrom (£65 for a set of three) are more obscure, sculptural items like Ludvig Lofgren's limited-edition Vanitas Disco Skull. The store also has modernist plates by People Will Always Need Plates (£155 for a set of six). The gallery downstairs hosts some well-curated shows, displaying everything from specially commissioned one-off pieces to themed exhibitions. Vessel's wedding-list service is a popular choice.

Also check out...

Ceramica Blue

10 Blenheim Crescent, W11 1NN (7727 0288/www.ceramicablue.co.uk). Ladbroke Grove or Notting Hill Gate tube. **Open** 10am-6.30pm Mon-Sat; noon-5pm Sun. **Credit** MC, V.
Eclectic collection of ceramics from around the world.

La Cuisiniere

81-83 & 91 Northcote Road, SW11 6PL (7223 4409/www.la-cuisiniere.co.uk). Clapham Junction rail. **Open** 9am-5.30pm Mon-Sat. **Credit** AmEx, MC, V.

David Mellor

4 Sloane Square, SW1W 8EE (7730 4259/www.davidmellordesign.com). Sloane Square tube. **Open** 9.30am-6pm Mon-Sat; 11am-5pm Sun. **Credit** MC, V.
Classy tableware and kitchen essentials from the 'Cutlery King'. Mellor's cutlery is all manufactured in the UK.

Emma Bridgewater

739 Fulham Road, SW6 5UL (7371 5264/ www.bridgewaterpottery.co.uk). Parsons Green tube. **Open** 10am-6pm Mon-Sat; 11am-4pm Sun. **Credit** AmEx, MC, V.
Specialises in high-quality, nostalgic crockery. Personalised mugs, plates and pet bowls are ever-popular gifts.
For branch see index.

Gill Wing Cook Shop

190 Upper Street, N1 1RQ (7226 5392/ www.gillwing.co.uk). Highbury & Islington tube. **Open** 9.30am-6pm Mon-Sat; 10am-6pm Sun. **Credit** MC, V.
For branch see index.

Oggetti

135 Fulham Road, SW3 6RT (7581 8088). South Kensington tube. **Open** 10am-6pm Mon-Sat; noon-5pm Sun. **Credit** MC, V.
Good selection of sleek modernist classics.

Reject Pot Shop

56 Chalk Farm Road, NW1 8AN (7485 2326). Chalk Farm tube. **Open** 11am-5.30pm Tue-Sun. **Credit** AmEx, MC, V.
Classic kitchen basics at knock-down prices.

Richard Dare

93 Regent's Park Road, NW1 8UR (7722 9428). Chalk Farm tube. **Open** 9.30am-6pm Mon-Fri; 10am-6pm Sat. **Credit** MC, V.
Smart Primrose Hill cookshop selling top-notch kitchenware and attractive crockery.

Villeroy & Boch Factory Shop

267 Merton Road, SW18 5JS (8875 6006/ www.villeroy-boch.com). Southfields tube. **Open** 10am-5pm Mon-Sat; 11am-5pm Sun. **Credit** AmEx, MC, V.
Discontinued ranges at discounts that range from 25% to 80%. Expect to find all manner of crockery, glassware as well as canteens of cutlery.

Wedgwood

173-174 Piccadilly, W1J 9EL (7629 2614/ www.wedgwood.com). Green Park tube. **Open** 9.30am-6.30pm Mon-Sat; 11am-5pm Sun. **Credit** AmEx, DC, MC, V.
As well as its own iconic brand, the store also sells china and crystal by Waterford, Royal Doulton and others. Head here during sale time when stock is reduced by 50%.

China & glass restoration

China Repairers

The Old Coach House, King Street Mews, off King Street, N2 8DY (8444 3030). East Finchley tube. **Open** 10am-4pm Mon-Thur. **No credit cards.**
Specialist repairer of antique and modern glassware, porcelain and pottery.

Tablewhere?

4 Queen's Parade Close, N11 3FY (8361 6111/www.tablewhere.co.uk). Bounds Green tube then 221 bus. **Open** 9am-5.30pm Mon-Fri; 9.30am-4pm Sat. **Credit** AmEx, MC, V.
A discount retail store that can source discontinued china to replace lost or broken items in sets.

Lighting

Artemide

106 Great Russell Street, WC1B 3NB (7631 5200/www.artemide.com). Tottenham Court Road tube. **Open** 10am-5.30pm Tue-Sat. **Credit** AmEx, DC, MC, V.
Founded in Italy in 1959 by aeronautics engineer Ernesto Gismondi and architect Sergio Mazza, the company continues to develop its classic products, such as the Tizio and Tolomeo family of lamps, as well as industrial projects at the cutting edge of optical technology (it illuminated the Shanghai Formula One racetrack). Gismondi's totem pole-like Metacolor emits an ethereal fluorescent light whose colour can be changed to suit your mood via remote control. Classic, quirky, space age, it's all here. Artemide continues to win prestigious prizes such as the Compasso d'Oro and Red Dot design awards.

London Lighting Co

135 Fulham Road, SW3 6RT (7589 3612/www.londonlighting.co.uk). South Kensington tube. **Open** 9.30am-6pm Mon-Sat; noon-5pm Sun. **Credit** MC, V.
For 35 years, this well-organised showroom has been providing an extensive choice of

contemporary lighting. You'll find most modern lamps currently in mass production here, including classics like a Jacques Adnet chrome desk lamp, the iconic Wilhelm Wagenfeld glass and nickel lamps and the much-copied steel and marble Arco floor lamp by Achille Castigliono. There are contemporary favourites like Philippe Starck, Jasper Morrison and Christopher Pillet. The store also provides staples for the bathroom and outdoors, as well as picture lights and spots.

Rocco Borghese

59 Park Road, N8 8DP (8348 0456/www.futuraneon-artlight.com). Finsbury Park tube then W9 bus. **Open** 10am-7.30pm Mon-Sat; 11am-4pm Sun. **Credit** AmEx, MC, V.

Rocco Borghese trained on the Venetian island of Murano before settling in London, and his workshop and showroom add a little Venetian sparkle to N8, with delicate and intricate lights that look like spun sugar or tenticled sea creatures. The designs may not be to everybody's taste, but the distinctive pieces certainly offer an alternative to antique chandeliers and minimalist contemporary lights. His long chandeliers look particularly impressive at the top of a staircase. Borghese works mostly on commissions, with each light created by one of the sculptors in his studio. Prices start at £800.

SKK

34 Lexington Street, W1F OLH (7434 4095/www.skk.net). Oxford Circus tube. **Open** 10am-6.30pm Mon-Fri. **Credit** AmEx, MC, V.

You're sure to find a light to match your mood here; from a calm green Buddha to a haunting halogen skull. There are also rather wonderful dogs and rabbits (£49). Lighting designer Shiu Kay Kan, who started out making a Kite Lite for the Conran Shop in 1979, covers serious high-tech lighting too in his Soho studio and showroom. He works with the domestic market as well as commercial and museum sectors, providing architectural lighting components, energy saving lighting and a customised service. He boasts a variety of high-profile clients.

W Sitch & Co

48 Berwick Street, W1F 8JD (7437 3776/www.wsitch.co.uk). Oxford Circus tube. **Open** 8am-6pm Mon-Fri; 8am-1pm Sat. **No credit cards.**

This strangely old-fashioned shop has been trading in this Soho townhouse for more than 100 years. Managed by Ronald Sitch and his sons James and Laurence, its business is the reproduction and restoration of antique lights, though there are also fittings for sale. The company's own range of wall lights and lanterns are made using traditional methods. This may be a small-scale operation, but its prestige and skill are far-reaching – W Sitch supplied the light fittings for the film *Titanic* and it also looks after the wall brackets that grace the state dining room at No.10. For the rest of us, W Sitch will repair, rewire and repolish most period lighting or convert a favourite vase into a lamp.

Also check out...

Christopher Wray

591-593 King's Road, SW6 2EH (7751 8705/www.christopherwray.com). Fulham Broadway tube. **Open** 9.30am-6pm Mon-Sat. **Credit** AmEx, MC, V.

More than 3,000 lighting designs, covering all areas from bathroom to garden, and chandeliers to desk lamps.

For branch see index.

John Cullen Lighting

585 King's Road, SW6 2EH (7371 5400/www.johncullenlighting.co.uk). Fulham Broadway tube. **Open** 9.30am-5.30pm Mon-Fri; 10am-4pm Sat. **Credit** MC, V.

Uplighters, downlighters, dimmers and exterior lighting. John Cullen knows how lighting can transform a room. The design team will visit your home and devise a plan.

The Light Store

11 Clifton Road, W9 1SZ (7286 0233/www.thelightstore.co.uk). Warwick Avenue tube. **Open** 9am-6pm Mon-Fri; 10am-5pm Sat. **Credit** MC, V.

An extensive range from Philippe Starck, Jasper Morrison, Artemide and Egoluce.

Mathmos

96 Kingsland Road, E2 8DP (7549 2700/www.mathmos.com). Old Street tube/rail. **Open** 9.30am-5.30pm Mon-Fri; 10.30am-6pm Sat. **Credit** MC, V.

The home of the original lava lamp also stocks a range of projector lights and other clever lighting.

Mr Light

279 King's Road, SW3 5EW (7352 8398/www.mrlight.co.uk). Sloane Square tube then 11, 19, 22 bus. **Open** 10.30am-6pm Mon-Sat. **Credit** MC, V.

General lighting store with a particularly good selection of wall lights.

For branch see index.

Wilkinson

35 Dover Street, W1S 4MQ (7495 2477/repairs 8314 1080/www.wilkinson-plc.com). Green Park tube. **Open** 9.30am-5pm Mon-Fri. **Credit** AmEx, MC, V.

Restoration and glass-repair service for chandeliers and light fittings.

For branch see index.

Mirrors & frames

John Jones

4 Morris Place, off Stroud Green Road, N4 3JG (7281 5439/www.johnjones.co.uk). Finsbury Park tube/rail. **Open** by appointment 9.30am-6pm Mon-Fri. **Credit** MC, V.

John Jones has been in the business for 40 years, and most of the top London commercial galleries send works here for framing. It's not cheap, but you can be assured of a quality frame and a great finish. The studio offers virtually any kind of frame from timber and welded metal to perspex boxes, with skilled craftsmen at hand to recommend and advise. Based in a warehouse just behind Finsbury Park tube station, John Jones also offers a photographic department, which can shoot original artworks for reproduction, plus a great range of art materials including panels, papers and canvases, a fine-art printing service and frame conservation.

Also check out...

Alec Drew

5-7 Cale Street, SW3 3QT (7352 8716/www.alec-drew.co.uk). Sloane Square tube. **Open** 9am-6pm Mon-Fri; 9.30am-1pm Sat. **Credit** AmEx, DC, MC, V.

A wide choice of frames and museum-quality glass. It will also mount objects such as textiles – or even your dearly departed dog's collar – in perspex box frames.

Arch One Studio

12 Percy Street, W1T 1DW (7636 8241/www.archonestudio.co.uk). Goodge Street tube. **Open** 9.30am-5.30pm Mon-Fri. **Credit** AmEx, DC, MC, V.

This picture framers recently moved from Bounds Green to this central location; it offers a good range of high-quality services.

Art & Soul

G14 Belgravia Workshops, 157 Marlborough Road, N19 4NF (7263 0421/www.artandsoulframes.com). Archway tube. **Open** 9am-1pm, 2-5pm Tue-Fri; by appointment Sat. **No credit cards.**

Workshop-based, offering framing and mounting using conservation techniques.

Darbyshire Framemakers

19-23 White Lion Street, N1 9PD (7812 1200/www.darbyshire.uk.com). Angel tube. **Open** by appointment 9am-5.30pm Mon-Fri. **Credit** MC, V.

Prestigious firm with a host of high-profile, Brit Art clients such as Damien Hirst and Tracey Emin. Book ahead.

Fix-a-Frame

280 Old Brompton Road, SW5 9HR (7370 4189). Earl's Court tube. **Open** 10am-6.30pm Tue-Sat. **Credit** AmEx, MC, V.

Bespoke framing and related services.

Frame Emporium

123-129 Pancras Road, NW1 1UN (7387 6039). King's Cross tube/rail. **Open** 9.30am-6pm Mon-Fri; 9.30am-5.30pm Sat. **Credit** AmEx, MC, V.

Large artworks framing specialist, used by galleries.

For branch see index.

Frame Factory

20 Cross Street, N1 2BG (7226 6266). Angel tube/Highbury & Islington tube/rail. **Open** 9.30am-5.30pm Mon-Fri; 10am-5.30pm Sat. **Credit** MC, V.

Friendly and helpful bespoke service, with reasonable prices.

Frame, Set & Match

113 Notting Hill Gate, W11 3LB (7229 7444/www.framesetandmatch.com). Notting Hill Gate tube. **Open** 9.15am-6pm Mon-Wed, Fri, Sat; 9.15am-7.30pm Thur. **Credit** MC, V.

Framing and conservation services. They will even frame football shirts.

For branch see index.

House of Mirrors

597 King's Road, SW6 2EL (7736 5885/ www.houseofmirrors.co.uk). Fulham Broadway tube. **Open** 10am-6pm Mon-Fri; 10am-4pm Sat. **No credit cards.**
A plethora of gilded antique mirrors, though you may need to strike gold to afford them. A restoration service is also available.

Overmantels

66 Battersea Bridge Road, SW11 3AG (7223 8151/www.mirrors.co.uk). Bus 49, 239, 319, 345. **Open** 9.30am-5.30pm Mon-Sat. **Credit** MC, V.
A large range of traditional and giltwood mirrors. English and French antique pieces are a forte. The bespoke reproduction service lets you choose from over 50 styles.

Posters & prints

Museum and gallery gift shops often provide a fruitful hunting ground for unusual art posters, *see p204* **Museum pieces**. There are also several photographic copying and printing services you can rely on to turn your own masterpieces into posters; *see p220.*

55max

6 Lonsdale Road, NW6 6RD (7625 3774/ www.55max.com). Queens Park tube. **Open** 10am-6pm Mon-Fri; 11am-5pm Sat. **Credit** MC, V.
Choose from around 3,000 images from its archive, then select the size, frame and printing (on paper or canvas) you fancy. It's not strictly £55 max, as the name suggests – more £55 min. That will buy you a framed 14 x 11in print from the archive or a 12 x 12in print on canvas. Images are mostly photographs, but it also has graphics and illustrations. If you prefer your own photographs to someone else's, a canvas montage of ten will cost £65, going up to £630 for 100.

Limelight Movie Art

135 King's Road, SW3 4PW (7751 5584/ www.limelightmovieart.com). Sloane Square or South Kensington tube. **Open** 11.30am-5.30pm Mon-Sat. **Credit** AmEx, MC, V.
Limelight Movie Art sells original movie artwork from all over the world. The clientele includes collectors looking for the work of a particular graphic artist, such as Saul Bass or Ercole Brini, as well as film buffs or fans hunting down images of their favourite star. Buying a piece of movie artwork can prove a wise investment, as it's a product that never seems to go out of fashion (ten years ago, an original poster of *It's a Wonderful Life* cost around £1,500; today it could go for up to £15,000). Foreign posters can be less expensive – *Certains l'aiment chaud* (rather than *Some Like It Hot*) can be bought for £375. All the posters, lobby cards and inserts on sale are in excellent condition.

Also check out...

Reel Poster Gallery

72 Westbourne Grove, W2 5SH (7727 4488/www.reelposter.com). Bayswater or Queensway tube. **Open** 11am-7pm Mon-Fri; noon-6pm Sat. **Credit** AmEx, MC, V.
A large collection of original, vintage film posters from around the world with an emphasis on classics and film noir. Hepburn, Hitchcock and Bond are faves.

Rugs

Deirdre Dyson Contemporary Handmade Carpets

554 King's Road, SW6 2DZ (7384 4464/ www.deirdredyson.com). Fulham Broadway tube. **Open** 10am-6pm Mon-Fri; 10am-5pm Sat. **Credit** AmEx, MC, V.
Deirdre Dyson may be married to James Dyson of vacuum cleaner fame, but she's obviously more concerned with designing carpets than vacuuming them. Her art school background means she sees rugs as artistic centrepieces in their own right. Arranged over three floors, her King's Road shop displays a range of 30 graphic designs. Choose from hand-knotted rugs, made in Nepal using Chinese or Indian silk with Tibetan wool, or home-grown versions using New Zealand wool. Bespoke carpets can be commissioned from Dyson's design team.

Helen Yardley

28-29 Great Sutton Street, EC1V 0DS (7253 9242/www.helenyardley.com). Barbican tube/rail. **Open** 10.30am-5.30am Tue-Fri; also by appointment. **No credit cards.**
Helen Yardley's rugs and wall hangings have attracted international attention; her works grace the floors of buildings such as the London Stock Exchange and the Metropolitan Hotel in Bangkok. You can see her collections at her airy Clerkenwell gallery, which is a perfect backdrop for her rugs, runners and wall hangings. The hand-tufted collection features some subtle linear designs in a spectrum of different colours and textures, while the hand-knotted rugs make up the Japanese

Labour & Wait. *See p129.*

inspired Jutan collection. One-off pieces can be made to any size and shape with felt and needlepoint extras. Rugs start at £1,800 for 180x240cm.

Loophouse

88 Southwark Bridge Road, SE1 OEX (7207 7619/www.loophouse.com). Borough tube/344 bus. **Open** 9.30am-5.30pm Mon-Fri; also by appointment. **Credit** MC, V.
Loophouse's handmade patterned rugs work in both traditional and contemporary interiors. Founder Lorraine Stratham has had commissions from a wide ranging clientele – everything from a converted chicken shed in Wiltshire to a trendy boutique hotel in Edinburgh. Collections allow you to choose from subtle linear designs in neutral tones or bold colourful patterns such as the red and gold Suiren rug inspired by Japanese waterlilies. If you need a perfect colour match, you should find it here, as it has a palette of 360 shades. The funky Urban Pets range has beanbags, throws and cushions made from lambskin in a range of colours.

The Rug Company

124 Holland Park Avenue, W11 4UE (7229 5148/www.therugcompany.info). Holland Park tube. **Open** 10am-6pm Mon-Wed, Fri, Sat; 10am-8pm Thur; 11am-5pm Sun. **Credit** MC, V.
The designer collection here reads more like a fantasy wardrobe than a selection of rugs, with collaborations from Vivienne Westwood, Paul Smith and Matthew Williamson among others. Grown-up girls will love Lulu Guinness's Glamour Girl rug and Diane von Furstenberg's Leopard. Founded in 1997 by Christopher and Suzanne Sharp, the Rug Company is dedicated to traditional methods of rug-making; the hand-knotting is done by weavers in Nepal, Turkey and China, using hand-spun wool from Tibet and northern India. It also sells antique rugs, sourced from around the globe. Bespoke commissions are undertaken.

Stepevi

274 King's Road, SW3 5AW (7376 7574/ www.stepevi.com). Sloane Square tube. **Open** 10am-6pm Mon-Wed, Fri, Sat; 10am-7pm Thur. **Credit** AmEx, DC, MC, V.
This Turkish company began life in Istanbul and is now an international brand with 35 showrooms worldwide. It set up its London business in 2005 in this glitzy King's Road showroom. An array of incredibly tactile modern-design rugs in bold colours line the floors and walls of the ground floor, while downstairs a bespoke rug service offers you a quiet corner, Turkish tea or coffee and the guidance of a rug expert as you pick your own patterns, colours and sizes. Compared to many other high-end rug showrooms, Stepevi offers a competitive price tag (plain wool ones from £200/sq m). Its Noble Fibres collection, introduced in 2008, is made in silk, linen and wool with an earthy palette and subtle easy-to-live-with designs.

Also check out...

Charlotte Gaskell Oriental Carpets

183 Trinity Road, SW17 7HL (8672 3224/ www.charlottegaskell.com). Tooting Bec tube/Wandsworth Common rail. **Open** by appointment only. **Credit** MC, V.
Persian, Afghan and Turkish oriental rugs with prices starting at £150.

Joss Graham Oriental Textiles

10 Eccleston Street, SW1W 9LT (7730 4370). Victoria tube/rail. **Open** 10am-6pm Mon-Sat. **Credit** AmEx, MC, V.
Carpets and textiles from India, Central Asia and Africa.

Richard Morant

27 Chepstow Corner, W2 4XE (7727 2566/ www.richardmorant.com). Notting Hill Gate tube. **Open** 10am-6pm Mon-Fri; 11am-6pm Sat. **No credit cards**.
Custom-made kilims, cotton dhurries from India and antique carpets; services include cleaning, moth-proofing and repair work.

Roger Oates Design

1 Monro Terrace, Riley Street, SW10 0DL (7351 2288/www.rogeroates.com). South Kensington tube. **Open** 10am-5pm Mon-Sat. **Credit** MC, V.
Smart, striped wool runners for stairs and halls in bold or neutral tones. Handmade rugs come in wool, cotton and abaca.

Top Floor

2-6 Chelsea Harbour Design Centre, Lots Road, SW10 OXE (7795 3333/ www.topfloorrugs.com). Earl's Court tube/C3 bus. **Open** 9am-5.30pm Mon-Fri. **No credit cards**.
Designer Esti Barnes's rugs are tactile and nature-inspired. Not the sort to go unnoticed under a coffee table.

Tribe Contemporary Rugs

52 Cross Street, N1 2BA (7226 5544/ tribe-london.com). Angel tube/Highbury & Islington tube/rail. **Open** 11am-6pm Tue-Sat; noon-5pm Sun. **Credit** AmEx, MC, V.
Hand-woven rugs from around the world. **For branch see index**.

Interiors

DIY & tools

For more decorating supplies, *see below* **Timber & builders' merchants** and *p146* **Paint & wallpaper**.

B&Q

Mini warehouse: 524 Old Kent Road, SE1 5BA (7252 0657/www.diy.com). South Bermondsey rail. **Open** 7am-9pm Mon-Fri; 7am-8pm Sat; 10am-4pm Sun. **Credit** MC, V. *Supercentre: 304-322 Norwood Road, SE27 9AF (8761 1236/www.diy.com). West Norwood rail.* **Open** 8am-8pm Mon-Sat; 10am-4pm Sun. **Credit** MC, V.
Branches: throughout the city.

Buck & Ryan

Unit 4, Victoria House, Southampton Row, WC1B 4DA (7430 9898/www.buckandryan.co.uk). Holborn tube. **Open** 8am-6pm Mon-Fri; 9am-5pm Sat. **Credit** MC, V.

Clerkenwell Screws

109 Clerkenwell Road, EC1R 5BY (7405 1215/www.screwfastfix.com). Chancery Lane tube/Farringdon tube/rail. **Open** 8am-5.30pm Mon-Fri; 9am-1pm Sat. **Credit** MC, V.
For branch see index.

Decorator's Mate

76-80 Streatham Hill, SW2 4RD (8671 3643/www.thedecoratorsmate.co.uk). Streatham Hill rail. **Open** 7.30am-5.30pm Mon-Fri; 8am-5.30pm Sat. **Credit** AmEx, MC, V.

Focus DIY

Highams Park Industrial Estate, Hickman Avenue, Chingford E4 9JG (0844 800 1437/www.focusdiy.co.uk). Highams Park rail. **Open** 8am-8pm Mon-Sat; 10am-4pm Sun. **Credit** AmEx, MC, V.

Grizard

84A-C Lillie Road, SW6 1TL (7385 5109/www.grizard.co.uk). West Brompton tube/rail. **Open** 9am-5pm Mon-Fri; 9am-4pm Sat. **Credit** AmEx, MC, V.

Homebase

195 Warwick Road, W14 8PU (7603 6397/www.homebase.co.uk). West Kensington tube. **Open** 8am-9pm Mon-Fri; 8am-8pm Sat; 11am-5pm Sun. **Credit** MC, V.
Branches: throughout the city.

HSS Hire

95 Tower Bridge Road, SE1 4TW (7357 9207/www.hss.com). London Bridge tube/ rail. **Open** 7am-5.30pm Mon-Fri; 8am-1pm Sat. **Credit** AmEx, MC, V.
Branches: throughout the city.

London Power Tool Centre

188-190 Lower Road, SE16 2UN (7237 9884). Surrey Quays tube. **Open** 7.30am-5.30pm Mon-Fri; 8.30am-3pm Sat. **Credit** AmEx, MC, V.

Robert Dyas

123 Tottenham Court Road, W1T 5AR (7388 0183/www.robertdyas.co.uk). Warren Street tube. **Open** 8am-7pm Mon-Fri; 9am-6pm Sat; 11am-5pm Sun. **Credit** AmEx, DC, MC, V.
Branches: throughout the city.

Wickes

317 Cricklewood Broadway, NW2 6JN (8450 9025/www.wickes.co.uk). Kilburn tube. **Open** 7am-9pm Mon-Fri; 7am-8pm Sat; 10am-4pm Sun. **Credit** MC, V.
Branches: throughout the city.

Plasterwork & mouldings

Butcher Plasterworks

Chalcot Yard, 8 Fitzroy Road, NW1 8TX (7722 9771/www.butcherplasterworks.com). Chalk Farm tube. **Open** 8am-5pm Mon-Fri. **Credit** MC, V.
From domestic cornicing refurbs to bespoke designs, Butcher can tackle all sorts of plaster-based projects.

Thomas & Wilson

903 Fulham Road, SW6 5HU (7384 0111/www.thomasandwilson.com). Parsons Green tube. **Open** 9am-6pm Mon-Fri; 10am-4pm Sat. **Credit** MC, V.
Thomas and Wilson is an old-established fibrous plaster specialist whose inspirational showroom displays more than 120 different styles of cornice, panel mouldings, wall friezes and ceiling centres. Its range of accessories and supports include corbels, brackets and columns.

Winther Browne

75 Bilton Way, Enfield, Middx EN3 7ER (8344 9050/www.wintherbrowne.co.uk). Enfield Lock rail. **Open** 8.30am-8.30pm Mon-Fri. **Credit** MC, V.
A wide range of fireplaces, radiator covers, decorative screens and staircase parts, as well as decorative wood carving.

Stone suppliers & products

See also p149 **Tiles & mosaics**.

Limestone Gallery

Arch 47, South Lambeth Road, SW8 1SS (7735 8555/www.limestonegallery.co.uk). Vauxhall tube/rail. **Open** 8.30am-5.30pm Mon-Fri; 10am-4pm Sat. **Credit** MC, V.
This importer of onyx, limestone, marble, granite and reclaimed antique stone for flooring and other stonework has London's largest stone showroom underneath the arches in Vauxhall. The gallery also runs a bespoke stone manufacturing service in the factory. It's solid carved bathtubs (made from a single block) and its made-to-order shower trays are a speciality.

Stonetheatre

Newnham Terrace, Hercules Road, SE1 7DR (7021 0020/www.stonetheatre.com). Lambeth North tube. **Open** 9am-5.30pm Mon-Sat. **Credit** MC, V.
Granite, marble, limestone, onyx, slate, travertine… you name it, it's all on display here under the railway arches, waiting to be converted into luxurious floors, kitchen surfaces, wetrooms and other objects of desire by the resident stonemasons and designers. There are over 300 samples to look at and you can have small items made to order. Stonetheatre designs, supplies and installs the stone and provides advice on maintenance.

Also check out…

Stone Age

Unit 3, Parsons Green Depot, Parsons Green Lane, SW6 4HH (7384 9090/www.estone.co.uk). Parsons Green tube. **Open** 9am-5.30pm Mon-Fri; 10am-4pm Sat. **Credit** AmEx, MC, V.
More than 100 types of limestone and sandstone, as well as basalt, slate, granite and marble.

Stone Federation Great Britain

01303 856123/www.stone-federationgb.org.uk. **Phone enquiries** 9.30am-5pm Mon-Fri.
Phone or visit the website for details of Stone Federation members and for domestic technical advice.

Stonell

521-525 Battersea Park Road, SW11 3BN (7738 0606/www.stonelldirect.com). Clapham Junction rail. **Open** 9.30am-5.30pm Mon-Fri; 9.30am-5pm Sat. **Credit** MC, V.
Has an impressive variety of natural stone, marble, limestone, travertine, granite and slate in stock.
For branch see index.

Timber & builders' merchants

To find an outlet near you, contact the **Builders Merchants Federation** (7439 1753, www.bmf.org.uk).

AW Champion

2 Hartfield Crescent, SW19 3SD (8542 1606/www.championtimber.com). Wimbledon tube/rail. **Open** 8am-5.30pm Mon-Fri; 8am-5pm Sat. **Credit** MC, V.
Champion sources and cuts quality wood for fencing, roofing, decking and other projects. It can also provide all the requisite tools you'll need.
For branches see index.

General Woodwork Supplies

76-80 Stoke Newington High Street, N16 7PA (7254 6052). Stoke Newington rail. **Open** 8am-5.30pm Mon-Wed, Fri; 8am-4pm Thur; 9am-5.30pm Sat. **Credit** AmEx, MC, V.
GWS cuts timber and board materials and sells the tools for would-be cabinet-makers.

Jewson

Baltic Sawmills, Carnwath Road, SW6 3DS (7736 5511/www.jewson.co.uk). Parsons Green tube. **Open** 7.30am-5pm Mon-Fri; 8am-noon Sat. **Credit** MC, V.

Jewson is the UK's biggest timber and builders' merchant, but it also sells kitchens, bathrooms, tools and accessories. There's also an online tool hire service and a brick library too.
Branches: throughout the city.

Keyline
Cody Business Centre, South Crescent, off Cody Road, E16 4SR (7511 5171/ www.keyline.co.uk). Canning Town tube/ rail/DLR. **Open** 7.30am-5pm Mon-Fri; 8am-noon Sat. **Credit** MC, V.
This chain supplies trade and domestic DIYers with everything from construction materials to decorating supplies.
For branches see index.

Moss & Co
Dimes Place, 104 King Street, W6 0QW (8748 8251/www.mosstimber.co.uk). Hammersmith tube. **Open** 8am-noon, 1-5pm Mon-Fri; 8-11.30am Sat. **Credit** MC, V.
Moss & Co's range of top-quality sheet materials, hardwoods and softwoods – air seasoned or kiln dried – explains its near-on 125 years of popularity.

Nu-line
305-317 Westbourne Park Road, W11 1EF (7727 7748/www.nu-line.net). Ladbroke Grove or Westbourne Park tube. **Open** 7am-5.30pm Mon-Fri; 8am-1pm Sat. **Credit** MC, V.
An impeccably polite, family-run builders' merchant just off the Portobello Road stocking kitchen equipment, electrical goods, tools and architectural ironmongery, with plumbing and building materials kept at its new bathroom showroom (12 Malton Road, W10 5UP, 8206 5177).

Travis Perkins
763 Harrow Road, NW10 5NY (8969 2000/www.travisperkins.co.uk). Kensal Green tube. **Open** 7.30am-5pm Mon-Fri; 8am-noon Sat. **Credit** MC, V.
With 600 branches and more to come, TP proves that people are making do with DIY in these straitened times.
Branches: throughout the city.

Curtains, blinds & shutters

The industry's representative, the **British Blind & Shutter Association** (01827 52337, www.bbsa.org.uk), has a useful list of over 390 firms on its online database. The **Association of Master Upholsterers & Soft Furnishers** (*see p143*) lists a number of curtain and blind suppliers.

New England Shutter Company
16 Jaggard Way, SW12 8SG (8675 1099/ www.tnesc.co.uk). Wandsworth Common rail. **Open** 9am-5pm Mon-Fri; by appointment Sat. **Credit** MC, V.
In search of privacy, aesthetics or light control? The range of window covers here, both custom-made and off-the-peg, is an eye-opener. As well as classic wooden finishes, you can have them stained to suit the decor, or covered with other materials, such as suede or fabric. NESC can also rustle up venetian blinds of the highest order.

Curtain Exchange
129-131 Stephendale Road, SW6 2PS (7731 8316/www.thecurtainexchange.net). Fulham Broadway tube then 28, 295 bus. **Open** 10am-5pm Mon-Sat. **Credit** MC, V.
This is one of the original London branches of the hugely successful curtain specialist. The bulk of the business is new drapes in designer fabrics by the big cheeses of interior design (Nina Campbell, Colefax & Fowler, Andrew Martin and Zoffany). A range of accessories such as curtain tie-backs, lamps, cushions and throws is also stocked, as are exclusive items of furniture. The 'Exchange' bit refers to the second-hand curtain service, but only top-quality, almost new curtains are considered.
For branch see index.

Also check out...

City Blinds
273 Hackney Road, E2 8NA (7739 6206/ www.cityblinds.co.uk). Liverpool Street tube/ rail then 26, 48, 55 bus. **Open** 9.30am-5.30pm Mon-Fri; 10am-5pm Sat; 10am-3pm Sun. **Credit** MC, V.
Wood, faux wood and aluminium venetian blinds, plus high-quality roller ones, both ready-made and made to measure.

Curtain Workshop
39 Amwell Street, EC1R 1UR (7278 4990). Angel tube. **Open** 9am-6pm Mon-Fri. **No credit cards.**
Allow about four weeks between taking in the fabric and drawing your new curtains, made by this bespoke manufacturer.

Eclectics
01843 608780/www.eclectics.co.uk. **Phone enquiries** 9am-5.15pm Mon-Fri. **Credit** AmEx, MC, V.
Aspirational window coverings include beautiful blinds and trendy Kyoto sliding panels and curtains. It's all available online or can be checked out in a variety of stockists across the country.

Plantation Shutters
131 Putney Bridge Road, SW15 2PA (8871 9333/www.plantation-shutters.co.uk). East Putney tube. **Open** 9am-5.30pm Mon-Fri. **Credit** MC, V.
Traditional slatted shutters custom-made from high-quality renewable wood.

Sanderson. *See p143.*

HOME

Doors, fixtures & fittings

See also p140 **DIY & tools** and **Timber & builders' merchants** and *p146* **Ironmongers**.

Chloe Alberry

84 Portobello Road, W11 2QD (7727 0707/ www.chloealberry.com). Notting Hill Gate tube. **Open** 9am-6pm Mon-Sat; 10am-5pm Sun. **Credit** AmEx, MC, V.
Blissful to browse around. Door handles, knobs, knockers, latches, hooks, lightpulls and chandelier drops in nickel, brass, wood, porcelain, crystal and coloured glass.

Clayton Munroe

01803 865700/www.claytonmunroe.com.
Cool-looking door hardware made at the Dange St-Romain foundry in France can be ordered by phone or via the website.

Cotswood

5 Hampden Way, N14 5DJ (8368 1664/ www.cotswood-doors.co.uk). Southgate tube. **Open** 9am-5.30pm Mon-Fri; 9am-4pm Sat. **Credit** MC, V.
Internal or external domestic doors and fittings using sustainably sourced materials.

Forbes & Lomax

205A St John's Hill, SW11 1TH (7738 0202/www.forbesandlomax.co.uk). Clapham Junction rail. **Open** 9am-5pm Mon-Fri; 9am-1pm Sat. **Credit** MC, V.
Light switches and wall plates that blend into their surroundings; in various finishes.

Haute Déco

556 King's Road, SW6 2DZ (7736 7171/ www.doorknobshop.com). Fulham Broadway tube. **Open** 10am-6pm Mon-Sat. **Credit** MC, V.
Luxury door handles and drawer pulls for fans of high-quality knobs, in glass, crystal, nickel and other funky materials.

London Door Company

155 St John's Hill, SW11 1TQ (7801 0877/www.londondoor.co.uk). Clapham Junction rail. **Open** 9.30am-5pm Mon-Sat. **Credit** MC, V.
Distinctive hardwood doors tailored to customers' specifications.

Fabrics & soft furnishings

For a list of upholsterers, contact the **Association of Master Upholsterers & Soft Furnishers** (029 2077 8918, www.upholsterers.co.uk). For more fabric shops, *see also p205* **Art & craft supplies** and **Fabrications** on *p208. See also p133* **Repairs & re-upholstery**.

Celia Birtwell

71 Westbourne Park Road, W2 5QH (7221 0877/www.celiabirtwell.com). Royal Oak or Westbourne Park tube. **Open** 10am-1pm, 2-5pm Mon-Fri; by appointment 10am-1pm, 2-5pm Sat. **Credit** AmEx, MC, V.
The work of this celebrated textile designer has long been in vogue. Her latest foray into bright, breezy colourful interiors, Pop Story, keeps her in the trendy bracket, while the delightful classic lines Beasties, and Kew are hardy perennials. This lovely little shop is all about the textile collection, launched in partnership with her former husband, fashion designer Ossie Clarke, in the 1960s, and which later became a witty range of furnishing fabrics and wallpapers. Classic collection prints cost from £40/m, and voiles, silk cushions (£100 each) and upholstered chairs are also available, as is a bespoke upholstery service.

Cloth Shop

290 Portobello Road, W10 5TE (8968 6001). Ladbroke Grove tube. **Open** 10am-6pm Mon-Sat. **Credit** AmEx, MC, V.
Proprietor Sam Harley prides himself on stocking an excellent range of natural fabrics – cotton, muslin, wool, linen – as well as a fantastic array of antique fabrics. The Swedish linen, available in 27 colours, is good value at £15/m. Also on sale are French rustic tea towels in blue and white (£6-£18) and antique or cashmere throws.

Sanderson

Unit G9, Chelsea Harbour Design Centre, Lots Road, SW10 0XE (08708 300066/ www.sanderson-online.co.uk). Earl's Court tube then C3 bus/Sloane Square tube then 11, 22 bus. **Open** 9am-5pm Mon-Fri. **Credit** MC, V.
A byword for posh furnishings, Sanderson, established in 1860, is all about classic, English-inspired designs for gracious homes. It's a timeless look, but there's also a line in bold, bright florals that sit well in modern homes. Drawing inspiration from nature and its own archive of prints, the collections also include the Morris & Co brand – Arts and Crafts designs based on original William Morris documents. Wallpapers, bedlinen, paint, furniture and blinds are also sold. Fabric starts at £18/m.

Also check out...

Beaumont & Fletcher

261 Fulham Road, SW3 6HY (7352 5594/ www.beaumontandfletcher.com). South Kensington tube. **Open** 9.30am-5.30pm Mon-Fri; 10.30am-5.30pm Sat. **Credit** AmEx, MC, V.
This range of fabrics, wallpapers, furniture and mirrors based on 18th- and 19th-century designs is definitely eye-catching.

Clarissa Hulse

132 Cavell Street, E1 2JA (7375 1456/ www.clarissahulse.com). Whitechapel tube. **Open** by appointment Mon-Fri. **Credit** MC, V.
Colourful, botanical prints are this young textile designer's hallmark; they come on bedding, cushions, throws, lampshades and wallpaper.

Fabric Warehouse

Unit F2, Felnex Trading Estate, 190 London Road, Hackbridge, Surrey SM6 7EL (8647 3313/www.fabricwarehouse.co.uk). Hackbridge rail. **Open** 9am-5.30pm Mon-Wed, Fri; 9am-7pm Thur; 9am-6pm Sat; 10am-4pm Sun. **Credit** MC, V.
Fabrics, linings, nets, blinds and all sorts of haberdashery at hugely discounted prices.

Fabric World

287-289 High Street, Sutton, Surrey SM1 1LL (8643 5127/www.fabricworld london.co.uk). Morden tube/Sutton rail. **Open** 9am-5.30pm Mon-Sat. **Credit** MC, V.
An extensive, 4,000-strong collection of fabrics. Look out for prints by Cath Kidston, Liberty and Colefax & Fowler. It also offers a local interior design service.
For branch see index.

George Spencer

33 Elystan Street, SW3 3NT (7584 3003/ www.georgespencer.com). Sloane Square tube. **Open** 9.30am-5.30pm Mon-Fri. **Credit** AmEx, MC, V.
A quintessentially English company that stocks glorious woven fabrics from mills in England, Scotland and across the Channel, in cool, modish designs. The UK block-printed wallpaper is one to look out for.

Ian Mankin Natural Fabrics

109 Regent's Park Road, NW1 8UR (7722 0997/www.ianmankin.com). Chalk Farm tube. **Open** 10am-5.30pm Mon-Fri; 10am-4pm Sat. **Credit** MC, V.
Nearly all of the distinctive ticking, stripes, checks and plains here are woven at a Lancashire cloth mill, and all fabrics are either 100% cotton or linen or a mix of both. Classy new designs are brought in regularly.
For branch see index.

Osborne & Little

304-308 King's Road, SW3 5UH (7352 1456/www.osborneandlittle.com). Sloane Square tube then 19, 22 bus. **Open** 10am-6pm Mon-Sat. **Credit** AmEx, MC, V.
Big names in fashionable interiors since their 1980s paint-effect wallpaper heyday, Peter Osborne and Anthony Little have moved on with the times. These days the fabrics, wallcoverings and trimmings follow a bold, dramatic line in flowers and feathery whorls. O&L also distributes the work of Nina Campbell, Liberty and French company Lorca and sells furniture by Michael Reeves.

Pierre Frey

251-253 Fulham Road, SW3 6HY (7376 5599/www.pierrefrey.com). South Kensington tube. **Open** 9.30am-6pm Mon-Fri; 10.30am-5.30pm Sat. **Credit** AmEx, MC, V.
Pure French style from a *maison de luxe*: sumptuous prints and jacquards are sold alongside modern stripes and abstracts.

Wall to Wall

549 Battersea Park Road, SW11 3BL (7585 3335). Clapham Junction rail. **Open** 10am-5pm Mon-Fri. **Credit** MC, V.
A nicely contrasting range of designer end-of-line, seconds and discounted fabrics, from as little as a tenner a metre.

Warris Vianni

85 Golborne Road, W10 5NL (8964 0069/ www.warrisvianni.com). Ladbroke Grove tube. **Open** 10am-5pm Mon-Sat. **Credit** MC, V.
Rich colours and unusual weaves make WV's fabrics stand out from the crowd.

Fireplaces & heating

The **National Fireplace Association** (0121 288 0050, www.nfa.org.uk) publishes a number of free leaflets with advice on installation. Period fireplaces can be obtained through architectural salvage dealers (*see p158*); for a list of reclamation dealers in England or France, contact **Salvo** (8400 6222, www.salvoweb.com). For information on engineers and installers of wood-burning stoves, contact www.hetas.co.uk.

To get chimneys swept, tested or lined, try Andrew Taylor from the **Guild of Master Sweeps** (01733 330449, www.guild-of-mastersweeps.co.uk). Alternatively, contact the **National Association of Chimney Sweeps** (01785 811732, www.nacs.org.uk); you could also check the association's website for details of registered members in your area. **HG Lockey & Son** (8 Halton Cross Street, N1 2ET, 7226 7044) can deliver smokeless coal, kindling and firelighters to addresses within the London area.

Chesney's

194 Battersea Park Road, SW11 4ND (7627 1410/www.chesneys.co.uk). Clapham Junction rail then 344 bus. **Open** 9am-5.30pm Mon-Fri; 10am-5pm Sat. **Credit** AmEx, MC, V.

An international fireplace empire that began when Paul Chesney and his brother Nick realised the value of discarded antique fireplaces 25 years ago. Chesney's Battersea showroom stretches over four shopfronts, providing ample space to display an impressive variety of antique and reproduction chimneypieces. Manufactured in China from limestone and marble, there are over 50 period-inspired styles (£500-£25,000) to choose from. Contemporary designs come courtesy of partnerships with designers such as Jasper Conran and Jane Churchill. Chesney's also has a licence to recreate a collection of chimmneypiece replicas from the archives of Sir John Soane's Museum. A bespoke service is also available; call for details.

For branch see index.

Also check out...

Amazing Grates

61-63 High Road, N2 8AB (8883 9590/ www.gatwoodandelcombe.com). East Finchley tube. **Open** 10am-5.30pm Mon-Sat. **Credit** MC, V.

A selection of fine mantelpieces in solid stone and marble, 90% of which are made in the Barnet workshops.

Arbon Interiors

80 Golborne Road, W10 5PS (8960 9787/ www.arboninteriors.com). Ladbroke Grove tube. **Open** 9am-5pm Mon-Sat. **No credit cards**.

It's worth visiting the showroom to see the Buddha water feature, as well as a whole load of antique and repro fireplace surrounds, grates and inserts.

Bisque

244 Belsize Road, NW6 4BT (7328 2225/ www.bisque.co.uk). Kilburn Park tube. **Open** 9am-5pm Mon-Fri; 10am-4pm Sat. **Credit** AmEx, MC, V.

Whacky radiators by top supplier Bisque will help you forget the pain of the central heating bill. We adore the Priestman Goode Hot Spring. Supplies electric and central-heating models.

Original Features

155 Tottenham Lane, N8 9BT (8348 5155/ www.originalfeatures.co.uk). Finsbury Park tube/rail then W3 bus/41 bus. **Open** 9am-5pm Mon-Wed, Fri, Sat. **Credit** MC, V.

The main supplier in the UK of classic geometric and encaustic floor tiles, this company can also source your fireplaces and related spare parts.

Platonic Fireplace Company

Phoenix Wharf, Eel Pie Island, Twickenham, Middx TW1 3DY (8891 5904/www.platonicfireplaces.co.uk). Twickenham rail. **Open** 9am-5pm Mon-Fri; by appointment Sat. **Credit** MC, V.

Henry Harrison, who in 1984 pioneered the Geolog gas fire, now presides over a huge range of glamorous fireplace designs in gleaming stainless steel and concrete.

Renaissance

193-195 City Road, EC1V 1JN (7251 8844/ www.renaissancelondon.com). Old Street tube/rail. **Open** 9am-5pm Mon-Fri; 10am-5pm Sat. **Credit** MC, V.

Antique and reproduction mantels in marble, stone and wood alongside grates, stoves and period radiators. Also good for mirrors, doors and stone urns.

Flooring

The **Carpet Foundation** (01562 755568, www.comebacktocarpet.com) provides details of registered carpet retailers in your local area. If you're after a local cleaner, contact the **National Carpet Cleaners' Association** (0116 271 9550, www.ncca.co.uk). Also, the **National Institute of Carpet & Floorlayers** (0115 958 3077, www.nicfltd.org.uk) can provide lists of approved carpet fitters. *See also p149* **Tiles & mosaics**.

Abbott's

470-480 Roman Road, E3 5LU (0800 716783/www.abbottscarpets.co.uk). Bethnal Green tube/rail. **Open** 8.30am-5.30pm Mon-Fri; 8.30am-5pm Sat. **Credit** AmEx, MC, V.

A 12-year-old family business offering a massive range of carpets, vinyl and laminate flooring at excellent prices.

Carpet Man

7A Putney Bridge Road, SW18 1HX (8875 0232/www.carpetman.co.uk). Wandsworth Town rail. **Open** 8am-6pm Mon-Thur, Sat; 8am-5pm Fri. **Credit** AmEx, MC, V.

Vinyls, seagrass, sisal, jute, coir, laminate flooring and wood at bargain prices.

Crucial Trading

79 Westbourne Park Road, W2 5QH (7221 9000/www.crucial-trading.com). Royal Oak tube. **Open** 10am-5.30pm Tue-Sat. **Credit** MC, V.

Crucial, one of the trendiest names in natural floor coverings, promises an 'all-round sensory experience'. There's an inspirational range of materials to help you fall in love with your floor, from jute and sisal to wool and paper. Crucial also runs a 'design your own rug' service.

For branch see index.

Fired Earth

117-119 Fulham Road, SW3 6RL (7589 0489/www.firedearth.com). South Kensington tube. **Open** 9.30am-6pm Mon, Tue, Thur-Sat; 10am-6pm Wed; noon-5.30pm Sun. **Credit** MC, V.

With its farmhouse beginnings, Fired Earth is synonymous with rustic tiles and the warm glow of the Aga (its mother company since 2001), but contemporary marbles and limestones are available too, as well as a design service. Side issues in the Home Collection cover furniture, fabric, flooring and paints.

Branches: throughout the city.

First Floor

174 Wandsworth Bridge Road, SW6 2UQ (7736 1123/www.firstfloor.uk.com). Fulham Broadway or Parsons Green tube. **Open** 10am-5.30pm Mon-Fri; 10am-2pm Sat. **Credit** MC, V.

Bright, warm Dalsouple rubber floor tiles, Marmoleum marbled linoleum, Amtico's vinyl woods, plus a range of cork and natural flooring, make this Wandsworth fixture first choice for those after an affordable, statement-making base for kitchens and bathrooms.

Floor Warming Company

Domoteck House, Eskdale Road, Uxbridge, Middx UB8 2RT (01895 257995/www.floorwarmingcompany.co.uk). Uxbridge tube. **Open** 9am-5pm Mon-Fri. **Credit** MC, V.

'If your floor's warm enough you don't need radiators,' says this electrical underfloor heating specialist, which provides the equipment to make it possible.

Hardwood Flooring Company

31-35 Fortune Green Road, NW6 1DU (7328 8481/www.hardwoodflooring company.com). West Hampstead tube/rail. **Open** 8.30am-5.30pm Mon-Fri. **Credit** AmEx, MC, V.

The largest hardwood flooring showroom in London has a huge range of woods to lay, all from sustainable sources.

Harvey Maria

0845 680 1231/www.harveymaria.co.uk. **Phone enquiries** 9am-5.30pm Mon-Fri. **Credit** MC, V.

Funky-looking vinyl floor tiles in a huge range of photographic designs, including jolly florals, cool grass, soft feathers and disconcerting water.

Natural Wood Flooring Company (eco)

20 Smugglers Way, SW18 1EG (8871 9771/ www.naturalwoodfloor.co.uk). Wandsworth Town rail. **Open** 9am-6pm Mon-Fri; 9am-4pm Sat. **Credit** MC, V.
Beautiful floors in beech, cherry, oak, elm, teak, maple and walnut come in strip, board, laminate, decking, pre-finished and parquet woodblock formats. Sustainably sourced woods and reclaimed timber are used.

S&M Myers

100-106 Mackenzie Road, N7 8RG (7609 0091/www.myerscarpets.co.uk). Caledonian Road tube. **Open** 8am-5.30pm Mon, Wed, Fri; 8am-5pm Tue, Thur; 9.30am-2pm Sat. **Credit** MC, V.
This north London carpet expert of 190 years' standing started as a government surplus contractor. Its old-school service and good-quality wool carpets, naturals, modern berbers (more hardwearing than wool) and rugs at reasonable prices have proved irresistible over the decades.
For branch see index.

Sinclair Till

791-793 Wandsworth Road, SW8 3JQ (7720 0031/www.sinclairtill.co.uk). Wandsworth Road rail. **Open** 9.30am-5.30pm Mon-Fri. **Credit** MC, V.
There's a massive range of floor coverings for all eventualities here – we particularly like the patterned and plain naturals: sisal, seagrass, coir, paper and bamboo choices – the biggest we've seen in London. Runners and rugs, wool carpet, rubber, cork, vinyl, wooden and laminate flooring are all available, and consultation pre-installation is taken seriously.
For branch see index.

Solid Floor

53 Pembridge Road, W11 3HG (7221 9166/www.solidfloor.co.uk). Notting Hill Gate tube. **Open** 10.30am-6pm Mon-Fri; 10.30am-5pm Sat. **Credit** MC, V.
Founded by a Dutch designer, Eelke Jan Bles, the seamless wooden floors exhibited in the London showrooms are a world away from the flimsy veneers that followed. Timber in light, mid and dark tones, produced to the customer's requirements and grown from sustainably managed wood. Embellishments include natural fibre rugs and carpets.
For branches see index.

Türgon Hardwood Flooring

955 Fulham Road, SW6 5HY (7751 0541/ www.turgon.co.uk). Putney Bridge tube. **Open** 10am-5pm Mon-Fri; 10am-4pm Sat. **Credit** AmEx, MC, V.
With more than 300 colours and finishes, there's sure to be a floor that suits your tastes here. Most are crafted from high-quality woods from forests in the Ukraine.
For branch see index.

Victorian Wood Works

Redhouse, Lower Dunton Road, Upminster, Essex RM14 3TD (8534 1000/www. victorianwoodworks.co.uk). Laindon rail. **Open** 8.30am-5.30pm Mon-Fri; call for details Sat. **Credit** AmEx, MC, V.
Deeply polished antique wooden flooring, such as Parquet de Versailles, and replica antique versions in hardwood.
For branch see index.

West End Carpets

928 High Road, N12 9RW (7224 6635/ www.westendcarpets.co.uk). Woodside Park tube. **Open** 9am-5.30pm Mon-Fri; 10am-4pm Sun. **Credit** MC, V.
Personal service and expert knowledge have made a famous name of this specialist in ready-to-lay and bespoke carpets, wood and laminate flooring.

Glass & windows

The **Glass & Glazing Federation** website (www.ggf.org.uk) has a list of local glaziers.

Classic Window Company

8275 0770/www.classicwindow.co.uk. **Phone enquiries** 9am-5pm Mon-Fri. **Credit** MC, V.
Wooden sashes – refurbs and bespoke – are the speciality, but noise-reducing glass and security products are in demand too.

Original Box Sash Window Company

0800 783 4053/www.boxsash.com. **Phone enquiries** 9am-5.30pm Mon-Fri. **Credit** AmEx, MC, V.
Handsome, traditional and energy efficient, Original's made-to-order oak sash windows have had praise heaped upon them.

Philip Bradbury Glass

83 Blackstock Road, N4 2JW (7226 2919/ www.philipbradburyglass.co.uk). Finsbury Park tube/rail. **Open** 9.30am-5.30pm Mon-Fri; 9.30am-1.30pm Sat. **Credit** MC, V.
Hand-made period etched glass, stained glass and brilliant-cutting in Victorian and Edwardian reproduction styles.

Sash Window Workshop

0800 597 2598/www.sashwindow.com. **Phone enquiries** 8.30am-5pm Mon-Thur; 8.30am-4.30pm Fri. **Credit** MC, V.
After a free site visit, the window-makers here can give you a quote for restoring, replacing, sealing, soundproofing or double-glazing sash windows.

Stained Glass Guild/ Stained Glass House

4 Grosvenor Gardens, Kingston-Upon-Thames, Surrey KT2 5BE (8274 1562/ www.stainedglassguild.co.uk). Wandsworth Town rail. **Open** by appointment only. **No credit cards.**
Victorian, Edwardian, art deco, art nouveau, Mackintosh and contemporary styles for your windows and doors.

Ironmongers

See also p140 **DIY & tools** and **Timber & builders' merchants** and *p143* **Doors, fixtures & fittings**.

Allgood

297 Euston Road, NW1 3AQ (7255 9321/ www.allgood.co.uk). Warren Street tube. **Open** 8.30am-5pm Mon-Fri. **Credit** MC, V.
Good-looking metal bits for bathrooms, kitchens and doors include handles, hinges, locks, snib turns, flush pulls, knob furniture and panic hardware. Yes, really.

B Levy & Co (Patterns)

37 Churton Street, SW1V 2LT (7834 1073/www.metalstaircases.com). Victoria tube/rail. **Open** 9am-5pm Mon-Fri. **No credit cards.**
Stunning wrought-iron gates, railings, balustrades, staircases and more, made and installed to order.

FW Collins & Son

14 Earlham Street, WC2H 9LN (7836 3964). Covent Garden or Tottenham Court Road tube. **Open** 8am-5pm Mon-Fri; 11am-5pm Sat. **Credit** AmEx, MC, V.
A good old-fashioned ironmonger in the heart of the West End.

Romany's

104 Arlington Road, NW1 7HP (7424 0349). Camden Town tube. **Open** 8am-5pm Mon-Fri; 9am-5pm Sat. **Credit** MC, V.
Assorted architectural ironmongery.

Locksmiths & security

To find a qualified locksmith in your area, as well as useful contacts for security and alarm-system companies, contact the **Master Locksmiths' Association** (5D Great Central Way, Daventry, Northants NN11 3PZ, 0800 783 1498, 01327 262255, www.locksmiths.co.uk).

National Security Inspectorate (NSI)

0845 006 3003/www.nsi.org.uk. **Phone enquiries** 9am-5pm Mon-Fri.
Supplies details of recommended installers of security systems and burglar alarms.

Paint & wallpaper

See also p140 **DIY & tools** and *p143* **Fabrics & soft furnishings**. The **Designers Guild** (*see p121*), **Places & Spaces** (*see p125*), **Supernice** (*see p125*) and **Beyond the Valley** (*see p19*) all produce their own wallpaper; the latter is currently stocking exclusive lines produced collaboratively with Cole & Son and Jenny Wilkinson.

The **Wallpaper History Society** (89 Lifford House, 199 Eade Road, N4 1DN, www.wallpaperhistory society. org.uk), is an invaluable resource for anyone who wants to date or trace period wallpaper, or is interested in the preservation of period items.

Cole & Son
Ground Floor, Unit 10, Chelsea Harbour Design Centre, Lots Road, SW10 0XE (7376 4628/www.cole-and-son.com). Sloane Square tube then 19 bus. **Open** 10am-5.30pm Mon-Fri. **Credit** MC, V.

Distinctive, detailed and handprinted wallpaper has been Cole & Son's remit since 1875 (when it was known as John Perry Ltd), so finding something suitable for your period home shouldn't be too much trouble. The modern styles, including designs from Tom Dixon and David Easton, are also stunners. *See also p9* **From London, with love**.

Farrow & Ball
249 Fulham Road, SW3 6HY (7351 0273/ www.farrow-ball.com). South Kensington tube. **Open** 8.30am-5.30pm Mon-Fri; 10am-5pm Sat. **Credit** MC, V.

Traditionally produced, environmentally safe paints and wallpapers have been F&B's big selling point since the 1930s, and it's still all about quality, depth of colour and superlative definition.

For branches see index.

Francesca's Paints (eco)
34 Battersea Business Centre, 99-109 Lavender Hill, SW11 5QL (7228 7694/ www.francescaspaint.com). Clapham Junction rail. **Open** by appointment 10am-5pm Mon-Fri. **Credit** MC, V.

The greenest thing in paint since, er, green paint is Francesca's Eco Emulsion, a water-based, breathable, matt paint, with a velvety finish, which comes in 162 colours. Free from solvents, it covers well, wipes clean and has a citrus fragrance. What's not to like? Colours can be made to order.

Hamilton Weston
Marryat Courtyard, 88 Sheen Road, Richmond, Surrey TW9 1UF (8940 4850/ www.hamiltonweston.com). Richmond tube/ rail. **Open** 10am-5.30pm Tue-Sat. **Credit** MC, V.

Georgina Hamilton and Robert Weston have been producing historic (from 1690) wallpapers for period settings for 27 years, and run an interior design service.

Jocelyn Warner
7375 3754/www.jocelynwarner.com. **Phone enquiries** 10am-5pm Mon-Fri. **Credit** MC, V.

Wallpaper designer Warner creates thrilling, botanically inspired, bang up to date prints for wall coverings. Lampshades and rugs complement the themes.

Malabar
31-33 The South Bank Business Centre, Ponton Road, SW8 5BL (7501 4200/www. malabar.co.uk). Vauxhall tube/rail. **Open** 9am-4.30pm Mon-Fri. **Credit** MC, V.

Inspired by the weavers and spinners of stunning fabrics in Kerala, Peter Sterck has created a range of fabrics and rugs that recall the Indian vibrancy, as well as a 105-colour palette of paints to work with them.

Paint & Paper Library
5 Elystan Street, SW3 3NT (7823 7755/ www.paintlibrary.co.uk). Sloane Square tube. **Open** 9am-5pm Mon-Fri; 10am-5pm Sat. **Credit** MC, V.

David Oliver, design director of this enterprise and author of *Paint & Paper, A Masterclass of Colour and Light*, has been described as a colour addict. His dedication to chromatics is evidenced in the subtle gradations of architectural tones in the paint collection held here in his Chelsea showroom. His services as personal designer will cost you from £4,500 per project, but more modest (from £150/hr) consultations in your home can help you get the pigments right for harmonious visual arrangements in every room. There's also a delightful collection of wallpapers by David Oliver and Allegra Hicks.

For branch see index.

Pickwick Papers & Fabrics
6 Nelson Road, SE10 9JB (8858 1205/ www.pickwickpapers.co.uk). Cutty Sark DLR. **Open** 9.30am-5pm Mon-Sat. **Credit** MC, V.

Wallpaper, paints, blinds, trimmings, tracks and fabrics are sold in this well-regarded shop, which is replete with designer names. Head-turning interiors can be created from the design work of Nina Campbell, Paint & Paper Library, Liberty, Cole & Son, Osborne & Little, Florence Broadhurst, Brian Yates, Harlequin Kuboaa and Zoffany. Paints include Farrow & Ball, William Morris Colours, Sanderson, Fired Earth, the Little Greene Paint Company and Designers Guild. There's a quick turnaround on orders, with most things in stock within two or three days and curtains taking six weeks from ordering to hanging. An interior design consultation costs £62/hr, and wallpapers start at around £15 per roll.

Criterion Tiles. *See p149.*

Siecle

Unit B2, St Leonards Road, NW10 6ST (8961 9632/www.sieclecolours.com). Park Royal tube. **Open** 8am-6pm Mon-Fri. **No credit cards.**

A bright and light palette of lead-free paint colours, around 200 in all, are made to a unique recipe for Siecle, a specialist in paint, bespoke wallpapers and colour consultations. At the shop you can see all the colours and take your selection away with you, or just samples if you can't make up your mind; you can also browse wallpapers printed with water-based inks.

Paint House

52 Northcote Road, SW11 1PA (7924 5118). Clapham Junction rail. **Open** 9am-5.30pm Mon-Fri; 10am-5.30pm Sat. **Credit** MC, V.

At Paint House you can choose from around 4,000 paint colours (including some great eco options), plus fabrics, wallpapers, tiles and mosaics.

Sally Bourne Interiors

10 Middle Lane, N8 8PL (8340 3333/ www.sallybourneinteriors.co.uk). Finsbury Park tube/rail then W7 bus. **Open** 10am-6pm Mon-Sat; noon-5pm Sun. **Credit** MC, V.

Creator of designer paints, handmade tiles and home accessories.

For branch see index.

Simpsons

122-124 Broadley Street, NW8 8BB (7723 6657). Edgware Road tube. **Open** 7.30am-5pm Mon-Fri; 8am-4pm Sat. **Credit** AmEx, MC, V.

Interior design showroom stocks paints and wallcoverings by the likes of Farrow & Ball and Osborne & Little.

Stencil Library

01661 844844/www.stencil-library.com. **Phone enquiries** 9am-5.30pm Mon-Sat. **Credit** AmEx, MC, V.

An enormous range of stencil designs, plus accessories and painting tools.

Tiles & mosaics

Criterion Tiles

196 Wandsworth Bridge Road, SW6 2UF (7736 9610/www.criterion-tiles.co.uk). Fulham Broadway tube then 295 bus. **Open** 9.30am-5.30pm Mon-Fri; 9.30am-5pm Sat. **Credit** MC, V.

A *Homes & Gardens* favourite for classic and decorative tiles, Criterion's *haute couture* selection is at this branch, and its quality tiles at low prices at the branch at 178 Wandsworth Bridge Road (Criterion #2, 7731 6098). The breadth of stock is fabulous.

For branches see index.

Dominic Crinson

27 Camden Passage, N1 8EA (7704 6538/www.crinson.com). Angel tube. **Open** 10am-6pm Mon-Fri; 11am-6pm Sat. **Credit** MC, V.

Dominic Crinson's amazing creations, displayed here in the showroom, blow traditional tile design out of the water. The pink and green-hued Jafleur range, for example, references the colours and forms of traditional Japanese kimono textiles and Moroccan tile design, while the Incredible Edibles range shows cross-sections of fruit and veg. Many of Crinson's designs can be applied to wallpaper too, which is made to the customer's specification in one to two weeks (£11.02/m, with one-off imaging fee of £34). The bespoke service Digitile (www.digitile.co.uk) specialises in producing digital images on wall tiles (as well as wallpaper, floor and carpet tiles), either drawn from Crinson's own selection or created to the client's personal specifications.

Material Lab

10 Great Titchfield Street, W1W 8BB (7436 8629/www.material-lab.co.uk). Oxford Circus tube. **Open** 9am-5.30pm Mon-Fri. **Credit** MC, V.

Ostensibly a showroom for H&R Johnson tiles, Material Lab is also a great place to browse the company's full ceramic tile range, with both matt and gloss architectural colours, non-slip, decorative, textural and floor tiles displayed full size. The stunning range of printed tiles includes the Artile bespoke photographic collection. Customers can choose from a range of images or supply their own ideas in the form of photos or sketches.

Milagros

61 Columbia Road, E2 7RG (7613 0876/ 07931 705 202/www.milagros.co.uk). Liverpool Street tube/rail then 26, 48 bus. **Open** 9am-4pm Sun; also by appointment. **Credit** MC, V.

If you're looking to add some vibrancy to your bathroom or kitchen, head to Milagros; its colourful range of wall tiles are all handmade in Mexico and have a lovely folk-art quality to them due to their slightly uneven surfaces. Tiles measure 10.5cm square and are available in 16 colours, including terracotta, cherry, Mexican green and canary yellow. Prices start at £21.60/sq m, or you can buy single tiles for between 30p and 70p. The shop also stocks a colourful range of hand-blown recycled glassware, Day of the Dead papier mâché wall art, laundry baskets and Mexican ceramics. A charming spot.

Paris Ceramics

583 King's Road, SW6 2EH (7371 7778/ www.parisceramics.com). Fulham Broadway tube. **Open** 9.30am-5pm Mon-Fri; 10am-4pm Sat. **Credit** MC, V.

Impressive stones and marbles for floors and walls are displayed seductively in these cool Chelsea showrooms: the US company's only London outlet. There's newly quarried limestone from the Balkans, mosaic floors from grand old buildings earmarked for demolition in France, antique Jerusalem stone or fancy Spanish black marble. The stone is processed in Farmville, Virginia, where the head office is based, and each showroom has a design studio attached.

Reed Harris

27 Carnwath Road, SW6 3HR (7736 7511/ www.reedharris.co.uk). Parsons Green or Putney Bridge tube. **Open** 8am-5.30pm Mon-Fri; 9am-5.30pm Sat. **Credit** AmEx, MC, V.

Much-lauded bathroom tile specialist, Reed Harris does handmade English glass tiles by Rupert Scott, flooring tiles in a wide palette from earthy and understated to bright and bold, as well as a huge range of ceramic, glass, mosaic and stone tiles in co-ordinating wall and floor options.

Tower Ceramics

97 Parkway, NW1 7PP (7485 7192/ www.towerceramics.co.uk). Camden Town tube. **Open** 9am-5.30pm Mon-Fri; 10am-5pm Sat. **Credit** MC, V.

Miles of tiles, from plain ceramics and terracottas to fanciful glass mosaic patterns and the iridum range of metallic glazed finishes, are packed into this space. Other stylish materials in tile form include granite, marble and slate. Tiles kept in stock – and a lot of those ordered in – have no minimum order policy, so you can mix and match styles and quantities to suit.

Also check out...

Elon

12 Silver Road, W12 7SG (8932 3000/ www.elon.co.uk). White City tube. **Open** 9am-5pm Mon-Fri. **Credit** MC, V.

Elon offers imported wall and floor tiles with a Mediterranean feel.

Mosaik

10 Kensington Square, W8 5EP (7795 6253/www.mesguichmosaik.co.uk). High Street Kensington tube. **Open** noon-6.30pm Mon-Fri; noon-6pm Sat; also by appointment. **No credit cards.**

Architect Pierre Mesguich creates bespoke mosaics in marble and glass.

Stone & Ceramic Warehouse

51-55 Stirling Road, W3 8DJ (8993 5545/ www.stoneandceramicwarehouse.co.uk). Acton Town tube. **Open** 8.30am-5.30pm Mon-Wed, Fri; 8.30am-7pm Thur; 10am-5pm Sat; 11am-4pm Sun. **Credit** MC, V.

Supplies textured or smooth, ceramic and limestone tiles, in materials sourced from all over the world. Glamorous looks can be achieved with Indian sandstone and Persian grey.

For branch (Walton Ceramics of Knightsbridge) see index.

Terrazzo Tiles

70 Chalk Farm Road, NW1 8AN (7485 7227/www.terrazzo-tiles.co.uk). Chalk Farm tube. **Open** 9.30am-5.30pm Mon-Sat; 11am-4pm Sun. **Credit** MC, V.

Well-known supplier of Italian porcelain and glass tiles, as well as marble, slate, travertine, limestone and terracotta tiles from British and continental factories.

World's End Tiles

British Rail Yard, Silverthorne Road, SW8 3HE (7819 2100/www.worldsendtiles.co.uk). Battersea Park or Queenstown Road rail. **Open** 9am-6pm Mon-Sat; 11am-5pm Sun. **Credit** MC, V.

A growing tile concern that remains at the cutting edge of design trends – tumbled marble, natural stones and clays, stoneskin and, in contrast, vibrant aqua colours.

For branch see index.

Useful contacts

Avoid the cowboys by making sure you hire a registered contractor. The **London Tradesmens Directory** (www.thetradesmensdirectory.co.uk) is a list of tradesmen recommended by the general public, from builders, plumbers and electricians to interior designers, cleaners or craftsmen. However you find someone, it's always better to employ a member of a trade association that demands adherence to a code of practice, so make a point of checking before you commit to a specific service.

If you have any legal concerns, contact the **Office of Fair Trading** (08457 224499, www.oft.gov.uk).

For furniture-makers, *see p131* **Out of the woodwork...**

Asbestos Removal Contractors Association

ARCA House, 237 Branston Road, Burton-upon-Trent, Staffs DE14 3BT (01283 531126/www.arca.org.uk). **Phone enquiries** 9am-5pm Mon-Fri.

Association of Building Engineers

Lutyens House, Billing Brook Road, Northampton NN3 8NW (0845 126 1058/ www.abe.org.uk). **Phone enquiries** 9am-5pm Mon-Fri.
ABE can connect you to builders, surveyors and structural designers.

Association of Plumbing & Heating Contractors

14 Ensign House, Ensign Business Centre, Westwood Way, Coventry, Warks CV4 8JA (024 7647 0626/www.aphc.co.uk). **Phone enquiries** 9am-5pm Mon-Fri.

British Association of Removers

Tangent House, 62 Exchange Road, Watford, Herts WD18 0TG (01923 699480/www.removers.org.uk). **Phone enquiries** 9am-5pm Mon-Thur; 9am-4pm Fri.

British Interior Design Association

Units 109-111, The Chambers, Chelsea Harbour, SW10 0XF (7349 0800/www.bida.org). Earl's Court tube then C3 bus. **Open** 9am-5pm Mon-Fri.

British Woodworking Federation

55 Tufton Street, SW1P 3QL (0870 458 6939/www.bwf.org.uk). **Phone enquiries** 9.30am-5.30pm Mon-Fri.

Council for Registered Gas Installers (CORGI)

1 Elmwood, Chineham Park, Crockford Lane, Basingstoke, Hants RG24 8WG (0800 915 0480/www.trustcorgi.com). **Phone enquiries** 9am-5.30pm Mon-Thur; 9am-5pm Fri.

Electrical Contractors' Association

ESCA House, 34 Palace Court, W2 4HY (7313 4800/www.eca.co.uk). **Phone enquiries** 9am-5pm Mon-Fri.

Energy Saving Trust

21 Dartmouth Street, SW1H 9BP (0800 512012/www.est.org.uk). **Phone enquiries** 9am-5.30pm Mon-Fri.
A non-profit-making organisation that deals with all aspects of energy saving and conservation.

Heating & Ventilating Contractors' Association

ESCA House, 34 Palace Court, W2 4JG (7313 4900/www.hvca.org.uk). **Phone enquiries** 9am-5pm Mon-Fri.

Low Carbon Buildings Programme

0800 915 0990/www.lowcarbonbuildings.org.uk.
A website and helpline offering consumers a host of tips and other useful information on how to make their homes more environmentally friendly.

National Access & Scaffolding Confederation

4th floor, 12 Bridewell Place, EC4V 6AP (7822 7400/www.nasc.org.uk). **Phone enquiries** 9am-5pm Mon-Fri.

National Inspection Council for Electrical Installation Contracting (NICEIC)

0870 0130382/www.niceic.com. **Phone enquiries** 8.30am-5.30pm Mon-Fri.
A useful resource to help you find a reliable electrician: members must adhere to strict rules.

Painting & Decorating Association

02476 353776/www.paintingdecorating association.co.uk. **Phone enquiries** 9am-5pm Mon-Fri.

Royal Institute of British Architects

66 Portland Place, W1B 1AD (7580 5533/www.architecture.com). Great Portland Street or Oxford Circus tube. **Open** *Exhibitions* 10am-6pm Mon-Fri; 10am-5pm Sat.

Royal Institution of Chartered Surveyors

RICS Contact Centre, Surveyor Court, Westwood Way, Coventry, Warks CV4 8JE (0870 333 1600/www.rics.org). **Phone enquiries** 8.30am-5.30pm Mon-Fri.

Timber Decking Association

5 Flemming Court, Castleford, West Yorks WF10 5HW (01977 558147/ www.tda.org.uk). **Phone enquiries** 9am-5pm Mon-Fri.
Members listed on the website include deck designers and installers.

Bathrooms & Kitchens

The **Kitchen Bathroom Bedroom Specialists Association** (01623 818808, www.kbsa.co.uk) can direct you to your nearest design specialist – all have been vetted and follow an approved code of practice. For bathroom and kitchen tiles, *see p149* **Tiles & mosaics**.

Wigmore Street brims with bathroom and kitchen showrooms.

All-rounders

For **Fired Earth**, *see p144.*

Alternative Plans

4 Hester Road, SW11 4AN (7228 6460/ www.alternative-plans.co.uk). Sloane Square tube. **Open** 9am-5.30pm Mon-Fri; 10am-4pm Sat. **Credit** MC, V.
Alternative Plans has worked on some of London's most prestigious developments. It fitted out 80 kitchens in the Panoramic building, for instance. But it caters for individuals too. Finishes for kitchens are sophisticated and subtle – graphite oak, stainless steel, ebony macassar, aluminium and grey polyester. Norbert Wangen's Mono-block with stainless-steel top that slides across to reveal a hob, prep area and sink is particularly impressive and designers are on hand to manage your project. Kitchens with appliances and fitting start at £30,000. Bathrooms are equally minimalist.
For branch see index.

Smallbone of Devizes

220 Brompton Road, SW3 2BB (7581 9989/ www.smallbone.co.uk). South Kensington tube. **Open** 9.30am-5.30pm Mon-Fri; 10am-5pm Sat. **Credit** AmEx, MC, V.
Smallbone's grown-up kitchens ooze class. The new Macassar kitchen is inspired by the architect Sir John Soane, and is elegant and timeless in rich macassar ebony, or in hand-painted finishes. The interconnecting rooms of the showroom lead you through the Smallbone range. There's the iconic Original hand-painted kitchen inspired by Irish Georgian dressers and launched 30 years ago, the grander Pilaster, the Arts and Crafts-inspired Mandarin, the loft-style Metropolitan and the sophisticated Walnut & Silver with its mirrored plinths, black granite-topped island and faux ostrich-lined drawers. Pop down the road to the company's bedroom and bathroom showroom (6-7 Thurloe Road, SW7 2RX) to see the Alchemy and Shagreen collections. All pieces are made to order in the company's Devizes workshops. Kitchens start at £30,000 and bathrooms £17,000.
For branches see index.

Smirk

Unit 2 & 5 Morie Street, SW18 1SL (8870 5557/www.smirk.co.uk). Wandsworth Town rail. **Open** 9am-6pm Mon-Fri; by appointment 10am-4pm Sat. **Credit** AmEx, MC, V.

Smirk's two showrooms are practically neighbours, making it easy to see the range of kitchens and bathrooms on offer from the likes of Effeti, Boform, Milldue Karol and Catalano. Unit 2 – the newer showroom – is kitchen-focused and there's even a cookery school next door where you can check out the latest appliances in action. Kitchens cost from £15,000 to £60,000 depending on size, appliances and finishes. Exclusively available from Smirk is Simplicity, a unique glass kitchen designed by Ennio Arosio where the hob unit alone costs £8,000. If you like glass house living, there's also a glass bed, bookcase and table.
For branch see index.

Also check out...

Chalon

The Plaza, 535 King's Road, SW10 0SZ (7351 0008/www.chalon.com). Fulham Broadway tube. **Open** 9am-5.30pm Mon-Fri; 10am-4pm Sat. **Credit** AmEx, MC, V.
Handmade furniture inspired by 18th- and 19th-century designs. Kitchens start at £30,000, excluding appliances, while a freestanding bathroom might cost £25,000.

Greenwich Wood Works

Friendly Place, Lewisham Road, SE13 7QS (8694 8449/www.greenwichwood works.co.uk). Lewisham rail. **Open** by appointment 9am-5pm Mon-Fri; 10am-2pm Sat. **No credit cards.**
Bespoke kitchens and furniture.

Holloways of Ludlow

121 Shepherd's Bush Road, W6 7LP (7602 5757/www.hollowaysofludlow.com). Hammersmith tube. **Open** 9.30am-6pm Mon-Sat; 11am-4pm Sun. **Credit** MC, V.
Contemporary and period fixtures and fittings for kitchens and bathrooms.

In Design

Kiran House, 53 Park Royal Road, NW10 7LQ (8963 5841/www.indesignuk.co.uk). North Acton tube. **Open** 9.30am-5.30pm Mon-Fri; 10am-4pm Sat. **Credit** MC, V.
SieMatic and Villeroy & Boch showroom for kitchens and bathrooms.

MC Stone

2C Chippenham Mews, W9 2AW (7289 7102/www.mcstone.co.uk). Westbourne Park tube. **Open** 9am-5pm Mon-Fri; by appointment 10am-2pm Sat. **Credit** MC, V.
Stockist of contemporary fixtures, fittings and surfaces for kitchens and bathrooms. Suppliers include Alape and Durat.

MFI

339 The Hyde, Edgware Road, NW9 6TD (0844 800 8734/www.mfi.co.uk). Colindale tube. **Open** 10am-8pm Mon-Fri; 9am-6pm Sat; 10am-4pm Sun. **Credit** AmEx, MC, V.
Affordable kitchens and bathrooms.
Branches: throughout the city.

Newcastle Furniture Company

79 Moore Park Road, SW6 2HH (7371 0052/www.newcastlefurniture.com). Fulham Broadway tube. **Open** 9.30am-5.30pm Tue-Fri; 10am-4pm Sat. **No credit cards**.
Timeless fitted and freestanding furniture for kitchens, bedrooms and bathrooms.

Nicholas Anthony

44-48 Wigmore Street, W1U 2RY (7935 0177/www.nicholas-anthony.co.uk). Bond Street tube. **Open** 9.30am-6pm Mon-Fri; 10am-4.30pm Sat. **Credit** MC, V.
Award-winning bespoke bathrooms and kitchens; from concept to installation. On our last visit only kitchens were on display.
For branch see index.

Porcelanosa

Wandsworth Bridge Road, SW6 2TY (0870 8110 345/www.porcelanosa.co.uk). Wandsworth Bridge rail then 28 bus. **Open** 9am-6pm Mon-Fri; 9am-5pm Sat; 11am-4pm Sun. **Credit** MC, V.
Kitchens, bathrooms and tiles.

Tsunami

27 Wigmore Street, W1U 1PN (7408 2230/www.tsunamiuk.com). Bond Street tube. **Open** 9.30am-5.30pm Mon-Fri; 10am-4pm Sat. **Credit** MC, V.
Designers of clean, streamlined kitchens and bathrooms. Its ethos? 'The absence of ornament is proof of spiritual power'.

Underwood

34 Beauchamp Place, SW3 1NU (7590 6611/www.underwood-kitchens.co.uk). Knightsbridge tube. **Open** 9.30am-5.30pm Mon-Fri; 10am-5pm Sat. **Credit** MC, V.
Bespoke furniture for kitchens, bathrooms and living spaces. There's a 'Celebrity Chef' kitchen, should your cooking skills merit it.

Bathrooms

The members of the **Independent Bathroom Specialist Association** (0870 240 8028, www.ibsa.org.uk) are all selected for their high standards, and their work is covered by an insurance-backed guarantee. For information on everything from water efficiency to whirlpool baths, visit the **Bathroom Manufacturers Association** (01782 747123, www.bathroom-association.org).

Aston Matthews

141-147A Essex Road, N1 2SN (7226 7220/www.astonmatthews.co.uk). Angel tube/Essex Road rail. **Open** 8.30am-5pm Mon-Fri; 9.30am-5pm Sat. **Credit** AmEx, MC, V.
This bathroom emporium has been trading since 1823 and the showroom, stretched over several shopfronts on the Essex Road, is packed floor to ceiling with a huge selection of bathroomware, showerheads, screens, taps and accessories. Every taste is catered for from Empire-style cast-iron baths, such as the Brunel, through to art deco-inspired taps and the latest Philippe Starck-designed bidet. You'll also find cloakroom-sized basins and, for very bijou spaces, corner WCs. The extensive range means anyone with lavatory pretentions will be happy here, yet the store maintains the reassuring, competent feel of an old-fashioned plumber's merchants.

CP Hart

Arch 213, Newnham Terrace, Hercules Road, SE1 7DR (7902 5250/www.cphart.co.uk). Lambeth North tube/Waterloo tube/rail. **Open** 9am-5.30pm Mon-Sat. **Credit** MC, V.
A visit to CP Hart's flagship showroom underneath the Waterloo arches is rather like going on an exciting outing. Filled with gleaming room-sets, a fountain of shower heads and sanitaryware that is more Salvador Dali than Thomas Crapper – this is a place like no other. Here, bathrooms are courtesy of Starck, Foster, Massaud, Hayón and Citterio. For boutique hotel style decadence, there's the Hayon freestanding bath, which, with its dark tapered legs and integral tray, looks more like a piece of antique furniture. Walk up steps to the Seaside Waterfall bath and you could be in an Indian Ocean spa. Showering has possibilities you never knew existed: FeOnic sound technology turns glass shower screens into speakers, and Power Glass has invisibly wired LED lights that appear to float. If your main bathroom concerns are to wash and go, there are simple classics such as CP Hart's own London range – ideal for period homes. Our only gripe is that nothing is priced, not even on the website, but for products alone, expect to pay from £8,000 for an average bathroom. The design service is £500, redeemable if you spend over £7,000.
For branch see index.

Czech & Speake

39C Jermyn Street, SW1Y 6DN (7439 0216/www.czechspeake.com). Green Park or Piccadilly Circus tube. **Open** 10am-6pm Mon-Fri; 10am-5pm Sat. **Credit** AmEx, MC, V.
Located on the street that's renowned for purveying the finer things in life to gentlemen of means – shirts, cologne, cigars – Czech & Speake is perhaps the poshest bathroom shop in London. Its bathroom furniture is terribly smart and includes a mahogany Edwardian-style range of fittings and bath panels. From its art deco-inspired Cubist range, an octagonal black lacquer-framed mirror costs £1,400 plus VAT, while a set of chrome basin taps will set you back £705 plus VAT (more for the platinum option, obviously). We spotted a chrome toilet brush for £315 plus VAT and a pair of robe hooks for £150 plus VAT – both beautifully designed, but you'd have to spend a lot of time in your smallest room to justify it. If you can't afford the hardware, you can always treat yourself to some of the elegant own-brand lotions and potions, including the No. 88 bath oil in a chic black frosted bottle for £40. Also stocks Edwardian kitchen fittings.

Drummonds

78 Royal Hospital Road, SW3 4HN (7376 4499/www.drummonds-arch.co.uk). Sloane Square tube. **Open** 9am-5pm Mon-Fri; 10am-4pm Sat. **Credit** MC, V.
Every one of Drummonds' elegant free-standing baths is a traditionally handmade copy of an original antique tub. It takes around eight weeks to make each bath and every one is stamped with a unique number. The finished products – they can either be painted, metallic-painted and lacquered, or polished – are splendidly

indulgent. The Usk bateau bath (from £3,450) looks stunning in copper and the Spey bath (£3,450), copied from a double-ended 1950s original, is one of the biggest cast-iron baths currently being produced in the world. The London showroom, recently redesigned by Sophie Conran, also displays shower roses, WCs, cisterns, taps and accessories; Drummonds' HQ in Hindhead, Surrey, specialises in architectural salvage, should you prefer the genuine article.

Ripples

138 Wigmore Street, W1U 3SG (7935 6112/www.ripples.ltd.uk). Marble Arch tube. **Open** 9am-5.30pm Mon-Fri; 9.30am-5pm Sat. **Credit** MC, V.
Ripples moved to this new store on central London's kitchen and bathroom street in January 2008. The family business, which began in Bath, now has 20 shops in the UK. Inspirational displays showcase bathroom basics, luxuries such as designer radiators and finishing touches from the likes of Grohe, Bette, Dornbracht, Gessi, Hüppe, Bisque and Keramag. Tiles can also be supplied and stone, glass and mirrors templated to fit. Ripples has embraced the trend for boutique hotel-style bathrooms with elegant contemporary freestanding baths and quirky pieces, such as its heart-shaped basins. The design service is free (but you have to make an order first). An average bathroom will set you back around £15,000 including lighting, heating and flooring.
For branch see index.

Water Monopoly

16-18 Lonsdale Road, NW6 6RD (7624 2636/www.watermonopoly.com). Queens Park tube/rail. **Open** 9am-6pm Mon-Thur; 9am-5pm Fri. **Credit** MC, V.
The Water Monopoly certainly has the wow factor. The company, based in a converted stables, specialises in restored English and French antique sanitaryware. Choose from over 200 baths and basins, from copper tubs to polished-iron wash stands, all expertly restored to your chosen finish. Our last visit unearthed a French 1930s art deco double basin and an Edwardian canopy shower bath complete with body sprays. There's no need to worry about dodgy old plumbing – each item comes complete with fittings converted for modern pipes, and smart new taps in classic designs, such as its Bistrot range, work perfectly with the antique baths and basins. As well as original pieces, there's a selection of reproductions such as the beautiful freestanding Paris bath based on a French stone tub (from £5,200 plus VAT). Children – or exhibitionists – will appreciate the Porthole bath (£3,250 plus VAT) with its two glazed portholes on the side.

West One Bathrooms

45-46 South Audley Street, W1K 2PY (7499 1845/www.westonebathrooms.co.uk). Bond Street or Green Park tube. **Open** 9am-6pm Mon-Fri; 10am-6pm Sat. **Credit** AmEx, MC, V.
For those who like the gold tap variety of bathroom luxury, West One, with its showrooms in Knightsbridge, Mayfair and Cannes, is undeniably glitzy. There's a huge gold-plated 'waterfall' bath tap in the shape of a falcon, or a gold-plated toilet brush, finished in a choice of semi-precious veneers such as malachite and jasper. The Venus marble sink is supported by a nude woman, who also kneels behind the Venus toilet bowl where the cistern would be. Contemporary minimalists should pop downstairs to the basement where you'll find a modern world that's more typical of the company's Battersea and Wandsworth showrooms, and which includes Hansgrohe's Raindance shower system, Kohler's Sok infinity-edge bath and Geberit's Balena 8000 remote-controlled 'shower toilet' (£3,500) which reaches the parts other bidets cannot reach. There's even an inbuilt drier.
For branches see index.

Also check out…

Bathroom Discount Centre

297 Munster Road, SW6 6BW (7381 4222/www.bathroomdisc.co.uk). Fulham Broadway tube then 211, 295 bus. **Open** 8am-6pm Mon, Tue, Thur, Fri; 8am-8pm Wed; 9am-5pm Sat, Sun. **Credit** MC, V.
Discounted, non-designer bathroom gear.

Bathroom Heaven

144 York Way, N1 0AY (7812 1300/ www.bathroomheaven.com). King's Cross tube/rail. **Open** 9.30am-6pm Mon-Fri; 9am-5pm Sat; 10am-4pm Sun. **Credit** MC, V.
Simple bathrooms at affordable prices.

Bathrooms International

4 Pont Street, SW1X 9EL (7838 7788/ www.bathroomsint.com). Knightsbridge tube/Sloane Square tube. **Open** 10am-6pm Mon-Thur; 10am-5.30pm Fri. **Credit** MC, V.
Luxury products in designer settings.

Bathstore

62-82 Commercial Road, E1 1NU (7702 9898/www.bathstore.com). Aldgate East tube. **Open** 9.30am-6pm Mon-Fri; 9am-6pm Sat; 11am-5pm Sun. **Credit** MC, V.
Bathstore sells cheap and cheerful suites, particularly good for compact bathrooms.
Branches: throughout the city.

British Bathroom Centre

Oxgate House, Oxgate Lane, NW2 7HU (8453 7000/www.bathcentre.com). Cricklewood rail. **Open** 9am-6pm Mon-Fri; 10am-4pm Sat, Sun. **Credit** MC, V.
Vast showroom with small prices.
For branch see index.

Burge & Gunson

13-27 High Street, SW19 2JE (8543 5166/ www.burgeandgunson.co.uk). Colliers Wood tube. **Open** 8am-5.30pm Mon-Fri; 8am-4pm Sat. **Credit** MC, V.
Independent specialist stocking bathrooms from leading manufacturers.

Colourwash Bathrooms

223-225 Westbourne Park Road, W11 1EB (7243 3300/www.colourwash.co.uk). Westbourne Park tube. **Open** 9am-5.30pm Mon-Fri; 10am-5pm Sat. **Credit** AmEx, MC, V.
From budget-friendly collections to ranges by the likes of Grohe and Kaldewei.
Branches: throughout the city.

Edwins

17, 19, 21 & 26 All Saints Road, W11 1HE (7221 3550/www.edwinsbathrooms.co.uk). Westbourne Park tube. **Open** 8am-5pm Mon-Fri; 9am-4pm Sat. **Credit** MC, V.
A plumbers' merchant (no.17) plus stylish showrooms (nos.19, 21 and 26).

Just Add Water

202-228 York Way, N7 9AZ (7697 3161/ www.justaddwater.co.uk). King's Cross tube/ rail. **Open** 8am-5pm Mon-Fri; 9am-4pm Sat. **Credit** MC, V.
Design-led bathrooms in a loft-style setting. You'll find everything from spa baths to wet room displays.
For branches see index.

Kitchens

Alno Store

120 Wigmore Street, W1U 3LS (7486 3080/www.halcyon-interiors.co.uk). Bond Street tube. **Open** 10am-5.30pm Mon-Fri; 10am-4pm Sat. **Credit** MC, V.
This German company has over 30 ranges in its cool, calm showroom. From shiny to Shaker, in wood veneer, high-gloss and laminate finishes, its most successful look is probably its high-gloss monochrome lacquer kitchen. The Alno Sign range in quartz grey combined with a granite top has a seamless, sophisticated appeal. Likewise, the all-white Arnoart Pro kitchen is dazzlingly contemporary. The sleek displays are set off with chandelier-like Elica extractors and appliances from Miele, Gaggenau, Viking and Siemens. Alno will manage your project from specification to installation, including structural work and right down to the lighting scheme and bar stools. Door handles and drawer closing mechanisms are not quite up to the same standard as über-kitchen makers Bulthaup or chic Pedini, but Alno's prices are considerably lower – kitchens start at £15,000 with fitting and appliances on top.
For branch see index.

John Lewis of Hungerford

156-158 Wandsworth Bridge Road, SW6 2UH (7371 5603/www.john-lewis.co.uk). Fulham Broadway or Parsons Green tube. **Open** 9am-5.30pm Mon-Sat. **Credit** MC, V.
John Lewis of Hungerford has been making its homely, high-quality kitchens for 17 years. The Cool kitchen manages to be both contemporary and retro, and can be finished in either high gloss or eggshell. The original kitchen – the Artisan – is still going strong, thanks to a classic design perfect for a London house or country cottage. In addition, there's the can't-go-wrong Shaker kitchen in wood, or with painted finishes, and the beach house-inspired Steamer Bay design, which has freestanding units and a fresh breezy palette. The Crème de la Crème range is more seriously retro, inspired by the 1950s 'English Rose' design manufactured by the company who also happened to make nose cones for Spitfires. We thought the pink version, with its curvy lines, just perfect for Nigella Lawson, along with a Cool refrigerator (a unique range, styled after early iceboxes and fridges).
For branch see index.

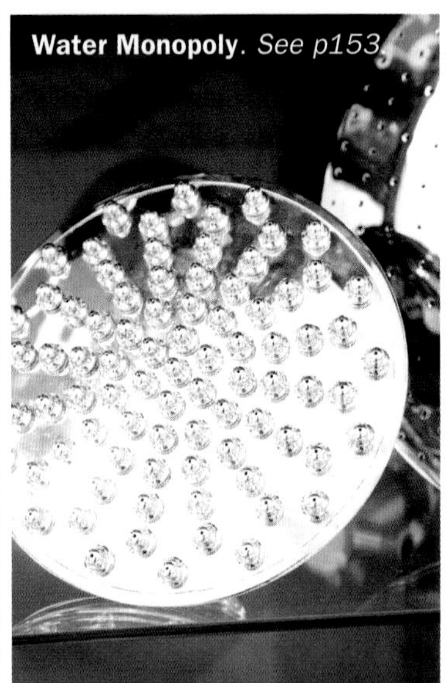

Water Monopoly. See p153.

Kitchen Central

19 Carnwath Road, SW6 3HR (7736 6458/ www.kitchencentral.co.uk). Parsons Green tube. **Open** 9.30am-5.30pm Mon-Fri; 10am-4pm Sat. **No credit cards.**

The Kitchen Central showroom brings together kitchens from a selection of Italian and Spanish manufacturers, with around 20 different designs on display. The emphasis is on unfussy, minimalist forms, sleek lines and the latest materials. Designers will guide you through the whole process from initial brief to final installation. Kitchens start at £10,000, and go up to £100,000 or more. You can have worktops to match your height, a plasma screen to watch Gordon and crew as you cook, a steam oven, a larder fridge – whatever you desire. The (kitchen) devil is in the detail here.

Mowlem & Co

555 King's Road, SW6 2EB (7610 6626/www.mowlemandco.co.uk). Fulham Broadway tube. **Open** 9.30am-5.30pm Mon-Fri; 10am-4pm Sat. **No credit cards.**

This smart set-up has five branches in the UK – this is the only London branch – and it offers a bespoke service rather than a menu of kitchen ranges. There are, of course, showroom displays here to fire your imagination, but then it will be up to you and your own dedicated hands-on designer to create a truly one-off kitchen that suits you and your home perfectly. Woods such as walnut, oak, maple, cherry and wenge are used to make the stylish contemporary kitchens, as well as other high gloss materials such as Parapan. All this doesn't come cheap, fo course, with kitchens costing from around £25,000. Mowlem & Co also make bespoke furniture for all living spaces.

Pedini

25 Wigmore Street, W1U 1PN (7491 4020/ www.pedini.co.uk). Bond Street tube. **Open** 9am-6pm Mon-Fri; 9.30am-6pm Sat. **No credit cards.**

Pedini's elegant showroom is housed in a former bank on the corner of Wigmore and Wimpole streets. The high-ceilinged space, with its arched windows is a perfect setting for these ultra-glam Italian kitchens. In comparisom with some of its kitchen retail neighbours, Pedini feels like couture. There's a cascading Giogali chandelier and shimmering Bisazza mosaics – and we haven't even started on the kitchens yet. There are six ranges available – all minimalist, all luxurious. The Outline kitchen in lacquered ebony macassar has masculine appeal and is so unkitcheny it could extend seamlessly into a dining or living room. In fact, you wouldn't want to shut the door on any of these kitchens. Take the Integra island units and 'peninsulas' – they are so sleek that your guests would just assume they were leaning on a rather glamourous bar. With looks like these, prices start at around £50,000. Ideal for open plan living, or for people who are always in the kitchen at parties.

Plain English

41 Hoxton Square, N1 6PB (7613 0022/ www.plainenglishdesign.co.uk). Old Street tube/rail. **Open** 10am-5pm Tue-Sat. **Credit** MC, V.

Plain English's beautiful kitchens are based on 17th- and 18th-century examples and handmade in Suffolk. Designs are beautifully simple; the London-popular Spitalfields is timeless without being olde worlde, and adapted to suit contemporary living. The Shaker kitchen was designed for the Shaker Shop in London while the Longhouse was inspired by a Georgian butler's pantry. The designs differ slightly, but are very much in the same restrained – and yes, plain – mould. Look around and the displays ooze craftmanship and longevity. Drawers are dovetailed and cupboards can have 'Wapping holes' or a 'Spitalfields hole fret' for ventilation. Three coats of Farrow & Ball paint are applied before installation plus a final coat once the kitchen is in place. You'll pay £35,000 for an average kitchen, including appliances and fitting.

Roundhouse

857 Fulham Road, SW6 5HJ (7736 7362/ www.roundhousedesign.com). Fulham Broadway or Parsons Green tube. **Open** 9.30am-6pm Mon-Fri; 10am-5pm Sat. **Credit** MC, V.

The Roundhouse partnership of architects and designers will take you through a step-by-step plan to build your perfect kitchen. The initial planning and design service is free of charge and Roundhouse will liaise with builders and architects to ensure all goes smoothly. Choose from a selection of doors, such as the Shaker-style Classic that's available in four types of timber or can be painted in any colour from Dulux or Farrow & Ball. For a more contemporary look, there's the minimalist Metro and Urbo styles. Here's where it helps to be a good decision maker; in the matt lacquer finish you have a choice of 4,000 colours, and in high-gloss lacquer, 20 colours, not including stainless steel or multiple veneered options. Then, of course, you need a worktop (50 types of granite, 50 colours of Corian, 20 colours of glass). An average-sized kitchen costs £25,000 to £30,000, including appliances.

For branches see index.

Also check out...

Aga

5 Beauchamp Place, SW3 1NG (7589 6379/www.aga-web.co.uk). Knightsbridge tube. **Open** 9.30am-6pm Mon, Tue, Thur-Sat; 10.30am-6pm Wed. **Credit** AmEx, MC, V.

Aga and Rayburn cookers, refrigeration, Shaker kitchens and accessories. Prices start at £6,600 for the cream-coloured Aga.

For branch see index.

Andrew Macintosh Furniture

293 New King's Road, SW6 4RE (7371 7288/www.andrewmacintoshfurniture.co.uk). Parsons Green tube. **Open** 9am-5.30pm Mon-Sat. **No credit cards.**

Painted kitchens in Shaker and English country designs are complimented by more unusual and contemporary lines.

For branch see index.

Bulthaup

37 Wigmore Street, W1U 1PP (7495 3663/ www.bulthaup.co.uk). Bond Street tube. **Open** 9.30am-5.30pm Mon-Thur; 9.30am-4pm Fri. **No credit cards.**

German manufacturer with an emphasis on functionality and longevity. Its clever minimalist kitchens start at around £35,000.

For branch see index.

Buyers & Sellers

120-122 Ladbroke Grove, W10 5NE (7243 5400/www.buyersandsellersonline.co.uk). Ladbroke Grove tube. **Open** 9.30am-5.30pm Mon-Wed, Fri; 10am-5.30pm Thur; 10am-4.30pm Sat. **Credit** AmEx, MC, V.

Stocks a range of leading-brand appliances at highly competitive prices.

Connaught Kitchens

2 Porchester Place, W2 2BS (7706 2210/ www.connaughtkitchens.co.uk). Marble Arch tube. **Open** 9am-5.30pm Mon-Thur; 9am-5pm Fri; 10am-5pm Sat. **Credit** MC, V.

Specialists in Leicht contemporary kitchens.

Crabtree Kitchens

17 Station Road, SW13 0LF (8392 6955/ www.crabtreekitchens.co.uk). Barnes rail. **Open** 9.30am-5.30pm Mon-Fri; 10am-4pm Sat. **No credit cards.**

Family firm making quality, custom-built kitchens in Bristol from £30,000.

Harvey Jones

137-139 Essex Road, N1 2NR (7354 9933/ www.harveyjones.com). Angel tube. **Open** 9.30am-6pm Mon-Thur; 9.30am-5pm Fri; 10am-5pm Sat. **Credit** MC, V.

Quality, classic timber or painted kitchens starting from £15,000 incuding appliances.

For branches see index.

Interior Arts

7737 0533/www.theinteriorarts.com.

Bespoke kitchens.

In-toto

11 St Mary's Road, W5 5RA (8840 5005/ www.intoto.co.uk). Ealing Broadway tube. **Open** 9am-5pm Mon-Sat. **Credit** AmEx, MC, V.

In-toto supplies German kitchens, worktops, appliances and furniture that cover a range of differnt styles.

For branches see index.

Kitchen Clinic

149 St John's Hill, SW11 1TQ (7924 7877/www.kitchenclinic.com). Clapham Junction rail. **Open** 9am-5pm Mon-Fri; 10am-5.30pm Sat. **No credit cards.**

Kitchen design company creating bespoke, fitted and free-standing kitchens in both contemporary and traditional styles.

For branch see index.

Kitchens Italiana

72B George Lane, E18 1JJ (8518 8415). South Woodford tube. **Open** 9.30am-5pm Mon-Wed, Fri, Sat; 9.30am-1pm Thur. **No credit cards.**

This is a mid-market Italian and French kitchen supplier that also has planning and installation services.

Living in Style

Unit 1, 162 Coles Green Road, NW2 7HW (8450 9555/www.livinginstyle.co.uk). Brent Cross tube. **Open** 10am-6pm Mon-Fri; 10am-4pm Sat. **Credit** MC, V.

Beam me up, Scottie. Futuristic, high gloss kitchens worthy of a space station.

Magnet

78-80 Wigmore Street, W1U 2SL (7486 8711/www.magnet.co.uk). Bond Street tube. **Open** 9am-6pm Mon-Fri; 10am-5pm Sat. **Credit** AmEx, MC, V.

Off-the-peg, affordable kitchens.

Branches: throughout the city.

Matrix

10 Thurloe Place, SW7 2RZ (7808 0340/ www.matrixkitchens.co.uk). South Kensington tube. **Open** 9.30am-5.30pm Mon-Fri; 10am-5pm Sat. **No credit cards.**

The UK flagship showroom for the SieMatic range of kitchens.

Neil Lerner

487 Finchley Road, NW3 6HS (7433 0705/ www.neillerner.com). Finchley Road tube. **Open** 9am-5.30pm Mon-Fri; 10am-4pm Sat. **Credit** MC, V.

Sir Terence Conran cooks in one of these custom-made, cool, uncluttered kitchens.

Robinson & Cornish

245 Munster Road, SW6 6BS (7385 9666/ www.robinsonandcornish.co.uk). Fulham Broadway tube then 211, 295 bus. **Open** 9am-5.30pm Mon-Sat. **Credit** MC, V.

Refined, quality, bespoke kitchens.

Schiffini

33 Parkgate Road, SW11 4NP (7228 8088/ www.designspacelondon.com). Sloane Square tube. **Open** 9am-6pm Mon-Fri; by appointment 9am-6pm Sat. **No credit cards.**

This Italian, design-led company has been making sleek kitchens since the 1940s. The average spend is around £35,000.

For branch see index.

Antiques

Andrew Bewick

287 Lillie Road, SW6 7LL (7385 9025). West Brompton tube/rail/74 bus. **Open** 10.30am-5.30pm Mon-Sat. **Credit** AmEx, MC, V.

The star attraction here is the elegant English and French furniture, reupholstered in subtle monochrome linens, especially the 19th-century day beds. Bewick also has an eye for the unusual; on our last visit, we saw a 10ft-long upholstered stool (£950) and an 18th-century lead dove for the garden (£340). There is also a good stock of convex mirrors. Textile dealer Katherine Pole, who shares the space with Bewick, specialises in 18th- and 19th-century French quilts and fabric. Quilts start at around £150.

Andrew Nebbett Antiques

35-37 Church Street, NW8 8ES (7723 2303/www.andrewnebbett.com). Edgware Road tube/Marylebone tube/rail. **Open** 10am-5.30pm Mon-Sat. **Credit** AmEx, DC, MC, V.

Nebbett's stock – bold, masculine and statement-making – never fails to impress. If you have the space (and the budget) for a big piece of furniture with an interesting provenance, this is the place to come. Large tables are always available: just in when we last dropped by was an 8ft circular oak boardroom table from a shipping company, with an inlaid compass rose and 12 drawers for each of the partners. OK, it was £24,000, but we've never seen anything quite like it in such good condition. There was also a 12ft deco satinwood table, ideal for dining in style, and some 1960s nickel-plated bar stools from a London hotel (£850 each). You'll also find sleek 1960s Swedish leather sofas, sturdy garden benches and industrial wall clocks. The 'live shop webcam' allows you to browse before you visit in person.

Antique Trader at Millinery Works

85-87 Southgate Road, N1 3JS (7359 2019/ www.millineryworks.co.uk). Old Street tube/ rail then 76, 141 bus. **Open** 11am-6pm Tue-Sat; noon-5pm Sun. **Credit** MC, V.

A former Victorian hat factory, this large showroom is packed with Arts and Crafts and Aesthetic Movement furniture and objects from Gothic Reform to the Cotswold School – all of which can be picked up at reasonable prices. Even the most basic dining tables and chairs are sturdy and of good quality. Expect to pay £1,500 for an oak Arts and Crafts table and four chairs by an unknown maker. Specialised pieces that you wouldn't be surprised to see in the V&A are a real draw – and some are strictly POA. Top-drawer makers include Godwin, Dresser, Rennie Mackintosh and 'Mouseman' Thompson. Heal's bedroom furniture is often in stock – 1920s oak wardrobes start from £950 and go up to £6,000 for examples from around 1900. Look out too for smaller items in the cabinets, such as Liberty & Co dressing-table sets and Glasgow Style ceramics. There are regular exhibitions as well as excellent Arts and Crafts shows twice a year, in June and November.

B&T Antiques

47 Ledbury Road, W11 2AA (7229 7001/ www.bntantiques.co.uk). Notting Hill Gate tube. **Open** 10am-6pm Mon-Sat. **Credit** AmEx, MC, V.

On her regular visits to France, Bernadette Lewis returns with treasures for the boudoir and beyond. The French-born owner claims to have introduced mirrored furniture to the UK, and there are lots of good examples from the 1930s and '40s here. The stock is not exclusively French; stealing the show on our last visit was a 1930s aluminium bedroom suite, stripped of its original, institutional paint and now shining like a vintage Airstream caravan. Look out for smaller items such as '30s coat racks and '40s chrome standing ashtrays and there is always a good selection of French lighting, and mirrors of all shapes and sizes around the £1,000 mark. The shop offers a wedding list service.

Bentley's

204 Walton Street, SW3 2JL (7584 7770/ www.bentleyslondon.com). South Kensington tube. **Open** 10am-6pm Mon-Sat. **Credit** AmEx, DC, V.

Where does one find a cigar cutter fashioned from a boar's tusk? Or a Victorian crocodile-skin cigar case? A *Boy's Own* world filled with vintage Dunhill lighters, stout leather bags for shotgun cartridges, magnificent aircraft propellers, and even a spirit decanter with a padlock to stop the servants stealing your booze, Bentley's in Brompton Cross excels at this kind of gentlemanly paraphernalia. Owner Tim Bent prides himself on sourcing well-made, unusual and luxurious items from the 1880s to the 1930s – and he had the foresight to buy classic brands before they were revived. Opulent vintage luggage from Hermès, Louis Vuitton and Goyard is still a highlight at the shop.

Bloch & Angell Antiques

22 Church Street, NW8 8EP (7723 6575). Edgware Road tube/Marylebone tube/rail. **Open** 10am-5.30pm Tue-Sat. **Credit** AmEx, MC, V.

'Decorative without being fussy' is how Tony Bloch describes his stock. He also 'doesn't do small' , so it's just as well he has a large, attractive space to house his expansive collection of furniture and objects. He specialises in Scandinavian, French and English pieces from the Georgian era to the 1950s. Typical items include 18th-century rustic farmhouse tables alongside bold pieces of sculpture. You'll also find pairs of 1930s leather armchairs for around £2,200 and good-quality chaises longues. Bloch shares the space with Andrew Angell, who specialises in old shop fittings, vintage advertising signs and tins.

Core One

The Gas Works, 2 Michael Road, SW6 2AD. Fulham Broadway tube. **Open** 10am-6pm Mon-Fri; 11am-4pm Sat. **Open** varies. **Credit** varies.

This large industrial building is an unlikely setting for a group of antique and 20th-century furniture dealers. Head through the gates, keep going past the rusting gasometer, and you're there. Dean Gipson, whose Dean Antiques (7610 6697/www.deanantiques.co.uk) covers 2,000sq ft of Core One, has a great eye. Everything has a solid feel and a wow factor, from a 19th-century French oak workshop table to a pair of stone obelisks. Mirrors are another strength, from Regency convex to French brasserie-style. DNA Design has a mixture of antique and later furniture. Elegant pieces include dining tables, marble-topped consoles and Venetian mirrors. Other dealers here include Jamb (fine chimney pieces, 7736 3006) and Roderic Haugh Antiques Ltd (English and French furniture and objects, 7371 5700). De Parma, the 20th-century furniture dealer (*see p161*), is also here.

Cristobal

26 Church Street, NW8 8EP (7724 7230/ www.cristobal.co.uk). Edgware Road tube/ Marlyebone tube/rail. **Open** 10.30am-5pm Tue-Sat; by appointment Mon, Sun. **Credit** MC, V.

Cristobal specialises in jewellery from classic 20th-century names like Miriam Haskell and Stanley Hagler, as well as furniture. It may sound like an unusual mix but it works: the masculine look of some of the furniture is a good foil for the decorative jewellery. There is always something big, arresting and unusual to catch your eye. It might be a pair of French café mirrors from 1900, a large exterior clock, a Viennese Secessionist cabinet or a Gothic Revival table. Leather club armchairs are usually in stock, priced from around £1,800 for a pair, as well as early 20th-century French Venetian-style mirrors (£450).

Dining Room Shop

62-64 White Hart Lane, SW13 0PZ (8878 1020/www.thediningroomshop.co.uk). Hammersmith tube/Barnes Bridge rail. **Open** 10am-5.30pm Mon-Sat. **Credit** AmEx, DC, MC, V.

It does what the name says: this is dining room central, with everything you need, from the table itself to napkins. You can choose from antique stock – on a recent visit we saw a French 19th-century eight-seater farmhouse table for £1,700 – or use the bespoke service and select the wood and dimensions yourself. Glassware, dinner services, tablecloths and silver round off the stock. Victorian dinner services start at £450, and single wine glasses and vintage damask napkins at £10 each. Meat plates, cake stands and Georgian decanters all hark back to the time when dinner was a nightly event. The shop also provides a furniture restoration service and can mend glass, china and silver. Staff can even copy an existing chair or glass so that you can complete your set.

Floral Hall

Corner of Crouch Hill & Haringey Park, N8 9DX (8348 7309/www.floralhall antiques.co.uk). Finsbury Park tube/ rail then W7 bus/91 bus. **Open** 10am-5pm Tue-Sat; also by appointment. **No credit cards.**

With its old-fashioned window, Floral Hall is a constant in Crouch End, its shop floor creaking with faded French grandeur. Gilt overmantel mirrors may not be in top-notch nick but, with prices starting from around £300, they are ideal for those in search of the battered look – and a bargain. Early 20th-century chandeliers range from £250 to £2,000 and on our last visit we admired a large 19th-century inlaid mahogany bookcase, priced at £5,500, which is top of the range for Floral Hall. Call before visiting in August as, in true French style, the shop usually closes.

French House

41-43 Parsons Green Lane, SW6 4HH (7371 7573/www.thefrenchhouse.co.uk). Parsons Green tube. **Open** 10am-6pm Mon-Sat. **Credit** MC, V.

The French House has the sort of stock you'd like to discover in France yourself, if only you had a van, the time and the know-how. Most of the furniture is displayed in its original state with two prices: restored and as seen. The on-site workshop has been integrated into the showroom so you can watch the experienced upholsterer at work; for your own piece, you can choose from a selection of lovely French fabrics, exclusive to the shop. A restored 1860s chaise longue will cost around £1,800. Not everything needs work, though – large gilt mirrors are good enough to hang as they are. Thanks to monthly buying trips to France, there's always something new and unusual to check out. If you want to add a bit of *je ne sais quoi* to your child's bedroom, pretty 19th-century single bed prices start at £600, more masculine lits bateaux from around £950.

Gallery 1930

18 Church Street, NW8 8EP (7723 1555/ www.susiecooperceramics.com). Edgware Road tube/Marylebone tube/rail. **Open** 10am-5pmTue-Sat. **Credit** MC, V.

The shop is a must for deco enthusiasts and a particularly good hunting ground for those furnishing small flats, with dinky occasional tables and silver or chrome deco photograph frames, nostalgically filled with pictures of silver screen stars like Grant and Garbo (from £65). The drinks trays from the 1920s and '30s – mirrored or in black Vitriolite – make classy wedding gifts. For more movie glamour, there's 1930s polished steel film-set lighting on wheels – some lights are huge (prices range from £700 to £1,500) and all are reconditioned and rewired. Susie Cooper ceramics are always in stock, as are other big names such as Clarice Cliff and Lalique.

Henry Gregory

82 Portobello Road, W11 2QD (7792 9221/www.henrygregoryantiques.com). Notting Hill Gate tube. **Open** 10am-5pm Mon-Fri; 8am-5pm Sat; 11am-4pm Sun. **Credit** AmEx, MC, V.

No blue blood or family heirlooms? Then head here to buy all the trappings of old money, from antique silver to vintage sporting equipment and luggage. A purveyor of class, Henry Gregory feels rather like below stairs at Brideshead, with Louis Vuitton trunks and plenty of silver for the butler to buff. Mahogany cabinets line the walls, filled with silver sporting trophies, champagne buckets, hip flasks and cigar boxes, engraved with the initials of bygone gents. If a vintage Vuitton or Hermès steamer trunk doesn't float your boat, the shop also makes trunks using leather from old luggage that's beyond repair. Almost all the stock is British: there are 1920s pond yachts (£500), wooden propellers from WWI planes (£2,800) – you can even buy old polo balls for £4. Now all you need is a stately home.

Josephine Ryan Antiques & Interiors

63 Abbeville Road, SW4 9JW (8675 3900/ www.josephineryanantiques.co.uk). Clapham Common tube. **Open** 10am-6pm Mon-Sat; 11am-4pm Sun. **Credit** MC, V.

Ryan stocks the sort of things you might come across if you were nosing around an old French country house: a 19th-century carved Madonna and child, a French zinc potting table or a pile of monogrammed linen sheets. Furniture is gently restored and reupholstered, so it's more chic than shabby, and therefore priced accordingly. Nineteenth-century armchairs are a speciality (from £695), as are large, painted buffets and bookcases, priced at around £1,500. Ryan also has an interesting line in unusual lamp bases that she has made from old French pillars, balusters and even table legs. Among the more affordable items we noticed were Italian 18th-century painted candlesticks (from £195). The monogrammed sheets (£125) and mercury glass candlesticks (£48) are also worth looking out for.

La Maison

107-108 Shoreditch High Street, E1 6JN (7729 9646/www.lamaisonlondon.com). Liverpool Street tube/rail/26, 48, 149, 242 bus. **Open** 10am-6pm Mon-Sat. **Credit** DC, MC, V.

This classy shop makes you want to get under the sheets – and stay there. The beds here are the stuff of French costume dramas and perfect for *liaisons dangereuses*. If you don't know your Louis XVI from your Louis Philippe, the charming staff will guide you through some bedroom history. Don't be put off by the rather cramped dimensions of the antique doubles; La Maison provides a seamless extension service. Single Louis XVI beds go for £500 and doubles from £700. Armoires start at £900 and bedside tables at £350. The shop also sells its own reproduction beds – expect to pay around £2,000 for a simple Louis XV-style double.

Lacquer Chest & Lacquer Chest Too

71 & 75 Kensington Church Street, W8 4BG (7937 1306/www.lacquerchest.com). Notting Hill Gate or Kensington High Street tube. **Open** 9.30am-5.30pm Mon-Fri; 10.30am-4.30pm Sat. **Credit** AmEx, MC, V.

Gretchen Anderson and her husband Vivian have been in the business for well over 40 years and the ordered clutter of their 18th- and early 19th-century household antiques creates a more intimate atmosphere than that found in the shop's smarter neighbours. Think William Morris rush chairs, Welsh milking stools and early 19th-century, three-legged cricket tables (£500-£2,000). Gretchen is passionate about her stock – she loves pieces with an intriguing tale. When we last visited, she had decided to sell her personal collection of 19th-century Scottish metal piggy banks, engraved with messages such as 'Dinna spare the cream mither'. Most of the business is carried out behind the scenes, however; five floors hold an extraordinary library of antiques, with pieces hired out to film makers and stylists.

Stephen Sprake

283 Lillie Road, SW6 7LL (7381 3209). Fulham Broadway tube/West Brompton tube/rail/74 bus. **Open** 10.30am-5.30pm Mon-Sat. **Credit** MC, V.

You never know quite what you'll happen upon at Sprake's Lillie Road shop. His 18th- to 20th-century tastes are all-encompassing. In the past we've been greeted with a stuffed horse's head and a painted panel from a 1970s soft porn film. The panel (from *The Erotic Diary of a Lumberjack*) was still waiting for Mr Right when we last visited, but it had been joined by a job lot of old City of Westminster street signs. Downstairs, the basement has a touch of Transylvania about it, with heavy iron chandeliers and outsize candlesticks. The large stylish tables by 1960s French and Scandinavian designers are good value. The shop keeps casual hours in August so call before you visit.

Also check out...

Bazar

82 Golborne Road, W10 5PS (8969 6262). Ladbroke Grove or Westbourne Park tube. **Open** 10am-5.30pm Tue-Thur; 9.30am-5.30pm Fri, Sat. **No credit cards.**

Rustic, decorative French furniture from the 1850s to the 1950s.

Les Couilles du Chien

65 Golborne Road, W10 5NP (8968 0099/ www.lescouillesduchien.co.uk). Ladbroke Grove tube. **Open** 9.30am-5.30pm Mon-Thur; 8am-5pm Fri; 9.30am-5.30pm Sat. **Credit** AmEx, MC, V.

Recent stock at this bastion of eccentricity has included fittings from an entire 1970s Belgian chemist's shop as well as taxidermy, skulls and chandeliers.

Furniture Cave

533 King's Road, SW10 0TZ (7352 2046/www.furniturecave.co.uk). Fulham Broadway tube. **Open** 10am-6pm Mon-Sat; 11am-5pm Sun. **Credit** AmEx, MC, V.

There are 17 dealers showcasing a mix of antique and repro furniture and accessories here, with everything from Georgian door knobs to aeroplane ejector seats.

Myriad Antiques

131 Portland Road, W11 4LW (7229 1709). Holland Park tube. **Open** 11am-6pm Tue-Sat. Closed Aug. **Credit** MC, V.

This spacious shop stocks a multitude of mirrors, reupholstered 19th-century chairs and garden furniture.

Nine Schools

Unit 9, Ferrier Street, SW18 1SW (8874 6296/www.thenineschools.com). Wandsworth Town rail. **Open** 10am-6pm Tue-Sat. **Credit** AmEx, MC, V.

Antique and modern Chinese furniture.

Old Cinema

160 Chiswick High Road, W4 1PR (8995 4166/www.theoldcinema.co.uk). Turnham Green tube. **Open** 10am-6pm Mon-Sat; noon-5pm Sun. **Credit** MC, V.

A former picture palace that is home to 15 dealers over two floors. Lots of Victorian and Edwardian furniture as well as 1950s, '60s and '70s items.

Strand Antiques

46 Devonshire Road, W4 2HD (8994 1912). Turnham Green tube. **Open** 10.30am-5.30pm Tue-Sat. **Credit** MC, V.

Five dealers occupy this Victorian shop, providing a mix of decorative and useful furniture of varying styles and ages. Good for mirrors and lighting.

Architectural, industrial & shop fittings

Ben Southgate

4 The Courtyard, Ezra Street, E2 7RH (07905 960792/www.bsouthgate.co.uk). Old Street tube/rail/26, 48, 55 bus. **Open** 9am-2.30pm Sun. **Credit** MC, V.

Ben Southgate spent over a decade as a furniture restorer before opening this stylish grown-up boys' paradise among the blooms of Columbia Road. Stock includes vintage board games from around £30, the kind of 1950s football tables you see in French bars and cafés, clubby 1930s and '40s leather armchairs, oak filing cabinets and steel desk lamps. Prices are reasonable; huge 1940s eight-drawer plan chests sell for £595. As well as restoring the items he sells, Southgate will take on a range of private restoration commissions, including French polishing, upholstery, cane repairs and desk leathering.

Castle Gibson

106A Upper Street (7704 0927/www.castlegibson.com). Angel or Highbury & Islington tube. **Open** 10am-5.30pm Mon-Fri. **Credit** DC, MC, V.

Castle Gibson owns the location – a 19th-century London depository – where the TV series *Dragon's Den* is filmed and it also provided the leather chairs on which the 'dragons' deliberate. If you like the 'industrial comfort' look, then you'll love this Upper Street shop filled with 1940s steel desks, filing cabinets and lovely nutty brown leather armchairs. Small desks are priced at around the £950 mark and chairs at £850, but it's the more unusual pieces that are the draw here. When we last dropped by, a wall of 1940s steel lockers – with 32 compartments – had just arrived (£1,650). From the same era was a huge industrial cheval mirror, perfect for a large loft bedroom, and architects' chairs (£250) to give your breakfast bar some edge.

D&A Binder

34 Church Street, NW8 8EP (7723 0542/ www.dandabinder.co.uk). Edgware Road tube/Marylebone tube/rail. **Open** 10am-6pm Tue-Sat. **Credit** MC, V.

D&A Binder looks rather like the ghost of Grace Brothers past. You can almost hear a ghostly cry of 'I'm free!' when you step inside. This is where old shop fittings come to rest, no longer needed for perfumery, haberdashery and wigs. David Binder sells to the likes of Hackett and Agent Provocateur but private individuals shop here too – the huge 1920s mahogany shirt cabinets are perfect for the shirted man about town and seem a snip at £1,250. Chrome and glass display cabinets from the 1940s work well in modern bathrooms. Museum cabinets are often in stock too. Not everything is large scale – look out for 1920s hat moulds and corsetry advertising figures for manufacturers like Regent Corsetry. And, of course, chrome shoe stands will do a fine job displaying your treasured Manolos.

For branch see index.

LASSCo

Brunswick House, 30 Wandsworth Road, SW8 2LG (7394 2124/www.lassco.co.uk). Vauxhall tube/rail. **Open** 10am-5pm Mon-Sat. **Credit** MC, V.

You can buy your very own piece of London from LASSCo. The 18th-century Vauxhall mansion and its vast warehouse are packed with architectural relics from the capital and beyond, such as a pair of Victorian stained-glass windows from a Kentish Town church (£8,200), large 'Coolican' enamelled downlighters from the Rover factory in north London (£135 plus VAT) and a cell door from the Clerkenwell House of Detention (£975 plus VAT). There are entire rooms, such as an early 20th-century oak-panelled room from Lord Victor Rothschild's Mayfair mansion (£8,500), and the Portland stone entrance to the Mappin & Webb building in the City (£45,000 plus VAT). The stunning first-floor 'saloon' of the house is the flooring department. Baltic pine floorboards from

Sales & events

The cream of the auction houses and antiques fairs.

Bonhams

101 New Bond Street, W1S 1SR (7447 7447/www.bonhams.com). Bond Street or Oxford Circus tube. **Open** 9am-5.30pm Mon-Fri. **Credit** MC, V.

Christie's

8 King Street, SW1Y 6QT (7839 9060/www.christies.com). Green Park tube. **Open** 9am-5pm Mon-Fri; noon-5pm Sat, Sun (during auction season). **Credit** AmEx, MC, V.
For branch see index.

Criterion Auctioneers

53 Essex Road, N1 2SF (7359 5707/ www.criterion-auctioneers.co.uk). Angel tube/38, 73 bus. **Open** *Viewing* 10am-5pm Mon; 2-7pm Fri; 10am-6pm Sat, Sun. *Sales* 5-8.30pm Mon. *Collections & valuations* 9.30am–7pm Tue; 9.30am-1pm, 1.30-6pm Wed, Thur. *Auctions* 5pm Mon. **Credit** MC, V.
For branch (Riverside Criterion Auctions) see index.

Decorative Antiques & Textiles Fair

Battersea Park, SW11 4NJ (7624 5173/www.decorativefair.com). Sloane Square tube then free bus. **Dates** 20-24 Jan, 21-26 Apr, 29 Sept-4 Oct 2009.
Antiques and vintage textiles fair featuring around 140 exhibitors.

Grosvenor House Art & Antiques Fair

Le Meridien Grosvenor House Hotel, Park Lane, W1K 7TN (7399 8100/ www.grosvenor-antiquesfair.co.uk). Hyde Park Corner or Marble Arch tube. **Date** 11-17 June 2009.
Celebrating its 75th anniversary, there's everything from antiquities and master paintings to 20th-century iconic pieces, jewellery and furniture.

Lots Road Auctions

71-73 Lots Road, SW10 0RN (7376 6800/www.lotsroad.com). Fulham Broadway tube. **Open** *Viewing* 6-8pm Wed; 10am-6pm Thur; 9am-4pm Fri; 10am-4pm Sat, Sun. *Sales* 1pm (contemporary and traditional), 4pm (antiques) Sun. **Credit** AmEx, MC, V.
Around 550 to 600 lots per week; homeware, furniture and fine art.

Midcentury.Modern

Dulwich College, nr College Road, SE21 7LD (8761 3405/ www.ourshowhome.com). West Dulwich rail. **Date** 16 Nov 2008, 29 Mar & 15 Nov 2009.
Admission £6.
A one-day selling event at Dulwich College curated by Lucy Ryder Richardson and Petra Curtis, which brings together 20th-century and contemporary design, with the focus on Scandinavian furniture.

Olympia Fine Art & Antiques Fairs

Olympia Exhibition Halls, Hammersmith Road, W14 8UX (tickets 0870 126 1725/info 7370 8211/www.olympia-antiques.com). Kensington (Olympia) tube/rail. **Dates** 10-16 Nov 2008; 4-14 June, 9-15 Nov 2009.
A vast array of items from many periods; the summer fair is the biggest, with around 260 dealers from all over the world.

Sotheby's

34-35 New Bond Street, W1A 2AA (7293 5000/www.sothebys.com). Bond Street or Oxford Circus tube. **Open** 9am-5pm Mon-Fri. Open for viewings some weekends.
Credit AmEx, MC.

an ex-Salvation Army building were £38/ sq m. The Parlour houses baths and basins of the sort Hercule Poirot might have used and there are also ornate art nouveau radiators (around £780 plus VAT). Head downstairs for butlers' sinks and 1930s free-standing larders.

Retrouvius

2A Ravensworth Road, NW10 5NR (8960 6060/www.retrouvius.com). Kensal Green tube. **Open** 10am-6pm Mon-Sat.
Credit MC, V.
Aptly, for an architectural salvage and design business, Retrouvius was renovating a premises on Harrow Road when we visited. This will give it a shopfront for the first time, which will be linked to the current warehouse. Work should be completed by the beginning of 2009. Look out for such features as a wall made from wooden bookshelves reclaimed from the British Museum. We spotted factory chairs (from £175 plus VAT), drapers' mirrors (from £75 plus VAT), cinema seats (£40 each plus VAT) and enamelled lamps from the Dunlop factory (£205 plus VAT). You'll also find pedestal desks, large school tables and library cabinets.

SALVO

www.salvo.co.uk.
SALVO produces lists of architectural salvage dealers in the UK and France.

Willesden Green Architectural Salvage

189 High Road, NW10 2SD (8459 2947/ www.willesdensalvage.com). Willesden Green tube. **Open** 9am-6pm Mon-Sat.
No credit cards.
Willesden Green sells fireplaces, doors and other small-scale domestic salvage.

Clocks

Russell Callow

7 Sunbury Workshops, Swanfield Street, E2 7LF (7729 1211/www.londontimepiece.co.uk). Old Street tube/rail. **Open** by appointment 10am-6pm daily. **Credit** MC, V.
Callow restores and sells 19th- and 20th-century wall clocks, both traditional and industrial, fitted with new batteries or electric mechanisms for ease of use. Prices range from £75 to £1,200.

Glass & ceramics

Hope & Glory

131A Kensington Church Street, W8 7LP (7727 8424). Notting Hill Gate tube. **Open** 10am-5pm Mon-Sat. **Credit** MC, V.
This fascinating little shop specialises in commemorative ceramics, spanning two centuries. Prices range from £20 to £2,500 depending on date, maker and rarity. A good Queen Victoria diamond jubilee mug from 1897 costs around £125. When it comes to modern day royals, however, collectors are fickle – Diana items have 'cooled off' a bit, but Charles and Camilla wedding mugs with the original 'wrong' date on them (£30) are still selling well. William and Harry mugs commemorating their 18th and 21st birthdays are also popular, ranging in price from £35 to £65. Queen Victoria, Winston Churchill and Margaret Thatcher remain top sellers.

Jeanette Hayhurst

32A Kensington Church Street, W8 4HA (7938 1539/www.antiqueglass-london.com). High Street Kensington tube. **Open** 10am-5pm Mon-Fri; noon-5pm Sat. **Credit** AmEx, MC, V.
Known as 'the decanter lady' thanks to her well-stocked window, Jeanette Hayhurst has been a glass specialist for a quarter of a century. Decanters make reliable wedding gifts: Victorian ones start at £70 and good Georgian examples go for £200, which, Hayhurst points out, is considerably cheaper than the modern equivalent. Her other main speciality is 18th-century English drinking glasses 'for use'. Georgian port glasses start at £15 and a plain-stemmed glass from 1730 will cost £110; but for something really special and

collectable, like a 1690 heavy baluster goblet, you can pay as much as £4,250. Centuries of butter-fingers mean that sets of glasses are not easy to come by, but Hayhurst often has sets of Victorian Champagne saucers (£120 for six).

Lighting

The Facade

99 Lisson Grove, NW1 6UP (7258 2017/ www.thefacade.co.uk). Edgware Road tube/Marylebone tube/rail. **Open** 10.30am-5pm Wed-Sat. **Credit** AmEx, MC, V.

A stalwart of Westbourne Grove for almost 30 years, walking into the Facade feels like entering a sort of a crystal hanging garden. Specialising in decorative antiques from 1890 to 1950, there is a definite emphasis on lighting. Its ceilings drip with chandeliers of all sizes – some supremely elegant, some coloured, tasselled and bordering on the kitsch. At floor level there are stacks of gilded and painted mirrors and the odd piece of furniture, including the kind of overstuffed, oversized and over-gilded chairs that you imagine might appeal to a dictator. At the back of the shop there are weird and wonderful standard lamps – churchy plaster angels holding lights, bronze rose bushes with light bulbs in their blooms and mad pineapple wall sconces. If you find most lighting shops bland, the Facade will put a smile on your face.

Jones Lighting

194 Westbourne Grove, W11 2RH (7229 6866/www.jonesantiquelighting.com). Notting Hill Gate tube. **Open** 10am-5pm Mon-Fri; 10am-6pm Sat. **Credit** AmEx, MC, V.

The majority of the original, restored and rewired lights on display here are Victorian, but there's a good selection of decorative lighting from 1850 to 1940.

Turn On Lighting

11 Camden Passage, N1 8EA, (020 7359 7616) Angel tube. **Open** 10.30am-5.30pm Tue-Sat. **Credit** DC, MC, V.

After 25 years in the Angel Arcade (all 25 traders were evicted when Lombok acquired the arcade in 2007), Janet Holdstock moved to this smaller shop across the way. She specialises in mostly English antique lighting from 1850 to 1950. Expect to pay from £400 for a 1920s desk lamp or ceiling pendant.

Silver

London Silver Vaults

Chancery House, 53-64 Chancery Lane, WC2A 1QT (7242 3844/www.thesilver vaults.com). Chancery Lane tube. **Open** 9am-5.30pm Mon-Fri; 9am-1pm Sat. **Credit** AmEx, MC, V.

London toffs once stored their valuables in guarded strong-rooms at the Chancery Lane Safe Deposit. Gradually, silver dealers began to trade in the underground vaulted premises and the current structure (rebuilt in 1953) today houses around 30 dealers, many of whom have been here for three generations. Not all that sparkles is sterling silver – silver plate and Sheffield plate are also on sale – but all the dealers here are part of an accredited association, which means that all stock must be accurately described. R Feldman specialises in the sort of silver table centrepieces that you would expect the royals to wheel out for state banquets (from £1,500 for simpler pieces). You can pick up smaller, more affordable items too, like pretty, 19th-century triple cake stands and Victorian silver-topped perfume bottles (around £200). Stephen Kalms has bowls brimming with early 20th-century silver-plated napkin rings (from £30); John Hamilton specialises in cutlery; and Langfords provides good inspiration for gifts – we spotted a Victorian silver hip flask by a London maker (£600)).

Vincenzo Caffarella. *See p162.*

Arcades & covered markets

Alfie's Antique Market

13-25 Church Street, NW8 8DT (7723 6066/www.alfiesantiques.com). Edgware Road tube/Marylebone tube/rail. **Open** 10am-6pm Tue-Sat. **Credit varies.**

Alfie's occupies a building that started life as the Edwardian department store, Jordan's. After falling into disrepair, it reopened as an antique market in 1976 and is now home to around 60 dealers. On the ground floor, highlights include the vintage clothes shops Tintin Collectables (1920s and '30s English rose chic) and The Girl Can't Help It ('40s and '50s Hollywood glamour, *see p58*). For 20th-century furniture, venture into the area known as the Quad as well as Decoratum's vast space in the basement. On the first floor, don't miss Dodo for '20s and '30s advertising posters and signs, and Louise Verbier, who has mirrors, lighting and mercury glass. Vincenzo Caffarella's impressive showroom of 20th-century Italian lighting takes up the second floor mezzanine. Finally, rest up at the pleasant rooftop café, before one last rummage through the vintage trimmings at the charming Persiflage.

Antiquarius

131-141 King's Road, SW3 5PH (7823 3900/www.antiquarius.co.uk). Sloane Square tube, then 11, 19, 22, 319, 211 bus. **Open** 10am-6pm Mon-Sat. **Credit** varies.

The space is being partly redeveloped, so there are fewer dealers here than before, but still plenty of variety. Ferguson Antiques has sporting collectibles: gun cases and foxy things aplenty. Islamic art is Aysen's speciality: orientalist paintings, Ottoman ceramics and crystal nargileh bottles. You'll find Louis Vuitton trunks at XS Baggage and truncheons, helmets and militaria at Chelsea Military Antiques. Jasmin Cameron has a good selection of English and Irish 18th- and 19th-century glassware and there's a café at the back, should you need a cuppa while you consider a purchase.

Bermondsey Square Antiques Market

Corner of Bermondsey Street & Long Lane, SE1 (7525 6000). Borough tube/ London Bridge tube/rail. **Open** 6am-2pm Fri. **No credit cards.**

Bermondsey Square is currently being redeveloped. The plan as we went to press was for the market area to include food, fashion and craft stalls, but the antiques market, traditionally good for china and silver, will carry on in an expanded space accommodating 200 stalls.

Camden Passage/ Pierrepont Arcade

Camden Passage, off Upper Street, N1 5ED (www.camdenpassageislington.co.uk). Angel tube. **Open** General market 7am-6pm Wed, Sat. **Credit** varies.

Boutiques and estate agents have now encroached on this once-thriving antiques enclave, with the Mall being the latest casualty to developers, its future uncertain. But some antiques dealers remain: for a good old rummage, turn off the Passage and explore the antique and vintage clothes shops in the still bustling Pierrepont Arcade. Aquamarine Antiques (www.aquamarineantiques.co.uk) has military costumes and taxidermy. Key Leyshon (7226 8955/www.kays-canteen.com), at no.15, has well-priced silver-plated flatware. For antique maps and prints, check out Finbar Macdonell (www.finbarmacdonnell.co.uk) at no.10.

Grays Antique Market & Grays in the Mews

58 Davies Street, W1K 5LP & 1-7 Davies Mews, W1K 5AB (7629 7034/www.grays antiques.com). Bond Street tube. **Open** 10am-6pm Mon-Fri. **Credit** varies.

Stalls in this smart covered market – housed in a terracotta building that was once a 19th-century lavatory showroom – sell everything from antiques, art and rare books to jewellery and vintage fashion. The place was set up in 1977 and is now home to around 200 dealers – making it one of the world's largest and most diverse markets of its kind. There's a good café on site. *See also p184* **Bernard J Shapero** and **Biblion** – two of the antiquarian booksellers here.

20th-century Design

Birgit Israel

301 Fulham Road, SW10 9QH (7376 7255/ www.birgitisrael.com). South Kensington tube. **Open** 10am-6pm Mon-Sat. **Credit** AmEx, DC, MC, V.

Birgit Israel's smart, timeless 20th-century furniture store attracts collectors, interior designers and stylists looking for period pieces in mint condition. Lights are a particular passion, on our last visit we spotted a dazzling Murano glass tiered chandelier (£7,900) and a pair of Venini glass disk wall lights (£3,750). Furniture is understated – what Israel calls 'casual luxury' – encompassing, for example, a pair of Pierre Paulin CM190 1950s armchairs (£1,600), and a 1960s stainless steel and glass coffee table by Italian designer Willy Rizzo. An interior design consultancy is available and you can arrange a wedding list here. Israel's clothing boutique is just along the road; *see p57.*

Boom! Interiors

115 Regent's Park Road, NW1 8UR (7722 6622/www.boominteriors.com). Chalk Farm Road tube. **Open** 11am-6pm Tue-Sat; noon-5pm Sun. **Credit** MC, V.

Phil Cowan specialises in good-quality English and Danish furniture from the 1950s to '70s. Pieces by Merrow Associates, the British engineering company that branched into furniture design in the 1960s, are always in stock, and are extremely well made. Sideboards, Merrow's best-known product, sell for £4,000 to £5,000, while sleek coffee tables are £1,950 and drinks trolleys £995. Lighting is French or Italian, with an emphasis on 1960s Murano glass lamps and chandeliers, and everything is displayed in tasteful room settings (you could almost move in), giving ample inspiration for those seeking the perfect modern interior. Cowan also offers an interior design service.

Caira Mandaglio

Arch 18, Kingsdown Close, Bartle Road, W10 6SW (07836 354632/7243 6035/ www.cairamandaglio.co.uk). Latimer Road or Ladbroke Grove tube. **Open** 10.30am-6pm Fri-Sat, and by appointment. **Credit** MC, V.

Anna Mandaglio and Sharon Moore-Daniel (née Caira) specialise in quality 20th-century design, focusing on mainly French and Italian furniture, lighting and objects from 1920 to 1960. Head here for good pieces by Italian names, such as Fontana Arte, Ico Parisi and Venini, and French designers including Adnet and Guariche. You'll also find good-quality anonymous pieces: when we last dropped by we saw a pair of 1950s French armchairs with those tubular legs so distinctive to the era (£2,200) and an Italian 1940s maplewood cocktail cabinet with original parchment-covered doors (£2,900). Good examples of lighting and mirrors are always in stock. Expect to pay around £950 for chic 1970s Italian table lamps. The duo also regularly exhibit at fairs, such as the Olympia International Art and Antiques Fair in the summer.

Decoratum

Alfie's Antique Market, 13-25 Church Street, NW8 8DT (7724 6969/www.decoratum.com). Marylebone tube/Edgware Road tube/rail. **Open** 10am-6pm Tue-Sat. **Credit** AmEx, MC, V.

This vast showroom – 5,000sq ft in all – takes up the entire basement of Alfie's Antique Market, displaying 20th-century furniture in a series of room sets. You can step quickly from super-stylish to super-ugly (the chunky Brazilian furniture somehow screams 'yabadabadoo!'). Good European and North American designers include Gio Ponti, Willy Rizzo and Paul Evans and there's an interesting selection of lighting and mirrors – the latter range from Spanish 1920s gilt sunbursts to 1960s perspex models.

De Parma

The Gas Works, 2 Michael Road, SW6 2AN (7736 3384/www.deparma.com). Fulham Broadway tube. **Open** 10am-6pm Mon-Fri; 11am-4pm Sat. **No credit cards.**

Gary de Sparham concentrates on mid 20th-century design in this hip white space. Almost everything is Italian and, in the main, by well-known designers such as Ico Parisi, Gio Ponti and Fornasetti. We've seen special pieces such as a 1969 Maurice Calka fibreglass 'Boomerang' desk, one of only 35 (£24,000), and a 1940s Osvaldo Borsani commode in black lacquer and sycamore (£5,200). But there are more affordable items, such as a chic 1940s black lacquered armchair (£1,450). De Sparham has a branch at Domus Gallery, 15 Needham Road, W11 2RP.

Fandango

2 & 50 Cross Street, N1 2BA (7226 1777/ www.fandangointeriors.co.uk). Angel tube/ Highbury & Islington tube/rail. **Open** noon-6pm Tue-Sat; by appointment Sun, Mon. **Credit** AmEx, MC, V.

The selection of 20th-century furniture and objects at Fandango is so thoughtful that even the shop's dog – a smokey grey whippet – complements the surroundings. The shop specialises in post-war design from the 1950s and '60s. When we last visited, we saw leather safari chairs by Arnie Norrell (£850 each) and you'll find pieces by well-known designers such as Arne Jacobsen. But it's not all about names here. Stock is interesting even if it is anonymous. We also saw attractive 1940s Murano glass chandeliers that had been resin-coated to bring them up to date and give them more masculine appeal (£1,400). Fandango has a restoration workshop, and will email you images of pre-madeover pieces before they arrive in the shop.

Gordon Watson

28 Pimlico Road, SW1W 8LJ (7259 0555/ www.gordonwatson.co.uk). Victoria or Sloane Square tube. **Open** 11am-5pm Mon-Sat. **Credit** MC, V.

Watson started his business 30 years ago, and is now a leading authority on 20th-century design. In 2006, he relocated to Pimlico Road after selling the contents of his Fulham Road shop, as well as pieces from his private collection, for a cool £2.7 million at a Sotheby's sale. In his ultra-chic new premises he continues to deal in fine furniture, objects, lighting and silver. You'll find superb pieces from collectable makers of the 20th century. Even the experts turn to Watson: in 2007 he curated a sale at Sotheby's entitled 20th-Century Decorative Arts Selected by Gordon Watson, attended by an arty *Who's Who* including architect John Pawson and artist Gillian Wearing.

Origin Modernism

25 Camden Passage, N1 8EA (7704 1326/ www.origin101.co.uk). Angel tube. **Open** 10am-6pm Wed, Sat; noon-6pm Thur, Fri; also by appointment. **No credit cards.**
People always have room for a chair, Chris Reen believes, which is why you'll always find a good selection of seating in his Camden Passage shop. Reen will happily talk you through the interesting modernist stock here and explain why, for instance, a deliberate mistake might be visible in a design. Furniture and lights dating from 1930 to 1950 are usually Scandinavian, American or British and well-preserved examples of the period. Expect to find names such as Eames and Breuer. When we last dropped by, a Herman Miller 1970s Eames lounger was on sale for £3,200. We also spotted a Hans Peik chair for Morris of Glasgow (£1,200) and Alvar Alto Type 51 Swedish production chairs. Take care if you want to try one for size – a metal jeans button on a back pocket can ruin a collectable chair. Ouch.

Park59

59B Park Road, N8 8SY (8341 6556). Finsbury Park tube/rail then W7 bus. **Open** 10am-6pm Tue-Sat. **Credit** AmEx, MC, V.
Gino Coen's Crouch End shop keeps a consistent stock of pieces from the 1950s through to the '70s, with emphasis on good leather chairs and interesting lighting. On our last visit, we spotted good collectable pieces such as a 1957 Cherner chair (£1,250) and a 1955 Arne Jacobsen dining suite with four 'Series 7' chairs (£1,700). We also admired lighting from the likes of Vistosi, Stilnovo and Verner Panton. If, however, a designer name is not a priority, you can pick up elegant Danish leather sofas for £1,250 and 1960s teak plywood dining chairs for around £65.

Paul Smith

9 Albemarle Street, W1S 4BL (7493 4565). Green Park tube. **Open** 10.30am-6pm Mon-Wed, Fri; 10.30am-7pm Thur; 10am-6pm Sat. **Credit** AmEx, DC, MC, V.
Since opening his first shop in 1970, this most British of designers has evolved and expanded his now-global brand. Smith often dressed his shops using art and furniture from his own collection and eventually he took to selling art and furnishings too. As you would expect, the look is quirky – 20th-century with a 21st-century twist. A collaboration with the long-established fabric firm Gainsborough has breathed new life into faded furniture. Using the company's archive, the designer selected vintage fabric designs but changed the colours to make them brighter and more 'Smith'. So chairs are recovered in a floral jacquard with his distinctive stripe through the fabric and smithed-up 1950s armchairs are priced at around £3,800 a pair. Not everything is reworked, though; there is a changing stock of original furniture, art and lighting. On recent visits, in addition to American and Italian furniture from the 1960s and '70s, we've seen exhibitions of the 1960s fashion photographer Gian Paolo Barbieri and the photographer-turned-furniture designer Willy Rizzo.

Planet Bazaar

397 St John Street, EC1V 4LD (7278 7793/www.planetbazaar.co.uk). Angel tube/19 bus. **Open** noon-6.30pm Mon-Sat; also by appointment. **Credit** MC, V.
Maureen Silverman says people pop into her shop if they need cheering up, and you can see why. The place is crammed with everything from 1950s to '70s telephones (from £65) to funky '60s Danish wooden lamps (from £95). Downstairs you'll find rosewood coffee tables and sideboards of the kind that would have been laden with platters of cheese and pineapple in *Abigail's Party*. We spotted a 1960s teak sideboard by John and Sylvia Reid for Stag (£850) and there's a variety of lighting priced from £65. Pop art is usually in stock, with prints by Jamie Reid, who did iconic artwork for the Sex Pistols.

Talisman

79-91 New King's Road, SW6 4SQ (7731 4686/www.talismanlondon.com). Fulham Broadway tube/22 bus. **Open** 10am-6pm Mon-Sat. **Credit** AmEx, MC, V.
This art deco building is the perfect location for Ken Bolan's show-stopping 20th-century furniture and garden statuary. He relocated his long-established interiors business from Dorset in 2006 and his stock, spanning three floors and four decades (1950s to '80s), is impressive. Everything is handpicked during Bolan's buying trips to America and Europe. From across the pond are '70s tables by the likes of Karl Springer and Paul Evans. On our last visit, we saw a large 1978 Milo Baughman dining table with a steel base and polished top (£6,500), and a pair of 1960s nickel-plated armchairs by the same designer (£2,750). Upstairs you might find a good pair of 1970s American lucite table lamps for £1,100 and don't miss the second floor, with its stunning display of stone and marble garden statuary.

Themes & Variations

231 Westbourne Grove, W11 2SE (7727 5531/www.themesandvariations.com). Notting Hill Gate tube. **Open** 10am-1pm, 2-6pm Mon-Fri; 10am-6pm Sat. **Credit** AmEx, MC, V.
Liliane Fawcett's enduringly chic gallery has a strong focus on Scandinavian and Italian decorative arts and furniture. It takes its name from Italian designer Piero Fornasetti's series and is the exclusive UK agent for the Fornasetti studio. Plates from the series, featuring a woman's head in one of 365 positions, are £75. Stylish post-war and contemporary furniture is a speciality. When we last dropped in, a 1970s sideboard – from the Gucci showroom in Rome – had just arrived. There's also usually some excellent lighting and the gallery has an annual themed exhibition, bringing together 20th-century pieces with furniture and objects from contemporary designers.

Two Columbia Road

2 Columbia Road, E2 7NN (7729 9933/ www.twocolumbiaroad.com). Old Street tube/rail/26, 48, 55 bus. **Open** noon-7pm Tue-Fri; noon-6pm Sat; 10am-3pm Sun. **Credit** MC, V.
Well-selected pieces are the order of the day here, whether it's 1970s chrome pendant lights or collectable Charles Eames wooden chairs. Some 20th-century shops can feel like a bit of a mixed bag, but there's a definite style here. Perhaps that's because this appealing corner site is owned by Tommy Roberts, who made his name with the cult Carnaby Street interiors shop Kleptomania in the 1960s. Tommy still comes in at weekends, but his son Keith now runs the show. Expect to find well-known names such as Arne Jacobsen and Willy Rizzo among the stock as well as more affordable pieces (Danish 1960s leather sofas in slender, elegant shapes for around £850, and rosewood desks of the same period for £1,500). If you've visited Milk and Honey in Soho, you may have perched on a sofa or two from the shop – it provided most of the furniture.

Also check out...

Century

58 Blandford Street, W1U 5JB (7487 5100/www.centuryd.com). Baker Street tube. **Open** 10.30am-6pm Tue-Sat; by appointment Mon, Sun. **Credit** AmEx, MC, V.
Mid 20th-century furniture, with an emphasis on the mass market brands Stag, G-Plan and Ercol, as well as contemporary furniture and home accessories.

Past Caring

54 Essex Road, N1 8LR (07956 383510). Angel tube. **Open** noon-6pm Mon-Sat. **No credit cards.**
A chaotic jumble of all sorts from the owner of the vintage clothes shop Persiflage, in Alfie's Antique Market.

Lighting

Vincenzo Caffarella

Alfie's Antique Market, 13-25 Church Street, NW8 8DT (7724 3701/www.vinca.co.uk). Edgware Road tube/ Marylebone tube/rail. **Open** 10am-6pm Tue-Sat. **Credit** AmEx, MC, V.
As well as his ground-floor space at Alfie's, Vincenzo Caffarella has a huge showroom on the second floor. He specialises in Italian lighting from the 1950s to the '70s, including pieces by Arteluce, Venini and Vistosi. Indeed his stock is so vast, it's a wonder that Italy hasn't been plunged into darkness. Prices start at around £1,000, for which you could buy a trio of 1950s Stilnovo wall lights, like mini Mondrians. We also saw a 1950s Arredoluce brass lamp, with five lights drooping over the base like flowers, for £2,000. Then prices rise steeply: a beautiful 1970s Paul Walter wall light like a glittering piece of jewellery was £8,000. A certain amount of weirdness lurks among the elegance and the passionate Caffarella will be happy to tell you about any of the pieces.

Art & Craft

The arrival of the **Frieze Art Fair** has sealed London's reputation as a major player in the world of art. Of course, much of the work on sale is for serious collectors, but on the back of the fair's success, several smaller galleries have sprung up selling more affordable work. Along with the galleries listed here, London's art fairs and open-studio weekends (*see p164* **Sales & events**) are the best places to unearth emerging talent. Online, **Art Rabbit** (www.artrabbit.com) and **New Exhibitions** (www.newexhibitions.com) offer impressive listings of exhibitions, art fairs and open studios. The website **www.degreeart.com** is a great place to find out about degree shows and new college talent, while online marketplace **Etsy** (www.etsy.com) has taken the craft world by storm in 2008, selling handmade items from designers and craftspeople worldwide.

East End stalwart **Lorem Ipsum** (www.loremipsumgallery.com) was in the process of relocating as this guide went to press; see the website for details.

Art galleries

Cosh

69 Berwick Street, W1F 8SZ (7287 7758/ www.coshuk.com). Oxford Circus tube. **Open** 11am-6pm Mon-Wed, Fri, Sat; 11am-7pm Thur; noon-4pm Sun. **Credit** MC, V.

Part print house, part gallery, Cosh is a fascinating venture. Brothers Will and John Cossey work in collaboration with a young and hip selection of international artists and designers whose emphasis is firmly on illustration, graffiti and graphic art. All the limited-edition print runs are in-house, many are devised between the gallery and the artists, and the resulting archival Giclée prints on Da Vinci paper look fantastic. Changing shows and a selection of works enable you to get a sense of the quality as well as the range.

David Risley Gallery

45 Vyner Street, E2 9DQ (8980 2202/ www.davidrisleygallery.com). Bethnal Green tube/rail. **Open** noon-6pm Wed-Sun. **No credit cards.**

In the melee that is the Vyner Street art scene, David Risley stands out as an exciting, off-beat stable of artists presented with ceaseless invention and originality in monthly changing shows. Painting is well represented too; James Aldridge's intricate, sumptuous cut-outs and canvasses and Anna Bjerger's alluring oil paintings, for example. There's a nice line in wit at David Risley too: Helen Frick's full-size gold and diamond sculpture *Happy with Less* is bound to raise a smile: a stainless steel edition is just £135. In an art scene where much work either baffles or bemuses its audience, David Risley is a true gem.

Degree Art at the Empire Gallery

30 Vyner Street, E2 9DQ (8980 0395/ www.degreeart.com). Bethnal Green tube/ rail. **Open** by appointment Mon-Wed; noon-6pm Thur-Sun. **Credit** MC, V.

It's a tough haul trying to make all the big London college degree shows. That's where Empire Gallery comes in. As the home of www.degreeart.com, a longtime supporter of emerging talent from the UK's art schools, this recently opened permanent space is a great place to seek out new work. Founding partners Isobel Beauchamp and Elinor Olisa do all the hard work, sourcing the best new painting, photography, sculpture and prints, and inviting their creators in to represent them. Prices are keen – £120 to £5,000 – and the body of work is wide enough to offer something for most tastes.

Eagle Gallery/ Emma Hill Fine Art

159 Farringdon Road, EC1R 3AL (7833 2674/www.emmahilleagle.com). Farringdon tube/rail. **Open** 11am-6pm Wed-Fri; 11am-4pm Sat. **Credit** AmEx, MC, V.

Emma Hill's small but enjoyable gallery in Farringdon exhibits and sells an impressive range of limited-edition artists' books, graphics and photography, offering a great selection of original, provocative work by artists who crop up in many national collections. You'll find paintings by the likes of Matthew Burrows, and works on paper for sale from as little as £450. Elsewhere there are examples of Rebecca Sitar's gorgeous, delicate abstract canvasses, with prices starting at £250.

Eleven

11 Eccleston Road, SW1W 9LX (7823 5540/www.elevenfineart.com). Victoria tube/rail. **Open** 11am-6pm Tue, Wed, Fri; 11am-7pm Thur; 11am-4pm Sat. **Credit** AmEx, MC, V.

In a lovely old townhouse, Eleven shows a fine selection of work – much of it painting – by an impressive range of artists, among them hip celeb portrait painter Jonathan Yeo and photographer Norman Parkinson. The most recent addition to the collection of paintings, works on paper and prints are the arresting oil paintings of Romanian painter Marius Bercea. The gallery's strong track record – it was launched by Charlie Phillips, founder and former director of Haunch of Venison, and is managed by Laura Parker Bowles, once gallery manager at Space – means there's always something worth seeing. Prices can run into five figures, but you can own a print from around £200.

England & Co

216 Westbourne Grove, W11 2RH (7221 0417/www.englandgallery.com). Notting Hill Gate tube. **Open** 11am-6pm Mon-Sat. **Credit** AmEx, MC, V.

Jane England's gallery is a grand old dame of the London commercial art scene, having promoted modern British and contemporary work for more than two decades. England has brought together a great range of artists, many of them names you will see at the Tate and V&A. There are works by Patrick Caulfield, Peter Blake and Cornelia Parker, alongside works by Ken Grimes,

Shop talk Sam Chatterton Dickson

Gallerist Sam Chatterton Dickson spent 16 years at Flowers East before moving to West End contemporary gallery Haunch of Venison. He lives in Hackney.

'I've bought several things from **Seventeen Gallery** in Hackney (www.seventeengallery.com), which shows good young artists who are going to make it big, but haven't yet. It's affordable; you can buy for around £500. I like **Hales Gallery** (*see p165*) and **Keith Talent Gallery** (www.keithtalent.com) too.

'The new area for contemporary art is Fitzrovia. **Alison Jacques** (www.alisonjacquesgallery.com) first set the scene and now there are a lot of good galleries there, such as the **Approach** (www.theapproach.co.uk) and **One One One** (111 Great Titchfield Street, W1). **Crisp London Los Angeles** (www.crisplondonlosangeles.com) is another good new gallery. I also buy photography. I like Nobuyoshi Araki, whose work I've bought from **Michael Hoppen** (www.michaelhoppengallery.com).

'To get a flavour of the London art scene, I'd recommend **White Cube** (www.whitecube.com), **Hauser & Wirth** (www.ghw.ch) and **Haunch of Venison** (www.haunchofvenison.com) where I work. When it comes to art fairs, there is nothing like **Frieze**, but I do like the **London Art Fair** (for both, *see p164* **Sales & events**) for its mix of more conservative modern British art with quite interesting contemporary work.'

HOME

Sales & events

The pick of the bunch from the capital's art fairs and open studios.

The Londonwide **artsunwrapped** (www.artsunwrapped.com) open-studio event normally takes place over three consecutive summer weekends, while **Craft Central** (www.craftcentral.org.uk) allows the public to browse its Clerkenwell workspaces twice a year. The **Cockpit Arts** (www.cockpitarts.com) open-studio events, held at its two locations in Holborn and Deptford, are good for sourcing original gifts and art from more than 165 designers and makers. **Bridge Art Fair** (www.bridgeartfair.com) takes a year out in 2008, but promises to return to London in late 2009, when it will bring 60 contemporary American galleries to the capital.

Affordable Art Fair

Battersea Park, SW11 4NJ (8246 4848/www.affordableartfair.co.uk). Sloane Square tube then free shuttle bus. **Dates** 12-15 Mar 2009.
Contemporary art fair (featuring a curated annual 'Recent Graduates' exhibition) where all works cost from £50 to £3,000.

Art Car Boot Fair

Old Truman Brewery, 146 Brick Lane, E1 (www.artcarbootfair.com). **Admission** £3. **Dates** see website.
A one-day fair where small-scale art, ephemera and editions are flogged from art cars by the likes of Jessica Voorsanger, Le Gun and Gavin Turk.

artLONDON

Royal Hospital Chelsea, Royal Hospital Road, SW3 4SR (7259 9399/www.artlondon.net).
Dates Oct 2008 and 2009.
Dozens of galleries from around the world exhibit painting, sculpture, 3D works and photography at this fascinating four-day event.

Chocolate Factory Open Studios

Chocolate Factory One, Clarendon Road, N22 6XJ (8365 7500/www.chocolatefactoryartists.co.uk).
Date 14-16 Nov 2008.
One of the largest events of its kind, featuring over 220 diverse creators.

COLLECT

Saatchi gallery, County Hall, South Bank, SE1 (7806 2549/ www.craftscouncil.org.uk/collect). **Date** 25-29 Jan 2009.
Huge art fair for contemporary objects, featuring makers from all disciplines of applied and decorative arts, including ceramics, glass, jewellery and textiles. Europe's only event of its kind.

East London Design Show

Shoreditch Town Hall, 380 Old Street, EC1V 9LT (7038 3660/ www.eastlondondesignshow.co.uk).
Dates 4-7 Dec 2008.
Unique gifts from some of the UK's most exciting independent interior, product, textile and jewellery designers. This year the fabulous Stinkie Industries label joins the mix with its great range of accessories.

Free Range

Old Truman Brewery, 91 Brick Lane, E1 6QL (7770 6100/www.free-range.org.uk). Liverpool Street tube/rail. **Dates** June/ July 2009.
More than 3,000 graduate artists exhibit in weekly changing shows. With prices starting at a fiver for prints, it's a great chance to scout future stars.

Frieze Art Fair

Regent's Park (Tickets 0870 890 0514/www.frieze.com).
Dates Oct 2008 and 2009.
Named after the eponymous magazine, and not for the faint-hearted (ie poor), but nevertheless a fun opportunity to mingle with and view work by the movers and shakers of the contemporary creative world.

Great Western Studios Open Studios

The Lost Goods Building, Paddington New Yard, Great Western Road, W9 3NY (7221 0100/www.greatwesternstudios.com). Westbourne Park tube.
Dates 6-7 Dec 2008 & June 2009; see website for exact date.
Twice a year, Great Western Studios invites friends and the public to view the broad-ranging artwork of its resident designers and artists.

Hidden Art Fair/ Open Studios

7729 3800/www.hiddenartlondon.co.uk. **Dates** last wknd Nov & 1st wknd Dec; phone or consult website for exact dates.
Centralised fair selling applied arts and crafts-based work. The website offers a great directory of more than 300 UK designers and designer-makers, or you can buy online from www.hiddenartshop.com.

London Art Fair

Business Design Centre, 52 Upper Street, N1 0QH (7288 6736/www.londonartfair.co.uk). Angel tube.
Date 14-18 Jan 2009.
London's largest art fair offers affordable photography, video, paintings and print. Don't be put off by the size: smaller exhibitions within the fair make the whole thing feel more intimate and manageable.

Origin: The London Craft Fair

Somerset House, Strand, WC2R 1LA (7806 2500/www.craftscouncil.org.uk/origin). **Dates** Oct 2008 and 2009.
Around 300 contemporary craft-makers sell a deliciously broad and imaginative range of work within the lovely confines of Somerset House.

Secret Sale

Royal College of Art, Kensington Gore, SW7 2EU (7590 4186/ www.rca.ac.uk/secret). **Dates** 14-21 Nov 2008.
This hugely popular annual sale sees 2,500 postcard-sized works by RCA graduates and world-famous artists sold for £40 on a first-come-first-served basis.

20/21 British Art Fair

Royal College of Art, Kensington Gore, SW7 2EU (8742 1611/ www.britishartfair.co.uk). **Date** 16-20 Sept 2009.
Exclusive fair showing modern and contemporary British art from 1900 to the present day. 20/21's sister International Art Fair will take place from 19-22 February 2009.

Zoo Art Fair

Royal Academy of Arts, 6 Burlington Gardens, W1S 3EX (7247 8597/ www.zooartfair.com). Piccadilly Circus tube. **Dates** Oct 2008 and 2009.
Zoo may have swapped its London Zoo setting for a more traditional space, but the policy of only inviting galleries under six years old to exhibit means it's still one of the best places to buy emerging talent.

whose monochrome ink on paper pieces use the subject and symbols of extraterrestrial encounters. There's a strong line in prints and mixed media work too. Prices start at £100 and are on average around £10,000.

Flowers East

82 Kingsland Road, E2 8DP (7920 7777/ www.flowerseast.com). Old Street tube/rail. **Open** 10am-6pm Tue-Sat. **Credit** AmEx, MC, V.

With branches in Cork Street and New York and a pedigree spanning decades of premier artists – among them Eduardo Paolozzi and Nicola Hicks and photographers Edward Burtynsky and Robert Polidori – you'd be forgiven for assuming that Flowers East is prohibitively expensive. In fact, you'll find a vibrant exhibition programme and a great range of affordable drawings, prints, photography and mixed media pieces. The graphics department is particularly strong; with affordable prints, monoprints and etchings by established artists such as Trevor Sutton (£300 to £1,500), plus brooding etchings by Ken Currie (£400 to £150,000). **For branch (Flowers Central) see index**.

Hales Gallery

Tea Building, 7 Bethnal Green Road, E1 6LA (7033 1938/www.halesgallery.com). Liverpool Street tube/rail. **Open** 11am-6pm Wed-Sat; also by appointment. **Credit** AmEx, DC, MC, V.

Hales Gallery founders Paul Hedge and Paul Maslin have launched the career of many an emerging British artist, including Jake and Dinos Chapman, Mike Nelson and Sarah Jones. Since then the duo have represented international names like Tomoko Takahashi, Spencer Tunick and Hans Op de Beeck, and in their current Tea Building space they continue to show and represent artists from around the world. South African Trevor Appleson's arresting photographs uncover unseen lives, while Dutch artist Sebastiaan Bremer constructs poetic, ghostly abstracts and figurative mixed media works.

Lazarides

8 Greek Street, W1D 4DG (3214 0055/ www.lazinc.com). Piccadilly Circus tube. **Open** 11am-7pm Tue-Sat (closed bank holidays). **Credit** MC, V.

Lazarides has been going from strength to strength since opening this gallery; 2008 saw the creation of a permanent gallery and print room at Charing Cross Road. Between them, the London spaces show some of the best emerging and outsider art talent, everything from a solo show of new works by Jonathan Yeo, through the cream of International Street Art, including Banksy, Todd 'Reas' James and Mode 2, to the intricate black and white drawings of Erica Il Cane. There's a good range of prints; a limited-edition Yeo goes from £550.

Lorem Ipsum Gallery

12 Vyner Street, E2 9HE (07984 153375/ www.loremipsumgallery.com). Bethnal Green tube. **Open** noon-6pm Wed-Sun or by appointment.

Artist and gallery director Birthe Jørgensen set up this gallery in an old print shop with the aim of introducing solid emerging artists to the contemporary scene, and her excellent eye for all things new certainly stands out. Jørgensen's taste is eclectic and unexpected and includes delicate metal sculptures by Thomas Harrison (from £350) and striking wall pieces by Agnieszka Stone. Other arresting compositions can be found in the handmade photos of New York-based Viola Yesilac. The gallery is relocating into a larger space next door in October 2008.

Rebecca Hossack Gallery

2A Conway Street, W1T 6BA (7436 4899/ www.r-h-g.co.uk). Warren Street tube. **Open** 10am-6pm Mon-Sat. **Credit** DC, MC, V.

In this recently opened, light-filled three-storey space, Rebecca Hossack has two floors dedicated to group and solo shows by international contemporary artists and a top floor devoted to the Aboriginal art she's best known for. If this swish space is too *gallerista* for you, visit the smaller Charlotte Street gallery (8 Charlotte Street, W1T 2NA, 7255 282). Intimate and warmly inviting, it holds solo shows by the gallery's many artists whose work benefits from the more human dimensions. Hepzibah Swinford's whimsical oil paintings are here (from £900), so too are Charlotte Cary's strange and fabulous stuffed animal montage photos (around £600).
For branch see index.

Transition Gallery

Unit 25A, Regent Studios, 8 Andrews Road, E8 4QN (72544202/www.transition gallery.co.uk). Bethnal Green tube. **Open** noon-6pm Fri-Sun.

Run by artist Cathy Lomax, Transition specialises in themed group shows by a great range of emerging and established artists, with prices rarely rising above £1,000. It was here that Charles Saatchi discovered stripper turned artist Stella Vine. There are cute little oil paintings by Annabel Dover (£150) and a changing selection of small works by the likes of Roma outsider artist Delaine Le Bas (£400), various paintings by recent RCA painting graduate Tamara Dubnyckyj from £350 to £850, and prints by Susan Aldworth and Katherine Tuloh. Limited-edition works produced by artists who've shown at Transition include a bold-as-brass set of overpainted prints by Peter Lamb; framed and in editions of three, they're a bargain at £200. Lomax publishes a range of artist magazines and art ephemera (all available at the gallery and website), including *Garageland* and *Arty*. **For branch see index**.

Also check out...

Danielle Arnaud

123 Kennington Road, SE11 6SF (7735 8292/www.daniellearnaud.com). Lambeth North tube. **Open** 2-6pm Fri-Sun; also by appointment. **Credit** AmEx, MC, V.

A striking space showing an exciting range of video art and photography alongside painting, mixed media and sculpture.

Greenwich Printmakers

1A Greenwich Market, SE10 9HZ (8858 1569/www.greenwich-printmakers.org.uk). Greenwich rail/DLR. **Open** 10.30am-5.30pm daily. **Credit** MC, V.

Limited-edition etchings, lithographs, relief and silkscreen prints, from £40 to £300.

Plus One Gallery

89-91 Pimlico Road, SW1W 8PH (7730 7656/www.plusonegallery.com). Sloane Square tube. **Open** 10am-6.30pm Mon-Fri; 10am-3pm Sat. **Credit** AmEx, MC, V.

A broad range of realism and photorealism. Prices from £1,000 to £25,000.

Rocket Gallery

Unit G04, Tea Building, 56 Shoreditch High Street, E1 6JJ (7729 7594/www.rocket gallery.com). Liverpool Street or Old Street tube/rail. **Open** 10am-6pm Tue-Fri; noon-6pm Sat. **Credit** AmEx, MC, V.

Shows abstract, design-influenced art and photography, with the odd mid-century modern Danish furniture show thrown in.

Trolley

73A Redchurch Street, E2 7DJ (7729 6591/www.trolleybooks.com). Liverpool Street or Old Street tube/rail. **Open** noon-6pm Tue-Sat. **Credit** AmEx, MC, V.

One of the best artists' book publishers around offers imaginative and affordable limited-edition and short-run publications.

Will's Art Warehouse

Sadler's House, 180 Lower Richmond Road, SW15 1LY (8246 4840/www.wills-art.com). Putney Bridge tube then 22 bus. **Open** 10.30am-6pm daily. **Credit** MC, V.

The 'Oddbins of the art world' sells affordable art (from £50 to £3,000).

Crafts & applied art

For **Lesley Craze Gallery**, *see p81*.
For **Beyond the Valley**, *see p19*.

Barrett Marsden Gallery

17-18 Great Sutton Street, EC1V 0DN (7336 6396/www.bmgallery.co.uk). Barbican tube. **Open** 11am-6pm Tue-Fri; 11am-4pm Sat. **Credit** AmEx, MC, V.

Barrett Marsden shows six solo or two-person exhibitions a year alongside group shows by gallery artists, creating a range of works in glass, ceramics, wood, cloth and metal that span everything from museum-quality pieces to more affordable buys. Some of the biggest names in applied arts have shown here, among them Tord Boontje, Elizabeth Fritsch and Emma Woffenden. A nice range of limited editions, however, makes even the best artists' work available to all. The emphasis is firmly on the contemporary.

Contemporary Applied Arts

2 Percy Street, W1T 1DD (7436 2344/ www.caa.org.uk). Goodge Street or Tottenham Court Road tube. **Open** 10am-6pm Mon-Sat. **Credit** AmEx, MC, V.

The CAA is consistently inventive with its exhibitions of its 300-plus makers. The applied arts here embrace the functional in the form of jewellery, textiles and tableware (lustrous glass bowls from Gillies-Jones start at £145), but there are also purely decorative pieces like Cleo Mussi's wall hangings and ornaments made of recycled ceramic and mosaic shards. The ground-floor gallery space houses solo or themed exhibitions, while the large basement shop area has pieces for all pockets, from both established members and newcomers.

Flow

1-5 Needham Road, W11 2RP (7243 0782/ www.flowgallery.co.uk). Notting Hill Gate tube. **Open** 11am-6pm Mon-Sat. **Credit** AmEx, MC, V.

This Notting Hill gallery houses the work of more than 100 makers working across a broad array of styles and media, from ceramics, glass and paper to wood, textiles, metal and jewellery. The combination of six exhibitions a year as well as a permanent collection makes for an interesting and desirable selection of affordable items, such as Allison Wiffen's original vases that use old-fashioned anaglypta wallpapers as textures for moulds (£87.50 to £175), Alison Crowther's organic furniture and unusual objects carved from solid pieces of native hardwoods (from £1,200). Jewellery is particularly well represented here.

Ryantown

126 Columbia Road, E2 7RG (7613 1510/ www.misterrob.co.uk). Liverpool Street or Old Street tube/rail/26, 48, 55 bus. **Open** 1-4pm Sat; 9am-4.30pm Sun. **Credit** AmEx, MC, V.

Printmaker Rob Ryan opened this lovely gallery/shop in summer 2008. Tiles, printed tissue paper, screen-prints, paper cut-outs, cards, wooden keys, limited-edition prints, vases, even skirts and T-shirts, all bear his distinctive, fun graphics and words – with phrases such as 'I thought you didn't like me' printed on many of the covetable items.

Also check out...

Commissionacraftsman.com

www.commissionacraftsman.com.

An online commissioning service set up by former Christie's expert Gregory Page-Turner.

Contemporary Ceramics

William Blake House, 7 Marshall Street, W1F 7EH (7437 7605/www.cpaceramics.com). Oxford Circus or Piccadilly Circus tube. **Open** 10.30am-6pm Mon-Wed, Fri, Sat; 10.30am-7pm Thur. **Credit** AmEx, MC, V.

The Craft Potters Association gallery encompasses a range of prices and styles.

Design Nation

www.designnation.co.uk

The Design Trust's promotional wing has contacts for 130 member designers.

Frivoli

7A Devonshire Road, W4 2EU (8742 3255). Turnham Green tube. **Open** 10am-6pm Tue-Sat; 11am-5pm Sun. **Credit** MC, V.

Quality, often very affordable crafts.

Glass Art Gallery

7 The Leathermarket, Weston Street, SE1 3ER (7403 2800/www.londonglassblowing.co.uk). London Bridge tube/rail. **Open** 10am-5pm Mon-Fri. **Credit** AmEx, MC, V.

Glass works by Peter Layton and his team.

Hidden Art

www.hiddenart.com

Online directory of 300 designer-makers.

Thinking outside the box

There's something strange going on in the art world. Work we usually associate with the hallowed halls of the Tate and the Saatchi Gallery is making its way into the mainstream public domain: into shops, cafés, pubs and even hairdressing salons. This is great news for the serious galleryphobe, but it's a boon for the rest of us too. Who hasn't walked into a stark white space manned by an imperious pearl-clad gal and wanted to walk straight back out, too intimidated to enquire about the work? These new platforms for art are something that gallery owner and artist Cathy Lomax – who recently held an exhibition at new Primrose Hill beauty shop **Lost in Beauty** (*see p89*) – thinks can only be a good thing, for both artists and fledgling collectors. 'It can enhance the work to show it in a venue that has relevance to the work itself,' she says, 'at the same time giving viewers a great idea of how it will look in a space that's not purely dedicated to the work.'

This blurring of boundaries is nothing new to shops such as **Bermondsey 167** and **Beyond the Valley** (for both, *see p19*), where exhibitions have always been integral to the shops' concepts. But a growing number of other stores are now following suit, including London high fashion chain **Matches** (*see p36*). In 2008, its flagship Marylebone store hosted the first in a series of artists' collaborations curated by Karen Ashton, founder of the **Art Car Boot Fair** (*see p164*).

The 'For Your Pleasure' installation (*pictured above*) by Abigail Lane saw limited-edition works for sale, among them cufflinks, tables, plates and more traditional wall pieces starting at under £50 and rising to £10,000.

Similar approaches are taking place at **Patrick Lüdde Salon & Spa** (*see p110*) and **Stamp Hair** (www.stamphair.com), where exhibitions of works can be enjoyed while you're pampered, and bought for much less than you might pay at a gallery.

Cafés are another great place to catch exhibitions by local artists. Cultured coffee shops include gay and lesbian café **First Out** (52 St Giles High Street, WC2H 8LH, 7240 8042, www.firstoutcafebar.com), the delightful gallery above **Handmade Food** (40 Tranquil Vale, Blackheath, SE3 0BD, 8297 9966, www.handmadefood.com), the **London Review Cake Shop** in the eponymous bookshop (*see p178*) and several park cafés – including those in **Clissold Park** (Clissold Park Mansions, Stoke Newington Church Street, N16 9HJ, 7923 9797), **Dulwich Park** (off College Road, SE21 7BQ, 8299 1383) and **Springfield Park** (White Lodge Mansion, Springfield Park, Stamford Hill, E5 9EF, 8806 0444).

Your local pub is also worth scouring; if those prints on the wall look a bit more original than the usual sepia street scenes, it may be because they are – the **Herne Tavern** (2 Forest Hill Road, East Dulwich, SE22 0RR, www.theherne.net) recently showed photography by local artist Rebecca Milligan of plantlife in and around Dulwich Park, Peckham Rye Park, Brockley and Ladywell Fields. Limited to an edition of three, each framed print was available to take away for from just £30. That wouldn't even get you a framed poster at the Tate.

Gardens & Flowers

Our plots may be merely backyards, balconies and window boxes, but London gardeners have reasons to be cheerful. Firstly, our collective horticultural efforts add up to a significant greening of the city. Secondly, gardening in London does not throw up the challenges that provincial growers face: our plots are unravaged by rabbits, and usually escape the frost, which is why you see so many exotic palms, bamboos, olives and citrus trees in the city's garden centres.

Columbia Road Market (*see p22 and p174* **Streetwise**) is the best bet for variety, and as a dedicated plant market prices are keen, but your local street market is likely to sell you workaday bedding plants and blooms for even less. **New Covent Garden Flower Market** (Covent Garden Market Authority, Covent House, SW8 5NX, 7720 2211, www.cgma.gov.uk) covers three-and-a-half acres and sells blooms, in bulk only, from all over the world. Turn up before 7am for the best choice.

Many of the garden centres listed here have their own design and landscaping services. Otherwise, ask for a list of accredited designers in your area from the **Society of Garden Designers** (www.sgd.org.uk).

Green-fingered enthusiasts might want to join a national organisation, such as **Garden Organic** (024 7630 3517, www.gardenorganic.org.uk), the **Herb Society** (012 9576 8899, www.herbsociety.org.uk) or the **Royal Horticultural Society** (www.rhs.org.uk); these offer expert advice, access to demonstration gardens and monthly journals, as well as discounts from various shops and nurseries. And if you want advice on starting your own patch, the **National Society of Allotment & Leisure Gardeners** (www.nsalg.org.uk) will have lots of useful information and advice.

Garden centres & nurseries

Crocus (www.crocus.co.uk) is an online supplier of plants, tools and accessories. For herbs, including organic, biodynamic and medicinal specimens, it's well worth visiting the websites for **Iden Croft Herbs** (www.herbs-uk.com), **Jekka's Herb Farm** (www.jekkasherbfarm.com) – run by the many times Chelsea Gold-winner Jekka McVicar – and **Poyntzfield Herb Nursery** (www.poyntzfieldherbs.co.uk).

Other good nurseries with mail-order services are **Reads Nursery** (www.readsnursery.co.uk), which grows fruit bushes and trees, vines and conservatory plants, **Special Plants** (www.specialplants.net), specialising in tender perennials, and **Woottens of Wenhaston** (www.woottensplants.co.uk), growing auriculas, pelargoniums, grasses, hemerocallis and bearded iris. All of these offer mail order via their websites.

Alleyn Park Garden Centre

77 Park Hall Road, SE21 8ES (8670 7788/www.alleynpark.co.uk). West Dulwich rail. **Open** *Mar-July, Sept, Oct, Dec* 9am-6pm Mon-Sat. *Aug, Nov, Jan, Feb* 10am-4pm Mon-Sat; 10am-4pm Sun. **Credit** MC, V.

Flourishing in a fertile spot behind the villagey Croxted Road shopping hub, Alleyn Park is perfect for beginner growers, thanks to its engaging and interested proprietor. Prices are excellent, with large pots of hardy perennials, such as stachys and geraniums, for £2.95 and pot-grown herbs of many varieties for just £1.49 a pop. Everything is well tended and attractively laid out, and there's a lovely wooden indoor section for cards, seeds, vases and accessories. Alleyn Park is also well known for its olive trees, hand-picked in Tuscany. Keep an eye on the website for the exciting summer sale, when prices are pruned dramatically – we filled the garden with herbs for a few quid.

C Rassell

80 Earl's Court Road, W8 6EQ (7937 0481). Earl's Court or High Street Kensington tube. **Open** *Jan-Mar, mid July-Sept* 9am-5.30pm Mon-Wed, Fri, Sat; 9am-6.30pm Thur. *Apr-mid July, Oct-Dec* 9am-5.30pm Mon-Wed, Fri, Sat; 9am-6.30pm Thur; 11am-5.30pm Sun. **Credit** MC, V.

An old-school, central centre with a large plant stock, seeds, fertilisers, pots and tools. The central building has a certain antique charm and it's clearly run by proper gardening folk. A big board outside tells customers what they should be doing this month (chitting potatoes late winter, planting out sweet peas in spring) and each species in the beautiful shady garden that meanders down leafy walks has an informative, handwritten label. There are loads of bedding plants and plenty of specimens for dry shade and small terraces.

Camden Garden Centre

2 Barker Drive, NW1 0JW (7387 7080/www.camdengardencentre.co.uk). Camden Town tube. **Open** *Apr-Sept* 9am-5.30pm Mon, Tue, Fri, Sat; 9am-7pm Wed, Thur; 11am-5pm Sun. *Oct-Mar* 9am-5pm Mon-Sat; 10am-4pm Sun. **Credit** AmEx, DC, MC, V.

This acclaimed and inspirational garden centre near the canal towpath offers opportunities and training for the long-term unemployed, the homeless and those with learning disabilities. It also has a gardening services team that can transform your patch, but once you've toured the selection of healthy, well-priced specimens on show you'll be itching to get growing yourself. There's a great selection of bedding shrubs, old-fashioned and hybrid tea roses, exotic architectural plants such as tree ferns and a magnificent terracotta pot collection. Salad ingredients and individual kitchen garden favourites such as beans and marrows are also sold at this great centre.

Capital Gardens

Alexandra Palace, Alexandra Palace Way, N22 7BB (8444 2555/www.capitalgardens.co.uk). Alexandra Palace rail/Wood Green tube or Finsbury Park tube then W3 bus. **Open** 9am-6pm Mon-Sat; 10.30am-4.30pm Sun. **Credit** MC, V.

The W3 bus takes you straight to the garden centre gate, otherwise it's a hilly march round the Palace from the other stations. Capital is London's largest group of garden centres (there are six). It's good for a wide choice of vertical growers (always wise in a small plot), including climbing roses, clematis, jasmine and honeysuckles. Bedding standards and impact shrubs are all present and correct. Inside, there are ranks of seeds, tools, gifts, houseplants, outdoor furniture and the rest. The café has a rooftop terrace with lovely views of allotments, parkland and the city beyond.

For branches (Highgate Garden Centre, Morden Hall Garden Centre, Temple Fortune Garden Centre, Neal's Nurseries) see index.

Chelsea Gardener

125 Sydney Street, SW3 6NR (7352 5656/www.chelseagardener.com). South Kensington tube/14, 49 bus. **Open** 10am-6pm Mon-Sat; noon-6pm Sun. **Credit** AmEx, MC, V.

This fashionable centre is pretty enough to browse through and guarantees a personal service for those who are definite about the look they want for their terrace and are prepared to pay for it. Although common bedding species, such as lobelia and busy lizzie, cost much the same as those sold the same way in other centres, some items seem pricey. The statement exotics and houseplants in fashionable containers elicit a 'wow' and the selection of garden furniture and related accessories is second to none. Lily Simmons (7351 9611) handles the cut flowers here. Arbours and garden rooms can be made to order.

Clifton Nurseries

5A Clifton Villas, W9 2PH (7289 6851/www.clifton.co.uk). Warwick Avenue tube. **Open** *Apr-Sept* 8.30am-6pm Mon, Tue, Thur-Sat; 8.30am-8pm Wed; 10.30am-4.30pm Sun. *Oct-Mar* 8.30am-5.30pm Mon-Sat; 10.30am-4.30pm Sun. **Credit** AmEx, MC, V.

Visiting London's stateliest centre, established in 1851, fills the amateur gardener with longing and enthusiasm. From the gorgeous stucco mansions of Little Venice you enter a horticulturalist's paradise via a shady drive lined with topiarised box trees in lavish pots (average price of each tree: £300). Fortunately, good looks aren't Clifton's only selling point. Helpful and

knowledgeable staff are able to steer you toward sensible purchases for your patch. There's also a huge flowering shrub and perennial section. Take some time to sit on the bench in the fragrant rose garden collection and breathe deeply. The centre's impressive exotics are pampered in a large hothouse – head inside for carnivorous plants, fragrant gardenias, cacti and succulents and fleshy tender tropicals. Non-gardeners might like to enquire about the legendary Clifton design and landscaping service. Cut flowers, as well as tools and accessories, are sold and Clifton also runs a plantfinder service. What's more, there's a Daylesford organic café on site.

Clock House Nursery

Forty Hill, Enfield, EN2 9EU (020 8363 1016/ www.clockhousenursery.co.uk). Enfield tube. **Open** 9am-5pm daily. **Credit** MC, V.

Established in 1928 and run by the same family ever since, Clock House is the most venerable of the many large nurseries around the gardeners' Eden that is Enfield. We've been reliably informed by several keen gardeners and at least one professional landscaper that its flowers, plants and shrubs are consistently fresh – they're grown on site in the huge glasshouses – and of a very high quality. The nursery also offers horticultural advice. Best of all, though, is that prices are almost wholesale. Highly recommended, especially if you're planning a major restock or thinking of redesigning your garden.

Dulwich Garden Centre

20-22 Grove Vale, SE22 8EF (8299 1089). East Dulwich rail. **Open** 9am-5.30pm Mon-Sat; 10am-2pm Sun. **Credit** AmEx, MC, V.

A neat and orderly centre on a sloping site by East Dulwich station, DGC is strong on ready-made impact and edibles for the small south London garden. There are boxes of saladings and sweetcorn, mature showy lavenders, even showier standard roses and solanum and lollipop-cut variegated hollies – all of which will create an instant fix for the backyard, if you're willing to pay for the time it has taken to grow them. Those keener to get their green fingers dirty can survey the many racks of seeds (Johnsons, Geo and the Laura Ashley selections of cut flower seeds), fertilisers, propagators, hose systems and all the other gardening hardware set out in the large shop area. There's also a big range of tiny bonsai and a houseplant section. Prices have undergone quite a hoick over the last year. The herb deal we've always loved now stands at £14.99 for ten (£1.99 per herb – same as Clifton).

Fulham Palace Garden Centre

Bishop's Avenue, SW6 6EE (7736 2640/ www.fulhamgardencentre.com). Putney Bridge tube. **Open** 9.30am-5.30pm Mon-Thur; 9.30am-6pm Fri, Sat; 10am-5pm Sun. **Credit** AmEx, DC, MC, V.

A superb location – next door to the 16th-century former residence of various bishops of London, and near a glorious riverside walk – makes this garden centre impressively bucolic. It's run by a charity, Fairbridge, which supports disadvantaged young people. All the profits go to Fairbridge , which is as good a reason as any to fill your patch with the annuals, perennials, shrubs and trees sold here. When we visited, the fragrant calamondin

Columbia Road Market. See p167.

oranges, lime and lemon trees (from £24) were looking good. Bargain plants are often available in the sale area. Aromatherapy unguents, candles, cards and homewares are sold alongside the horticultural necessities in the shop. Planters range from coolly modish to snazzy and prettily traditional, and you can even have a filled planter made to order, using a wide variety of pots from the garden centre – or that old olive oil tin that's been knocking around your garden for years. Planting charge is £5.

Gingko Garden Centre

Railway arches, Ravenscourt Avenue, off King Street, W6 0SL (8563 7112/ www.gingkogardens.co.uk). Ravenscourt Park tube. **Open** *Mar-Dec* 9am-6pm Mon-Sat; 10am-5pm Sun. *Jan-Feb* 9am-5pm Mon-Sat; 10am-5pm Sun. **Credit** AmEx, MC, V.

Glamorous Gingko – well set out and beautifully tended – sits beside Ravenscourt Park, so pulls in fair-weather gardeners with its grandiloquent clipped box and bay trees and gorgeous climber and burgeoning cottage perennials. It's also strong on Mediterranean splendour for the sunny terrace; olives that would do well in big planters, little citrus trees and architectural spiky agaves give instant impact. For those all-important window boxes there are well-priced six-packs of petunias, marigolds and lobelia and individual pelargoniums for summer planting. The range of containers is impressive, as are the terrace and conservatory furniture and ornaments. Staff dispense advice and will also pot out containers to order; the Gingko design, landscape and maintenance business provides for larger projects.

Growing Concerns

2 Wick Lane (corner with Cadogan Terrace), E3 2NA (8985 3222/www.growingconcerns.org). Bow Road tube/DLR then 8, S2 bus. **Open** *Summer* 10am-4pm Tue; 10am-6pm Wed-Sun. *Winter* 9am-dusk Tue-Sun. **Credit** AmEx, MC, V.

With its flowery fulsomeness spreading out on to the banks of the Union Canal, this neat little centre is a pleasure to visit on a summer's day, especially as it sells Purbeck ice-cream and coffee. Growing Concerns is run by community gardeners who are serious about improving Hackney's environment. The plants it sells are all in very good nick – we were impressed by the ranked pots of morning glory and black-eyed Susan, as well as the affordable pelargonium and herb pots (£1.99 and £1.75 respectively). The accessories shop also has an encouraging line in organic vegetable seeds, including exotica from World Kitchen. You can sign up for one of its gardening classes that include learning how to plant up a hanging basket.

North One Garden Centre

The Old Button Factory, 25A Englefield Road, N1 4EU (7923 3553). Highbury & Islington tube/76, 141 bus. **Open** *Summer* 9.30am-6pm Mon-Wed, Fri-Sun; 9.30am-7pm Thur. *Winter* 9.30am-5pm Mon-Wed, Fri-Sun; 9.30am-7pm Thur. **Credit** MC, V.

A well-rounded centre, with a strong line in plants from specialist English growers. The stylish Islington location dictates a suitably fashionable look to the window box annuals, hardy perennials, architectural shrubs and gardenware, but the staff are ready with sensible advice. All the basics for urban terraces and balconies are here – French marigolds, viola, busy lizzies, pelargoniums and ever-popular lavenders to pop in a pot and leave to bloom. There's a trendy range of glazed ceramics and frost-proof planters and, for local young families, an impressive range of brightly coloured miniature gardening implements. Carefully topiarised architectural shrubs in pots are a speciality. North One also runs a garden design service.

Palm Centre

Ham Central Nursery (opposite Riverside Drive), Ham Street, Ham, Richmond, Surrey TW10 7HA (8255 6191/www.thepalmcentre.co.uk). Richmond tube/rail then 371 bus. **Open** 9am-5pm Mon-Sat; 10am-5pm Sun. **Credit** MC, V.

This extensive collection of exotica has a glorious riverside location near Ham House, and is as exciting to visit. It was founded by Martin Gibbons, a dedicated grower of palms, and has developed into the largest selection of the trees in the UK. There's a huge choice for all locations, from the lady palm suitable for dark indoor spaces to the hardy giant Chilean Wine palm, which can grow up to 21ft and is tolerant of dank London winters. And it's not just palms; there are also bamboos, banana plants, olives, ferns and cycads. The plants are displayed in hothouses as well as in a large plantation, where you can wander about and sit on antique benches to listen to the breeze rustling the ornamental foliage.

Petersham Nurseries

Church Lane, off Petersham Road, Petersham, Richmond, Surrey TW10 7AG (8940 5230/www.petershamnurseries.com). Richmond tube/rail. **Open** 11am-5pm Mon, Sun; 9am-5pm Tue-Sat. **Credit** MC, V.

There isn't a corner of this celebrated nursery that isn't ravishing, especially in its flowery summer garb. Idyllically set amid Petersham's pastures, the nurseries are a series of antique timber frame greenhouses around which pots and raised beds, old-fashioned hand carts and timber boxes filled with annuals, hardy perennials, shrubs, climbers and herbs put up a stunning cottage garden display. There are big blowsy dahlias and planters full of sweet peas and nasturtiums in high season, fruit trees and bushes for autumn planting and bulbs, conifers and evergreens for winter interest. It really is a feast for the eyes – and the stomach too, as Petersham Nurseries is home to Skye Gyngell's fantastic café. It's best to walk from the bus stop or the Twickenham ferry to get here, as Richmond Council will only give permanent consent for this treasure to remain if fewer people arrive by car. Be as green as your fingers and leave the motor behind.

Also check out...

Phoebe's Garden Centre

Penerley Road, SE6 2LQ (0870 443 5600/ www.phoebes.co.uk). **Open** 9am-5.30pm Mon-Fri, Sat; 10am-4pm Sun. **Credit** MC, V.

Good local pet and garden centre.

Tendercare Nurseries

Southlands Road, Denham, Uxbridge, Middx UB9 4HD (01895 835544/ www.tendercare.co.uk). Uxbridge tube then 300, 331, 724 bus. **Open** 8am-5pm Mon-Sat. **Credit** MC, V.

A vast nursery specialising in serious-sized mature specimen trees and shrubs.

Wheelers

Cato's Yard, Turnham Green Terrace, W4 1LR (8747 6776). Turnham Green tube. **Open** 9am-6pm daily. **Credit** MC, V.

An attractive centre specialising in mature shrubs, climbers and Mediterranean natives, like olives, in ornate pots.

Wyevale Garden Centre

Syon Park, Brentford, Middx TW8 8JG (8568 0134/www.wyevale.co.uk). Gunnersbury tube/rail/Syon Park rail/ 267 bus. **Open** 9am-6pm Mon-Sat; 10.30am-4pm Sun. **Credit** AmEx, MC, V.

A well-known garden centre chain.
For branches see index.

Garden shops

Daylesford Organic (30 Pimlico Road, SW1W 8LJ, 7730 2943, www.daylesfordorganic.com) has an achingly ideal garden shop for timber furniture, vintage garden tools, aged pots, organic seeds and cut flowers.

Hortus

26 Blackheath Village, SE3 9SY (8297 9439/www.hortus-blackheath.co.uk). Blackheath rail. **Open** 9.30am-6pm Mon-Wed, Fri, Sat; 9.30am-7pm Thur; 10am-4pm Sun. **Credit** MC, V.

A garden design and maintenance business is run from this rather lovely village store. Hortus aims to sell unique designs from small producers that are not available on the high street. The stock changes seasonally and includes the shop's own range of tools and accessories. Everything is functional first and beautiful second and the owners personally test the tools before they're put on sale. Trowels and secateurs from Burgon & Ball and Duchy, swings and containers made from recycled tyres, trug baskets, lamps, ceramics and glassware, picnicware and quality outdoor furniture, including hand-printed deckchairs, are stocked inside. In the fragrant garden at the rear you can buy a selection of roses, herbs, perennials and city-suitable shrubs, all well tended and healthy looking. Modern stone water features and bird-baths complete the look.

Judy Green's Garden Store

11 Flask Walk, NW3 1HJ (7435 3832). Hampstead tube. **Open** 10am-6pm Mon-Sat; noon-6pm Sun. **Credit** AmEx, MC, V.

This 'garden boutique' is Hampstead down to its delicate roots. Outside there's a tumble of pelargoniums, lavender, nemesias and angelonias, all of which will look artful in the designer pots you'll find indoors. Alongside these are a selection of orchids and an ever-changing range of accessories, including pretty floral things, handmade garden tools, outdoor furniture and bags and aprons from Cath Kidston.

Marston & Langinger

192 Ebury Street, SW1W 8UP (7881 5717/www.marston-and-langinger.com). Sloane Square tube. **Open** 10am-6pm Mon-Fri; 10am-5pm Sat. **Credit** MC, V.

M&L's upmarket shop window for superior bespoke timber conservatories, orangeries and greenhouses is a pleasure to fantasise in. Any number of accessories with which to embellish the outdoor rooms are also sold here. Frost-resistant planters, conservatory containers, vintage and new tools, wrought votive candle-holders, heavy glassware, benches and artfully arranged patio plants make lovely house-warming gifts. It can also supply paving, blinds, outdoor and indoor furniture and lighting.

RK Alliston

173 New King's Road, SW6 4SW (7731 8100/www.rkalliston.com). Parsons Green tube. **Open** 10am-5pm Mon, Wed, Fri. **Credit** AmEx, DC, MC, V.

Harriet Scott's garden design service operates from this exclusive showroom, where distinctive garden accessories are also sold. There are planters, pots, ornaments, gift-packed secateurs, designer twine, hand-turned yew dibbers and exclusive outdoor eating implements. Ideal if you need a gift for the gardener who has everything. At the time this guide went to press, RK Alliston was undergoing a refurbishment, due to be complete in September 2008.

Also check out...

Patio

100 Tooting Bec Road, SW17 8BG (8672 2251). Tooting Bec tube. **Open** 10am-5.30pm daily. **Credit** MC, V.

A friendly shop full of Mediterranean plants and mainly terracotta pots.

Bulbs & seeds

The following are all good online suppliers of bulbs and/or seeds, including for edible plants:

Avon Bulbs *www.avonbulbs.com*

Broadleigh Gardens *www.broadleighbulbs.co.uk*

Chiltern Seeds *www.chilternseeds.co.uk*

Jacques Amand *www.jacquesamand.com*

Marshalls *01480 443390/www.marshall-seeds.co.uk*

Mr Fothergill's Seeds *www.mr-fothergills.co.uk*

Organic Gardening Catalogue *www.organiccatalog.com*

Suttons *www.suttons.co.uk*

Thomas Etty *www.thomasetty.co.uk*

Thompson & Morgan *www.thompson-morgan.com*

Trees

Both the **Aboricultural Association** (01794 368717, www.trees.org.uk) and the **Tree Council** (7407 9992, www.treecouncil.org.uk) are useful contacts for anything tree-related. Good online suppliers include **Bluebell Nursery & Arboretum** (www.bluebellnursery.com), **Keepers Nursery** (www.keepers-nursery.co.uk) and **Thornhayes Nursery** (www.thornhayes-nursery.co.uk).

London Tree Centre

102 High Street, Tring, Herts HP23 4AF (01442 825401/www.civictrees.co.uk). **Open** by appointment. **Credit** DC, MC, V.

Mature trees for instant impact.

Furnishings & accessories

As well as the shops listed below, the **Conran Shop** (*see p121*) and **Heal's** (*see p123*) have attractive lines for the garden, and even big DIY chains like B&Q (*see p140*) have some stylish ranges. In spring and summer, check out **Habitat** (*see p122*) and **John Lewis** (*see p16*) too.

For pieces with more of a 'wow' factor, visit the websites of **David Harber Sundials** (www.davidharbersundials.com), for virtuoso sundials, sculpture and water features, **Lucy Smith Ceramic Garden Sculpture** (www.lucysmith.org.uk) – an east London-based sculptor who creates water features and garden ornaments – and the **Truggery** (www.truggery.co.uk), a century-old Sussex-based trug-maker. And fans of contemporary garden furniture and design should find much to enjoy at the **Modern Garden Company** (www.moderngarden.co.uk).

H Crowther

5 High Road, Chiswick, W4 2ND (8994 2326/www.hcrowther.com). **Open** 7.30am-4.30pm Mon-Fri. **No credit cards.**

The Crowther Foundry was established in 1908, making this company the first and last word in spectacular lead urns, planters, statuary and fountains.

Snapdragon

266 Lee High Road, SE13 5PL (8463 0503/www.snapdragonpots.co.uk). **Open** 10am-6pm Mon-Sat; 10am-4pm Sun. **Credit** AmEx, MC, V.

A great pot shop for glazed and terracotta containers at budget prices.

Conservatories

Bartholomew Conservatories

www.bartholomew-conservatories.co.uk

Bespoke designs for very contemporary glasshouses, which can be made from EC Smartglass (TM), the revolutionary new glass that can be tinted from clear to almost black at will (as seen on *Grand Designs*).

Glass Houses

www.glasshouses.com

This company creates conservatories, orangeries and other glass structures.

Landscaping

CED

www.ced.ltd.uk

Stone, gravel and aggregate supplier CED has everything from York stone to Indian sandstone. It even does standing stones 'to add a sense of mystery to your garden'.

Naybur Bros

www.nayburbros.co.uk

Suburban garden centres that are specialists in landscaping materials, such as ready-to-lay wooden decking and paving for paths. **For branch see index.**

Thompsons

www.thompsonsofcrewshill.com

Colin Thompson's hard landscaping business provides gardeners with rockery stones, paving, soil, fertilisers and mulches.

Harvest supper

Londoners, it seems, are once more being encouraged to dig – if not for victory – then for health and efficiency. In times of financial uncertainty, anything that cuts the grocery bill – and mitigates the effects of global warming – is a good thing. That was the feeling behind a City Hall conference 'Growing Food for London', which took place in the summer of 2008, and the reason why the Royal Parks started putting courgettes in their flowerbeds. Of course, not all the glorious floral displays in the prestigious parks have been turned into allotments, but the Royal Parks management is keen to show Londoners how their veg gardens could grow; hence the public potagers where once there were pelargoniums.

It's not just the horticulturalists of the Royal Parks that are waxing evangelical about home-grown vegetables. Numerous community initiatives are doing great work to encourage the growing of one's own. The most celebrated of these is the Hackney social enterprise **Growing Communities** (www.growingcommunities.org). This is a sustainable system of growing and selling seasonal organic veg that provides 450 local households with a fruit and veg box scheme and encourages volunteers to work on the land – a fabulous way to learn the ropes. It also runs its own farmers' market every Saturday.

Another scheme, **Food Up Front** (www.foodupfront.org), down Balham way, is all about turning your front garden over to vegetable growing. It's amazing the variety of crops you can fit into the three feet between the front door and the wheelie bin.

Growing Communities

Growing vegetables in this communal way, whether on an allotment (the waiting list for these often runs into years in London) or along with your neighbours, is a far more economical way of growing than going it alone. For a start, it avoids gluts. Packets of seeds often contain too many, so, unless you're growing food that can be sown frequently for regular harvesting (cut and come again salad leaves, radishes) you'll end up with an embarrassment of riches, or a half hundredweight of purple cabbage when you can only stomach a few. Sharing seeds, seedlings, cuttings and harvests with your fellow growers makes sense.

The best advice comes from your fellow mucker on the allotment or down the road, but the experts are easily on hand (or online) with answers to your questions. Joining the **Royal Horticultural Society** (*see p67*) gives access to the cream of the experts. Organic vegetable growers should consider the annual subscription to join **Garden Organic** (*see p67*). This gives you access to organic seeds and the expert advice on growing them. You can also attend courses at its Ryton headquarters – 'Starting an Organic Allotment' is a great favourite. It provides the inspiration, but the hard work will be all yours. Just think of the calories burned and help yourself to another buttery potato harvested from the compost-filled bin on your windowsill. They sure taste better than petunias.

Flowers

The **Flowers & Plants Association** (7738 8044, www.flowers.org.uk) is an excellent source of information and advice on flowers and house plants, from plant and flower care to florists.

Absolute Flowers

12-14 Clifton Road, W9 1SS (7286 1155). Warwick Avenue tube. **Open** 8am-7pm Mon-Sat; 10am-6pm Sun. **Credit** AmEx, MC, V.

Absolutely sumptuous arrangements are created by the artists bustling about the art deco tiled interior of this chic, black shop, which acts as a perfect backdrop to the richly coloured glass vases and containers stacked to the ceiling. The shop specialises in English blooms, and bouquets are kept simple with minimal foliage. Homewares and accessories are also sold.

Angel Flowers

60 Upper Street, N1 0NY (7704 6312/ www.angel-flowers.co.uk). Angel tube. **Open** 9am-7pm Mon-Sat; 11am-5pm Sun. **Credit** AmEx, MC, V.

Marco Wouters founded this bright and breezy shop in 1995. His blooms are imported from Dutch flower markets four times per week and there's always a massive variety with which to make a dramatic bunch. There are hot tropicals and orchids and buckets full of cottage garden lovelies in season. The shop is very handsome, with its vintage lights and containers filled with colour, so it's difficult to leave without at least a pretty posy. More elaborate hand-tied bouquets cost from about £35.

For branch (The Wings) see index.

Bloomsbury Flowers

29 Great Queen Street, WC2B 5BB (7242 2840/www.bloomsburyflowers.co.uk). Covent Garden tube. **Open** 9.30am-5pm Mon; 9.30am-5.30pm Tue-Fri. **Credit** AmEx, MC, V.

A classy shop opposite the Freemasons Hall, where seasonal flowers are carefully chosen to appeal to all the senses. Dramatic and unusual arrangements made up while you wait may involve scented herbs and shiny evergreens. Good-quality standards like orchids, lilies, roses, peonies and summer sweet peas stand alongside more unusual choices such as bergamot, allium and rosemary, part of an imaginative range that changes throughout the year. Day and evening flower design courses are on offer – see the website for details.

Jane Packer Flowers

32-34 New Cavendish Street, W1G 8UE (7935 2673/www.jane-packer.co.uk). Bond Street tube. **Open** 9am-6pm Mon-Sat. **Credit** AmEx, MC, V.

Jane Packer – the florist of choice for many stars – has now become something of a household name. This sleek Marylebone store fronts her equally successful school of floristry, for evening and one-day courses where students sit with their clippers and wire learning the tricks of the trade. There's a range of own-brand candles and toiletries, unusual plants in modern containers and vases, ready-assembled arrangements in boxes (from £45) and a selection of Packer's books. A classic and dependable choice.

La Maison des Roses

48 Webbs Road, SW11 6SF (7228 5700/ www.maison-des-roses.com). Clapham South tube/Clapham Junction rail. **Open** 10am-6pm Mon-Sat. **Credit** MC, V.

A beautiful and soothing shop, where our national flower scents the rarefied air. The rose wallpaper and soft furnishings, and the bouquets, nosegays and bushes of blooms wherever you look, add to the charm. Given the flower's short season in this country, imported flowers make up most of the stock – all of it in the winter – but there's always a heady variety of species, and a lovely range of bouquets, including stunning rose hearts. Scented candles, soaps, bath oils and room sprays add to the all-pervading aroma. Dried and preserved roses are also sold.

McQueens

70-72 Old Street, EC1V 9AN (7251 5505/ www.mcqueens.co.uk). Old Street tube/rail. **Open** 8.30am-6pm Mon-Fri; 9am-3pm Sat. **Credit** MC, V.

Drop-dead gorgeous arrangements are prepared on site by impossibly glamorous students studying at this floristry school. The shop and school is very Old Street industrial chic, with a huge tree trunk laden with coloured glass bottles in the window. There's usually an enormous range of stems that can be hand tied into a bunch, with the glamourpusses – strelitzia, protea et al – alongside the more stolid natives, such as molucella (bells of Ireland) and hydrangea.

Moyses Flowers

16 Motcomb Street, SW1X 8LB (7823 2684/www.moysesflowers.co.uk). Knightsbridge tube. **Open** 10am-6pm Mon-Fri. **Credit** AmEx, MC, V.

This long-established florist prides itself on its frightfully well-bred blooms and traditional style, but is committed to sustainability, organic flower growing and Fairtrade suppliers. It's full of seasonal gorgeousness: in high summer, when we visited, there was a wealth of lovely British blooms: sweet peas, peonies, hydrangeas, aliums and cymbidiums in lovely fresh-looking bouquets. There's a Moyses concession in the Symons Street entrance of Peter Jones.

Phillo

59 Chepstow Road, W2 5BP (7727 4555/ www.philloflowers.com). Westbourne Park tube. **Open** 9.30am-8pm Mon-Fri; 9.30am-7pm Sat; 11am-5pm Sun. **Credit** AmEx, MC, V.

As if to emphasise the exotic nature of the business, the sound of squawking parrots assails your ears as you enter. Phillo is home to a dozen parrots, and there are often a couple watching beadily from behind the counter. They can't be trusted to serve yet, that's left to the reserved but polite florist, whose striking bouquets can include protea, anthurium, canna and other hot-looking babes, as well as more temperate peonies, roses and hydrangea heads. Orchids are a speciality. The rare blooms come from Ivan's Orchids (www.ivansorchids.co.uk). Cacti in trendy containers are also displayed; candles and soaps are a fragrant sideline.

Rebel Rebel

5 Broadway Market, E8 4PH (7254 4487/ www.rebelrebel.co.uk). Bethnal Green tube then 26, 48, 55 bus/London Fields rail. **Open** 10am-6pm Tue-Fri; 9am-5pm Sat. **Credit** AmEx, MC, V.

Heady in summer with the scent of sweet peas and stocks, this flower shop is run by a delightful pair called Mairead Curtin and Athena Duncan. The pretty blooms, which make full use of the English cottage garden and potager in season (there's dill, lavender and blackberry stalks as well as the more conventional peonies, delphiniums, roses, goldenrod, harebells and nigella filling the containers) are worked into generous bouquets that are the talk of Hackney's burgeoning chattering classes. They do exotic too – strelitzia, kangaroo paw, orchids and calla lilies make vivid additions to the feast. The shop's trademark is bouquets, but the tied bunches are also lovely.

Wild at Heart

Turquoise Island, 222 Westbourne Grove, W11 2RH (7727 3095/www.wildatheart.com). Notting Hill Gate tube. **Open** 8am-6pm Mon-Wed, Sat; 8am-7pmThur-Fri; 11am-3pm Sun. **Credit** AmEx, MC, V.

The Ledbury Road Wild shop sells homewares, clothing and gifts with a floral theme. Pop around the corner to Westbourne Grove for the florist: in the middle of the street stands Turquoise Island, with a designer public loo on one side and Wild at Heart on the other. It's vibrant with peonies, delphiniums, hydrangeas and sweet peas in summer, daffs, tulips and anemones in spring. Traditional English blooms are close to the Wild heart, so it's a seasonal look you'll find in its fragrant tied bunches. A new branch of Wild at Heart opened in Pimlico in September 2008, as well as a concession in Liberty (*see p16*). There's also a concession in Liverpool Street's AN*d*AZ (formerly known as the Great Eastern Hotel).
For branches see index.

Wild Bunch

17-22 Earlham Street, WC2H 9LL (7497 1200). Covent Garden or Leicester Square tube. **Open** 9.30am-7pm Mon-Sat. **Credit** AmEx, MC, V.
This flower stall has a sprawling habit with bundles of exotica such as celosia, calla and strelitzia – which earn it a good deal of attention from office bods on their way home. A mixed bunch costs about £35 but you can put together a seasonal spray of sweet peas, stocks and anemones for much less.

Also check out...

Chez Michèle

7A Stoney Street, Borough Market, SE1 9AA (7357 6133). London Bridge tube. **Open** 9am-7.30pm Mon; 9.30am-7.30pm Tue-Fri; 9am-6pm Sat. **Credit** MC, V.
Sells some highly impressive stems. It's opposite the Market Garden, a mini garden centre at Borough Market (no phone).

Chiltern Flowers

Ground Floor, Oxo Tower, Barge House Street, SE1 9PH (7928 7400/www.chilternflowers.com). Southwark tube/Waterloo tube/rail. **Open** 8am-6pm Mon-Fri; 10am-4.30pm Sat. **Credit** MC, V.
Oxo Tower's trendy flowershop is now in the hands of the Chiltern chain. Expect crowd-pleasers such as lilies and roses.
For branches see index.

Dansk Flowers

St Mary's Church, Upper Street, N1 2TX (7354 5120). Angel tube. **Open** 8am-6pm Mon; 8am-9pm Tue-Sat; 9am-6pm Sun. **Credit** MC, V.
Flowers spill out of this big, old and dark church building. Fat hand-tied bunches of, say, peonies, ranuncula, veronica and roses with assorted greenery cost from £35.
For branch see index.

Harper & Tom's

73 Clarendon Road, W11 4JF (7792 8510/www.harperandtoms.co.uk). Holland Park tube. **Open** 9am-6pm Mon-Fri. **Credit** AmEx, MC, V.
A well-known florist with a penchant for seasonal English blooms.

Heart & Soul

73 Churchfield Road, W3 6AX (8896 3331/www.heart-n-soul.co.uk). Acton Central rail. **Open** 9.30am-6pm Mon-Fri; 10.30am-5pm Sat. **Credit** AmEx, MC, V.
Hot exotica from Covent Garden Market, plus cool containers to set them in.

JW Flowers

Unit E5-9, Westminster Business Square, 1-45 Durham Street, SE11 5JH (7735 7771/www.jwflowers.com). Vauxhall tube. **Open** 8.30am-5.30pm Mon-Fri. **Credit** AmEx, MC, V.

Angel Flowers. *See p171.*

This offshoot of Jane Wadham sends out contemporary bouquets from its studios.

Kensington Flowers

3 Launceston Place, W8 5RL (7937 0268/www.kensingtonflowers.co.uk). Gloucester Road tube. **Open** 8am-5.30pm Mon-Fri. **Credit** AmEx, MC, V.
A pretty, green place for floral bunches and backyard essentials such as made-to-order hanging baskets and pots.

Kenneth Turner

www.kennethturner.com.
Bouquets, fragrances and vases online, with concessions in Fortnum & Mason, Harvey Nicks, Harrods and Selfridges.

Louise Taylor Flowers

135 Dulwich Road, SE24 0NG (7737 6565/www.louisetaylor-flowers.co.uk). Herne Hill rail. **Open** 9am-6pm Mon-Fri; 10am-6pm Sat; 11am-3pm Sun. **Credit** AmEx, MC, V.
A large shop where florists show off their skills with displays for parties and weddings, but a bunch can be made up for you for £15.

Paula Pryke Flowers

The Flower House, 3-5 Cynthia Street, N1 9JF (7837 7336/www.paula-pryke-flowers.com). Angel tube. **Open** 8am-6pm Mon-Sat. **Credit** AmEx, MC, V.
Mostly events here, so not much to see, but there are concessions at Liberty, Selfridges and Michelin House (81 Fulham Road).

Pemizett

115 Parkway, NW1 7PS (7388 4466). Camden Town tube. **Open** 8am-7pm Mon-Sat. **Credit** MC, V.
Pem Izet runs this eye-catching store. He also creates bold designs for Harvey Nichols, hotels and society weddings.

Pesh Flowers

31-31A Denmark Hill, SE5 8RS (7703 9124/www.peshflowers.co.uk). Denmark Hill rail. **Open** 7.30am-5.30pm Mon; 8am-5.30pm Tue-Fri; 8am-5pm Sat. **Credit** MC, V.
Elaine Boon's pretty shop has been creating lovely bunches for about 40 years. Good for seasonal faves.

Stem & Petal Company

132 Northcote Road, SW11 6QZ (7924 3238). Clapham Junction rail. **Open** 9am-6pm Mon-Sat; 11am-3pm Sun. **Credit** AmEx, MC, V.
The eclectic collection of seasonal and exotic blooms is supplemented by thyme, rosemary and tomato plants in the summer.

William Clarke Flowers

26 Seymour Place, W1H 7NN (7402 3399/www.williamclarkeflowers.com). **Open** 9am-5pm Mon-Fri.
Glorious made-to-order bouquets and gifts.

Woodhams

45 Elizabeth Street, SW1W 9PP (7730 3353/www.woodhams.co.uk). Victoria tube/rail. **Open** 9am-6pm Mon-Fri; 10am-4pm Sat. **Credit** AmEx, MC, V.
An elegant shop for bunches, pot-grown orchids and architectural plants. Also offers a design and maintenance service.

Streetwise

Columbia Road

Come on a Sunday for the popular flower market and a winning array of quirky, one-off shops.

If you can drag yourself out of bed on Sunday morning and stagger down to Hackney's Columbia Road, you'll find London's sweetest-scented and most colourful market, with flower stalls, trendy locals and an excellent range of boutique-style shops. If you want to avoid the crowds and you're not after any blooms, many of the shops also open on Saturday afternoons – though the lively Sunday exchanges are often the best part of the experience.

The market is open from 8am until 2pm. Given the early start needed to bag the choicest bouquets, you might need sustenance first: starting from the Haggerston Park end of the street, turn right when you reach Ezra Street, next to the Royal Oak pub. Here is a delightful little square with a festival atmosphere. It's a great place to gather, eat delicious treats and listen to the buskers. Grab some breakfast at characterful **Jones Dairy Café**, next to the **Jones Dairy Provisions** store (*see p239*) or wander down to the yard where stalls tout vintage items – one stand serves up a hearty breakfast.

If you're looking for upmarket homewares, **Wawa** (*see p126*) sells customised handmade sofas, lamps and the ever desirable Mimi bags and purses. On your way back up Ezra Street to Columbia Road, you pass **Hot & Tottenham** (14 Ezra Street, 7729 9181) a small new studio-shop that sells photography books and prints.

You mustn't miss a mooch in the Courtyard, also on Ezra Street. There you can drool in **B Southgate** (4 The Courtyard, 07905 960792), which sells restored furniture and ephemera, and check out the art in **Columbia Road Gallery** (no.7, 07812 196257), where Sam Marshall's tiny framed etchings of classic British scenes start from £40.

Back on Columbia Road, you'll be swept along by the market throng. When you've had your fill of flower traders, check out the attractive shops that run either side of the street.

This end of Columbia Road is best for art. **Elphick's** (no.160, 7033 7891) deals in mixed media work; Rob Clarke's slightly unsettling bird paintings start at £188. **Nelly Duff** (no.156, www.nellyduff.com) has an affordable array of more graphic art, and **Start Space** (no.150, 7729 0522) showcases large-scale paintings and photography.

L'Orangerie is an accessories shop on the corner of Barnet Grove (no.162, 8983 7873). Gems, including chunky bead necklaces, trendy straw sun-visors and fat glass rings, can get a bit lost among the vast quantities of merchandise, but the staff are friendly and it's worth a rummage. At no.152 is **Open House** (07979 851593), a pretty shop selling reproduction home- and gardenwares. **Marcos & Trump** (no.146, *see p58*) has a gorgeous, decadent interior displaying carefully chosen vintage women's clothes and accessories. Sweet-toothers can indulge at old-fashioned sweetshop **Suck & Chew** (no.130, 8983 3504) and cup cake and retro kitchenware shop **Treacle** (nos.110-112, 7729 5657).

Columbia Road institution **Milagros** (no.61, *see p149*) offers a wonderful selection of Mexican curiosities and trinkets. Particularly covetable are the *retablos* (allegorical folk art) and the Day of the Dead paper banners.

Franklin & Alvarez is at no.53 (07737 517252). Bev and Jen make unique clothes and jewellery from mostly recycled sources. Jen's delicate silver necklaces (from £35) have tiny pendants of wooden mushrooms, while Bev uses vintage fabric to make her charming children's and womenswear.

Ryantown (no.126, *see p166*) is one of the newest – and loveliest – additions to the street. Rob Ryan's crafty motifs cover tiles, perspex keys, giant floor-standing rulers, screenprints and mugs. He's also teamed up with the ever-fabulous Clothkits, so you can even wear one of his beautiful designs. **Fred Bare** (no.118; *see p78*) has a lovely selection of hats, from quirky contemporary to classic.

Opposite Fred Bare at no.49 is the **Fleapit** café, which proffers delicious vegetarian food and organic juices. **Supernice** (no.106, 7613 3890) has Blik wall art (removable stickers for your walls; from £20) in a great range from robots to birds on telegraph wires. Thomas Paul melamine plates and trays sell from £6.

You're coming to the end of the main drag, but don't miss **Vintage Heaven** (no.82, 01277 215968, http://vintage heaven.co.uk) just before the junction with Cosset Street. Poke around to find vintage kitchen and garden treasures. Further on, past the residential flats, at the junction with Hackney Road, is **Two Columbia Road** (*see p162*), a stalwart for 20th-century furniture.

Leisure

Leisure

Playlounge. *See p209.*

Audio Gold. *See p199.*

Bridgewood & Neitzert. *See p215.*

Cass Art. *See p205.*

Gosh. *See p182.*

Design Museum. *See p204.*

Books

General & local

Central branches of the big chains include **Books etc** (263-265 High Holborn, WC1V 7EE, 7404 0261, www.bordersstores.co.uk), **Borders Books & Music** (203 Oxford Street, W1D 2LE, 7292 1600, www.bordersstores.co.uk), the massive **Waterstone's** flagship (203-206 Piccadilly, SW1Y 6WW, 7851 2400, www.waterstones.co.uk), which has a bar/restaurant, and the academic bookseller **Blackwell's** (100 Charing Cross Road, WC2H 0JG, 7292 5100, www.blackwell.co.uk).

Daunt (*see p188*) is also an excellent general bookseller, while the **British Library Bookshop** (British Library, 96 Euston Road, NW1 2DB, 7412 7735, www.bl.uk/bookshop) stocks some good literature and history titles based on the collections.

Big Green Bookshop

Unit 1, Brampton Park Road, Wood Green, N22 6BG (8881 6767/www.woodgreenbookshop.blogspot.com). Turnpike Lane tube. **Open** 9.30am-6pm Mon-Tue, Thur-Sat; 10.30am-6pm Wed; 11am-5pm Sun. **Credit** AmEx, MC, V.

A bookshop deserving of accolades, Big Green Bookshop is a community effort in every way. The owners decided to go it alone when the only bookshop in Wood Green, a Waterstone's, closed down. They enlisted locals to help them turn a defunct internet café into a bookshop in a little over two weeks, and when it launched in March 2008 decisions regarding the shop's name, stock and events were made by the customers themselves. In return, patrons have access to a comfy sofa, free coffee and wonderfully enthusiastic staff. As well as a fine stock of local bookshop usuals, it's strong on children's titles, multicultural books and fiction. There are weekly writer's workshops and children's author events, parent and toddler mornings and the odd festival (crime was the theme in 2008). The energy is infectious.

Bolingbroke

147 Northcote Road, SW11 6QB (7223 9344/www.bolingbrokebookshop.co.uk). Clapham Junction rail/319 bus. **Open** 9.30am-6pm Mon-Sat; 11am-5pm Sun. **Credit** AmEx, MC, V.

The latest big news at Bolingbroke (named after a local 18th-century political agitator) is the installation of a steam engine in the children's room. It's the sort of personal touch that has helped owner Michael Gibbs – who's also an amateur pilot and cellist – maintain a successful business for the past 27 years. His bookshop doubles up as a neighbourhood communications hub (there's a free noticeboard on the front window), and local reading groups receive discounts. Stock is varied, with much of it arranged by publisher – the *Pevsner Architectural Guides* to Britain, books from Eland Press and women's writing from Persephone (*see p188* and *p187* **Unique Selling Point**) are the source of some interesting titles here. There's also a large selection of coffee-table books and greetings cards.

Broadway Bookshop

6 Broadway Market, E8 4QJ (7241 1626/www.broadwaybookshophackney.com). London Fields rail/26, 55 bus. **Open** 10am-6pm Tue-Sat; 11am-5pm Sun. **Credit** MC, V.

This Broadway Market independent benefits from its position alongside the Saturday farmers' market and from its proximity to the canal. A smart layout and intelligently weighed stock boost its appeal further. The Broadway Bookshop is a thoughtful enterprise, promoting small publishers like Eland and stocking lots of *New York Review* titles, plus interesting reprints of forgotten gems. There's plenty of top-drawer literary fiction – among recent in-store signings are locals Ronan Bennet and Iain Sinclair – and a large travel section that's strong on London and local history. The second-hand collectibles have become more popular since last year, with punters keen to get their hands on old Penguins and 1930s and '40s hardbacks. The shop is also a permanent exhibition space, promoting local artists.

Crockatt & Powell

345 Fulham Road, SW10 9TW (7351 3468/www.crockattandpowell.com). South Kensington/Fulham Broadway tube. **Open** 9am-7pm Mon, Tue, Thur, Fri; 9am-9pm Wed; 10am-7pm Sat, Sun. **Credit** AmEx, MC, V.

While Crockatt & Powell's main branch is in Waterloo, there's a new kid on the block: the Chelsea store opened in May 2008, triggered by the closure of Pan Bookshop. Some of Pan's expert booksellers can now be found plying their trade a few doors away from the defunct shop, in this fine local. The branch boasts a great selection of mainly literary books, a dedicated children's room, a garden where you can sit and ponder at leisure and an excellent book ordering service. For monthly book groups, head to the Waterloo shop.

For branch see index.

Foyles

113-119 Charing Cross Road, WC2H 0EB (7437 5660/www.foyles.co.uk). Tottenham Court Road tube. **Open** 9.30am-9pm Mon-Sat; 11.30am-6pm Sun. **Credit** AmEx, MC, V.

Probably the single most impressive independent bookshop in London (and UK Bookseller of the Year 2008 according to the British Book Industry Awards), Foyles built its reputation on the sheer volume and breadth of its stock (with 56 specialist subjects in the flagship store). It boasts four stores in central London, following the recent opening of a branch at St Pancras International station, and a fifth is on its way to White City – due to open in December 2008. Its five hugely comprehensive storeys accommodate other shops too: there's Ray's Jazz and café and a fine concession of Unsworth's antiquarian booksellers. Fiction at Foyles should be lauded along with an impressive range of teaching materials, computing software and the comprehensive basement medical department. Elsewhere, there's an extensive music department, a large gay-interest section, an impressive range of foreign fiction, law and business, philosophy and sport. The shop hosts regular events featuring well-known faces like John Gray, Billy Bragg and Sophie Dahl (visit the website for more details).

For branches see index.

Hatchards

187 Piccadilly, W1J 9LE (7439 9921/www.hatchards.co.uk). Piccadilly Circus tube. **Open** 9.30am-7pm Mon-Sat; noon-6pm Sun. **Credit** AmEx, DC, MC, V.

Holding court with Fortnum & Mason and other Piccadilly royalty is London's oldest bookshop, dating back to 1797. Its old-school charm and refined aura have helped it maintain an ambience all its own and it's particularly good for travel and biography, new hardback fiction and signed editions. Benjamin Disraeli, Lord Byron and Oscar Wilde are former fans. These days, celebrated authors come to sign the books – recent visitors include Salman Rushdie and Michael Palin. Mowbray Religious booksellers is located on the third floor.

John Sandoe

10 Blacklands Terrace, SW3 2SR (7589 9473/www.johnsandoe.com). Sloane Square tube. **Open** 9.30am-5.30pm Mon, Tue, Thur-Sat; 9.30am-7.30pm Wed; noon-6pm Sun. **Credit** AmEx, DC, MC, V.

The paragon of independent local bookshops celebrated its 50th birthday in 2007, although John Sandoe, the founder, has sadly passed away. His legacy is one of the best local bookshops in London with a loyal and ever-growing clientele, professional staff and enviably broad stock. New and classic releases rub spines with more unusual items – books with no ISBN or that have been privately printed, for example. These are bought safe in the knowledge that certain customers will be interested – a testament to the personal relationship here between staff and visitors. There's a high proportion of quality hardbacks, a very full travel section upstairs and a fun children's section in the basement. Half the ground floor is devoted to art, photography and architecture.

Top ten Shop cafés

Aperture. *See p220.*
Books for Cooks. *See p181.*
Brill. *See p189.*
Coffee, Cake & Kink. *See p201.*
Bamford & Sons' Daylesford Organic Café. *See p28.*
London Review Bookshop. *See p178.*
Foyles' first-floor café. *See p177* and *p193.*
Rough Trade East's Progresso Café. *See p189.*
Dover Street Market's Rose Bakery. *See p19.*

Kew Bookshop

1-2 Station Approach, Richmond, Surrey TW9 3QB (8940 0030). Kew Gardens tube. **Open** 10am-6pm Mon-Sat; noon-6pm Sun. **Credit** AmEx, DC, MC, V.

Located on a charming crescent that connects Kew station to Kew Gardens, Kew Bookshop makes the most of its prime position and cultured locale (the National Archives is another near-neighbour). Manager Mark Brighton and his staff have a keen eye for literary quality and you can happily pop in and pass the time discussing the relative merits of recent publications. Given the suburban setting and pram-dense populace, it's no surprise that half the shop is dedicated to an impressive children's section. Brighton's partner runs the Barnes Bookshop in SW13 with much the same ethos.

For branch see index.

Kilburn Bookshop

8 Kilburn Bridge, Kilburn High Road, NW6 6HT (7328 7071). Kilburn High Road rail. **Open** 10am-6pm Mon-Sat. **Credit** MC, V.

Widely believed to be London's number one specialist in Irish literature, Kilburn Bookshop also orders in large quantities of African-American work. Its intrepid experimenting with new authors RM Johnson, Teri Woods and Brenda Jackson has gone down well with the customer base. There's also a good travel guides section that has expanded in the last few years. Located at the smarter end of Kilburn High Road, this shop has survived and prospered for 25 years, priding itself on friendliness and customer service; it's easy to see why it's a success.

For branch (Willesden Bookshop) see index.

Foyles. *See p177.*

London Review Bookshop

14 Bury Place, WC1A 2JL (7269 9030/ www.lrbshop.co.uk). Holborn or Tottenham Court Road tube. **Open** 10am-6.30pm Mon-Sat; noon-6pm Sun. **Credit** AmEx, MC, V.

London Review Bookshop celebrated half a decade's trading in 2008, proving itself the capital's most precociously intelligent and charming five-year-old. If you're looking for a place to inspire you to get reading then this is it, from the inviting and stimulating presentation to the clear quality of the books chosen. Politics, current affairs and history are well represented on the ground floor, while downstairs, books on CD lead on to thorough and exciting poetry and philosophy sections – everything you'd expect from a shop owned by the *London Review of Books*. The LRB's events programme has seen authors such as Martin Amis, Christopher Hitchens and Anne Enright visit, while all sorts of writers and journalists stop by at the adjoining London Review Cake Shop, a breezy coffeeshop that displays original art. The shop also sells second-hand books, mainly modern first editions, and co-publishes signed limited editions by writers such as Julian Barnes and Ian McEwan.

Owl Bookshop

209 Kentish Town Road, NW5 2JU (7485 7793). Kentish Town tube/rail. **Open** 9.30am-6pm Mon-Sat; noon-4.30pm Sun. **Credit** AmEx, MC, V.

A clever rearrange has made Kentish Town's Owl Bookshop easier to negotiate: classic fiction has been given room to expand and there are now some armchairs to help you relax while you mull over your choices. Trading for a good three decades, the shop covers food and drink, gardening, sport and fiction, with all stock judiciously laid out. There's a strong children's section to the right as you come in and a smart selection of stationery and magazines for sale. Owl also stocks some DVDs (mainly cult and classic films) and CDs, (particularly classical, world music and jazz). You can combine fiction and non-fiction in the popular four-for-three promotions. All in all, a valuable local resource in this part of north London.

Primrose Hill Books

134 Regent's Park Road, NW1 8XL (7586 2022/www.primrosehillbooks.co.uk). Chalk Farm tube. **Open** 9.30am-6pm Mon-Fri; 10am-6pm Sat; 11am-6pm Sun. **Credit** AmEx, MC, V.

One of the highlights of this enclave of independent shops and restaurants, Primrose Hill Books has been serving the local community for over 20 years. In that time, owner Jessica Graham has come to know many of her customers – some of whom end up signing the books: Alan Bennet, Martin Amis and Isabel Fonseca are all locals and visit on a regular basis. Journalists, authors and publishers make up much of the population in this area of London, and the shop's strengths – principally literary fiction,

biography and travel – mirror this. Handfuls of second-hand books in trolleys outside are dwarfed by the 10,000 second-hand items actually held here (out of sight in the basement). Visit the website for a catalogue.

Review

131 Bellenden Road, SE15 4QY (7639 7400). Peckham Rye rail. **Open** 10am-7pm Tue-Sat; 11am-6pm Sun. **Credit** MC, V.
Ultra-friendly Ros Simpson's small-but-perfectly-formed bookshop has become an essential Peckham resource in the three years since it opened. The bohemian atmosphere at Review has tapped into the community spirit, in an area populated by a good number of designers, artists and architects. Stock leans towards arts and design, though it also encompasses literary fiction and children's books and there's a solid stash of creative periodicals like *Cabinet* and *Ceramic Review*. The little garden area in front of the shop features backgammon and chess tables sculpted by the owner's artist partner. The coffee machine and resident whippet Gus add to the charm.

Village Books

1D Calton Avenue, SE21 7DE (8693 2808). North Dulwich rail. **Open** 9am-5.30pm Mon-Sat; 11am-5pm Sun.
Credit MC, V.
With two former Waterstone's directors at the helm, this Dulwich bookshop had a great start to life and has consistently built on those auspicious beginnings; indeed, it recently claimed the accolade of Best Bookshop in the South East at the British Book Industry Awards. Situated near six schools, Village Books' activity list caters for youngsters: as well as producing summer and Christmas reading lists for children, it organises a children's fair in April, with writers Andy Stanton and Helen Banmore making past appearances. The shop also promotes local comedians-cum-writers Jo Brand and Jenny Éclair, and knowledgeable staff are very happy to help with recommendations.
For branch see index.

West End Lane Books

277 West End Lane, NW6 1QS, (7431 3770/www.westendlanebooks.co.uk). West Hampstead tube. **Open** 9am-9pm Mon-Fri; 9.30am-6.30pm Sat; noon-6pm Sun. **Credit** AmEx, DC, MC, V.
This spacious and airy West Hampstead indie is a pleasure to browse in. A bookshop has stood here for over 14 years, but the current incarnation is the most impressive, with intelligent choices gracing the display tables and well-ordered shelves. The shop has strong holdings in poetry and – thanks to the local demographic – Jewish interest. It orders many of its books direct from America, so there's some stuff here you might not otherwise be able to find.

Art & design

London's main art galleries, such as **Tate Britain**, **Tate Modern**, the **Design Museum**, as well as the **National Gallery**, should also be first ports-of-call for books on art.

Artwords Bookshop

65A Rivington Street, EC2A 3QQ (7729 2000/www.artwords.co.uk). Old Street tube/rail. **Open** 10.30am-7pm daily. **Credit** AmEx, MC, V.
Partly thanks to its location in artist-dense Hoxton but also due to its knowledgeable staff, Artwords has its finger firmly on the pulse when it comes to contemporary visual arts publications. As well as offering a vast collection of up-to-date books from the UK, the shop regularly imports new works from Europe, North America and Australia. Stock relating to contemporary fine art dominates, but there are also plenty of architecture, photography, graphic design, fashion, advertising and film titles, plus a range of DVDs and industry and creative magazines – including the Eastern European import *Piktogram*, the painting-specialist *TurpsBanana* and the interdisciplinary *Cabinet*.

Blenheim Books

11 Blenheim Crescent, W11 2EE (7792 0777/www.blenheimbooks.co.uk). Notting Hill Gate tube. **Open** 9am-6pm Mon-Sat; noon-5pm Sun. **Credit** MC, V.
One of many pleasant semi-specialist bookshops in this well-heeled area (others include the Travel Bookshop, *see p188*, and Books for Cooks, *see p181*), the impressive collection of gardening books reminds visitors that this was formerly a gardening specialist. It's diversified since the current owner took over in 1996, and now has a

well-selected collection of books on graphics, interiors, architecture, fashion and photography. The shop promotes local authors – novelist Poppy Adams launched *The Behaviour of Moths* here.

Bookartbookshop
17 Pitfield Street, N1 6HB (7608 1333/ www.bookartbookshop.com). Old Street tube/rail. **Open** 1-7pm Wed-Fri; noon-6pm Sat. **Credit** MC, V.
A shop of books about artists' books: it's unique and we love it. This fascinating Hoxton shop aims to 'interrogate the conceptual and material form of the book' – and to have a lot of fun in the process. *The Soap Opera* sees sentences printed on linen and encased in blocks of soap – wash your hands to reveal parts of a story; *The Six Clubs* is a collection of prose about the blank page. And for the post-structuralist who has everything, how about some pop-up pornography or Sally Alatalo's 'alphabetised' Mills & Boon? Bookartbookshop was founded by artist Tanya Peixoto to provide a permanent outlet for small-press publishers and, though space is tight, the shop is the main UK supplier of Continental book art.

Koenig Books
80 Charing Cross Road, WC2 0BF (7240 8190/www.koenigbooks.co.uk). Leicester Square tube. **Open** 10am-8pm Mon-Wed, Fri, Sat; 10am-9pm Thur; noon-6pm Sun. **Credit** MC, V.
An inspiring, German-owned independent bookshop specialising in art, architecture and photography tomes. Koenig's first London branch is based in the Serpentine Gallery, and the other is the newest addition to the capital's traditional literary artery – Charing Cross Road. The latter shop is done out stylishly in black and every book is given respectful prominence – products are displayed with their covers rather than spines facing customers to ensure their full effect. Both branches of Koenig have full access to the stock of mammoth arts bookshop Buchhandlung Walther Koenig in Cologne, so can order you just about anything you can think of.
For branch see index.

Magma
117-119 Clerkenwell Road, EC1R 5BY (7242 9503/www.magmabooks.com). Chancery Lane tube/Farringdon tube/ rail. **Open** 10am-7pm Mon-Sat. **Credit** AmEx, MC, V.
There's all the design, architecture, graphics and creative magazines you could want here, but the main stock is large-format art and design books. Its objective is to blur the boundary between bookshop and exhibition space, making visits interactive and educational experiences. As well as the usual look-at-me coffee-table books, there are lots of in-depth essay collections, plus obscure and fun tomes. If you can visualise it, there's probably a book on it here, with stock covering everything from Banksy to less predictable items like *Custom Kicks* (about customised trainers). There are also numerous unbookish design-related items, such as the blank toys that you can make your own and a popular T-shirt range. Try the nearby arty products sister store for trendy bicycle clips, Moomin-print kitchenware or Hayao Miyazaki (*Spirited Away*) stuffed toys.
For branches see index.

Shipley
70 Charing Cross Road, WC2H 0BQ (7836 4872/www.artbook.co.uk). Leicester Square tube. **Open** 10am-6pm Mon-Sat. **Credit** AmEx, MC, V.
Until recently, Shipley's art bookshops were spread over two stores with slightly different emphases; two have become one with this branch. The original stock – books on fine art, architecture and antiques – has now been joined by highlights from the other collection – books on photography, graphic and interior design, film and fashion, plus photographers' monographs and scattered theory and technical books. The collection spans Tracey Emin right back to early rock art. The shelves, many of which are usefully labelled by country/region, carry stock that includes catalogue resumés and old exhibition books. The clientele includes students, critics and artists and staff are all artists in their own right, so you know you're in safe hands.

Also check out...

Dover Bookshop
18 Earlham Street, WC2H 9LG (7836 2111/www.doverbooks.co.uk). Covent Garden or Leicester Square tube. **Open** 10am-6pm Mon-Wed; 10am-7pm Thur-Sat; 1-5pm Sun. **Credit** AmEx, MC, V.
Copyright- and permission-free images.

Nog Gallery
182 Brick Lane, E1 6SA (7739 4134/ www.noggallery.com). Aldgate East tube. **Open** 11am-7pm daily. **Credit** AmEx, MC, V.
Alternative design bookshop/gallery hybrid.

Photo Books International
99 Judd Street, WC1H 9NE (7813 7363/ www.pbi-books.com). King's Cross tube/ rail. **Open** 11am-6pm Wed-Sat. **Credit** AmEx, MC, V.
Superb range of photography monographs.

Children

See chapter **Babies & Children**, *pp258-267*. For collectible children's books, head to **Marchpane** and **Nigel Williams** (for both, *see p186*) and **Ripping Yarns** (*see p188*). Many locals, such as the **Kew Bookshop** (*see p178*) devote large areas to children's books.

Cinema & theatre

David Drummond at Pleasures of Past Times (*see p188*) sells second-hand and rare books on theatre and performing arts.

Cinema Store
4B Orion House, Upper St Martin's Lane, WC2H 9NY (7379 7838/www. thecinemastore.co.uk). Leicester Square tube. **Open** 10am-6.30pm Mon-Wed, Sat; 10am-7pm Thur, Fri; 11am-5pm Sun. **Credit** AmEx, MC, V.
Books on all aspects of the silver screen.

French's Theatre Bookshop
52 Fitzroy Street, W1T 5JR (7255 4300/ www.samuelfrench-london.co.uk). Warren Street tube. **Open** 9.30am-5.30pm Mon-Fri; 11am-5pm Sat. **Credit** AmEx, MC, V.
Playscripts, stagecraft and theatre history.

Offstage Theatre & Cinema Bookshop
34 Tavistock Street, WC2E 7PB (7240 3883). Covent Garden tube. **Open** noon-6pm Mon-Fri. **Credit** AmEx, MC, V.
Eclectic collection of titles with a firm emphasis on the arts.

Cookery

Books for Cooks
4 Blenheim Crescent, W11 1NN (7221 1992/www.booksforcooks.com). Ladbroke Grove/Notting Hill Gate tube. **Open** 10am-6pm Tue-Sat. **Credit** MC, V.
The astute book shopper will have noticed the number of London bookshops opening coffeeshops to attract customers. Books for Cooks puts them all to shame – it has its own kitchen in the back, where recipes from a massive stock of cookery books are put to the test and sold from midday (no reservations). The most successful of them are compiled into the shop's own publications (£5.99 each). The front room is stacked high with books covering hundreds of cuisines, chefs and cookery techniques, as well as food-related fiction, culinary history, foodie biographies and nutrition. The Authors' Lunch series is going strong – the likes of Tessa Kiros, Jay Raynor and Mark Hix demonstrate how to make a three-course meal from one of their books; evening classes are another way to get stuck in (see website for details).

Fashion & magazines

RD Franks
5 Winsley Street, W1W 8HG (7636 1244/www.rdfranks.co.uk). Oxford Circus tube. **Open** 9am-6pm Mon-Fri. **Credit** AmEx, MC, V.
In business since 1877, RD Franks is beloved of the city's fashion students. Books cover everything from pattern-cutting techniques to sartorial history.

Vintage Magazine Store
39-43 Brewer Street, W1F 9UD (7439 8525/www.vinmag.com). Piccadilly Circus tube. **Open** 10am-8pm Mon-Thur; 10am-10pm Fri, Sat; noon-8pm Sun. **Credit** MC, V.
More than 250,000 vintage magazines from the 1930s onwards, plus memorabilia.

Gay & lesbian

Foyles (*see p177*) has a large gay-interest section.

Gay's the Word

66 Marchmont Street, WC1N 1AB (7278 7654/www.gaystheword.co.uk). Russell Square tube. **Open** 10am-6.30pm Mon-Sat; 2-6pm Sun. **Credit** AmEx, DC, MC, V.

Britain's only dedicated gay and lesbian bookshop – established in 1979 – has bounced back from the downer that was 2007, when it almost closed. The shop launched a shelf-sponsorship programme called Cash for Honours, which drew support from loyal customers including Sarah Waters, Ali Smith and Simon Callow. Stock covers fiction, history and biography, as well as more specialist holdings in queer studies, sex and relationships, children, and parenting. In addition to regular author readings and book-signings (think Adam Mars-Jones, Armistead Maupin, Neil Bartlett, Clare Summerskill), there are weekly lesbian and monthly trans discussion groups. Look out for a relaunch of the website in late 2008.

Genre fiction & comics

For **Forbidden Planet**, *see p209*.

Gosh!

39 Great Russell Street, WC1B 3NZ (7636 1011/www.goshlondon.com). Tottenham Court Road tube. **Open** 10am-6pm Mon-Wed, Sat, Sun; 10am-7pm Thur, Fri. **Credit** MC, V.

What with the Natalie Portman *V for Vendetta*, a slew of Marvel-hero movies and a *Watchmen* film in the pipeline, there's never been a better time to take up reading comics – and there's nowhere better to bolster your collection than at this Bloomsbury specialist. Half of the basement room is given over to comics while the other holds a fine stash of Manga. It's graphic novels that take centre stage, though, from early classics like *Krazy Kat* and *Little Nemo* to Alan Moore's recent Peter Pan adaptation *Lost Girls*. The legendary Moore is one of many high-profile authors to have signed here. Bryan Talbot (*Alice in Sunderland*) is another. Gosh! has begun to sell exclusive bookplated editions of some works – authors sign tip-in sheets that collectors can then add to their copies; plates upcoming when we visited included Mike Mignola and Duncan Fregredo's *Hellboy: Darkness Calls*, Nick Abadzis's *Laika* and Gilbert Shelton's *Complete Fabulous Furry Freak Brothers Omnibus*. Classic children's books, of the *This is London* vein, are also a plus point here.

Murder One

76-78 Charing Cross Road, WC2H 0BD (7539 8820/www.murderone.co.uk). Leicester Square tube. **Open** 10am-7pm Mon-Wed; 10am-8pm Thur-Sat; noon-6pm Sun. **Credit** AmEx, MC, V.

This distinctive Charing Cross Road bookshop celebrated its 20th anniversary

Collectomania

An American lady rang one London bookseller in 2008 to ask for a signed, first-edition *Harry Potter* for her nephew's eighth birthday; she paid a staggering £25,000, then rang again the next week to request another for her niece. We're not sure if this anecdote should be shelved under crime or horror, but we do know you can build up your own unique book collection using more sense than money.

The experts are unanimous in their advice: collect what you love, and what interests you. Bookseller **Simon Finch** (*see p186*) says: 'There will always be a market for a collection that is passionately and intelligently created, however obscure. Be driven by your passion and your collection will reflect that brilliance.' Sophie Williams from **Nigel Williams** (*see p186*) agrees: 'Books go in and out of fashion. If you are left with the works of Richmal Crompton at least you can be thrilled about that.' In other words, don't see your purchases as an investment: the best collections are created by genuine enthusiasts.

But how to get started? 'There's no substitute for handling items and talking to dealers,' advises Adam Douglas from **Peter Harrington** (*see p186*). Once you've visited the shops in this chapter, the next step is to head to one of London's book fairs, the most prestigious of which is the **Antiquarian Book Fair** (www.olympiabookfair.com), run by the **Antiquarian Booksellers' Association** (www.abainternational.com). The ABA also runs the **Chelsea Book Fair** (www.chelseabookfair.com) in November. You need to get a feel for the sorts of items that interest you, whether it's leather-bound Dickens pressings or illustrated children's books.

Simon Finch

Once you know your field, you can begin visiting auction houses like the approachable **Bloomsbury Auctions** (www.bloomsburyauctions.com, 7495 9494), and using websites such as **www.addall.com** (though the descriptions of books are not always entirely accurate online). Most dealers advise you to buy the best condition that you can afford, though some believe that any book in any condition is interesting.

From this point, a collection can be built up in a number of ways. You might shape it around a subject, a broad time period, an author, a publisher (Penguin has an avid fanclub at www.penguincollectorssociety.org), or even a particular printer. Alternatively, you could put together a collection of books from a certain year and see what happens when you create a cross-section of a time-specific event. You'll soon start to see interesting links emerging, which may in turn inform your next purchases, or lead you in new directions.

So it's not all about modern firsts and expensive famous titles. That said, Simon Finch interrupted his honeymoon to buy a copy of *Don Quixote*, which he later sold for a cool $2 million. It remains to be seen if young Potter will last this sort of distance.

in 2008 and remains almost certainly the largest bookshop of its kind in Europe. The specialism here is crime and detective fiction. The goal: to stock every crime title in print in the UK and US. An entire section is devoted to Agatha Christie on the ground floor, while downstairs there are miles of Sherlock Holmes-related books filling the shelves. Also in the basement are graphic novels, crime reference guides, periodicals and magazines. Anthologies, videos and DVDs are also available and the shop's smart layout makes everything easy to locate. Staff know their stuff, and are always up for a chat. A whole section is also given over to romance: let your heart lead you to such titles as *Bedding the Heiress* or *Dial M for Mischief*.

Also check out...

Fantasy Centre

157 Holloway Road, N7 8LX (7607 9433/ www.fantasycentre.biz). Holloway Road tube/Highbury & Islington tube/rail. **Open** 10am-6pm Mon-Sat. **Credit** MC, V.
Sci-fi, fantasy and horror specialists.

Mega City Comics

18 Inverness Street, NW1 7HJ (7485 9320/www.megacitycomics.co.uk). Camden Town tube. **Open** 10am-6pm Mon-Wed, Fri-Sun; 10am-7pm Thur. **Credit** MC, V.
Strong on comics, with lots of graphic novels too.

Orbital Comics & Collectibles

148 Charing Cross Road, WC2H 0LB (7240 7672/www.orbitalcomics.com). Tottenham Court Road tube. **Open** 10.30am-7pm Mon-Wed, Fri, Sat; 10.30am-7.30pm Thur; 11.30am-5pm Sun.
Credit AmEx, MC, V.
Underground comics and graphic novels. Alan Moore was signing on our latest visit.

International & languages

Arthur Probsthain

41 Great Russell Street, WC1B 3PE (7636 1096/www.oriental-african-books.com). Tottenham Court Road tube. **Open** 9.30am-5.30pm Mon-Fri; noon-4pm Sat. **Credit** AmEx, DC, MC, V.
Arthur Probsthain has specialised in books on African, Asian and Middle Eastern topics since as far back as 1903. The shop has recently undergone refurbishment and looks all the better for it: new floors and shelving give the store a more welcoming feel and the original Chinese paintings on the walls (for sale) have brightened the place up. This branch concentrates on art, religion, literature and language – it's the place to come if you want to learn Tibetan, Zulu or colloquial Yoruba. The branch within the nearby School of Oriental & African Studies (SOAS) stocks the more academic and political tomes. Book launches held at the Great Russell Street branch are primarily of academic and specialist interest, though display tables often tie in with exhibitions at the British Museum. Rumour has it a café may be up and running by early 2009.
For branch (SOAS bookshop) see index.

Grant & Cutler

55-57 Great Marlborough Street, W1F 7AY (7734 2012/www.grantandcutler.com). Oxford Circus tube. **Open** 9.30am-6.30pm Mon-Wed, Fri; 9.30am-7pm Thur; 9.30am-6pm Sat; noon-6pm Sun. **Credit** MC, V.
Offering an exhaustive collection (some 55,000 items) of foreign-language books, reference works and teaching aids in more than 150 languages, Grant & Cutler is an essential resource for language students and their profs. Much of the material is for hardcore study, but there are interesting translations too. French is still the biggest section, with Spanish snapping at its toes; the Eastern European languages section is also strong (and includes items like the UK driving theory test in Polish). Elsewhere there's Scrabble in several languages and international films on DVD. G&C was set up in 1936 as a lending library, which may explain its dull decor. Amuse yourself by working out how many languages your shop assistant speaks.

Also check out...

European Bookshop

5 Warwick Street, W1B 5LU (7734 5259/ www.eurobooks.co.uk). Piccadilly Circus tube. **Open** 9.30am-6pm Mon-Sat.
Credit AmEx, MC, V.
A massive range of European-language titles and language-learning textbooks.
For branch (the Italian Bookshop) see index.

French Bookshop

28 Bute Street, SW7 3EX (7584 2840/ www.frenchbookshop.com). South Kensington tube. **Open** 8.15am-6.30pm Mon-Fri; 10am-6.30pm Sat. **Credit** MC, V.
French authors and translations, including children's books and CD-Roms.

Librairie/Papeterie La Page

7 Harrington Road, SW7 3ES (7589 5991/www.librairielapage.com). South Kensington tube. **Open** 8.15am-6.30pm Mon-Fri; 10am-6pm Sat. **Credit** AmEx, MC, V.
French literature and kids' books, plus CDs and DVDs. Established in 1978, the shop was relaunched by a new owner in 2008.

Maghreb Bookshop

45 Burton Street, WC1H 9AL (7388 1840/ www.maghrebbookshop.com). Euston tube/rail. **Open** by appointment only.
No credit cards.
North Africa, the Arab world and Islam.

Mind, body & spirit

Atlantis Bookshop

49A Museum Street, WC1A 1LY (7405 2120/www.theatlantisbookshop.com). Holborn or Tottenham Court Road tube. **Open** 10.30am-6pm Mon-Sat. **Credit** AmEx, MC, V.
London's oldest independent bookshop on the occult sells new and second-hand titles.

Karnac Books

118 Finchley Road, NW3 5HT (7431 1075/www.karnacbooks.com). Finchley Road tube. **Open** 9.30am-6pm Mon-Sat.
Credit MC, V.
Stocks hundreds of titles on psychology, psychotherapy and related subjects.

Mysteries

9-11 Monmouth Street, WC2H 9DA (7240 3688/www.mysteries.co.uk). Covent Garden or Leicester Square tube. **Open** 10am-7pm Mon-Fri; 10am-6pm Sat; noon-6pm Sun. **Credit** AmEx, MC, V.
Books on crystal healing, astrology, dreams, yoga, meditation and religion. Psychic readings done in-house.

Music

Most musical instrument shops (*see pp211-216*) stock sheet music; **Foyles** (*see p177*) is very strong in this department too.

Travis & Emery

17 Cecil Court, WC2N 4EZ (7240 2129/ www.travis-and-emery.com). Leicester Square tube. **Open** 10.15am-6.45pm Mon-Sat; 11.30am-5pm Sun. **Credit** AmEx, MC, V.
Specialist second-hand music shops are low on the ground in London; it's no surprise that the best one should be in Cecil Court, home of antiquarian publications and convenient for customers popping in for a browse before going to the nearby Coliseum Opera House. It stocks mostly collectors' music: librettos for operas, music history and theory books and collectable programmes and play-bills. Travis & Emery has strong holdings in piano, violin, flute and organ music, but all music is catered for. Staff are musicians and very knowledgeable – ask them if you can't find something as they may have it in the basement storeroom. Upstairs is mainly sheet music, with reference works behind the counter. It's good for out-of-print music, and is popular with students; much of the second-hand stock is as good as new.

Politics

Bookmarks

1 Bloomsbury Street, WC1B 3QE (7637 1848/www.bookmarks.uk.com). Tottenham Court Road tube. **Open** noon-7pm Mon; 10am-7pm Tue-Fri; 10am-6pm Sat.
Credit MC, V.
From each according to his ability, to each according to his reads: Bookmarks is London's premier socialist bookshop, going strong for more than three decades, despite constant threats from, well, global capitalism (Amazon is 'the Starbuck's of the booktrade', say staff). Bookmarks (note the pun) sees itself as a home for ideas and an enabler of those ideas in a practical manner, regularly 'taking ideas to the movement' by setting up stalls at rallies, providing information about activism and hosting author events; in the past year Patrick Cockburn, Sara Paretsky and Melissa Benn (Tony's wife) have all been

guests. The shop's spacious, airy interior (replete with replica Soviet sculpture) holds a fabulous collection of left-wing writing – lots of history and politics of course, but also a small but well-chosen fiction section, left-wing second-handers and a great, thought-provoking children's section. As official bookshop for near-neighbour the TUC, there are also many trade union publications.

Also check out...

Freedom Press Bookshop

84B Whitechapel High Street (entrance on Angel Alley), E1 7QX (7247 9249/ www.freedompress.org.uk). Aldgate East tube. **Open** noon-6pm Mon-Sat. **No credit cards.**
The largest anarchist bookshop in Britain.

Housmans

5 Caledonian Road, N1 9DX (7837 4473/ www.housmans.com). King's Cross tube/ rail. **Open** 10am-6.30pm Mon-Fri; 10am-6pm Sat. **Credit** AmEx, MC, V.
Established in 1945, Housmans stocks books on progressive politics and pacifism.

Parliamentary Bookshop

12 Bridge Street, SW1A 2JX (7219 3890/www.bookshop.parliament.uk). Westminster tube. **Open** 9.30am-5.30pm Mon-Thur (9.30am-4.30pm during summer recess); 9am-4pm Fri (9.30am-4pm during summer recess). **Credit** MC, V.
Political titles, government publications (like Hansard) and acts of parliament.

Second-hand, rare & antiquarian

Useful websites include **www.abebooks.com**, **www.alibris.com**, **www.bibliofind.com** (an affiliate of Amazon) and **www.ibooknet.co.uk**, though bear in mind that bookshops pay hefty commission to these sites so, if you can, you should buy direct. **Twiggers** (www.twiggers.com) can track down out-of-print titles. The book stalls underneath **Waterloo Bridge**, near BFI Southbank, are a hotspot for browsers. For more on collecting books, *see p182* **Collectomania**. Many of the Cecil Court bookshops listed below have banded together to form their own website: www.cecilcourt.co.uk.

Amwell

53 Amwell Street, EC1R 1UR (7837 4891/ www.amwellbookcompany.co.uk). Angel tube/King's Cross tube/rail. **Open** 11am-6pm Tue, Thur-Sat. **Credit** MC, V.
Having beaten off threats from the local council, Amwell has retained its title as London's biggest seller of second-hand books on architecture. The owner and, it would seem, most of her family are trained in architecture, so there is something of a pedigree to the stock, which also includes art, photography, design, textiles, fashion and jewellery. It should be a first stop for architecture students, as there's a healthy stock of review copies of academic books at reduced prices. Local history is well-represented and there's a great children's section (perhaps aimed more at nostalgic adults than youthful bibliophiles?). Amwell also has a stall at Biblion (*see below*).

Any Amount of Books

56 Charing Cross Road, WC2H 0QA (7836 3697/www.anyamountofbooks.com). Leicester Square tube. **Open** 10.30am-9.30pm Mon-Sat; 11.30am-8.30pm Sun. **Credit** AmEx, MC, V.
This Charing Cross stalwart seems to have smartened up a little over the last year; fear not, the bare floorboards and wooden shelving remain, but the stock seems easier to negotiate than in times past. Specialising principally in arts and literature, Any Amount is jam-packed with decent quality books on all subjects. Prices range from £1 to £2,000 (including, amusingly, a 'medium-rare' section). The shop had a scoop in 2007 by acquiring the library of Angela Carter; more recently, the books of noted *bon viveur* Norman Douglas made their way here. Diversifying a little never hurts business either, and the shop has developed a sideline selling collections of leather bindings to interior decorators, set designers and posh drinking establishments.

Bernard J Shapero

32 St George Street, W1S 2EA (7493 0876/www.shapero.com). Bond Street or Oxford Circus tube. **Open** 9.30am-6.30pm Mon-Fri; 11am-5pm Sat. **Credit** AmEx, DC, MC, V.
Bernard J Shapero's interesting collection of antiquarian and out-of-print texts is enticingly displayed over four floors in these smart Mayfair premises. Specialisms here include travel (with a comprehensive collection of Baedeker guides), natural history, literature and colour-plate books. The shop's newest department deals with books from and about Russia and there are also rare maps and atlases and monographs of early photography. The shop began in Grays Antiques Market in 1979 and moved to Notting Hill before settling here just over a decade ago; the range, presentation and, above all, quality of its beautiful volumes are second to none. One for the serious collector – though by no means unapproachable to the rest of us.

Bertram Rota

31 Long Acre, WC2E 9LT (7836 0723). Covent Garden tube. **Open** 9.30am-5.30pm Mon-Fri. **Credit** MC, V.
Not many people know about Bertram Rota, though it seems a shame to use the cliché 'well-kept secret' about such a fine, august establishment, set up in 1923. Its relative anonymity (perhaps it's more an old-fashioned discretion) is not for want of location – the shop is right in the middle of Covent Garden and probably passed by thousands each day, who don't think to look up to the first floor, where the sign of the yellow book is on display. Pass the door buzzer and up a narrow staircase to a beautiful storehouse of antiquarian books, particularly strong in modern firsts (a collecting discipline the shop's founder is said to have invented), architecture, the applied arts and modern poetry. Author manuscripts are well represented – Bertram Rota brokered the sale of Harold Pinter's papers to the British Library – and private presses are a strong point, including The Golden Cockerel, Kelmscott and Nonesuch as well as contemporary British printers such as Parvenu Press.

Biblion

1-7 Davies Mews, W1K 5AB (7629 1374/ www.biblion.co.uk). Bond Street tube. **Open** 10am-6pm Mon-Fri. **Credit** MC, V.
A good idea was hatched in 1999: to set up a shop within Grays Antiques Market in which a number of national and international booksellers could all exhibit their wares – it turned out to be a great idea. Around 50 to 60 dealers currently deposit stock at this permanent bookfair, with around 20,000 titles on offer. There's room for even more, but some of that space is now occupied by a free gallery dedicated to book-related art. With such a large number of dealers the range of stock is unsurprisingly broad – and so are the prices; whether equipped with £10 or a lifetime's worth of savings, it's unlikely that any self-respecting bookworm will leave empty handed. Biblion is particularly strong on illustrated works, children's and travel books, titles on glass, modern first editions and finely bound volumes.

Fisher & Sperr

46 Highgate High Street, N6 5JB (8340 7244). Highgate tube. **Open** 10.30am-5pm Mon-Sat. **No credit cards.**
A bookshop has inhabited this four-storey building in genteel Highgate Village for over 100 years (and been in the same hands for the past 60). Stock ranges from valuable antiquarian sets (which are kept in a room behind a sliding door) to general stock priced under £10 on almost every topic imaginable, with especially strong pickings from the fields of history, literature, travel, art and philosophy. A big plus point here is the room dedicated to London-related books, often including valuable copies of the works of those distinguished Londoners, Pepys and Johnson. With low ceilings and cramped rooms, the shop, like the proprietor, is as traditional and characterful as they come.

Goldsboro

7 Cecil Court, WC2N 4EZ (7497 9230/ www.goldsborobooks.com). Leicester Square tube. **Open** 10am-6pm Mon-Sat. **Credit** AmEx, MC, V.
Goldsboro stands out from the crowd along this street of antiquarian booksellers. As the largest signed first-edition specialist in the UK, its premises may not bulge with the weight of stock as at most Cecil Court repositories, but everything here has been autographed by its author. Writers regularly sign consignments of first editions (mostly from the 1960s onwards), which often sell for the same price as unsigned editions elsewhere: there were around 200 such copies of Salman Rushdie's brand-new *The Enchantress of Florence* on our visit; other big names include Ian Rankin and Wilbur Smith. Goldsboro is also responsible for one

of the world's largest first-edition book clubs; there's a new title each month and many are exclusive to the store and bound in limited-edition slipcases.

Halcyon Books

1 Greenwich South Street, SE10 8NW (8305 2675/www.halcyonbooks.co.uk). Greenwich rail/DLR. **Open** 10am-6pm daily. **Credit** AmEx, MC, V.

Halcyon is renowned for its diverse range of affordable stock, with the focus less on collectable titles (although there's a small section of first editions and antiquarian books) and more on content. Although all subjects are covered, the art, philosophy and literature sections are particularly strong and the shop holds a large number of military titles – staff point out that Greenwich has a long-standing association with England's military history (indeed, the *Cutty Sark* is just a short stroll away). There are also children's books. Books sell from as little as 50p and rise into the hundreds; most are £5 to £10.

Henry Sotheran

2-5 Sackville Street, W1S 3DP (7439 6151/www.sotherans.co.uk). Green Park or Piccadilly Circus tube. **Open** 9.30am-6pm Mon-Fri; 10am-4pm Sat. **Credit** AmEx, DC, MC, V.

A fine old-fashioned antiquarian bookshop, Henry Sotheran combines its well-founded association with quality, class and tradition – established in York back in 1761, the business moved to London nearly two hundred years ago, in 1815 – with a surprisingly relaxed ambience. The extraordinary range of stock covers English literature (specialising in first and important editions of works from the 17th to the 20th centuries), children's and illustrated titles, travel and exploration, art and architecture, science and natural history. Departments are run by specialists, so novices can be assured of being guided by informed hands, while opportunities for collectors are abundant (past acquisitions have included the libraries of Laurence Sterne and Charles Dickens). Prices fittingly often run into the thousands here – a first edition of *The Origin of Species* had just sold for £82,000 on our last visit – though they start at around £20. In recent years greater emphasis has been placed on the shop's fine collection of prints and posters downstairs, where two or three

Gosh!. See p182.

LEISURE

exhibitions are put on per year – prints by William Blake were a recent attraction.

Jarndyce

46 Great Russell Street, WC1B 3PA (7631 4220/www.jarndyce.co.uk). Tottenham Court Road or Holborn tube. **Open** 10.30am-5.30pm Mon-Fri. **Credit** AmEx, MC, V.

Jarndyce and Jarndyce was the law case in Dickens's *Bleak House* that consumed all the money the litigants were fighting over. In contrast, the stock in this charming bookshop opposite the British Museum (which dates back to the 1860s) is most reasonably priced, with exciting finds from £20. The shop does maintain its links to the great man himself, though, with a suitably large collection of Dickens that had been freshly catalogued on our last visit. The owners believe strongly in the durability and good value of an 18th- or 19th-century hardback – the focus of this fine institution. Other specialisms here include pamphlets, street literature, women writers and chapbooks from the period. Proprietor Brian Lake is known for his publication *Fish Who Answer the Telephone* (co-edited with Russell Ash) and other amusingly titled publications.

Marchpane

16 Cecil Court, WC2N 4HE (7836 8661/ www.marchpane.com). Leicester Square tube. **Open** 11am-6pm Mon-Sat. **Credit** AmEx, MC, V.

London's longest-serving specialist for children's books, Marchpane is the only bookshop we know with its own 24-hour security guard – a 1980s BBC Dalek. Other features are signed photos of Russian cosmonauts, punk fanzines and circuit board fixtures. Since 2008, the shop has also housed a fully functional Scalextric track downstairs (the owner is making up for not having had one as a child). There are perhaps fewer recognisable items than you would find at Nigel Williams across the way (*see below*), but you don't need to be a serious collector to appreciate the stock, which starts at around £5 and includes some real gems, such as a complete run of the Waverley novels and some rare Peter Pan items for £200 to £300. Downstairs, near the gramophone and chaise-longue, are drawers housing periodicals from the 1930s to '60s.

Nigel Williams

25 Cecil Court, WC2N 4EZ (7836 7757/ www.nigelwilliams.com). Leicester Square tube. **Open** 10am-6pm Mon-Sat. **Credit** AmEx, MC, V.

Nigel Williams stocks mainly 20th-century first editions costing between £15 and £15,000. On the ground floor is a wonderful collection of rare children's books, including what staff call 'the three Bs' – Biggles, Bunter and Blyton – and a host of popular 20th-century authors and illustrators such as AA Milne, Arthur Rackham and Heath Robinson. There's also the 'Wodehouse Wall' – which staff conjecture is the largest collection of PG Wodehouse in the country – and a growing poetry section. Approximately 10% of the stock is signed. The owners believe that collecting first editions needn't be expensive and advise potential purchasers to collect the kind of thing they take pleasure in: a good place to start is the shop's pleasingly unpretentious basement collection, which places strong emphasis on popular genres like crime and detective fiction. Whether it's John Fowles or Dick Francis you're after, books here are all less than £250, sometimes as low as £10.

Oxfam Books

12 Bloomsbury Street, WC1B 3QA (7637 4610/www.oxfammarylebone.co.uk). Tottenham Court Road tube. **Open** 10am-6pm Mon-Sat; noon-5pm Sun. **Credit** MC, V.

Oxfam now claims to be the biggest retailer of second-hand books in Europe. This flagship is part of a general movement for Oxfam stores to become book specialists. In the airy, welcoming space, there's a good deal of brand-new, review and proof copies, as well as collectable and antiquarian titles, with a healthy stock of art, history and social sciences. Thanks to its location near the University of London the shop receives lots of academic books. Prices are not necessarily the best you could find, but you know where the money's going.

Branches: throughout the city.

Peter Harrington Antiquarian Bookseller

100 Fulham Road, SW3 6HS (7591 0220/ www.peterharringtonbooks.com). South Kensington tube. **Open** 10am-6pm Mon-Sat. **Credit** AmEx, MC, V.

Peter Harrington is as aesthetically pleasing to browse as it is strong in its stock. One of its specialities is library sets – 'complete set' style leather-bound beauties – giving the ground floor the feel of a gentleman's pad. The shop has its own bindery, where old books are restored and rebound (prices start at £420). It also houses antiquarian items; a fine example on our last visit included a first edition of *The Wealth of Nations* (£65,000), though more modest items also abound (modern firsts, £35 and up). Travel books are a new area of interest, displayed in their own room. The bookshop has started to integrate with its adjoining gallery (which also sells maps), meaning that modern art takes centre stage. Original Dr Seuss artwork and signed photographs of Churchill adorn the walls – look out also for odd gems like a framed, autographed Sylvia Plath poem (£7,500), written when she was just 12.

Quinto/Francis Edwards

48A Charing Cross Road, WC2H 0BB (7379 7669). Leicester Square tube. **Open** 9am-9pm Mon-Sat; noon-8pm Sun. **Credit** AmEx, DC, MC, V.

Two shops with different emphases, but united in purpose; Quinto is on Charing Cross Road, Francis Edwards just behind it on Great Newport Street. The former is shabby and ramshackle, but charming and deservedly famous for its monthly wholesale change of stock on the ground floor, with new books brought from Hay-on-Wye; lines of customers extend down the street at 2pm on the chosen Sunday. There's a rolling stock of around 50,000 titles, so you'll feel like you've earned your find, especially if you're rooting around the basement. The smaller, one-room Francis Edwards concentrates on military history. Quinto's branch near the British Museum closed in summer 2008; the stock has moved here.

Red Snapper

22 Cecil Court, WC2N 4HE (7240 2075). Leicester Square tube. **Open** 10.30am-6pm Mon-Sat. **No credit cards.**

This small Cecil Court shop specialises in Beat and counter-culture literature, attracting a cool clientele – the owner is happy to reminisce about selling Jude Law a copy of *Ham on Rye* signed by Bukowski (£2,500), while Patti Smith has been known to pop in too. Authors like William Burroughs and Hunter S Thompson are well represented. There are also books covering counter-culture spheres aside from literature – one item, the snappily titled *LSD & Sex & Censorship & Vietnam Cookbook*, rather sums it all up. We also found an unopened copy of Madonna's *Sex*, for £200. Stock is roughly 40% American, and sells for £20 and upwards.

Simon Finch Rare Books

53 Maddox Street, W1S 2PN (7499 0974/ www.simonfinch.com). Oxford Circus tube. **Open** 10am-6pm Mon-Fri. **Credit** MC, V.

The first impression of this tall, slender shop may be its staircase, but you'll leave remembering the books. Its six floors of printed material (only two of which are accessible to visitors) contain non-stop surprises, in the fields of English and European literature, science, early printing, art, photography and architecture. Simon Finch certainly has an eye for intriguing items, from HG Wells's *The First Men in the Moon* signed by the second man on the moon, Buzz Aldrin, to Twiggy's modelling card from 1968. The ground floor houses mainly 20th-century works, while older books are held on the first. Finch produces several catalogues a year; prices start at around £20 or £30, so it's worth popping in even if you're not a serious collector. Once you've got past the door buzzer, staff are welcoming.

Skoob

Unit 66, The Brunswick, WC1N 1AE (7278 8760/www.skoob.com). Russell Square tube. **Open** 10.30am-8pm Mon-Sat; 10.30am-6pm Sun. **Credit** AmEx, DC, MC, V.

Skoob returned to business in the Brunswick Centre just in time for our last edition, and we're delighted to say it's still going strong. The 2,500sq ft of floor space may be in a basement with concrete walls and exposed piping, but loses none of its ambition for that and remains light and airy. Recent reshuffles have made it more logical to navigate the 60,000 titles on display, which cover almost every subject imaginable – from philosophy, biography, maths and science to languages, literature and criticism, art, history, economics and politics. Holdings are regularly refreshed with stock from the 750,000-strong shop in Oxford that's also run by personable owner Chris Edwards, and as other bookshops

Unique Selling Point
Persephone Books

Virginia Woolf was, as usual, very insightful when she wrote that 'A woman must have money and a room of her own if she is to write fiction.' How else, she argued in her 1929 tract *A Room of One's Own*, could women find the freedom to express their imaginations? But could even Woolf have imagined a room like this?

The main office of publisher and bookseller Persephone Books (*see p188*) is piled high with lovingly restored reprints of unfairly neglected women writers, mainly from the interwar period. It's a testament to those women who did find their own creative space – even if their books were largely overlooked in their own time. They are beautiful objects, many gift-wrapped in bright pastels; but, more importantly, they make for fascinating reading.

Some are by well-known names: Penelope Mortimer, Katherine Mansfield and even Woolf herself, in a biography of Elizabeth Barrett Browning's dog Flush. Others offer the chance to get to know quick-witted women who, by virtue of the time in which they lived, were not given the respect they might otherwise have gained in their own lifetimes. There's *William – an Englishman*, Cicely Hamilton's 1919 exploration of war; or *Someone at a Distance* (1953), in which Dorothy Whipple traces the effects of a man's infidelity on his family. Persephone's bestseller is *Miss Pettigrew Lives for a Day* (1938) by Winifred Watson, which has just been made into a film by director Bharat Nalluri.

Rosie Ashworth from Persephone explains that many readers are drawn to the works because they offer a new perspective on really quite recent times: 'Customers like gaining insights into the periods of their mothers and grandmothers,' she says, 'the kinds of experiences they lived through and attitudes they faced. For older readers, the books even evoke their own childhoods.'

Persephone's books are all covered in identical plain eggshell blue, but each book's endpapers comprise wonderful re-creations of patterns – wallpapers, fabrics, clothing or suchlike – contemporary with the book. They are intelligently

matched too: EM Delafield's spiky *Consequences* (1919) is papered with a thistle print from 1896, the year the novel's protagonist would have been 'scratched by thickets of convention'.

To the Greeks, Persephone was the goddess of creativity and fecundity, and she certainly seems to be presiding over this operation. In business for nine years, it has occupied this spot on Lamb's Conduit Street since 2001, and opened a recession-mocking outpost in Kensington in summer 2008 (109 Kensington Church Street, 7221 2201). As Woolf put it, 'Odd how the creative power at once brings the whole universe to order.'

round the country collapse, Skoob buys their stock. Despite its name, Skoob is clearly not backward in coming forwards, and we hope it continues in the same vein for many more years to come.

Tim Bryars

8 Cecil Court, WC2N 4HE (7836 1901/ www.timbryars.co.uk). Leicester Square tube. **Open** 11am-6pm Mon-Fri; noon-5pm Sat. **Credit** MC, V.

Tim Bryars is secretary of the Cecil Court association (visit www.cecilcourt.co.uk) and works to promote all the shops on the street. His own shop has a unique emphasis – it's notable first and foremost for its collection of antiquarian maps. Every item here is original, from a first-edition 1933 London Underground map, back to some of the earliest maps on record. While prices rise into the thousands, there are treasures to be had for under £100. Dig a little deeper (or chat to the ebullient owner) and you'll find a selection of early printed matter, especially strong in the classics and their early translations. As you'd expect, there's also an emphasis on atlases.

Also check out...

Bernard Quaritch

8 Lower John Street, W1F 9AU (7734 2983/www.quaritch.com). Piccadilly Circus tube. **Open** 9am-6pm Mon-Fri. **Credit** AmEx, MC, V.

This grand store (est. 1847) specialises in rare architectural books and manuscripts.

Black Gull Books

70-71 West Yard, Camden Lock Place, NW1 8AF (7267 5005). Camden Town tube. **Open** 10am-6pm daily. **Credit** AmEx, DC, MC, V.

Small second-hander located in the middle of Camden Market.

For branch see index.

Book Mongers

439 Coldharbour Lane, SW9 8LN (7738 4225). Brixton tube/rail. **Open** 10.30am-6.30pm Mon-Sat. **Credit** MC, V.

This Brixton fave is packed with varied and inexpensive titles, covering literature, food and drink, comics and more.

Collinge & Clark

13 Leigh Street, WC1H 9EW (7387 7105). Russell Square tube. **Open** 11am-6.30pm Mon-Fri. **Credit** AmEx, MC, V.

This calming little shop sells illustrated books, private-press editions and historical works on engraving and printing.

David Drummond at Pleasures of Past Times

11 Cecil Court, WC2N 4EZ (7836 1142). Leicester Square tube. **Open** 11am-2.30pm, 3.30-5.45pm Mon-Fri; also by appointment. **Credit** MC, V.
Theatre, magic and performing arts.

Gekoski

Pied Bull Yard, 15A Bloomsbury Square, WC1A 2LP (7404 6676/www.gekoski.com). Holborn tube. **Open** 10am-5.30pm Mon-Fri; also by appointment. **Credit** MC, V.
Modern first editions and literary prints.

Gloucester Road Bookshop

123 Gloucester Road, SW7 4TE (7370 3503/www.gloucesterbooks.co.uk). Gloucester Road tube. **Open** 9.30am-10.30pm Mon-Fri; 10.30am-6.30pm Sat, Sun. **Credit** MC, V.
Second-hand booksellers with a good number of out-of-print titles.

Henry Pordes Books

58-60 Charing Cross Road, WC2H 0BB (7836 9031/www.henrypordesbooks.com). Leicester Square tube. **Open** 10am-7pm Mon-Sat; 1-6pm Sun. **Credit** AmEx, MC, V.
A family business, strong on Jewish books.

Judd Books

82 Marchmont Street, WC1N 1AG (7387 5333/www.juddbooks.com). Russell Square tube. **Open** 11am-7pm Mon-Sat; noon-6pm Sun. **Credit** AmEx, MC, V.
Two floors of mainly academic books.

Maggs Brothers

50 Berkeley Square, W1J 5BA (7493 7160/ www.maggs.com). Green Park tube. **Open** 9.30am-5pm Mon-Fri. **Credit** MC, V.
Expert dealers in rare books, first editions and manuscripts; established in 1853 and one of the world's largest antiquarian booksellers.

Maritime Books

66 Royal Hill, SE10 8RT (8692 1794/ www.navalandmaritimebooks.com). Cutty Sark DLR/Greenwich DLR/rail. **Open** 10am-6pm Tue-Sat. **Credit** MC, V.
Antiquarian and modern naval history.

Pickering & Chatto

144-146 New Bond Street, W1S 2TR (7491 2656/www.pickering-chatto.com). Bond Street tube. **Open** 9.30am-5.30pm Mon-Fri; also by appointment. **Credit** AmEx, MC, V.
Antiquarian and rare books – with most titles pre-20th century.

PJ Hilton

12 Cecil Court, WC2N 4HE (7379 9825). Leicester Square tube. **Open** 11am-5.30pm Mon-Sat. **Credit** MC, V.
Close attention is paid to English literature and historical Bibles (in fine condition).

Ripping Yarns

355 Archway Road, N6 4EJ (8341 6111/ www.rippingyarns.co.uk). Highgate tube. **Open** noon-5pm Tue-Fri, Sun; 10am-5pm Sat. **Credit** MC, V.
Collectible children's and illustrated books, including adventure stories, annuals, out-of-print fiction and British comics .

Stephen Foster

95 Bell Street, NW1 6TL (7724 0876/ www.95bellstreet.com). Edgware Road tube/Marylebone tube/rail. **Open** 10.30am-6pm Mon-Sat. *July, Aug* 10.30am-6pm Thur-Sat. **Credit** AmEx, MC, V.
Mixed range of stock that leans towards the arts; good for modern firsts.
For branch (Fosters' Bookshop) see index.

Tindley & Chapman

4 Cecil Court, WC2N 4HE (7240 2161). Leicester Square tube. **Open** 10am-5.30pm Mon-Fri; 11am-5pm Sat. **Credit** MC, V.
Reasonably priced modern first editions in good nick; also sells books on photography and architecture.

Walden Books

38 Harmood Street, NW1 8DP (7267 8146). Chalk Farm or Camden Town tube. **Open** 10.30am-6.30pm Thur-Sun. **Credit** AmEx, MC, V.
A good range of second-hand books, covering philosophy to fiction.

World's End Bookshop

357 King's Road, SW3 5ES (7352 9376). Sloane Square tube then 11, 19, 22 bus. **Open** 10am-6.30pm daily. **Credit** AmEx, MC, V.
Mixed bag of new and second-hand books.

Special interest

The café **Coffee, Cake & Kink** (*see p201*) has all sorts of books on 'special interest' sexual practices. At the opposite end of the spectrum are **Ian Allan's Transport Bookshop** (*see p210*) and, for books on chess, the **BCM Chess Shop** (*see p209*).

High Stakes

21 Great Ormond Street, WC1N 3JB (7430 1021/www.highstakes.co.uk). Russell Square tube. **Open** noon-6pm Mon-Fri. **Credit** MC, V.
Books about betting and gambling.

Motor Books

13/15 Cecil Court, WC2N 4AN (7836 5376/www.motorbooks.co.uk). Leicester Square tube. **Open** 9.30am-6pm Mon-Wed, Fri; 9.30am-7pm Thur; 10.30am-5.30pm Sat. **Credit** AmEx, MC, V.
Now in new premises, this shop still stocks a wide range of motoring, military, aviation and maritime titles.

Travel

Daunt Books

83-84 Marylebone High Street, W1U 4QW (7224 2295/www.dauntbooks.co.uk). Baker Street tube. **Open** 9am-7.30pm Mon-Sat; 11am-6pm Sun. **Credit** MC, V.
Though not strictly a travel bookshop, this beautiful Edwardian shop will always be seen first and foremost as a travel specialist thanks to its elegant three-level back room complete with oak balconies, viridian-green walls, conservatory ceiling and stained-glass window – home to row upon row of guide books, maps, language reference, history, politics, travelogue and related fiction organised by country. France, Britain, Italy and the United States are particularly well represented; go downstairs to find more far-flung destinations. Travel aside, Daunt is also a first-rate stop for literary fiction, biography, gardening and much more. James Daunt's commitment to providing proper careers for his workers ensures an informed and keen team of staff.
For branches see index.

Stanfords

12-14 Long Acre, WC2E 9LP (7836 1321/ www.stanfords.co.uk). Covent Garden or Leicester Square tube. **Open** 9am-7.30pm Mon, Wed, Fri; 9.30am-7.30pm Tue; 9am-8pm Thur; 10am-8pm Sat; noon-6pm Sun. **Credit** MC, V.
Escape the throngs of tourists on Long Acre by ducking for a breather into this inspirational travel shop. Stanfords is almost as essential to your trip as suntan lotion. In addition to every kind of travel guide, you'll find background literature on every conceivable destination, a specially selected fiction range, world music and cinema, a children's section and navigation software in the basement. The selection of equipment like medical kits, binoculars and torches (all upstairs) has also grown in recent years. Check out the giant maps on each shop floor, then go to the basement and have your very own customised map or aerial photograph printed out in poster form. Adding even more character, Stanfords stocks atlases and antique maps and guides. A café is now open at the back of the ground floor.

Travel Bookshop

13-15 Blenheim Crescent, W11 2EE (7229 5260/www.thetravelbookshop.com). Ladbroke Grove or Notting Hill Gate tube. **Open** 10am-6pm Mon-Sat; noon-5pm Sun. **Credit** MC, V.
Success hasn't gone to the head of this Blenheim Crescent establishment. Since finding fame as the inspiration for Hugh Grant's store in Richard Curtis's *Notting Hill*, it's continued to open up the world to residents of its chi-chi neighbourhood. At the front is the Europe room; turn right for the excellent UK and London room or go straight ahead for well-lit Africa, Asia, Australasia and Americas sections. All are filled with travel guides and background reading. There's a small but pretty children's section (featuring the likes of Sasek's *This is London*), a range of colourful cards, a decent selection of road maps and, as you would expect, a fab choice of coffee-table travel books. Knowledgeable staff display clippings of recent reviews to help with your choices. Collectors may wish to peruse the cabinets of first- and early-edition travel books.

Women

Persephone Books

59 Lamb's Conduit Street, WC1N 3NB (7242 9292/www.persephonebooks.co.uk). Holborn or Russell Square tube. **Open** 10am-6pm Mon-Fri; noon-5pm Sat. **Credit** AmEx, MC, V.
See p187 **Unique Selling Point**.

CDs & Records

General

If new releases and encyclopaedic selections are your main priority, then Oxford Street's **HMV** (no.150, W1D 1DJ, 7631 3423, www.hmv.co.uk) and **Zavvi** (nos.14-16, W1D 1AR, 7631 1234, www.zavvi.co.uk) are two of your best bets.

Brill

27 Exmouth Market, EC1R 4QL (7833 9757/www.musiccoffeebagels.com). Angel tube/Farringdon tube/rail. **Open** 7.30am-6pm Mon-Fri; 9am-6pm Sat. **Credit** AmEx, MC, V.

It's no misnomer: this small CD store/café has a strong local following and is a great place to add to your collection without being patronised by record fascists. Stock is CD-only; not all back-catalogue records make the cut and new releases only do if they're suitably interesting. You'll find a rock section that mixes classic albums by Pavement with newer releases from Fleet Foxes, a soul rack where the Marvin Gayes and Al Greens of this world snuggle up to the Corinne Bailey Raes and Marie Knights, and eclectic jazz, reggae, pop, country and world sections. Overseeing the operation is Jeremy Brill himself, as affable as he is informed, cheerfully dispensing fresh (Fairtrade) coffee, Brick Lane bagels and Flower Power bakery cakes for consumption at a smattering of outdoor and window seats.

Rough Trade East

Dray Walk, Old Truman Brewery, 91 Brick Lane, E1 6QL (7392 7788/www.roughtrade.com). Liverpool Street tube. **Open** 8am-9pm Mon-Thur; 8am-8pm Fri, Sat; 11am-7pm Sun. **Credit** AmEx, DC, MC, V.

This infamous temple to indie music has never looked more upbeat, its new-found impetus provided by its venture east in August 2007. Rough Trade East's truly inspiring 5,000sq ft loft-style store, café and gig space offers aural beats and treats for Shoreditch's scenesters. The café sells smoothies, sarnies and beer, and rock portraits are hung around the seating area, while nu-psychedelic pop often floats out of the speakers. Both the vinyl and CD collections are dizzying in their range, spanning punk, hardcore, American and British indie (such as Radiohead, who also played a not-so-secret-show here in early 2008), reggae, dub, funk, soul, post punk and new wave, with a large row of dance 12-inches, the highlight of which is the 'bastard pop' mash-up section. With 16 listening posts and a stage for live sets you cannot get much closer to music nirvana.

For branch see index.

Top five

Listening posts

BM Soho. *See p191.*
MDC. *See p191.*
Rough Trade East. *See p189.*
Sister Ray. *See p189.*
Sounds of the Universe. *See p193.*

Sister Ray

34-35 Berwick Street, W1F 8RP (7734 3297/www.sisterray.co.uk). Oxford Circus or Piccadilly Circus tube. **Open** 10am-7pm Mon-Sat; noon-6pm Sun. **Credit** AmEx, MC, V.

Previously Selectadisc, Sister Ray remains a mecca for Berwick Street's beat obsessives on their lunchbreaks, with its flat-screen TV, customer turntables and turquoise walls – not to mention a hugely broad stock. Much of the music is on vinyl (over 20,000 plates and counting) and the shop's dedication to back-cataloguing genres like drum'n'bass, gothic and industrial, hip hop (with UK talent well represented) and rock albums puts most megastores to shame. Staff are well informed and there are plenty of new release CDs, DVDs, T-shirts and books should the vinyl not appeal, as well as regular instores from hipster bands. If in doubt, check the tacky (and cheap!) Sleeve of the Week outside for inspiration.

Also check out...

All Ages Records

27A Pratt Street, NW1 0BG (7267 0303/www.allagesrecords.com). Camden Town tube. **Open** 11.30am-6pm daily. **Credit** MC, V.

Punk second-hand collectibles, seven-inches and CDs, from hardcore and ska to emo and anarcho-crust.

Banquet Records

52 Eden Street, Kingston-upon-Thames, Surrey KT1 1EE (8549 5871/www.banquetrecords.com). Kingston rail. **Open** 10am-6pm Mon-Wed, Sat; 10am-7pm Thur, Fri; noon-5pm Sun. **Credit** MC, V.

Rock and indie, punk, hardcore and emo at the alternative side of the spectrum, plus drum'n'bass, hip hop and house.

Sound 323

323 Archway Road, N6 5AA (8348 9595/www.sound323.com). Highgate tube. **Open** noon-5.30pm Tue-Sat. **Credit** MC, V.

Mainly deviant genres, from leftfield electronica to avant-garde jazz via electro-acoustic improv and spoken word.

Second-hand

Flashback

50 Essex Road, N1 8LR (7354 9356/www.flashback.co.uk). Angel tube then 38, 56, 73, 341 bus. **Open** 10am-7pm Mon-Sat; noon-6pm Sun. **Credit** AmEx, MC, V.

Just a stone's throw from the cavernous Haggle Vinyl (*see below*), but a million miles away aesthetically, Flashback's mostly second-hand stock is treated with utmost respect. There are usually a few boxes of bargain basement 12-inches going for pennies outside the front door, but inside stock is scrupulously organised. The ground floor is dedicated to CDs, with rock and pop alongside dance, soundtracks, soul, jazz and metal, while the new stock of urban and dance records, especially 1960s psych, garage and hip hop, is a well-kept secret among DJs. The basement, though, is vinyl only: an ever-expanding jazz collection jostles for space alongside soul, hip hop and an astonishing selection of library sounds (regularly plundered by producers looking for samples). Those not inclined to rummage can search out long lost gems on its website.

For branch see index.

Haggle Vinyl

114-116 Essex Road, N1 8LX (7704 3101/www.hagglevinyl.com). Angel tube then 38, 56, 73, 341 bus. **Open** 9am-7pm Mon-Sat; 9am-5pm Sun. **Credit** MC, V.

Tales of owner Lynn Alexander's grumpy eccentricity are legendary at this cluttered tomb of second-hand vinyl (Gilles Peterson was once asked to leave the store for 'pretentious behaviour' while younger staff looked on in horror). If other record shops take great pride in carefully editing their collection with stylish handwritten dividers, Haggle's stock is a ramshackle assortment. Some genres are organised to an extent (the hip hop and drum'n'bass sections are expansive, and folk, soul, psych-rock, house, jazz, rare reggae and 1980s pop are well-represented), while others – the many rare movie soundtracks, for example – get posted on the wall and the rest are left teetering in unmarked piles on the floor. To say it's the sort of place you could spend all day in is an understatement.

Intoxica!

231 Portobello Road, W11 1LT (7229 8010/www.intoxica.co.uk). Ladbroke Grove tube. **Open** 10.30am-6.30pm Mon-Sat; noon-5pm Sun. **Credit** AmEx, DC, MC, V.

One of London's most idiosyncratically decorated shops, Intoxica! – a vinyl-only store – is kitted out with bamboo wall coverings and glowering tribal masks. You wouldn't want to be the last person locking up here, but it makes for a browsing experience that's as big on character as it is on classic records. The ground-floor shelves are stacked with everything from reggae, funk and '60s beat to exotica and easy listening; there's also a good range of alternative and new wave from the 1970s to today and a great soundtrack selection. The basement is packed with soul, blues and jazz, the latter being especially big on British artists.

On the Beat

22 Hanway Street, W1T 1UQ (7637 8934). Tottenham Court Road tube. **Open** 11am-7pm Mon-Sat. **No credit cards.**

Put thoughts of Norman Wisdom's 1967 police comedy to one side: On the Beat is for record collectors of all stripes. Spend 15 minutes thumbing here and you'll definitely come out with something you'd forgotten you always wanted. The well-priced, mostly vinyl collection is crammed into a small room, walls lined with posters and dog-eared music mags that date back decades. In manager Tim Derbyshire's words, the large

Harold Moores

collection covers 'everything but classical' – you'll find a wealth of old funk and soul albums, a huge number of library sound compilations and a good range of jazz, country, folk, 'girl singers' and rock records, the latter covering everything from 1960s psychedelia to '90s pop.

Out on the Floor

10 Inverness Street, NW1 7HJ (7267 5989). Camden Town tube. **Open** 11am-6pm daily. **Credit** MC, V.

Think Camden and think music, from the Dublin Castle and the Camden Crawl to punks drinking cider by the canal – but you're unlikely to think of many good music stores. This three-level, three-shop operation is a sanctuary for serious record collectors in an area short on decent options. Out on the Floor itself is in the basement and stocks guitar music – there's a particularly interesting selection of heavy metal seven-inches and plenty of punk, prog and 1960s and '70s rock. The ground floor hosts Up at Out on the Floor, home to a well-chosen collection of 12-inch reggae and 1960s soul and a limited array of CDs. Despite the unwieldy name, hand-drawn psychedelic signs for the 12-inches give the place a particular charm. In between the two floors is Backroom Records, catering to the upper end of the collectors' market with a greater emphasis on poster art and silkscreen prints.

Also check out…

Beanos

1-7 Middle Street, Croydon, Surrey CR0 1RE (8680 1202/www.beanos.co.uk). East Croydon rail. **Open** 10am-6pm Mon-Sat; 11am-5pm Sun. **Credit** AmEx, MC, V.

Despite a recent scale-down, this shop still houses a huge choice of second-hand 1960s and '70s rock, dance, pop and classical records and CDs.

Cheapo Cheapo Records

53 Rupert Street, W1V 7HN (7437 8272). Piccadilly Circus tube. **Open** 11.30am-10pm Mon-Sat. **No credit cards.**

A wealth of 1970s and '80s vinyl across the genres from £2.50 upwards.

JB's Records

36 Hanway Street, W1T 1UP (7436 4063/www.myspace.com/jbsrecords). Tottenham Court Road tube. **Open** noon-7pm Mon-Sat; noon-6pm Sun. **Credit** AmEx, MC, V.

A colourful and cosy cavern, specialising in 1950s to the present blues, soul, funk, psychedelic and rock rarities.

Minus Zero Records

2 Blenheim Crescent, W11 1NN (7229 5424/www.minuszerorecords.com). Ladbroke Grove or Notting Hill Gate tube. **Open** 10.30am-6pm Wed-Sat; noon-4pm Sun. **Credit** MC, V.

This shop shares its premises with Stand Out Collectors Records (*see below*) and spans rare folk rock and psychedelia to punk and power pop.

Music & Video Exchange

38 Notting Hill Gate, W11 3HX (7243 8573/www.mveshops.co.uk). Notting Hill Gate tube. **Open** 10am-8pm daily. **Credit** AmEx, MC, V.
Great for those looking to sell their collection or bolster it with someone else's, with advice from its chirpy staff. Also on this strip: Soul & Dance Exchange (no.42), Classical Exchange (no.36) and Stage & Screen (no.34). **Branches**: throughout the city.

Record Detective Agency

492 Green Lanes, N13 5XD (8882 6278). Southgate tube/Palmers Green rail/329, W6 bus. **Open** noon-6pm Mon-Sat. **No credit cards**.
Derek Burbridge uses his sleuthing skills to fill tricky gaps in your vinyl collection.

Retrobloke.com

47 Church Road, NW4 4EB (8203 8868/ www.retrobloke.com). Hendon Central tube/ Hendon rail. **Open** 11am-6pm Mon-Sat. **Credit** MC, V.
Hard-to-find records spanning rock, reggae, blues, soul and funk classics on vinyl and CD. Also a hearty tape collection.

Revival Records

30 Berwick Street, W1F 8RH (7437 4271/ www.revivalrecords.co.uk). Oxford Circus or Piccadilly Circus tube. **Open** 10am-7pm Mon-Sat. **Credit** MC, V.
On the site of the defunct Reckless Records is this minimalist selection of used but quality CDs and vinyl, spanning rock, pop, soul and dance.

Sounds that Swing

46 Inverness Street, NW1 7HB (7267 4682/www.nohitrecords.co.uk). Camden Town tube. **Open** noon-6pm daily. **Credit** AmEx, DC, MC, V.
Vinyl rarities, reissues and compilations; mainly 1950s and '60s surf, rockabilly, rhythm 'n' blues and rock.

Stand Out Collectors Records

2 Blenheim Crescent, W11 1NN (7727 8406). Ladbroke Grove or Notting Hill Gate tube. **Open** 10.30am-6.30pm Wed-Sat; noon-4pm Sun. **Credit** MC, V.
Specialists in 1960s and '70s CDs and vinyl, with some excellent reissues and remasters.

Classical

Gramex

25 Lower Marsh, SE1 7RJ (7401 3830/ www.gramexlondon.com). Waterloo tube/rail. **Open** 11am-7pm Mon-Sat. **Credit** AmEx, DC, MC, V.
Browsing here is as comfy and laid-back as flicking through a friend's collection; battered sofas and cuppas abound. The vast selection of quality used LPs and CDs is so constantly in flux that hundreds of records are cluttered on the central table at any given time while they await sorting. This is done by affable owner Roger Hewland, whose alleged photographic memory is probably the only thing stopping the store sliding into chaos. The majority of the ground-floor CD stock is taken up with an alphabetised catalogue of composers past and present, with opera also well represented (both on CD and DVD) and an assortment of mainstream and modern jazz, comprising almost half the stock. Venture down to the shoebox basement and you'll find the home of the store's vinyl collection. There's a 10% discount on purchases over £100 too.

Harold Moores Records

2 Great Marlborough Street, W1F 7HQ (7437 1576/www.hmrecords.co.uk). Oxford Circus tube. **Open** 10am-6.30pm Mon-Sat; noon-6pm Sun. **Credit** AmEx, MC, V.
Harold Moores is not your stereotypical classical music store: young, open-minded staff (including Tim Winter of Resonance FM) and an expansive stock of new and second-hand music bolster its credentials. This collection sees some great old masters complemented by a range of eclectic contemporary music, including plenty of avant-garde and electronic work from independent labels like Touch. Soft lighting, carpets and wood panelling create a cosy atmosphere, and there's plenty to appeal to amateur enthusiasts as well as aficionados. There's a suitably studious basement dedicated to second-hand classical vinyl, including an excellent selection of jazz.

Les Aldrich

98 Fortis Green Road, N10 3HN (8883 5631/www.lesaldrich.com). 43, 134 bus. **Open** 9.30am-6pm Mon-Fri; 9am-5.30pm Sat; 11am-4pm Sun. **Credit** AmEx, MC, V.
Les Aldrich's charming blue façade hides the finest crammed-in range of classical music CDs in north London, with major names like Pavarotti and Maria Callas snuggled next to rising stars like Rolando Villazón, modern composers and a comprehensive selection of the old masters. On top of that there's a growing jazz section, a smattering of classic retro pop, plus film scores, nostalgia and, added most recently, a good world music department with an emphasis on African, Middle Eastern and Cuban artists. The store is very family friendly, boasting not only a unique collection of classical albums aimed at expectant mothers and young children (*Mozart for Babies, Bach for Newborns*), but also sheet music to get them thinking about performances of their own.

MDC Music & Movies

Unit 3, Level 1, Festival Riverside, Royal Festival Hall, South Bank, SE1 8XX (7620 0198/www.mdcmusicandmovies.co.uk). Waterloo tube/rail. **Open** 10am-10pm daily. **Credit** AmEx, MC, V.
MDC enjoys one of the most privileged shopping locations in London, a riverside installation on the South Bank. The white walls, reverent atmosphere and abundance of light lend the store a slightly sterile air, but it remains a top place to browse CDs. These include classical music in all its forms, with entire shelves dedicated to the likes of Wagner and Vaughan Williams, not to mention a huge range of albums from modern composers like Karl Jenkins, John Tavener and Hans Zender. There are improved jazz and world sections, plus a recently extended selection of foreign and arthouse DVDs, which have taken over half the store. Opera buffs, however, may be better off making a beeline for the branch by the English National Opera's Coliseum. **For branch see index**.

Jazz, soul & dance

BM Soho

25 D'Arblay Street, W1F 8EJ (7437 0478/ www.bm-soho.com). Oxford Circus tube. **Open** 11am-7pm Mon-Wed, Sat; 11am-8pm Thur, Fri; noon-6pm Sun. **Credit** AmEx, MC, V.
Junglist Nicky Blackmarket's BM Soho has kids queuing up to snag his latest promos. Don't come expecting anything other than upfront club music: the ground floor stocks house, minimal and techno, while the basement remains London's most reliable dispenser of new and pre-release drum'n' bass, with dubstep, bassline and UK garage represented too. Both are kitted out in futuristic black metallic that only amplifies the apocalyptic bass sounds emanating from the sound system. Come on a Friday afternoon when turntablists nod into their headphones trying out white labels for the weekend's sets and it can feel like you're already clubbing. DJs also head here for last minute equipment – slip mats, needles, mixers and speakers reside at the back.

Honest Jon's

278 Portobello Road, W10 5TE (8969 9822/www.honestjons.com). Ladbroke Grove tube. **Open** 10am-6pm Mon-Sat; 11am-5pm Sun. **Credit** AmEx, MC, V.
This legendary record shop's owner had the good foresight to lend former hired hand James Lavelle £1,000 to set up Mo' Wax records in the early 1990s. Prints of old blaxploitation posters crowd the technicolour walls, a sign that jazz, soul, revival reggae and global sounds remain the house specialities. Honest Jon's has also branched out into many of the genres that for years relied on this very store for their samples: hip hop is especially well represented and even more peripheral dance genres like dubstep get a look in. The majority of the store's CD and vinyl collection is reserved for luminaries such as Parliament, Prince and Burning Spear.

Phonica

51 Poland Street, W1F 7LZ (7025 6070/ www.phonicarecords.co.uk). Oxford Circus or Tottenham Court Road tube. **Open** 11.30am-7.30pm Mon-Wed, Sat; 11.30am-8pm Thur, Fri; noon-7.30pm Sun. **Credit** MC, V.
The doors are always flung open at this lively dance vinyl hubbub. Recline on the battered leather sofas and egg-shaped chairs that give the chic space a 1970s gangster feel, or finger through rack upon rack of pristinely selected records favouring the deeper and edgier side of club music. The balanced selection journeys around the world taking in nu jazz, krautrock, minimal techno, exotica, dubstep and nu disco flavours, but fluorescent-clad

kids best head for the front rack of French electro labels. CDs are displayed on antique wooden tables, boasting the latest alt-indie and electronic releases, from White Denim and Cut Copy to Appleblim and Jesse Rose. Box sets take pride of place in a glass cabinet, while tees suspend above the vinyl racks. The staff – regular DJs-about-town themselves – are more than happy to help you dig out a hard to find disc.

Pure Groove Records

6-7 West Smithfield, EC1A 9JX (7778 9278/www.puregroove.co.uk). Farringdon tube. **Open** 11am-7pm Mon-Fri. **Credit** MC, V.

Once Archway's tiny testament to all things indie, alternative and cutting edge in guitar and electronic music, Pure Groove has upped sticks to this minimalist space next to Smithfield Market. Its stylish, multimedia treasure trove of vinyl, poster art and CD gems will strike fire in the loins of London's chic elite. A visually stimulating jigsaw of record and CD cases connected with metal pincers suspends from one wall, displaying the shop's top 100 leftfield singles, 12-inches and CDs from acts like MGMT, Chromatics and Foals. Garish graphics by artist Kate Moross hang over the till while black and white photographs are exhibited in the centre of the shop, hanging over magazines stacked neatly on black cubes. The rear, housing T-shirts, cotton bags and posters, doubles as a stage for the regular live-band sets and film screenings. Simply stunning.

Ray's Jazz at Foyles

3rd Floor, Foyles Bookshop, 113-119 Charing Cross Road, WC2H 0EB (7440 3205/www.foyles.co.uk). Tottenham Court Road tube. **Open** 9.30am-9pm Mon-Sat; 11.30am-6pm Sun. **Credit** AmEx, MC, V.

Ray's Jazz, which used to share space with the café on the first floor, has moved up to the third floor alongside the rest of the music department. Gigs will still be held in the now expanded café. Ray's stock covers all corners of the jazz spectrum (blues, avant-garde, gospel, folk, world), although modern and avant-jazz is the main draw: legends like Charlie Parker, Bill Evans and Chet Baker enjoy rows of shelf space, but there's still room for lesser-known gems like Polar Bear. One corner of the store stacks plenty of jazz magazines and there's a substantial selection of second-hand vinyl and other rarities to the left of the counter. Details of regular in-store gigs and book signings can be found on the website.

Reds

500 Brixton Road, SW9 8EQ (7274 4476). Brixton tube/rail. **Open** 9am-8pm Mon-Sat; 11am-5pm Sun. **No credit cards**.

Reds is a musical fixture for Brixton's Jamaican community. The shop's sound system can usually be heard rumbling all the way from the tube station and at weekends the place is packed with DJs stocking up on party tunes. Accessories including stereos, slipmats and amps, and labels like New Era and Rocawear, are also on offer. Urban music in all its forms gets a look in – hip hop and R&B are well covered, as are soca, dancehall and more mainstream pop – while the first-class reggae section boasts CDs, vinyl and an excellent selection of DVDs. Staff are enthusiastic and capable of making even the most token of island hoppers feel like full-time dub stars.

Rhythm Division

391 Roman Road, E3 5 QS (8981 2203/ www.rhythmdivision.co.uk). Bethnal Green or Mile End tube. **Open** 11am-7pm Mon-Sat. **Credit** AmEx, MC, V.

Still a DJ stalwart 15 years after it first opened, this record shop specialises in tunes of an urban bent on vinyl and CD. Grime, garage and baseline are all well represented – and its stock of UK and US house keeps growing with the genre's popularity. You can try before you buy on one of its seven turntables or there's a mail order service.

Sounds of the Universe

7 Broadwick Street, W1F 0DA (7734 3430/www.soundsoftheuniverse.com). Tottenham Court Road tube. **Open** 11am-7.30pm Mon-Sat. **Credit** MC, V.

Bright and breezy, this sound store has universal appeal. Its affiliation with reissue kings Soul Jazz records means its remit is broad. This is especially true on the ground floor (new vinyl and CDs), where grime and dubstep 12-inches jostle for space alongside new wave cosmic disco, electro-indie re-rubs, Nigerian compilations and some electronic madness. Six listening posts offer insights into a diverse mix of new releases from Venetian Snares to Soul II Soul legend Jazzie B, while the second-hand vinyl basement is big on soul, jazz, Brazilian and alt-rock.

Rough Trade East. *See p189.*

Pure Groove Records.
See p193.

See p193.

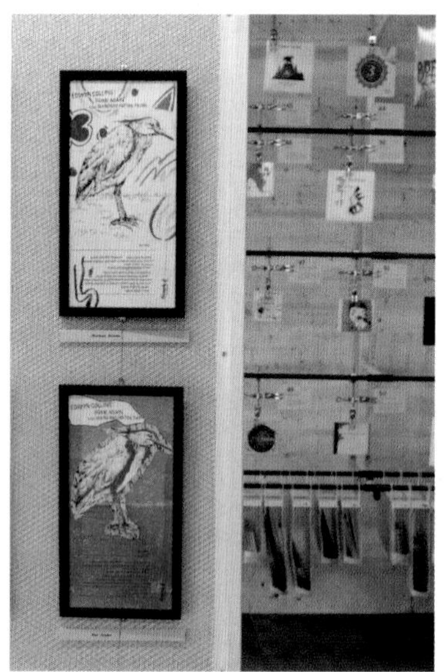

LEISURE

Uptown Records

3 D'Arblay Street, W1F 8DH (7434 3639/ www.uptownrecords.com). Oxford Circus tube. **Open** 10.30am-7pm Mon-Wed, Sat; 10.30am-8pm Thur, Fri. **Credit** AmEx, MC, V.

A stone's throw from moodier BM Soho (*see p191*), Uptown Records is a temple to the lighter side of undeground club culture, its well-versed staff only too pleased to guide vinyl junkies through the latest jams, which are posted on the wall behind a fleet of turntables for previewing tracks. The ground floor has its flag firmly in the house camp (funky and club, electro and tech, deep and soulful), while downstairs the specialities are hip hop, UK garage, grime, dubstep and bassline. There's little in the way of back-catalogue browsing potential (although the basement does stock CDs by major urban artists), and the place can feel eerily empty when DJs are doing whatever it is DJs do on weekday afternoons. Still, come the weekend it's packed to the rafters with potential Carl Coxes all eyeing up the latest bangers or nodding along to instore PAs by rising grime MCs.

Vinyl Junkies

94 Berwick Street, W1F 0QF (7439 2923/ www.vinyl-junkies.co.uk). Piccadilly Circus tube. **Open** 11am-7.30pm Mon-Sat; noon-5pm Sun. **Credit** AmEx, MC, V.

Vinyl Junkies takes the business of record buying very seriously indeed. The stock is on black plastic only – as the name suggests – and the extensive selections of battle records, breaks samples and a capella compilations is a sure sign of the place's affection for its male-heavy, DJ clientele. Eyes are initially drawn to the numerous reggae and dancehall seven-inches tacked to the walls, but there's also a comprehensive collection of house music in all its geographical subdivisions (New York, Chicago, Detroit, West Coast). And there's also a smattering of hip hop, disco, eclectic electronica and second-hand thrown in for good measure. Turntables are available for sampling potential purchases through headphones – which you'll definitely need, what with staff spinning deafening floor fillers that shake the walls all day.

Also check out...

Crazy Beat Records

87 Corbets Tey Road, Upminster, Essex RM14 2AH (01708 228678/www.crazy beat.co.uk). Upminster tube/rail. **Open** 10am-6pm Mon-Sat. **Credit** AmEx, MC, V.

Vinyl heavy, new and used soul, hip hop, house, reggae and R&B.

If Music...

Victory House, 99-101 Regent Street, W1B 4EZ (7437 4799/www.ifmusic.co.uk). Oxford Circus tube. **Open** by appointment 11.30am-9pm daily. **Credit** AmEx, MC, V.

An eclectic mix of upfront electro, dubstep, Brazilian, nu jazz, soul and hip hop rarities and new releases.

Kinetec

1C Darnley Road, E9 6QH (8533 1717/ www.kinetec.com). Bethnal Green tube/rail/ Hackney Central rail. **Open** noon-8pm Mon-Sat. **Credit** MC, V.

Underground dance specialist on an acid and hard house tilt.

Selectors Music Emporium

100B Brixton Hill, SW2 1AH (7771 2011/ www.selectorsmusic.co.uk). Brixton tube/rail. **Open** 11am-7pm Mon-Sat; 11pm-5pm Sun. **No credit cards.**

New and second-hand vinyl with an urban focus, including soul, reggae, roots and R&B.

Soul Brother Records

1 Keswick Road, SW15 2HL (8875 1018/ www.soulbrother.com). East Putney tube. **Open** 10am-7pm Mon-Sat; 11am-5pm Sun. **Credit** AmEx, MC, V.

Devoted to the smoother end of the spectrum, and catering to further-flung fanatics with a comprehensive online store.

Swag Records

42 Station Road, Croydon, Surrey CR0 2RB (8681 7735/www.swagrecords.com). West Croydon rail. **Open** 11am-7pm Mon-Wed, Fri, Sat; 11am-8pm Thur. **Credit** AmEx, DC, MC, V.

Sells a range of underground UK and US garage, plus techno, house and breaks.

Wyld Pytch

51 Lexington Street, W1F 9HL (7434 3472/www.wyldpytch.com). Oxford Circus tube. **Open** 11am-7pm Mon-Sat; noon-6pm Sun. **Credit** AmEx, DC, MC, V.

Mainly focusing on hip hop and R&B but also has a sprinkling of Afrobeat and Brazilian compilations.

Reggae

Dub Vendor

274 Lavender Hill, SW11 1LJ (7223 3757/ www.dubvendor.co.uk). Clapham Junction rail. **Open** 10am-7pm Mon-Thur, Sat; 10am-7.30pm Fri; 11.30am-5.30pm Sun. **Credit** AmEx, MC, V.

This polished practitioner of all things reggae actually began life as a market stall in the mid 1970s before setting up shop proper in 1983. Since then, a certain amount of diversification has seen the stock swell to take in hip hop and R&B. Sadly, its rear dub vinyl cave has been sealed off, bringing to the main floor its coveted albums, 12-inches and seven-inches, covering the entire reggae spectrum from dancehall to ska. Here, plenty of international artists are represented alongside UK talents like General Levy. There's also small range of DVDs, compilations, a top 20 R&B chart on disc and a reggae event ticket outlet.

Hawkeye Record Store

2 Craven Park Road, NW10 4AB (8961 0866). Willesden Junction tube/rail. **Open** 10am-7pm Mon-Fri; 10am-8pm Sat. **Credit** AmEx, MC, V.

Little has changed since reggae specialist Roy 'Hawkeye' Forbes-Allen opened this welcoming emporium of bass just over 30 years ago. It's pretty much all the same: the atmosphere, its approach to black music, hell, even the staff haven't moved on. So it must be doing something right. Various genres from blues and soul to gospel feature on a vast amount of vinyl, although hip

Shop talk Kieran Hebden

Londoner Kieran Hebden is best known as FourTet, his electronica guise on the Domino label, but he also works in other areas of music. He lives in Holloway.

'For all the joys of downloading music, one of the things I like about record shops is that you end up meeting people with a similar mindset. When I was 15 years old I took a long lunchbreak from school to buy a Tortoise record from **Rough Trade** (*see p189*). While there I got talking to another customer who suggested I contact a record company guy he knew. Within a few weeks I was in touch with a record label and my band Fridge were recording our first album.

'**Sounds of the Universe** (*see p193*) is a wonderful place to learn about great music, new and old. The owners run the Soul Jazz record label, one of the best labels in the world.

'**Honest Jon's** (*see p191*) is one of the great specialist record shops, and also a great record label. It's got incredible selections of African music, hip hop, Detroit techno, dub and more. It's a place where you can get turned on to records that no other shops seem to know about.

'**Phonica** (*see p191*) is my main stop in London for dance music, especially now that I'm doing more techno DJ-ing. There's a really fast turnover of fresh new releases, covering house, electro, dubstep and more. A great place to find amazing music that is not being written about in trendy magazines.'

Sounds of the Universe. See p193.

hop is notable by its diminutive presence. Reggae, needless to say, remains the biggest draw. It's a slog for more centrally located music-lovers, but well worth the pilgrimage, especially for fans of Sugar Minott's number one single 'Good Thing Going', originally released on the shop's own record label. The Hawkeye Soundsystem is also available for hire if you fancy feeling the riddims at your own event.

Also check out…

Body Music

261 High Road, N15 4RR (8802 0146). Seven Sisters tube/rail. **Open** 10am-8pm daily. **Credit** MC, V.
Reggae and music of black origin, namely soca, hip hop, urban house, R&B and gospel, plus DJ accessories.

Supertone Records & CDs

110 Acre Lane, SW2 5RA (7737 7761/ www.supertonerecords.co.uk). Brixton tube/rail. **Open** 11am-10pm Mon-Sat; 1-7.30pm Sun. **Credit** MC, V.
Owner Wally B takes his rare reggae, revival, soul, soca and gospel records very seriously indeed.

Soundtracks, shows & nostalgia

Dress Circle

57-59 Monmouth Street, WC2H 9DG (7240 2227/www.dresscircle.co.uk). Leicester Square tube. **Open** 10am-6.30pm Mon-Sat; noon-5pm Sun. **Credit** AmEx, DC, MC, V.
This OTT luvvy-magnet and temple to show tunes is still a West End hit after 30 years in business. It continues to wow professional thesps and drama queens alike with its staggering collection of show tunes on CD and DVD (featuring popular classics like *The Sound of Music* and plenty of more obscure gems for collectors). A range of posters celebrates productions past and present, from *Billy Elliot* to *Hairspray*; Stephen Sondheim, Barry Manilow and Barbara Cook are regulars here. The downstairs boasts a range of musical scores as comprehensive as you'll find anywhere in the capital, alongside a new book range from reference to autobiographies. There is a 10% discount for Equity members.

Also check out…

Sounds Original

169 South Ealing Road, W5 4QP (8560 1155/www.soundsoriginal.co.uk). South Ealing tube. **Open** 11am-5pm Wed-Sat. **Credit** AmEx, MC, V.
A selection of antique UK, US and Japanese LPs and singles from 1953 to 1970.

World, folk & country

Unfortunately, the Greenwich branch of **Bud's Country Music Store** has bitten the dust, but you can still get hold of its hallowed CD and DVD collection online at www.budscountrymusicstore.com.

Stern's Music

293 Euston Road, NW1 3AD (7387 5550/ www.sternsmusic.com). Euston Square or Warren Street tube. **Open** 10.30am-6.30pm Mon-Sat. **Credit** AmEx, MC, V.
With branches in London, New York and São Paulo, this world music store offers a comprehensive collection of global sounds, including mind-expanding genres of the Baltic Gypsy punk and Haitian voodoo jazz variety. Not that it's all niche market beats: the Fela Kutis and Ravi Shankars of this world are represented, as is reggae music in all its forms, Arabic rai and upbeat jazz from Brazil and Cuba. There's also a good range of African and Latin DVDs featuring performances by artists from Sly & Robbie to Amr Diab. Staff are hugely knowledgeable and more than capable of steering those overwhelmed by the sheer volume of stock in the direction of something special, or towards the shop's charming coffee and cake shop .

Also check out…

ABC Music

7 The Broadway, Southall, Middx UB1 1JR (8574 1319/www.abcmusicshop.com). Southall Broadway rail. **Open** 10.30am-7.30pm Mon-Fri; 10.30am-8pm Sat; 11am-8pm Sun. **Credit** AmEx, DC, MC, V.
Need a fix of India? Come here for everything from the latest Bollywood DVDs to bhangra CDs and plenty more besides.

Muzik Dunyasi

58 Green Lanes, N16 9NH (7254 5337). Manor House tube/141, 341 bus. **Open** noon-9pm Mon-Wed, Fri-Sun. **No credit cards**.
Pick up the latest Tarkan (Turkey's Justin Timberlake) single or traditional music.

Trehantiri Greek & Arabic Music

365-367 Green Lanes, N4 1DY (8802 6530/www.trehantiri.com). Manor House tube. **Open** 10.30am-7pm Mon-Sat; noon-4.30pm Sun. **Credit** AmEx, MC, V.
The largest collection of Greek music outside Greece, on vinyl and CD. Traditional musical instruments are also stocked.

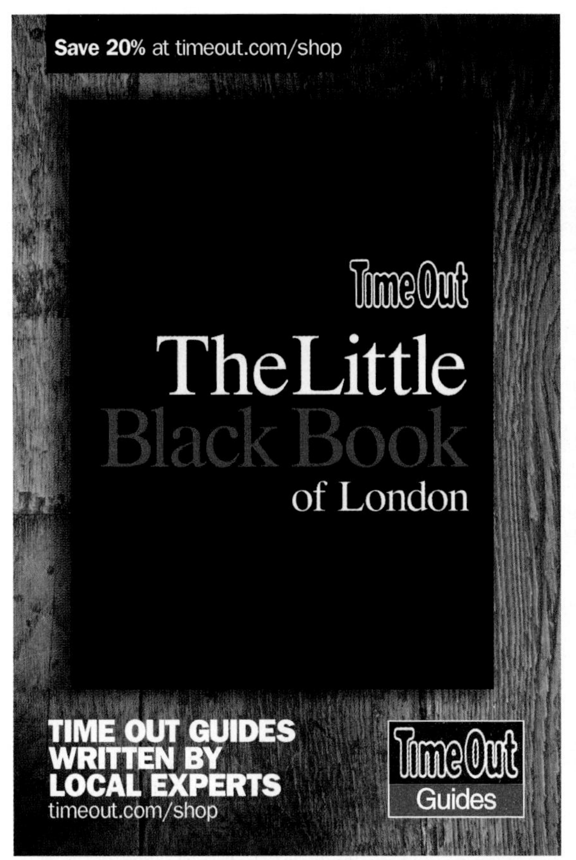
Save 20% at timeout.com/shop
Time Out
The Little Black Book of London
TIME OUT GUIDES WRITTEN BY LOCAL EXPERTS
timeout.com/shop
Time Out Guides

INTOXICA!
231 Portobello Road London W11 1LT
www.intoxica.co.uk intoxica@intoxica.co.uk
T: 0207 229 8010 F: 0207 792 9778
SECOND-HAND & NEW VINYL
originals - reissues - 45s - LPs
60s soul - beat - psych - jazz
70s funk - blues - beats & breaks
soundtracks - punk - weird stuff
nearest tube Ladbroke Grove
open 7 days a week

"the best record shop in the world" NME
ROUGH TRADE
EAST
Old Truman Brewery
91 Brick Lane, London
E1 6QL tel. 020 7392 7788
ROUGH TRADE
WEST
130 Talbot Road, London
W11 1JA tel. 020 7229 8541
WWW.ROUGHTRADE.COM

Electronics

General

Ask

248 Tottenham Court Road, W1T 7QZ (7637 0353/www.askdirect.co.uk). Tottenham Court Road tube. **Open** 10am-7pm Mon-Wed, Fri, Sat; 10am-8pm Thur; noon-6pm Sun. **Credit** AmEx, DC, MC, V.

Ask is a virtual palace in comparison with other shops along this stretch, offering four floors of stock, more staff than you can shake a stick at and a lofty feel. Boasting a clean online service, which allows you either delivery or a pick-up service, the company supplies some 10,000 different lines, with the emphasis on popular items like home-cinema packages, hi-fi equipment, laptops (no Apple Macs though), digital cameras, sat navs, MP3 players and DAB radios from big-name brands. Staff are helpful but not overly pushy – and they're trained by the manufacturers themselves so they're kept up-to-date with new technology and are always willing to impart their knowledge. Competitive prices, frequent special offers and a 'try before you buy' policy are further pluses.

For branches (including Harp, Kamla, McDonald) see index.

Blue Audio Visual

44 Duncan Street, N1 8BW (7713 6865/www.blueaudiovisual.co.uk). Angel tube. **Open** 10am-7pm Mon-Sat; noon-6pm Sun. **Credit** MC, V.

This old-school emporium stocks an eclectic range of cherry-picked second-hand and new audio-visual equipment, while offering competitive prices and exchanges for specialist items. Filmmakers – both amateur and pro – will be in their element here, with a Super 8 collection, cameras, viewers, projectors, 16mm cameras (including from Aaton, Bolex and Kinor), filmstock, lenses, tripods, splicers to lamps, film cement to clapperboards and cables to prop hire. Staff can even process your masterpiece for you, on Kodak Super-8, Extrachrome 64T, Tri-X and Plus-X films. The shop also has a great selection of electric and acoustic guitars (boasting Fender and Gibson models), pedals, mics, keyboards, drum machines, amps, samplers and PA systems, as well as DJ equipment. It's also a good bet for hard-to-find items such as analogue synthesisers, collectable guitars and used hi-fi parts. Anyone with an obsession for the non-digital world may not leave the store for hours.

Audio Gold. *See p199.*

Maplin

166-168 Queensway, W2 6LY (7229 9301/www.maplin.co.uk). Bayswater or Queensway tube. **Open** 9am-8pm Mon-Fri; 9am-6pm Sat; 10am-5pm Sun. **Credit** AmEx, MC, V.

The size of the shop often dictates the size of gear on offer, so expect plasma screens, speakers, satellite kits and hard drives aplenty at the 31 spacious Maplin stores located in the London area. Yet this only scratches the surface – the real beauty of the nationwide chain is the sheer scale of random kit available, from motherboards to computer cables, wireless phone line extenders to USB turntables and roll-up pianos. Turntables, mixers, amps and disco lighting do a roaring trade with the capital's DJs while gadget fiends are well catered for with metal detectors, a variety of flying toys, underwater CCTV surveillance systems (honestly) and solar-powered battery chargers. All in all, there's a mind-boggling choice, so use the power of the internet to narrow your preferences before setting off (the more central shops tend to be smaller).

Branches: throughout the city.

Also check out...

Gultronics

52 Tottenham Court Road, W1T 2EH (7637 1619/www.gultronics.co.uk). Goodge Street or Tottenham Court Road tube. **Open** 9.30am-6.30pm Mon-Wed, Fri, Sat; 9.30am-7pm Thur; 11am-5pm Sun. **Credit** AmEx, MC, V.

Gultronics was the first authorised UK supplier of Toshiba so laptops are a strength. Also lots of printers and scanners.

Shasonic

241 Tottenham Court Road, W1T 7QR (0845 634 0333/www.shasonic.co.uk). Tottenham Court Road tube. **Open** 9am-6pm Mon-Wed, Fri, Sat; 9am-7pm Thur; 11am-5pm Sun. **Credit** AmEx, DC, MC, V.

Annexed with the Sony Centre Galleria (*see below*), Shasonic is strong on laptops, digital cameras, DAB radios and large TVs.

Sony Centre Galleria

22-24 Tottenham Court Road, W1T 1BP (0845 634 0350/www.sonycentres.co.uk). Tottenham Court Road tube. **Open** 9am-6pm Mon-Wed, Fri, Sat; 9am-7pm Thur; 11am-5pm Sun. **Credit** AmEx, DC, MC, V.

The largest Sony Centre Gallery in Europe, with a wide range of equipment.

Branches: throughout the city.

Computers

See also p199 **CeX**.

Apple Store

235 Regent Street, W1B 2EL (7153 9000/www.apple.com). Oxford Circus tube. **Open** 10am-9pm Mon-Sat; noon-6pm Sun. **Credit** AmEx, DC, MC, V.

Apple's grandiose London flagship is as hip and beautiful as one might expect. All the latest Apple products can be found here – compact MacBook and MacBook Pro laptops, iMac desktops, the full range of iPods, Apple TV systems and covetable Apple Cinema HD display units. The new iPhone – a mobile phone, iPod and camera hybrid that also allows fast web browsing and email – has been joined in the 'must-own' category by the iPod touch and the breathtaking MacBook Air. Head up the imposing glass staircase to the 'Genius Bar', where you can get free one-to-one technical support. Rumours of a plan for a new three-storey Apple store in Covent Garden were circulating in summer 2008.

For branches see index.

Micro Anvika

245 Tottenham Court Road, W1T 7QT (7467 6000/www.microanvika.co.uk). Goodge Street or Tottenham Court Road tube. **Open** 9.30am-8pm Mon-Fri; 9.30am-6pm Sat; 11am-5pm Sun. **Credit** AmEx, MC, V.

Micro Anvika now has three shops along Tottenham Court Road, concessions in Harrods and Selfridges and a Mac-dedicated store at 13 Chenies Street. Like all the best places in this electronics-heavy part of the city, the draw is the presence of major suppliers such as Toshiba, Sony, Apple, Samsung and Hewlett Packard. Cameras, MP3 players, sat navs, PDAs and home-cinema systems are all to be found in-store, but the chain is most notable for its great range of laptops and LCD screens at competitive prices. The branch at 53-54 Tottenham Court Road also offers a trouble-shooting service upstairs in its 'digital life support' section. Service is far less hassly than in neighbouring stores.

For branches see index.

Also check out...

Apple Centre

78 New Oxford Street, WC1A 1HB (7692 6810/www.squaregroup.co.uk). Tottenham Court Road tube. **Open** 10am-5.30pm Mon, Fri; 10am-7pm Tue-Thur; 10am-5pm Sat. **Credit** MC, V.
This authorised Apple provider stocks Mac hardware, software and accessories, plus extended warranties for existing gear.

Morgan Computer Company

64-72 New Oxford Street, WC1A 1AX (7255 2115/www.morgancomputers.co.uk). Tottenham Court Road tube. **Open** 10am-6.30pm Mon-Fri; 10am-6pm Sat; 11am-5pm Sun. **Credit** AmEx, MC, V.
Surplus, overstock and closeout stocks; it operates on a pile-it-high, sell-it-low basis.

PC World

145 Tottenham Court Road, W1T 7NE (0870 242 0444/www.pcworld.co.uk). Warren Street tube. **Open** 9am-8pm Mon-Fri; 9am-6pm Sat; 11am-5pm Sun. **Credit** AmEx, MC, V.
Desktops, laptops, printers, monitors, PC peripherals, gaming and data storage.
Branches: throughout the city.

Yoyo Tech

30 Windmill Street, W1T 2JL (0871 855 3380/www.yoyotech.co.uk). Goodge Street tube. **Open** 9am-6.30pm Mon-Wed, Fri, Sat; 9am-7pm Thur; 11am-5pm Sun. **Credit** MC, V.
One of the largest online computer stores also boasts a shop in central London, so you can touch and try before you buy.

Computer games

Notting Hill Gate's **Computer Games Exchange** is being incorporated into a branch of the same-owned **Music & Video Exchange** (*see p191*); call for up-to-date information.

CeX

32 Rathbone Place, W1T 1JJ (0845 345 1664/www.cex.co.uk). Tottenham Court Road tube. **Open** 10am-7.30pm Mon-Wed, Sat; 10am-8pm Thur, Fri; 11am-7pm Sun. **Credit** MC, V.
CeX (Computer Exchange) sells up-to-the-minute gaming goods, with staff who are genuine, callous-thumbed gaming nuts. Expect the full range of consoles, such as Xbox 360, Nintendo Wii and PlayStation 3; hand-helds like the Nintendo DS; and all the latest games, including those for PCs. As the name suggests, cash and exchanges are offered for your games and DVDs and you get a year's warranty on everything bought. The Tottenham Court Road branch deals in electronics.
Branches: throughout the city.

Also check out...

Game

10 Victoria Place, Buckingham Palace Road, SW1W 9SJ (7828 9913/www.game.co.uk). Victoria tube/rail. **Open** 8am-8pm Mon-Fri; 9am-7pm Sat; 11am-5pm Sun. **Credit** MC, V.
The Game stores offer every new to newish console and an unrivalled range of games, either in-store or online (free UK delivery).
Branches: throughout the city.

Zavvi

14-16 Oxford Street, W1D 1AR (7631 1234/www.zavvi.co.uk). Goodge Street tube. **Open** 9am-10pm Mon-Sat; noon-6pm Sun. **Credit** MC, V.
Few can rival the game choice of this rebranded megastore. There are plenty of machines to try out the latest titles, though the space is often bombarded by kids.
Branches: throughout the city.

DJ & home-studio equipment

See pp211-216 **Music. Blue Audio Visual** and **Maplin** (for both, *see p197*) are also good bets.

Hi-fi

Many of the most respected hi-fi retailers are members of the **British Audio Dealers Association** (BADA, 8150 6741, www.bada.co.uk), meaning that they offer extended warranties and good exchange/return policies on hi-fi separates, as well as well-trained staff.

Audio Gold

308-310 Park Road, N8 8LA (8341 9007/www.audiogold.co.uk). Finsbury Park tube/rail then W7 bus. **Open** 10.30am-6.30pm Mon-Sat. **Credit** MC, V.
A mix of new, second-hand and hireable audio products, Audio Gold is one of the best places in London to track down old-school equipment – from ghetto blasters to gramophones, this store has it covered. The extensive 'prop hire' section celebrates all the 'strange and beautiful' machines the owners have picked up over the years, which is ideal for the media industry (film shoots or magazine articles especially) looking to set the scene with an original Walkman or a 1980s clock-radio. The list of manufacturers covered includes typical brands (Sony, Toshiba, Denon, Tivoli) but by and large they are names from a realm that's beyond the high street's vocabulary: turntables by Linn, speakers by Quad, amps by Sugden and so on. Audio Gold also buys your second-hand equipment – as long as it works, of course.

Cornflake.co.uk

37 Windmill Street, W1T 2JU (7323 4554/www.cornflake.co.uk). Goodge Street tube. **Open** by appointment 9am-5pm Mon-Fri. **Credit** MC, V.
When a music store requires you to book by appointment, you know you're in for an experience beyond the average superstore. Cornflake is the audiophile equivalent of a day spa. It's great, though cheap it is not. The company specialises in designing and building tightly integrated, multi-room audio (and home-cinema) set-ups, although that's not to say that it won't cater for buyers looking simply to buy a single-room system or even a single separate. The showroom has facilities for extensive consultation and testing of components to help you search for value. You shouldn't expect to be leaving here with a stereo system costing anything less than a four-figure sum (six figures at the top end). The range of manufacturers and components is relatively compact, but carefully and diligently chosen with an eye on superior quality.

Grahams

Unit 1, Canonbury Yard, 190A New North Road, N1 7BS (7226 5500/www.grahams.co.uk). Old Street or Highbury & Islington tube/rail then 271 bus. **Open** 10am-6pm Tue, Wed; 10am-8pm Thur; 9am-6pm Fri, Sat. **Credit** AmEx, DC, MC, V.
Secreted away in the backstreets of De Beauvoir Town, Grahams certainly won't be doing any casual business with passing pedestrians. Those who come here make the pilgrimage because they are ready to compile a hi-fi/home-cinema system with much care and deliberation – and spend a large sum of money in the process. Probably the longest-established of all competitors in town (its predecessor, Grahams Electrical, opened in Clerkenwell in 1929), the shop is guided by a policy of uncompromising quality, whatever the cost; consequently, the large majority of its components (amps, speakers, HD TV equipment, wireless streaming audio and so on) demand four-figure sums. The carefully crafted list of manufacturers includes B&W, Linn, Loewe, Miller & Kreisel, Spendor, Classe and many others of the same lofty and rarefied standard. The staff and owners are so proud of the company that their profiles can be found online so you can put names to faces before walking through the front door.

Listening Rooms

161 Old Brompton Road, SW5 0LJ (7244 7750/www.thelisteningrooms.com). Gloucester Road tube. **Open** 10am-6pm Mon-Sat. **Credit** AmEx, MC, V.
An audiophile's dream, the Listening Rooms offers a professional and well-informed service from the moment you step inside. The staff are extremely helpful, but bear in mind that they work primarily with the new-build market and full home installations (along the lines of those in *Grand Designs* showhouses). A wide range of suppliers is stocked, including Krell, Denon, Logitech and Yamaha.

Oranges & Lemons

61-63 Webb's Road, SW11 6RX (7924 2040/www.oandlhifi.co.uk). Clapham Junction rail. **Open** 11am-7pm Mon, Tue, Fri; 11am-9pm Thur (7-9pm by appointment only); 10am-6pm Sat. **Credit** AmEx, MC, V.
Laid-back and friendly, Oranges & Lemons is one of the best places in which to buy separates or home-cinema equipment in south London. It's keen to insist that hi-fi and home cinema are, fundamentally, about fun, and this is reflected in the store and its website. As with many of the other stores listed here, HD systems are available but, unlike some of the others, the new visual

technology has not overtaken the audio side of things. The test rooms are cosy, serving as both a pleasant environment for your shopping experience and a guide to how the audio set-up will work in an average living room. Systems of any size and complexity can be compiled – right up to a full, wireless multi-room AV solution – but you could also come here to upgrade just one component of an existing system. Bear in mind that the shop can often reach 'chaotic' proportions so you may not get a test room immediately – you can, however, book a demonstration in advance online, by phone or in-store.

Richer Sounds

2 London Bridge Walk, SE1 2SX (7403 1201/www.richersounds.co.uk). London Bridge tube/rail. **Open** 8am-7pm Mon-Fri; 10am-5pm Sat. **Credit** AmEx, MC, V.
Richer Sounds is a bit of a hi-fi phenomenon, boasting a personality (free lollipops are sometimes handed out to customers) alongside its fleet of stores (nine in London). The focus is on the more affordable end of the market; for £500 you could build a very respectable hi-fi system here, with components from manufacturers that are a cut above the high street regulars – brands such as Marantz, Denon, NAD, Yamaha and Teac. Speakers (of all conceivable sizes) come from Eltax, Mission, Mordaunt, TDL and Wharfedale and so on. Somehow, Richer manages to maintain its policy of slashing large sums off many goods; it's not unusual for £100 to be knocked off the RRP of a particular item. You can also happily extend your spree into the realms of home cinema (DVD players, plasma screens and freeview boxes), turntables and MP3 players. Free parking may be available – ask inside.
Branches: throughout the city.

Also check out...

Audio T

159A Chase Side, Enfield, Middx EBN2 0PW (8367 3132/www.audio-t.co.uk). Oakwood tube/Enfield Chase rail. **Open** 9.30am-5.30pm Tue-Sat. **Credit** MC, V.
Quality BADA member catering to the middle and top end of the market, and with a strong online presence.

Audio Venue

27 Bond Street, W5 5AS (8567 8703/ www.audiovenue.com). Ealing Broadway tube/rail. **Open** 10am-6pm Mon-Sat. **Credit** AmEx, MC, V.
Top end home-cinema and audio specialist, spanning individual components to full, professional installation.

KJ West One

26 New Cavendish Street, W1G 8TY (7486 8262/www.kjwestone.com). Baker Street or Bond Street tube. **Open** 10am-5.30pm Mon-Sat. **Credit** MC, V.
Premium hi-fi and home cinema equipment; consultation service available, either in-store or at your home.

Martin Kleiser

109 Chiswick High Road, W4 2ED (8400 5555/www.martin-kleiser.net). Turnham Green tube. **Open** 9am-5.30pm Tue-Sat. **Credit** AmEx, MC, V.
Good for large-scale home installations, offering consultation.

Musical Images

173 Station Road, Edgware, Middx HA8 7JX (8952 5535/www.musicalimages.co.uk). Edgware tube. **Open** 9.30am-6pm Mon-Sat. **Credit** DC, MC, V.
The Covent Garden branch of this highly acclaimed audio specialist has closed, but its extensive range is available here.
For branches see index.

Robert Taussig

59 Blandford Street, W1U 7HP (7487 3455). Baker Street tube. **Open** 9am-5pm Mon-Fri; 10am-5pm Sat. **Credit** MC, V.
Specialist in design and installation of high end, bespoke multi-room systems.

Sevenoaks Sound & Vision

144-148 Grays Inn Road, WC1X 8AX (0800 587 9909/www.ssav.com). Chancery Lane tube. **Open** 10.30am-6.30pm Mon-Fri; 11am-5pm Sat. **Credit** MC, V.
Mid-range and connoisseur manufacturers; specialises in hi-fi/home-cinema systems.
Branches: throughout the city.

The Studio

28 Aylmer Parade, Aylmer Road, N2 0PE (8348 0990/www.thenaimshop.dsl.pipex.com). Highgate tube/43, 134, 263 bus. **Open** by appointment Mon-Sat 11am-5pm. **Credit** AmEx, MC, V.
Catering to serious audiophiles and staffed with enthusiasts.

Erotic

Forget the stiff upper lip and British prudery; if it's latex, bondage and fetish gear you're after – London is the place to unleash your wildest fantasies. Visit the monthly **London Fetish Fair** (www.londonfetishfair.co.uk) for the last word in fetish fashion, dungeon design and pretty much everything else in between, or celebrate your sexual freedom at the **London Alternative Market** (www.londonalternativemarket.com). Fetish fashionistas never miss the annual **Erotica** (www.eroticauk.com), an exhibition that attracts around 80,000 visitors; you can relish a Monmouth coffee at **Coffee, Cake & Kink** (61 Endell Street, WC2H 9AJ, 7419 2996, www.coffeecakeandkink.com) while browsing through their collection of saucy books, prints and gifts; and the high-end lingerie brand **Agent Provocateur** (*see p67*) also has a continually expanding range of accessories (crystal whips, nipple tassles, metal cuffs) for sale in store and online.

Breathless

131 King's Cross Road, WC1X 9BJ (7278 1666/www.breathless.uk.com). King's Cross tube/rail. **Open** 11am-7pm Mon-Sat. **Credit** AmEx, MC, V.

Owner and designer Dolenta and her team continue to expand the house label and explore beyond fetishwear essentials. The ranges lie somewhere between glam street and vintage-inspired couture – and there's plenty to choose from with ten new designs emerging each year and a made-to-measure service. New women's lines nod to London's obsession with burlesque shapes, featuring black and lilac mini-dresses with contrasting flared red petticoats and bow belts, and black and white striped Cruela DeVil-esque tailored jackets that look divine with the Vogue range of latex miniature top hats. Classics include the 1930s-style baby doll dresses with latex rose detail and the bestselling straight and flared-leg catsuits in a cornucopia of colours. For men, new label DVote offers a latex black and red pleated kilt with button-up jacket, but Breathless's own white latex zoot suit and floor-length 'Hellraiser' skirt remain the most striking outfits. They also stock corsetry and lingerie from What Katie Did and Leg Avenue.

Coco de Mer

23 Monmouth Street, WC2H 9DD (7836 8882/www.coco-de-mer.co.uk). Covent Garden tube. **Open** 11am-7pm Mon-Wed, Fri, Sat; 11am-8pm Thur; noon-6pm Sun. **Credit** AmEx, MC, V.

This erotic emporium is London's most glamorous introduction to kink. The boudoir aesthetic creates an unmistakeable vibe of refined naughtiness, while a revamp last year has given the place a lighter, brighter and more museum-like feel, with quirky displays such as wall-mounted wooden hands cupping massage oils. Trying items on is a particular highlight, what with the peepshow-style velvet changing rooms that allow your lover to watch you undress from a 'confession box' next door. Stock has an ethical, artisan-led twist; you can be sure your dildo is made from WWF-endorsed wood (owner Sam Roddick clearly inherited her mother Anita's green credentials) or that part of the price includes a charity donation (Bondage for Freedom donates to Burmese charities). The jewelled nipple clips, jade cock rings and rose-decorated ceramic butt plugs and dildos are among the most intriguing new pieces. There's a deliciously large lingerie selection, with pieces from Afterwear, Louise Feuillère, Fifi Chachnil, La Perla and Coco de Mer's own range and an array of leather masks, locking gauntlets and corseted belts by Paul Seville and Ilya Fleet. The female-oriented book range now includes an exclusive rare vintage selection, where you can find 1920s pornography and fiction originals, like *Lolita*.

For branch see index.

Expectations

75 Great Eastern Street, EC2A 3RY (7739 0292/www.expectations.co.uk). Old Street tube/rail. **Open** 11am-7pm Mon-Fri; 11am-8pm Sat; noon-5pm Sun. **Credit** AmEx, MC, V.

Part of the gay Millivres Prowler Group empire (which owns *Gay Times* and *Diva* magazines), Expectations – a leather, rubber and fetish store – has an industrial, boiler-house setting that evokes a club-like vibe. Pass the cage at the bottom of the stairs, where you may find 'players' locked up during late-night shopping sessions, and you'll find plenty to wear to the ball. Premium jock straps, vivid rubber wrestling suits and cycling shorts, kilts and army surplus togs (such as combat pants) all make a statement, as do the 'high visibility' suits that glow in UV light, the sleek black rubber Adonis pouches (£45) and the new neoprene chaps, rubber jeans and streetwear from Nasty Pig. For private play, there are over 100 electro-stimulation accessories, ranging from butt plugs to cock rings, in stainless steel and conductive plastic, and masked men can choose from a multiplicity of hoods in breath control, executioner or Hannibal styles, to name just a few. Other hardware includes restraints, collars, slings, new harnesses, hogties, a quality metalwork series from Fuck Pig Dungeons, and the new in-house range of stimulation aromas and herbal sex aids.

Fettered Pleasures

90 Holloway Road, N7 8JG (7619 9333/www.fetteredpleasures.com). Holloway Road tube/Highbury & Islington tube/rail. **Open** 11am-7pm Mon-Sat. **Credit** MC, V.

There are few kinks that this friendly fetish monolith doesn't cater for, but for bondage enthusiasts it's deviant paradise: chain and rope by the metre; whips, canes, floggers and paddles; and a vast playground of high-quality restraints and contraptions to ensure your dungeon is the best equipped in town. The impressive 2008 menswear collection incorporated a large selection of 'playing sportswear', surplus army gear, including East German tank and flight suits, camouflage trousers as well as a variety of respiratory masks. Womenswear flails in comparison but there is a good number of latex uniforms and some decent corsets. The vast shop is still rich in niche lines, with a large display of electrics, dildos, horse-hair butt plugs, worship pants, puppy masks, hoods in over 80 styles, mitts and cages – and staff will try their utmost to source specific items.

Honour

86 Lower Marsh, SE1 7AB (7401 8219/www.honour.co.uk). Waterloo tube/rail. **Open** 10.30am-7pm Mon-Fri; 11.30am-5pm Sat. **Credit** AmEx, MC, V.

Honour's wide-ranging stock has something to suit all budgets, with clothing starting at

Coco de Mer

£5 for G-strings. The ground level is home to a wealth of PVC and latex fashion, from tops, skirts and catsuits to classic uniforms such as nuns, maids and even secretaries outfits (complete with waistcoat and shirt ensemble) to the 'Dirty & Flirty' selection featuring saucy 1950s-esque shirts in semi-transparent pink and black rubber. Much of this is available up to size 26 – and a new range of plus-size PVC and rubber was launched in September 2008. The latex menswear line includes a metallic red and blue fireman's costume and new olive-green military suit. Fetish magazine *Skin Two*'s sartorial offshoot, the popular, good-value rubber and PVC clothing range, is also available in store – fantastic for mistresses in the making. High, high heels, other shoes and boots are stocked up to size 11. Hardcore guys and girls should venture upstairs to the 'bondage attic', where there's a no-nonsense display of toys, cuffs and collars, restraints and clamps.

House of Harlot

90 Holloway Road, N7 8JG (7700 1441/ www.houseofharlot.com). Holloway Road tube/Highbury & Islington tube/rail.
Open 11am-6pm Mon-Fri; 11am-7pm Sat. **Credit** AmEx, MC, V.
Don't let this tiny boutique deceive you – the displays only represent a fraction of the sartorial wonders that this leading hydra-headed latex monster can produce. Kinky cobbler Natacha Marro and corset queen Miss Katie also have wares on display. Eye-catching accessories include Marro's six-inch thigh-high boots and Prong's latex boa. Other garments range from basic T-shirts and trousers to handmade stockings (£70), rubber corsets to catsuits (starting at £280), and rubberised uniforms – with themes like military muscle or kinky air hostess. Torture Garden's range is stocked, but the shop's own new lines have a more hardcore and retro-oriented feel, giving seasoned fetishists the extreme clothing they crave in times when fetishwear has been watered down for the Ann Summers crowd. Prices may be commensurate with workmanship involved, but service is friendly and professional. Clothing can be cut to measure at no extra cost, or created from scratch in around three to four weeks.

Liberation

49 Shelton Street, WC2H 9HE (7836 5894/ www.libidex.com). Covent Garden tube.
Open 11am-7pm Mon-Sat; also by appointment. **Credit** MC, V.
The flagship store for latex couturiers Libidex has considerably extended its range of glossy clothing delights, but you can still find intriguing accessories, all in *Little Shop of Horrors*-like surrounds. Pick up a hand-carved wooden cane (£35-£75), antique ivory dildos (£650) or a World War I operating table with original straps (and blood stains!). Downstairs you'll find clothing, accessories and hardware lines from Radical Rubber, Bondinage, hot new designer Bordello, Scarlet Diva, Prong, Beautiful & Damned and a new women's Libidex range, covering classic fetish staples and 1940s Hollywood glamour puss and army-inspired couture. For men, ponytailed Leigh Bowery-esque hoods, extreme catsuits and shirts with vintage pin-up and intricate Japanese bondage designs feature, plus the usual collars, cuffs and neck corsets.

Sh!

57 Hoxton Square, N1 6HD (7613 5458/www.sh-womenstore.com). Old Street tube/rail. **Open** noon-8pm daily. **Credit** MC, V.
You don't necessarily need to be a woman to pass through the hallowed pink portals of London's only female-oriented sex shop, but you'll need to be chaperoned by one. The capital's best sex shop for toys, Sh!'s strongest feature is its friendly staff who give honest advice. Books, gifts and new kinky artworks are displayed alongside strap-on harnesses and a penis-shaped sex toy demo desk that includes own-range clitoral pumps, dildos and vibrators in numerous materials, styles and prices (our fave is the iPod-activated vibrator, £50, that pulsates in time to your tunes). The Sh! Lil' Softee vibrator is a bargain at £7. Even the fetish and lingerie lines downstairs in the basement have the feminine touch: handcuffs are suede-lined, collars are fit for a princess and bondage tape, crops and whips (some, vibrating!) are candy-coloured.

Showgirls

64 Holloway Road, N7 8JL (7697 9072/ www.showgirlslatexboutique.com). Holloway Road tube/Highbury & Islington tube/rail.
Open 10.30am-7pm Mon-Sat. **Credit** AmEx, MC, V.
This small but stylish fetish boutique is going from strength to strength with a supreme selection of latex fashion from Jane Doe, Inner Sanctum and more. Stock ranges from the briefest of briefs to slinky dresses, in striking colourways (like red and gold or blue and silver) as well as in classic black. The shop's true selling point is as London's only retail outlet for latex couturier, *Vogue* favourite and fetish award-winner Atsuko Kudo, whose glamorous 'Hitchcock heroine' take on latex means a range boasting stylish lace-print jacket-and-pencil skirt ensembles and accessories like her signature veiled pillbox hat, driving gloves and latex blinkers. A new, select menswear line in the basement offers alternatives to staple rubber shorts and kilts, from top hats and ties to braces and there's an ample sale rale.

The best Erotic shops

For vibrators and sex toys
Coco de Mer (*see p201*) and **Sh!** (*see p202*).

For bondage gear
Fettered Pleasures (*see p201*) and **Honour** (*see p201*).

For latex fashion and corsetry
Breathless (*see p201*), **House of Harlot** (*see p202*) and **Liberation** (*see p202*).

For erotic literature
Coco de Mer (*see p201*) and **Coffee, Cake & Kink** (*see p201*).

For kinky but stylish lingerie
Agent Provocateur (*see p67*), **Coco de Mer** (*see p201*) and **Miss Lala's Boudoir** (*see p67*).

Also check out...

Clone Zone

64 Old Compton Street, W1D 4UQ (7287 3530/www.clonezone.co.uk). Leicester Square or Piccadilly Circus tube. **Open** 11am-9pm Mon-Sat; noon-8pm Sun. **Credit** AmEx, DC, MC, V.
Gay-oriented accessories, underwear, DVDs, magazines, books and sex toys.
Branches: throughout the city.

Fairy Gothmother

15 Lamb Street, Old Spitalfields Market, E1 6EA (7377 0370/www.fairygoth mother.com). Camden Town tube.
Open 11am-6pm Tue-Sat; 11am-5pm Sun. **Credit** MC, V.
This ever-morphing shop (its Camden branch is no more) stocks some 520 corset styles. A Victorian cincher starts at £70.

Harmony

167 Charing Cross Road, WC2H 0EN (7439 6261/www.harmonyxxx.com). Tottenham Court Road tube. Open 8am-midnight Mon-Fri; 10am-midnight Sat; 11am-11pm Sun. Credit AmEx, MC, V.
Sex superstore, with a tacky feel.
For branches see index.

Leatherworks

Unit 8, Stephen House, 1B Darnley Road, E9 6QH (8533 5599/www.leatherworks. co.uk). Hackney Central rail. **Open** 9am-5.30pm Mon-Fri; 9am-12.30pm Sat.
Credit MC, V.
East London kinky boot and shoe seller.

Natacha Marro

33 Marshall Street, W1F 7EX (7494 4044/ www.natachamarro.com). Oxford Circus tube. **Open** 11.30am-6.30pm Mon-Sat or by appointment. **Credit** MC, V.
Celebrity-favoured vertiginous, cartoonish heels share shelf space with vintage Victim clothing. A bespoke service is available.

Regulation

17A St Alban's Place, N1 0NX (7226 0665/www.regulation-london.co.uk). Angel tube. **Open** 10.30am-6.30pm Mon-Sat; noon-5pm Sun. **Credit** AmEx, MC, V.
Dedicated to the art of control. Around 4,000 items (paddles, harnesses, clubwear).

Zeitgeist

66 Holloway Road, N7 8JL (7607 2977/www.fetishcentral.net). Highbury & Islington tube/rail. **Open** 10am-6pm Mon-Fri; 10am-7pm Sat. **Credit** AmEx, MC, V.
PVC heaven at wallet-friendly prices.

Gifts

The term 'gift shop' has rather tacky connotations, often bringing to mind touristy souvenir shops; the shops listed here, however, have all been included by virtue of their wide range of quality products covering various categories, including accessories, jewellery, homeware, collectibles and beauty products – in other words, places you can visit to buy several gifty items at once.

Lots of the shops sell greetings cards, as do many of the places listed in the **Books** and **Stationery** chapters; *see pp177-188 and p231* respectively. **Supernice** on Columbia Road (*see p174* **Streetwise**) also sells original, witty cards.

For recommended flower shops, *see p171*. **Fabrications** (*see p208*), on Broadway Market, is also good for unusual gifts.

After Noah

121 Upper Street, N1 1QP (7359 4281/ www.afternoah.com). Angel tube. **Open** 10am-6pm Mon-Sat; noon-5pm Sun. **Credit** MC, V.

Islington's After Noah began life as an antique furniture restorer; now the shop is better known for its covetable selection of collectibles, homeware and toys. Industrial lamps that once hung in Smithfields and Billingsgate markets can be had for around £200; old-fashioned acrylic dial phones go from £85; and toys – for adult collectors as well as kids – include tin robots and racing cars. Vintage, antique and contemporary furniture remains a strong point: the wide, comfy Boho sofa has proved a particular hit (£1,850). There's also a concession in Harvey Nichols.

For branch see index.

Cat's Pyjamas of Marylebone

69 York Street, W1H 1QD (7723 7537/ www.thecatspyjamasofmarylebone.com). Baker Street or Edgware Road tube. **Open** 9am-7pm Mon-Fri; 10am-6pm Sat. **Credit** AmEx, MC, V.

You'd be hard pushed not to find a charming gift in this cleverly edited shop, where the stock is regularly renewed. 'Girly' gifts include butter-soft clutches and handbags, as well as chunky resin jewellery and pretty trinkets designed by Lisbeth Dahl. Homeware is on the quirky side: Lucy Tom's cotton and linen doorstop pigs cost from £30. The children's section boasts an array of gorgeous clobber, including Albetta's retro-style range, plus equipment, such as Charlie & Lola milk and biscuits sets (£14.95). Nostalgic Peter Pan types will love the Build Your Own Aeroplane and Pocket Kite kits (from £4.95).

Edwards & Todd

25A Museum Street, WC1A 1JU (7636 4650). Holborn tube or Tottenham Court road tube. **Open** 9.30am-6.30pm Mon-Sat. **Credit** AmEx, MC, V.

Whoever said that London's shops are not welcoming? Bloomsbury stalwart Edwards & Todd will always lift flagging spirits, with its eclectic, impossible-to-pigeonhole array of gifts and goods for the home. Some items are quintessentially British – a dozen wooden dolly pegs for £1.50, or gorgeous baby booties hand-knitted by the co-owner's mum in Wales – others have notched up a few more miles, such as the Zimbabwean tin giraffes recycled from old soda cans (£10). In the costume jewellery collection, big, bright beads jostle for attention with silver pieces and the prices start at a mere fiver. Retro space-hoppers and ginger-beer kits are also a hit.

Family Tree

53 Exmouth Market, EC1R 4QL (7278 1084/www.familytreeshop.co.uk). Angel tube/Farringdon tube/rail/19, 38, 341 bus. **Open** 11am-6pm Mon-Sat. **Credit** MC, V.

Another gem on hip Exmouth Market, Family Tree offers a carefully chosen selection of designer-made gifts, homeware and accessories sourced from around the globe. Owner Takako Copeland makes sure the shop's wares have an eco slant, with plenty of Fairtrade and organic cotton represented, but the main draw is her delicate lamps, made from Japanese rice paper. A diminutive version costs £19.80; £65 will get you the tallest shade plus the base. A few pretty pieces point to Copeland's past as a jeweller – like the rice paper patterns of birds and butterflies encased in resin (from £15).

Grace & Favour

35 North Cross Road, SE22 9ET (8693 4400). East Dulwich rail/176, 185 bus. **Open** 10am-6pm Mon-Sat; 11am-5pm Sun. **Credit** AmEx, MC, V.

One of East Dulwich's best-loved retail haunts, Rose Ratcliffe's lovely shop is the first port-of-call for clueless gift buyers. As jam-packed with covetable stuff for the home, garden and body as ever, new designer stationery brand Rosehip has been going down a storm. Illumens is another new name on the shelves: fragrant candles and room sprays start at £9.95. Bigger home accessories include a new range of striking, crackle-glaze vases in contrasting shades of shocking yellow, olive-green and stone (from £7.95). Meanwhile, the selection of mirrors has expanded: an ornate gold Regency-style winner is an affordable £45.

Lucas Bond

45 Bedford Hill, SW12 9EY (8675 9300/ www.lucasbond.com). Balham tube/rail. **Open** 10am-6pm Mon-Sat; noon-5pm Sun. **Credit** AmEx, MC, V.

Combining elegance with prettiness and chucking in a dollop of individuality for good measure, Lucas Bond has become something of an institution on Bedford Hill. Ceramics and British-designed treasures are the strong points: Andrew Tanner's simple white plates with the shapes of birds and butterflies cut out look charming displayed high on the wall; meanwhile, Snowden Flood's mugs (from £11.95) capture stylised views of London from the Thames. The vintage tiered cake stands are perfect for a retro tea party (£39 plus).

Rosie Brown

224-228 Fortis Green Road, N10 3DU (8883 5385). East Finchley tube/43 bus. **Open** 10.30am-6pm Mon-Sat; noon-5pm Sun. **Credit** MC, V.

Slightly off the beaten track from Muswell Hill's chi-chi shops, Lin Rosie Brown's appealing East Finchley boutique is worth the detour. As the eponymous owner says herself, the shop sells 'a bit of everything', from boudoir-style chandeliers dripping with crystal shards (from £90) to affordable beachwear (there's a great casual bargain line with everything below £30). Reflected in decadent Venetian-style mirrors (£80 upwards) is a well-edited range of vintage-look clothes from brands such as Lipsy.

Something...

58 Lamb's Conduit Street, WC1N 3LW (7430 1516/www.something-shop.com). Holborn or Russell Square tube. **Open** 10.30am-6pm Mon-Fri; 11am-5pm Sat. **Credit** AmEx, MC, V.

On one of London's best independent-dominated shopping roads, Toni Horton's light and bright shop full of keepsakes and accessories stands out. Girlish rather than girly bags range from practical holdalls to pay-day treats in candy colours and complete with bows, such as the roomy Amore scarf bags (£45). Jewellery is similarly diverse, with a highlight being the gobstopper-sized cocktail rings. High-end beauty and bath goodies include solid bars of fine Provençal soap (£5.50). In the summer months, head out to the back garden for a selection of pots and furniture.

Space EC1

25 Exmouth Market, EC1R 4QL (7837 1344). Angel tube/Farringdon tube/rail/ 19, 38, 341 bus. **Open** 10.30am-6pm Mon-Fri; 11am-5pm Sat. **Credit** AmEx, MC, V.

This friendly shop does novelty with humour and class. A set of three flying ducks in either black, silver or gold is a witty take on the suburban ceramic classic for just £15, while the origami kits will have you creating prom dresses and space rockets in no time (£7.50). A particular bestseller is the Mysterio baby T-shirt range (£12.50); each one comes in a sealed bag – unwrap it to reveal, printed across the front, your child's future profession. Other gifts include Ella Doran's Routemaster range of placemats, and there's a top-notch collection of cards.

Stardust

294 Milkwood Road, SE24 0EZ (7737 0199/www.stardustkids.co.uk). Herne Hill rail. **Open** 9.30am-6pm Mon-Sat; 11am-5pm Sun. **Credit** MC, V.

This funky shop prescribes a lighthearted dose of 'urban rebellion' among south London's edgier mums, dads and their little nippers. Pretty sundresses for girls come with a twist, including a cotton black number embroidered with cherries in the shape of skulls (£20), while stripy Tees for tots are emblazoned with ironic slogans such as 'The Future is Unwritten' (£15). Parents can choose matching sets of T-shirts – the Che Guevara set is £32 for both mother and child sizes. Toys, unusual greetings cards and and children's musical instruments are also up for grabs.

Tessa Fantoni

73 Abbeville Road, SW4 9JN (8673 1253/ www.tessafantoni.com). Clapham Common or Clapham South tube. **Open** 10am-6pm Mon-Sat; 10am-2pm Sun. **Credit** MC, V.
Tessa Fantoni began designing her stylish photograph albums back in 1978. Now sold exclusively at her peaceful Abbeville Road shop they are still bound in buckram and exquisitely patterned paper (from £26.50). The store is known for its pretty cards and wrapping paper, as well as toiletries (Floris, Neal's Yard) and furniture.

Whippet

71 Bedford Hill, SW12 9HA (8772 9781). Balham tube/rail. **Open** 11am-7pm Mon-Sat; noon-5pm Sun. **Credit** AmEx, MC, V.
Previously a textile designer in the fashion business, owner Vincent Wainwright's bold, graphic aesthetic is evident as soon as you cross the threshold. Wainwright admits to a bias towards Scandinavian design so there are bags from the house of Marimekko along with striking cased glass from Holmegaard. Vintage ceramics include hand-painted Royal Copenhagen from the 1970s (£75 for a large platter).

Wilton & Noble

9 Goldhurst Terrace, NW6 3HX (7624 2742/www.wiltonandnoble.com). Finchley Road tube. **Open** 9am-7pm Mon-Fri; 9am-6pm Sat; 11am-5pm Sun. **Credit** AmEx, MC, V.
Thanks to regularly evolving stock that showcases more difficult-to-find brands, it's very easy to find something individual at this friendly shop. Those with a sweet tooth will be delighted by the offerings from traditional English chocolatiers Ackerman's – the bestseller (£6 bags you 100g) – though the array of handmade Belgian chocs from Chocolate on Chocolate will also be tempting. The dining and kitchenware section is substantial, with glasses and cocktail-making equipment from Zak Designs and Invotis, and good-quality china from France. The newest branch is at St Pancras International.
For branch see index.

Also check out...

American Retro

35 Old Compton Street, W1D 5JX (7734 3477/www.americanretrolondon.com). Leicester Square tube. **Open** 10.30am-7pm Mon-Fri; 11am-7.30pm Sat; 1-6pm Sun. **Credit** AmEx, DC, MC, V.
Vintage clothes, gift ideas and other *Happy Days*-style ephemera, plus menswear from Fred Perry, Penguin and Kangol.

The Ark

161 Stoke Newington Road, N16 8BP (7275 9311/www.thearkgifts.com). Rectory Road rail/67, 76, 149, 243 bus. **Open** 11am-6pm Tue-Sat. **Credit** AmEx, DC, MC, V.
Plenty of classy gift ideas for him, her, the kids or even those awkward teens.

Chain Reaction

208 Chalk Farm Road, NW1 8AB (7284 2866). Camden Town tube. **Open** 10am-7pm daily. **Credit** AmEx, MC, V.
A plethora of fun gifts and collectibles.

Dulwich Trader

9-11 Croxted Road, SE21 8SZ (8761 3457/ www.dulwichtrader.com). West Dulwich rail. **Open** 9.30am-6pm Mon-Sat; 11am-5pm Sun. **Credit** AmEx, MC, V.
Quality womenswear, French furniture and smaller treasures for the home.
For branches (Ed and Tomlinsons) see index.

Farrago

25-27 Lacy Road, SW15 1NH (8788 0162). Putney Bridge tube/Putney rail. **Open** 10am-6pm Mon-Sat; noon-5pm Sun. **Credit** MC, V.
Eclectic goods: baby gifts to modern lamps.

Huttons

29 Northcote Road, SW11 1NJ (7223 5523/www.huttonsdirect.co.uk). Clapham Junction rail. **Open** 9.30am-6.30pm Mon-Fri; 9.30am-6pm Sat; 11am-5pm Sun. **Credit** AmEx, DC, MC, V.
Indispensable for emergency present ideas.
For branch see index.

Mint Source

23 Church Road, SW19 5DQ (8944 9580/ www.mintsource.com). Wimbledon tube/rail. **Open** 10am-6pm Mon-Sat; noon-5.30pm Sun. **Credit** MC, V.
Traditional and sporting gifts.

Multipazz

27 Rathbone Place, W1T 1EP (7462 0064/ www.multipazz.com). Tottenham Court Road tube. **Open** 10.30am-7pm Mon-Fri; noon-6pm Sat. **Credit** AmEx, MC, V.
An eclectic collection of jewellery, handbags, cards, candles and beauty products.

Oliver Bonas

137 Northcote Road, SW11 6PX (7223 5223/ www.oliverbonas.com). Clapham Junction rail. **Open** 10am-6.30pm Mon-Fri; 10am-6pm Sat; 11am-5pm Sun. **Credit** MC, V.
Attractive gifts, clothes and accessories.
Branches: throughout the city.

Tintin Shop

34 Floral Street, WC2E 9DJ (7836 1131/ www.thetintinshop.uk.com). Covent Garden tube. **Open** 10am-5.30pm Mon-Sat. **Credit** AmEx, DC, MC, V.
Tintin obsessives will find whatever they're after in this diminutive shop.

Treehouse

7 Park Road, N8 8TE (8341 4326). Finsbury Park tube then W7 bus or Highgate tube then W5 bus. **Open** 10am-5.30pm Mon-Sat; noon-4pm Sun. **Credit** MC, V.
Unusual gift ideas from far and wide.

Museum pieces

Many of the city's museums and galleries have gift shops that are destination-visits in their own right.

First up for style fiends is the **Design Museum** (28 Shad Thames, SE1 2YD,7940 8753, www.designmuseumshop.com), which stocks slick gifts ranging from modern design classics – the Campanas brothers' Citrus Basket, for example (£95) – to the innovative; we particularly like the eco Sun Jar light (£19.95) and the retro-style timepieces. Keeping with things technological, the **Science Museum** (Exhibition Road, SW7 2DD, 7942 4994, www.sciencemuseum.org.uk) sells gizmos aimed mainly at kids – from useful, like wind-up torches (£19.99), and fun, like the space ice-cream (from £3). Children and nostagic adults alike love the shop at the **V&A Museum of Childhood** (Cambridge Heath Road, E2 9PA, 8983 5200, www.museumofchildhood.org.uk), which stocks great retro-inspired toys, games and posters.

London's art galleries are also well worth a look. The gift shop at **Tate Modern** (Bankside, SE1 9TG, 7401 5167, www.tate.org.uk/shop) has a huge range of books, gadgets, prints, homeware and accessories; the Designers for Tate range sells stylish products made especially for the Tate – check out the bags by Ally Capellino, Mimi and Orla Kiely and exclusive jewellery lines from Tatty Devine and Terry Frost. The bookshops at the **Serpentine Gallery** (Kensington Gardens, W2 3XA, 7402 6075, www.serpentinegallery.org) and the **Photographers' Gallery** (5 & 8 Great Newport Street, WC2H 7HY, 7831 1772, www.photonet.org.uk) are good places to pick up coffee-table art books as well as hard-to-find and trendy imported magazines; the latter is also excellent on novelty gadgets. The **National Portrait Gallery** (2 St Martin's Place, WC2H OHE, 7306 0055, www.npg.org.uk) also has a good selection of books as well as posters and postcards – many relating to current shows. If that sounds a bit serious, then head to the **Museum of London** (150 London Wall, EC2Y 5HN, 0870 444 3851) for a fluffy toy plague rat (£11.99) or a cockney rhyming slang teapot (£25.99). It also has a selection of tube map paraphernalia, though the shop at the **London Transport Museum** (39 Wellington Street, WC2E 7BB, 7379 6344) has the best range of iconic Underground goods.

Art & Craft Supplies

Art supplies

Cass Art

66-67 Colebrooke Row, N1 8AB (7354 2999/www.cassart.co.uk). Angel tube. **Open** 10am-7pm Mon-Wed, Fri; 10am-6.30pm Sat; 11.30am-5.30pm Sun. **Credit** MC, V.
Cass Art's flagship store in Islington spans three floors and sells everything for the artist from a huge supply of sketchbooks and papers to a comprehensive stock of easels, canvases and portfolios. Inks, paints, pastels and brushes are sold in abundance and there is a good craft section downstairs.
For branches see index.

Green & Stone

259 King's Road, SW3 5EL (7352 0837/ www.greenandstone.com). Sloane Square tube. **Open** 9am-6pm Mon-Fri; 9.30am-6pm Sat; noon-5pm Sun. **Credit** AmEx, MC, V.
Browsing around this old-fashioned and wonderfully tranquil shop is like taking a step back in time. It is one of Chelsea's longest-standing retailers (first established in 1927), and the emphasis is on quality and authenticity: you'll find only the best fine and antique art supplies here. As well as Georgian watercolour boxes and inkwells, there's a comprehensive selection of calligraphy tools and paper. A picture-framing and mounting service is also available. Downstairs in the basement you'll find a huge selection of easels (both wood and metal) as well as rolls of canvases and unprimed linens, a craft section and a good selection of portfolios. At the time of writing, a new prop hire service for film and TV companies had just been set up (check the website for details).

L Cornelissen & Son

105 Great Russell Street, WC1B 3RY (7636 1045/www.cornelissen.com). Tottenham Court Road tube. **Open** 9.30am-5.30pm Mon-Sat. **Credit** MC, V.
With its stoppered glass jars and original antique shop fittings, this beautifully quaint shop resembles an old apothecary and is one of a dying breed. Established in 1855, Ford Maddox Brown, Dante Gabriel Rosetti and, more recently, Damien Hirst have all passed through its doors to peruse its impressive range of colourful pigments and pastels. Specialising in restoration, gilding and printmaking materials, it also sells calligraphy equipment, painting sets and feather quills.

London Graphic Centre

16-18 Shelton Street, WC2H 9JL (7759 4500/www.londongraphics.co.uk). Covent Garden or Leicester Square tube. **Open** 10am-6.30pm Mon-Fri; 10.30am-6pm Sat; noon-5pm Sun. **Credit** AmEx, MC, V.
The mother of all art shops. Whether you're a keen novice or established professional, you'll find all you need in the way of fine art supplies, graphics materials, light boxes, papers, portfolios and bags, books and magazines, spray paint – the list goes on. The shop also houses sporadic exhibitions.
For branches see index.

Also check out...

Alec Tiranti

27 Warren Street, W1T 5NB (7380 0808/ www.tiranti.co.uk). Great Portland Street or Warren Street tube. **Open** 9am-5.30pm Mon-Fri; 9.30am-1pm Sat. **Credit** MC, V.
Everything for the sculptor and ceramicist, including a good range of tools, materials and studio equipment.

AS Handover

Unit 8, Leeds Place, Tollington Park, N4 3RF (7272 9624/www.handover.co.uk). Finsbury Park tube/rail. **Open** 8.30am-5pm Mon-Fri. **Credit** AmEx, MC, V.
A comprehensive range of paints, brushes, decorating tools and stencilling supplies housed in a warehouse-style unit.

Atlantis European

7-9 Plumbers Row, E1 1EQ (7377 8855/ www.atlantisart.co.uk). Aldgate East tube. **Open** 9am-6pm Mon-Sat; 10am-5pm Sun. **Credit** AmEx, MC, V.
Warehouse space selling all manner of art materials, but specialising in painting.

Bird & Davis

45 Holmes Road, NW5 3AN (7485 3797/ www.birdanddavis.co.uk). Kentish Town tube/rail. **Open** 8am-5pm Mon-Fri. **Credit** MC, V.
Huge range of fine art materials – canvases, easels, modelling clays and pastels. There's a bargain box of primed canvas fabrics.

Cowling & Wilcox

26-28 Broadwick Street, W1F 8HX (7734 9556/www.cowlingandwilcox.com). Oxford Circus tube. **Open** 9.30am-6.30pm Mon-Sat. **Credit** AmEx, MC, V.
A fave with art students and designers. As well as fine art and graphic supplies, it stocks a wide variety of portfolios and bags.
For branch see index.

Jackson's Art

Arch 66, Putney Bridge, Station Approach, SW6 3UH (7384 3055/www.jacksonsart.co.uk). Putney Bridge tube. **Open** 9am-6pm Mon-Thur; 9am-5.30pm Fri; 9am-5pm Sat. **Credit** MC, V.
A compact but comprehensive art supplies shop with helpful, knowledgeable staff and an ever-expanding craft section.

Paintworks

99-101 Kingsland Road, E2 8AG (7729 7451/www.paintworks.biz). Old Street tube/ rail/26, 35, 67, 149, 242 bus. **Open** 9.30am-5.30pm Mon-Thur, Sat; 9.30am-6.30pm Fri. **Credit** MC, V.
This well-located shop (in arty Hoxton) stocks a large selection of paints and papers. Picture-framing is also available.

Partridge's

295-297 Lavender Hill, SW11 1LP (7228 7271/www.partridgesonline.com). Clapham Junction rail. **Open** 9am-6.30pm Mon-Fri; 9.30am-6.30pm Sat. **Credit** AmEx, MC, V.
A good general selection of arts and crafts materials at reasonable prices.

Russell & Chapple

68 Drury Lane, WC2B 5SP (7836 7521/ www.randc.net). Covent Garden or Holborn tube. **Open** 9am-5.30pm Mon-Fri. **Credit** AmEx, MC, V.
Russell & Chapple is the capital's oldest supplier of both canvases and fabrics to theatrical designers; upstairs, its sister company (Brodie & Middleton, 7836 3289) sells brushes and scenic paints.

Beading & jewellery-making

Bead Shop

21A Tower Street, WC2H 9NS (7240 0931/www.beadshop.co.uk). Covent Garden or Leicester Square tube. **Open** 1-6pm Mon; 10.30am-6pm Tue-Fri; 10.30am-5pm Sat. **Credit** MC, V.
This long-established and hugely popular shop attracts professional designers and bead enthusiasts from around the globe. A huge variety of beads is stocked, from humble resin varieties to the more ostentatious Swarovski crystal pearls. Beads made from precious metals, glass, bone and carved lacquer are just a small example of the vast stock housed here. Threads, wires and tools for putting it all together are also available as well as bargain packs of mixed beads. Classes are offered for beginners or those who need to brush up on their skills.

Buffy's Beads

Unit 2.3, Kingly Court, W1B 5PW (7494 2323/www.buffysbeads.com). Oxford Circus tube. **Open** 11am-7pm Mon-Sat; noon-6pm Sun. **Credit** AmEx, MC, V.
This minimalist, airy shop is tucked away on the top floor of a shopping emporium and seems only to attract those in the know. A favourite with discerning designers, all the beads are of the finest quality and are housed in lovely-looking antique drawers. Husband and wife team Rosie (a jewellery maker herself) and Andrew Pollard sell a hand-picked selection of tiaras, rings, chains and ribbons. Staff are all jewellery-makers and are on hand to offer friendly, informative service.

R Holt & Co

98 Hatton Garden, EC1N 8NX (7405 5286/www.rholt.co.uk). Chancery Lane tube/Farringdon tube/rail. **Open** 9.30am-5.30pm Mon-Fri; occasional Sat (call for info). **Credit** AmEx, DC, MC, V.
This well-known Hatton Garden outlet has recently been renovated and is now all sleek modern styling and glass interiors. It stocks an even larger selection of precious gemstones than before and is a great place to browse around if you're looking for a bit of inspiration. Endless trays of exquisite precious stones such as corals, turquoise, sapphires and carnets are great for ideas and adding colour. Prices start from as low as £1 and a small selection of ready-strung necklaces in a variety of colours and materials is on offer for those in a hurry. Jewellery designers on the premises can offer a sketching service and advice if you're feeling too spoilt for choice.

Also check out...

Creative Beadcraft

20 Beak Street, W1F 9RE (7629 9964/ www.creativebeadcraft.co.uk). Oxford Circus or Piccadilly Circus tube. **Open** 9am-5.15pm Mon-Fri; 10am-5.15pm Sat. **Credit** DC, MC, V.

Beads, sequins, imitation pearls, semi-precious stones and diamantés from around the globe, plus Swarovski crystals.

London Bead Co/ Delicate Stitches

339 Kentish Town Road, NW5 2TJ (0870 203 2323/www.londonbeadco.co.uk). Kentish Town tube/rail. **Open** 9.30am-5.30pm Mon-Sat. **Credit** AmEx, MC, V.

Housed in the same shop (beads at the front, needlecraft at the back), these companies complement each other perfectly.

Bookbinding

Shepherds Bookbinders (*see p231*) also sells bookbinding materials.

Wyvern Bindery

56-58 Clerkenwell Road, EC1M 5PX (7490 7899/www.wyvernbindery.com). Farringdon tube/rail. **Open** 9am-5pm Mon-Fri. **Credit** MC, V.

For a slice of 19th-century London, this Dickensian shop is hard to beat. Popular with art students and collectors alike, the Wyvern Bindery offers a good, old-fashioned personal service with the emphasis firmly where it should be: on quality bookbinding. Rolls of binding in an array of different fabrics are littered around the shop and friendly, knowledgeable staff are on hand to give advice. A book restoration service is also offered for those lovingly thumbed old tomes as well as the binding of presentation documents, theses, photo albums and boxes. Fabrics used range from silks in a variety of vibrant colours and textures to goatskin and pigskin.

Ceramics & mosaics

Mosaic Workshop

Unit 2, 1 Harry Day Mews, 1 Chestnut Road, SE27 9EZ (8670 4466/www.mosaic workshop.com). **Open** 10am-6pm Mon-Fri; 10am-1pm Sat. **Credit** MC, V.

This shop's new site still stocks everything for beginner and expert alike, though its workshop activity is now concentrated in Holborn. The Chestnut Road spot sells glass tiles of all shapes and sizes as well as books, kits, tools and other materials. Ring for details of mosaic courses.

For branch see index.

Fabrics

For more fabric and textile shops, including the **Cloth Shop**, *see p143* **Fabric & soft furnishings.** For **Fabrications**, *see p208.*

A1 Fabrics

50 & 52 Goldhawk Road, W12 8DH (8740 7349/www.a1fabrics.com). Goldhawk Road tube. **Open** 9am-6pm Mon-Sat. **Credit** MC, V.

A vast array of fabrics over two premises, plus trimmings and invisible zips.

Berwick Street Cloth Shop

14 Berwick Street, W1F 0PP (7287 2881). Oxford Circus or Piccadilly Circus tube. **Open** 9am-6pm Mon-Fri; 9am-5pm Sat. **Credit** AmEx, MC, V.

Large, ecletic selection of fake furs, rubber and latex, denims, jerseys and silks.

Bhopal Textile

98 Brick Lane, E1 6RL (7377 1886). Aldgate East tube. **Open** 9am-6pm daily. **Credit** AmEx, MC, V.

Bargain bolts of fabric, including luxurious silks, satins and linens.

Borovick Fabrics

16 Berwick Street, W1F 0HP (7437 2180/www.borovickfabricsltd.co.uk). Oxford Circus tube. **Open** 8.15am-6pm Mon-Fri; 8.15am-5pm Sat. **Credit** MC, V.

A stomping ground for stylists and fashionistas who flock here for the wide selection of fabrics.

Broadwick Silks

9-11 Broadwick Street, W1F 0DB (7734 3320). Oxford Circus or Piccadilly Circus tube. **Open** 9am-6pm Mon-Fri; 9am-5pm Sat. **Credit** AmEx, MC, V.

Sells a stunning selection of silks, from shantung to chiffon.

Cass Art. *See p205.*

Cloth House

47 Berwick Street, W1F 8SJ (7437 5155/ www.clothhouse.com). Oxford Circus or Tottenham Court Road tube. **Open** 9.30am-6pm Mon-Fri; 10.30am-6pm Sat. **Credit** DC, MC, V.

Has a good selection of pretty, patterned fabrics – everything from Laura Ashley styles to Liberty-esque lines.

For branches see index.

Joel & Son Fabrics

75-83 Church Street, NW8 8EU (7724 6895/www.joelandsonfabrics.com). Edgware Road tube. **Open** 9am-5pm Mon-Sat. **Credit** AmEx, MC, V.

High-end designer fabrics from the likes of Loro Piana, Ermenegildo Zegna and Valentino, plus well-priced printed cottons, silks, embroidered chiffons and lace.

Silk Society

44 Berwick Street, W1F 8SE (7287 1881). Oxford Circus tube. **Open** 9am-6pm Mon-Fri; 9am-5pm Sat. **Credit** AmEx, MC, V.

Large selection of silks for bridalwear and special occasions.

Soho Silks

22 D'Arblay Street, W1F 8ED (7434 3305). Oxford Circus tube. **Open** 9.30am-6pm Mon-Sat. **Credit** AmEx, DC, MC, V.

Textile King

81 Berwick Street, W1F 8TW (7437 7372). Oxford Circus tube. **Open** 10am-5pm Mon-Fri 11am-6pm Sat. **Credit** MC, V.

A bustling and cheerful shop that specialises in suiting and coating fabrics mainly for menswear.

Haberdashery, trimmings & buttons

John Lewis (*see p15*) has a strong haberdashery department, **Cloth House** (*see p207*) and **Persiflage** (*see p59*) have a great selection of vintage buttons and trimmings.

All the Fun of the Fair

Unit 2.8, Kingly Court, W1B 5PW (7287 2303/www.allthefunofthefair.biz). Oxford Circus tube. **Open** 11am-7pm Mon-Sat; noon-5pm Sun. **Credit** MC, V.

Cute, quirky shop that stocks an interesting and colourful range of yarns and threads for all your knitting, crocheting and sewing needs. Owner Buzz Stokes calls her shop a 'haberdashery boutique' and vintage knitting patterns and patterns are sold here together with some original gift ideas like knitted flowers and hot cross buns and even plastic aprons for washing-up bottles.

Button Queen

19 Marylebone Lane, W1U 2NF (7935 1505/www.thebuttonqueen.co.uk). Bond Street tube. **Open** 10am-5pm Mon-Fri; 10am-2pm Sat. **Credit** MC, V.

A long-established retailer with a great reputation for knowledge and expertise, Button Queen is an Aladdin's cave of buttons of all shapes and sizes (from 1920s antique art nouveau buttons to oversize contemporary styles). Shelves are filled with boxes of different buttons – made from horn, glass and plastic. If you've lost an unusual or antique button, these guys will try to source it for you or suggest alternative solutions. A button-covering service is also offered.

Fabrications (eco)

7 Broadway Market, E8 4PH (7275 8043/ www.fabrications1.co.uk). London Fields rail/26, 55, 106, 277, 394 bus. **Open** noon-5pm Tue-Fri; 10am-5.30pm Sat. **Credit** MC, V.

Barley Massey's studio/shop/gallery is an outlet for her distinctive textile designs, which focus on recycled materials. Among the regularly changing offerings, you might find Massey's cushions made from vintage fabrics (from £20) and knitted lambswool creatures by Donna Wilson (£20-£45). There's a quirky haberdashery section, with a small but unusual selection of wool, needles and patterns, and the shop also does a good line in seasonal items (Valentine's Day sees a riot of quirky love tokens), cards and gifts. Massey is happy to undertake interior accessories commissions; a new 'Remember Me' service enables you to bring clothing and textiles that hold sentimental value, such as your child's outgrown clothing, to be remade into furnishings, artworks and gifts. Massey's items are also stocked in new shop Eco (*see p121*) as well as EcoCentric (www.ecocentric.co.uk).

MacCulloch & Wallis

25-26 Dering Street, W1S 1AT (7629 0311/www.macculloch-wallis.co.uk). Bond Street or Oxford Circus tube. **Open** 10am-6pm Mon-Wed, Fri; 10am-7pm Thur; 10.30am-5pm Sat. **Credit** AmEx, DC, MC, V.

A legend in the eyes of the many designers and tailors that frequent this long- established shop, MacCullock & Wallis stocks a huge selection of fabrics, zips, thread and buttons as well as millinery supplies and dressmaker's dummies. Upstairs, there's also a good selection of sewing machines (mainly Bernina).

VV Rouleaux

102 Marylebone Lane, W1U 2QD (7224 5179/www.vvrouleaux.com). Bond Street tube. **Open** 9.30am-6pm Mon-Wed, Fri, Sat; 9.30am-6.30pm Thur. **Credit** AmEx, MC, V.

A great place to visit when you're in need of some visual inspiration, this shop is a staple favourite of designers and stylists alike and is best known for its huge variety of vibrantly coloured ribbons, trimmings, feathers and hatpins. The light, airy shop houses a fine selection of accessories like the delicate-looking fabric butterflies that dangle above colourful corsages. There's also a good selection of masks and vintage brooches and pins. Downstairs you'll find furnishing trimmings, including ties, tassles and fringing for edgings as well as vintage bridal headdresses, veils and flowers. The shop's a popular choice for wedding designers and bridal magazines.

For branch see index.

Also check out...

Barnett Lawson

16-17 Little Portland Street, W1W 8NE (7636 8591/www.bltrimmings.com). Oxford Circus tube. **Open** 9am-5.30pm Mon-Fri. **Credit** MC, V.

A functional-looking shop (press buzzer for entry) that stocks a wide selection of tassels, trimmings, braid and diamanté.

JT Morgan

128 Railway Arches, behind Macfarlane Road, W12 7LA (8222 6711/www.jt morganhaberdasher.co.uk). Shepherd's Bush tube. **Open** 2-7pm Mon-Fri; also by appointment. **No credit cards.**

Over 19,000 lines of stock and millions of button designs. Covered-button, pattern-cutting and alterations services are available.

Kleins

5 Noel Street, W1F 8GD (7437 6162/ www.kleins.co.uk). Oxford Circus tube. **Open** 10am-5pm Mon-Fri. **Credit** MC, V.

A good, comprehensive range of trimmings with a craft supplies section downstairs.

Taylor's Buttons

22 Cleveland Street, W1T 4JB (7436 9988). Goodge Street tube. **Open** 11am-4pm Mon-Fri. **No credit cards.**

Vintage and contemporary styles. Buttons, belts and buckles can also be covered and in some cases, dyed to order.

Hides & leather

Walter Reginald

Unit 6, 100 The Highway, E1W 2BX (7481 2233/www.walterreginald.com). Shadwell tube/DLR. **Open** 9am-5pm Mon-Fri. **Credit** MC, V.

Leather and suede for garments, footwear, upholstery and general crafts.

Knitting & needlecraft

For woolly fashion boutique **House of Weardowney**, *see p31*.

I Knit London

106 Lower Marsh, SE1 7AB (7261 1338/ www.iknit.org.uk). Waterloo tube/rail. **Open** 11am-9pm Tue-Thur; 11am-7pm Mon, Fri, Sat. **Credit** AmEx, MC, V.

Since relocating last year from bohemian Bonnington Square to a more central location in Waterloo, this cool, quirky haberdashery shop has gone from strength to strength. A laid-back atmosphere (with the help of big leather sofas and a drinks fridge) coupled with an amazing selection of wools and yarns makes this salon-style shop a one-off in the knitting world. Owners Gerard Allt and Craig Carruthers sell a wide range of yarns with special emphasis on British independent producers. More unusual types of yarn such as recycled sari silk from India are also available; 1950s and '60s knitting patterns are stocked, as well as a decent range of how-to books. With regular film screenings, knitting get-togethers, beginners' classes and even a knitting night for the discerning male, what more could you ask for?

Loop

41 Cross Street, N1 2BB (7288 1160/www. loop.gb.com). Angel tube. **Open** 11am-6pm Tue-Sat; noon-5pm Sun. **Credit** DC, MC, V.

Tucked away in a corner of Islington's trendy Cross Street, this shop is a joy to browse. An array of yarns in a kaleidoscope of colours awaits you and textures vary from the softest kid mohair to the chunkier Misti Alpaca wool for more heavyweight knits. You'll also find eco-friendly, hand-dyed yarns by brands such as Be Sweet as well as velvety chenilles by Touch Me. Other products on offer include rosewood knitting needles, crochet and knitting kits and dupion silk ribbons. A small selection of colourful tea-cosies and other knitted accessories by new, young designers is also on sale. Classes for beginners and improvers are available.

Prick Your Finger

260 Globe Road, E2 0JD (8981 2560/ www.prickyourfinger.com). Bethnal Green tube/rail. **Open** noon-7pm Tue-Fri; 11am-6pm Sat. **Credit** DC, MC, V.

A funky little shop set up by two Central St Martin graduates to promote all things knitted; yarns, needles, patterns and kits.

Stash Yarns

213 Upper Richmond Road, SW15 6SQ (8246 6666/www.stashyarns.co.uk). East Putney tube/Putney rail/337, 430 bus. **Open** 10am-5pm Tue-Fri; 11am-5pm Sat. **Credit** AmEx, MC, V.

A huge range of colourful, carefully sourced yarns can be found in this cosy informal shop with regular customers dropping in for tips, hints or just to check out the new stock. Hand-dyed wool by Canadian company Handmaiden can be found here as well as more unusual brands from around the world. Knitting patterns, magazines and needles are also available and owners Michelle Lieberson and Nathalie Giauque are often on hand to offer helpful advice. A drop-in knitting group happens every Wednesday and classes are available throughout the year.

Also check out...

Creative Quilting

32 Bridge Road, Hampton Court, East Molesey, Surrey KT8 9HA (8941 7075/ www.creativequilting.co.uk). Hampton Court rail. **Open** 9.30am-5.30pm Mon-Sat; noon-4pm Sun. **Credit** MC, V.
A quilt-maker's paradise, Creative Quilting has over 1,000 bolts of fabric, as well as literature, threads and tools in stock. Staff are all quilters. Quilting classes are also held.

Wools & Crafts

169 Blackstock Road, N4 2JS (7359 1274/ www.woolsandcrafts.co.uk). Finsbury Park tube/rail. **Open** 10am-5pm Mon-Wed, Fri, Sat. **Credit** MC, V.
A traditional haberdashery shop selling yarns, crochet cottons, needles, patterns, books and general knitting supplies.

Sewing machines

See also p208 **MacCulloch & Wallis**. The following sell and service new and second-hand machines.

Chapman Sewing Machines *80 Parkway, NW1 7AN (7485 0140). Camden Town tube.* **Open** 9am-5pm Mon-Fri; 10.30am-5pm Sat. **Credit** AmEx, MC, V.

Lewisham & Deptford Sewing Machines *181 Deptford High Street, SE8 3NT (8692 1077/www.sewing machinesuk.co.uk). Deptford Bridge DLR.* **Open** 10am-5.30pm Mon-Wed, Fri, Sat. **Credit** MC, V.

Olympic Sewing Machines *1B Shepherd's Bush Road, W6 7NA (8743 6683). Shepherd's Bush or Goldhawk Road tube.* **Open** 10am-5.30pm Mon-Sat. **Credit** AmEx, MC, V.

Sew Amazing *80 St Stephen's Road, E3 5JL (8980 8898/www.sewamazingltd. co.uk). Bethnal Green tube/rail/8 bus.* **Open** 9.30am-5pm Mon-Sat. **Credit** (over £10) MC, V.

Sewing Centre *266 Battersea Park Road, SW11 3BP (7228 3022/www. directsewingmachines.co.uk). Sloane Square tube then 219, 319 bus/Clapham Junction rail.* **Open** 10am-5.30pm Mon-Sat. **Credit** AmEx, MC, V.

Spinning & weaving

Fibrecrafts

www.fibrecrafts.com
A range of materials and supplies for paper-making, spinning, felting, weaving, batik, fabric-dying and painting. Knitting and crochet equipment is also sold.

Hobbies & Games

For computer games, *see p199*.

Board & fantasy games

BCM Chess Shop/ Bridge Shop

44 Baker Street, W1U 7RT (7486 8222/ www.bcmchess.co.uk). Baker Street tube. **Open** 10am-6pm Mon-Sat. **Credit** AmEx, MC, V.
As the base of *British Chess* magazine it's perhaps not surprising that this chess shop is so well stocked with equipment: computer chess, books, videos plus a selection of other board games can all be bought here. It also sells decorative chess sets; pick up a Staunton mahogany chest for £595.
For branch see index.

Compendia

10 Greenwich Market, SE10 9HZ (8293 6616/www.compendia.co.uk). Cutty Sark DLR. **Open** 11am-5.30pm Mon-Fri; 10am-5.30pm Sat, Sun. **Credit** MC, V.
A specialist in traditional games such as dominoes and jigsaws, Compendia also has some obscure titles. There's mancala (an African game often compared to chess), the Japanese board game Go and Mexican train dominoes (a Latin American variant on the classic game). On other shelves, there are traditional pub games like skittles and shove ha'penny. Board games include Pass the Bomb, Treasure Island and Settlers of Catan.
For branch see index.

Playin' Games

33 Museum Street, WC1A 1JR (7323 3080). Holborn or Tottenham Court Road tube. **Open** 10am-6pm Mon-Wed, Fri, Sat; 10am-7pm Thur; noon-6pm Sun. **Credit** AmEx, MC, V.
A handsome boutique in which traditional board games, war and fantasy role-playing games, puzzles and books sit side-by-side. Names like Twister, Monopoly and Cluedo will spark nostalgia; others – like the War on Terror and the Hungry Caterpillar game – are new offerings. If you're inspired to start playing again, try the Champagne Murder dinner party set at £18.99.
For branch see index.

Also check out...

Chess & Bridge

369 Euston Road, NW1 3AR (7388 2404/ www.chess.co.uk). Great Portland Street tube. **Open** 10am-6pm Mon-Sat; 11am-5pm Sun. **Credit** AmEx, MC, V.
Chess & Bridge holds all sorts of goodies. Chess sets go from £15 to £1,500. It also sells playing cards and Scrabble.
For branch see index.

Games Workshop

The Plaza, 116-128 Oxford Street, W1D 1LT (7436 0839/www.games-workshop.com). Oxford Circus tube. **Open** 10am-7pm Mon-Wed, Fri, Sat; 10am-8pm Thur; noon-6pm Sun. **Credit** AmEx, MC, V.
Games Workshop supplies *Warhammer* battle games, miniature models and collectable artefacts.
Branches: throughout the city.

Orc's Nest

6 Earlham Street, WC2H 9RY (7379 4254/www.orcsnest.com). Leicester Square tube. **Open** 11am-6.30pm Mon-Wed, Fri; 11am-7pm Thur; 11am-6pm Sat. **Credit** AmEx, MC, V.
The UK's largest independent retailer of role-playing collectibles and accessories.
For branch see index.

Village Games

65 The West Yard, Camden Lock, NW1 8AF (7485 0653/www.villagegames.com). Camden Town tube. **Open** 10am-6pm Wed-Sun. **Credit** AmEx, MC, V.
Brain-boggling logic games, 3D jigsaws, mechanical puzzles and traditional toys.
For branch see index.

Models & model-making

Forbidden Planet

179 Shaftesbury Avenue, WC2H 8JR (7420 3666/www.forbiddenplanet.com). Covent Garden or Tottenham Court Road tube. **Open** 10am-7pm Mon-Wed, Fri, Sat; 10am-8pm Thur; noon-6pm Sun. **Credit** AmEx, DC, MC, V.
Geeks get together at London's mega-store for sci-fi, fantasy and comic-related memorabilia. The term 'Super Hero' is used imaginatively here: among the collection is an 18in-high model of Tony *Scarface* Montana for £39.99 and a Kurt Cobain figure at £29.99. On other shelves you'll find good company with Rocky, He-Man and armies of Transformers. You can also pick up signed books and DVDs, and even buy disguises if you really want to get into character.
For branch see index.

Model Zone

202 High Holborn, WC1V 7BD (7405 6285/8592/www.modelzone.co.uk). Holborn tube. **Open** 9.30am-6pm Mon-Sat; 11am-5pm Sun. **Credit** AmEx, MC, V.
Painted statuettes, model railways and Scalextric will set your imagination ticking. Buy a miniature Enzo Ferrari for £19.99 if you can't stretch to the Real McCoy, or, if you don't think it's politically incorrect, get yourself a British Infantry Tank for £17.99.
For branches see index.

Playlounge

19 Beak Street, W1F 9RP (7287 7073/ www.playlounge.co.uk). Oxford Circus or Piccadilly Circus tube. **Open** 10.30am-7pm Mon-Sat; noon-5pm Sun. **Credit** AmEx, MC, V.
Compact but fun filled, this groovy little shop has action figures, gadgets, books and comics, e-boy posters, T-shirts and clothing that appeal to children and adults alike. Pick from a full set of Gorillaz statuettes (£63) or a box of Tragic Toys for Girls & Boys

Playlounge. See p209.

figurines (£14.95), the product of Tim Burton's twisted imagination. For soft toys, how about a huge Plush Moomin (£24.95) or a character from the Uglydoll range (including a good selection of Little Uglies for £9.95). Those nostalgic for illustrated children's literature shouldn't miss out on the selection of *Dr Seuss PopUps* and *Where the Wild Things Are* books. The website – designed like a game of snap – is a hit too.
For branch see index.

Also check out…

Comet Miniatures
44-48 Lavender Hill, SW11 5RH (7228 3702/www.comet-miniatures.com). Clapham Common tube or Clapham Junction rail. **Open** 9am-5.30pm Mon-Sat. **Credit** MC, V.
Models and toys of film, TV and sci-fi characters, plus magazines and model kits.
For branch see index.

Hobby's
Knights Hill Square, SE27 0HH (8761 4244/www.hobby.uk.com). West Norwood rail. **Open** 9am-5pm Mon-Fri; 9am-1pm Sat. **Credit** AmEx, MC, V.
This doll's house specialist also sells a range of kits, tools and materials for general model-making.
For branch see index.

Ian Allan's Transport Bookshop
45-46 Lower Marsh, SE1 7RG (7401 2100/www.ianallanpub.co.uk). Waterloo tube/rail. **Open** 9am-5.30pm Mon-Fri; 9am-5pm Sat. **Credit** MC, V.
Models of vehicles, plus books and videos.
For branch see index.

My Hobbies
706 High Road, E11 3AJ (8539 9009/www.myhobbies.co.uk). Leytonstone tube. **Open** 9am-5.30pm Mon-Sat. **Credit** MC, V.
A specialist in radio-controlled vehicles; also stocks Matchstick kits and radio sets.
For branch see index.

Stamps & coins

Stampex stamp fairs are held twice a year; see www.stampex.ltd.uk.

Argyll Etkin Gallery
27 Regent Street, SW1Y 4UA (7437 7800/www.argyll-etkin.com). Piccadilly Circus tube. **Open** 9am-5.30pm Mon-Fri. **Credit** MC, V.
Autographs, royal memorabilia, stamps and historic postal documents.
For branch see index.

Coincraft
44-45 Great Russell Street, WC1B 3LU (7636 1188/www.coincraft.com). Holborn or Tottenham Court Road tube. **Open** 9.30am-5pm Mon-Fri; 9.30am-2.30pm Sat. **Credit** AmEx, DC, MC, V.
In the trade since 1899, this elegant shop sells coins, banknotes, and medals as well as antiquities from ancient Rome and Greece.
For branch see index.

Collector's Centre
79 Strand, WC2R 0DE (7836 2341/www.stampcentre.co.uk/www.scificollector.co.uk). Embankment tube/Charing Cross tube/rail. **Open** 9.30am-5pm Mon-Sat. **Credit** AmEx, MC, V.
First-day covers, signed covers and prints, stamps and sci-fi collectibles.
For branch (Royale Stamp Company) see index.

Simmons Gallery
www.simmonsgallery.co.uk
World coins, medals and tokens online.

Stanley Gibbons
399 Strand, WC2R 0LX (7836 8444/www.stanleygibbons.com). Embankment tube/Charing Cross tube/rail. **Open** 9am-5.30pm Mon-Fri; 9.30am-5.30pm Sat. **Credit** AmEx, MC, V.
The world's largest stamp shop, established in 1856, has over three million stamps. Upstairs, Frasers specialises in autographs.
For branch see index.

Music

Most shops listed in this section deal in second-hand as well as new equipment. Many music shops are clustered around **Denmark Street** (commonly known as 'Tin Pan Alley') and **Charing Cross Road**.

Barbican Chimes Music Shop

Silk Street, EC2Y 8DD (7588 9242). Barbican tube/Moorgate tube/rail. **Open** 9am-5.30pm Mon-Fri; 9am-4pm Sat. **Credit** DC, MC, V.

An invaluable resource for Guildhall students and soloists performing at the Barbican, Chimes – at the base of Cromwell Tower, right next to the main entrance of the Barbican – has a large stock of sheet music, manuscript paper, reeds, strings, bows, mouthpieces, classical CDs and more. There's also a limited selection of guitars and ukes, plus rhythm instruments and novelty children's items. The South Ken branch has more for-hire instruments, while the Royal Academy branch is something of a tourist museum shop.

For branches see index.

Chappell of Bond Street

152-160 Wardour Street, W1F 8YA (7432 4400/www.chappellofbondstreet.co.uk). Tottenham Court Road tube. **Open** 9.30am-6pm Mon-Fri; 10am-5.30pm Sat. **Credit** AmEx, MC, V.

It's retained its old name, but in 2006 Chappell moved from Bond Street (its home for nearly 200 years) to this amazing three-storey temple in Soho. The shop is the leading Yamaha stockist in the UK, with a great range of digital and acoustic pianos, guitars, brass, woodwind and electronic equipment. Prices start at around £20 for a recorder and £550 for a violin and go up to £19,000 for a double bass. The collection of sheet music is reputedly the largest in Europe.

Umbrella Music

2 Greenleaf Road, E17 6QQ (8520 2163/www.umbrellamusic.co.uk). **Open** 10am-6pm Mon-Sat. **Credit** MC, V.

A long-established local music shop with a very reasonable collection of new electronic keyboards and guitars, plus plenty of beginners-level brass, woodwind, strings, percussion, amplifiers, recorders, ukes and banjos. It also stocks sheet music, runs a 'hire and try' scheme, hosts education courses and has an on-site workshop for basic repairs.

Also check out...

Gigsounds

86-88 Mitcham Lane, SW16 6NR (8769 3206/www.gigsounds.co.uk). Tooting Broadway tube then 57 bus/Streatham Common rail. **Open** 10am-6.30pm Mon-Fri; 10am-6pm Sat. **Credit** AmEx, MC, V.

An amazingly comprehensive stock, from kazoos to studio electronics.

Mill Hill Music Mart

Unit 7, Bunns Lane, Mill Hill, NW7 2AJ (8906 9991). Mill Hill Broadway rail.

Bridgewood & Neitzert. *See p215.*

LEISURE

Open 11am-11pm Mon-Fri, Sun; 11am-6pm Sat. **Credit** MC, V.
This rehearsal mecca is also a music store, with drums, guitars, gear hire, and more.

Drums & percussion

Diamond UK

Unit G4, Lea Valley Business Centre, 1 Horley Road, Edmonton, off the A406, nr Cooks Ferry Interchange, N18 3SB (8803 3345). Angel Road rail/34 bus. **Open** 10am-5pm Mon-Sat. **Credit** MC, V.
Very competitively priced own-brand drum kits (£290-£600), hand percussion, stands and accessories, plus Istanbul cymbals and Remo heads. There's also a small selection of brass and woodwind.

Foote's

10 Golden Square, W1F 9JA (7734 1822/ www.footesmusic.com). Piccadilly Circus tube. **Open** 9am-6pm Mon-Fri; 10am-6pm Sat. **Credit** AmEx, MC, V.
This long-established store concentrates on percussion and drums, with big names including Yamaha, Ludwig and Zildjian. World and Latin percussion, glockenspiels, electronic drums and a huge assortment of accessories are also sold alongside a good selection of woodwind, brass and string instruments, and a rent-to-buy scheme is available. Learners can browse a decent stock of books, DVDs and CDs covering a wide range of instruments; hands-on tuition is also offered on request in an in-store demo room.

Also check out...

Professional Percussion

205 Kentish Town Road, NW5 2JU (7485 4434/www.propercussion.co.uk). Kentish Town tube/rail. **Open** 10am-6pm Mon-Sat. **Credit** MC, V.
Aimed at professionals and beginners, this place boasts many a celebrity customer.

Wembley Drum Centre

Unit 7-8, Metro Trading Centre, Fifth Way, Wembley, Middx HA9 0YJ (8795 4001/ www.wembleydrumcentre.com). Wembley Park tube. **Open** 10am-6pm Mon-Sat. **Credit** AmEx, MC, V.
A drum paradise with a range of Pearl, Yamaha, Sabian, DW and Zildjian products.

Guitars & banjos

Bass Cellar

22 Denmark Street, WC2H 8NG (7240 3483/www.denmarkstreetonline.co.uk). Tottenham Court Road tube. **Open** 10am-7pm Mon-Sat; 11am-5pm Sun. **Credit** MC, V.
Bass guitar legend selling well-worn 1960s and '70s Fenders and Rickenbackers, five-, six- and seven-string bass guitars, semi-acoustics and acres of Warwick and Fender.

Chandler Guitars

300-302 Sandycombe Road, Kew, Surrey TW9 3NG (8940 5874/www.chandler guitars.co.uk). Kew Gardens tube/rail. **Open** 9.30am-6pm Mon-Sat. **Credit** MC, V.
The fact that Chandler has survived for long in its remote, sleepy Kew Gardens locale is a testament to the quality of the service and instruments here. The catalogue covers new electric guitars from Paul Reed Smith and Fender as well as a superb range of vintage models. Chandler is the servicing workshop of choice when the Red Hot Chili Peppers or Dave Gilmour are in town.

Duke of Uke

22 Hanbury Street, E1 6QR (7247 7924/ www.dukeofuke.co.uk). Liverpool Street tube/rail. **Open** noon-7pm Tue-Sun. **Credit** MC, V.
See right **Unique selling point**.

London Guitar Studio/ El Mundo Flamenco

62 Duke Street, W1K 6JT (7493 0033/ www.londonguitarstudio.com/www.elmundo flamenco.co.uk). Bond Street tube. **Open** 9.30am-6pm Mon-Sat; 10am-5pm Sun. **Credit** AmEx, MC, V.
Acoustic models for classical and flamenco; plus essential extras like castanets.
For branches see index.

Music Ground

27 Denmark Street, WC2H 8NJ (7836 5354/www.musicground.com). Tottenham Court Road tube. **Open** 10am-7pm Mon-Sat. **Credit** AmEx, MC, V.
Interesting top-of-the-range vintage guitar shop, which also houses the London Pedal Company, a specialist in high-end 'boutique pedals' including Keely, Fulltone, Z-Vex, Electro-Harmonix and T-Rex.

Regent Sounds

4 Denmark Street, WC2H 8LP (7379 6111). Tottenham Court Road tube. **Open** 10am-7pm Mon-Sat. **Credit** AmEx, MC, V.
Europe's largest Fender dealer, also stocks Gretsch, Music Man, Squier, Vox, Tokai, Hofner and Danelectro guitars, basses, amps and accessories. The Rolling Stones recorded their first album here.

Rhodes Music

21 Denmark Street, WC2H 8NA (7836 4656). **Open** 10am-7pm Mon-Sat. **Credit** AmEx, MC, V.
Legendary establishment where Jeff Beck, Eric Clapton, Pete Townsend, the Strokes and Oasis have all bought guitars. Rhodes specialises in Gibson guitars, guitar amps and lots of guitar effects and demo areas.

Rockers Guitars

5 Denmark Street, WC2H 8LP (7240 2610). Tottenham Court Road tube. **Open** 10am-7pm Mon-Sat; 11am-5pm Sun. **Credit** AmEx, MC, V.
Electric guitars, basses, amplifiers, acoustics and accessories, as well as a dedicated workshop for set-ups and repairs. It stocks guitars by Gibson, Epiphone, Fender, Dean, Pignose, ESP, Ibanez, BC Rich and many others, amps by Marshall and HiWatt, and basses by Cort, Aria, Fender, OLP and Ibanez.

Vintage & Rare Guitars

6 Denmark Street, WC2H 8LX (7240 7500/ www.vintageandrareguitars.com). **Open** 10am-6pm Mon-Sat; noon-4pm Sun. **Credit** MC, V.
An atmospheric shop bursting with collectibles from the likes of Fender, Gibson and Gretsch alongside a few pre-war numbers. At the back is the room that used to be the Sex Pistols' rehearsal studio.

Wild Guitars

393 Archway Road, N6 4ER (8340 7766/ www.wildguitars.com). Highgate tube. **Open** 10am-7pm Mon-Sat. **No credit cards**.
A favourite with north London's rock aristos (including members of Coldplay, Babyshambles and Pink Floyd), Dave Wild's shop specialises in rare, vintage and often bizarre second-hand guitars, amps, effects and echo machines. An Eastern Bloc Jonala Tornado will set you back £900, a 1967 Rickenbacker £2,800. There are also old valve amps by Gibson, Fender and Gretsch.

Also check out...

Bass Centre

9 Morocco Street, SE1 3HB (7357 7704/ www.basscentre.com). London Bridge tube/rail. **Open** by appoinment. **Credit** MC, V.
Online-based shop specialising in bass guitars and accessories.

Bryant

126 Charing Cross Road, WC2H 0LA (7836 4723). Tottenham Court Road tube. **Open** 10am-6pm Mon-Sat; 11am-5pm Sun. **Credit** MC, V.
Sells electric, acoustic and vintage guitars, banjos, mandolins, accessories and amps.

Hanks

24 Denmark Street, WC2H 8NJ (7379 1139/www.hanksguitarshop.com). Tottenham Court Road. **Open** 10am-7pm Mon-Sat; 11am-5pm Sun. **Credit** MC, V.
New and vintage acoustic guitar, banjo, mandolin and ukulele dealer.

Ivor Mairants Musicentre

56 Rathbone Place, W1T 1JT (7636 1481/ www.ivormairants.co.uk). Tottenham Court Road tube. **Open** 9.30am-6pm Mon-Sat. **Credit** AmEx, MC, V.
High-end specialist in acoustic, jazz and classical guitars, and the odd mandolin.

Rock Around The Clock

11 Park Road, N8 8TE (8348 2311). Crouch Hill rail. **Open** 10am-6pm Mon-Sat; noon-5pm Sun. **Credit** AmEx, MC, V.
Specialist in guitars, amps, keyboards, pedals, strings and FX pedals.

Spanish Guitar Centre

36 Cranbourn Street, WC2H 7AD (7240 0754/0800 371 339/www.spanishguitar centre.com). Leicester Square tube. **Open** 10.30am-6pm Mon-Sat. **Credit** MC, V.
This shop specialises in handmade classical and flamenco guitars.

Wunjo Guitars

20 Denmark Street, WC2H 8NE (7379 0737/www.wunjoguitars.com). Tottenham Court Road tube. **Open** 10am-7pm Mon-Sat; noon-5pm Sun. **Credit** AmEx, DC, MC, V.
Wunjo sells new, second-hand and vintage guitars, custom-built guitars and also offers on-site repairs.

Unique Selling Point
Duke of Uke

Three years ago, eccentric musician Matthew Reynolds decided that what London desperately needed was a specialist ukulele shop. There was, after all, only one such outlet in the world – and that was in Japan – so there wasn't much competition. And so he ploughed his life savings into Duke of Uke (*see p212*).

Located halfway between Old Spitalfields Market and Brick Lane, the shop stocks a fair few banjos, guitars, mandolins and harmonicas, but its USP is its baffling range of ukuleles. In this, Matt Reynolds certainly pre-empted a trend. Artists such as Arcade Fire, Conor Oberst, Patrick Wolf, Beirut, Jeremy Warmsley and Stephin Merrit have all brandished ukes on stage, and you'll even hear one on the latest Portishead album. The shop has become popular for its jam sessions, with recent visitors including Kitty Daisy & Lewis, Le Volume Courbe, Vincent Vincent and the Villains, the Duke Spirit, Dylan Bates and, of course, the Ukulele Orchestra of Great Britain. It also organises workshops, starting at £15 for a beginner's two-hour class, and you can hire out the shop between 6.30pm and 9.30pm for £30.

Ukes come in four sizes: the 21-inch soprano ukes are the small, entry-level models. Slightly larger are concert ukes (23 inches) and tenors (26 inches), which are tuned to the same pitch but have a richer tone, while the 30-inch baritone ukes are pitched a fourth lower. Sopranos start at £20 for the brightly coloured Mahalo plywood models made in China. 'They sound OK, and are fine for kids or as jokey presents,' says Reynolds. 'But you only have to step up to about £40 or £50 to get a really good instrument.' Prices can rise to £600 for the top handmade models, or up to £1,000 for distinctive vintage pieces.

Zach Condon from Beirut has described his uke as 'a portable songwriting machine', and Matthew Reynolds is equally evangelical: 'It's a genuinely versatile instrument that lends itself to so many genres. It's unintimidating and easy to learn, and perfect for small-fingered children.'

Duke of Uke now attracts Shoreditch hipsters and City boys alike, with celebrity customers including Tracey Emin, Gilbert & George and Pete Doherty. Two years ago Doherty got the shop into the tabloids when a member of his entourage left the place with a £120 ukulele and a harmonica. 'I worry about the company Pete keeps,' laughs Reynolds. 'But we were easy on him because he spends a lot of money here.'

Pianos & organs

Allodi Accordions

143-145 Lee High Road, SE13 5PF (8244 3771/www.accordions.co.uk). Lewisham DLR/rail then 122, 178, 261, 321 bus. **Open** 10.30am-6pm Tue, Thur, Fri; 10.30am-5pm Sat. **Credit** AmEx, MC, V.
Founded in 1953 by Bruno Allodi and now run by his son Emilio, this Lewisham store heaves with hundreds of (mainly second-hand) piano accordions, button accordions, continental chromatics and bandoneons. There is also an on-site repairs workshop.

J Reid & Sons

184 St Ann's Road, N15 5RP (8800 6907/ www.jreidpianos.co.uk). Seven Sisters tube/ South Tottenham rail. **Open** 8am-5.30pm Mon-Fri; 10am-5pm Sat. **No credit cards.**
At Britain's largest piano store you'll find brand new Bluthners, Bosendorfers, Kawais and Yamahas; reconditioned Steinways and Bechsteins; shiny new Czech uprights (Petrof, Weinbach, Zeidel, Riga Kloss); and scores of restored second-hand models. Reid's own brand pianos – Reid & Sohn – are built in Korea, but the company also runs a busy workshop repairing and restringing pianos. It also does rentals and hire-to-buy schemes.

Kensington Pianos

288 Kensington High Street, W14 8NZ (7602 7566/www.kensingtonpianos.com). High Street Kensington tube. **Open** 10am-6pm Mon-Sat; 10am-5pm Sun. **Credit** AmEx, DC, MC, V.
Two floors of brand-new Yamaha, Kawai and Zieder pianos plus a large range of second-hand, reconditioned and digital models.

Markson Pianos

8 Chester Court, Albany Street, NW1 4BU (7935 8682/www.marksonpianos.com). Great Portland Street tube/C2 bus. **Open** 9.30am-5.30pm Mon-Sat; 10am-4pm Sun. **Credit** AmEx, DC, MC, V.
As well as selling pianos, this family-run business has been providing restoration, polishing and tuning services since 1910. Pianos from the British manufacturer Kemble are sold alongside Bechstein's high-end professional uprights and grands. Designer pieces from makers like Sauter and Pleyel cost well into the thousands, although there are plenty from around £500.

Piano Warehouse

30 Highgate Road, NW5 1NS (7267 7671/ www.piano-warehouse.co.uk). Kentish Town tube/rail. **Open** 10am-6pm Mon-Sat. **Credit** AmEx, DC, V.
Large upstairs warehouse selling brand-new Yamaha, Steinmayer, Weber, Kemble and Seiler plus second-hand and digital. The shop also runs a rental scheme: new uprights cost £396 for a year.
For branches see index.

Pro audio/ electronics

Digital Village

14 The Broadway, Gunnersbury Lane, W3 8HR (8992 5592/www.dv247.com). Acton Town tube. **Open** 9.30am-5.30pm Mon-Fri; 10am-5pm Sat. **Credit** MC, V.
Claiming to sell 'everything you need to make and record music', the bright and spacious stores located all over London and nationwide certainly offer a massive range of stock, from studio, pro-audio and recording equipment, to amps, guitars, keyboards and MIDIs, microphones, mixers and sample CDs.
For branches see index.

Sapphires Sound & Light

4-6 Burlington Parade, Edgware Road, NW2 6QG (8450 2426/www.decks.co.uk). Kilburn tube. **Open** noon-7pm Mon-Wed; 11am-7pm Thur, Fri; 10am-7pm Sat. **Credit** AmEx, MC, V.
With a strong online persona, Sapphires virtually encourages customers into its fully stocked showroom on the Edgware Road. The staff are, in the main, experienced DJs so you can expect decent advice before you choose from a wide range of DJ-related equipment, including decks, mixers, amps and speakers.

Westend DJ

10-12 Hanway Street, W1T 1UB (7637 3293/www.westenddj.com). Tottenham Court Road tube. **Open** 9.30am-6.30pm Mon-Sat; noon-6pm Sun. **Credit** AmEx, MC, V.
An exhaustive range of cutting-edge DJ and audio-visual equipment and accessories is stocked at Westend DJ. The complete hardware catalogues for all of the leading brands, including Technics and Pioneer, are all available, plus industry names like Stanton, Numark and Denon. As well as the latest turntables, mixers, CD decks, video decks, effects units, amplifiers and speakers, you can pick up headphones, slipmats, styli, microphones, stands, record boxes and a whole lot more. Service is informative and not pushy; and it may well be possible to barter for a deal if you're buying a package of several items. It's worth browsing the comprehensive website before you visit (or if you're too lazy to leave the house).
For branches see index.

Also check out...

BEM

395 Coldharbour Lane, SW9 8LQ (7733 6821/www.bem-music.com). Brixton tube/ rail. **Open** 10am-6.30pm Mon-Sat. **Credit** AmEx, MC, V.
General music store with good electronic equipment for studio and live work.

Rose Morris Pro Audio

8, 10, 11 Denmark Street, WC2H 8TD (nos.8 & 10 7836 0991/no.11 7632 3950/www.rosemorris.com). Tottenham Court Road tube. **Open** 10am-6.30pm Mon-Fri; 10am-6pm Sat; noon-5pm Sun. **Credit** MC, V.
There are three Rose Morris branches – no.8 deals with pro audio and pianos, no.10 acoustic guitars and no.11 sheet music.

Walrus Systems

11 New Quebec Street, W1H 7RW (7724 7224/www.walrus.co.uk). Marble Arch tube. **Open** 10.30am-5.30pm Mon-Sat. **Credit** MC, V.
A must for analogue junkies in search of top-quality vinyl and valve equipment.

Stringed instruments

Bridgewood & Neitzert

146 Stoke Newington Church Street, N16 0JU (7249 9398/www.londonviolins.com). Stoke Newington rail/73 bus. **Open** 10am-6pm Mon-Fri; 10am-4pm Sat. **Credit** MC, V.
This respected duo sells violins, violas, cellos and double basses in both modern and classical styles. Prices for a modern violin start at around £200, rising to the thousands for high-end models. Bows start at £20. Five full-time members of staff deal with repairs.

Ealing Strings

4 Station Parade, Uxbridge Road, W5 3LD (8992 5222/www.ealingstrings.info). Ealing Common tube. **Open** 9.15am-6pm Mon-Sat. **No credit cards.**
This long-standing, friendly neighbourhood shop takes pride in selling high-quality, top of the range violins, violas and cellos, aimed at professional and high-end amateur players. All products are handmade, which is why prices start at £1,500 for violins and rise to the hundreds of thousands. There are no factory-made or Chinese instruments here. The workshop also offers a repair service for damaged instruments.

Holywell Music

58 Hopton Street, SE1 9JH (7928 8451/ www.holywellmusic.co.uk). Blackfriars or Southwark tube/rail. **Open** 10am-5pm Mon-Fri. **Credit** MC, V.
London's long-established premier harp retailer has more than 50 instruments made by Salvi and Lyon & Healy on display. Prices start at around £750 for the smallest lever harp and rise to over £59,000 for the most expensive Salvi model. Beginners can take advantage of the three-month rental scheme before deciding to buy.

John & Arthur Beare

30 Queen Anne Street, W1G 8HX (7307 9666/www.beares.com). Bond Street tube. **Open** (preferably by appointment) 10am-5pm Mon-Fri. **Credit** MC, V.
With over 140 years' experience in selling Stradivaris, Guarneris and other Italian masters, Beare's collection of instruments is of the highest calibre. Many of the world's top musicians (Nathan Milstein and Isaac Stern included) frequent the place. The majority of the violins, violas and cellos are antiques, but there are a few new items. Experts are on hand for repairs.

Also check out...

Dulwich Music Shop

2 Croxted Road, SE22 9BN (8693 1477/ www.dulwichmusic.com). East Dulwich rail then 12, 185 bus. **Open** 2-5.30pm Mon; 9.30am-5.30pm Tue-Sat. **Credit** AmEx, MC, V.
Specialises in beginner- and student-oriented violins, classical guitars, stringed instruments and their accessories.

Frederick Phelps
34 Conway Road, N14 7BA (8482 3887/ www.phelpsviolins.com). Arnos Grove or Southgate tube. **Open** by appointment only. **Credit** MC, V.
Specialising in 'investment brand' violins, violas, cellos and bows.

JP Guivier
99 Mortimer Street, W1W 7SX (7580 2560/ www.guivier.com). Oxford Circus tube. **Open** 9am-6pm Mon-Fri; 10am-5pm Sat. **Credit** MC, V.
World-renowned dealer with workshop.

Portobello Music
13 All Saints Road, W11 1HA (7221 4040/ www.portobellomusic.co.uk). Westbourne Park tube. **Open** 10.30am-8pm Mon; 10.30am-6pm Tue-Sat. **Credit** MC, V.
Aimed at the amateur market.

Woodwind & brass

All Flutes Plus
60-61 Warren Street, W1T 5NZ (7388 8438/ www.allflutesplus.co.uk). Warren Street tube. **Open** 10am-6pm Mon-Fri; 10am-4.30pm Sat. **Credit** MC, V.
New and second-hand flutes, from beginners to specialist models, with lots of sheet music, heads, piccolos and a two-man repairs workshop too.

Paxman Musical Instruments
Unit B4, Linton House, 164-180 Union Street, SE1 0LH (7620 2077). Southwark tube. **Open** 9.30am-5.30pm Tue-Fri; 10am-5pm Sat. **Credit** AmEx, MC, V.
Paxman is London's only French horn specialist, attracting everyone from complete beginners to world-class orchestral soloists. Also does repairs and a good line in sheet music. Second-hand French horns start at around £600, while new models can cost up to £6,500.

Phil Parker
106A Crawford Street, W1H 2HZ (7486 8206/www.philparker.co.uk). Baker Street tube. **Open** 10am-5.30pm Mon-Fri; 10am-4.30pm Sat. **Credit** MC, V.
Phil Parker is an excellent brass specialist selling trombones, tubas, trumpets and various other instruments. Dizzy Gillespie once visited this brass instrument temple, as have hundreds of jazz and classical performers over the last 50 years. It has an unrivalled range of trumpets, trombones and tubas.

Top Wind
2 Lower Marsh, SE1 7RJ (7401 8787/ www.topwind.com). Waterloo or Lambeth North tube/rail. **Open** 8.30am-6pm Mon-Fri; 9am-5pm Sat. **Credit** AmEx, MC, V.
Opened in 1991, Top Wind prides itself on only employing flautists and stocks a broad range of beginners and specialist models.

TW Howarth
31-35 Chiltern Street, W1U 7PN (7935 2407/www.howarth.uk.com). Baker Street tube. **Open** 10am-5.30pm Mon-Fri; 10am-4.30pm Sat. **Credit** AmEx, MC, V.
Britain's leading outlet for all woodwind instruments and accessories is spread across three separate storefronts, each specialising in clarinets, saxophones, bassoons and oboes. It stocks specialist CDs, accessories and plenty of sheet music, and has four full-time members of staff who look after repairs. Yamaha remains the market leader, but the best saxes and clarinets are French (Selmer, Buffet, LeBlanc), while the best bassoons tend to be German (Gebrüder Mönnig, Oscar Adler and the like).

Michael White
11 Queens Parade, Queens Drive, W5 3HU (8997 4088/www.michaelwhitewind.co.uk). North Ealing tube. **Open** 9.30am-5.30pm Mon, Tue, Thur, Fri; 9.30am-1pm Wed; 9.30am-5pm Sat. **Credit** MC, V.
White has been specialising in flutes, oboes, clarinets, bassoons, saxophones and cors anglais for 27 years, stocking all the big brands, new and second-hand, along with accessories, cases and music. There are also two on-site staff doing repairs.

World, early music & folk

Bina Musicals
31-33 The Green, Southall, Middx UB2 4AN (8571 5904/www.binaswar.com). Southall rail. **Open** 10am-7pm Mon-Sat; 11am-7pm Sun. **Credit** AmEx, MC, V.
Specialises in sitars, veenas, flutes and drums from around the world, plus made-to-order harmoniums.

Early Music Shop/ London Recorder Centre
34 Chiltern Street, W1U 7QH (7486 9101/ www.earlymusicshop.com). Baker Street tube. **Open** 10am-5pm Mon-Sat. **Credit** AmEx, DC, MC, V.
You can pay a tenner here for a plastic Yamaha soprano recorder, and up to £3,500 for a Paetzold cherrywood sub great bass model, moving through handmade wooden recorders by Blezinger, Kobliczek, Moeck, Mollenhauer, Netsch, Ran, von Huene, Aura, Kung and Coolsma. Also stocks harps, viols, flutes, baroque cellos, zithers, crumhorns and folk and world instruments.

Hobgoblin
24 Rathbone Place, W1T 1JA (7323 9040/ www.hobgoblin.com). Tottenham Court Road tube. **Open** 10am-6pm Mon-Sat. **Credit** AmEx, MC, V.
The diverse stock at this remarkable folk shop covers a mix of traditional, world and folk instruments including banjos, mandolins, ukuleles, bagpipes, harmonicas, whistles, flutes and hand percussion. More unusual finds like the Irish bodhrán drum (from £32), a double-reed Chinese flute (£50) or the Spanish cajon (from £95) make this shop unique. Vintage and second-hand items are for sale and a luthier makes lutes, ouds and guitars and does repairs.

Jas Musicals
124 The Broadway, Southall, Middx, UB1 1QF (8574 2686/www.jas-musicals.com). Southall rail or Ealing Broadway tube, then 207, 607 bus. **Open** 11am-7pm daily. **Credit** AmEx, DC, MC, V.
Jimmy Page, Talvin Singh, John McLaughlin, Asha Bhosle, Zakir Hussain and David Gray have all visited this fantastic Southall shop, which recently opened West End premises. It's run by Harjit Singh Shah, who applies high-class Western technology to traditional Indian instruments. Prices are still amazingly inexpensive compared to most Western musicial instruments: a pair of 'junior-sized' tabla drums start at around £30, a student sitar is only £130.
For branches see index.

Ray Man
54 Chalk Farm Road, NW1 8AN (7692 6261/www.raymaneasternmusic.co.uk). Camden Town or Chalk Farm tube. **Open** 10.30am-6pm Tue-Sat; 11am-5pm Sun; 1-5pm Mon. **Credit** MC, V.
A family-run business for over 30 years, Ray Man sells a unique variety of traditional instruments from all over Asia, Africa, the Middle East and South America. More recognisable items like sitars and darbuka drums share the space with Chinese zithers and Indian fiddles. There are also several smaller and more affordable objects such as the Vietnamese frog box (£3) and Indian monkey drums (£7.50), gongs, cymbals and shakers. The Vietnamese jaw harps (as heard on Morricone spaghetti western soundtracks) fit nicely into your pocket (£6). Ray Man also runs a service that tracks down specialist overseas instruments.

Sheet music

See also p211 **Chappell of Bond Street** and *p183* **Travis & Emery**. **Foyles** (*see p177*) also has a good selection of sheet music, as do many of the general music shops listed in this chapter.

Argent's
19 Denmark Street, WC2H 8NA (7379 3384/www.musicroom.com). Tottenham Court Road tube. **Open** 9am-6pm Mon-Fri; 10am-6pm Sat; 11am-5pm Sun. **Credit** AmEx, MC, V.
An array of classical and pop printed music, instructional DVDs and a few general music spares (stands, guitar strings, etc).

Equipment hire

Peter Webber Hire
110-112 Disraeli Road, SW15 2DX (8870 1335/www.peterwebberhire.com). East Putney tube/Putney rail. **Open** 10am-6pm Mon-Fri. **Credit** AmEx, MC, V.
Peter Webber hire provides a host of musical equipment (guitars, drum kits and PA systems) plus rehearsal studios.

Systems etc
Unit 8, Print Village, Chadwick Road, SE15 4PU (7732 3377/www.systemsetc.co.uk). Peckham Rye rail. **Open** 10am-6.30pm Mon-Fri. **Credit** MC, V.
Systems etc offers a high-quality array of hire equipment for DJs and live gigs.

Parties

For celebration cakes, such as **Daisy Cakes Bake Shop** and **Konditor & Cook**, *see pp235-236*.

Fancy dress & party supplies

For theatrical make-up, *see p91* **Screenface**.

Angels

119 Shaftesbury Avenue, WC2H 8AE (7836 5678/www.fancydress.com). Leicester Square or Tottenham Court Road tube. **Open** 9.30am-5.30pm Mon, Tue, Thur, Fri; 10.30am-7pm Wed. **Credit** AmEx, MC, V.

Angels is the undisputed doyenne of fancy dress hire for adults and children in the capital. The range – spanning everything from splendid Tudor robes to a sequinned showgirl outfit from *Octopussy* – and quality are unparalleled. Some of the costumes have even found their way to the six-floor hire shop from the massive collection of handmade costumes Angels has created for films over the years. The expanding range of packet costumes, sold via the website, are also very good, with Playboy bunnies, sumo wrestlers and Marie Antoinette lookalikes new for 2008. There's also a selection of cheap superhero costumes for sale (Superman, Spider Man), starting at £30.99. Outfits for hire from the shop start at £80 plus VAT and include matching accessories, plus £100 deposit

Contemporary Wardrobe

The Horse Hospital, Colonnade, WC1N 1HX (7713 7370/www.contemporary wardrobe.com). Russell Square tube. **Open** *Viewings* noon-6pm Mon-Sat. Hire by appointment. **Credit** MC, V.

Established in 1978 by stylist and costume designer Roger Burton, this specialist hire company has a collection of over 15,000 garments dating from 1945 to the present day and includes vintage Yves Saint Laurent and Givenchy pieces, as well as rock and pop outfits worn by both the über-iconic establishment (the Beatles, Annie Lennox) and more recent stars (Kanye West). For inspiration, there's also a public-access collection of European street fashion and culture, a style magazine archive, and taped interviews with people from the worlds of fashion, style and culture. Hire prices for a complete outfit are around £75 plus VAT.

Party Party

9-13 Ridley Road, E8 2NP (7254 5168). Dalston Kingsland rail/67, 76, 149 bus. **Open** 9am-5.30pm Mon-Thur; 9am-6.30pm Fri, Sat. **Credit** MC, V.

This cheap and cheerful three-floored party shop – the area's best – is packed to the brim with dressing-up outfits and props (wigs, gorilla outfits, hats, masks, fat suits) and party supplies. There's a large area dedicated to equipment for cake-making and decorating and a massive range of balloons, glitter and decorations.

For branch see index.

So High Soho

96 Berwick Street, W1F 0QQ (7287 1295/ 6387/www.sohighsoho.co.uk). Oxford Circus or Tottenham Court Road tube. **Open** 10am-6pm Mon-Wed; 11am-7pm Thur-Sat. **Credit** AmEx, MC, V.

For 12 years, friendly So High in the heart of Soho has been sourcing a stash of cheap costumes, wigs (including the 'mother of all afros' for £20), jewellery, accessories and make up. Office workers looking for party gear can pick up vampire, superhero and belly dancer outfits. Every budget is catered for – from a pirate's eye-patch costing just £1.50 to a Victorian frock coat priced at £75. (Note that there isn't a hire service.)

Also check out...

Balloon & Kite Company

613 Garratt Lane, SW18 4SU (8946 5962/www.balloonandkite.com). Earlsfield rail. **Open** 9am-6pm Mon-Fri; 9am-5.30pm Sat. **Credit** AmEx, MC, V.

Charles H Fox

22 Tavistock Street, WC2E 7PY (7240 3111/www.charlesfox.co.uk). Covent Garden tube. **Open** 9.30am-5.45pm Mon-Wed; 9.30am-6.45pm Thur, Fri; 10am-5.45pm Sat. **Credit** AmEx, MC, V.

The place to go for both professional and standard wigs and theatre make-up.

Costume Studio

Montgomery House, 159-161 Balls Pond Road, N1 4BG (7923 9472/www.costume studio.co.uk). Highbury & Islington tube/ rail/30, 38, 56, 277 bus. **Open** 9.30am-6pm Mon-Fri; 10am-5pm Sat. **Credit** MC, V.

Period costumes of all kinds for hire, from Edwardian dandies to swashbuckling pirates. Sci-fi films are well represented.

Escapade

150 Camden High Street, NW1 0NE (7485 7384/www.escapade.co.uk). Camden Town tube. **Open** 10am-7pm Mon-Fri; 10am-6pm Sat; noon-5pm Sun. **Credit** AmEx, MC, V.

Hire and retail service, covering everything from a *South Park* Satan outfit to bumble bees to 1920s-style flapper dresses.

Harlequin

254 Lee High Road, SE13 5PR (8852 0193). Hither Green rail/Lewisham rail/DLR. **Open** 10am-5.30pm Mon, Tue, Thur-Sat; 10am-1pm Wed. **Credit** MC, V.

Garish 1970s outfits, such as Bay City Roller-style tartan suits and Abba jumpsuits.

Non-Stop Party Shop

214-216 Kensington High Street, W8 7RG (7937 7200/www.nonstopparty.co.uk). High Street Kensington tube. **Open** 9.30am-6pm Mon-Sat; 11am-5pm Sun. **Credit** AmEx, MC, V.

Party gear and a variety of balloon services.

Oscar's Den

127-129 Abbey Road, NW6 4SL (7328 6683/www.oscarsden.com). Swiss Cottage tube/West Hampstead tube/rail. **Open** 9.30am-5.30pm Mon-Sat; 10am-2pm Sun. **Credit** AmEx, MC, V.

Everything for all sorts of parties – bar mitzvahs, Diwali and hen nights. Plus bubble machines and bouncy castles.

Party Plus

4 Acton Lane, W4 5NB (8987 8404/ www.partiesbypost.co.uk). Chiswick Park tube station. **Open** 9.30am-5pm Mon-Fri; 9am-5pm Sat. **Credit** AmEx, MC, V.

An enormous choice of partyware, great for theme parties. Its online store offers an equally enormous range.

Party Superstore

268 Lavender Hill, SW11 1LJ (7924 3210/ www.partysuperstores.co.uk). Clapham Junction rail. **Open** 9am-6pm Mon-Wed, Sat; 9am-7pm Thur-Fri; 10.30am-4.30pm Sun. **Credit** AmEx, MC, V.

Costumes for sale and hire, plus masks, wigs and a range of party novelties like piñatas.

For branch see index.

Prangsta Costumiers

304 New Cross Road, SE14 6AF (8694 9869/www.prangsta.com). New Cross Gate tube/rail. **Open** 11am-7pm Mon-Sat. **Credit** MC, V.

All of the outfits here have been made from scratch using vintage textiles and fabrics.

Preposterous Presents

262 Upper Street, N1 2UQ (7226 4166). Highbury & Islington tube/rail. **Open** 10am-6pm Mon-Sat. **Credit** MC, V.

An old-school jape player's paradise, full of novelties such as fake blood, stick-on moustaches and eye-patches.

Sparkling Strawberry

www.sparklingstrawberry.com

An emphasis on sexy saloon-girl frills (via some slightly dubious erotic/clubwear) plus *Wizard of Oz* tin man jumpsuits.

Magic & novelties

Davenports Magic Shop

7 Charing Cross Underground Shopping Arcade, WC2N 4HZ (7836 0408/www. davenportsmagic.co.uk). Charing Cross tube/rail. **Open** 9.30am-5.30pm Mon-Fri; 10.15am-4pm Sat. **Credit** AmEx, MC, V.

Established in 1898, staff at Davenports are professional magicians able to demonstrate the most suitable magic for your level of experience and budget. The equipment for beginners, such as trick card decks, starts from £6; for more advanced magicians, there's everything from trick Top Hats (£25) to craftytables (£108). There's also a wide range of how-to instruction manuals and DVDs, most costing around £15.

Also check out...

International Magic

89 Clerkenwell Road, EC1R 5BX (7405 7324/www.internationalmagic.com). Chancery Lane tube. **Open** 11.30am-6pm Mon-Fri; 11.30am-4pm Sat. **Credit** AmEx, MC, V.

Playing cards, garish silks, arcane books, lengths of white rope, DVDs and boxes of assorted tricks, props and gimmicks.

Jugglemania/Magic Circus

www.magiccircus.co.uk

Clubs for jugglers and pocket money-friendly magic tricks for novice magicians.

Pets

Accessories designer **Bill Amberg** (*see p76*) also does a Pampered Pets line.

Aquatic Design Centre

109 Great Portland Street, W1W 6QG (7580 6764/www.aquaticdesign.co.uk). Great Portland Street tube. **Open** 10am-8pm Mon-Thur; 10am-7pm Fri; 10am-6pm Sat; 11am-5pm Sun. **Credit** MC, V.

A welcoming royal blue hue greets visitors to this fancy fish emporium boasting over 300 tanks of marine, tropical and freshwater fish, from white cloud mountain minnow (90p) to the popular neon tetras (£1.45). If it's not bread and butter fish you want you can take home a pair of rare giant gourami (£600 for two). Clued-up staff offer comprehensive advice; they're hot on all the equipment you'll need to keep your scaly pals happy, from java moss, filters and algae cleaners to the tanks themselves (starting at £15, rising to the thousands for large aquariums).

City & East Grooming Services

423 Roman Road, E3 5QX (07828 953944/www.grooming-services.co.uk). Bethnal Green tube/rail, then 8, D6 bus. **Open** 7am-4.30pm Tue-Sat. **Credit** MC, V.

This East End salon opened in April 2008 and has been fully booked ever since – mostly from word-of-mouth recommendations. The modern, bright space allows owners to watch every part of their pet's treatment, from grooming to bathing. Owner/dog-lover Mark spent years learning his craft – and it shows; our little pooch was a nervous grooming 'virgin' but Mark's firm but reassuring manner ensured she looked happy and relaxed during the shampoo and slightly noisy drying. A quick squirt of Calvin Klein's K9 PawFume meant she hit the street running. Grooming starts at £20 for a whippet rising to £80 for a St Bernard. Doggy accessories include leads, grooming tools and treats.

Holly & Lil

103 Bermondsey Street, SE1 3XB (07811 715452/www.hollyandlil.co.uk). London Bridge tube/rail. **Open** 11.30am-7pm Thur; 10.30am-5pm Fri, Sat; also by appointment. **Credit** MC, V.

Holly & Lil's dog collars and leads are all handmade and luxurious – think of the brand as the Jimmy Choo of canine fashion. The limited-edition collection should meet the needs of any trend-conscious pooch, in leather, tartan, Harris tweed and other wear and tear materials. For a bit of bling, there are 'charm collars' (neckwear adorned with beads), tiny multicoloured dice, or semi-precious stones such as freshwater pearls and black onyx. Prices start at around £40, rising to £120 for the heavily adorned Boho models. Cats can get vain here too with their own line of collars. If nothing seems quite fancy enough, owners can commission something ultra outrageous themselves. The shop also sells a range of doggie knick-knacks commissioned from British designers.

Kings Aquatic & Reptile World

26 Camden High Street, NW1 0JH (7387 5553). Mornington Crescent tube. **Open** 10am-6pm daily. **Credit** MC, V.

Reptile expert Simon King set up this exotic pet shop, supplying arachnids, snakes, amphibians, invertebrates and reptiles, in 1997. Any squeamish readers out there can relax, though – all the creatures are safely ensconced in their cages. Prices vary widely depending on the rarity of the specimen; a tarantula will set you back between £10 and £200, lizards go for £8 to £800 and baby corn snakes are £45. Kings also breeds rare monitor lizards and runs a pet-sitting service. Crickets, locusts and frozen mice are for sale for pets' snacks, and there are all sorts of cages. A modest selection of cold-water and tropical fish is available downstairs.

Mungo & Maud

79 Elizabeth Street, SW1W 9PJ (7952 4570/www.mungoandmaud.com). Sloane Square tube/Victoria tube/rail/ 11 bus. **Open** 10am-6pm Mon-Sat. **Credit** AmEx, MC, V.

A boutique with a touch of French sophistication, this is the ultimate 'dog and cat outfitters'. Fed up with her dog's outmoded accessories clashing with her modern home, dog-lover Nicola Sacher decided to design her own to fill the niche. Stylish and minimalist, pooch products include washable dog beds (£90-£195), and the 'petite amande dog fragrance' (£38); for kitty, there's catnip (£8) and embroidered wool cat blankets (£175). Humans won't feel left out and can browse over book titles like *Pug Therapy* and *Is Your Dog Gay?* There are also concessions at Selfridges Oxford Street and Fortnum & Mason.

Mutz Nutz

221 Westbourne Park Road, W11 1EA (7243 3333/www.themutznutz.com). Ladbroke Grove or Westbourne Park tube. **Open** 10am-6pm Mon, Fri, Sat; 10am-7pm Tue-Thur; noon-5pm Sun. **Credit** AmEx, MC, V.

As the name suggests, the treats from this attractive boutique will drive cats and dogs (or their owners) crazy. On the shelves you'll find toys, leads, handmade jewel-encrusted collars (£50-£200), organic nibbles, toothbrushes – even dog nappies. There are also special dog car seats and, bizarrely, wedding dresses with veils (£19.95). Cats are equally well catered for, with catnip spray and a three-sided 'scratch lounge'. The nearby same-owned Dog Spa (22 Powis Terrace, W11 1JH, 7243 3399) offers Italian baths: pets are tended to by personal groomers and leave fully coiffed, perfumed and ribbon clad. At the pet supermarket, goodies and tit-bits can be taken away.

Primrose Hill Pets

132 Regent's Park Road, NW1 8XL (7483 2023/www.primrosehillpets.co.uk). Chalk Farm tube. **Open** 9am-6pm Mon-Sat; 11am-5pm Sun. **Credit** MC, V.

Quality leads, collars, coats, beds, airline-approved pet carriers and a range of grooming products are all available here, plus there's a treatment service for cats and dogs (by appointment). Informed staff give advice on diets, food, supplements and treats and although pets themselves are not sold here, they'll readily point you in the direction of local breeders and shelters.

Pugs & Kisses

183 New King's Road, SW6 4SW (7731 0098/www.pugsandkisses.com). Parsons Green tube. **Open** 10am-6pm Mon-Sat. **Credit** AmEx, MC, V.

This hip boutique was set up by a New York pug-lover to offer stylish products (beds, toys, carriers, bowls, health and beauty products) and a grooming 'spa', as well as walk-in appointments for 'touch-ups' (nail clipping, ear cleaning, brush out, wash and dry). Products range from leather collars (£10) and khaki leads (£34) to luxury dog-carrying bags (£130).

Also check out...

Animal Fair of Kensington

17 Abingdon Road, W8 6AH (7937 0011). High Street Kensington tube. **Open** 9.30am-6pm Mon-Sat; 11am-5pm Sun. **Credit** MC, V.

Expect an attractive selection of canaries, budgies, fish and small domestic animals like rabbits and hamsters.

Chiswick Pets

32-34 Devonshire Road, W4 2HD (8747 0715/www.devonshireroad.com). Turnham Green tube. **Open** 9am-6pm Mon-Sat; 11am-4pm Sun. **Credit** MC, V.

Here you'll find cats, dogs, rabbits and birds roaming freely during business hours, returning to their cages at night. Exotic friends like geckos can also be found.

Dog About Town

196 Bellenden Road, SE15 4BW (7358 9709). Peckham Rye rail. **Open** 9.30am-5pm Tue-Sat. **No credit cards.**

A long-established grooming parlour that will bath, groom and trim your small dog from about £30.

Fish Bowl

133-135 Dawes Road, SW6 7EB (7385 6005). Parsons Green tube. **Open** 10am-6pm Mon-Wed, Fri, Sat. **Credit** AmEx, MC, V.

Alongside the fish, Fish Bowl also sells small domestic animals, as well as snakes, lizards and birds.

Pets at Home

100 Blackheath Road, SE10 8DA (8469 9130/www.petsathome.co.uk). Deptford Bridge DLR. **Open** 9am-8pm Mon-Fri; 9am-6pm Sat; 10am-4pm Sun. **Credit** MC, V.

A one-stop pet shop and advice centre.

Poochie Amour

www.poochieamour.com.

The accessories 'for stylish dogs' on sale here range from leads and collars to scarfs and jumpers.

Wow Bow

www.wowbow.co.uk.

Luxury brand of contemporary acrylic beds, doggy dining tables and cat scratchers.

Photography

As well as the shops listed here, it's worth checking out online options; **Camera King** (www.cameraking.co.uk) and the award-winning **Warehouse Express** (www.warehouseexpress.com) offer an impressive range of equipment at competitive prices.

For photograph albums, *see p231* **Stationery** (**Tessa Fantoni** in particular); **Liberty** (*see p16*) also has a very good selection.

Note that underwater photography specialist **Ocean Optics** (www.oceanoptics.co.uk) has recently relocated to Essex.

Calumet

93-103 Drummond Street, NW1 2HJ (7380 1144/www.calumetphoto.co.uk). Euston tube/rail. **Open** 8.30am-5.30pm Mon-Fri; 9am-5.30pm Sat; 10am-4pm Sun. **Credit** AmEx, MC, V.

Calumet's bright, spacious showroom caters mainly for professional snappers, students and darkroom workers. Lights, power packs, gels, tripods, printing and storage stock complement top-end digital gear plus medium- and large-format cameras. There's a selection of high-quality film, a repairs service and an extensive rental section.
For branches see index.

Kingsley Photographic

93 Tottenham Court Road, W1T 4HL (7387 6500/www.kingsleyphoto.co.uk). Goodge Street or Warren Street tube. **Open** 9am-5.30pm Mon-Fri; 10am-5.30pm Sat. **Credit** MC, V.

This tiny shop squeezes in a surprisingly extensive range. Nikons are to the fore, though there's also a selection of Leicas and a diverse mix of second-hand gear. But it's the staff that make this such a highly-regarded place. They are all keen, knowledgeable photographers who discuss products with genuine enthusiasm rather than as a sales pitch. There's a large selection of photographic accessories, including bags, tripods and albums, plus binoculars and telescopes. Catering to film loyalists, it still stocks photographic paper as well as digital accessories and printers.

Mr Cad

68 Windmill Road, Croydon, Surrey CRO 2XP (8684 8282/www.mrcad.co.uk). East Croydon or West Croydon rail. **Open** 9am-5pm Mon-Fri; 10am-4pm Sat. **Credit** MC, V.

Though slightly hindered by its suburban location, Mr Cad is still Britain's biggest independent photographic store and claims to have the largest stock of second-hand equipment in Europe. You'll also find Multiblitz studio flashes and, on the more idiosyncratic side, cult cameras from Holga and Lomo. Around 90% of the stock is second-hand, the constant turnover always keeping stock fresh – expect to find everything from Horizon panoramics to Hasselblads and vintage 35mm equipment. A repairs service is also available.

Nicholas Camera Company

15 Camden High Street, NW1 7JE (7916 7251/www.nicholascamera.com). Mornington Crescent tube. **Open** 10am-6pm Mon-Sat. **Credit** AmEx, MC, V.

An interestingly shambolic shop with mountains of stock, Nicholas sells all sorts of old and modern cameras dating back to the 1800s. It's best to have a clear idea before you go in of what you want – rather than browsing you have tell the shopkeeper what you want and he goes and looks. In addition to the more familiar SLR names, you'll find large-format cameras by the likes of Linhof, Sinar, Horseman and medium-format giants such as Hasselblad and Mamiya. There are also accessories, darkroom kits and a growing array of used digital equipment.

Pro Centre

5-6 Mallow Street, EC1Y 8RS (7490 3122/www.procentre.co.uk). Old Street tube/rail. **Open** 8am-6pm Mon-Thur; 8am-7pm Fri. **Credit** AmEx, MC, V.

As the name makes clear, this outfit is pitched at the professional market. It has a focus on Hasselblad, which owns the shop. In addition to a wide range of 'Blads, however, the store also rents out gear by other major manufacturers, including the latest top-end digital cameras from Canon and Nikon. Other rental options include Profoto lighting, scanning gear and hi-spec laptops for digital processing. There's also a growing range of second-hand equipment from Nikon, Canon and Mamiya. Orders can also be couriered from just £7 (free for orders over £150 – or the option of having your congestion charge refunded if picking up in person).

Teamwork

41-42 Foley Street, W1W 7JN (7323 6455/www.teamworkphoto.com). Goodge Street tube. **Open** 9am-5.30pm Mon-Fri. **Credit** AmEx, MC, V.

Teamwork specialises in high-end digital camera backs and medium- to large-format models, as well as meters, lighting and many other accessories. Although it caters mainly to a professional market, the knowledgeable vendors are more than happy to advise and help amateurs too – just not where compact cameras are concerned.

Classic Camera. *See p220.*

Top five Second-hand camera shops

Aperture Photographic. *See p220.*
Classic Camera. *See p220.*
Mr Cad. *See p219.*
Nicholas Camera Company. *See p219.*
York Cameras. *See p220.*

York Cameras
18 Bury Place, WC1A 2JL (7242 7182/ www.yorkcameras.co.uk). Holborn tube. **Open** 9am-5pm Mon-Fri; 10am-3pm Sat. **Credit** MC, V.
Staffed by a team of seasoned experts, York Cameras is a Canon Pro Centre, and stocks an impressive selection of both new and used cameras as well as lots of accessories. A smaller selection of used Nikon gear is also for sale, including some interesting rarities. Factor in the attentive service, and it's little wonder the shop attracts a loyal, discerning clientele.

Also check out…

Cameras Underwater
Ocean Leisure, 11-14 Northumberland Avenue, WC2N 5AQ (7839 1991/www.camerasunderwater.co.uk). Embankment tube. **Open** 10am-7pm Mon-Fri; 10am-5pm Sat. **Credit** AmEx, MC, V.
Europe's biggest underwater camera dealer; cheapos to broadcast-quality.

Gemini
58 High Road, N2 9PM (8883 6152). East Finchley tube/102 bus. **Open** 10am-6pm Mon-Sat. **Credit** AmEx, MC, V.
One of the UK's main Minolta dealers.

Jacobs
74 New Oxford Street, WC1A 1EU (7436 5544/www.jacobsdigital.co.uk). Tottenham Court Road tube. **Open** 9am-6pm Mon-Wed, Fri, Sat; 9am-8pm Thur. **Credit** AmEx, MC, V.
Stocks a decent selection of new and used cameras with an emphasis on digital models and accessories.
Branches: throughout the city.

Jessops
63-69 New Oxford Street, WC1A 1DG (7240 6077/www.jessops.com). Tottenham Court Road tube. **Open** 9am-7pm Mon-Wed, Fri, Sat; 9am-8pm Thur; 11am-5pm Sun. **Credit** AmEx, DC, MC, V.
The flagship of this major chain has user-friendly departments covering all areas, including processing and repairs.
Branches: throughout the city.

London Camera Exchange
98 Strand, WC2R 0EW (7379 0200/ www.lcegroup.co.uk). Charing Cross tube/rail. **Open** 9am-5.30pm Mon-Fri; 11am-5.30pm Sat. **Credit** AmEx, MC, V.
New and second-hand film cameras, digital compacts and SLRs, plus accessories.

Percival Cameras
207 Eltham High Street, SE9 1TX (8859 7696/www.percivalcameras.org.uk). Eltham or New Eltham rail. **Open** 9am-5.30pm Mon-Sat. **Credit** AmEx, DC, MC, V.
Percival stocks new and used cameras, as well as other accessories and equipment including filters, darkroom gear, camcorders and telescopes.

RG Lewis
29 Southampton Row, WC1B 5HL (7242 2916/www.rglewis.co.uk). Holborn tube. **Open** 8.30am-5.30pm Mon-Fri; 9.30am-3.45pm Sat. **Credit** AmEx, DC, MC, V.
Camera buffs here offer advice on specialist equipment, especially Leica models.

Antique & collectable

Aperture Photographic
44 Museum Street, WC1A 1LY (7242 8681/www.apertureuk.com). Holborn or Tottenham Court Road tube. **Open** 11am-7pm Mon-Fri; noon-7pm Sat. **Credit** AmEx, MC, V.
Frequented by camera enthusiasts and paparazzi downloading their latest scoops, this camera shop-cum-café has a great atmosphere. The photographic side centres on an excellent selection of vintage Nikons, Leicas and Hasselblads, along with a sprinkling of other makes. Prices are reasonable too, while offers for unwanted gear are among the more generous in town.

Camera City
16 Little Russell Street, WC1A 2HL (7813 2100/www.cameracity.co.uk). Holborn or Tottenham Court Road tube. **Open** 10am-5.30pm Mon-Fri; 10am-2pm Sat. **Credit** MC, V.
One of a cluster of second-hand photography outlets within a stone's throw of each other, this tiny shop is a good place to look for hard-to-find vintage accessories ranging from flash adaptors to small-but-important things like a replacement tripod bush. It also stocks old Nikon, Canon, Olympus and Pentax cameras, and has a postal service if you can't come personally. Repairs also undertaken – to digital and film cameras.

Classic Camera
2 Pied Bull Yard, off Bury Place, WC1A 2JR (7831 0777/www.theclassiccamera.com). Holborn tube. **Open** 9.30am-5pm Mon-Fri; 10am-4.30pm Sat. **Credit** AmEx, DC, MC, V.
This isn't the place for anyone on a tight budget, since 90% of the stock is Leica, and the rest is a mix of Voigtlander and Nikons. Accessories include Billingham bags and Gitzo tripods, plus there's a nice selection of photographic books by famed Leica users such as Korda and Brassai.

MW Classic Cameras
Unit 3K, Leroy House, 436 Essex Road, N1 3QP (7354 3767/www.mwclassic.com). Angel tube then 38, 73, 341, 476 bus. **Open** 11am-6pm Mon-Fri; 11am-4pm Sat. **Credit** MC, V.
The enthusiastic staff at this ten-year old shop sell rare and collectable photographic equipment. A wide range of brands are stocked, with lots of old Leica models, as well as cameras, lenses and accessories from the likes of Rollei and various other rare and unusual makes. A mail-order service is also available.

Repairs

Camera City (*see above*) in Holborn offers a good repairs service.

Camera Clinic
26 North End Crescent, W14 8TD (7602 7976/www.kensingtoncamera.co.uk). West Kensington tube. **Open** 9am-6pm Mon-Fri; 9am-1pm Sat. **Credit** MC, V.
On-site repairs mean a fast turnaround at this respected shop. Cameras are guaranteed for six months, camcorders for three.
For branch see index.

Fixation
Unit C, 250 Kennington Lane, SE11 5RD (7582 3294/www.fixationuk.com). Vauxhall tube/rail. **Open** 8am-5.30pm Mon-Thur; 8am-4.30pm Fri. **Credit** MC, V.
An official service centre for Nikon and Canon, Fixation will tackle anything from sensor cleaning to more major overhauls (no compact repairs though). They also sell and rent a selection of cameras.

Sendean
Shop 2, 9-12 St Anne's Court, W1F 0BB (0871 750 2463/www.sendeancameras.com). Tottenham Court Road tube. **Open** 10.30am-6pm Mon-Fri. **Credit** AmEx, MC, V.
This long-standing camera repair centre offers customers free estimates and six-month guarantees on repairs (three months for camcorders).

Copying

Learn to Dream
Coate House, Ground Floor East, 1-3 Coate Street, E2 9AG (0845 456 4033/www.learntodream.co.uk). Bethnal Green tube/rail. **Open** by appointment 9am-6pm Mon-Fri. **Credit** MC, V.
Have your own photos turned into works of art on a variety of media, either via the website or by appointment. Sister company Ltd Limited's clients include the Science Museum and RIBA.

Point 101
7241 1113/www.point101.com
This web-based bespoke printers will print your personal photos on to good-quality cotton canvas. Prices are very reasonable.

Tapestry
51-52 Frith Street, W1D 4SH (7896 3000/ www.tapestry.co.uk). Tottenham Court Road tube. **Open** 8.30am-6.30pm Mon-Fri. **Credit** AmEx, MC, V.
This production agency offers a host of services, including reprinting from original photos, to a mainly professional clientele.

Darkroom hire & accessories

It is possible to hire darkrooms at the following places: **Camera Club** (16 Bowden Street, SE11 4DS, 7587 1809, www.thecameraclub.co.uk); **Four Corners** (121 Roman Road, E2 0QN, 8981 6111, www.fourcornersfilm.co.uk); **Islington Arts Factory** (black and white only; 2 Parkhurst Road, N7 0SF, 7607 0561, www.islingtonartsfactory.org.uk); **Photofusion** (17A Electric Lane, SW9 8LA, 7738 5774, www.photofusion.org); **Rapid Eye** (79 Leonard Street, EC2A 4QS, 0871 873 1257, www.rapideye.uk.com). In most cases you will be asked to pay a membership fee.

Silverprint

12 Valentine Place, SE1 8QH (7620 0844/www.silverprint.co.uk). Southwark tube or Waterloo tube/rail. **Open** 9.30am-5.30pm Mon-Fri. **Credit** MC, V.

An excellent range of photographic papers and darkroom materials, as well as digital equipment, inks, portfolios and books.

Processing & printing

All of the places listed below offer a professional and/or specialised processing and printing service.

Bayeux Ltd *78 Newman Street, W1T 3EP (7436 1066/www.bayeux.co.uk). Tottenham Court Road tube.* **Open** 8am-7pm Mon-Fri. **Credit** AmEx, DC, MC, V.

C3 Imaging *81-84 Scoresby Street, SE1 0XN (7833 9100/www.C3imaging.com). Southwark tube/rail.* **Open** 8am-6pm Mon-Fri. **Credit** MC, V.

Chaudigital *19 Rosebury Avenue, EC1R 4SP (7833 3938/www.chaudigital.com). Farringdon tube/19, 38, 341 bus.* **Open** 9am-6pm Mon-Fri. **Credit** AmEx, MC, V.

Image *24-25 Foley Street, W1P 7LA (7580 5020/www.imageblackandwhite.com). Oxford Circus tube.* **Open** 9am-6pm Mon-Fri. **Credit** MC, V.

Metro Imaging *32 Great Sutton Street, EC1V 0NA (7865 0000/www.metroimaging.co.uk). Farringdon tube/rail.* **Open** 8am-7pm Mon-Fri. **Credit** AmEx, MC, V. **For branch see index.**

Panther Professional *87 Clerkenwell Road, EC1R 5BX (7405 8833/www.panther-imaging.com). Chancery Lane or Farringdon tube/rail.* **Open** 8am-7pm Mon-Fri; 10am-4pm Sat. **Credit** MC, V.

Photo Professional *123 Lower Clapton Road, E5 0NP (8986 9621). Hackney Central rail/38 bus.* **Open** 9am-6.30pm Mon-Fri; 10.30am-5.30pm Sat. **Credit** MC, V.

Plastic fantastic

These days, the word 'camera' is often taken to mean 'digital camera', and flawless pictures and instant 'photographers' are the new reality. But with technical advancement and the resulting democratisation of high-quality photography, a yearning has arisen for imperfect images and less predictable outcomes. As a result, cheap, low-fidelity plastic cameras of the 1960s, '70s and '80s are enjoying something of a renaissance, with reissued models from the likes of Holga and Lomo being sold in growing numbers. Those seeking to escape the brave new world of mexapixels and crisp images are snapping up these technically basic – and, in many cases, technically problematic – but more romantic cameras of yesteryear.

Fuelled by nostalgia for the good old days of cut-off heads, unfocused shots and faded corners – when Polaroid cameras were considered super-advanced technology – some people are being seduced by these old-school plastic medium-format cameras that have become part of the so-called 'toy' camera movement. These cameras are now valued for the inadvertent surreal effects caused by the models' inherent quality problems: light leaks, blurring and resulting distortions are utilised creatively rather than being seen as problems to be solved.

The phenomenon grew out of the Lomography movement of the 1990s, which started when a group of art students from Austria rediscovered the Lomo LC-A 35mm Soviet-era compact. It evolved in parallel with the rise in digital photography, eventually becoming an official organisation as well as a manufacturing company (www.lomography.com). The company has been behind the 'cloning' over the last few years of some cult models – meaning that toy camera enthusiasts no longer have to go in search of the original versions. The **Diana** (which retails for around £42.99) is the latest model to be reissued. Like the Chinese **Holga** and Russian **Lomo** cameras, the Diana – which hadn't been manufactured in its native Hong Kong for 25 years – is a cute-looking plastic 120 medium-format camera featuring the now-desired technical deformaties such as vignetting and over saturation. Lomography still attracts a large following (2007 saw hundreds of 'Lomo-graphers' descend on central London), yet some toy camera aficionados are critical of the company, seeing it as a monopolising commercial venture and the movement as more than a tad pretentious.

If you feel like taking the leap (back) into the unpredictable world of shoddy lenses and real film (quite an adjustment once you're used to digital), then head over to stockists such as **Mr Cad** (*see p219*; Holgas only), **West End Cameras** (160a Tottenham Court Road, 7387 0787), the **London Graphic Centre** (*see p205*), **Urban Outfitters** (*see p20*) or the **Photographers' Gallery** or **Design Museum** (for both, *see p204* **Museum pieces**); prices start from around £25. And if you really want to get to grips with the creative possibilities of using toy cameras, Central St Martins (www.csm.arts.ac.uk) runs an instructional short course.

Sport & Fitness

Of the major department stores, **Harrods** (*see p15*) has the biggest selection of sports and fitness equipment. **John Lewis** (*see p16*) stocks table tennis, snooker and pool tables as well as exercise machines and accessories for other sports. **Selfridges** (*see p16*) has concessions for Cycle Surgery, Powerhouse Fitness and Speedo.

General & local

Ace Sports & Leisure

341 Kentish Town Road, NW5 2TJ (7485 5367). Kentish Town tube. **Open** 9.30am-6.00pm Mon-Sat. **Credit** AmEx, DC, MC, V.

A proper old-school sports shop, established in 1949, covering all sports but with an emphasis on football gear. Stock includes a small rack of boxing gloves and accessories, a rugby section, a set of walking and hiking boots, a few snooker cues and cricket whites, gloves and pads.

Capstick Sports

84 Northcote Road, SW11 6QN (7228 7814/www.capsticksports.co.uk). Clapham South tube. **Open** 10am-5.30pm Mon; 9.30am-5.30pm Tue-Fri; 9am-5.30pm Sat; 11am-4pm Sun. **Credit** AmEx, DC, MC, V.

Every bit the traditional family-run sports shop, with tennis as a strong suit. You can get equipment and advice on anything from lacrosse and golf to rugby and basketball.

Decathlon

Canada Water Retail Park, Surrey Quays Road, SE16 2XU (7394 2000/www.decathlon.co.uk). Canada Water tube. **Open** 10am-8pm Mon-Fri; 9am-7pm Sat; 11am-5pm Sun. **Credit** MC, V.

The warehouse-sized London branch of this French chain offers London's biggest single collection of sports equipment. You'll find a vast array of reasonably priced equipment and clothing for all mainstream racket and ball sports as well as for swimming, running, surfing, fishing, horse riding, mountaineering, ice skating, skiing and more. Separate premises host bicycle sales and repairs along with all sorts of cycling paraphernalia.

Furley & Baker

69 High Street, Beckenham, Kent BR3 1AW (8650 2761/www.furleyandbaker.co.uk). Beckenham Junction rail. **Open** 9.30am-5.30pm Mon-Fri; 9am-5.30pm Sat. **Credit** MC, V.

A professionally and lovingly run local. There's top-quality equipment for a number of sports, including racket sports, cricket and rugby, but it's hockey where the stock and advice on offer are most impressive. The shop is run by a keen hockey coach who will gladly help you find the right stick, clothing and accessories from an extensive range. **For branch see index.**

Sheactive

21-22 New Row, WC2N 4LA (7836 6222/www.sheactive.co.uk). Covent Garden tube. **Open** 11am-7.30pm Mon-Fri; 11am-8pm Thur; 10.30am-7.30pm Sat; noon-6pm Sun. **Credit** AmEx, DC, MC, V.

The people behind stylish Sheactive insist all their products are designed specifically for women. The shop's sports bra range is unparalleled and there are plenty of sport-specific items such as tennis skirts; for fashion-led sportswomen there's the Adidas by Stella McCartney range. Staff are trained in biomechanics and footwear engineering.

Sports Centre

4 Turnham Green Terrace, W4 1QP (8995 6482). Turnham Green tube. **Open** 10am-6pm Mon-Sat; 11am-5pm Sun. **Credit** MC, V.

The cramped feel of the premises is testament to the high volume of products squeezed in here, representing countless sports. You'll need to have a sharp eye, or ask one of the helpful staff, to spot some of the equipment racked up along the narrow aisles, although balls for numerous sports are easy to find, as are the racket sports and cricket sections. There's a notably good choice of swimwear too.

Also check out...

Adidas Performance Store

415-419 Oxford Street (7493 1886/www.adidas.com). Bond Street tube. **Open** 10am-8pm Mon-Sat; noon-6pm Sun. **Credit** AmEx, DC, MC, V.

Clothing, trainers and football boots only at the sportswear giant's London flagship. **For branches see index.**

Euro Sports

1 New College Parade, Finchley Road, NW3 5EP (7722 1775/7586 5897). Swiss Cottage tube. **Open** 9.30am-6pm Mon-Sat; 11am-5pm Sun. **Credit** AmEx, MC, V.

Stands out in particular for its range of tennis, squash and badminton rackets.

JJB Sports

Unit 3C, Staples Corner Retail Park, Geron Way, NW2 6LW (8208 2155/www.jjb.co.uk). Kilburn tube then 32 bus. **Open** 9am-8pm Mon-Fri; 9am-6pm Sat; 11am-5pm Sun. **Credit** AmEx, MC, V.

JJB's larger stores like this one still resemble traditional sports shops (the smaller ones now concentrate on clothing). **Branches**: throughout the city.

Len Smith's

1-15 Heath Road, Twickenham, Middx TW1 4DB (8892 2201/www.lensmiths.com). Twickenham rail. **Open** 9am-5.30pm Mon-Sat. **Credit** MC, V.

Specialises, among other things, in rugby, cricket, lacrosse, hockey and netball.

Lillywhites

24-36 Lower Regent Street, SW1Y 4QF (0870 333 9600/www.sportsdirect.com). Piccadilly Circus tube. **Open** 10am-9pm Mon-Sat; noon-6pm Sun. **Credit** AmEx, DC, MC, V.

Once a landmark sports shop, most of the six floors are now crammed with fashion, but you can still find football boots, racket sports equipment and cricket gear.

Millet Sports

60 The Broadway, NW7 3TE (8959 5539/www.milletsports.co.uk). Edgware tube. **Open** 9am-5.30pm Mon-Sat; 9am-1.30pm Sun. **Credit** MC, V.

Particularly strong on cricket, tennis, squash and badminton. A wide range is available online, including basketball backboards.

Nike Town

236 Oxford Street, W1W 8LG (7612 0800/www.nike.com). Oxford Circus tube. **Open** 10am-7pm Mon-Sat; 11.30am-6pm Sun. **Credit** AmEx, MC, V.

Big on clothing, low on equipment, but an excellent selection of football boots and a well-stocked running department.

Puma

52-55 Carnaby Street, W1F 9QE (7439 0221/www.puma.com). Oxford Circus tube. **Open** 10am-7pm Mon-Wed, Fri, Sat; 10am-8pm Thur; noon-6pm Sun. **Credit** AmEx, MC, V.

Predominantly a sports fashion store and a trainer enclave. The motorsports and sailing departments are unusual surprises.

Basketball

See also above **Millet Sports** and *p229* **Sweatband.com**.

Bowls

Valence Bowls

76 Valence Avenue, Dagenham, Essex RM8 1TL (8590 6980/www.valence-bowls.co.uk). Chadwell Heath rail. **Open** 9.30am-4.45pm Mon, Tue, Thur; 9.30am-1pm Wed, Fri. **Credit** MC, V.

A full selection of Taylor, Drakes Pride and Henselite bowls, along with used bowls.

Cricket

Both the **Lords** and **Brit Oval** cricket grounds have decent shops selling equipment and accessories. *See also p225* **Pro Shop**.

Beckenham Cricket Specialists & Soccer Shop

181A High Street, Beckenham, Kent BR3 1AE (8663 3582/www.beckenhamcricketspec.com). Beckenham Junction rail. **Open** 9.30am-5.30pm Mon-Fri; 9am-5.30pm Sat. **Credit** MC, V.

A cricket shop that also stocks an excellent range of football gear. There's also some rugby and hockey equipment in stock.

Fordham Sports

81 Robin Hood Way, Kingston Vale, SW15 3PW (8974 5654/www.fordhamsports.co.uk). Putney Bridge tube. **Open** 10am-6pm Mon-Fri; 9am-5pm Sat. **Credit** AmEx, MC, V.

Authoritative staff and a comprehensive stock of cricket clothing and equipment make this shop a good choice for serious cricketers. The breadth and depth of stock set it apart, but the professional 'knocking in' service (£30-£40), which allows you to take your bat away 'match ready', gives this place a dimension that most other cricket gear suppliers simply can't compete with. Rugby gear is also stocked.

Cycling

See also p226 **Recyled rides**.

Apex Cycles

40-42 Clapham High Street, SW4 7UR (7622 1334/www.apexcycles.com). Clapham North tube. **Open** 9am-6pm Mon-Fri; 9.30am-6pm Sat. **Credit** AmEx, MC, V.

One of the most reliable bike repair services in south London. The helpful front-of-house staff won't make you feel stupid if you don't know your hybrids from your road bikes. Marin, Ridgeback and Specialized feature heavily among the models for sale; Brompton folders and Pashley traditional-style bikes are also available.

Bikefix

48 Lamb's Conduit Street, WC1N 3LJ (7405 1218/www.bikefix.co.uk). Holborn tube. **Open** 8.30am-7pm Mon-Fri; 10am-5pm Sat. **Credit** MC, V.

If you're looking for a machine that'll make fellow cyclists stop and stare, or need a three-wheeler to take your ice-cream business into the parks, head for Bikefix. The fantastically quirky and original selection of bikes includes utility models, recumbents and folding bikes. There's also an excellent choice of more familiar-looking bikes from lesser-known manufacturers such as Fahrrad Manufaktur, and a repair and maintenance workshop too.

Brick Lane Bikes

118 Bethnal Green Road, E2 6DG (7033 9053/www.bricklanebikes.co.uk). Bethnal Green tube. **Open** 9am-7pm Mon-Fri; 11am-7pm Sat; 11am-6pm Sun. **Credit** AmEx, MC, V.

Fixed-wheel and single-speed bikes have become essential urban-hipster accessories in recent years, and Brick Lane Bikes is where you'll find London's widest selection. The stock includes Charge Plugs and Surly Steamrollers, but the kit that gets die-hards drooling will be hanging above your head: new frames from esteemed Leeds firm Bob Jackson, plus a variety of vintage track and road frames in most shapes and sizes, all of which can be built to order. Prices for custom-builds are highish and customer service can range from fairly helpful to crushingly indifferent; it helps to have some idea what you're after before going in.

Brixton Cycles

145 Stockwell Road, SW9 9TN (7733 6055/www.brixtoncycles.co.uk). Brixton tube. **Open** 9am-6pm Mon-Wed, Fri, Sat; 10am-7pm Thur. **Credit** MC, V.

A Brixton fixture since the 1980s, this co-operative offers a fine range of bicycles and a well-regarded workshop. Bikes from Trek and Specialized keep commuters happy, as do the Bromptons. The workshop can also undertake custom-builds, including fixed-wheel and single-speed machines. It offers a daily on-the-spot repair service in the first hour of opening, otherwise you'll need to book up a month in advance.

Condor Cycles

51 Gray's Inn Road, WC1X 8PP (7269 6820/www.condorcycles.com). Chancery Lane tube. **Open** 9am-6pm Mon, Tue, Thur, Fri; 9am-7.30pm Wed; 10am-5pm Sat. **Credit** MC, V.

The USP of this family-run London legend, in business since 1948 and still in excellent health, is its own range of road bikes, built to order on a bespoke basis. Having chosen a model, prospective purchasers are propped on a fitting jig and measured for the correct frame and components, with clued-up staff adding appropriate parts according to the buyer's budget. But while Condor is heaven for the serious road cyclist, there's plenty for casual riders too. The basement showroom also has some off-the-peg bikes from other manufacturers, and the range of accessories on the main floor is perhaps the best in town.

Herne Hill Bicycles

83 Norwood Road, SE24 9AA (8671 6900/ www.hhbikes.co.uk). Herne Hill rail. **Open** 9am-6pm Tue-Fri; 10am-5pm Sat. **Credit** MC, V.

This little south London bike shop exudes all the positive virtues associated with independent local businesses: courteous, friendly and down-to-earth staff with an enthusiastic and in-depth knowledge of their subject. The store specialises in Ridgeback and Brompton bicycles.

Mosquito Bikes

123 Essex Road, N1 2SN (7226 8765/ www.mosquito-bikes.co.uk). Angel tube/ Essex Road rail. **Open** 8.30am-7pm Mon-Fri; 10am-6pm Sat. **Credit** AmEx, MC, V.

Stockist of high-end road and mountain bikes, Mosquito Bikes is a dream shop for the serious cyclist. Not only can you find top-spec models from such frame-building masters as Pegoretti, Colnago and Merlin, but you can get your bike professionally and perfectly fitted to your own specifications.

Also check out...

Action Bikes

23-26 Embankment Place, WC2N 6NN (7930 2525/www.actionbikes.co.uk). Embankment tube. **Open** 8am-7pm Mon-Fri; 9.30am-5.30pm Sat. **Credit** AmEx, MC, V.

One of the best located bike workshops for West End puncture sufferers; staff'll get you back on the road for just £10.

For branches see index.

Bicycle Workshop

27 All Saints Road, W11 1HE (7229 4850/ www.bicycleworkshop.co.uk). Westbourne Park tube. **Open** 10am-2pm, 3-6pm Tue-Sat. **Credit** MC, V.

This business has been built on an expert, efficient and fairly priced repair service.

Bikefix

LEISURE

Time Out
Online

Cycle Surgery

Spitalfields Market, 12-13 Bishops Square, E1 6EG (7392 8920/www.cyclesurgery.com). Liverpool Street tube/rail. **Open** 10am-7pm Mon-Fri; 10am-6pm Sat; noon-6pm Sun. **Credit** AmEx, MC, V.
This nationwide chain stocks all the well-known brands, from kids' bikes and BMX to road racers and specialist triathlon models.
Branches: throughout the city.

Cyclefit

11-13 Macklin Street, WC2B 5NH (7430 0083/www.cyclefit.co.uk). Holborn tube. **Open** 9.30am-6pm Mon-Fri; 10am-3pm Sat. **Credit** MC, V.
A highly professional bike-fitting service; staff scientifically modify a bike set-up to your optimum level of comfort and efficiency.

Evans Cycles

77-79 The Cut, SE1 8LL (7928 4785/www.evanscycles.com). Southwark tube/Waterloo tube/rail. **Open** 8am-8pm Mon-Fri; 9am-6pm Sat; 11am-5pm Sun. **Credit** MC, V.
This excellent chain has managed to retain the feel of an independent business.
Branches: throughout the city.

London Fields Cycles

281 Mare Street, E8 1PJ (8525 0077/www.londonfieldscycles.co.uk). Hackney Central rail. **Open** 8am-6pm Mon-Fri; 10am-6pm Sat; 11am-5pm Sun. **Credit** AmEx, MC, V.
This superb East End independent is one of the only London stockists of the Gazelle brand's practical no-nonsense city bikes.

London Recumbents

Rangers Yard, Dulwich Park, College Road, SE21 7BQ (8299 6636/www.londonrecumbents. com). North Dulwich or West Dulwich rail. **Open** 10am-5pm daily (closes earlier in winter; phone to check). **Credit** MC, V.
A hire specialist with kids' bikes, recumbents, tandems, and normal bikes for hire and sale.

Moose Cycles

48 High Street, SW19 2BY (8544 9166/www.moosecycles.com). Colliers Wood tube. **Open** 9.30am-7pm Mon-Fri; 9.30am-5pm Sat. **Credit** MC, V.
A wide range of mountain bikes.

Dance

Also see **Porselli** (www.dancewear.co.uk) and *p227* **Freddy**.

Bloch

35 Drury Lane, WC2B 5RH (7836 4777/www.blochworld.com). Covent Garden tube. **Open** 10am-6pm Mon-Sat. **Credit** MC, V.
Retail outlet for this renowned dance footwear and apparel manufacturer.

Dancia International

168 Drury Lane, WC2B 5QA (7831 9483/www.dancia.co.uk). Covent Garden tube. **Open** 10am-6pm Mon-Wed, Fri, Sat; 10am-7pm Thur; 11am-4pm Sun. **Credit** AmEx, MC, V.
One of London's widest ranges of specialist dancewear and shoes.
For branch see index.

Freed of London

94 St Martin's Lane, WC2N 4AT (7240 0432/www.freedoflondon.com). Leicester Square tube. **Open** 9.30am-5.30pm Mon-Fri; 9.30am-3.30pm Sat. **Credit** AmEx, MC, V.
The world's most famous pointe shoe maker is the official supplier of dance shoes to plenty of internationally famous ballet companies. As well as ballet shoes, there are ballroom, jazz and Latin shoes plus a range of clothing. All products are Freed-branded.

Gandolfi

150 Marylebone Road, NW1 5PN (7935 6049/www.gandolfi.co.uk). Baker Street tube. **Open** 10am-5pm Mon-Sat. **Credit** AmEx, MC, V.
Another dancewear specialist with a rich London history, this manufacturer and retailer of tap and ballet shoes has an extensively stocked store stacked high with racks of leotards, tutus and the like.

Equestrian

For riding accessories and clothing, *see p79* **Swaine Adeney Brigg** and **Harrods**' sport section (*see p15*).

Fencing

Leon Paul Equipment

Unit 14, Garrick Industrial Centre, NW9 6AQ (0845 388 8132/www.leonpaul.com). Hendon Central tube/rail. **Open** 9am-5pm Mon-Fri; 10am-3pm Sat. **Credit** MC, V.
The only British manufacturer of fencing equipment stocks everything from starter kits to masks and all three types of sword.

Fishing & angling

Farlows

9 Pall Mall, SW1Y 5NP (7484 1000/www.farlows.co.uk). Piccadilly Circus tube. **Open** 9am-6pm Mon-Wed, Fri; 9am-7pm Thur; 10am-6pm Sat. **Credit** AmEx, DC, MC, V.
A trademark name in the world of fly-fishing, Farlows is the country gentleman's choice for fishing gear and shooting apparel.

Gerry's of Wimbledon

170 The Broadway, SW19 1RX (8542 7792/www.gerrysofwimbledon.co.uk). Wimbledon tube/rail. **Open** 9am-6pm Mon-Sat; 10am-3pm Sun. **Credit** AmEx, MC, V.
Every inch of this huge family-run store is filled with a dizzying array of rods, reels, darts and baits, plus outdoor clothing, wellies, tents, fishing luggage, chairs and bags.

Football

See also p222 **Beckenham Cricket Specialists** and **Soccer Shop**.

Soccer Scene

56-57 Carnaby Street, W1F 9QF (7439 0778/ www.soccerscene.co.uk). Oxford Circus tube. **Open** 10am-8pm Mon-Wed; 10am-9pm Thur, Fri; 10am-7pm Sat; noon-6.30pm Sun. **Credit** AmEx, MC, V.
Replica kits are the big sellers here, but there's also a wide selection of goalkeeping gloves and clothing, and training DVDs. Naturally, football boots and astros are here too – and not just the mainstream brands: come here for Lotto, Uhlsport and Joma.
For branches see index.

Golf

American Golf Centre

12-14 Ashbourne Parade, 1277 Finchley Road, NW11 0AD (8458 9212/www.americangolf.co.uk). Finchley Central tube. **Open** 9.30am-6.30pm Mon-Wed, Fri; 9.30am-8pm Thur; 9am-6pm Sat; 10am-4pm Sun. **Credit** AmEx, DC, MC, V.
A humungous selection of equipment from this branch of the chain.
For branches see index.

Nevada Bob's

The Rotunda, Broadgate Circle, EC2M 2BN (7628 2333/www.nevadabobs.co.uk). Liverpool Street tube/rail. **Open** 9.30am-7pm Mon-Fri; 10am-4pm Sat. **Credit** AmEx, DC, MC, V.
A vast choice of equipment from a nationwide chain. Also has Taylormade, Callaway and Cobra custom-fitting systems.
For branch see index.

Hockey

See also p222 **Furley & Baker**.

The Hockey Shop

Old Loughtonians Hockey Club, Roding Sports Centre, Luxborough Lane, Chigwell, Essex IG7 5AB (8505 3388/www.thehockeyshopatolhc.co.uk). Chigwell tube. **Open** 9am-7pm Mon-Thur; 9am-5pm Sat. **Credit** MC, V.
Everything from umpire warning cards and stick rings to sticks and specialist hockey shoes, bags and protective equipment.

Pro Shop

Unit E, 30 Commerce Road, Brentford, Middx TW8 8LE (8568 9929/www.proshopsport.com). Syon Lane rail. **Open** 10am-5.30pm Mon-Fri; 9.30am-5pm Sat. **Credit** MC, V.
Run by serious sportspeople for serious sportspeople, Pro Shop specialises in rugby, hockey and cricket equipment. There are indoor, outdoor and mini balls; ball bags, kit bags and tour bags; coaching packs, rules books and first aid kits, plus a wide choice of sticks, footwear and clothing. There's even a hitting area for bashing balls into.

Martial arts & boxing

See also **Powerhouse Fitness** and **Totally Fitness** *on p229*.

Blitzsport

Unit 10, The IO Centre, Duke of Wellington Avenue, Royal Arsenal, SE18 6SR (8317 8280/www.blitzsport.com). Woolwich Arsenal rail. **Open** 9.30am-5.45pm Mon-

Thur; 8am-4.15pm Fri; 10am-4.45pm Sun. **Credit** MC, V.
A huge range of clothing, weapons, bags, books and DVDs for all the principal martial arts, as well as boxing equipment.

Shaolin Way

10 Little Newport Street, WC2H 7JJ (7734 6391/www.shaolinway.com). Leicester Square tube. **Open** 11am-6.30pm Mon-Sat; 11am-5.30pm Sun. **Credit** AmEx, MC, V
A pokey martial arts shop in Chinatown with an authentic backstreet feel, expert staff and a jumble of stock piled all over the place. Specialist equipment includes rare handmade Iado swords from Japan (£200-£500), wooden training dummies and 8ft kung fu staffs.

Tao Sports

523 Green Lanes, N4 1AN (8348 0870/ www.taosport.co.uk). Turnpike Lane tube. **Open** 9.30am-5.30pm Mon-Fri; 10am-4pm Sat. **Credit** MC, V.
Much of the stock – which covers a number of martial arts – is the Taogear own brand. Boxing is particularly well covered too.

Vader Sports

865 Forest Road, E17 4AT (8531 0288/ www.vadersports.co.uk). Blackhorse Road or Walthamstow Central tube. **Open** 10.30am-5.30pm Mon-Fri; 11am-4pm Sat. **Credit** MC, V.
A neatly organised and compact shop specialising in boxing, kickboxing and Thai boxing gear. There's a fantastic range of gloves, and you can pick up leather shin and instep guards for £25.99, groin guards for £14.99 and head guards from £19.99, as well as useful training accessories.

Pilates, yoga & gymwear

See also p229 **Weight training**.

Devotion

15 Hildreth Street, SW12 9RQ (8675 7069/ www.devotion.co.uk). Balham tube/rail. **Open** 10am-5.30pm Mon-Sat. **Credit** MC, V.
Yoga accessories from a husband and wife team of Kundalini Yoga teachers.

Recycled rides

Second-hand bikes come with dodgy reputations: many of the bikes that turn up at markets in London have been stolen. But markets are not the only source of second-hand bikes; if you buy sensibly you can be confident of your bike's provenance and quality. Rule number one, if you want peace of mind, is to go to a specialist.

Dealers in used bikes are usually very discerning about where they source their stock – often from auctions (commonly police auctions) and sometimes from manufacturers selling off end-of-line bikes. The more professional second-hand shops offer a free repair and review service after the first month or two. Also, bike hire shops periodically renew stock and sell off old bikes.

Gumtree (www.gumtree.com) has one of the largest selections of used bikes, while **Loot** (www.loot.com) has far fewer but is still worth a look. By using **eBay** (www.ebay.co.uk) you can narrow your search by wheel size, frame colour and brand. Or try one of the recycling and reconditioning initiatives run predominantly by voluntary groups and local councils .

WHAT TO LOOK FOR

Buying second-hand means you need to be doubly careful about your choice. The main defects to look for are rust (especially deep rust); dents and cracks in the frame and forks, particularly around the joins; buckled wheels and broken or missing spokes; loose pedals or handlebars; worn chain, cogs or tyres; and poor response from braking and gear changing. Most importantly, it pays to take a trial ride on the bike, making sure the frame is the right size and that the brakes and gears are in order.

Also look for the bike's unique frame number, usually found etched on to the underside of the main frame or on the rear fork ends. Some bikes are tagged with the previous owner's postcode and house number, again often etched on the underside of the frame. If it looks as though any numbers on the frame have been scratched off, chances are that the bike is stolen property.

BIKE SHOPS

Camden Cycles (251 Eversholt Street, NW1 1BA, 7388 7899, www.camdencycles.co.uk) specialises in reconditioned bikes. All bikes are sold with a one-month free service period. At **Everything Cycling** in Walthamstow (530 Forest Road, E17 4NB, 8521 5812), owner Tom Gilley has decades of experience in repairing bikes and is prepared to deal with all makes and models. **Station Cycles** (Arch 1-4, Upper Walthamstow Road, E17 3QG, 8520 6988, www.stationbicycles.co.uk), offers a huge selection of reconditioned bikes, with prices as low as they come. Children's bikes go for as little as £10; adult's start at around £50.

In the south, **Pedal It** (18 Newington Causeway, SE1 6DR, 7407 9115) sells a good choice of second-hand bikes and is endorsed by the local branch of the London Cycling Campaign. Another option is **Recycling** (110 Elephant Road, SE17 1LB, 7703 7001, www.re-cycling.co.uk); claiming to have 'London's largest selection of reconditioned bicycles', this place is always choc-a-bloc. Staff encourage you to try before you buy and offer a month's free service. Finally, **Smith Bros** (14 Church Road, SW19 5DL, 8946 2270) is a bicycle sale and repair shop with a decent range of second-hand bikes.

RECYCLING SCHEMES

Lunar Cycles (PO Box 13995, W9 2FL, 07935 241928, www.lunar-cycles.com) in Islington run a bike refurb scheme in partnership with the council. In Tower Hamlets, **Bikeworks** (Gun Wharf, 241 Old Ford Road, E3 5QB, 8980 7998, www.bikeworks.org.uk) is a social enterprise that organises sales of new and second-hand bikes. Refurbished bikes typically cost £40-£100 and all recycled bikes come with a one-month guarantee.

In Leyton, the **Low Hall Depot** (Argall Avenue, E10 7AS, 07948 060473 Friday and Saturday only or phone Waltham Forest Council on 8496 3000) has recycled bikes available on the first Saturday of each month between 1pm and 3pm, for a donation starting from £45. Children's bikes start at £20. You can donate old bicycles to the workship, and learn bike maintenance on every third and fourth Saturday of the month.

Another noble scheme is in operation in Wandsworth, at the **Alma Road Resource Training Centre** (Alma Road, SW18 1AA, 8871 8530), where unwanted bikes can be taken for the youth offending team bike recycling project every Thursday between 5pm and 8pm. The refurbished bikes are given to victims of crime.

OTHER CONTACTS

The **London Cycling Campaign** (www.lcc.org.uk) has local branches in every borough and a superb website offering sound advice on buying second-hand.

Freddy

30-32 Neal Street, WC2H 9PS (7836 5291/ www.freddy.it). Covent Garden tube. **Open** 10am-7pm Mon-Wed, Sat; 10am-8pm Thur; noon-6pm Sun. **Credit** AmEx, MC, V.

The official outfitter to the Italian Olympic team and La Scala Ballet, Freddy has also been Italy's essential label for aerobics fans since the 1980s. Its first UK branch offers three floors of own-label sportswear. Think slouchy sweats, with simple jersey shirting, footless tights and cute legwarmers, as well as vintage-looking sports equipment and a range of Renoir-esque tutus.

King's Road Sporting Club

38-42 King's Road, SW3 4UD (7589 5418/ www.krsc.co.uk). Sloane Square tube. **Open** 10am-6.30pm Mon-Sat; noon-6pm Sun. **Credit** AmEx, MC, V.

An independent specialist in women's activewear and swimwear, which also sells yoga accessories. Much of the stock is imported from the US, with brands such as USA PRO and Venice Beach.

Sweaty Betty

21 Beak Street, W1F 9RR (7287 5128/ www.sweatybetty.com). Oxford Circus or Piccadilly Circus tube. **Open** 11am-7pm Mon-Sat; noon-5pm Sun. **Credit** MC, V.

Female sportswear boutique chain where the focus is on looking good while you sweat. Yoga and Pilates accessories and clothing are for sale, as well as running and tennis clothes and pregnancy sportswear.

Branches: throughout the city.

Yogamatters

32 Clarendon Road, N8 0DJ (8888 8588/ www.yogamatters.com). Turnpike Lane tube. **Open** 9.30am-5.30pm Mon-Sat. **Credit** MC, V.

The large selection of yoga mats, starting at £13.99, includes pricier eco-friendly natural versions. Numerous accessories include yoga belts and resistance bands, and an impressive range of CDs, DVDs and books.

Skiing & outdoor pursuits

Covent Garden is the spot for hikers, climbers, campers and snowsports enthusiasts. For snowboards, *see also p228* **Slick Willies**, *p229* **LCB Surf Store** and *p228* **Profeet**.

Boardwise

146 Chiswick High Road, W4 1PU (8994 6769/www.boardwise.com). Turnham Green tube. **Open** 10am-6pm Mon-Sat; noon-5pm Sun. **Credit** AmEx, MC, V.

Boardwise caters to all board sports, including skateboarding and surfing. The best selection is in the snowboard section, where you can find a number of brands including Burton and K2. Boardwise makes a point of not stocking skis.

Ellis Brigham

Tower House, 3-11 Southampton Street, WC2E 7HA (7395 1010/www.ellis-brigham.com). Covent Garden tube. **Open** 10am-7pm Mon-Wed, Fri; 10am-8pm Thur; 9.30am-6.30pm Sat; 11.30am-5.30pm Sun. **Credit** AmEx, MC, V.

With countless racks of outdoor clothing upstairs and climbing, hiking, skiing and snowboarding equipment downstairs in the basement, this is the largest of the mountain sports shops on Southampton Street. It also houses London's only ice-climbing wall, 8m (26ft) high. Two people can climb at any one time for £40 per person per hour, £20 if you have your own kit and don't need instruction. Book at least a day ahead for weekdays, and around six weeks in advance for weekends. A new branch is opening in Westfield London (*see p17*) in autumn 2008.

For branches see index.

Nomad

40 Bernard Street, WC1N 1LJ (7833 4114/ www.nomadtravel.co.uk). Russell Square tube. **Open** 10.30am-7pm Mon-Fri; 10am-6pm Sat; 11am-5pm Sun. **Credit** MC, V.

The target market is independent travellers rather than outdoor pursuits enthusiasts, but climbers and hikers will find useful stock here, including carriers and specialist footwear like waterproof shoes and hiking boots. Invaluable items you never knew you needed are here too, like doorguards for those dodgy hotel rooms and jet lag tablets. This branch has its own vaccination clinic, where you can also pick up anti-malarial medicines and specialised medical kits. A fantastic resource on the website is the kit list section, a set of checklists of items you shouldn't leave home without.

For branches see index.

Rock On

Mile End Climbing Wall, Haverfield Road, E3 5BE (8981 5066/www.rockonclimbing.co.uk). Mile End tube. **Open** noon-9pm Mon-Fri; 10am-6pm Sat, Sun. **Credit** MC, V.

Mountaineering shops don't come any more specialist than this fantastic little place, unmatched in London for the expertise of its staff, all of them active climbers determined that you should get the right gear for your needs. There's no superfluous stock either: the excellent selection of harnesses, helmets, footwear, ice axes, carabiners and such are all vital to some aspect of climbing.

Snow + Rock

4 Mercer Street, WC2H 9QA (7420 1444/ www.snowandrock.com). Covent Garden tube. **Open** 10am-7pm Mon-Wed, Fri, Sat; 10am-8pm Thur; 11.30am-5.30pm Sun. **Credit** AmEx, MC, V.

Not sure if you're cut out for mountain sports? Try tackling the staircase at this six-floor branch of Snow + Rock. All bases are covered in this vast store, so whether it's climbing, hiking, trekking, skiing, running, cycling, swimming, snowboarding or camping, you'll find a section dedicated to it. There's even a sports rehabilitation clinic offering physiotherapy, sports massage, osteopathy and a personal trainer service.

For branches see index.

Also check out...

Blacks

10-11 Holborn, EC1N 2LE (7404 5681/ www.blacks.co.uk). Chancery Lane tube. **Open** 8.30am-7.30pm Mon-Fri; 9.30am-5.30pm Sat; 11am-5pm Sun. **Credit** AmEx, MC, V.

Competitively priced walking, hiking and camping specialist.

Branches: throughout the city.

Cotswold Outdoor

23-26 Piccadilly, W1J 0DJ (7437 7399/ www.cotswoldoutdoor.com). Piccadilly Circus tube. **Open** 10am-8pm Mon-Fri; 10am-6pm Sat; 11am-5pm Sun. **Credit** AmEx, MC, V.

Camping equipment, outdoor clothing and an excellent selection of hiking boots.

For branches see index.

Field & Trek

42 Maiden Lane, WC2E 7LJ (0870 333 9622/www.fieldandtrek.com). Covent Garden tube. **Open** 10am-8pm Mon-Sat; 10am-8pm Thur; 11am-6pm Sun. **Credit** AmEx, MC, V.

Two tightly packed floors of outdoor equipment at lower than average prices.

For branches see index.

47 Degrees

907-909 Fulham Road, SW6 5HU (7731 5415/www.47degrees.com). Parsons Green or Putney Bridge tube. **Open** *Apr-Sept* 10am-6pm Mon-Wed, Fri, Sat; 10am-7pm Thur; 11am-5pm Sun. *Oct-Mar* 10am-7pm Mon-Wed, Fri; 10am-8pm Thur; 10am-6pm Sat; 11am-5pm Sun. **Credit** AmEx, MC, V.

Skiwear rental and sale specialist.

For branches see index.

North Face

30-32 Southampton Street, WC2E 7HA (7240 9577/www.thenorthface.com/eu). Covent Garden tube/Charing Cross tube/ rail. **Open** 10am-7pm Mon-Wed, Fri; 10am-7.30pm Thur; 9.30am-6.30pm Sat; 11am-5pm Sun. **Credit** AmEx, MC, V.

All the own-brand outdoor clothing that you'd expect, plus hiking and climbing equipment such as Suunto watches and altimeters, GPS systems and headlamps.

Urban Rock

Westway Sports Centre, 1 Crowthorne Road, W10 6RP (8964 0185/www.urbanrock.com). Latimer Road tube. **Open** noon-10pm Mon-Fri; 10am-8pm Sat, Sun. **Credit** MC, V.

One of the few stores of this ilk to specialise solely in climbing equipment. Both branches are based at climbing centres.

For branch see index.

Racket sports

See also *p229* **Sweatband.com**.

PWP

273 Wimbledon Park Road, SW19 6NW (8780 3062/www.pwp.com). Southfields tube. **Open** *Mar-Oct* 10am-7pm Mon-Fri; 9am-6pm Sat; 10am-5pm Sun. *Nov-Apr* 10am-6pm Mon-Fri; 9am-6pm Sat; 10am-5pm Sun. **Credit** MC, V.

One branch of a small chain of superb racket sport stores, this shop offers good deals on professional standard equipment.

Wigmore Sports

39 Wigmore Street, W1U 1QQ (7486 7761/www.wigmoresports.com). Bond Street tube. **Open** 10am-6pm Mon-Wed,

Fri, Sat; 10am-7pm Thur; 11am-5pm Sun. **Credit** AmEx, MC, V.
If it's got strings and it swings, you can buy it here. The most impressive racket sports specialist in London, Wigmore Sports has a whole room stacked full of tennis, squash and badminton rackets. This is high-end gear so don't expect to find more than a dozen tennis rackets among the hundreds on display for much under £50; most are over £100. All the extras are here, plus specialist clobber like tennis-specific sunglasses with teal tinted lenses that mute all light except optic yellow. The footwear choice is also extensive, with something for every surface. There's a 24-hour stringing service and an in-store practice wall so you can try before you buy. There's also a concession in Harrods.
For branch see index.

Rugby

See also p225 **Pro Shop** and *p222* **Fordham Sports**.

Rugby Scene
1st Floor, 56-57 Carnaby Street, W1F 9QF (7287 9628/www.rugbyscene.co.uk). Oxford Circus tube. **Open** 10am-8pm Mon-Sat; noon-6pm Sun. **Credit** AmEx, MC, V.
One of London's very few rugby-only shops is located above Soccer Scene (*see p225*) and stocks training equipment, a huge selection of balls, a fairly large number of boots and body armour and a wide range of replica kits. One of the best places to get rugby DVDs.

Rugby Store
15-19 York Street, Twickenham, Middx TW1 3JZ (8892 9250/www.rfu.com/therugbystore). Twickenham rail. **Open** 10am-6pm Mon-Fri; 9am-5pm Sat. **Credit** AmEx, MC, V.
Boots, balls, replica kit and memorabilia.
For branch see index.

Running

Profeet
592 Fulham Road, SW6 5NT (7736 0046/www.profeet.co.uk). Parsons Green tube. **Open** 1-8pm Tue, Thur; 10am-6pm Wed, Fri; 9am-5pm Sat; 10am-3pm Sun. **Credit** MC, V.
If you're looking for perfect performance running shoes or ski boots, or you want a more precise fit from your existing sports shoes and are prepared to go the extra mile – and cost – to get it, then Profeet is the shop for you. Using its highly scientific 3D Fit System, which involves video-imaging and foot-pressure mapping, it designs customised insoles based on analysis of your individual foot type and gait; they can help in injury prevention and recovery. The only footwear actually stocked is running shoes and ski boots; however, staff can fit insoles to a wide variety of shoes and advise on footwear for other sports. The cost of the running analysis is £40 and if you choose to have the insoles made you'll pay an additional £95. The ski analysis and insole package is £119 (only at the Ski Boot Lab).
For branches (including Ski Boot Lab) see index.

Run & Become
42 Palmer Street, SW1H 0PH (7222 1314/www.runandbecome.com). St James's Park tube. **Open** 9am-6pm Mon-Wed, Fri, Sat; 9am-8pm Thur. **Credit** MC, V.
The experienced staff here, most of them enthusiastic runners, are determined to find the right pair of shoes for your particular physique and running style. The full gamut of running kit, from clothing to speed monitors, is also available.

Runners Need
34 Parkway, NW1 7AH (7267 7525/www.runnersneed.co.uk). Camden Town tube. **Open** 10am-6pm Mon, Tue, Thur-Sat; 10am-7pm Wed; noon-5pm Sun. **Credit** AmEx, MC, V.
Sports therapists, personal trainers and sport science degree graduates are among the staff at Runners Need, so expert advice is always on hand. Treadmills are used to analyse your running gait (except at the Camden store where staff still use the pavement outside), and video equipment allows you to see for yourself how your feet behave once in full stride. Accessories like hydration packs, MP3 player arm wallets and nipple guards are also stocked.
For branches see index.

Also check out...

London City Runner
10 Ludgate Broadway, EC4V 6DU (7329 1955/www.londoncityrunner.com). St Paul's tube. **Open** 9.30am-6pm Mon-Wed, Fri; 9.30am-7pm Thur; noon-4pm Sat. **Credit** AmEx, DC, MC, V.
A small range of discounted running shoes can usually be found at this family-run store. Full-price stock includes off-road and fell running shoes.

Runnersworld
139 Field End Road, Eastcote, Pinner, Middx HA5 1QH (8868 6997/www.runnersworld.ltd.uk). Eastcote tube. **Open** 9.30am-6pm Mon, Tue, Thur, Fri; 9.30am-7pm Wed; 9am-6pm Sat. **Credit** MC, V.
An ample selection of running shoes, apparel and accessories.
For branches see index.

Skating

See also p227 **Boardwise** and *p229* **LCB Surf Store**.

London Skate Centre
27 Leinster Terrace, W2 3ET (7706 8769/www.lonskate.com). Queensway tube. **Open** noon-6.30pm Wed-Fri; 11am-5pm Sat, Sun. **Credit** MC, V.
Ice figure, ice hockey, inline and good old-fashioned roller skates are all for sale in this small independent shop run by an ex-pro ice-skating coach. Rollerblade rental is also available.

Skate Attack
72 Chase Side, N14 5PH (8886 7979/www.skateattack.co.uk). Southgate tube. **Open** 9am-6pm Tue-Sat. **Credit** DC, MC, V.
A big store specialising in all things skating – it's a great place for ice-hockey equipment.

Slam City Skates
16 Neal's Yard, WC2H 9DP (7240 0928/www.slamcity.com). Covent Garden tube. **Open** 11am-7pm Mon-Sat; noon-5pm Sun. **Credit** AmEx, MC, V.
Slam City is a legendary name on the British skate scene, as much a part of the London skateboarding identity as the South Bank. It's also the best-stocked shop for decks, trucks, wheels and almost any skateboard accessory, as well as footwear and clothing, including the shop's own unique T-shirt and hoodie range. All the staff are skaters.

Slick Willies
12 Gloucester Road, SW7 4RB (7225 0004). Gloucester Road tube. **Open** 10am-6.30pm Mon-Sat; noon-5pm Sun. **Credit** AmEx, MC, V.
Friendly staff are equally at home advising on skateboarding as on inline skating at this hip veteran of the London skate shop scene. Shopping here can help you get the balance right between looking good and having the right equipment.

Tuesday
118 Camden Road, NW1 9EE (7284 4515/www.tuesdayskateshop.blogspot.com). Camden Town tube/Camden Road rail. **Open** 11.30am-6.30pm Tue-Sat; noon-4pm Sun. **Credit** MC, V.
If this skate shop was any more laid-back it'd be closed. Indeed, Sunday's opening hours do slightly depend on the calibre of Saturday night's partying. Its Camden Road location means it draws a lot of business from Cantelowes skatepark; folk pop by for hard-to-find lines of shoes from NikeSB and Vans, as well as Lakai and DVS. Apparel comes from Insight, 4Star and Volcom. DVDs, wheels, trucks and decks are all stocked, and chirpy owner Jonathan will talk you through the merits of the different woods.

Snooker, pool & billiards

Hunt & Osborne Cues
124 Himley Road, SW17 9AQ (8767 9944/www.robertosbornecues.com). Tooting Broadway tube. **Open** 11am-6pm Mon, Tue, Thur-Sat; by appointment Wed. **Credit** MC, V.
Expertly crafted, handmade cues for snooker and pool are manufactured at this showroom and workshop, which has a table set up for trying out the finished products. A made-to-measure service is available and you can get repairs done too.

Swimming

See also p227 **King's Road Sporting Club**, *p229* **Bike & Run** and **SBR**.

Speedo
41-43 Neal Street, WC2H 9PJ (7497 0950/www.speedo.com). Covent Garden tube. **Open** 10am-7.30pm Mon-Wed; 10am-8pm Thur; 10am-7pm Fri, Sat; noon-6pm Sun. **Credit** AmEx, MC, V.
Swimwear including goggles, caps and the latest bonded-seams swimsuits.

Freddy. *See p227.*

Table tennis

See below **Sweatband.com** and *p222* **Decathlon**.

Target sports

If you're after darts equipment, *see p225* **Gerry's of Wimbledon**.

Quicks Archery Centre

Apps Court, Hurst Road, Walton-on-Thames, Surrey KT12 2EG (01932 232211/www.quicksarchery.co.uk). Hampton Court or Walton-on-Thames rail. **Open** 9.30am-5pm Mon-Sat. **Credit** MC, V.

This branch of a four-store chain of archery equipment shops features both indoor and outdoor shooting ranges.

Triathlon

Bike & Run

125 High Road, N2 8AG (8815 1845/www.bikeandrun.co.uk). East Finchley tube. **Open** 9.30am-6pm Mon-Fri; 9.30am-5.30pm Sat. **Credit** AmEx, MC, V.

Stock includes such specialist items as elastic laces, race number belts, triathlon-specific shoes, tri suits and tri shorts.

SBR

917-919 Fulham Road, SW6 5HU (7731 5005/www.sbrsports.com). Putney Bridge tube. **Open** 10am-7pm Mon-Fri; 9am-7pm Sat; 11am-5pm Sun. **Credit** MC, V.

A comprehensive stock range for runners, cyclists and swimmers as well as specialist triathletes. Tri-specific wetsuits are also available for hire for a day, week or month.

Watersports

For windsurfing and surfboards, *see also p227* **Boardwise**.

Arthur Beale

194 Shaftesbury Avenue, WC2H 8JP (7836 9034). Tottenham Court Road tube. **Open** 9am-6pm Mon-Fri; 9.30am-1pm Sat. **Credit** AmEx, MC, V.

It may look old-fashioned, but the stock at this long-standing yacht chandler is as useful now as it ever was. On the ground floor you'll find everything from reels of rope, ship's bells, barometers and brass navigation lights to basic boating hardware such as cleats, fairleads and lacing hooks. On the first floor you'll find books, boots and lifejackets.

LCB Surf Store

121 Bethnal Green Road, E2 7DG (7739 3839/www.lcbsurfstore.com). Liverpool Street tube/rail. **Open** 8am-7pm Mon-Fri; 10am-7pm Sat, Sun. **Credit** AmEx, DC, MC, V.

LCB's laid-back vibe and colourful, light interior hit just the right note for a surf shop. The store's owners design and manufacture their own distinctive surfboards, the LCB Eseries (£440-£475), as well as their own line of clothing. Rip Curl wetsuits, Burton snowboards and a range of skateboards round out the stock. There is also an instore café with internet access. A Clapham branch is opening at the end of 2008.

Ocean Leisure

11-14 Northumberland Avenue, WC2N 5AQ (7930 5050/www.oceanleisure.co.uk). Embankment tube. **Open** 10am-7pm Mon-Fri; 10am-5pm Sat. **Credit** MC, V.

A marine superstore selling gear for every imaginable watersport, from sailing, kayaking, kitesurfing and windsurfing to scuba diving, snorkelling and plain old swimming. Stock includes wetsuits, marine electronics, underwater cameras, life jackets, clothing, footwear, swimsuits and goggles. Wakeboards, kneeboards, surfboards, waterskis and canoes are here too. The store also contains a chandlery and a large book department, plus yachting charts and DVDs.

Mike's Waterfront Warehouse

113 Power Road, W4 5PY (8994 6006/www.mikesdivestore.com). Gunnersbury tube. **Open** 10am-6pm Mon-Fri; 10am-5.30pm Sat. **Credit** AmEx, MC, V.

Next door to the London School of Diving, this store (a branch of a nationwide chain) is a one-stop shop for diving equipment.

Weight training & fitness equipment

Decathlon (*see p222*) has own-brand weight training equipment at below average prices.

Powerhouse Fitness

Charing Cross Underground, Strand, WC2N 4HZ (7240 1363/www.powerhouse-fitness.co.uk). Charing Cross tube. **Open** 9am-7pm Mon-Fri; 9am-6pm Sat; 11am-5pm Sun. **Credit** AmEx, MC, V.

Pick up free weights and weights machines at this spacious store, as well as treadmills, rowing machines, boxing equipment and nutrition supplements.

For branches see index.

Sweatband.com

42 Clipstone Street, W1W 5DW (7927 8101/www.sweatband.com). Great Portland Street tube. **Open** 9.30am-6pm Mon-Fri. **Credit** MC, V.

A shop/showroom for a web-based company with lots more stock online than can be displayed at the shop. There are around 20 fitness machines – treadmills, cross trainers and exercise bikes – plus bits and pieces for other sports, including racket sports kit, basketball stands, backboards and balls, and snooker, pool and table tennis tables.

Totally Fitness

108 Crawford Street, W1H 2JB (7467 5925/www.totallyfitness.co.uk). Baker Street tube. **Open** 9am-6pm Mon-Fri; 10am-4pm Sat; noon-4pm Sun. **Credit** AmEx, MC, V.

An upmarket showroom for this expanding chain of top-quality fitness equipment. This is a reliable place to get set up with a home gym, or buy a treadmill or exercise bike. Simpler items such as dumbbells, yoga mats and benches are also available.

Stationery

Liberty is great for diaries and photo albums and **John Lewis** has well-priced stationery; for both, *see p16*.

Blade Rubber Stamps

12 Bury Place, WC1A 2JL (7831 4123/ www.bladerubber.co.uk). Holborn tube. **Open** 10.30am-6pm Mon-Sat. **Credit** AmEx, MC, V.

A shrine to wooden-handled rubber stamps, there's something for everyone here: Y-fronts, art deco roses, Henry VIII, London buses and telephone boxes are all up for grabs, plus celtic insignia, homework stamps ('Check spelling', 'Keep trying'), adorable love-letter writing kits and all the animals in Noah's ark. The resurrections of old postmarks are fun and quaint: 'Too late for the morning mail' or 'Paid Penny Post, Brick Lane' and Blade also offers unmounted sheets of rubber stamps, ink pads in every imaginable shade, glitters, glues, stencils and stickers.

For branch see index.

Mount Street Printers & Stationers

4 Mount Street, W1K 3LW (7409 0303/ www.mountstreetprinters.com). Bond Street or Green Park tube. **Open** 9am-6pm Mon-Fri. **Credit** AmEx, MC, V.

With a whiff of glue and ink permeating up from the printworks downstairs, this shop means business and claims to be the fastest stationery turnaround in town. You'll find everything from classy white invitation cards to thank-you notes with matching lined envelopes. Even the most imaginative commissions are affordable, and the company takes particular pride in its special design techniques including ornate die-stamping and engraving. There's also a small selection of ready-made stationery including visitors' books, cards and office supplies.

For branches see index.

Nemeta

10 Great Newport Street, WC2H 7JL (7379 7898/www.nemeta.com). Leicester Square tube. **Open** 9.30am-7.15pm Mon-Sat; 12.30-6.30pm Sun. **Credit** AmEx, MC, V.

Shopping for pens has never been so enjoyable, and all for just a few pence more than WH Smith. Nemeta supplies stationery in every shape and colour, unveiling papers, journals, albums and portfolios from all over the world. Clairefontaine is one of the leading brands stocked – its quality, unique design and affordability suiting the shop to a tee. Filofaxes can be had cheaply if you catch a seasonal sale, as can Nava computer bags and Antonio Miro shoulder bags. Recycled-tyre mousemats and bog standard files in pretty shades are displayed at the entrance.

For branch see index.

Paperchase

213-215 Tottenham Court Road, W1T 7PS (7467 6200/www.paperchase.co.uk). Goodge Street tube. **Open** 9.30am-7pm Mon-Wed, Fri, Sat; 9.30am-8pm Thur; noon-6pm Sun. **Credit** AmEx, MC, V.

You'll find everything from jiffy bags to wooden linen boxes at Paperchase. It's a reference point for greetings cards and also sells all the equipment for making them. The flagship celebrates dots, lines and sweet-shop colours on own-brand diaries, albums, folders and writing paper. Upstairs, prices climb, with luxury Filofaxes, pens, leather bags and a select homewares range. The top floor stocks top-notch art materials.

Branches: throughout the city.

Penfriend

Bush House Arcade, Strand, WC2B 4PH (7836 9809/www.penfriend.co.uk). Temple tube. **Open** 9.30am-5.15pm Mon-Fri. **Credit** AmEx, MC, V.

This pen specialist stocks quality brands like Parker, Waterman, Yard-o-Led, Pelikan and Montegrappa, has a repair, restoration and engraving service, and their nibs can be shaped to suit individual writing styles. The vintage selection includes De La Rue, Conklin and limited-edition Conway Stewart, and you'll also find antique silver penknives, old stamps and assorted curios.

For branches see index.

Shepherds Bookbinders

76 Southampton Row, WC1B 4AR (7831 1151/www.bookbinding.co.uk). Holborn or Russell Square tube. **Open** 10am-6pm Mon, Tue, Thur, Fri; 11am-6pm Wed; 10.30am-5.30pm Sat. **Credit** MC, V.

Previously Falkiner Fine Papers, this shop changed its name in 2008; the old-fashioned timber space with tall shelves crammed full make it a romantic's haven. Wrapping paper comes in all sorts of formats, like the Bengali Fairtrade papers in sari-like colours, and Japanese prints are recycled into albums and notepads. In the basement there's also a bookbinding workshop; get a photograph album bound for £55 in one of 150 choices of book cloth. If you want to do the binding yourself, you can find the sewing thread, glue and tools you'll need here as well as paper-making equipment.

For branch see index.

Smythson

40 New Bond Street, W1S 2DE (7629 8558/www.smythson.com). Bond Street or Oxford Circus tube. **Open** 9.30am-6pm Mon-Wed, Fri; 10am-7pm Thur; 10am-6pm Sat. **Credit** AmEx, DC, MC, V.

This profoundly posh English stationers has been around since 1887. Its trademark is pale blue featherweight paper, bound in stunning polished leather: recent collections include a black calfskin design and a 1950s-style bold graphic print. The themed notebook range contains titles such as 'Yummy Mummy' and 'Forget Me Not' (from £38). Smythson also makes personalised wallets and bags and there's a bespoke correspondence card and writing paper service. The shop is a discreet affair (no price tags) with friendly staff.

For branches see index.

Also check out...

Aspinal of London

0845 052 6900/www.aspinaloflondon.com

Leather bags, notebooks and stationery.

For branch see index.

City Organiser

40 Bow Lane, EC4M 9DT (7248 8326/ www.cityorg.co.uk). Mansion House tube. **Open** 9.30am-6pm Mon-Fri. **Credit** AmEx, DC, MC, V.

For branches see index.

Filofax

68 Neal Street, WC2H 9PF (7836 1977). Covent Garden tube. **Open** 9.30am-6pm Mon-Wed; 10am-7pm Thur, Fri; 10am-6pm Sat. **Credit** AmEx, DC, MC, V.

For branches see index.

Hazlitz

www.hazlitz.com

The Coulson Street shop and bespoke service are no longer, but Hazlitz still sells its 100% cotton ready-to-write range online.

JM Pennifeather

4 Flask Walk, NW3 1HE (7794 0488). Hampstead tube. **Open** 10.30am-5.30pm Mon-Fri; 10.30am-5.30pm Sat; 11am-5.30pm Sun. **Credit** MC, V.

For branch see index.

Pen Shop

199 Regent Street, W1B 4LZ (7734 4088/ www.penshop.co.uk). Oxford Circus tube. **Open** 9.30am-6pm Mon, Tue, Fri, Sat; 10am-6pm Wed; 9.30am-7pm Thur; 11am-5pm Sun. **Credit** AmEx, DC, MC, V.

For branches see index.

Scribbler

15 Shorts Gardens, WC2H 9AT (7836 9600/www.scribbler.co.uk). Covent Garden tube. **Open** 9am-7pm Mon-Sat; noon-6pm Sun. **Credit** AmEx, MC, V.

Branches: throughout the city.

Blade Rubber Stamps

Streetwise

Mount Street

New arrivals have injected some glamour into this traditional Mayfair enclave.

Significant swathes of W1 have always been known for their rather stuffy atmosphere. Doormen – that is, men who open doors for a living – are prone to sneer at potential customers who might rank below viscount. Mount Street, with its dignified Victorian terracotta facades and by-appointment-only art galleries, still harbours a superior Mayfair elite; consider, for example, traditional vendors such as master butcher **Allens Butchers of Mount Street** (no.117, *see p236*), cigar shop **Sautter** (no.106, 7499 4866), with its dusty collection of antique crocodile skin cigar cases, and **Purdey** (7499 1801), the traditional gunsmith that has stood aloof at 57 South Audley Street since 1882.

But Mount Street has recently become home to a raft of top-notch new openings that have given the area's traditional luxury aesthetic a youthful, less exclusive twist – but without compromising on quality.

Towards the east end of the street, near the newly refurbished Connaught Hotel, sits the **Balenciaga** flagship (no.12, 7317 4400), its super-chic clothing set against a glowing sci-fi interior. Next door, you can splurge on a Moser wristwatch at Asprey offshoot **William & Son** (no.10, 7493 8385) – or buy a rifle at their branch at no.14.

Across the road, gentlemen's tailor **Rubinacci** (no.96, 7499 2299) sits near the **Mount Street Galleries** (no.94, 7493 1613), one of several fine art dealers in the area. Antiques dealers, perhaps unsurprisingly, also feature, including **Kenneth Neame** (no.27, 7629 0445) just up the street. Indeed, just round the corner on South Audley Street are neighbours **Adrian Alan** (nos.66-67, 7495 2324,) and **Emanouel** (nos.64-64A, 7493 4350), both selling extremely impressive items.

They hold court with **Edi B** (no.29, 7629 4650), purveyor of fine linens; the exquisite china and glass of **Thomas Goode & Co** (no.19, 7499 2823); and **Spa Illuminata** (no.63, *see p99*), a lovely luxury day spa.

But it's back on Mount Street where the new lease of life is most in evidence, with **Marc Jacobs**' first UK boutique (nos.24-25, *see p42*), one of the first of the superbrands that was cherry-picked by boutique real-estate consultants Wilson McHardy, who were put in charge of reinvigorating the area in 2006. Life-size shots of Victoria Beckham and other celebrities – all stark naked – line the windows. A stand-alone **Marc by Marc Jacobs** store is due to open at no.44 in spring 2009. Another of the red-hot names is revered shoe designer **Christian Louboutin** (no.17, *see p70*), whose storefront display features a woman prancing nonchalantly out of a giant gilded egg. Parisian perfumer **Annick Goutal** has opened shop at no.109, and contemporary jeweller **Fiona Knapp** will move in next door soon. You'll also find niche Australian skin, hair and body brand **Aesop** (no.91, 7409 2358) and the best highlights in London at **Jo Hansford** (no.19, *see p109*).

High-end fashion brands may be opening up on this previously sleepy stretch, then, but it's the deliberate absence of brash, ultra-luxe fashion houses like Louis Vuitton and Gucci that is giving Mount Street its real cachet. The idea behind the renaissance has been to source the best of everything – and not necessarily the most expensive or best known. Some of the biggest brands are conspicuous by their absence. So there's no chance of this becoming another Bond Street, at least for now.

Other new shops are set to open imminently: the icing on the cake will be reserved for the unveiling of a **Lanvin** store (no.128), bridal and cocktail dress shop **Jenny Packham** (3 Carlos Place), men's shoe store **Harry's of London** (no.56), and **Wunderkind** (no.15), a youthful diffusion line from German label Joop!

When the luxury gets too much for you (if it ever does), take some time out in Mount Street Gardens, which snakes behind the south side of the street. Founded in 1889, this green space is a prime lunchbreak location. You can sit and watch long-term residents of this history-loaded area puzzle over its new-found popularity with fashionable young upstarts.

Local dining options include afternoon tea at the Connaught Hotel's **Gallery at the Connaught** or a drink at its opulent **Coburg Bar** (voted the pick of London's bars by *Time Out* magazine in 2008). There's also long-running, recently refurbished fish restaurant **Scott's** (no.20). Or sneak down the road to the **Audley** pub (no.41) for a pint of Young's and some pork scratchings.

Food & Drink

Food & Drink

Unpackaged (and bottom left and right). *See p238.*

Algerian Coffee Stores. *See p256.*

Paul (and right). *See p236.*

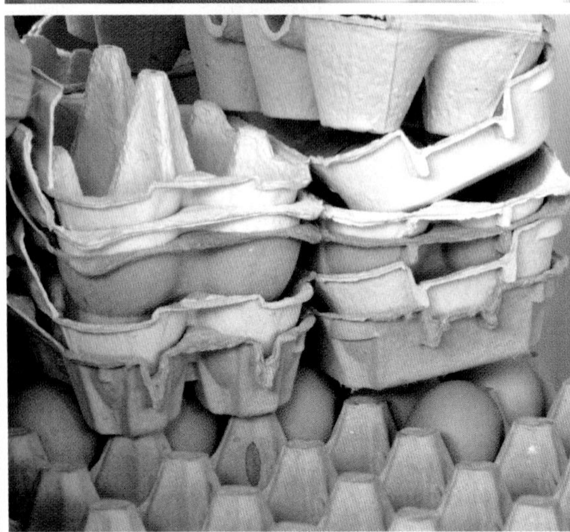

Food

Bakeries & pâtisseries

Baker & Spice

75 Salusbury Road, NW6 6NH (7604 3636/www.bakerandspice.com). Queen's Park tube. **Open** 7am-7pm Mon-Sat; 8am-5pm Sun. **Credit** MC, V.

Baker & Spice is admired for loaves such as caramelised garlic bread, seed-studded ficelle (very thin baguette), Westphalian rye bread and pain de mie (a soft white French loaf made from enriched dough), but this small chain rises souffle-like above most of the competition when it comes to the sweet stuff. Muffins, rugalachs, pecan slices, fruit tarts, cheesecakes and some really sensational physalis-topped chocolate fondants stand there just begging to be smeared over your hips. Not everything is organic, but sustainable sourcing of quality seasonal ingredients is taken very seriously and goes some way to explaining the jaw-clenching prices.

For branches see index.

Breads Etcetera

127 Clapham High Street, SW4 7SS (7720 3601/www.breadsetcetera.com). Clapham Common tube. **Open** 2-7pm Mon; 10am-6pm Tue, Wed; 10am-10pm Thur-Sat; 10am-4pm Sun. **No credit cards.**

We love visiting this bakery-café for leisurely breakfasts featuring the local butcher (Moen's) cumberland sausages and bacon from free-range Plantation Pigs in Surrey, along with Breads Etcetera's own distinctive, ecologically minded products. A wholesale supplier to top restaurants and bars, Troels Bendix and Kurt Anderson's outfit produces some memorable organic sourdough loaves: bestseller is the six-seed but do try the original white or walnut breads, and the tangy Danish rye. Muffins, macaroons and the like are also available.

De Gustibus

53 Blandford Street, W1U 7HL (7486 6608/www.degustibus.co.uk). Baker Street tube. **Open** 7am-4pm Mon-Fri. **No credit cards.**

Dan and Annette Schickentanz started this highly esteemed bakery business in the kitchen of their Oxfordshire home. While the shops tend to look like sandwich joints (and the sandwiches are indeed terrific), it's the modest displays of expertly made breads that really shine. The huge rounds of Six Day Sour are worth a trip across town as this deliciously tangy, even-textured white bread keeps well and upgrades your daily toast and sarnies to gourmet status. A choice of rye loaves and others in the American and Italian traditions mean everyone will find something to satisfy.

For branches see index.

Euphorium Bakery

211 Haverstock Hill, NW3 4QN (7431 8944/www.euphoriumbakery.com). Belsize Park tube. **Open** 7.30am-9pm Mon-Fri; 8am-9.30pm Sat, Sun. **Credit** MC, V.

This shiny Belsize Park branch of the popular Islington bakery-café features the neon brights of the new corporate logo. Modern apparently, but hardly soothing. Still, the Czech master baker Jan Hanzl produces some fine loaves here, including pain de campagne, sourdough, muesli, rye and rosemary. Of course, there are plenty of less virtuous ways to spend your money at Euphorium: éclairs, brownies, biscotti and – the stars of the range – frangipane and bitter chocolate tarts. You can pick up hampers here for scoffing on nearby Hampstead Heath, and the bakery also provides special-occasion cakes: think chocolate curls and fresh berries rather than the Tottenham Hotspur shield.

For branches see index.

Konditor & Cook

22 Cornwall Road, SE1 8TW (7261 0456/ www.konditorandcook.com). Waterloo tube/rail. **Open** 7.30am-6.30pm Mon-Fri; 8.30am-3pm Sat. **Credit** AmEx, MC, V.

Gerhard Jenne caused a stir when he opened this bakery on a South Bank side street in 1993, selling rudie gingerbread people for grown-ups and lavender-flavoured cakes. It's now a mini chain with a few branches (including a swanky café in the Gherkin). The distinctive folds of the whisky and orange bombe make it one of the best-known cakes in the range. Look out especially for seasonal treats such as pumpkin pie in October and mince pies in December, and don't miss the terrific hot chocolate, made with double cream and Valrhona couverture. Quality prepacked lunchtime salads, sandwiches and sausage rolls are also available.

For branches see index.

Macaron

22 The Pavement, SW4 0HY (7498 2636). Clapham Common tube. **Open** 7.30am-8pm Mon-Fri; 9am-8pm Sat, Sun. **No credit cards.**

Young French pâtissier Nicholas Houchet works from the kitchen at the rear of this shop/café, producing cutting-edge culinary creations that combine seemingly disparate flavours – sherry, thyme and pistachios, say, or Earl Grey tea, caramel, coconut and apricot. You'll also find classics such as éclairs, fruit tarts, macaroons and Paris-Brest, plus a fine range of ice-cream by an artisan producer in nearby Vauxhall.

Allens Butchers of Mount Street. *See p236.*

Primrose Bakery

69 Gloucester Avenue, NW1 8LD (7483 4222/www.primrosebakery.org.uk). Camden Town or Chalk Farm tube. **Open** 8.30am-6pm Mon-Sat; 10am-5pm Sun. **Credit** MC, V.

A pretty cake shop in pastel colours with retro kitchenette tables and chairs for eating in, plus a selection of girly gifts, toys and stationery. Martha Swift's cupcakes (from simple vanilla to lime and coconut) and layer cakes (carrot, victoria sponge, chocolate) command a seriously A-list following, including Kate Moss and U2.

Poilâne

46 Elizabeth Street, SW1W 9PA (7808 4910/www.poilane.fr). Sloane Square tube/ Victoria tube/rail. **Open** 7.30am-7pm Mon-Fri; 7.30am-6pm Sat. **Credit** MC, V.

Founded in Paris in 1932 by Pierre Poilâne, this company achieved international repute under his son Lionel and is now run by granddaughter Appollonia. The London branch produces bread satisfyingly similar to that made in Paris and distributes to many other shops in the capital, including Selfridges and Waitrose. Although prices are premium, the chewy, dense and remarkably sour loaves have long keeping qualities, so score on value. Try the rye and raisin as a lively alternative to the signature pain au levain.

Also check out...

Brick Lane Beigel Bake

159 Brick Lane, E1 6SB (7729 0616). Liverpool Street tube/rail/8 bus. **Open** 24hrs daily. **No credit cards**.

Join the fast-moving queue snaking around the counter of this East End institution.

Carmelli Bakery

128 Golders Green Road, NW11 8HB (8455 2074/www.carmelli.co.uk). Golders Green tube. **Open** 6am-1am Mon-Wed; 6am Thur-1hr before sabbath Fri; 1hr after sabbath Sat-1am Mon. **Credit** MC, V.

One of north London's best options for bagels, filled or plain. Sweet things include mini rugelachs (Jewish pastries) and heart-decorated cakes.

Daisy Cakes Bake Shop

11 Turnpin Lane, SE10 9JA (3248 3047/ www.daisycakesbakeshop.com). Cutty Sark or Greenwich DLR. **Open** 11am-5.30pm Tue-Sun. **Credit** AmEx, MC, V.

Bespoke novelty cakes for all sorts of special occasions, plus cupcakes and a cute range of bridal figurines.

Gail's

64 Hampstead High Street, NW3 1QH (7794 5700/www.gailsbread.co.uk). Hampstead tube. **Open** 7am-9pm Mon-Fri; 8am-9pm Sat, Sun. **Credit** MC, V.

From the team behind Baker & Spice and the wholesale Bread Factory, Gail's impresses with consistent high quality.

For branches see index.

Hummingbird Bakery

47 Old Brompton Road, SW7 3JP (7584 0055/www.hummingbirdbakery.com). South Kensington tube. **Open** 10.30am-7pm daily. **Credit** AmEx, MC, V.

Tarek Malouf's homage to the American-style bake sale. Cupcakes are the bestsellers; layer cakes are made to order.

For branch see index.

Louis' Pâtisserie

32 Heath Street, NW3 6DE (7435 9908). Hampstead tube. **Open** 9am-6pm daily. **No credit cards**.

You'll find Hungarian cream cakes, chocolate croissants and breads piled high as you enter this evocative tea room.

Maison Blanc

37 St John's Wood High Street, NW8 7NG (7586 1982/www.maisonblanc.co.uk). St John's Wood tube. **Open** 8am-7pm Mon-Sat; 9am-6.30pm Sun. **Credit** MC, V.

Jenny Blanc, ex-wife of Raymond, founded this smart pâtisserie specialising in breads, gateaux, viennoiserie and savouries in 1989.

Branches: throughout the city.

Old Post Office Bakery

76 Landor Road, SW9 9PH (7326 4408/ www.oldpostofficebakery.co.uk). Clapham North tube. **Open** 8.30am-7pm Mon-Fri; 8.30am-5pm Sat; 8.30am-2pm Sun. **No credit cards**.

This long-established organic bakery produces robust loaves, wholesome hippy cakes and vegetable-laden savouries.

Paul

29 Bedford Street, WC2E 9ED (7836 5321/www.paul-uk.com). Covent Garden or Leicester Square tube. **Open** 7.30am-9pm Mon-Fri; 9am-8pm Sat, Sun. **Credit** MC, V.

This French chain has spread faster than tuile batter on a hot baking sheet. Best bets are pain ancien, croissants and fruit tarts.

Branches: throughout the city.

St John

26 St John Street, EC1M 4AY (7251 0848/ www.stjohnrestaurant.com). Farringdon tube/rail. **Open** 9am-midnight Mon-Fri; 10am-midnight Sat; 10am-10.30pm Sun. **Credit** AmEx, MC, V.

Wonderful sourdough breads, custard-filled doughnuts and world-famous eccles cakes; breads tend to sell out by 5pm.

For branch (St John Bread & Wine) see index.

Butchers

Allens Butchers of Mount Street

117 Mount Street, W1K 3LA (7499 5831). Bond Street or Green Park tube. **Open** 6am-6pm Mon-Fri; 6am-2pm Sat. **Credit** MC, V.

Michael Winner (gourmand) is among the loyal customers of this Mayfair institution operating for nearly 180 years from the same site, though not with the same owners – Justin Preston and David House (both butchers by trade) saved the business from imminent closure when they bought it in spring 2006. Beef and game remain the fortes; in season you'll find snipe, teal and widgeon as well as more common species such as pheasant and grouse, and for a small charge Allens will process birds you have acquired. This year saw meat boxes added to the range, including a gourmet weekend selection and a weekly meat box for two or four people. *See also p232* **Streetwise**.

C Lidgate

110 Holland Park Avenue, W11 4UA (7727 8243). Holland Park tube. **Open** 7am-7.30pm Mon-Fri; 7am-6.30pm Sat. **Credit** MC, V.

See p245 **Enduring loves**.

Frank Godfrey

7 Highbury Park, N5 1QJ (7226 2425/ www.fgodfrey.co.uk). Highbury & Islington tube/rail. **Open** 8am-6pm Mon-Fri; 8am-5pm Sat. **Credit** MC, V.

A clean and inviting store, where the logo on the dark green awning proudly proclaims membership of the Q Guild and availability of free-range and additive-free meats. Godfrey's used to own the right to graze animals in Clissold Park and local sourcing remains a priority – pork comes from Plantation Pigs in Surrey, poultry from Temple Farm in Essex. Amid the expertly trimmed racks and legs of lamb, you'll see chimichurri (Argentinian), bhoona (Indian) and creamy peppercorn (French) cooking sauces to add international culinary panache to your purchases.

Ginger Pig

99 Lauriston Road, E9 7HJ (8986 6911/ www.thegingerpig.co.uk). Mile End tube then 277, 425 bus/London Fields rail. **Open** 9am-5.30pm Tue; 9am-6.30pm Wed-Fri; 9am-6pm Sat; 9am-3pm Sun. **Credit** MC, V.

A new outlet for the celebrated farm-based butcher of rare breed meats that came to national attention via Borough Market; this one has a downstairs deli. You'll find cuts from longhorn cattle, Swaledale and Black Face sheep, Gloucester Old Spot and Tamworth pigs, plus own-made bacon, sausages, pork pies and terrines.

For branches see index.

Highland Butchers

14 Bittacy Hill, NW7 1LB (8346 1055/ www.organicbutcher.net). Mill Hill tube. **Open** 8am-5.30pm Mon-Sat. **Credit** MC, V.

If there's a butcher in London with a more diverse range than this, we've yet to find it. Organic Welsh beef and poultry (not just chicken and turkey but capons and geese), Japanese wagyu, salt beef and Clonakilty black pudding line up alongside an astonishing choice of sausages and burgers including kangaroo, emu, crocodile and bison. Impressive spears of biltong hang in a display cabinet like black icicles.

Kingsland, the Edwardian Butchers

140 Portobello Road, W11 2DZ (7727 6067). Notting Hill Gate tube. **Open** 8.30am-5.30pm Mon-Sat. **Credit** MC, V.

Parchment-wrapped blocks of Britannia beef dripping are displayed in the window like a mission statement at this respected butcher and member of the Rare Breed Trust. The decor is charmingly vintage, yet the young staff aren't at all stuffy. In addition to salt-marsh lamb, Gloucester Old Spot pork, Hereford beef and Sutton Hoo chickens, you'll find wild boar and apple sausages and organic fresh veg.

Wyndham House

339 Fulham Road, SW10 9TW (7352 7888). Fulham Broadway tube. **Open** 7am-7pm Mon-Fri; 7am-5.30pm Sat; 10am-4pm Sun. **Credit** MC, V.

Wyndham is certainly on-trend in terms of its careful sourcing, with poultry from the company's own farm in Essex. It also offers sophisticated recipe dishes and upmarket cookbooks. Wondering what to have for dinner? There's an elegant lamb roast with redcurrant and rosemary glaze that needs just 30 minutes in the oven. Or try the sweet triangular lamb burgers dusted with herbs; ribeye steaks marinated in garlic and parsley; fat gourmet sausages made of pork, chicken and lamb – and don't miss the Label Anglais chicken, a cross between traditional Red Cornish and White Rock birds.

For branch see index.

Sheepdrove Organic Farm Family Butcher

5 Clifton Road, W9 1SZ (7266 3838/ www.sheepdrove.com). Warwick Avenue tube. **Open** 9am-7pm Mon-Fri; 9am-5pm Sat; 10am-4pm Sun. **Credit** AmEx, MC, V.

The books on sale at this Soil Association-accredited butcher say it all: *The New Complete Book of Self Sufficiency – A Guide for Realists and Dreamers* and *Barbecue*, co-authored by a member of the owners' family – the Kindersleys of Dorling Kindersley book publishing fame, now major players in the organic movement. This London outpost of their mixed Berkshire farm, Sheepdrove, sells their own chickens and honey, plus sausages made on the premises, South Devon Aberdeen Angus beef and an array of prepared lines such as minted lamb chops. Jute shopping bags and bicycle delivery underline the green theme.

Also check out...

A Dove & Son

71 Northcote Road, SW11 6PJ (7223 5191). Clapham Junction rail. **Open** 8am-4pm Mon; 8am-5.30pm Tue-Sat. **Credit** MC, V.

Game in season, free-range Bronze turkeys at Christmas, salt belly pork, suckling pig, own-made sausages and renowned pies.

Butcher & Grill

39-41 Parkgate Road, SW11 4NP (7924 3999/www.thebutcherandgrill.com). **Open** 8am-9pm Mon-Sat; 9am-4pm Sun. **Credit** MC, V.

This combo of butcher shop and brasserie has recently opened a branch in Wimbledon. Both British and French cutting is available.

For branch see index.

GG Sparkes

24 Old Dover Road, SE3 7BT (8355 8597). Westcombe Park rail. **Open** 8am-5.30pm Tue-Fri; 8am-5pm Sat. **Credit** AmEx, MC, V.

This family-run butcher specialises in rare-breed, free-range and organic meat and shares the premises with an Italian deli.

M Moen & Sons

24 The Pavement, SW4 0JA (7622 1624/ www.moen.co.uk). Clapham Common tube. **Open** 8am-6.30pm Mon-Fri; 8am-5pm Sat. **Credit** MC, V.

Like a mini food hall, this gloriously Victorian shop displays an inviting range of fresh meat, sausages and game.

Macken Bros

44 Turnham Green Terrace, W4 1QP (8994 2646). Turnham Green tube. **Open** 7am-6pm Mon-Fri; 7am-5.30pm Sat. **Credit** AmEx, MC, V.

A range of quality meats that includes Romney Marsh lamb and Orkney Island Gold beef.

Randalls Butchers

113 Wandsworth Bridge Road, SW6 2TE (7736 3426). Fulham Broadway tube. **Open** 8am-5.30pm Mon-Fri; 8am-4pm Sat. **Credit** MC, V.

Tidy shop selling organic meat; one of the few butchers in London that can obtain lamb or sheep's brains at a few days' notice.

William Rose

126 Lordship Lane, SE22 8HD (8693 9191/www.williamrosebutchers.com). East Dulwich rail. **Open** 8am-5.30pm Tue-Fri; 8am-5pm Sat. **No credit cards.**

Established in Vauxhall back in 1862, this family butcher has been supplying trendy East Dulwich residents since it relocated in 2005.

Cheese shops

La Cave à Fromage

24-25 Cromwell Place, SW7 2LD (0845 108 8222/www.la-cave.co.uk). South Kensington tube. **Open** 10am-7pm Mon-Sat; 11am-5pm Sun. **Credit** MC, V.

Founded by Eric Charriaux and Amnon Paldi, owners of the esteemed restaurant supplier Premier Cheese (Tom Aikens and Le Manoir aux Quat'Saisons are among its clients), this elegant shop is not as flag-wavingly French as the name may suggest. British varieties that are worth a look include the 12-month-old berkswell (a hard sheep's milk variety from the West Midlands reminiscent of manchego) and cerney (goat's milk cheese from the Cotswolds). Take a seat at one of the tall tables to enjoy a cheese platter. Tasting events are held fortnightly.

Cheeseboard

26 Royal Hill, SE10 8RT (8305 0401/ www.cheese-board.co.uk). Greenwich rail/ DLR. **Open** 9am-5pm Mon-Wed, Fri; 9am-1pm Thur; 8.30am-4.30pm Sat. **Credit** AmEx, MC, V.

Now running over 20 years, this little gem offers over 100 varieties of cheese, many of which are artisan-made. Temptations include a fresh Piedmontese goat's cheese topped with black truffle shavings, and ubriaco rosso ('drunken red'), which is washed in red wine then matured in grape must. Breads range from rye and pumpkin seed to simple bloomers, then there's pasta from Benedetto Cavaliera, preserves from Rosebud, as well as honey and antipasti from Seggiano. Free local delivery is available.

Cheeses

13 Fortis Green Road, N10 3HP (8444 9141). Highgate tube. **Open** 9.30am-5.30pm Tue-Thur; 9.30am-6pm Fri, Sat. **Credit** MC, V.

Behind a chainmail curtain, this tiny tiled shop offers a small but astutely edited range of cheeses and other good things. Support the home team with Appleby's farmhouse cheshire, Devon Oke and Colston Bassett stilton, or sample specimens from further afield such as livarot (France), gjetost (Norway) and the wonderfully buttery Old Amsterdam (Netherlands). Accompany them with Vallebona rosemary carta di musica (crisp flatbread), herb-flavoured Shropshire oatcakes or Bath Olivers. The superb chutneys from Corvedale Preserves and St John & Dolly Smith's Indian pickles are worth a little trip in themselves.

La Fromagerie

2-6 Moxon Street, W1U 4EW (7935 0341/ www.lafromagerie.co.uk). Baker Street or Bond Street tube. **Open** 10.30am-7.30pm Mon; 8am-7.30pm Tue-Fri; 9am-7pm Sat; 10am-6pm Sun. **Credit** AmEx, MC, V.

A large window piled with regal wheels of comté, gouda, emmenthal, unpasteurised cheddar and more offers but a taster of the delicious delights to be found beyond the black wooden door of this chic deli-café with refrigerated cheese room. Patricia Michelson and team hand-select cheeses from small artisan makers for sale alongside speciality seasonal produce (Brogdale heritage apples, Roscoff onions, San Marzano tomatoes), sweet things (orange and almond cake, brownies with Piedmontese hazelnuts) and traiteur dishes made on the premises.

For branch see index.

Jeroboams

96 Holland Park Avenue, W11 3RB (7727 9359/www.jeroboams.co.uk). Holland Park tube. **Open** 8am-8pm Mon-Fri; 8.30am-7pm Sat; 10am-6pm Sun. **Credit** AmEx, MC, V.

Jeroboams made its name as a superior London affineur of French cheeses, and quality wine supplier, but this outlet is very much a general fine food store. Of course, the long dresser-style chiller near the front holds an array of fine cheeses in yellow, bone, white, blue, orange and grey hues, but also tubs of sheep's milk yogurt, anchovies and cartons of Spanish gazpacho. Gastronauts can fly by for Poilâne bread, Swedish rhubarb cordial, organic muesli and Clam's cakes. If you're looking for gifts there are some sensual olive wood boards and elegant bottles of olive oil.

Branches: throughout the city.

Neal's Yard Dairy

17 Shorts Gardens, WC2H 9UP (7240 5700/www.nealsyarddairy.co.uk). Covent Garden tube. **Open** 11am-7pm Mon-Thur; 10am-7pm Fri, Sat. **Credit** MC, V.

A thoroughly British shop with a traditional French attitude to cheese retailing in that, like an affineur, Neal's Yard buys from small farms and creameries and matures the

Unique Selling Point
Unpackaged

'I got cross about the amount of supermarket packaging I was throwing away. It just seemed such a waste, when all I wanted was to fill up a jar with stuff,' says Catherine Conway, the brains behind **Unpackaged** (*see p247*) in Islington.

On discovering lots of her friends felt the same way, she decided to take action: in 2007, a local shop with a difference was unveiled. Buy only what you need, reduce what you use, reuse old containers and recycle all you can – that seems to be the mission statement behind Conway's store – and it's a concept its customers are hooked on.

Locals, as well as others from beyond the borough, bring in their own jars, pots, Tupperware and bags and fill them with fruit and veg – all strictly organic and Fairtrade. What's more, everyone who brings his or her own container is rewarded with a 50p discount; alternatively, buy a reusable container (the excellent Lock'n'Lock ones, which are always worth owning) from the store. 'It's all very well being environmental when you have time to think ahead,' former charity worker Conway notes. Unpackaged makes supporting biodegradables and cutting down on waste both possible and affordable.

Vats of olive oil are on tap for refills, and you can take your fill of the pulses, nuts, pasta, rice and cocoa beans arranged in stylish square containers. Barrels of environmentally friendly washing-up liquid, fabric softener and multi-surface cleaner by Ecover can be poured straight into containers brought from home.

There are also toiletries by Love The Planet, loose loo roll made from recycled paper and water filters by Charcoal People. Consumable liquids like juice, trendy cordials (try the wild bilberry from Sweden), wine and cider (by Sam Smith) so far remain packaged, but there are plans to introduce barrels soon. There are also takeaway lunchtime salads – but bring your own lunchbox, of course.

The entrepreneurial shopkeeper has also set up a special service for offices, delivering washing-up liquid and hand soap. In time, Conway hopes Unpackaged will branch out into a cultural-enterprise franchise giving everybody access to quality food. In a city where the average person is said to use around 213 plastic bags a year (on the last count), making an eco-friendly gesture has never been so easy. It could save you money as well.

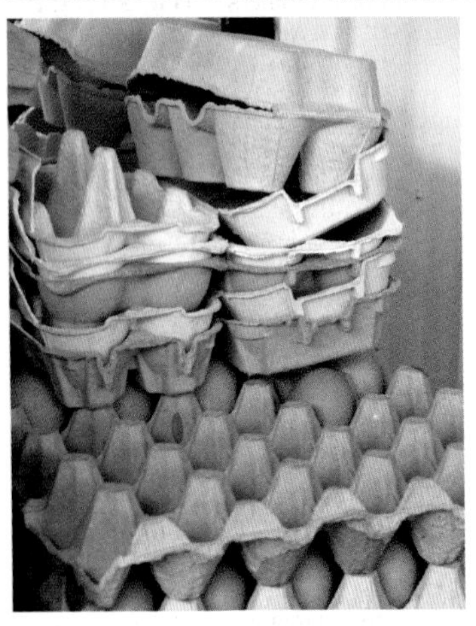

cheeses in its own cellars until ready to sell in peak condition. It's best to walk in and ask what's good today – you'll be given various tasters by the well-trained staff. The company also has a sizeable shop just off Borough Market.
For branch see index.

Paxton & Whitfield

93 Jermyn Street, SW1Y 6JE (7930 0259/ www.paxtonandwhitfield.co.uk). Piccadilly Circus or Green Park tube. **Open** 9.30am-6pm Mon-Sat. **Credit** MC, V.
See p245 **Enduring loves**.

Also check out...

Cheese at Leadenhall

4-5 Leadenhall Market, EC3V 1LR (7929 1697/www.cheeseatleadenhall.co.uk). Bank tube/DLR. **Open** 9am-5pm Mon, Tue; 9am-7pm Wed; 9am-9pm Thur, Fri. **Credit** AmEx, MC, V.
Innovative cheese shop and wine bar with over 200 varieties. Platters and sandwiches can be enjoyed at the bar or at outdoor tables.

Hamish Johnson

48 Northcote Road, SW11 1PA (7738 0741). Clapham South tube/Clapham Junction rail. **Open** 9am-6pm Mon-Sat; 11am-4pm Sun. **Credit** MC, V.
A good balance of farmhouse cheeses from Britain and abroad, along with many other delicious things at this charming local.

Jones Dairy

23 Ezra Street, E2 7RH (7739 5372/ www.jonesdairy.co.uk). Bus 26, 48, 55. **Open** 9am-3pm Fri, Sat; 8am-3pm Sun. **No credit cards**.
Artisanal farmhouse cheeses, plus a wide range of fresh breads, apple juice, dried fruit and nuts and teas and coffees.

International Cheese Centre

Unit 5, Marylebone Station, NW1 6JJ (7724 1432/www.cheesecentres.co.uk). Marylebone tube/rail. **Open** 7am-8pm Mon-Wed; 7am-8.30pm Thur, Fri; 10.30am-6.30pm Sat. **Credit** AmEx, MC, V.
Unpretentious shops situated in mainline rail stations so you can grab some cheese, bread and wine for supper on the way home.
For branches see index.

Rippon Cheese Stores

26 Upper Tachbrook Street, SW1V 1SW (7931 0628/www.ripponcheese.com). Pimlico tube/Victoria tube/rail. **Open** 8.15am-5.15pm Mon-Sat. **Credit** MC, V.
Around 500 different varieties of cheese are available from this neighbourhood shop and respected wholesaler.

Confectioners

Ambala Sweet Centre

112-114 Drummond Street, NW1 2HN (7387 3521/www.ambalasweets.com). Euston Square tube. **Open** 9am-9pm daily. **Credit** MC, V.
The flagship branch of this hit chain sells an impressive array of Indian eye-candy– and as the queues indicate, floral flavours, calorie-laden ghee (Asian clarified butter) and kilos of sugar won't be falling from fashion anytime soon. You'll need to be seriously sweet-toothed to enjoy the fruits of the halwais' (sweet-makers') labours, but you can expect to find soft cheese dumplings immersed in rose-scented syrup, fudgy blocks of cashew paste, marzipan-style rolls and toasted balls of gram flour on offer.
Branches: throughout the city.

L'Artisan du Chocolat

89 Lower Sloane Street, SW1W 8DA (7824 8365/www.artisanduchocolat.com). Sloane Square tube. **Open** 10am-7pm Mon-Sat. **Credit** AmEx, MC, V.
L'Artisan du Chocolat's Gerard Coleman and Anne Weyns launch a new collection each season as well as special designs for festive occasions such as Valentine's Day, Christmas, Easter and Halloween, making this an ideal destination for those occasions when you want to give something original and tasteful but lack inspiration. Best known for liquid salted caramels and chocolate 'pearls', they also offer a line of bars, made from scratch in Kent using ground cocoa beans, cane sugar and cocoa butter. The green tea bar is particularly innovative. A central London branch is in the pipeline for autumn 2008.

Cocomaya

35 Connaught Street, W2 2AZ (7706 2770/www.cocomaya.co.uk). Marble Arch tube. **Open** 11am-7pm Mon-Sat. **Credit** AmEx, MC, V.
Sheets of white chocolate studded with Asian crispy pancake highlight the creative aspirations of this new boutique, a pretty explosion of colourful butterflies, gilt, olive green and schiaparelli pink on an upmarket cut-through between Edgware Road and Lancaster Gate. We liked the smooth green tea ganaches, in which a strong tea taste gave way to a clean, dark chocolate flavour. Other on-trend chocolate flavours included pomegranate, rose and maple.

Demarquette Fine Chocolates

285 Fulham Road, SW10 9PZ (7351 5467/www.demarquette.com). South Kensington tube. **Open** 11am-6pm Tue-Thur; 11am-7pm Fri, Sat. **Credit** AmEx, MC, V.
Despite a French-Chinese background, savvy chocolatier Marc Demarquette hasn't let the trend to British produce pass him by, adding Surrey blackcurrant, Kentish pear and Yorkshire rhubarb, among others, to his range of exquisitely made chocolates in 2008. Still, it's the inspired fusion combinations (Tunisian bharat; Nile cumin; Japanese cherry blossom) that distinguish this premium-priced operation. Connoisseurs of single origin bars should check out the chocolates made from 'wild cocoa' grown in Amazonian Bolivia.

Hope & Greenwood

20 North Cross Road, SE22 9EU (8613 1777/www.hopeandgreenwood.co.uk). East Dulwich rail. **Open** 10am-6pm Mon-Sat; 11am-5pm Sun. **Credit** AmEx, MC, V.
Saturday queues are almost inevitable at this small vacuum for pocket money. Everything from chocolate gooseberries to sweetheart candies is prettily displayed in plastic beakers, cellophane bags, glass jars, illustrated boxes, porcelain bowls and cake tins. Gift possibilities include retro gumball machines, and the refills for them. Ice-cream is available in the warmer months. There is a second branch in Covent Garden.
For branch see index.

Melt

59 Ledbury Road, W11 2AA (7727 5030/ www.meltchocolates.com). Notting Hill Gate tube. **Open** 9am-6pm Mon-Sat; 11am-4pm Sun. **Credit** AmEx, MC, V.
Watch the chocolates being made in the pristine white open kitchen at the rear of this pretty boutique. Melt's bars are all made by hand and come in inspired flavours such as milk chocolate with raspberry and black pepper, or sesame, as well as modern favourites such as dark chocolate with chilli, orange candy or sea-salted caramel. Love bars (silky milk chocolate with creamy filling) have a secret pocket in the pack for your own private messages. The takeaway hot chocolate is superbly dark and reviving.

Minamoto Kitchoan

44 Piccadilly, W1J 0DS (7437 3135/ www.kitchoan.com). Piccadilly Circus tube. **Open** 10am-7pm Mon-Fri, Sun; 10am-8pm Sat. **Credit** AmEx, MC, V.
For years this serene place has held its own against the posh chocolate shops around Piccadilly, yet the lovely sweets on sale are made with ingredients such as red beans, chestnuts, sweet potato, rice flour and miso. Wagashi are Japanese cakes, biscuits, jellies and other types of confectionery eaten as afternoon snacks. Although displayed like jewellery in elegant glass cabinets, those on sale here are imported and packaged to ensure a long shelf life. Illustrated leaflets and labels help describe the myriad options but some things still get lost in translation.

Paul A Young Fine Chocolates

33 Camden Passage, N1 8EA (7424 5750/ www.payoung.net). Angel tube. **Open** 11am-6pm Wed, Thur, Sat; 11am-7pm Fri; noon-5pm Sun. **Credit** AmEx, MC, V.
A gorgeous boutique with almost everything – chocolates, cakes, ice-cream – made in the downstairs kitchen and finished in front of customers. Young is a respected pâtissier as well as chocolatier and has an astute chef's palate for flavour-combining. Valrhona and Amedei are his favoured couvertures, which he combines in different blends and origins to match his other ingredients. Even in summer there are plenty of temptations, such as Pimm's cocktail truffles featuring cucumber, strawberry and mint flavours, and white chocolate blondies made with raspberries and blueberries. *See also p85* **Streetwise**.
For branch see index.

Prestat

14 Princes Arcade, SW1Y 6DS (7629 4838/www.prestat.co.uk). Green Park tube. **Open** 9.30am-6pm Mon-Fri; 10am-5pm Sat. **Credit** AmEx, MC, V.
England's oldest chocolatier is up-to-the-minute when it comes to promoting the health advantages of chocolate. Prestat's

Choxi bars (dark, milk, ginger, orange, mint) are processed gently to maximise antioxidant content – the claim is that they contain two to three times more of these nutrients than standard milk or dark chocolate. This bijou boutique also offers unusual and traditional chocolates in brightly coloured gift boxes.

Rococo

321 King's Road, SW3 5EP (7352 5857/ www.rococochocolates.com). **Open** 10am-6.30pm Mon-Sat; noon-5pm Sun. **Credit** AmEx, MC, V.

Don't be fooled by the novelty bags of chocolate maize and mushrooms, Rococo is a serious chocolatier, pioneering artisan manufacture, unusual flavour combinations and ethical practices in the UK. Don't miss the Grenada 71% bar, which betters other 'fairly traded' products both in terms of quality, and the fact that the factory is attached to the estate, ensuring that the growers benefit from adding value to their beans themselves. Beautiful hand-painted eggs made of high-quality couverture are sold at Easter.

For branch see index.

Theobroma Cacao

43 Turnham Green Terrace, W4 1RG (8996 0431/www.theobroma-cacao.co.uk). Turnham Green tube. **Open** 9am-6pm Mon-Sat; 10am-5pm Sun. **Credit** AmEx, MC, V.

Philip Neal hand-makes a wide variety of chocolates, which are spread over the counter and adjacent dresser of this cosy shop. Individual chocolates include large truffles, fruit-flavoured whips in chocolate cups and good marzipan options, but our favourites are the cocoa-dusted chocolate 'sticks', rich enough to serve as dessert in themselves. Look at the rear shelves for the discreetly boxed Erotique range including 'decolletage', stilettos and gold-tipped phalluses.

Also check out...

Charbonnel et Walker

1 The Royal Arcade, 28 Old Bond Street, W1S 4BT (7491 0939/www.charbonnel.co.uk). Green Park tube. **Open** 10am-6pm Mon-Sat. **Credit** AmEx, DC, MC, V.

Rose and violet creams are the speciality of this royal warrant holder.

For branches see index.

La Maison du Chocolat

45-46 Piccadilly, W1J 0DS (7287 8500/ www.lamaisonduchocolat.co.uk). Green Park or Piccadilly Circus tube. **Open** 10am-7pm Mon-Sat; noon-6pm Sun. **Credit** AmEx, MC, V.

A prestigious French artisan manufacturer of chocolates using Valrhona couverture. Baked goods and ice-cream too.

Montezuma's Chocolates

51 Brushfield Street, E1 6AA (7539 9208/ www.montezumas.co.uk). Liverpool Street tube/rail. **Open** 10am-6pm daily. **Credit** MC, V.

Chocolates with bright packaging, quirky names and fun but sometimes also quite challenging flavours. Much of the range is organic and Fairtrade.

Mrs Kibble's Olde Sweet Shoppe

57A Brewer Street, W1F 9UL (77346633). Piccadilly Circus tube. **Open** 10am-6pm Mon-Wed; 10am-7pm Thur, Fri; 11am-7pm Sat; noon-6pm Sun. **Credit** AmEx, MC, V.

Handy West End source of pear drops, clove rock, soor plooms and swirly lollipops.

For branch see index.

William Curley

10 Paved Court, Richmond, Surrey TW9 1LZ (8332 3002/www.williamcurley.co.uk). Richmond tube/rail. **Open** 9.30am-8.30pm Mon-Sat; 10.30am-6.30pm Sun. **Credit** MC, V.

Best British Chocolatier according to the Academy of Chocolate, William Curley produces a sophisticated range of truffles, pâtisserie and ice-cream.

Delicatessens

Adafina

67 Abbey Road, NW8 0AE (7624 2013/ www.adafina.co.uk). St John's Wood tube/ Kilburn High Road or South Hampstead rail. **Open** 8.30am-7pm Mon-Thur; 8.30am-4pm Fri; 9.30am-1.30pm Sun. **Credit** AmEx, MC, V.

Named after a traditional Sephardi Jewish Sabbath meal from medieval Spain, this chic kosher deli offers a wide range of prepared dishes in pouches and tubs, including its namesake and various Moroccan dishes, plus old favourites like chopped liver and roast chicken. Freshly baked pâtisserie is available every day with a good selection of challot every Thursday and Friday. You'll also find cheffy lines such as a kosher balsamic vinegar glaze.

Blend

2 Barmouth Road, SW18 2DN (8871 2586/www.cafeblend.co.uk). Southfields tube/Wandsworth Town rail. **Open** 7.30am-7.30pm Mon-Sat; 8.30am-4pm Sun. **Credit** MC, V.

Will Oakley's much-loved local (formerly known as Ditto) offers an eclectic range of foods from the UK and the rest of the world – everything from Incan amaranth to Spanish charcuterie, and gourmet crisps to honeycomb ice-cream. Grab a table for a coffee or light meal, or pick up one of the own-made ready meals for a speedy supper. There is now a branch on zhooshy Wandsworth Common; Blend also runs a restaurant-tapas bar and catering service.

For branch see index.

East Dulwich Deli

15-17 Lordship Lane, SE22 8EW (8693 2525). East Dulwich rail. **Open** 9am-6pm Mon, Tue, Sat; 9am-7pm Wed-Fri; 10am-4pm Sun. **Credit** MC, V.

Walls lined with superior groceries lend a gourmet warehouse vibe to this sassy multi-room affair that sells everything from posh choc-hazelnut spread to Italian wines. Come late in the day and you may have the bonus of bread (from esteemed sister company Born & Bread) offered at knockdown prices – great for filling the freezer. Newby teas, True Story biscuits, Pink's sausages, Country Monkey muesli, Stokes' sauces and the large range of fine oils and vinegars are also very much worthy your attention.

L'Eau à la Bouche

49 Broadway Market, E8 4PH (7923 0600/www.labouche.co.uk). London Fields rail/26, 55, 106, 277, 394 bus. **Open** 8.30am-7pm Mon-Fri; 8.30am-5pm Sat; 10am-4pm Sun. **Credit** MC, V.

Everything is tempting at this Hackney deli. Meats include usuals like serrano ham, but also lines such as Jesus de Lyon, a type of salami cut from a rugby ball-shaped sausage. The wide range of cheeses includes ash-covered selles sur cher, creamy saint marcellin and, from April to October, etivaz, a raw-milk Swiss mountain cheese. Plus there's ground coffee, Hoxton sourdough breads and pastries, olives and tinned and dry goods – and sandwiches and salads for consumption at the small tables.

L'Epicerie@56

56 Chatsworth Road, E5 0LS (7503 8172/ www.lepicerie56.com). Homerton rail/ 242 bus. **Open** 8.30am-7.30pm Mon-Fri; 8.30am-5.30pm Sat, Sun. **Credit** MC, V.

Homerton's delightful new French deli-café gets its viennoisserie, breads and quiches delivered daily from Boulangerie Jade in Blackheath. Owner Rémy Zentar has also sourced a broad range of cheese, wine and groceries (mustards, vinegars, sauces, cassoulet, pasta, ice-cream). There's a seating area in which to enjoy soup of the day, a Moroccan wrap or bastilla, or one of the pretty tarts. A catering service is available.

Farm W5

19 The Green, W5 5DA (8566 1965/ www.farmw5.com). Ealing Broadway tube. **Open** 8am-7.30pm Mon-Fri; 9am-7pm Sat; 11am-5pm Sun. **Credit** MC, V.

The aim here is to support local producers and, while many delis make the claim, Farm W5 takes it literally with honey from Harrow and the wonderful St John & Dolly Smith pickles made in Ealing. If the foods are not produced nearby or on a British farm, they're likely at least to be organic. An open kitchen churns out strong coffee and delicious milkshakes but nabbing a table can be a challenge.

Flâneur Food Hall

41 Farringdon Road, EC1M 3JB (7404 4422/www.flaneur.com). Farringdon tube/ rail. **Open** 8.30am-10pm Mon-Fri; 10am-10pm Sat. **Credit** AmEx, MC, V.

Gourmet groceries line the walls of this beautifully designed food hall, which is also a café-restaurant, but aims collide when you find you can't get to the sea salt because there's a couple sitting in front of it having brunch. Goodies for taking away include a choice of aged French vinegars and honeys from the royal parks, carefully chosen jams (including Rosebud preserves), Lebanese nougat, Domori chocolate and exquisite-looking pastries and organic bread. If you prefer savoury things, look to the superb Italian and Spanish charcuterie. Takeaway salads and soups make this a useful spot for breakfast and lunch.

Food Hall

374-378 Old Street, EC1V 9LT (7729 6005). Old Street tube/rail. **Open** 9am-7pm Mon-Fri; 10am-5pm Sat, Sun. **Credit** (over £10) MC, V.

A bountiful display of pizzas, salads, cakes and other lunchtime chow greets visitors to this impressive shop set in a former Victorian dairy. Prices are at a premium, but the cheese range, sold (along with tempting fruit and veg) from a dedicated cold room, is particularly worth a look. Ice-creams, smoothies and yoghurts come from the esteemed Helsett Farm in Cornwall, among others. There's a sensational choice of luxury chocolate bars too, including Artisan du Chocolat, Maglio, New Tree and Feeding Your Imagination.

Grocer on Elgin

6 Elgin Crescent, W11 2HX (7221 3844/ www.thegroceron.com). Ladbroke Grove or Notting Hill Gate tube. **Open** 8am-8pm Mon-Fri; 8am-6pm Sat, Sun. **Credit** MC, V.

Here the word 'grocer' is used somewhat loosely. You won't find cans of baked beans and tuna (though Australians will love the range of Arnott's biscuits). Instead the draw is the long chiller cabinets lined with pouches of delicious things for dinner: everything from soups and vegetable side dishes to an atlas of spicy stews.

For branch (Grocer on King's) see index.

Hand Made Food

40 Tranquil Vale, SE3 0BD (8297 9966/ www.handmadefood.com). Blackheath rail. **Open** 9am-5pm Mon-Fri; 9am-6pm Sat; 9am-4.30pm Sun. **Credit** MC, V.

Chefs are busy working in the kitchen at the back of this bustling traiteur in Blackheath. Staff help you to the enticing array of freshly prepared meals – perhaps slow-roast pork with apricot and sage, pappa al pomodoro, bastilla or plump tarts, and summer pudding; a rifle through the freezer reveals crespelle and aubergine parmigiana. A concise selection of top-notch groceries is on the shelves: load up on the likes of moscatel vinegar, Laudemio olive oil and Stokes horseradish.

Leila's

17 Calvert Avenue, E2 7JP (7729 9789). Liverpool Street or Old Street tube/rail/26, 48, 55, 242 bus. **Open** 10am-6pm Wed-Sat; 10am-4pm Sun. **Credit** AmEx, MC, V.

Leila McAlister's eclectic store has the nous to distinguish between crusty and gooey brownies and offer customers the choice. French sunflower oil is sold from large plastic bottles. We picked up huge bags of marcona almonds for £16/kg. At front is a small selection of fresh produce including, on our last visit, radishes and thin-skinned lemons. Among the packaged groceries are Chegworth Valley apple juice (sold without the labels, because Leila doesn't like them) and chutneys, jellies and the like from Tracklements in Wiltshire.

Melbury & Appleton

271 Muswell Hill Broadway, N10 1DE (8442 0558/www.melburyandappleton.com). Bus 43, 134. **Open** 9am-6pm Mon, Tue; 9am-8pm Wed-Fri; 9.30am-6pm Sat; noon-6pm Sun. **Credit** MC, V.

Fans of British food will find much to delight them at this jam-packed high street deli. The flag-waving meat selection includes Shropshire Black, Alderton and York hams. Ice-creams come from highly regarded Alder Tree in Suffolk (try the gooseberry and elderflower). A small chiller is piled with fine British cheeses, plus a gourmet gouda. Posh ready meals, proper Cornish pasties and corn-fed free-range chickens cater to those wanting dinner. Tea connoisseurs will appreciate the well-edited range of leaves and blends, including Ronnefeldt and Jing varieties. Look to the display tables and it's clear a sweet tooth is at work: home-made fairy cakes, tiramisu, canoli, crispy Italian pastries, hand-cut shortbread, spelt and hazelnut cookies, plus jars of vintage mints and humbugs, ensure each visit ends on a sugar high.

Melrose & Morgan

42 Gloucester Avenue, NW1 8JD (7722 0011/www.melroseandmorgan.com). Chalk Farm tube. **Open** 8am-8pm Mon-Fri; 8am-6pm Sat; 9am-4pm Sun. **Credit** AmEx, MC, V.

Sophisticated suppers become dreamily low-effort when you shop at this ultra-foodie set-up. Made-on-the-premises dishes range from roast aubergine dip to fish cakes, beef Wellington, and fresh peaches in lavender syrup. The array of cakes, brownies, pasties and sausage rolls that covers the large table running down the centre of the store is simply spectacular. While there, pick up some Newby teas, Sir Hans Sloane chocolates, Regent's Park honey (in season) and M&M's wonderful own-made blueberry and thyme jam. Oh, and Flour Station bread to go with it.

Mortimer & Bennett

33 Turnham Green Terrace, W4 1RG (8995 4145/www.mortimerandbennett.com). Turnham Green tube. **Open** 8.30am-6pm Mon-Fri; 8.30am-5.30pm Sat. **Credit** AmEx, MC, V.

Dan Mortimer sources unique speciality foods by visiting artisan producers on his travels – yet you'll also find first-rate British stuff here, such as Ouse Valley jellies. Rare-breed salami from Tuscany, Spanish foie gras macerated in grape juice and duck pâté in Gewürztraminer are typical meat options. There's a mind-boggling selection of preserves (think French greengage, Lebanese mulberry, and wild-rose jams), while new lines include a range of Greek sauces from Lesvos.

Ottolenghi

63 Ledbury Road, W11 2AD (7727 1121/ www.ottolenghi.co.uk). Notting Hill Gate or Westbourne Park tube. **Open** 8am-8pm Mon-Fri; 8am-7pm Sat; 8.30am-6pm Sun. **Credit** AmEx, MC, V.

This glam, bright white shop-café always looks like it's been prepared for a photographic shoot. You may find the window decked with fresh aubergines, lemons and oranges, but eyes inevitably dart straight to the bodacious baked goods – hazelnut and cinnamon meringues, herb-topped focaccia, cute strawberry financiers and individual lemon and polenta cakes, for example. Colourful salads, with Middle Eastern, Mediterranean and a few oriental influences are prepared daily and show off chickpeas, lentils and other nutritious foods to their best effect.

For branches see index.

Panzer's

13-19 Circus Road, NW8 6PB (7722 8596/www.panzers.co.uk). St John's Wood tube. **Open** 8am-7pm Mon-Fri; 8am-6pm Sat; 8am-2pm Sun. **Credit** MC, V.

A St John's Wood fixture for more than 50 years, this deli-supermarket is an essential address for every food stylist seeking perfect-looking fruit and vegetables for photo shoots. Despite the workaday decor, quality is a priority; prestige breads from Clarke's and Poilâne are stocked and people travel from across London specifically for Panzer's smoked salmon. Also noteworthy is the large choice of kosher lines and international groceries.

Le Péché Mignon

6 Ronalds Road, N5 1XH (7607 1826/ www.lepechemignon.co.uk). Holloway Road tube/Highbury & Islington tube/rail. **Open** 8am-7pm Mon-Fri; 9am-6pm Sat; 9am-5pm Sun. **Credit** (over £10) MC, V.

Who'd have guessed that such a chic enclave of fine food could be found just off the Holloway Road? Smart locals have understandably embraced this young chocolate-fronted deli-café with orchids in the window and tables at front and back for enjoying coffee and pastries. Posh staples include Poilâne bread, tins of McCann's oatmeal, free-range eggs and Kusmi teas – essential luxuries rather than guilty pleasures, we reckon.

Raoul's Deli

8-10 Clifton Road, W9 1SS (7289 6649/ www.raoulsgourmet.com). Warwick Avenue tube/6, 414 bus. **Open** 7.30am-8.30pm Mon-Fri; 7.30am-8pm Sat; 9am-7pm Sun. **Credit** AmEx, MC, V.

A smart local deli split into two rooms roughly along savoury and sweet lines. Fridges hold own-made sauces and soups, plus ritzy cheeses. The fresh fruit and veg display typically includes good-looking herbs, Italian lemons and beefy aubergines. Also of note: Devon Rose bacon, Criterion ice-creams and Sharpham Park pearled spelt (for stirring up some delicious alternatives to risotto). The popular café-bistro opposite is owned by the same people.

St Helen's Foodstore

55 St Helen's Gardens, W10 6LN (8960 2225). Latimer Road tube. **Open** 8am-7pm Mon-Fri; 8am-6pm Sat; 8am-5.30pm Sun. **Credit** AmEx, MC, V.

A mouthwatering display of dishes greets customers as they enter this terrific combo of deli, traiteur and café. The upright chiller lines up Innocent smoothies and organic pomegranate juice alongside considerably less innocent chocolate mousse, trifles and blueberry jelly that's made on the premises. St Helen's packaged grocery selection is concise but takes in worthwhile purchases such as McCann's Irish oatmeal, Bone Suckin' rib sauce, quinoa, polenta, Dragonfly teas and Demarquette chocolate bars. Happy locals relax at the tables with a coffee or lunch on generous plates of caesar salad and the like.

Paul A Young Fine Chocolates. *See p239.*

Tavola

155 Westbourne Grove, W11 2RS (7229 0571). Notting Hill Gate tube. **Open** 10am-7.30pm Mon-Fri; 10am-6pm Sat. **Credit** AmEx, MC, V.

The name here is meant to suggest all the things you might want to put on the table as well as in to your mouth, so in addition to the delicious foods produced under the tutelage of chef Alastair Little you'll find Circulon cookware and hand-painted crockery. A large central table groans with the day's offerings: perhaps a harissa-crusted roast chicken, a chunky patatas bravas, or a pot of broad beans, minted artichokes and whole poached peaches. Bought-in goodies include Alba Gold ice-creams and Vallebona Italian groceries, plus speciality produce such as ox-heart tomatoes and unwaxed lemons.

W Martyn

135 Muswell Hill Broadway, N10 3RS (8883 5642/www.wmartyn.co.uk). Highgate tube then 43, 134 bus.. **Open** 9.30am-5.30pm Mon-Wed, Fri; 9.30am-1pm Thur; 9am-5.30pm Sat. **Credit** MC, V.

The scent of coffee emanates from this charming traditional store where beans are roasted on the premises, and old-fashioned products such as Epicure peach nectar and Sunsweet prune juice are considered suitable window display material. But Martyn's doesn't reject newfangled ideas entirely: coffee comes in flavours like cinnamon, choc mocha and amaretto, and you'll find bottles of A-list favourite AriZona iced tea on sale. Dried fruit (including fat muscatel raisins), muesli, myriad preserves from Cottage Delight and Tiptree, fudge, and Moore's Dorset biscuits make Martyn's a fun place to browse.

Also check out...

& Clarke's

122 Kensington Church Street, W8 4BU (7229 2190/www.sallyclarke.com). Notting Hill Gate tube. **Open** 8am-8pm Mon-Fri; 8am-4pm Sat. **Credit** AmEx, MC, V.
See p252 **A piece of the pie**.

Barnsbury Grocer

237 Liverpool Road, N1 1LX (7607 7222/ www.thebarnsbury.co.uk). Angel tube. **Open** 8am-8pm Mon-Fri; 8am-6pm Sat; 10am-4pm Sun. **Credit** MC, V.
See p252 **A piece of the pie**.

Bayley & Sage

60 High Street, SW19 5EE (8946 9904/ www.bayley-sage.co.uk). Wimbledon tube/ rail. **Open** 8am-9pm daily. **Credit** AmEx, MC, V.

This specialist food hall is crammed with over 2,000 high-quality unprocessed food items, including fresh line-caught fish that last tasted the salt of the sea around the shores of Cornwall.

Bluebird Epicerie

350 King's Road, SW3 5UU (7559 1140/ www.danddlondon.com). Sloane Square tube then 11, 19, 22, 49, 319 bus. **Open** 8am-8pm Mon-Fri; 8am-7pm Sat; 9am-5pm Sun. **Credit** AmEx, MC, V.
See p252 **A piece of the pie**.

Feast on the Hill

56 Fortis Green Road, N10 3HN (8444 4957). East Finchley or Highgate tube then 43, 134 bus. **Open** 8am-5pm Mon-Sat; 9am-5pm Sun. **Credit** AmEx, MC, V.

This friendly traiteur and deli offers a terrific range of antipasti, cheeses, sweet and savoury baked goods and groceries.

Fernandez & Wells

43 Lexington Street, W1F 9AL (7734 1546/www.fernandezandwells.com). Oxford Circus or Piccadilly Circus tube. **Open** 11am-10.30pm Mon-Sat. **Credit** MC, V.

Hams are the speciality of this sophisticated Spanish deli and sandwich shop; also a superb wine selection.
For branch see index.

Food Inc

Ground Floor, Whiteley's, Queensway, W2 4YN (7792 6020/www.food-inc.com). Bayswater tube. **Open** 9am-8pm Mon-Wed; 9am-9pm Thur-Sat; noon-6pm Sun. **Credit** AmEx, MC, V.

Imagine someone decided to relocate Harvey Nichols Foodmarket to the ground floor of Whiteley's – that's Food Inc, and the comparison with Harvey Nics food hall is no accident: both were set up by Dominic Ford, co-owner of the butcher-cum-brasserie Butcher & Grill (*see p237*).

Mr Christian's

11 Elgin Crescent, W11 2JA (7229 0501/ www.mrchristians.co.uk). Ladbroke Grove tube. **Open** 6am-7pm Mon-Fri; 6am-6.30pm Sat; 7am-5pm Sun. **Credit** MC, V.

Much-loved local delicatessen with loyal celebrity customers, and robust dishes made in the downstairs kitchen.

Modern Pantry

47-48 St John's Square, EC1V 4JJ (7250 0833/www.themodernpantry.co.uk). Farringdon tube/rail. **Open** 7.30am-7.30pm Mon-Sat. **Credit** AmEx, MC, V.
See p252 **A piece of the pie**.

Partridges

2-5 Duke of York Square, King's Road, SW3 4LY (7730 0651/www.partridges.co.uk). Sloane Square tube. **Open** 8am-10pm daily. **Credit** AmEx, MC, V.

Partridges is a huge food hall selling mass-market brands to seasonal specialities. On Saturdays it hosts a lovely food market.
For branch see index.

Rosslyn Delicatessen

56 Rosslyn Hill, NW3 1ND (7794 9210/ www.delirosslyn.co.uk). Hampstead tube. **Open** 8.30am-8.30pm Mon-Sat; 8.30am-8pm Sun. **Credit** AmEx, MC, V.

Rosslyn Delicatessen stocks a large range of fine foods, plus American brands for homesick expats.

Spoon

48 New Park Road, SW2 4UN (8674 6572). Brixton tube/rail then 45, 59, 159, 250 bus. **Open** 9.30am-7pm Mon-Fri; 9.30am-6pm Sat. **Credit** AmEx, MC, V.

Just over a year old, Nell Murphy's little deli is a breath of fresh air (scented with the sweet smell of baking) in Brixton.

Trinity Stores

5-6 Balham Station Road, SW12 9SG (8673 3773/www.trinitystores.co.uk). Balham tube/rail. **Open** 8am-8pm Mon-Fri; 9.30am-5.30pm Sat; 10am-4pm Sun. **Credit** MC, V.

Neighbourhood deli, perfectly situated on the way home from the station.

Verde & Co

40 Brushfield Street, E1 6AG (7247 1924). Liverpool Street tube/rail. **Open** 10am-6pm Mon-Sat; 10am-5pm Sun. **Credit** MC, V.

Vintage-chic deli-grocer and caterer.

Vivian's

2 Worple Way, Richmond, Surrey TW10 6DF (8940 3600/www.viviansdeli.co.uk). Richmond tube/rail. **Open** 9am-7pm Mon-Fri; 9am-6pm Sat; 9am-2pm Sun. **Credit** MC, V.

Established in 1991, this attractive fine food store specialises in food and drink from small producers in the West Country.

Fish

Covent Garden Fishmongers

37 Turnham Green Terrace, W4 1RG (8995 9273/www.coventgardenfishmongers.co.uk). Turnham Green tube. **Open** 8am-5.30pm Tue, Wed, Fri; 8am-5pm Thur, Sat. **Credit** MC, V.

This fishmongers has a commitment to the preservation of fish stocks; all the cod, haddock and plaice comes from sustainable sources in Iceland. The sandwich board outside advertises new seasonal varieties, products such as potted crab, or species with healthy omega-3s, such as sardines, herring and mackerel. On the shelves are the likes of Stokes creamed horseradish, Crustamor soupe de poisson and tempura batter mix.

Fish Shop at Kensington Place

199A Kensington Church Street, W8 7LX (7243 6626/www.danddlondon.com). Notting Hill Gate tube. **Open** 9am-7pm Tue-Fri; 9am-5pm Sat; 10am-4pm Sun. **Credit** MC, V.

A giant swordfish guards the entrance to this sparkling offshoot of Kensington Place restaurant. Most of the fish comes from Brixham, Cornwall or Scotland and, while there are premium lines such as live lobsters and langoustines, staff are also happy to suggest less expensive options such as sand sole or sardines. The range of ready meals (fish pies, crayfish tails in mayo and garlic, fish skewers in herb marinade) has recently expanded. You'll also find ingredients for paella, sushi and other classic fish dishes.

Sandys

56 King Street, Twickenham, Middx TW1 3SH (8892 5788/www.sandysfish.net). **Open** 7.30am-6pm Mon-Sat. **Credit** MC, V.

Easily one of London's best fishmongers, this large and popular high street store offers a wide range of species, fom Cornish sardines and lemon sole to Sri Lankan red snapper. Smoked produce comes from prestigious Scottish company Inverawe. You'll also find own-made sausages and game in season.

Classic London shops

Enduring loves

Good food never goes out of date.

Sell-by-dates. They may be good for food, but they aren't always necessary for the shops that sell food: true quality can prove itself over the years. These food shops have stood the test of time, and we hope they'll still be peddling edibles to our grandchildren.

50 years old

Behind this 1950s green ceramic Soho frontage is **Lina Stores** (*see p250*), an iconic family-run Italian deli that's been in business for over half a century. Indeed, Jane Grigson used to buy spagetti in blue wax paper here years before celebrity chefs coasted the streets on scooters. Besides dried pastas (stored in beautiful wooden crates), there's a deli counter chock-full of cured meats, hams, salamis, olives, cheeses, marinated artichokes and fresh pastas. Imported items run from breads to chestnut honey, and Lina is one of the best places to buy truffles in season.

120 years old

Unassumingly nestled in the heart of Soho, **Algerian Coffee Stores** (*see p256*) has traded from its Old Compton Street site for over 120 years and, remarkably, is still using the original wooden counter, shelving and display case. The range of coffees here is improbably large, with a high number of house blends alongside single-origin beans, flavoured beans, rarities and Fairtrade coffees, most costing £3.20-£5/250g. It also sells some serious teas and brewing hardware. If you're just passing by, the take-away option is the best coffee deal in London: 70p for an espresso, 95p for a cappuccino or latte; both delicious, and both available with an extra shot for no extra charge.

150 years old

The butchers at **C Lidgate** (*see p236*) have run this store for over 150 years – and have kept the cleavers in the same family's hands for four generations. That's right: the Lidgates truly have butchery in their blood. The meat here is organic and free range, and a great deal of it is sourced from prestige estates, including Prince Charles's Highgrove. But the family have also kept with the times; the window is crammed with tempting dishes like saddle of lamb with pesto, and the shelves hold jars of mayonnaise and cassoulet. New for 2008 are the scotch eggs made with quail eggs and wrapped in Lidgate's own cumberland sausage mince.

200 years old

In business for over 200 years, the last 100 of those on this site, **Paxton & Whitfield** (*see p239*) sells a wide range of British and continental European cheeses, plus excellent hams, biscuits and real ale. Service is exemplary and delightfully unstuffy – a rare pleasure on Jermyn Street. Among the unusual English varieties to look out for are Oxford isis (washed in mead), caradon blue from Cornwall and naturally smoked 'ceodre' cheddar.

300 years old

After a really good vintage? Try 1698, the year when a small wine merchants was set up by a London widow. **Berry Bros & Rudd**'s (*see p254*) impressive list of discerning patrons includes Lord Byron, William Pitt and Queen Elizabeth II (though probably not personally), all drawn by the heady atmosphere, highly knowledgeable staff and consistently high-quality wines.

Lina Stores

Steve Hatt

88-90 Essex Road, N1 8LU (7226 3963). Angel tube. **Open** 8am-5pm Tue-Thur; 7am-5pm Fri, Sat. **No credit cards.**

A wet fish display stretching along the wide front window affords queuing customers plenty of opportunity to check out what's available. Labels highlight deals, such as sea trout 'lowest price of the season'. Expect prime examples of wild Scottish halibut, bluefin tuna, gilt head bream, prawns, scallops and fresh samphire. Frozen fish is available, but extras are kept to a minimum.

Also check out...

Applebee's Café

5 Stoney Street, SE1 9AA (7407 5777/ www.applebeesfish.com). London Bridge tube/rail. **Open** 9am-6pm Tue-Sat. **Credit** MC, V.

Premium lines on offer here include excellent turbot but you'll also find the makings of a fine fish pie.

B&M Seafood

258 Kentish Town Road, NW5 2AA (7485 0346). Kentish Town tube/rail. **Open** 7.30am-5.30pm Mon-Sat. **Credit** MC, V.

We've bought fabulous prawns here, but the service can be very offhand.

Copes Seafood Company

778 Fulham Road, SW6 5SJ (7371 7300). Parsons Green or Putney Bridge tube. **Open** 9.30am-7.30pm Mon-Fri; 9am-7pm Sat; noon-5pm Sun. **Credit** AmEx, DC, MC, V.

Cornish fish are the speciality at Copes Seafood Company and we've been known to fall for the fat scallops. Ready-made fish cakes are often available.

Cape Clear Fish Shop

119 Shepherds Bush Road, W6 7LP (7751 1609). Hammersmith tube. **Open** 8am-7pm Tue-Fri; 8am-5pm Sat. **Credit** AmEx, DC, MC, V.

Now under new ownership, this smart west London store (being refurbished until November 2008) has spawned a Herne Hill branch that's been warmly welcomed.

For branch see index.

FishWorks

6 Turnham Green Terrace, W4 1QP (8994 0086/www.fishworks.co.uk). Turnham Green tube. **Open** 8.30am-10.30pm daily. **Credit** AmEx, MC, V.

This chain incorporates a traditional fish counter, seafood café and cookery school in each outlet.

Branches: throughout the city.

France Fresh Fish

99 Stroud Green Road, N4 3PX (7263 9767). Finsbury Park tube/rail. **Open** 9am-6.45pm Mon-Sat; 11am-5pm Sun. **No credit cards.**

Exotic species from the Seychelles and West Indies are a speciality.

Golborne Fisheries

75 Golborne Road, W10 5NP (8960 3100). Ladbroke Grove tube. **Open** 8am-6pm Mon-Sat. **Credit** MC, V.

Conch meat, live eels and frogs' legs are available; more approachable species include clams and langoustines.

Moxon's

149 Lordship Lane, SE22 8HX (8299 1559). East Dulwich rail. **Open** 9am-5.30pm Tue-Sat. **Credit** MC, V.

Sashimi-grade tuna, razor clams, oysters, lobster, wood-smoked salmon steaks and fresh samphire, plus groceries like dill sauce.

For branches see index.

Walter Purkis & Sons

17 The Broadway, N8 8DU (8340 6281/ www.purkis4fish.co.uk). Finsbury Park tube/rail then W7 bus. **Open** 8.30am-5pm Tue-Thur, Sat; 8.30am-5.30pm Fri. **Credit** AmEx, MC, V.

The Purkis family runs these traditional fishmongers in Muswell Hill and Crouch End, where there's a century-old smokehouse.

For branch see index.

Grocers & health food

Alara Wholefoods

58-60 Marchmont Street, WC1N 1AB (7837 1172). Russell Square tube. **Open** 8am-7pm Mon-Fri; 9.45am-6pm Sat. **Credit** MC, V.

This long-established shop and café is the birthplace of a popular range of organic mueslis that you'll find on sale in many of the other stores listed here. Our recent visit saw some café refurbishment taking place. On the shelves: Alara muesli, of course, but also breads from Celtic and South London Bakers, Organico pastas and grissini, tofu passion pudding, cranberry flavour aloe vera juice, 'incan' berries (dried physallis/cape gooseberries given the South American superfood spin) and a sizeable range of nutritional supplements.

Bumblebee

30, 32 & 33 Brecknock Road, N7 0DD (7607 1936/www.bumblebeenatural foods.co.uk). Kentish Town tube/rail/29, 253, 390 bus. **Open** 9am-6.30pm Mon-Sat. **Credit** AmEx, MC, V.

Sprawled over four units on both sides of Brecknock Road, this local favourite sells all manner of organic and natural health foods, plus supplements and remedies. The food-to-go outlet features cakes galore and a wide selection of chilled drinks. An everyday dairy selection is at the back of the greengrocer unit, which has an attractive display of fruit and veg.

Chegworth Farm Shop

221 Kensington Church Street, W8 7LX (7229 3016/www.chegworthvalley.com). Notting Hill Gate tube. **Open** 7.30am-7pm daily. **Credit** MC, V.

Stawarts of many a farmers' market, the producers from this Kent-based organic fruit farm opened their first stand-alone store in 2008. Known especially for the tangy and pure apple and pear juices as well as special blends using raspberries, strawberries, blackcurrants, blackberries and rhubarb, the shop also stocks organic fruit and veg and other essentials such as milk and bread. Best of all, there's a free (if you spend £15, which isn't hard) same-day delivery service.

Daylesford Organic

44B Pimlico Road, SW1W 8LP (7881 8060/www.daylesfordorganic.com). Sloane Square tube. **Open** 8am-8pm Mon-Sat; 10am-4pm Sun. **Credit** AmEx, MC, V.

Everyone shopping at this pristine white marble food hall is likely to be thinner, blonder and richer than you, but pootle about the shelves long enough and you too could take on that serene glow. Daylesford confidently sets its own rules regarding healthfulness, so while you'll find macca powder on the shelves there are also fat sausages and salamis, cakes and rustic breads. A typical summer veg display includes white and green asparagus, knobbly green tomatoes and bunches of beetroot. Much is from Daylesford's own organic estates (cheddar, soups, meat, quail eggs) but then, a lot is not, like the unusual varieties of rice, posh French and Italian cheeses and pasta and matching sauces.

For branches (including Daylesford Organic The Butcher, Daylesford Organic The Garden) see index.

Earth Natural Foods

200 Kentish Town Road, NW5 2AE (7482 2211/www.earthnaturalfoods.co.uk). Kentish Town tube/rail. **Open** 8.30am-7pm Mon-Sat. **Credit** MC, V.

Not just organic but vegetarian too, this ordered mini-supermarket nevertheless offers plenty of mouthwatering foods, from early morning croissants and seeded loaves, to lunchtime takeaway dishes, pasta for supper and tubs of Booja Booja's excellent vegan ice-creams to scoff in front of the telly. The range of quality oils, vinegars and condiments is impressive. It even sells teff flour.

The Grocery

54-56 Kingsland Road, E2 8DP (7729 6855/www.thegroceryshop.co.uk). Liverpool Street tube/rail then 26, 149, 242 bus. **Open** 8am-10pm daily. **Credit** MC, V.

Large enough to compete with the organic supermarket chains, the Grocery aims to offer the residents of east London around 70% organic produce and 30% conventional, including various household items like toothpaste. On the shelves you will find a wide selection of Payne's honeys from the South Downs and further afield, dry good basics like wholewheat pastas, grains and pulses, loads of Dr Karg's and similar crispbreads, plus trendy superfoods such as cacao nibs.

Hive Honey Shop

93 Northcote Road, SW11 6PL (7924 6233/www.thehivehoneyshop.co.uk). Clapham Junction rail. **Open** 10am-5pm Mon-Sat. **Credit** MC, V.

Owner James Harnill has been beekeeping since he was a boy and maintains around 150 hives in London and south-west England – including one inside this store. Varieties include Wandsworth, Wimbledon and Hampstead. Also here are a wealth of bee-related products including mead, pollen, propolis, beeswax and royal jelly.

Just Natural

304 Park Road, N8 8LA (8340 1720/ www.justnaturalshop.co.uk). Bus W3, W7. **Open** 9am-7pm Mon-Fri; 10am-7pm Sat; 11am-4pm Sun. **Credit** MC, V.

Whether you are looking for indulgent groceries (organic nitrate-free salamis, chocolate-coated fruit and nuts, Duchy Originals giftpacks) or some cutting-edge health foods (hemp oil, aloe vera juice), this rambling and spacious store is a viable alternative to the capital's organic supermarkets. Included in the tempting bakery section are some super sourdough loaves from the All Natural bakery in Suffolk and spelt croissants. At back is a garden area for enjoying home-made vegetarian lunches.

Natural Kitchen

77-78 Marylebone High Street, W1U 5JX (7486 8065/www.thenaturalkitchen.com). Baker Street or Bond Street tube. **Open** 8am-8pm Mon-Fri; 8am-6pm Sat; 11am-5pm Sun. **Credit** AmEx, MC, V.

The regal joints of richly coloured organic beef will probably be the first things to catch your eye as you walk into this food hall with café tables – not brown rice. Co-founder Keith Bird's definition of 'natural' sees authentic, unadulterated foods produced by artisans in the traditional manner placed firmly at the top of Natural Kitchen's shopping list, so you'll find fine cheeses and wines here as well as organic fruit, vegetables, milk and oats. Their lime and coriander chicken sausages are popular and a high-rise passion fruit cheesecake calls from the takeaway counter like a siren.

Unpackaged

42 Amwell Street, EC1R 1XT (7713 8368/ www.beunpackaged.com). Angel tube. **Open** 10am-7pm Mon-Fri; 10am-6pm Sat. **Credit** (over £10) MC, V.

See p238 **Unique Selling Point**.

Also check out...

As Nature Intended

201 Chiswick High Road, W4 2DR (8742 8838/www.asnatureintended.uk.com). Turnham Green tube. **Open** 9am-8pm Mon-Fri; 9am-7pm Sat; 10.30am-6.30pm Sun. **Credit** MC, V.

As Nature Intended stocks an ambitious range of organic products, plus a few gourmet and health fetishist lines à la Gillian McKeith.

For branches see index.

Bushwacker Wholefoods

132 King Street, W6 0QU (8748 2061). Hammersmith tube. **Open** 9am-6pm Mon-Sat. **Credit** AmEx, MC, V.

Organic foods and natural remedies.

Don't Panic Go Organic

49 Cavell Street, E1 2BP (7780 9319/ www.dontpanicgoorganic.co.uk). Whitechapel tube/Shadwell DLR. **Open** 8.30am-7.30pm Mon-Sat; 10am-5pm Sun. **Credit** MC, V.

This is a small shop with a loyal local fanbase and a vegetable box scheme.

Dragonfly Wholefoods

24 Highgate High Street, N6 5JG (8347 6087/www.dragonflywholefoods.co.uk). Highgate or Archway tube. **Open** *Term-time* 8am-8pm Mon-Fri; 9.30am-6pm Sat, Sun. *Holidays* 9am-8pm Mon-Fri; 9.30am-6pm Sat, Sun. **Credit** MC, V.

Many superb products are crammed into this tiny new shop with juice bar-cum-café discreetly hidden at the rear.

Fresh & Wild

49 Parkway, NW1 7PN (7428 7575/ www.wholefoodsmarket.com). Camden Town tube. **Open** 8am-9pm Mon-Sat; 10am-8pm Sun. **Credit** AmEx, MC, V.

This popular organic supermarket chain is now owned by Whole Foods Market (*see p248*). There's a juice bar on site at this branch.

For branches see index.

Here

Chelsea Farmers' Market, 125 Sydney Street, SW3 6NR (7351 4321). South Kensington tube. **Open** 9.30am-8pm Mon-Sat; 10am-6.30pm Sun. **Credit** MC, V.

Streamlined supermarket selling organic and biodynamic food and drink with its own butcher selling sausages made on the premises.

Oliver's Wholefoods Store

5 Station Approach, Kew, Surrey TW9 3QB (8948 3990/www.oliverswholefoods.co.uk). Kew Gardens tube/rail. **Open** 9am-7.30pm Mon-Sat; 10am-7.30pm Sun. **Credit** MC, V.

Oliver's Wholefoods Store is an excellent wholefoods supermarket with organic produce and grocery items, plus alternative therapy treatments.

Planet Organic

42 Westbourne Grove, W2 5SH (7727 2227/www.planetorganic.com). Bayswater tube. **Open** 8.30am-9pm Mon-Sat; noon-6pm Sun. **Credit** AmEx, MC, V.

The past year has seen this organic supermarket add two high-profile branches in Muswell Hill and Islington to its list.

For branches see index.

Whole Foods Market

63-97 Kensington High Street, W8 5SE (7368 4500/www.wholefoodsmarket.co.uk). High Street Kensington tube. **Open** 8am-10pm Mon-Sat; 10am-6pm Sun. **Credit** AmEx, DC, MC, V.

The American superstore approach to health food retailing, selling everything from banana chips to organic charcuterie.

International

A Gold

42 Brushfield Street, E1 6AG (7247 2487). Liverpool Street tube/rail. **Open** 9.30am-5.30pm Mon-Fri; 11am-6pm Sat; 10am-6pm Sun. **Credit** AmEx, MC, V.

A Gold was flying the flag for British foods long before it became fashionable to do so. Resembling a village shop from a bygone era, it appeals to tourists with its jars of clotted-cream fudge and coconut ice, Cornish saffron cakes and Welsh cakes. However, there are gourmet, artisan-produced lines here too, including Forman's smoked salmon, Richard Woodall's bacon, and Colston Bassett stilton.

Al-Abbas

258-262 Uxbridge Road, W12 7JA (8740 1932). Shepherd's Bush tube. **Open** 7am-midnight daily. **Credit** MC, V.

One of our favourite Middle Eastern stores in west London, Al-Abbas in fact stocks groceries from all corners of the globe, with Polish, African and Indian essentials. The range of grains and pulses is astonishing and includes the hard-to-find freekeh and moth beans. Spice up your cooking with the jalapeños and other fresh chillies or speciality herbs such as methi. Teetotallers will appreciate exotic cordials of tamarind and mint and the crates of fresh falafel sitting by the till are hard to resist too.

Andreas Michli & Son

405-411 St Ann's Road, N15 3JL (8802 0188). Manor House tube. **Open** 10am-7pm Mon-Sat; 11am-3.30pm Sun. **No credit cards.**

Although this looks something like a quirky antiques shop, in fact it's one of London's best Cypriot food stores. Among the family photos and religious objects you'll find buckets of olives, tubs of Varkas spices, yellow dates, fresh black-eyed beans and piles of ceramic cooking pots. Fresh produce comes from Cyprus or Michli's own farm in Hertfordshire.

Athenian Grocery

16A Moscow Road, W2 4BT (7229 6280). Bayswater tube. **Open** 8.30am-7pm Mon-Sat; 9.30am-1pm Sun. **No credit cards.**

This Greek delicatessen has provided the local community with Greek essentials for over 40 years. Out front are seasonal rarities such as green almonds and desirables such as fat, juicy figs. Inside you'll find *trahanas* (a dried mixture of yoghurt and wheat used for making soup), a chiller packed with feta, expat faves such as Kean fruit nectars in sour cherry and peach, a wide range of traditional sweets made with grape juice, and biscuits from Hornsey's specialist Melissa bakery.

Blue Mountain Peak

2A-8 Craven Park Road, NW10 4AB (8965 3859/www.bluemountainpeak.co.uk). Willesden Junction tube. **Open** 7am-6pm Mon-Fri; 7am-6.30pm Sat. **Credit** MC, V.

Willesden's favourite source of fresh yams, callaloo, jackfruit and sugar cane, this huge Afro-Caribbean shop has a comprehensive range of products from staples such as fufu (root vegetable starch) and jerk seasoning, to interesting drinks including herbal bitters and the likes of guava fruit syrup.

Brindisa

32 Exmouth Market, EC1R 4QE (7713 1666/www.brindisa.com). Angel tube/ Farringdon tube/rail. **Open** 9.30am-6pm Mon-Sat. **Credit** MC, V.

Brindisa has been seeking out Spain's best producers for around 20 years. Shelves are stacked with tinned and bottled goods, wines, sherries, paella pans and Spanish cookery books. There's a great selection of Iberico and serrano hams, which are expertly carved to order, plus sandwiches, salads and soups to take away.

For branch see index.

Centre Point Food Store

20-21 St Giles High Street, WC2H 8LN (7836 9860/www.cpfs.co.uk). Tottenham Court Road tube. **Open** 10am-10.30pm Mon-Sat; noon-10pm Sun. **Credit** (over £5) MC, V.

We love this Korean and Japanese supermarket for the fresh tubs of kimchi (Korean pickles), terrific served as appetisers before a Far Eastern supper. The uninitiated may want to go easy on the chilli-laden pickled perilla leaves (like eating fiery tobacco), but the sesame-seasoned seaweed salad, boiled eggs in soy sauce and orange-hued strips of chewy spiced squid are healthily moreish. Upstairs is a very decent sushi restaurant.

Food Hall

22-24 Turnpike Lane, N8 0PS (8889 2264). Turnpike Lane tube. **Open** 8.30am-7pm Mon-Sat; 9.30am-3pm Sun. **Credit** MC, V.

You'll have heard of Ethiopian coffee, but what other gustatory delights come from this and other parts of Africa? Plenty, as this well-stocked shop proves. Treat yourself to some niter kebbeh (aged spice butter), used for flavouring stews, some grains of paradise (a pungent, peppery West African spice) and the freshly milled flours of rice, millet and maize.

Fortune Foods

387-389 Hendon Way, NW4 3LP (8203 9325). Hendon Central tube. **Open** 10am-10pm daily. **No credit cards.**

Just north of Brent Cross, this deli sells imported produce from Lithuania, Russia, Poland and Slovakia.

Fruity Fresh

111-113 Ealing Road, Wembley, Middx HA0 4BP (8902 9797). Alperton tube. **Open** 9am-10pm Mon-Fri; 9am-11pm Sat, Sun. **Credit** MC, V.

One of the best Indian greengrocers in the area, Fruity Fresh's outdoor canopy allows for an expansive display, featuring, among other oddities, huge black watermelons and kantola (a vivid green fruit with spiky skin). You'll also find a range of Indian groceries, snacks such as cassava chips and cans of Foco coconut juice.

Chegworth Farm Shop. *See p247.*

Fuji Foods

167 Priory Road, N8 8NB (8347 9177). Bus W7. **Open** 11am-8pm Tue-Fri; 11am-7pm Sat; 11am-5pm Sun. **Credit** MC, V.

Run by a former chef from Atari-ya (*see p253*) and his wife, this charming Japanese delicatessen offers organic lines alongside the usual array of noodles, soy sauces and wacky soft drinks. It's worth seeking out for own-made sushi and miso-marinated black cod, plus specialities such as sea urchin paste, haiga rice (a semi-pearled variety retaining some of the wheatgerm), kimchi base and Minghella's black sesame and green tea ice-creams.

Funchal Bakery

141 Stockwell Road, SW9 9TN (7733 3134). Stockwell tube/Brixton tube/rail. **Open** 7am-7pm daily. **No credit cards**.

Some of London's best custard tarts and bolo con arroz (rice cakes) can be found in this friendly, if rather scruffy, Portuguese café-deli. Look out for the high quality yet inexpensive Gallo olive oils and honey from Funchal (on the island of Madeira). Expats can pick up Portuguese cookery magazines and newspapers, Compal juices and cases of Super Bock lager.

Gennaro's

23 Lewis Grove, SE13 6BG (8852 1370). Lewisham rail/DLR. **Open** 9am-6pm Mon-Thur, Sat; 9am-5.30pm Fri. **Credit** MC, V.

This beloved neighbourhood deli brings the authentic taste of Italy to south-east London and manages to keep the prices reasonable too. Grissini, biscotti and panettone hang from the ceiling, the counter is packed with antipasti, cheeses and cured meats, while shelves hold passata, grains, jars of anchovies and artichokes, coffee and Gennaro's own Sicilian olive oil, made by an artisan producer. Delicious.

German Deli

127 Central Street, EC1V 8AP (7250 1322/www.germandeli.co.uk). Barbican tube/Old Street tube/rail. **Open** 11am-7pm Mon-Fri; 11am-6pm Sat. **Credit** MC, V.

Cured meats and sausages are something the Germans do well, not least because of their rigid laws on product purity, and here at the German Deli, you'll find impressive stocks of Thuringian bratwurst, Hausmacher leberwurst (a kind of spreading sausage a bit like pâté), smoked hams from Westphalia, the Black Forest and north Germany, landjaeger (think gourmet Pepperami) and brawn. Of course, you'll also need the superior mustard, sauerkraut and rye bread it stocks as well, along with German chocolates for afters.

Giacobazzi's

150 Fleet Road, NW3 2QX (7267 7222/ www.giacobazzis.co.uk). Belsize Park tube/ Hampstead Heath rail. **Open** 9.30am-7pm Mon-Fri; 9.30am-6pm Sat. **Credit** AmEx, MC, V.

Customers queue patiently at this beloved Hampstead Heath deli to get their hands on Giacobazzi's selection of own-made dishes. Products, from all over Italy, have helpful labels to explain the difference between, say, the various types of pecorino, or Sicilian and Puglian quince pastes. The antipasti counter has more than the usual suspects with options like grilled radicchio and marinated carrot. Filled pastas are made on site, as is truffle butter and desserts.

Green Valley

36-37 Upper Berkeley Street, W1H 5QF (7402 7385). Marble Arch tube. **Open** 8am-midnight daily. **Credit** MC, V.

One of London's best Middle Eastern food halls, Green Valley has a comprehensive meze counter offering myriad possibilities for quick, after-work suppers. The fresh produce area includes squat, round Lebanese pears, dainty aubergines, stumpy cucumbers, plus the likes of dragon fruit, guava and young coconuts. In the freezer you'll find molokhia (a high-nutrient green vegetable used especially in soups and stews) and ready-made kibbeh in chicken, lamb and almond varieties. In addition to the eye-catching display of baklava, the sizeable pâtisserie section includes thickly layered gateaux and tubs of rice pudding.

Japan Centre

212 Piccadilly, W1J 9HG (7255 8255/ www.japancentre.com). Piccadilly Circus tube. **Open** 10am-9pm Mon-Sat; 11am-7pm Sun. **Credit** MC, V.

Japan Centre's basement grocery has taken over next door's premises, allowing for the expansion of the grocery and fresh meat, fish and vegetable ranges, plus the addition of a new trend-setting bakery. Sweet, creamy edamame gateau? It hardly sounds possible but you'll find it here, along with cakes flavoured with red beans and sesame, organic herbs, meats cut specially for shabu-shabu, takeaway sushi, myriad types of rice, snack foods and Fuji apples.

Kalinka

35 Queensway, W2 4QP (7243 6125). Bayswater or Queensway tube. **Open** 11am-8pm Mon-Sat; noon-6.30pm Sun. **Credit** MC, V.

Named after a famous Russian song, Boris Gofman's bright and cheerful shop is a community focal point with its flat-screen TVs, magazines and DVDs. The chiller cabinets hold all manner of cured fish, an astonishing variety of roe, tvarog and other curd cheeses, layered cakes, Ukrainian pig fat and more Russian essentials. In the freezer are delicious ready-made pelmeni (ravioli-like dumplings).

Korea Foods

Unit 5, Wyvern Industrial Estate, Beverley Way, New Malden, Surrey KT3 4PH (8949 2238/www.koreafoods.co.uk). New Malden or Raynes Park rail. **Open** 9am-9pm Mon-Sat; noon-6pm Sun. **Credit** MC, V.

Some distance from New Malden town centre, this warehouse-style Korean supermarket at the rear of an industrial estate nevertheless attracts plenty of custom making parking difficult at times. But it's a superb one-stop shop with fresh and frozen meats and fish, a wide choice of kimchi (Korean pickles), grains, beans, noodles, snacks and staple Korean veg such as beansprouts, taro and fragrant greens.

Shop talk Fergus Henderson

Londoner Fergus Henderson, owner of restaurants St John (*see p236*) and St John Bread & Wine, in Smithfields and Spitalfields respectively, has been a driving force in the British cuisine revival.

'I live in central London and, despite spending most of my time cooking in my restaurants, I still cook at home and buy most of the ingredients. I find supermarkets profoundly depressing, so I tend to go to specialist food shops.

'**I Camisa & Sons** (*see p252*) is my favourite. I probably pick up stuff here about twice a week. I've tried every style of their wonderful pasta, their cheese, their home-made ravioli, their olives and all their Italian sausages. My favourite is zampino, which is a spicy Italian sausage with a pig's trotter at one end. Yum.

'I'm also a huge fan of **Neal's Yard Dairy** (*see p237*), although I'll admit to the fact that I often get cheese rage when in delis. I go in and know exactly what I want, and I start fuming when people in front of me are like, hmm, now what do you have that tastes like that? Grrr! But all that aside, it's a wonderful shop with an incredible range of cheeses.

'The one London institution I can't praise enough is shoemaker **John Lobb** (www.johnlobb.com). I hate shoe shopping and could never find anything until I found Lobb. I have a couple of pairs of brogues in brown and black. And that's it. They cost a fortune, but it means that I don't have to worry about shoes ever again. They will last me forever.'

Lina Stores
18 Brewer Street, W1R 3FS (7437 6482). Piccadilly Circus tube. **Open** 8am-6.30pm Mon-Fri; 8am-5.30pm Sat. **Credit** AmEx, MC, V.
See p245 **Enduring loves**.

Lisboa
54 Golborne Road, W10 5NR (8969 1586). Ladbroke Grove tube. **Open** 9.30am-7.30pm Mon-Sat; 10am-5pm Sun. **Credit** MC, V.
Among the packaged groceries at this friendly Portuguese deli are tins of sweet potato and guava paste, beans, pastas and the essential strong coffee. You'll also find white anchovies in vinegar, Iberian oils, pasteis de bacalhau (salt cod fritters) and pasteis de nata (custard tarts).
For branches (including Lisboa Pâtisserie) see index.

London Star Night Supermarket & Video
203-213 Mare Street, E8 3QE (8985 2949). Hackney Central or London Fields rail/26, 48, 55, 253 bus. **Open** 10am-10pm daily. **Credit** MC, V.
A maze of weird and wonderful sights and smells, this spot supplies many of Hackney's Vietnamese restaurants with key fresh ingredients such as saw-leaf herb, perilla leaves and Asian red basil. The selection of fish and shellfish is unmissable and there is a good range of exotic South-east Asian fruits including rambutans, durian and dragon fruit, plus essentials like fish sauce and shrimp paste. If you need a particular Vietnamese cooking utensil, (maybe a clay pot for caramel fish?), you'll probably find it here too.

Luigi's Delicatessen
349 Fulham Road, SW10 9TW (7352 7739). Fulham Broadway tube. **Open** 9am-9.30pm Mon-Fri; 9am-7pm Sat. **Credit** MC, V.
Inevitably crowded, this hit Italian deli has a terrific range of basics and specialities including linguine with rosemary and olives, lardo di colonnata (seasoned rendered pork fat), free-range Italian chicken and own-made cooked dishes.

Manila Supermarket
11-12 Hogarth Place, SW5 0QT (7373 8305). Earl's Court tube. **Open** 9am-9pm daily. **Credit** MC, V.
There are many Filipino supermarkets in Earl's Court, but this large venue with friendly English-speaking staff is the best. You'll find row upon row of brightly coloured sauces, curry pastes, pickles, seasonings, instant mixes, snacks and confectionery, plus fresh produce, and chilled and frozen foodstuffs. Oriental beers and wines are also sold.

Maroush Deli
45-49 Edgware Road, W2 2HZ (7723 3666/www.maroush.com). Marble Arch tube. **Open** 8am-midnight daily. **Credit** AmEx, DC, MC, V.
An enjoyable shop with plenty of corners to browse, this tiny food hall is owned by Lebanese entrepreneur Marouf Abouzaki, who also runs the acclaimed restaurants of the same name. Come for big feathery bunches of dill, beautiful baklava, halal meat, unusual grains such as ble, and specialist dairy drinks and cheeses. The range of fresh and dried fruits is particularly tempting, including huge fat dates and frosted figs.

Monte's
23 Canonbury Lane, N1 2AS (7354 4335/ www.montesdeli.com). Highbury & Islington tube/rail. **Open** 10am-7pm Mon-Fri; 10am-6pm Sat; 10.30am-4pm Sun. **Credit** MC, V.
Despite the Italian flag on the fascia, Monte's sells plenty of good things from elsewhere, such as James's chocolates, Hill Station ice-cream, and London's own Kentish flute bread. But there are superb Italian lines here too, particularly in the meat counter where you'll find excellent mortadella, bresaola and ventricana salami. Intrigues in the cheese range include quadrello di bufala and semi-hard sheep's milk cheese brinata.

Olga Stores
30 Penton Street, N1 9PS (7837 5467). Angel tube. **Open** 8.30am-8pm Mon-Sat; 10am-4pm Sun. **Credit** (over £5) MC, V.
This unpretentious shop looks like many other Italian delis in London, but venture in and you'll find everything from canned tomatoes to whole fresh foie gras. Since our last visit it's become a welcome source of creamy burrata cheese. Check the pristine veg and herb section for wonderfully buttery fuerte avocados; and Olga sells Italian plant seeds too. Welcoming staff are patient while customers try to choose between trays of meat and vegetable lasagnes, and fresh pasta sauces for supper.

Persepolis
28-30 Peckham High Street, SE15 5DT (7639 8007). Peckham Rye rail/36 bus. **Open** 10.35am-10pm daily. **Credit** MC, V.
Music, handicrafts and shisha pipes are stocked alongside edibles at Sally Butcher's colourful Iranian store, an inspiration for food-lovers from the local area and beyond. The Western perspective she brings to proceedings – such as recommending rose petals not just for Persian ice-cream but for pretty party ice cubes – is undoubtedly part of the appeal. And it's a great place to stock up on the likes of fresh Persian dates, sumak, dried limes and verjus.

Phoenicia Mediterranean Food Hall
186-192 Kentish Town Road, NW5 2AE (7267 1267/www.phoeniciafoodhall.co.uk). Kentish Town tube/rail. **Open** 9am-8pm Mon-Sat; 10am-4pm Sun. **Credit** MC, V.
A clean and spacious food hall offering a comprehensive range of products from Lebanon, Greece, Turkey and Italy, plus some mass market convenience lines and household goods. Adjacent to the halal meat counter (great for hard-to-find offally bits) is a selection of semi-prepared dishes such as marinated swordfish steaks, lamb chops and chicken skewers. The spice section features Jordanian thyme and dried molokhia (a green vegetable) along with every Asian spice you can think of. There's an impressive display of fresh Portuguese and Lebanese pastries too, and the choice of exotic breads is the best in the area.

Red Pig
57 Camden High Street, NW1 7LJ (7388 8992). Mornington Crescent tube. **Open** 8am-9pm Mon-Fri; 9am-9pm Sat; 10am-6pm Sun. **Credit** (over £10) MC, V.
One of the new wave of Polish delis in the capital, Red Pig looks like a newsagent-cum-chemist at the front: you have to head through to the larger rear section for the food. The cold meat counter is better than most, offering a wide choice of sausages and luncheon meats, such as slaska, tourunska, hunter's sausage and jellied terrines. But with rice cakes, organic pasta, pizza bases, jars of antipasto and tapas, it's a useful stop-off for non-Polish locals too.
For branch see index.

R García & Sons
248-250 Portobello Road, W11 1LL (7221 6119). Ladbroke Grove or Westbourne Park tube. **Open** 9am-6pm daily. **Credit** MC, V.
One of London's largest Spanish grocer-delis, García's meat counter is a joy to peruse, as is the excellent range of sherries. Tins of smoked paprika, marcona almonds, olive oils, sherry vinegar and slabs of turron line the shelves, while the cheese selection includes manchego, mahon, cabralles and tetilla.

Reza Pâtisserie
345 Kensington High Street, W8 6NW (7603 0924). High Street Kensington tube. **Open** 9.30am-9.30pm daily. **Credit** MC, V.
Despite the name, Reza sells much more than the excellent Iranian biscuits, cakes and sweets that are baked on the premises. Fragrant herbs, fresh fruit and vegetables are enticingly displayed out front (look for fresh green almonds in season), while inside you'll find everything from halal meat to Iranian caviar, and pickles to rosewater.

Ryad Halal Way Butchers & Deli
248 Wandsworth Road, SW8 2JS (7738 8811). Vauxhall tube/rail. **Open** 9am-9pm daily. **Credit** (over £10) MC, V.
A small shop featuring an eclectic variety of foods. Moroccan and Middle Eastern ingredients are the mainstay but you'll also find some Indian, Turkish, Slovenian and Nigerian groceries. Good fresh produce is displayed out front.

Salvino
47 Brecknock Road, N7 0BT (7267 5303). Kentish Town tube/rail/29, 253, 390 bus. **Open** 8.30am-6.30pm Mon-Sat. **Credit** MC, V.
The range of *prodotti tipici* at this small but long-established Italian delicatessen is extremely well edited. Own-made Sicilian sausages (pizzaiola, fennel, or lemon zest) star on the impressive meat and cheese counters, while tempting fresh savouries (arancini), breads (muffaletta rolls) and pastries (cannoli) also offer a taste of that sun-drenched isle. Seriously posh pastas range from elegant crab and saffron ravioli to superior renditions of basics likes ricotta and spinach tortellini. Alba Gold ice-creams and Gli Aroni rices earn Salvino further kudos among gastronauts, and there's a small machine behind the counter producing takeaway Illy coffees.

Scandinavian Kitchen

61 Great Titchfield Street, W1W 7PP (7580 7161/www.scandikitchen.co.uk). Oxford Circus tube. **Open** 8am-7pm Mon-Fri; 10am-6pm Sat. **Credit** MC, V.

A cheerful shop and café providing the necessities of Scandinavian life to expats as well as a large number of health food enthusiasts drawn by gourmet wheat-products and superb herring. The choice of artisan-made rye and oat crackers puts supermarkets to shame. You'll also find Gevalia coffee, rosehip syrup, Lofoten fish soup, tubes of smoked fish roe and a range of Swedish cheeses that, while of the firm-rubbery-buttery school, are delicious for breakfast and sandwiches.

Sintra Delicatessen & Tapas

146 & 148 Stockwell Road, SW9 9TQ (7733 9402/www.sintradeli.co.uk). Stockwell tube. **Open** 8.30am-8pm daily. **No credit cards.**

Intriguing products are crammed into this small, thin Portuguese and Brazilian deli adjacent to a popular café and informal restaurant. The freezer cabinet holds salt cod, veal croquettes, hake and tiger prawns; elsewhere you'll find pretty jars of tomato and mango jams, quince paste, morcilla and a range of dried beans.

Spice Shop

1 Blenheim Crescent, W11 2EE (7221 4448/www.thespiceshop.co.uk). Ladbroke Grove tube. **Open** 10am-6pm Mon-Sat; noon-5pm Sun. **Credit** MC, V.

Birgit Ergat's tiny shop holds over 2,500 different spices, herbs, essential oils, aromatics, seasonings, flavourings and spice blends – everything from fresh barberries and curry leaves to zedoary medieval ginger and Indonesian white muntok peppercorns. Also stocks ingredients like agar agar, gelatine and crystallised angelica. There's an online mail-order service too.

Suroor Market

101-113 Robin Hood Way, SW15 3QE (8974 6088). Kingston rail then 85, K3 bus. **Open** 8.30am-8pm Mon-Sat; 8.30am-7pm Sun. **Credit** (over £10) MC, V.

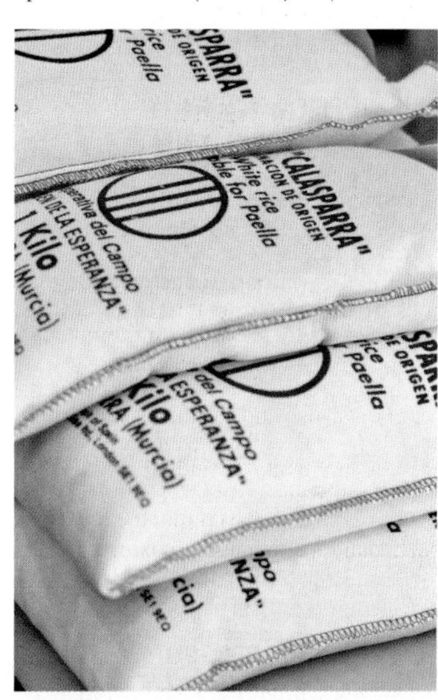

Brindisa. *See p248.*

A piece of the pie

Jenni Muir lifts the lid on the growing trend of restaurant-owned delis.

The dishes of London's finest restaurants were once accessible only to those with deep pockets, expense accounts and the foresight to book a table weeks in advance. But today's top chefs want everyone to enjoy their food, so their new must-have kitchen accessory is a delicatessen selling gourmet delights at democratic takeaway prices. Whether you enjoy traditional French and Italian cooking, great British grub, Japanese cuisine, or the inventive creations of fusion exponents, London now has more restaurant shops than there are days in the week to try them.

It all started with **& Clarke's** (122 Kensington Church Street, W8 4BH, 7229 2190, www.sallyclarke.com), the offshoot of Clarke's restaurant in Kensington, which opened (as many do) when the property next door to the restaurant became vacant. Well before 9am each day, Sally Clarke herself is regularly seen bustling around the shop, which sells a discerning selection of everyday luxuries (Lescure butter, Maldon sea salt, fruit and veg worthy of a photo shoot) alongside Clarke's own products from the restaurant kitchen and her wholesale bakery. While all is lovely, it's the dishes-to-go that make it individual – carrot and orange soup, fresh lemon mayonnaise, parsley pesto, bags of ravioli, chickpea salad.

'I should in theory spend a third of my time in each part of the business, but it's all too easy to go into the shop and spend three hours ordering and sorting out the display,' says Clarke. Which highlights a key issue: running a restaurant is notoriously hard, does running both mean double trouble?

Not for fusion chef Anna Hansen, who has included a shop in her new multi-faceted eaterie the **Modern Pantry** (47-48 St John's Square, EC1V 4JJ, 7250 0833, www.themodernpantry.co.uk). 'One of my first food-related jobs was in a deli that did catering and I loved dealing with the punters and produce. I love the idea that people can come into the building and we can satisfy anything they want, whether it's to sit down and eat, or take food away. The restaurant, café and shop all complement and publicise each other, so people who come by and enjoy the shop might decide they want to visit the restaurant another time, and vice versa.'

It also helps with stock control, she reveals. Andy Needham, executive chef of swish Knightsbridge Italian restaurant **Zafferano** and its adjacent deli (16 Halkin Arcade, Motcomb Street, SW1X 8JT, 7838 9995, www.zafferanorestaurant.com), agrees. 'We use a lot of fine cheeses and charcuterie in the restaurant and offering them for sale in the deli too helps keep everything turning over, maximising freshness,' he explains.

The deli also made it easy for Zafferano to satisfy diners' frequent requests for ingredients, wines and ready-made dishes to enjoy at home, or on their private jets. 'We have always spent a lot of time sourcing ingredients that are a bit different and have longstanding relationships with our suppliers,' says Needham. 'This shop is a way to let those artisan producers shine.'

But the main reason the restaurant shop trend is here to stay is pure economics: on both sides of the equation. Smart restaurateurs who've invested in a pro kitchen and have the staff available want to optimise their resources – and customers faced with tight budgets want to do the same. At **Bluebird** restaurant (350 King's Road, SW3 5UU, 7559 1000, www.danddlondon.com), for example, you can enjoy Mark Broadbent's salmon fish cakes for £11 a plate, or eat them at home for £3.50 each. In the restaurant, the wild mushroom risotto with porcini, chanterelles and truffle is £15.50, from the shop it's just £3 a tub.

It's a similar story over at the **Barnsbury Grocer** (237 Liverpool Road, N1 1LX, 7607 7222, www.thebarnsbury.co.uk) in Islington, not an offshoot of a restaurant, but of a gastropub. Here the home-made pies in reusable enamel dishes have become locals' favourite midweek supper choice, offered in flavours as homely and rustic as beef and Guinness, or inspired combinations like chicken and chorizo. Forget the highly processed flavours of supermarket ready-meals, this is upgraded comfort food at reasonable prices, and all you have to do is turn on the oven. What's not to savour?

& Clarke's

We think this friendly, family-run Iraqi supermarket (spread across four shop units and out on to the pavement) is one of the capital's best Middle Eastern suppliers. Whether you are looking for a simple tub of houmous or speciality cooking ingredients such as kashk (whey), golpar (the ground seeds of Persian hogweed), roast chickpea and sour grape powders, you will probably want to leave with much more than is on your shopping list. As well as a halal meat counter, fresh produce includes unusual gourds, wonderful avocados, five or six different types of chillies, kohlrabi, okra, baby aubergines, tiny apples and apricots, and much more.

Taj Stores

112-114A Brick Lane, E1 6RL (7377 0061/www.tajstores.co.uk). Aldgate East tube/Liverpool Street tube/rail. **Open** 9am-9pm daily. **Credit** (over £10) MC, V.
This Bangladeshi supermarket, founded in 1936, is still doing a brisk trade in its fresh naan and samosas, herbs and spices, pulses, grains, halal meat and Bangladeshi fish. The extensive range of fresh fruit and vegetables includes rarities such as lata and danga (leaf and stem vegetables). You'll also find bargain-priced tiffin boxes and cooking utensils.

Talad Thai

326 Upper Richmond Road, SW15 6TL (8789 8084/www.taladthai.co.uk). Putney rail. **Open** 9am-8pm daily. **Credit** (over £10) MC, V.
Hairy, holy and sweet Thai basil, cockroach berries, pea aubergines, toddy palm seeds, mooli and green papaya are among the authentic fresh ingredients you will find in the chiller cabinet of this long-established Thai grocery. The smart blue and gold fronted shop is owned by Sa-ard and Thanaporn Kriangsak, who also own the restaurant a couple of doors down, and fly in produce from Thailand on a weekly basis. There's a sizeable range of curry pastes, rice and noodles plus frozen foods, and groceries from other Asian culinary traditions including sauces from Lee Kum Kee and Amoy, and wasabi peas.

Totally Swedish

32 Crawford Street, W1H 1LS (7224 9300/www.totallyswedish.com). Baker Street tube. **Open** 10am-6pm Mon-Wed, Fri, Sat; 10am-7.30pm Thur; noon-4pm Sun. **Credit** MC, V.
Set in the Little Stockholm area of Marylebone, this small, powder-blue shop holds all the classic Swedish lines. Look in the freezer cabinet for delicious ready-made marzipan gateaux, and in the deli-counter for meatballs and cognacsmedwurst (salami-style sliced sausage). On the shelves you will find exotic treats like cloudberry jam, rosehip soup, cucumber relish, wholegrain rye flour and crispbreads, plus a selection of Swedish-language cookbooks as well as waffle makers. A mail-order service is also available.

Turkish Food Centre

89 Ridley Road, E8 2NH (7254 6754/ www.tfcsupermarkets.com). Dalston Kingsland rail/30, 56, 236 bus. **Open** 8am-9pm daily. **Credit** MC, V.
Now with ten branches stretching from Catford to Tottenham, this supermarket has fresh fruit and veg flown in weekly from Greece, Cyprus and Turkey. You'll find okra, prickly pears, swiss chard, herbs and kolngasi (similar to yam or sweet potato), plus olives in huge vats. An in-house bakery churns out baklava, breads and pastries.
Branches: throughout the city.

Also check out...

Atari-ya

7 Station Parade, Noel Road, W3 DS (8896 1552/www.atariya.co.uk). North Ealing tube. **Open** 11am-6.30pm Tue; 10am-6.30pm Wed-Fri; 9am-7pm Sat; 10am-7pm Sun. **Credit** MC, V.
Thriving Japanese grocery chain featuring excellent fish counters.
For branches see index.

Comptoir Gascon

61-63 Charterhouse Street, EC1M 6HJ (7608 0851/www.comptoirgascon.com). Farringdon tube/rail. **Open** 9am-7pm Tue-Sat. **Credit** AmEx, MC, V.
Foie gras is the speciality at this hip deli-bistro, though the exquisite pâtisserie and sourdough breads are hard to resist.

I Camisa & Son

61 Old Compton Street, W1D 6HS (7437 7610). Leicester Square tube. **Open** 8.30am-6pm Mon-Sat. **Credit** MC, V.
An old Soho stalwart, this rustic Italian deli is well worth visiting for its fresh pasta and accompanying sauces.

Manicomio

85 Duke of York Square, King's Road, SW3 4LY (7730 3366/www.manicomio.co.uk). Sloane Square tube. **Open** 8am-7pm Mon-Fri; 9am-7pm Sat; 10am-6pm Sun. **Credit** AmEx, MC, V.
Owned by the prestigious Italian foods wholesaler Machiavelli, this smart deli is a treasure trove of Italy's finest edibles.

Le Maroc

94 Golborne Road, W10 5PS (8968 9783). Ladbroke Grove tube. **Open** 9am-9pm Mon-Sat. **No credit cards**.
Le Maroc stocks halal and prepared meat, including kibbeh and merguez sausages, plus a wide range of delicatessen products. Free local delivery.

Mleczko Polish Delicatessen

362 Uxbridge Road, W12 7LL (8932 4487). Shepherd's Bush tube. **Open** 8am-10pm daily. **No credit cards**.
At rear is a comprehensive range of Polish cold meats and dairy products.

Naama

384 Uxbridge Road, W12 7LL (8740 0004). Shepherd's Bush tube. **Open** 9am-10pm daily. **Credit** MC, V.
Good-looking Lebanese deli serving halal meat, preserves, pickles and groceries.

New Loon Moon

9A Gerrard Street, W1D 5PP (7734 3887). Leicester Square tube. **Open** 10.30am-8pm daily. **Credit** AmEx, MC, V.
Expansive supermarket, including cooking equipment, in the heart of Chinatown.

Parade Delicatessen

8 Central Buildings, The Broadway, W5 2NT (8567 9066). Ealing Broadway tube/rail. **Open** 10am-7pm Mon-Fri; 10am-5pm Sat; 10am-4pm Sun. **Credit** MC, V.
Long-lived Polish deli serving all the trad delicacies such as smoked pork loin.

Polsmak

39 Balls Pond Road, N1 4BW (7275 7045/ www.polsmak.co.uk). Dalston Kingsland rail/38 bus. **Open** 9am-8pm Mon-Fri; 9am-6pm Sat, Sun. **Credit** MC, V.
Popular with young Polish expats, with a deli cabinet full of classic Polish meats.

St Marcus Fine Foods

1 Rockingham Close, SW15 5RW (8878 1898). Barnes rail/337 bus. **Open** 9am-6pm daily. **Credit** (over £10) MC, V.
A global range of sausages plus South African meats, condiments and sweets.

Sri Thai

56 Shepherd's Bush Road, W6 7PH (7602 0621). Hammersmith or Shepherd's Bush tube. **Open** 9.30am-7pm daily. **No credit cards**.
Family-run Thai shop with delicious own-made curry pastes and takeaway meals, plus fresh fruit, vegetables and herbs.

Tawana

18-20 Chepstow Road, W2 5BD (7221 6316). Notting Hill Gate tube. **Open** 9.30am-8pm daily. **Credit** MC, V.
Long-established Notting Hill store that's one of the largest importers of fresh Thai produce in London.

Turkish Food Market

385-387 Green Lanes, N4 1EU (8340 4547). Manor House tube/Harringay Green Lanes rail. **Open** 24hrs daily. **Credit** (over £10) AmEx, MC, V.
Top-quality herbs, veg, fruits and nuts flown in from Turkey, plus specialities such as vine leaves, breads and Turkish rice.

VB & Sons

147 Ealing Road, Wembley, Middx HA0 4BU (8795 0387/www.vbandsons.net). Alperton tube. **Open** 9.30am-6.30pm Mon-Fri; 8am-7pm Sat; 10.30am-5pm Sun. **Credit** MC, V.
Gujarati-owned store stocking dried herbs and spices rarely found in London.
For branches see index.

Wing Yip

395 Edgware Road, NW2 6LN (8450 0422/ www.wingyip.com). Cricklewood rail/16, 32, 316 bus. **Open** 9.30am-8pm Mon-Sat; 11.30am-5.30pm Sun. **Credit** MC, V.
Thriving chain with around 2,500 Chinese products, along with produce from Japan, Malaysia, Korea, Vietnam and Singapore.
For branch see index.

Zafferano Delicatessen

16 Halkin Arcade, SW1X 9EY (7838 9995). Knightsbridge tube. **Open** 10am-7pm Mon-Sat; 11am-5pm Sun. **Credit** AmEx, MC, V.
See p252 **A piece of the pie**.

Drink

Wine

Waitrose's wine selection rivals those of many independents, and for choice and quality it beats all the other supermarkets hands-down; visit www.waitrose.com to find your nearest branch or www.waitrosewine.com to order online from WaitroseWineDirect.

Bedales

5 Bedale Street, SE1 9AL (7403 8853/ www.bedalestreet.com). London Bridge tube/rail. **Open**; noon-8.45pm Tue; noon-10.15pm Wed-Fri; 8.30am-5.30pm Sat. **Credit** AmEx, MC, V.

Wine retailing runs in the bloodstreams of the two families that own Bedales. Their shops offer a globetrotting list of uniformly high quality, and they sell it with pride and enthusiasm. The unique attraction both at the original shop in Borough and the newer one in Spitalfields is the opportunity to try the wines in combination with simple and immaculately sourced food. The mark-up on every bottle is fixed at £8: the higher you go the better the bargain.

For branch see index.

Berry Bros & Rudd

3 St James's Street, SW1A 1EG (7396 9600/www.bbr.com). Green Park tube. **Open** 10am-6pm Mon-Fri; 10am-5pm Sat. **Credit** AmEx, DC, MC, V.

Visit Berry at least once, just to sniff the history. The company has been selling wine here since William III was king, and the cellars are ancient. Berry excels at the traditional favourites of the well heeled, with prices to match. There's ample choice under £10, and its own-label wines (clarets especially) are superb. Creaky floorboards and excellent staff add to the appeal.

Green & Blue

36-38 Lordship Lane, SE22 8HJ (8693 9250/www.greenandbluewines.com). East Dulwich rail/37, 40, 176, 185 bus. **Open** 9am-11pm Mon-Thur; 9am-midnight Fri, Sat; 11am-10.30pm Sun. **Credit** MC, V.

Green & Blue has been in Lordship Lane for three years now, and it's great to see such an individualistic merchant thriving. Its wine bars, where customers can sample anything from the list at a small mark-up, have proved popular too. Those buying to drink at home won't be disappointed either – the compact list is exemplary. You won't get much for a fiver, but if you can go up to £10 you'll have good choice, and over half the non-sparkling wines cost under £15. Every country is represented by a worthy bottle or two.

For branch see index.

Handford Wines

105 Old Brompton Road, SW7 3LE (7589 6113/www.handford.net). South Kensington tube. **Open** 10am-8.30pm Mon-Sat; noon-4pm Sun. **Credit** AmEx, MC, V.

Prices at this outstanding merchant start at around £7 and reach dizzying heights. Spend a little bit extra and you'll have plenty of choice from a quality list. Clarets from France are said to 'fly out the door', though the stock from Italy makes up one of the most interesting selections. The locked EuroCave cabinet is the place to head for if you want a bottle of something seriously splendid with which to impress your oenophilic guests.

Haynes Hanson & Clark

7 Elystan Street, SW3 3NT (7584 7927/ www.hhandc.co.uk). South Kensington tube. **Open** 9am-7pm Mon-Fri; 9am-4.30pm Sat. **Credit** MC, V.

Haynes Hanson & Clark is best known as a Burgundy specialist, though staff pride themselves on running a local shop where regulars pop in for everyday bottles – in addition to costly rarities there's ample choice under £8. Knowledgeable, helpful staff ensure you don't feel intimidated despite the ritzy neighbourhood.

Jeroboams

6 Pont Street, SW1X 9EL (7235 1612/ www.jeroboams.co.uk). Knightsbridge or Sloane Square tube. **Open** 10am-8pm Mon-Fri; 10am-7pm Sat. **Credit** AmEx, DC, MC, V.

Jeroboams has grown a lot in recent years through acquisitions of other independent merchants, including Milroy's (*see p255*). Its core business is still good wines with a heavy emphasis on France. Though often viewed as an old-fashioned merchant catering for big spenders, it has surprisingly good offerings under £10, with lots of New World gems. The main shop has recently been refurbished to give it a more contemporary look.

Branches: throughout the city.

Lea & Sandeman

170 Fulham Road, SW10 9PR (7244 0522/ www.londonfinewine.co.uk). Gloucester Road tube. **Open** 10am-8pm Mon-Sat. **Credit** AmEx, MC, V.

Lea & Sandeman is so good, you may not know where to start. Charles Lea and Patrick Sandeman only buy wines they are really excited about, whether it's a Vin de Pays d'Oc or a £60 red Burgundy. Here, Europe is king, but the coverage is global, and there's always the same attention paid to good buying. What's more, the prices here are far lower than you would expect for this part of town. It's no wonder that so many critics regard L&S as the finest wine shop in London.

For branches see index.

Philglas & Swiggot

21 Northcote Road, SW11 1NG (7924 4494/www.philglas-swiggot.com). Clapham Junction rail. **Open** 11am-7pm Mon-Fri; 10am-6pm Sat; noon-5pm Sun. **Credit** AmEx, MC, V.

Long regarded as one of London's finest, Philglas & Swiggot is pre-eminently a shop for francophiles. Italy and Australia follow France in size and there are well-chosen South Africans and excellent wines from Spain. Quality often comes at a price though: you'll get much more choice if you can spend between £10 and £15 however, but even below a tenner there's pleasure to be had.

For branches see index.

Roberson

348 Kensington High Street, W14 8NS (7371 2121/www.robersonwinemerchant.co.uk). High Street Kensington tube/ Kensington (Olympia) tube/rail. **Open** 10am-8pm Mon-Sat; noon-6pm Sun. **Credit** AmEx, MC, V.

Roberson is a Kensington institution, providing an affluent clientele with a gobsmacking selection, heavily dominated by France. Bordeaux and Burgundy account for well over a third of the still wines, with Champagne in abundance and smaller offerings from the Loire and the Rhône at similarly exalted levels. If you love France, and you want something special, Roberson is a top choice in west London.

Sampler

266 Upper Street, N1 2UQ (7226 9500/ www.thesampler.co.uk). Angel tube/Highbury & Islington rail/tube. **Open** 11am-9pm Mon-Sat; 1-8pm Sun. **Credit** MC, V.

The Sampler is unique in London: a shop where you can taste 80 wines out of the 1,000 on offer. You buy a card (minimum £10), then use it to buy 25ml tastes. Samples cost from 30p to £10-plus for the costliest bottles. The wines are terrific at every level. There are around 100 under £10 and the upper reaches include mature classics.

Uncorked

Exchange Arcade, Broadgate, EC2M 3WA (7638 5998/www.uncorked.co.uk). Liverpool Street tube/rail. **Open** 10am-7pm Mon-Fri. **Credit** MC, V.

This City-based merchant excels in all the regions popular with wealthy drinkers – Bordeaux, Burgundy, Champagne, to name but a few – and the Rhône selection is outstanding. Everything is well chosen, and though you'll find very little for under a tenner, what is here is real value for money. Watch this space to see how it fares in these difficult economic times.

Wimbledon Wine Cellar

4 The Boulevard, Imperial Wharf, SW6 2UB (7097 5090/www.wimbledonwine cellar.com). Fulham Broadway tube then 391, C3 bus. **Open** 10am-9pm Mon-Sat; 11am-6pm Sun. **Credit** AmEx, MC, V.

One of London's best wine merchants: you'll look in vain for any weakness in the

Top five
Online wine merchants

Berry Bros & Rudd
www.bbr.com. *See also pxxx.*

Stone, Vine & Sun
www.stonevine.co.uk.

Swig
www.swig.co.uk.

Vinceremos
www.vinceremos.co.uk.

The Wine Society
www.thewinesociety.com.

Wimbledon list. At every price level it buys with a keen eye for quality and value. For those with a big budget and a taste for mature wines, there are several decade-old Piemontese heavyweights. For the rest of us, there are good things starting at a fiver. France and Italy make up most of the list, but some of the most interesting stuff comes from Australia.
For branches see index.

Winery

4 Clifton Road, W9 1SS (7286 6475/www.thewineryuk.com). Warwick Avenue tube. **Open** 11am-9.30pm Mon-Sat; noon-8pm Sun. **Credit** MC, V.
The Winery thinks small and personal: small producers, and personal relationships developed over years of trading. You'll look in vain for famous names – the emphasis is on individuality and quality, not brand recognition. It specialises in often forgotten German wines and Burgundy is another major strength here.

Also check out...

Balls Brothers Wine Merchants

313 Cambridge Heath Road, E2 9LQ (7739 1642/www.ballsbrothers.co.uk). Bethnal Green tube/rail. **Open** 9am-5.30pm Mon-Fri. **Credit** AmEx, MC, V.
A long-established merchant with its roots in France.

Friarwood

26 New King's Road, SW6 4ST (7736 2628/www.friarwood.com). Parson's Green tube. **Open** 10am-7pm Mon-Sat. **Credit** AmEx, DC, MC, V.
Majoring on Bordeaux and Burgundy, with smaller efforts in the rest of France, some good Italians and quite a decent collection from South Africa, Friarwood is a good place for a special bottle if you live in the area and don't mind spending £15 or more.
For branch see index.

Majestic

63 Chalk Farm Road, NW1 8AN (7485 0478/www.majestic.co.uk). Chalk Farm tube. **Open** 10am-8pm Mon-Fri; 9am-7pm Sat; 10am-5pm Sun. **Credit** AmEx, DC, MC, V.
Minimum purchase is one case; multi-buy prices are a strong feature.
Branches: throughout the city.

Nicolas

157B Great Portland Street, W1W 6QR (7580 1622/www.nicolas-wines.com). Great Portland Street tube. **Open** 10am-8pm Mon-Fri; noon-7pm Sat. **Credit** AmEx, MC, V.
France is a speciality – as you would expect from a French-owned company.
Branches: throughout the city.

Six Wines Eight

100-102 Tower Bridge Road, SE1 4TP (7231 4477/www.sixwineseight.com). London Bridge tube/rail. **Open** 11am-8pm Mon; 11am-9pm Tue-Fri; 11am-8pm Sat. **Credit** MC, V.
Like Wine of Course (*see below*) this tiny new shop in Bermondsey stocks only 48 wines at any time, and they're divided by taste and style rather than country or grape. Categories include, for example, 'crisp aromatic, vibrant' or 'juicy, round, easy'. Tastings are held every Tuesday evening.

Theatre of Wine

75 Trafalgar Road, SE10 9TS (8858 6363/www.theatreofwine.com). Cutty Sark DLR/Maze Hill rail. **Open** 10am-9pm Mon-Sat; noon-6pm Sun. **Credit** AmEx, DC, MC, V.
An enterprising shop with a sizeable and interesting list, much of it over £10.

El Vino

47 Fleet Street, EC4Y IBJ (7353 6786/www.elvino.co.uk). Chancery Lane or Temple tube/Blackfriars tube/rail. **Open** 8.30am-9pm Mon; 8.30am-10pm Tue-Fri. **Credit** AmEx, MC, V.
Attached to the renowned wine bar, there's a pretty good choice here under £8.
For branches see index.

Wine of Course

216 Archway Road, N6 5AX (8347 9006/www.zelas.co.uk/www.easy-wine.co.uk). Highgate or Archway tube. **Open** 11am-9pm Mon-Sat; noon-7pm Sun. **Credit** AmEx, MC, V.
This sleek little place stocks just 48 well-chosen wines, organised stylistically.

Spirits & beer

Cadenhead's Whisky Shop London

26 Chiltern Street, W1U 7QF (7935 6999). Baker Street tube. **Open** 11am-8pm Mon-Wed; 11am-6.30pm **Credit** DC, MC, V.
Cadenhead's is an independent whisky bottler, choosing top barrels of aged single malts from all over Scotland and bottling them separately. They're also bottled at cask strength (without dilution) so alcohol levels can be as high as 60%.

Gerry's

74 Old Compton Street, W1D 4UW (7734 4215/www.gerrys.uk.com). Leicester Square or Piccadilly Circus tube. **Open** 9am-6.30pm Mon-Thur; 9am-8pm Fri; 9am-9pm Sat. **Credit** MC, V.
A London institution with a warehouse-worth of spirits packed into its tiny Soho quarters. It has all the names you know, and dozens that you don't, including 200 vodkas and rums, plus 120 tequilas. And its selection of oddities is unrivalled. English elderflower vodka? Bulgarian rakia? The fun is in the browsing.

Milroy's of Soho

3 Greek Street, W1D 4NX (7437 9311/www.milroys.co.uk). Tottenham Court Road tube. **Open** 10am-7pm Mon-Sat. **Credit** AmEx, MC, V.
Milroy's is a whisky-lover's heaven. The range is enormous, with around 400 from Scotland alone. There's a large selection from £14.95 and fine and rare whiskies can cost up to £2,500 including some of Milroy's own bottlings. Other spirits are covered too, with carefully selected Cognac and Armagnac. Milroy's is now part of the Jeroboams group (*see p254*).

Algerian Coffee Stores. *See p256.*

FOOD & DRINK

Real Ale Shop

371 Richmond Road, Twickenham, Middx TW1 2EF (8892 3710/www.realale.com). Richmond tube or Twickenham rail. **Open** noon-8pm Mon-Thur; 11am-9pm Fri; 10am-9pm Sat; 11am-7pm Sun. **Credit** MC, V.

This shop sells a compact but outstanding sampling – around 100 beers, ales, ciders and perries – that takes in not just Europe but the USA as well. Join its Ale Club to have a case delivered to your door each month.

Vintage House

42 Old Compton Street, W1D 4LR (7437 2592/www.vintagehouse.co.uk). Leicester Square or Piccadilly Circus tube. **Open** 9am-11pm Mon-Fri; 9.30am-11pm Sat; noon-10pm Sun. **Credit** AmEx, DC, MC, V.

The country's largest selection of Scotch whisky. There are some 1,300 lines and a dazzling range is covered. The selection stretches to fine groups of Bourbon and rum, an excellent wine list, and liqueurs.

Also check out...

Fuller, Smith & Turner

The Griffin Brewery, Chiswick Lane South, W4 2QB (8996 2085/www.fullers.co.uk). Turnham Green tube. **Open** 10am-6pm Mon-Fri; 10am-5pm Sat. **Credit** AmEx, MC, V.

London's best beers, direct from the brewers.

Royal Mile Whiskies

3 Bloomsbury Street, WC1B 3QE (7436 4763/www.royalmilewhiskies.com). Holborn or Tottenham Court Road tube. **Open** 10am-6pm Mon-Sat; noon-5pm Sun. **Credit** MC, V.

A small Scottish enclave in Bloomsbury, Royal Mile has an enormous selection of single malts at every price level.

Tea & coffee

Algerian Coffee Stores

52 Old Compton Street, W1V 6PB (7437 2480/www.algcoffee.co.uk). Leicester Square or Piccadilly Circus tube. **Open** 9am-7pm Mon-Wed; 9am-9pm Thur, Fri; 9am-8pm Sat. **Credit** AmEx, DC, MC, V.

See p245 **Enduring loves**.

Camden Coffee Shop

11 Delancey Street, NW1 7NL (7387 4080). Camden Town tube. **Open** 9.30am-5.30pm Mon-Wed, Fri, Sat; 9.30am-2.30pm Thur. **No credit cards.**

The Camden Coffee Shop's been here since 1978. Roasting is done on the premises by owner George Constantinou, who sticks to a small range of six or seven coffees at a time. Prices are low, atmosphere is low-key. A lovely little bit of old London.

HR Higgins

79 Duke Street, W1K 5AS (7629 3913/ www.hrhiggins.co.uk). Bond Street tube. **Open** 9.30am-5.30pm Mon-Fri; 10am-5pm Sat. **Credit** AmEx, MC, V.

HR Higgins is a family-run firm with a deep commitment to quality in both tea and coffee. Teas include some Chinese rarities alongside a full range of both loose tea and teabags. Prices are on the steep side, as you would expect from a holder of a royal warrant (for coffee) operating in Mayfair.

Monmouth Coffee House

27 Monmouth Street, WC2H 9EU (7379 3516/www.monmouthcoffee.co.uk). Covent Garden tube. **Open** 8am-6.30pm Mon-Sat. **Credit** DC, MC, V.

Founded 30 years ago, Monmouth sets itself daunting standards for quality and ethical trading, and meets them consistently. This is pre-eminently a place for single-estate and co-operative coffees. You'll always be able to find a good Kenyan coffee here, and Central and South America are represented by excellent ranges. Founder Anita Le Roy is an industry leader in the campaign to help growers improve quality and earn higher prices. The original shop-café in Covent Garden is tiny and cosy; the Borough space is larger.

For branch see index.

Postcard Teas

9 Dering Street, W1S 1AG (7629 3654/ www.postcardteas.com). Bond Street or Oxford Circus tube. **Open** 10.30am-6.30pm Tue-Sat. **Credit** AmEx, MC, V.

Whether you're looking for black, white or green tea, you'll find intriguingly unusual examples here. Postcard takes pride in its support for high-quality estates in Sri Lanka and elsewhere. Also check out the interesting teas from China and Japan. You can sit and have a pot while you choose.

Also check out...

Angelucci Coffee Merchants

472 Long Lane, East Finchley, N2 8JL (8444 9211/www.angeluccicoffee.co.uk). East Finchley tube. **Open** 9am-4pm Mon-Fri. **No credit cards.**

A tiny, old-fashioned survivor selling a large range of beans. Angelucci supplies the renowned Bar Italia.

Drury Tea & Coffee Company

3 New Row, WC2N 4LH (7836 1960/ www.drury.uk.com). Leicester Square tube. **Open** 9am-6pm Mon-Fri; 11am-5pm Sat. **Credit** MC, V.

Founded in 1936, Drury is strongest on blends in every style of roasting, from light to high. Its range of teas is outstanding.

R Twining

216 Strand, WC2R 1AP (7353 3511/ www.twinings.com). Temple tube. **Open** 9am-5pm Mon-Fri. **Credit** AmEx, MC, V.

The retail outlet for this ancient firm (founded in 1706) includes a tea museum.

Tea & Coffee Plant

180 Portobello Road, W11 2EB (7221 8137/www.coffee.uk.com). Ladbroke Grove tube. **Open** 9am-4.30pm daily. **Credit** MC, V.

The emphasis is on organic and Fairtrade.

Whittard of Chelsea

203-205 Brompton Road, SW3 1LA (7581 4767/www.whittard.co.uk). Knightsbridge or South Kensington tube. **Open** 10am-7.30pm Mon-Sat; 10am-7pm Sun. **Credit** AmEx, DC, MC, V.

A smallish selection of coffees, a more extensive choice of teas. Everything is good.

Branches: throughout the city.

Cigars & tobacco

Davidoff of London

35 St James's Street, SW1A 1HD (7930 3079/www.davidoffoflondon.com). Green Park tube. **Open** 9am-6pm Mon-Fri; 9.30-6pm Sat. **Credit** AmEx, DC, MC, V.

The quintessential London cigar store, stocking the widest range of Habanos. There are some 17 lines of Cubans here such as Cohiba Robustos (£19.50 each) and Montecristo No.4s (£9.20 each); also popular is the Romeo y Julieta Corona (£11.50 each). The Davidoff handmade range is worth sampling: try the 2000 Tubos (£12.20 each).

G Smith & Sons

74 Charing Cross Road, WC2H 0BG (7836 7422). Leicester Square tube. **Open** 9am-6pm Mon-Fri; 9.30am-5.30pm Sat. **Credit** AmEx, MC, V.

The smoking ban hasn't stopped business from booming at G Smith. Established in 1869, it was the first licensed tobacconist on this road and its site can legally only house a tobacconist. The walk-in humidor holds a plethora of cigars including the Carlos Torano and La Invicta brands plus Puros Indios and Te-Amo lines. Pipe and roll-your-own smokers can choose from 50 blends of loose tobacco; snuff is also sold.

JJ Fox

19 St James's Street, SW1A 1ES (7930 3787/www.jjfox.co.uk). Green Park tube. **Open** 9am-6pm Mon-Fri; 9am-5.30pm Sat. **Credit** AmEx, DC, MC, V.

A prestigious, family-owned tobacconist with expert and enthusiastic staff. Among the 20 Cuban brands are the popular Montecristo No.4s (£10 each) and Bolivar Belicosos (£15 each). The great pipe selection features Dunhill and Meerschaum models.

Also check out...

La Casa del Habano

100 Wardour Street, W1F 0TN (7314 4001/www.lacasadelhabano.co.uk). Tottenham Court Road tube. **Open** noon-11pm Mon-Sat. **Credit** AmEx, DC, MC, V.

Elegant cigar shop/cocktail bar with a walk-in humidor housing one of the biggest ranges of Cuban cigars in the UK.

Segar & Snuff Parlour

27A The Market, Covent Garden, WC2E 8RD (7836 8345/www.davy.co.uk/segarandsnuffparlour). Covent Garden tube. **Open** 10.30am-7pm Mon-Wed; 10.30am-8pm Thur-Sat; 11am-5pm Sun. **Credit** AmEx, DC, MC, V.

This tiny shop features over 70 variations of Havana cigar – and four kinds of snuff.

Shervingtons

337-338 High Holborn, WC1V 7PX (7405 2929). Chancery Lane tube. **Open** 9am-6pm Mon-Fri. **Credit** AmEx, DC, MC, V.

Tobacco and accessories.

Tomtom

63 Elizabeth Street, SW1W 9PP (7730 1790/ www.tomtom.co.uk). Sloane Square tube/ Victoria tube/rail. **Open** 10am-6pm Mon-Fri; 10am-5pm Sat. **Credit** AmEx, MC, V.

Tomtom stocks the best of Cuban cigars.

Babies & Children

Babies & Children

Petit Aimé (also left). *See p265.*

Victoria Park Books (also right). *See p261.*

Puppet Planet (also right). *See p268.*

Babies & Children

All-rounders & gifts

Bump to 3 (0844 557 3007/www.bumpto3.com) sells a range of great products for pregnant mums and suckling babes, **Aspen & Brown** (0845 371 1171, www.aspenandbrown.com) is the place to head for baby-welcoming and christening gifts and **Couverture** (*see p19*) sells stylish clothes for children, as well as accessories and toys.

Bob & Blossom

140 Columbia Road, E2 7RG (7739 4737/www.bobandblossom.com). Old Street tube/rail/55 bus. **Open** 9am-3pm Sun. **Credit** MC, V.

Dear little knitted and crocheted animals, smart toy cars, spinning tops and bike horns, romper suits and sweetly logoed T-shirts – the selection at B&B is eclectic. The shop does a roaring trade despite being open just six hours a week to coincide with the popular Sunday flower market.

Buggies & Bikes

23 Broadway Market, E8 4PH (7241 5382/www.buggiesandbikes.net). London Fields rail. **Open** 10am-6.30pm Mon-Sat; 11am-5pm Sun. **Credit** MC, V.

Broadway Market – the most bohemian of Hackney's streets – attracts young families in their droves (particularly on Saturdays, when the market's in full swing), so this pleasant little shop makes the most of passing trade. As well as the buggies and bikes referenced in the shop's name – consisting of innovative double buggies and wooden, pedal-free starter bikes – the stock is made up of unusual pieces of nursery equipment, clothes for babies to 12-year-olds and a range of covetable toys. The proprietor is keen to display the knitwear and needlework of local designers; there are some delightful little cardigans for babies, fine print dresses for toddlers and colourful silky sarongs for small girls. Downstairs, the basement is given over to baby and toddler activities (drama, yoga, baby massage) and can be hired out for parties, along with the little courtyard garden.

Finnesse (eco)

453 Roman Road, E3 5LX (8983 9286/www.finnesselifestyle.com). Bethnal Green tube/rail, then 8 bus. **Open** 9.30am-6pm Mon-Sat. **Credit** AmEx, MC, V.

Finnesse houses a dainty selection of both organic and fair trade children's clothes and toys from around the world alongside womenswear and a small selection of home furnishings. Designs and materials hail from all over the place: Sri Lanka, South Africa, Bangladesh, Peru and Finland are some of the locations for interesting labels including Marimekko, Lanka, Leela, Kade, Noo Noo and Turquaz stocked alongside higher profile names like Nomads, People Tree and Hug.

Igloo

300 Upper Street, N1 2TU (7354 7300/www.iglookids.co.uk). Angel tube/Highbury & Islington tube/rail. **Open** 10am-6.30pm Mon-Wed; 10am-7pm Thur; 9.30am-6.30pm Fri, Sat; 11am-5.30pm Sun. **Credit** AmEx, MC, V.

Igloo's highly original range of toys, clothes and accessories is sourced by two mothers with limitless savoir-faire. Shelves of toys reach to the ceiling. Indoor favourites include inventive educational ideas for bright sparks, such as ant and worm farms and telescopes. Make your way through these plus bundles of lovely and wearable clothes for babies and children up to eight, to the back of the shop. Here there's a spacious Start-rite shoe corner with plenty of seating and another area with more clothes from the likes of Petit Bateau and Mini-a-Ture, plus fancy-dress outfits. There's a mirrored area for children's haircuts, a table for reading and drawing, party essentials and a gift-wrapping service too.

For branch see index.

JoJo Maman Bébé (eco)

68 Northcote Road, SW11 6QL (7228 0322/www.jojomamanbebe.co.uk). Clapham Junction rail. **Open** 9.30am-5.30pm Mon-Sat; 11am-5pm Sun. **Credit** MC, V.

This is still primarily a catalogue-based retailer, but its small network of boutiques (selling clothing, accessories, equipment and furniture) operates in child-dense areas. The distinctive pregnancy and childrenswear is relaxed and affordable, and includes bright, stripey fleeces, sweatshirts and easy-wash cottons, plus a great range of maternity wear. The company adheres to a strong code of ethical practice, exemplified by the organic cotton baby clothes and the Polartec fleeces made from recycled plastic bottles. JoJo also supports Nema, a charity in Mozambique.

For branches see index.

Little White Company

90 Marylebone High Street, W1U 4QZ (7486 7550/www.thewhitecompany.com). Baker Street or Bond Street tube. **Open** 10am-7pm Mon-Sat; 11am-5pm Sun. **Credit** AmEx, MC, V.

Snowy cotton soft furnishings, achromatic nightwear and bedlinen and icy-white painted wooden nursery furniture provide a suitably pure background for classic striped towelling beach hoodies in navy and pink, floral quilts, daisy swimwear and cute babygros and rompers. Baby sleeping bags in pink or blue are a popular line, as are the gift bags for newborns, containing a snowy babygro, swaddling blanket and hat, all stowed away in a little organza bag (£28). One of the nicest lines for babies and children around.

For branch see index.

Semmalina-Starbags

225 Ebury Street, SW1W 8UT (7730 9333/www.starbags.info). Sloane Square tube. **Open** 9.30am-5.30pm Mon-Sat. **Credit** AmEx, MC, V.

Semmalina's starbags are fantasy party bags wrapped in crackling cellophane and garlanded with bright ribbons. The stuff to fill them is arranged all around this shop. The neon-lit sweetie selection catches the eye on entering, but party bags can have more than sweets – bubbles, putty, bouncy balls, hair trinkets, stationery and more. Out of party bag territory there are gift boxes for new babies, Mamma Mio hospital pampering kits for women reaching the nine-month deadline, Mini-a-Ture fashions for children and nostalgic toys.

For branch see index.

Soup Dragon

27 Topsfield Parade, Tottenham Lane, N8 8PT (8348 0224/www.soup-dragon.co.uk). Finsbury Park tube/rail, then 41, W7 bus. **Open** 9.30am-6pm Mon-Sat; 11am-5pm Sun. **Credit** AmEx, MC, V.

The original, happy, hippie, splendidly tot-friendly all-rounder consists of a long, antique space with a stained-glass skylight and wonky wooden floors. The Dragon continues to draw in the majority of Crouch End's young families, and its frequent warehouse sales (see website for details) are not be missed. There's a lovely little play area and toy kitchen, a wide range of toys and dressing-up kit and attractive and affordable stripy knits for both babies and toddlers. To add to the Soup Dragon label there are rompers and play clothes from Katvig, Salty Dog and Freoli. Classic toys from LaMaze, Pintoy and Tomy, plus covetable one-offs such as rocking horses and dolls' houses, look the part in a typical Crouch End dwelling.

For branch see index.

Trotters

34 King's Road, SW3 4UD (7259 9620/www.trotters.co.uk). Sloane Square tube. **Open** 9am-7pm Mon-Sat; 10.30am-6.30pm Sun. **Credit** AmEx, MC, V.

Aways a pleasure to trot round, this children's shop of many parts has clothes, toys, accessories, toiletries, shoes, books and a hairdressing station (from £13). The clothes are adorable, with print dresses from Chelsea Clothing Company and stripy tops and cotton shorts from Petit Breton. There are insulated lunch packs and wheelie suitcases, Nitty Gritty headcare treatments and organic suncreams; the shoes at the back are Start-rite and the hairdressing station has a large tank of fish to distract the small clients.

For branches see index.

Top five Old-school toys

Cheeky Monkeys: Noah's Arks. *See p267.*

Honeyjam: wooden Agas. *See p267.*

Kristin Baybars: dolls' houses. *See p268.*

Petit Chou: wooden bricks. *See p267.*

Ringinglow Rocking Horse Company: rocking horses. 0800 074 6104, www.dapplegrey.co.uk.

Victoria Park Books

Also check out…

Mothercare

526-528 Oxford Street, W1C 1LW (7629 6621/www.mothercare.com). Marble Arch tube. **Open** 10am-8pm Mon-Sat; noon-6pm Sun. **Credit** AmEx, MC, V.

A three-floored branch of the parents' saviour where you will find all the basics, including a wide range of inexpensive baby clothes, everything for that first mad dash and most of the things you'll need later.

Branches: throughout the city.

Pure Baby

208 Fulham Road, SW10 9PJ (7751 5544/www.purebaby.co.uk). Fulham Broadway or South Kensington tube, then bus. **Open** 10am-6.30pm Mon-Wed, Fri, Sat; 10am-7pm Thur; noon-6pm Sun. **Credit** AmEx, MC, V.

Pricey but gorgeous baby clothes, prams, nursery furniture, accessories, toys and a lovely selection of gifts are beautifully laid out in this gleaming, shop.

Books

Many of the bookshops listed in the **Books** chapter stock children's titles; *see p177.*

Bookworm

1177 Finchley Road, NW11 0AA (8201 9811/www.thebookworm.uk.com). Golders Green tube. **Open** 9.30am-5.30pm Mon-Sat; 10am-1.30pm Sun. **Credit** MC, V.

This is a much-loved specialist children's bookshop with private spaces conducive to sampling and testing the merchandise. The stock is exemplary, and twice-weekly storytelling sessions for under-fives are held on Tuesdays and Thursdays (2pm), when badges and stickers are handed out.

Children's Bookshop

29 Fortis Green Road, N10 3HP (8444 5500). Highgate tube, then 43, 134 bus. **Open** 9.15am-5.45pm Mon-Sat; 11am-4pm Sun. **Credit** AmEx, MC, V.

Everyone was eagerly awaiting a visit from Maisy when we last visited this top specialist bookshop, renowned for its knowledgeable and interested staff. The celebrity mouse is just one of many famous characters and authors from the world of children's literature who drop by for book signings.

Lion & Unicorn

19 King Street, Richmond, Surrey TW9 1ND (8940 0483/www.lionunicornbooks.co.uk). Richmond tube/rail. **Open** 9.30am-5.30pm Mon-Fri; 9.30am-6pm Sat; 11am-5pm Sun. **Credit** MC, V.

'The Roar', the quarterly newsletter produced by this lovely bookshop, is an invaluable source of news about upcoming book signings, special author (and other) events as well as book reviews. The reading matter, crammed into the various rooms of this exciting shop, is diverse, and caters for all ages. Jacqueline Wilson and Anthony Horowitz are just two names that have popped in for signings.

Victoria Park Books

174 Victoria Park Road, E9 7HD (8986 1124/www.victoriaparkbooks.co.uk). Mile End tube/Bethnal Green tube/rail. **Open** 10am-5.30pm daily. **Credit** MC, V.

This amiable bookshop has a true community feel, with one wall featuring book reviews from local school children. Books are categorised by look and feel as well as content – there's a section for interactive titles, and children can get their hands on cloth, bath and buggy books. Teenagers and adults are also catered for – there's a strong range of parenting books, for example. Everybody's welcome to take a turn in the outside patio, and there are reading events for pre-schoolers on Tuesdays and Fridays.

Also check out...

Golden Treasury

29 Replingham Road, SW18 5LT (8333 0167/www.thegoldentreasury.co.uk). Southfields tube. **Open** 9.30am-6pm Mon-Fri; 9.30am-5.30pm Sat; 10.30am-4.30pm Sun. **Credit** MC, V.

An infant-friendly bookshop, with themed cabinets full of favourites. There's plenty of reading matter for teens too.

Never Ending Story Bookshop

59 North Cross Road, SE22 9ET (8693 0123/www.theneverendingstorybookshop.com). East Dulwich rail. **Open** 10am-5.30pm Tue-Fri; 10am-6pm Sat. **Credit** MC, V.

This neat bookshop is also the HQ of Future Matters, a family welfare consultancy for parenting programmes and play therapy.

Tales on Moon Lane

25 Half Moon Lane, SE24 9JU (7274 5759/www.talesonmoonlane.co.uk). Herne Hill rail/3, 37, 68 bus. **Open** 9.15am-5.45pm Mon-Fri; 9.30am-6pm Sat;11am-4pm Sun. **Credit** MC, V.

This lovely shop's storytelling sessions are a sweet affair. The back room has substantial reading matter for older children.

Equipment & accessories

Good website and mail-order sites include **lula sapphire** (0870 850 7541, www.lulasapphire.com), which sells eco-friendly, design-conscious items; the **Children's Furniture Company** (7737 7303, www.thechildrensfurniturecompany.com), for kids' study furniture; and **Urchin** (0844 573 6006, www.urchin.co.uk), selling fab accessories.

Aspace

140 Chiswick High Road, W4 1PU (8994 5814/www.aspaceuk.com). Turnham Green tube. **Open** 10am-6pm Mon-Sat; 11am-5pm Sun. **Credit** AmEx, MC, V.

This range of distinctive, co-ordinating furniture can be seen in all its glory here. The nursery can be kitted out Aspace-wise with beds (first, raised, bunk, sleepover truckles), handsome wardrobes, chests of drawers and bedroom furnishings. There's a concession in Heal's.

Born (eco)

168 Stoke Newington Church Street, N16 0JL (7249 5069/www.borndirect.com). Finsbury Park tube/rail, then 106 bus/ 73, 393, 476 bus. **Open** 9.30am-5.30pm Tue-Sat; noon-5pm Sun. **Credit** MC, V.

A calm, nurturing space with kind staff, specialising in pregnancy products, plus baby equipment, toys and clothes, Born has an organic and fair trade ethos, right down to cotton nappies. Attractions include organic baby clothes (Star range by Kate Goldsmith); toiletries and massage oils by Weleda, Green People and Born Naked (Born's own brand). Toys are made from renewable materials, products include the attractive Keptin-Jr Organic Comforter, and trendy baby transport systems include the Stokke Xplory buggy, Phil & Ted's Explorer, Bugaboo and Bee, plus Cameleon and Gecko. There's plenty of play space for lively tots, and a comfy sofa for breastfeeding. Born's network of support extends to a weekly mother's meeting on Mondays, plus parenting and breastfeeding groups.

Chic Shack

77 Lower Richmond Road, SW15 1ET (8785 7777/www.chicshack.net). Putney Bridge tube, then 14, 22 bus. **Open** 9.30am-6pm Mon-Sat. **Credit** MC, V.

The romantic and refined white-painted furniture and soft furnishings for children's rooms smack of clean living but without overdosing on formality. There are pink and pale blue floral or striped accessories and linens, but nothing is too sugary. Little extras, such as knitted bears and linen bags, pile on the charm.

Dragons of Walton Street

23 Walton Street, SW3 2HX (7589 3795/ www.dragonsofwaltonstreet.com). Knightsbridge or South Kensington tube. **Open** 9.30am-5.30pm Mon-Fri; 10am-5pm Sat. **Credit** AmEx, MC, V.

Rosie Fisher's hand-painted furniture for the nursery comes with all sorts of child favourites: bunnies, boats, soldiers, fairies, pirate mice and vintage roses. Customers are also encouraged to come up with their own ideas for designs. Dragons is a pleasant place to visit; staff are friendly, the mood relaxed and personal service is guaranteed. Curtains, cots, sofas, chaises longues and tiny chairs are made to order, as are the special artwork beds, for which you can expect to pay around £2,000. Personalised chairs and pretty quilts are more affordable. Handsome, traditional toys are also sold.

Lilliput

255-259 Queenstown Road, SW8 3NP (7720 5554/0800 783 0886/www.lilliput.com). Queenstown Road rail. **Open** 9.30am-5.30pm Mon, Tue, Thur, Fri; 9.30am-7pm Wed; 9am-6pm Sat; 11am-4pm Sun. **Credit** MC, V.

An extensive (900sq ft) one-stop baby shop underneath the railway arches, Lilliput has the biggest range of stock around, with collections from Mamas & Papas, Phil & Ted, Britax, Stokke and Bugaboo. As well as the latest crazes in inline buggies for double trouble, there are simple strollers and buggies for quick-folding. All the baby bathing, changing, dressing, entertaining, feeding and sleeping paraphernalia that parents feel they need are present. In fact, Lilliput and latest baby guru Gina Ford have put together a Baby Needs List for those last heady shopping days before the birth. A Crave maternity wear concession ensures a well-dressed bump.

Mamas & Papas

256-258 Regent Street, W1B 3AF (0845 268 2000/www.mamasandpapas.co.uk). Oxford Circus tube. **Open** 10am-8pm Mon-Wed, Fri; 10am-9pm Thur; 9am-8pm Sat; noon-6pm Sun. **Credit** AmEx, MC, V.

Always a calm and collected place to shop, the ylang-ylang scented air of the M&P flagship soothes anxious parent-to-be shoppers. It has a delightfully friendly team of staff and presents an irresistible picture of nursery bliss. There are large changing rooms for bump and buggy manoeuvres while trying on the modish and affordable range of maternity fashions and lingerie. A large selection of baby transport options, the company's stock in trade, range from simple strollers to complete systems (about £399). A series of 'dream nursery' room sets displays useful furniture in all shapes and sizes. Cibo, the soothing café on the first floor, has terrific coffee and pastries, as well as a popular lunch menu for parents and children, loads of high chairs and yet more delightful, patient staff.

For branch see index.

Mini Kin (eco)

22 Broadway Parade, N8 9DE (8341 6898). Finsbury Park tube/rail, then 41, W7 bus. **Open** 9.30am-5.30pm Mon-Sat; 10.30am-4.30pm Sun. **Credit** MC, V.

Your little darling can be tricked out and primped in sustainable, organic fashion at this well-established and reliable infant all-rounder. The atmosphere is heady with the scent of eco-friendly bathtime unguents by Organic Babies, Aviva and Burt's Bees. Primping is done in the colourful and fun hairdressing salon. Clothing-wise, Mini Kin is strong on the range by Dutch company Imps & Elfs, which was committed to sustainably produced fashion long before it became fashionable; quirky little rompers, dresses, sweats and knits in attractively muted colours make up the collection. A range by Baby Organic uses only 100% organic cotton.

Natural Mat Company (eco)

99 Talbot Road, W11 2AT (7985 0474/ www.naturalmat.co.uk). Ladbroke Grove or Notting Hill Gate tube. **Open** 10am-6pm Mon-Fri; 10am-4pm Sat. **Credit** MC, V.

Renowned for mattresses made of all natural materials, such as organic coir, latex straight from the rubber tree and unbleached cotton, Natural Mat makes for a toxin-free nursery environment. Infants may safely snooze under quilts, sheets and pillows in duck down and lambs' wool and unbleached cotton, babies can forget about kicked-off sheet misery in sleeping bags that come in pink, blue, white and natural in lightweight organic cotton or cotton fleece for winter. There are also lambskin fleeces, Welsh wool blankets and West Country willow cribs.

Blue Daisy

13 South End Road, NW3 2PT (7681 4144/www.blue-daisy.com). Hampstead Heath rail or Belsize Park tube. **Open** 9.30am-5.30pm Mon-Fri; 10am-5.30pm Sat. **Credit** AmEx, MC, V.

A typically stylish Hampstead baby boutique, Blue Daisy has adorable clothes (Mokopuna, Blue Day, Swaddle Designs, Togz), toys and accessories for babies to toddlers. The stock – organic and Fairtrade where applicable – is loaded with style and ingenuity. It's also well presented; children make straight for the toys alcove to play with the traditional wooden cookers by Tiny Love. Innovative home accessories include the new Kaboost chair booster, the bestselling Cuddledry towels and the Mini-Micro Scooters.

Nursery Window

83 Walton Street, SW3 2HP (7581 3358/ www.nurserywindow.co.uk). Knightsbridge or South Kensington tube. **Open** 10am-6pm Mon-Sat. **Credit** AmEx, MC, V.

Soft, beautiful furnishings for the new arrival's room, including cots, rocking chairs, Moses baskets, pillowcases and cashmere blankets. The enchanting cashmere matinée jackets, little trousers, boottees and dresses hand-knitted by Sue Hill make superior welcome presents.

Rub a Dub Dub

15 Park Road, N8 8TE (8342 9898). Finsbury Park tube/rail, then 41, W7 bus. **Open** 10am-5.30pm Mon-Fri; 9.30am-5.30pm Sat; 11.30am-4pm Sun. **Credit** AmEx, MC, V.

Nature's Nest, the dangling travelcot loved by celebrity parents, is a bestseller at RaDD, always up to the minute with its stock. The knowledgeable owner dispenses advice about the latest fashions in baby transport and nursery equipment with alacrity. Top pram systems are still the ever-popular Mountain Buggy and the Phil & Ted double decker. The last word in weather protection is Outlook's Shade-a-babe, a pushchair cover offering UV protection. For indoors there's the posture-reforming Tripp Trapp high chair (£145) and fun things like wheely bugs in ladybird and bumblebee shapes. Every conceivable brand of eco-friendly nappy and bottom cream is stocked. Look out for the always reliable Kooshies and and typically green German Moltex nappies: 30% gel, 70% biodegradable and entirely free of bleach.

Also check out...

Babyworld

239 Munster Road, SW6 6BT (7386 1904). Fulham Broadway tube, then 211, 295 bus. **Open** 10am-6pm Mon-Wed, Fri; 10am-5.30pm Sat. **Credit** AmEx, MC, V.

Cutting edge chic baby transport systems (Bugaboo convertibles, mountain buggies, dual systems), plus nursery equipment.

Velorution

18 Great Titchfield Street, W1W 8BD (7637 4004/www.velorution.biz). **Open** 9am-7pm Mon-Fri; 10.30am-6.30pm Sat. **Credit** MC, V.

Clever name, brilliant attitude, this family transport specialist shows that two wheels (sometimes three) are most definitely good.

Petit Aimé. *See p265.*

Fashion

Blossom Mother & Child (*see p66*) is a good bet for baby clothes while **Planet Boo** (01847 611777, www.planetboo.co.uk) does band T-shirts for rocker sprogs; **Snuglo** (7267 8533, www.snuglo.com) and **No Added Sugar** (7226 2323, www.noaddedsugar.co.uk) also sell a bold range of statement Tees, or you can head for the **Woolshed** (8444 8529, www.woolshed.co.uk) for hand-knitted clothes made from natural fibres. **Young England** (0845 055 9722, www.youngengland.com) kits out bridesmaids, page boys and children celebrating their first holy communion – you can visit the showroom by appointment.

Many high street clothes stores have decent children's lines, with reliable favourites including **Gap Kids**, **H&M**, **Jigsaw Junior**, **Monsoon**, **Zara** and **Comptoir des Cotonniers**; *see pp45-47*.

Many shops listed in the **Maternity** chapter sell baby togs; *see p66*.

Amaia

14 Cale Street, SW3 3QU (7590 0999/ www.amaia-kids.com). Sloane Square or South Kensington tube. **Open** 10am-6pm Mon-Sat. **Credit** MC, V.

'Fresh, elegant, easy to wear' is the Amaia theme. Clothes for children up to eight are unmistakeably continental (French/ Spanish in equal measure) and simplicity and classicism is key; there's no room for mini-me swank here. Hence you'll find shift dresses with four pretty buttons and piping, delicate cardies and skirts for the girls and cotton shorts and button-down shirts for boys. Winter brings in warm, woollen coats and soft jumpers and cords. Prices are middling to expensive. A cotton dress for a five-year-old costs between £40 and £60.

Aravore Babies (eco)

31 Park Road, N8 8TE (8347 5752/ www.aravore-babies.com). Highgate tube/ Crouch Hill rail/41, 91, W5, W7 bus. **Open** 10am-5.30pm Mon-Sat; noon-4.30pm Sun. **Credit** MC, V.

Distinctive, delectable fashions for babies from Aravore aren't cheap, but they'll be much appreciated as gifts for new parents. The crocheted and knitted organic clothes go up to age five. A visit to the shop reveals much to coo over: beautiful handcrafted cream knits in merino wool include gorgeous tops, dresses, mittens and booties, nestling alongside soft shawls and blankets. The spring/summer range is all organic cotton. Aravore also stocks other organic ranges like Green Baby, Tatty Bumpkin and Bamboo Baby. There are skincare products from Earth Mama Angel Baby, and a baby wish-list service too.

Biff

41-43 Dulwich Village, SE21 7BN (8299 0911). North Dulwich rail/P4 bus. **Open** 9.30am-5.30pm Mon-Fri; 10am-6pm Sat. **Credit** AmEx, MC, V.

Wide-ranging stock and a family-friendly café next door make this a village hub. It takes up two shops. At no.41 there's a wide shoe selection for all ages from many brands, including Lelli Kelly, Ricosta, Crocs, Geox and Start-rite. Clothes for boys aged two to 12, with the 14-16 age group catered for at the back, are also sold here. Expect labels such as Bench, O'Neill, Quiksilver, French Connection and Roxy for the girls. In no.43 it's the babies' turn. There are Grobags, socks, babysuits and swimwear (including confidence floats). Clothes for children aged up to two include IKKS, Weekend a la Mer, Freoli and Catimini, with top togs from Pepe Jeans, Powell & Craft as well as Roxy and French Connection for the girls (2-12).

Bonpoint

15 Sloane Street, SW1X 9NB (7235 1441/ www.bonpoint.com). Knightsbridge tube. **Open** 10am-6pm Mon-Sat. **Credit** AmEx, MC, V.

This shop looks as gorgeous as a French farmhouse, with tasteful floorboards, faded woven rugs and vintage chairs and tables for children to crayon on. The distinctive clothes echo the enchanting Gallic fantasy. It is, naturellement, far from cheap. The beautiful knitwear, baby dresses with matching bloomers, sundresses, linen shorts, denims and floppy cotton print shirts have an effortless charm, however, with tiny jumpers costing from about £60.

For branches see index.

Bunny London

7627 2318/www.bunnylondon.com.

Debbie Bunn sews glorious children's clothes in distinctive colours, patterns and textures that make these limited-edition garments must-haves among both celebrity and ordinary parents. Pictures of Ms Moss's daughter Lila Grace in a Bunny faux fur jacket caused the most recent feeding frenzy. Items are available in baby sizes and child sizes, with dresses starting at £60. Designs are available online or at Harvey Nichols and Paul Smith.

Caramel Baby & Child

77 Ledbury Road, W11 2AG (7727 0906/ www.caramel-shop.co.uk). Notting Hill Gate or Westbourne Park tube. **Open** 10am-6pm Mon-Sat; noon-5pm Sun. **Credit** AmEx, MC, V.

The bewitching Caramel brand was started by Eva Karayiannis, whose distaste for 'mass-produced clothing covered in logos' led her to open her own shop. Her foray into designing togs for children aged 0-12 has paid dividends. The look is relaxed, not aggressively trendy but obviously well finished and fun to wear. In summer 2008, we fell in love with the Kiki cotton print sundress in a variety of colours (from £66) and striped sweaters for boys (from £54). Haircuts are available on Saturdays and Wednesdays, but should be booked ahead.

For branches see index.

Carry Me Home

Unit 2.9, Kingly Court, Carnaby Street, W1B 5PW (7434 1840/www.carryme home.co.uk). Oxford Circus tube. **Open** 11am-7pm Mon-Sat; noon-5pm Sun. **Credit** AmEx, MC, V.

It's easy to get carried away by the stock of cute and carefully eccentric baby clothes in this delightful little shop. Stocks excellent quirky knits from All the Fun of the Fair, witty babywear from Oh Baby London, glorious rompers from Brights and Stripe, dresses by Minimod and, of course, its own Carry me Home label. Some of the lines are available in bigger sizes for children up to six years old.

Elias & Grace

158 Regent's Park Road, NW1 8XN (7449 0574/www.eliasandgrace.com). Chalk Farm tube. **Open** 10am-6pm Mon-Sat; noon-6pm Sun. **Credit** MC, V.

Modish, smart and effortless, Elias & Grace has a stylish mix of high fashion, luxury accessories, lush natural products, organic remedies and perfect gifts. As well as cool maternity wear, there's a great range of designer labels from children aged 0-10. Fashion and accessories from around the world include Chloé, Marni, Quincy, Bonton, plus quality basics. Toys and books are also sold. A relaxed atmosphere, with plenty of room for pushchairs, a mini play area and friendly assistants make it a pleasure to visit.

Frère Jacques

121 Stoke Newington Church Street, NW6 0UH (7249 5655). Finsbury Park tube/rail, then 106 bus/73, 393, 476 bus. **Open** 11am-6pm Tue-Sat. **Credit** AmEx, MC, V.

The emphasis here is on both stylish but also durable design – rather than cute or delicate offerings – with equal weight being given to boys' and girls' clothing. The stock includes Scandinavian labels Norlie, Minymo and Freoli, plus French names Petit Bateau, Trois Pommes and Confetti, and a newer collection from Deglingos. The colourful animal-themed mackintoshes and brightly patterned wellies from Kidorable are stand-out items, while footwear from Italian labels Ecco and Primigi, US brand Pedi Ped and Canada's Robeez forms a sturdy shoe range.

Frogs & Fairies

69A Highbury Park, N5 1UA (7424 5159). Highbury & Islington tube/rail. **Open** 10am-5.30pm Mon-Sat; 10am-4pm Sun. **Credit** AmEx, MC, V.

A little ray of sunshine in an otherwise unremarkable parade of shops, F&F has clothes, toys, cards, presents and shoes in large measure. The shoe department has large magnetic board games as a diversion while parents choose between Start-rite, Ecco or Converse for their tots. Clothes for babies and childen up to age six include classics by Petit Bateau and more quirky delights from Katvig and Imps & Elfs. There's also the full range of Aromakids aromatherapy oils for young'uns (including the all-important, all-natural lice-splicing products) and some lovely picture books and toys. Haircuts are offered on a Saturday.

Guys & Dolls

172 Walton Street, SW3 2JL (7589 8990/ www.guysanddollsuk.com). Knightsbridge or South Kensington tube. **Open** 10am-6pm Mon-Fri; 11am-6pm Sat. **Credit** AmEx, MC, V.

It's much easier to find luxury baby and toddler wear than designer stuff for the eight to 14 age group, which is why this eclectic boutique, with its Chloé, Missoni, Sonia Rykiel, Simonetta and Little Marc Jacobs designs, goes down well with girls aged up to 14 and boys to about 12 (they can choose from Rare, Simple Kids and Joe Black). The shop has a space-age layout, with clothes attractively laid out on spiral rails. There's a garden full of beanbag chairs out back.

Jakss

463 & 469 Roman Road, E3 5LX (8981 2233/www.jakss.co.uk). Bethnal Green tube/rail, then 8 bus. **Open** 10am-5.30pm Tue-Sat. **Credit** AmEx, MC, V.

A treat to visit, Jakss has been stocking designer fashion for newborns to teens since 1977. There are two stores: no.463 is for babies to six-year-olds, with top labels; new additions include Missoni Kids, Juicy Couture Kids and Chloé Kids. Oilily is a highlight with bold accessories including covetable (and washable) changing bags, plus travel bags you'd never miss on the carousel. The two to 14 age group is catered for at no.469.

Notsobig

31A Highgate High Street, N6 5JT (8340 4455). Archway or Highgate tube. **Open** 10am-6pm Mon-Sat; 11am-5pm Sun. **Credit** AmEx, MC, V.

An adorable confection, Notsobig's current highlights include chic separates by Cacherel and cosy Woolrich arctic parkas, Pedi Ped baby shoes and trainers, and T-shirts and dresses by American Outfitters. The basement yields further favourites like pretty dresses by Antik Batik and funky printed pyjamas from Mini-a-Ture. There isn't the space to display everything available, so customers order ahead from the catalogue with prices from £40.

Oh Baby London

162 Brick Lane, E1 6RU (7247 4949/ www.ohbabylondon.com). Liverpool Street tube/rail. **Open** 11am-6pm Mon-Fri; 10am-6pm Sat, Sun. **Credit** AmEx, MC, V.

'Been inside for 9 months' reads the logo on Oh Baby's bestselling black-and-white striped babygros for newborns. The witty brand was started as 'an allergic reaction to pastels', on a mission to introduce more jaunty kit for babies and children aged to about four. That said, the new baby gift sets (bib, towel, toy, £22) come in conventional pastel pink and blue – but they're very sweet all the same. We love the stripped leggings and pack of toddler pants in bright cotton.

Olive Loves Alfie

84 Stoke Newington Church Street, N16 0AP (7241 4212/www.olivelovesalfie.co.uk). Finsbury Park tube/rail, then 106 bus/73, 393, 476 bus. **Open** 9am-5.30pm Mon-Fri; 10am-6pm Sat; 10am-5pm Sun. **Credit** AmEx, MC, V.

A boutique with a strong aesthetic, Olive Loves Alfie houses design-led clothing for newborns, children and teens. There's no clichéd kids stuff in here and the gorgeous stock is wonderfully decorative – the walls are adorned with bestselling babygros from Scandinavian designers Katvig in stylish prints evoking Orla Kiely, which fly out of the shop. The cool educational toy range includes lots of puzzles, jigsaws and games by Djeco. Fabulous monkey-print pink lampshades illuminating the shop are also for sale.

Quackers

155D Northcote Road, SW11 6QB (7978 4235). Clapham Junction rail, then 319 bus. **Open** 9.30am-5.30pm Mon-Fri; 10am-5.30pm Sat. **Credit** MC, V.

A jolly atmosphere prevails in this cheerful little children's boutique run by Veronica McNaught. A wide range of fashions and toys for babies and children aged up to ten includes smart labels such as German brand Kanz and Whoopi, with cosy coats and cardies for winterwear and Blue Fish rainwear. Toys include floppy favourites by Moulin Roty and attractive wooden pull-alongs and trikes.

Rachel Riley

82 Marylebone High Street, W1U 4QW (7935 7007/www.rachelriley.com). Baker Street or Bond Street tube. **Open** 10am-6.30pm Mon-Sat; 10.30am-5.30pm Sun. **Credit** AmEx, MC, V.

Designed by Ms Riley from her atelier in France, the children's clothes sold here have a rarefied and timeless look. Gorgeous little smocked, print cotton dresses with matching bloomers, ruched bathing suits and rosebud pyjamas for little girls; manly stripes for little boys; cargo pants and cotton hoodies for casualwear; party frocks and tailored trousers for best – it's all top quality stuff that speaks of a country childhood idyll. The shop has a nostalgic air too: the floorboards creak as you creep about, and dark-wood glass cabinets and a retro chandelier light set off the clothes beautifully.

Roco

6 Church Road, SW19 5DL (8946 5288). Wimbledon tube/rail. **Open** 10am-6pm Mon-Sat; noon-5pm Sun. **Credit** AmEx, MC, V.

A smart boutique for newborns to 16-year-olds, this double-fronted store is bursting with bright clothes and gifts. Split level, the ground floor is divided into two areas for noughts to threes and four-to-eight-year olds. It's a complete shopping experience where all ages can browse at their leisure, although the cartoons playing on the store's TV are a great distraction for the tinier tots. In the basement, the Roco Star teen boutique has clothes for boys and girls aged ten to 16. Brands feature Guess, Polo, Ralph Lauren, French Connection, O'Neill, Ted Baker and Miss Sixty, as well as swimwear from Okay Brasil and Sea Folly.

Sasti

8 Portobello Green Arcade, 281 Portobello Road, W10 5TZ (8960 1125/www.sasti.co.uk). Ladbroke Grove tube. **Open** 10am-6pm Mon-Sat; 11am-5pm Sun. **Credit** AmEx, MC, V.

Named after the Hindu goddess who looks after all children and small creatures, Sasti is our favourite affordable children's boutique. This season we've been going a bundle on the cherry-print skirts and polka-dot cut-offs and the printed shirts for boys – festooned with grazing Friesian cows and fringed red cowboy trousers. Perennial bestsellers include the little leopard-print furry jackets and siren-suits with dragon tails for babies and toddlers. Small girls look very fetching in the sticky-out net skirts. Toys incude character lunchboxes and knitted toys by Anne-Marie Petit.

Their Nibs

214 Kensington Park Road, W11 1NR (7221 4263/www.theirnibs.com). Ladbroke Grove or Notting Hill Gate tube. **Open** 10am-6pm Mon-Sat; noon-5pm Sun. **Credit** AmEx, MC, V.

With an impressively spacious play area with blackboard, toys and books, a small hairdressing salon (ring for details of shearing sessions) and racks of original clothes, Their Nibs is a top shop for tots. There's a tree of fairies on the front desk and central tables filled with sweet accessories; fashions are pretty reasonably priced. You can pick up a distinctive cream crocheted party dress for a five-year-old for £39, and lovely velour collared T-shirts for boys in chocolate and turquoise cost £20. The alarming vintage rail is perhaps best avoided: the 1970s kids' clothes are polyester and crimplene rich, make no mistake. Would you pay £25 to squeeze your nine-year-old into an acid-green jumpsuit in synthetic fibres?

For branch see index.

Tots Boutique

39 Turnham Green Terrace, W4 1RG (8995 0520/www.totschiswick.com). Turnham Green tube. **Open** 10am-6pm Mon-Sat; noon-5pm Sun. **Credit** AmEx, MC, V.

Turnham Green is a shopping mecca for those with children and Tots is one of the original players on the scene, often praised for the breadth of its designer stock. Small and packed with labels, it has a frequently changing label cache. Look out for: Jottum, Mini-pi, Roxy, Ralph Lauren and Catimini Atelier.

Also check out...

Adams

Unit 26-27, Wandsworth Shopping Centre, SW18 4TE (8874 1820/www.adams.co.uk). Wandsworth Common rail. **Open** 9am-5.30pm Mon-Wed, Fri, Sat; 9am-7pm Thur; 11am-5pm Sun. **Credit** AmEx, MC, V.

Stocking affordable playwear, babywear and school uniforms.

Branches: throughout the city.

Brora

344 King's Road, SW3 5UR (0845 659 9944/www.brora.co.uk). Sloane Square tube. **Open** 10am-6pm Mon-Sat; noon-5pm Sun. **Credit** AmEx, MC, V.

Glorious cashmere clothes and cot blankets in tiny sizes alongside quality 100% cotton babywear and children's casuals.

Branches: throughout the city.

Catimini

52 South Molton Street, W1Y 1HF (7629 8099/www.catimini.com). Bond Street tube. **Open** 10am-6.30pm Mon-Wed, Fri, Sat; 10am-7pm Thur; 11am-5.30pm Sun. **Credit** AmEx, MC, V.

Vibrant, colourful and distinctive shift dresses, cardigans and cotton jackets.

For branch see index.

Felix & Lilys

3 Camden Passage, N1 8EA (7424 5423/ www.felixandlilys.com). Angel tube. **Open** 10.30am-6pm Mon-Sat; 11am-5pm Sun. **Credit** AmEx, MC, V.

A luxury baby shop with a range of bold, bright designer clothes and handsome toys.

Jake's

79 Berwick Street, W1F 8TL (7734 0812/ www.jakesofsoho.co.uk). Oxford Circus tube. **Open** 11am-7pm Mon-Sat. **Credit** AmEx, MC, V.

Jake's childrenswear range, mainly for boys, consists of distinctive slogan T-shirts ('Lucky 7'), polo shirts, sweatshirts and combat trousers.

Litkey

2A Devonshire Road, W4 2HD (8994 4112). Turnham Green tube. **Open** 10am-5.30pm Mon-Fri; 10am-6pm Sat; 11am-4pm Sun. **Credit** MC, V.

Mostly Hungarian, with some Italian and French fashions for boys and girls.

Marie-Chantal

148 Walton Street, SW3 2JJ (7838 1111/ www.mariechantal.com). Knightsbridge or South Kensington tube. **Open** 10am-6pm Mon-Sat. **Credit** AmEx, MC, V.

Exclusive clothes for babies and infants designed by mother-of-four Marie-Chantal, Crown Princess Pavlos of Greece.

Membery's

1 Church Road, Barnes, SW13 9HE (8876 8075/www.specialdresscompany.co.uk). Barnes Bridge rail. **Open** 10am-5pm Mon-Sat. **Credit** AmEx, MC, V.

Special-occasion outfits for small boys and girls; the shop is particularly good for wedding outfits.

Petit Aimé

34 Ledbury Road, W11 2AB (7221 3123/ www.aimelondon.com). Notting Hill Gate tube. **Open** 10.30am-6.30pm Mon-Sat. **Credit** AmEx, DC, MC, V.

Aimé's new children's boutique stocks an adorable range of French clothes labels for children and babies.

For branch (Aimé) see index.

Petit Bateau

106-108 King's Road, SW3 4TZ (7838 0818/www.petit-bateau.com). Sloane Square tube. **Open** 10am-6.30pm Mon, Tue, Fri, Sat; 10am-7pm Wed, Thur; noon-6pm Sun. **Credit** AmEx, MC, V.

Classic French baby and childrens' (up to 12 years' old) clothes, both floral, plain and in trademark milleraies stripes.

For branches see index.

Ralph Lauren

143 New Bond Street, W1S 2TP (7535 4600/www.ralphlauren.com). Green Park tube. **Open** 10am-6pm Mon-Wed, Fri, Sat; 10am-7pm Thur; noon-5pm Sun. **Credit** AmEx, DC, MC, V.

The traditional shop interior, complete with rocking horses, is so attractive you wistfully turn price labels longer than you should.

Second-hand

Little Angel Exchange

249 Archway Road, N6 5BS (8340 8003/www.littleangelexchange.co.uk). Highgate tube. **Open** 11am-5pm Mon-Fri; 11am-5.30pm Sat. **Credit** MC, V.

There's always a ready supply of nearly new or unused clothes, toys and equipment at the Little Angel Exchange. Prices start from a couple of quid for a mid-range label T-shirt (such as H&M) to a few more for designerwear. If you want to sell through Little Angel, you can leave clothing here in the hope of obtaining half the sale price (if the item sold is over £10), or one third (if the item sells for less than £10).

Shoes

One Small Step One Giant Leap

3 Blenheim Crescent, W11 2EE (7243 0535/www.onesmallstepone giantleap.com). Ladbroke Grove or Notting Hill Gate tube. **Open** 10am-6pm Mon-Fri; 9am-6pm Sat; 11am-5pm Sun. **Credit** MC, V.

You should count your blessings if there is a branch of this specialist children's shoe chain – and consistent winner of the Shoe Retailer of the Year gong – in your neighbourhood. It is a blissful place to take your children for all their footwear needs from Crocs and sandals to sensible schoolwear. The best thing is that there's space to spread out, the shoes are displayed with care and the highly regarded Bannock Device is used for fitting. Expect to pay about £12 for a jolly pair of One Small Step canvas sandals and about £36 for Start-rite school shoes.

For branches see index.

Papillon

43 Elizabeth Street, SW1W 9PP (7730 6690/www.papillon4children.com). Sloane Square tube or Victoria tube/rail. **Open** 10am-6pm Mon-Fri; 10am-5pm Sat. **Credit** MC, V.

Bright ballet-style pumps in a rainbow of colours and prints are a big part of the stock here. As well as the pumps, there are school shoes and beach sandals, flip flops, moccasins, bridesmaids' shoes, Hunter gumboots, socks, tights and kaftans.

Red Shoes

30 Topsfield Parade, N8 8QB (8341 9555/www.theredshoes.co.uk). Finsbury Park tube/rail, then W7, 41 bus. **Open** 10am-5.30pm Mon-Sat; noon-4.30pm Sun. **Credit** MC, V.

The cheerful staff at this spacious general shoe shop have winning ways with children, and the toys thoughtfully left out on the shop floor garner frequent fulsome praise from fraught parents. The junior shoe collection (there are adult shoes too) include Naturino, Start-rite, Birkenstock, Ricosta and Converse. New walkers can choose Bobux to aid their soft little foot bones. All kinds of ballet kit, UV resistant swimwear and babyclothes are also sold.

Shoe Tree

1 Devonshire Road, W4 2EU (8987 0525). Turnham Green tube. **Open** 9.30am-5.30pm Mon-Sat; 11.30am-4.30pm Sun. **Credit** AmEx, DC, MC, V.

Smart and comfortable, with decking and child-sized chairs and tables out the front and plenty of goodies inside. Children can be measured up and coaxed into a wide range of Start-rite, Bopi, Angulus, Ricosta and Aster designs while they watch the DVDs and CBeebies on the widescreen television. Dancewear, including tap and jazz shoes, is also sold. There's a cushiony sofa for them to sit on and crayoning for fun.

Also check out...

Brian's Shoes

2 Halleswelle Parade, Finchley Road, NW11 0DL (8455 7001/www.briansshoes.com). Finchley Central or Golders Green tube. **Open** 9.15am-5.30pm Mon-Sat; 10.30am-1.30pm Sun. **Credit** MC, V.

Calm, spacious, unfussy and a centre of excellence for foot-measuring services.

John Barnett

137-139 Lordship Lane, SE22 8HX (8693 5145). East Dulwich rail. **Open** 9.30am-5.30pm Mon-Sat. **Credit** AmEx, V.

Long-established Dulwich shoe shop with a great section for children.

For branch see index.

Little Me

141 Hamilton Road, NW11 9EG (8209 0440). Brent Cross tube. **Open** 10.30am-6.15pm Mon-Thur; 11am-4pm Sun; by appointment Fri. **Credit** MC, V.

Wide range of continental children's shoes; staff use the Swiss shoe measuring system for precision fitting.

Merlin Shoes

44 Westow Street, SE19 3AH (8771 5194/ www.merlinshoes.com). Crystal Palace rail. **Open** 9.30am-5.30pm Mon-Fri; 9.30am-6pm Sat. **Credit** MC, V.

Fab local shoe shop and shoe-fitting centre of excellence.

Shoe Station

3 Station Approach, Kew, Surrey TW9 3QB (8940 9905/www.theshoestation.co.uk). Kew Gardens tube. **Open** 9am-6pm Mon-Sat. **Credit** MC, V.

Children's shoes for every occasion; football boots, ballet shoes, slippers, gumboots, and more. Staff are trained Start-rite fitters.

Stepping Out

106 Pitshanger Lane, W5 1QX (8810 6141). Ealing Broadway tube. **Open** 9.30am-5.30pm Mon-Sat. **Credit** MC, V.

Start-rite, Ricosta, Mod8, Lelli Kelly and Geox are sold. Assistants can advise on shoes for children with mobility problems.

Vincent Shoe Store

19 Camden Passage, N1 8EA (7226 3141/www.vincentshoestore.com). Angel tube. **Open** 11am-6pm Tue-Fri; 10am-6pm Sat; noon-4pm Sun. **Credit** MC, V.

A household name in Sweden, Vincent purveys perky, affordable footwear.

Puppet Planet. *See p268.*

Toys & games

Interesting toys and trinkets can often be found in general gift shops; *see pp203*. Our favourite website/ mail-order companies are educational and the nostalgia experts **Alphabet Cat** (8693 6010, www.alphabetcat.com); as well as the new-born baby and christening gift vendors **Aspen & Brown** (0845 371 1171, www.aspenandbrown.com); and **Bright Minds** (0844 412 2250, www.brightminds.co.uk), whose sparky ideas make learning fun. **Ptolemy Toys** (01280 843000, www.ptolemytoys.co.uk) is a good bet for dressing-up gear.

See also p209 **Hobbies & games**.

Art Stationers/ Green's Village Toy Shop

31 Dulwich Village, SE21 7BN (8693 5938). North Dulwich rail. **Open** 9am-5.30pm Mon-Sat. **Credit** MC, V.

The shop space at the front has all manner of paints, pastels, pencils, paper, stationery and craft materials, but it's the big TOYS sign that gets the children excited: Brio, Sylvanian Families (it's an official collectors' shop), Playmobil, Crayola, Lego, Warhammer and other play giants are stocked and unusual companies such as Tantrix and Wow are also represented. The huge pocket money-priced range goes from your 25p rubber goldfish to £2.25 for a magnetic car racer.

Cheeky Monkeys

202 Kensington Park Road, W11 1NR (7792 9022/www.cheekymonkeys.com). Notting Hill Gate tube, then 52 bus. **Open** 9.30am-5.30pm Mon-Fri; 10am-5.30pm Sat; 11am-5pm Sun. **Credit** MC, V.

Attractive, tasteful and educational toys are Cheeky Monkey's business. Adults enjoy admiring the stock almost more than the childen. There are beautiful wooden painted Noah's Arks and Pirate Ships, castles and dolls' houses by Le Toy Van and Plan, as well as role-play toys, such as wooden kitchen mixers, china tea sets and play food. Animal rockers, the ever-entertaining Wheeliebugs for toddlers and colourful ride-on buses and cars all make great birthday presents for toddlers. Then there are all sorts of puppets and their theatres, dressing-up costumes, pirate ships and art kits. Trinkets cost from about £1.99.

Education Interactive

10 Staplehurst Road, SE13 5NB (8318 6380/www.education-interactive.co.uk). Hither Green rail. **Open** 9.30am-5.30pm Mon-Wed, Fri, Sat; 9.30am-6.30pm Thur. **Credit** AmEx, MC, V.

High-quality educational resources are the thing in this Hither Green shop. The goal: to provide games that stimulate thinking through intrigue and engagement. Games, puzzles and activities, great for individuals, families and schools, include delights such as electronic sudoku, Fraction Action snap and the ever-popular Polydron. Phone to check EI is open before visiting.

Fun Learning

Bentall's Centre, Clarence Street, Kingston-upon-Thames, Surrey KT1 1TP (8974 8900). Kingston rail. **Open** 9am-6pm Mon-Wed, Fri; 9am-6.30pm Sat; 9am-8pm Thur; 11am-5pm Sun. **Credit** MC, V.

Fun Learning covers all types of play: creative, quiet, thoughtful, raucous and computer-based (the computer games are mostly of an educational bent). There are large sections devoted to puzzles and number games, art and craft activities and science experiments. Affordable pocket-money-priced items include balloon-making gunk, bouncy balls, puzzles, magnifying glasses and other curiosities. Buggy and disabled access is available.

For branch see index.

Hamleys

188-196 Regent Street, W1B 5BT (0870 333 2455/www.hamleys.com). Oxford Circus tube. **Open** 10am-8pm Mon-Fri; 9am-8pm Sat; noon-6pm Sun. **Credit** AmEx, DC, MC, V.

Both a tourist attraction, with regular school-holiday events for children (check the website), and a ginormous toy shop, Hamleys has all the must-have toys, attractively displayed to boot. Arranged on five noisy floors, with perky demonstrators showing off certain wares on every one, you'll be lucky if you can spend less than an hour in here if you're accompanied by children. There's much to see: the basement has interactive toys, the ground floor is soft toys, floor one is all games, two is for pre-schoolers, three is girls' stuff, four hobbies and five is boys' toys with a newly refurbished café attached.

Happy Returns

36 Rosslyn Hill, NW3 1NH (7435 2431). Hampstead tube. **Open** 10am-5.30pm Mon-Fri; 10am-6pm Sat; noon-5.30pm Sun. **Credit** MC, V.

A pleasantly retro shop stocking toys old and new, with, as the name hints, much stock geared towards parties. Fill up on the celebration essentials then hunt for presents. There are products and prices to suit everyone: glow-stars, Etch-A-Sketch, Jellycat, Sylvanian Families, Schleich, Playmobil and Galt. The epic Gormiti game is a current bestseller.

Honeyjam

267 Portobello Road, W11 1LR (7243 0449/www.honeyjam.co.uk). Ladbroke Grove tube. **Open** 9.30am-5.30pm Mon-Sat; 11am-4pm Sun. **Credit** AmEx, MC, V.

Honeyjam is one of those fashionable toy shops that's still full of fun, and has a strong line in vintage playthings. There are Fisher Price classics that parents will remember from their own childhood, as well as some seriously aspirational role-playing toys, the apotheosis of which has to be the famous toy Aga (made to order). It's all beautifully laid out, with glories to catch the eye at every turn: tea sets, tiddly winks, anatomically correct dolls, forts and dragon castles and traditional wooden toys from companies like Bigjigs and Le Toy Van. Toys and baby and infant clothes are set out around the till.

Just Williams

18 Half Moon Lane, SE24 9HU (7733 9995). Herne Hill rail. **Open** 9.30am-6pm Mon-Sat. **Credit** MC, V.

A bright blue child's paradise, Williams has top names in toys, most particularly Brio, Sylvanians, Schleich and Playmobil; there are also traditional wooden playthings from Big Jigs, Plan, Pin Toy and Santas. Games Workshop is well represented for all those prep school boys and there's dressing-up stuff for rooky fairies.

Mystical Fairies

12 Flask Walk, NW3 1HE (7431 1888/ www.mysticalfairies.co.uk). Hampstead tube. **Open** 10am-6pm Mon-Sat; 11am-6pm Sun. **Credit** MC, V.

An all-out pretty-pink and sparkly retail experience. The shop is a glittery grotto dedicated to dreams of fairies, princesses and ballerinas, where fairy toys, flower fairies, pixies and elfin toys hang from silver branches overhead. It's hard to see the wood for the fairies but there are around 2,000 products including fairy bedwear, fairy and princess books and stickers and, at the back of the shop, fairy costumes, including various types of wings, plus wizard and pirate outfits for boys. Mystical Fairies runs themed parties in the shop's Enchanted Garden basement.

For branch see index.

Patrick's Toys & Models

107-111 Lillie Road, SW6 7SX (7385 9864/www.patrickstoys.co.uk). Fulham Broadway tube. **Open** 9.30am-5.30pm Mon-Sat. **Credit** MC, V.

Going on 60 years old and still game for anything, Patrick's is one of London's biggest toy and model shops, and the main service agent for Hornby and Scalextric. The model section specialises in rockets, planes, cars, military and sci-fi. The general toy department has traditional wooden toys, dolls' houses and their accessories.

Play

89 Lauriston Road, E9 7HJ (8510 9960/ www.playtoyshops.com). Bethnal Green or Mile End tube/277, 388 bus. **Open** 10am-6pm Mon-Sat; 11am-5pm Sun. **Credit** AmEx, MC, V.

A treasure trove located in a pretty part of Hackney, Play lives up to its name. Currently a hit with little customers are the Miffy soft toys, plus the Sylvanian Families range, along with the Brio Trains and Tobar bath toys in the basement. There's something for everyone and every room here with musical instruments by New Classic Toys, fun natty fabric wall-hangers from Fiesta Crafts, mobiles by Flensted and even a sweet organic clothes range by Green Eyed Monster (www.green-eyed-monster.co.uk. There's also dressing-up stuff and messy play products (glitter, glue, dough, beads and paints), alongside trinkets by Jellycat, jewellery boxes from Rousellier and party paperware.

Route 73 Kids

92 Stoke Newington Church Street, N16 0AP (7923 7873). Bus 73, 393, 476. **Open** 10am-5.30pm Tue-Sun. **Credit** AmEx, MC, V.

Guess which bus route this jolly toy shop is on? With a party-bag perfect pocket-money toy table, and a great selection of traditional toys from Brio and Galt, Route 73 comes recommended. Of the wide range of wooden toys, those by Plan are all the rage. There are also books, jigsaws, word games and craft packs, as well as Jellycat soft toys, and, for babies, soft leather shoes by Starchild and Out of the Blue.

Also check out...

Early Learning Centre

36 King's Road, SW3 4UD (7581 5764/ www.elc.co.uk). Sloane Square tube. **Open** 9.30am-7pm Mon-Fri; 9.30am-6pm Sat; 11am-6pm Sun. **Credit** AmEx, MC, V.
Dedicated to imaginative play for babies and young children; everything is sturdy, brightly coloured and reasonably priced.
Branches: throughout the city.

Disney Store

360-366 Oxford Street, W1N 9HA (7491 9136/www.disneystore.co.uk). Bond Street tube. **Open** 10am-9pm Mon-Sat; noon-6pm Sun. **Credit** AmEx, MC, V.
The family film of the moment spawns figurines, stationery, toys and costumes at these most animated of toy shops. Enduring favourites are the character dolls, costumes and classic DVDs.
For branches see index.

Fagin's Toys

84 Fortis Green Road, N10 3HN (8444 0282). East Finchley tube, then 102 bus. **Open** 9am-5.30pm Mon-Sat; 10am-3pm Sun. **Credit** MC, V.
Favourites from Galt, Orchard, Brio, Lego, Playmobil and Sylvanian Families, outdoor toys and a central table of penny dreadfuls.

Goody Gumdrops

128 Crouch Hill, N8 9DY (8340 3484/ www.goodygumdrops.co.uk). Finsbury Park tube/rail, then W7 bus/Crouch End rail. **Open** 10am-5.30pm Tue-Sat. **Credit** MC, V.
Pocket-money toys, books, dressing-up gear, role-play toys such as tin tea sets and lovely hessian-covered, 'house' toy boxes.

Hawkin's Bazaar

46 Ealing Broadway Centre, The Broadway, W5 5JY (0870 942 7312/ www.hawkin.com). Ealing Broadway tube. **Open** 9am-6pm Mon-Sat; 11am-5pm Sun. **Credit** MC, V.
Pocket money-priced toys, tricks and treats.

Lark

www.larkmade.com.
Lark sells vintage toys, gifts and decorations, including sweet knitted rattles and cuddly toys. Stockists include Their Nibs (*see p265*).
For branch see index.

Little Rascals

140 Merton Road, SW19 1EH (8542 9979). South Wimbledon tube. **Open** 9am-5.30pm Tue-Sat. **Credit** AmEx, MC, V.
A friendly, family-run local full of unusual wooden toys, clothes and gifts for babies.

Pedlars

128 Talbot Road, W11 1JA (7727 7799/ www.pedlars.co.uk). Notting Hill Gate tube. **Open** 10am-6pm Mon-Fri; 9am-6pm Sat; 11am-5pm Sun. **Credit** AmEx, DC, MC, V.
Children love the mix of toys, games, party packs, music, books and more.

QT Toys

90 Northcote Road, Clapham, SW11 6QN (7223 8637/www.qttoys.co.uk). Clapham Junction rail. **Open** 9.30am-5.30pm Mon-Sat, 9.30am-5pm Sun. **Credit** MC, V.
All the big name toy brands, as well as craft kits, modelling toys, stationery, and educational toys.

Snap Dragon

56 Turnham Green Terrace, W4 1QP (8995 6618). Turnham Green tube. **Open** 9.30am-6pm Mon-Sat; 11am-5pm Sun. **Credit** MC, V.
A good toy shop for big-name brands.
For branch see index.

Sylvanian Shop

68 Mountgrove Road, N5 2LT (7226 1329/ www.sylvanianfamilies.com). Finsbury Park tube. **Open** 9.30am-5.30pm Mon-Fri; 9am-6pm Sat; 10am-4pm Sun. **Credit** AmEx, MC, V.
This tiny outpost of Sylvania has been hidden away in this quiet London street for about 17 years.

Toys R Us

760 Old Kent Road, SE15 1NJ (7732 7322/ www.toysrus.co.uk). Elephant & Castle tube/ rail, then 21, 56, 172 bus. **Open** 9am-8pm Mon-Fri; 9am-7pm Sat; 11am-5pm Sun. **Credit** AmEx, MC, V.
All branches stock industrial quantities of the toy of the moment.
For branches see index.

Toy Station

6 Eton Street, Richmond, Surrey TW9 1EE (8940 4896). Richmond tube/rail. **Open** 10am-6pm Mon-Fri; 9.30am-6pm Sat; noon-5pm Sun. **Credit** (over £8) MC, V.
An old-fashioned, two-storey toy shop full of model animals, knights and soldiers, forts and castles, remote-control vehicles and traditional wooden toys.

Traditional toys

Benjamin Pollock's Toy Shop

44 The Market, Covent Garden, WC2E 8RF (7379 7866/www.pollocks-coventgarden.co.uk). Covent Garden tube. **Open** 10.30am-6pm Mon-Sat; 11am-4pm Sun. **Credit** AmEx, MC, V.
Climb the creaky stairs past Hobbs and into this shrine to playthings from the past. Toy theatres make up a good part of the stock, and cost from a couple of quid for one in a matchbox to much more for the really complicated set-ups. If miniature stages aren't your thing, there are more nostalgic toys, such as china tea sets, spinning tops, Matryoshka dolls, vintage-style board games, toy pianos and music boxes.

Kristin Baybars

7 Mansfield Road, NW3 2JD (7267 0934). Kentish Town tube/Gospel Oak rail/C2, C11 bus. **Open** 11am-6pm Tue-Sat. **No credit cards.**
A mysterious pink shop just across from Gospel Oak station, Ms Baybars's emporium is for careful collectors of dolls' houses and their contents, and children who know how to look without touching. There's no room for pushchairs as every inch of the shop seems to be laden with tiny attractions. Accompanied children are welcome to browse through the affordable miniaturised household items, furniture, equipment and food (a tiny plate of biscuits is £1.80) in the front part of the shop. Tucked away in the inner sanctum are the more expensive British-made items.

Never Never Land

3 Midhurst Parade, Fortis Green, N10 3EJ (8883 3997/www.never-never-land.co.uk). East Finchley tube. **Open** 10am-5pm Tue, Wed, Fri, Sat. **Credit** MC, V.
This splendid little toy shop has dolls' houses (from £99) and their accessories, as well as soft-bodied dolls, Heimess pram toys, tea sets, wooden firemen and fire stations, soldiers with forts and cars with garages. Great for toys for babies.

Petit Chou

15 St Christopher's Place, W1U 1NR (7486 3637/www.petitchou.co.uk). Bond Street tube. **Open** 10.30am-6.30pm Mon-Sat; noon-5pm Sun. **Credit** AmEx, MC, V.
A tasteful wooden toy enclave, where you can buy a gigantic tray of wooden blocks (£100) that will keep a child occupied until his or her GCSEs, or buy aesthetically pleasing pull-alongs, skittles, soldiers and animals in warm painted wood.

Puppet Planet

787 Wandsworth Road (corner of the Chase), SW8 3JQ (7627 0111/07900 975276/www.puppetplanet.co.uk). Clapham Common tube. **Open** 9am-4pm Tue-Sat; also by appointment. **Credit** AmEx, DC, MC, V.
A specialist marionette shop that's run by Lesley Butler, whose passion for stringed characters is all too evident in the range of stock hanging about here. There are classic Pelham characters, traditional Indian and African marionettes, Balinese shadow puppets and vintage figures. Best to call in advance if you're making a special trip to the shop as Butler occasionally closes it to put on puppet shows for children's parties.

Also check out...

Farmyard

63 Barnes High Street, SW13 9LF (8878 7338/www.thefarmyard.co.uk). Barnes or Barnes Bridge rail. **Open** 10am-5.30pm Mon-Fri; 9.30am-5.30pm Sat. **Credit** MC, V.
Personalised wooden toys and games for newborns to eight-year-olds, plus nursery gifts and dressing up.

Traditional Toys

53 Godfrey Street, SW3 3SX (7352 1718/ www.traditionaltoy.com). Sloane Square tube, then 11, 19, 22 bus/49 bus. **Open** 10am-6pm Mon-Sat; noon-4pm Sun. **Credit** AmEx, MC, V.
It's the beautiful wooden toys that really grab you here, like the tell-the-time clock face and the wooden Noah's Arks.

Indexes & Map

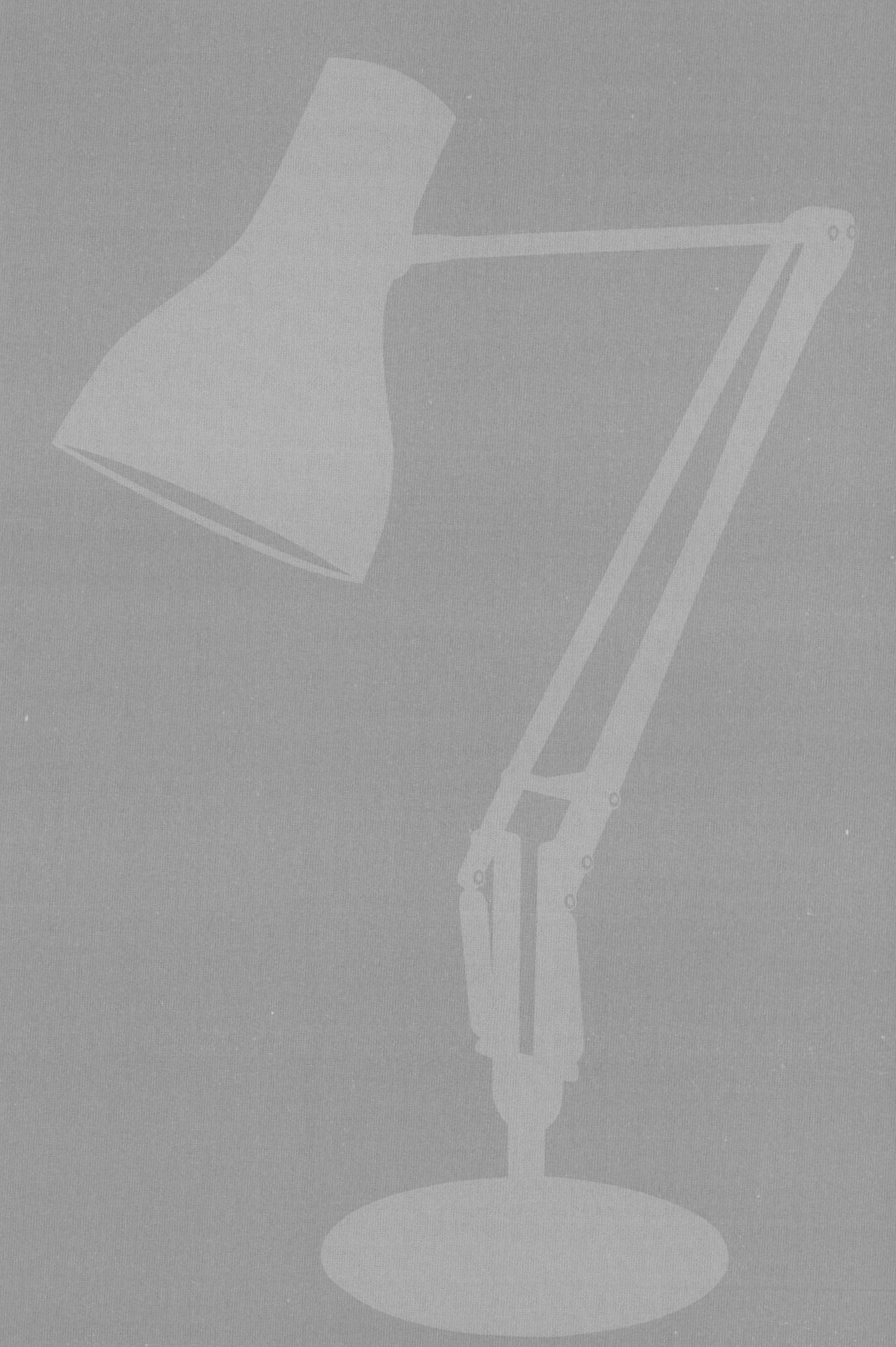

Subject Index

Note: Figures in **bold** refer to the main listings for the product or service.

SUBJECT INDEX

SUBJECT INDEX

SUBJECT INDEX

SUBJECT INDEX

A-Z index

Names with capital letters are listed at the front of each alphabetical section; for example, B Levy is at the start of 'B', followed by BM Soho and BCM Chess Shop. Numbers are listed as if spelled out.

A

B

C

D

E

F

G

H

I

L

M

N

Q

R

S

T

Advertisers' index

Please refer to relevant sections for addresses / telephone numbers

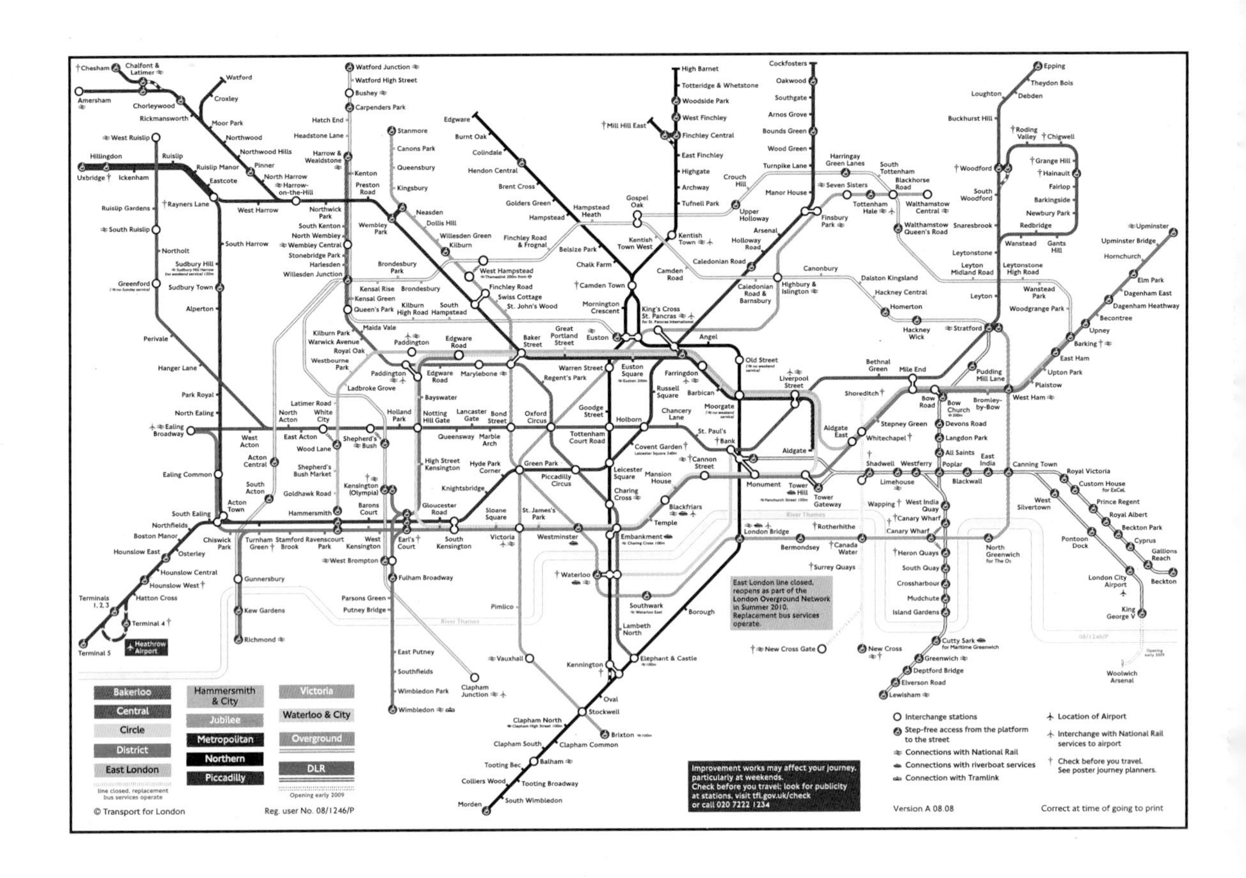
Chesham
Chalfont & Latimer
Watford
Croxley
Amersham
Chorleywood
Rickmansworth
Moor Park
Northwood
Northwood Hills
Pinner
North Harrow
Harrow-on-the-Hill
West Ruislip
Ruislip
Hillingdon
Uxbridge
Ickenham
Ruislip Manor
Eastcote
Rayners Lane
West Harrow
Ruislip Gardens
South Ruislip
Northolt
South Harrow
Sudbury Hill
Sudbury Town
Greenford
Alperton
Perivale
Hanger Lane
Park Royal
North Ealing
Ealing Broadway
Ealing Common
West Acton
North Acton
East Acton
Acton Central
South Acton
Acton Town
South Ealing
Northfields
Boston Manor
Osterley
Hounslow East
Hounslow Central
Hounslow West
Hatton Cross
Terminals 1, 2, 3
Terminal 4
Terminal 5
Heathrow Airport
Watford Junction
Watford High Street
Bushey
Carpenders Park
Hatch End
Headstone Lane
Harrow & Wealdstone
Kenton
Preston Road
Northwick Park
South Kenton
North Wembley
Wembley Central
Stonebridge Park
Harlesden
Willesden Junction
Wembley Park
Stanmore
Canons Park
Queensbury
Kingsbury
Neasden
Dollis Hill
Willesden Green
Kilburn
Kensal Rise
Brondesbury
Brondesbury Park
Kensal Green
Queen's Park
Kilburn Park
Maida Vale
Warwick Avenue
Royal Oak
Westbourne Park
Paddington
Ladbroke Grove
Latimer Road
White City
Wood Lane
Shepherd's Bush
Shepherd's Bush Market
Goldhawk Road
Hammersmith
Kensington (Olympia)
Holland Park
Notting Hill Gate
Bayswater
Edgware Road
Edgware
Burnt Oak
Colindale
Hendon Central
Brent Cross
Golders Green
Hampstead
Belsize Park
Chalk Farm
Camden Town
Mornington Crescent
Finchley Road
Finchley Road & Frognal
West Hampstead
Swiss Cottage
St. John's Wood
Kilburn High Road
South Hampstead
Hampstead Heath
Gospel Oak
Kentish Town West
Kentish Town
Camden Road
Caledonian Road
Caledonian Road & Barnsbury
High Barnet
Totteridge & Whetstone
Woodside Park
West Finchley
Mill Hill East
Finchley Central
East Finchley
Highgate
Archway
Tufnell Park
Crouch Hill
Upper Holloway
Holloway Road
Arsenal
Cockfosters
Oakwood
Southgate
Arnos Grove
Bounds Green
Wood Green
Turnpike Lane
Manor House
Harringay Green Lanes
South Tottenham
Seven Sisters
Blackhorse Road
Walthamstow Central
Tottenham Hale
Walthamstow Queen's Road
Finsbury Park
Highbury & Islington
Canonbury
Dalston Kingsland
Hackney Central
Homerton
Hackney Wick
Stratford
Epping
Theydon Bois
Debden
Loughton
Buckhurst Hill
Roding Valley
Chigwell
Grange Hill
Hainault
Fairlop
Barkingside
Newbury Park
Woodford
South Woodford
Snaresbrook
Redbridge
Gants Hill
Wanstead
Leytonstone
Leytonstone High Road
Leyton Midland Road
Leyton
Wanstead Park
Woodgrange Park
Upminster
Upminster Bridge
Hornchurch
Elm Park
Dagenham East
Dagenham Heathway
Becontree
Upney
Barking
East Ham
Upton Park
Plaistow
West Ham
Pudding Mill Lane
Bromley-by-Bow
Bow Church
Bow Road
Mile End
Bethnal Green
Shoreditch
Stepney Green
Whitechapel
Devons Road
Langdon Park
All Saints
Poplar
East India
Blackwall
Canning Town
Royal Victoria
Custom House
Prince Regent
Royal Albert
Beckton Park
Cyprus
Gallions Reach
Beckton
West Silvertown
Pontoon Dock
London City Airport
King George V
Woolwich Arsenal
North Greenwich
West India Quay
Canary Wharf
Heron Quays
South Quay
Crossharbour
Mudchute
Island Gardens
Cutty Sark for Maritime Greenwich
Greenwich
Deptford Bridge
Elverson Road
Lewisham
New Cross
New Cross Gate
Surrey Quays
Canada Water
Rotherhithe
Wapping
Shadwell
Limehouse
Westferry
Bermondsey
London Bridge
Tower Hill
Tower Gateway
Aldgate
Aldgate East
Liverpool Street
Old Street
Moorgate
Bank
Monument
Cannon Street
Mansion House
St. Paul's
Barbican
Farringdon
Chancery Lane
Holborn
Russell Square
Euston Square
Euston
King's Cross St. Pancras
Angel
Great Portland Street
Baker Street
Marylebone
Regent's Park
Warren Street
Goodge Street
Tottenham Court Road
Oxford Circus
Bond Street
Marble Arch
Lancaster Gate
Queensway
Covent Garden
Leicester Square
Piccadilly Circus
Green Park
Hyde Park Corner
Knightsbridge
High Street Kensington
Gloucester Road
Earl's Court
West Kensington
Barons Court
Ravenscourt Park
Stamford Brook
Turnham Green
Chiswick Park
Gunnersbury
Kew Gardens
Richmond
West Brompton
Fulham Broadway
Parsons Green
Putney Bridge
East Putney
Southfields
Wimbledon Park
Wimbledon
South Kensington
Sloane Square
Victoria
St. James's Park
Westminster
Embankment
Charing Cross
Temple
Blackfriars
Waterloo
Southwark
Borough
Lambeth North
Elephant & Castle
Kennington
Pimlico
Vauxhall
Oval
Stockwell
Brixton
Clapham Junction
Clapham North
Clapham Common
Clapham South
Balham
Tooting Bec
Tooting Broadway
Colliers Wood
South Wimbledon
Morden
River Thames
East London line closed, reopens as part of the London Overground Network in Summer 2010. Replacement bus services operate.
Bakerloo
Central
Circle
District
East London
line closed, replacement bus services operate
Hammersmith & City
Jubilee
Metropolitan
Northern
Piccadilly
Victoria
Waterloo & City
Overground
DLR
Opening early 2009
Improvement works may affect your journey, particularly at weekends.
Check before you travel: look for publicity at stations, visit tfl.gov.uk/check or call 020 7222 1234
Interchange stations
Step-free access from the platform to the street
Connections with National Rail
Connections with riverboat services
Connection with Tramlink
Location of Airport
Interchange with National Rail services to airport
Check before you travel. See poster journey planners.
© Transport for London
Reg. user No. 08/1246/P
Version A 08.08
Correct at time of going to print

GREEN HANDBAG,
BOUGHT WHEN I DIDN'T
GET THAT PROMOTION
BECAUSE APPARENTLY
I WASN'T
"CREATIVE ENOUGH."
"WELL,"
I TOLD MYSELF,
"THIS'LL SHOW THEM HOW
OUTSIDE
THE BOX I CAN BE.
THEY'LL SEE A NEW
ALICE BENNETT-GRANT
COME MONDAY."
AND ANYWAY,
EVERYONE'S BANGING
ON ABOUT
HOW WE SHOULD
ALL GO GREENER: £230
KEEPING THE RECEIPT:
PRICELESS
MasterCard
There are some things money can't buy.
For everything else there's MasterCard.